SPECIAL EDITION

USING
Mac® OS X, v10.3 Panther™

Brad Miser

que®

800 E. 96th Street
Indianapolis, Indiana 46240

CONTENTS AT A GLANCE

SPECIAL EDITION USING MAC® OS X, V10.3 PANTHER™

International Standard Book Number: 0-7897-3075-8

Library of Congress Catalog Card Number: 2003114782

Printed in the United States of America

First Printing: January 2004

07   06   05   04   4   3   2   1

Trademarks

Warning and Disclaimer

Bulk Sales

Que Publishing offers excellent discounts on this book when ordered in quantity for bulk purchases or special sales. For more information, please contact

U.S. Corporate and Government Sales
1-800-382-3419
corpsales@pearsontechgroup.com

For sales outside of the United States, please contact

International Sales
1-317-428-3341
international@pearsontechgroup.com

Publisher
Paul Boger

Associate Publisher
Greg Wiegand

Acquisitions Editor
Laura Norman

Development Editor
Laura Norman

Managing Editor
Charlotte Clapp

Project Editor
Tricia Liebig

Production Editor
Megan Wade

Indexer
Chris Barrick

Proofreader
Tracy Donhardt

Technical Editor
Brian Hubbard

Publishing Coordinator
Sharry Gregory

Interior Designer
Anne Jones

Cover Designer
Anne Jones

Page Layout
Michelle Mitchell

CONTENTS

II Mac OS X: Connecting to the World

ABOUT THE AUTHOR

Brad Miser has written extensively about all things Macintosh, with his favorite topics being OS X and the amazing "i" applications that empower Mac OS X users to unleash their digital creativity. In addition to *Special Edition Using Mac OS X Panther*, Brad has written many other books, including *Mac OS X and iLife: Using iTunes, iPhoto, iMovie, and iDVD*; *iDVD 3 Fast & Easy*; *Special Edition Using Mac OS X v10.2*, *Mac OS X and the Digital Lifestyle*; *Special Edition Using Mac OS X*; *The iMac Way*; *The Complete Idiot's Guide to iMovie 2*; *The Complete Idiot's Guide to the iMac*; and *Using Mac OS 8.5*. He has also been an author, development editor, or technical editor on more than 50 other titles. He has been a featured speaker on various Macintosh-related topics at Macworld Expo, at user group meetings, and in other venues.

Brad is the senior technical communicator for an Indianapolis-based software development company. Brad is responsible for all product documentation, training materials, online help, and other communication materials. He also manages the customer support operations for the company and provides training and account management services to its customers. Previously, he was the lead engineering proposal specialist for an aircraft engine manufacturer, a development editor for a computer book publisher, and a civilian aviation test officer/engineer for the U.S. Army. Brad holds a Bachelor of Science degree in mechanical engineering from California Polytechnic State University at San Luis Obispo (1986) and has received advanced education in maintainability engineering, business, and other topics.

In addition to his passion for Macintosh computers, Brad likes to run and play racquetball; playing with home theater technology is also a favorite pastime. He has also been a volunteer with the Zionsville Eagles High School football team.

Once a native of California, Brad now lives in Brownsburg, Indiana with his wife Amy; their three daughters, Jill, Emily, and Grace; and their guinea pig, Buddy.

Brad would love to hear about your experiences with this book (the good, the bad, and the ugly). You can write to him at bradmacosx@mac.com.

DEDICATION

To those who have given the last full measure of devotion so that the rest of us can be free.

ACKNOWLEDGMENTS

To the following people on the *Special Edition Using Mac OS X Panther* project team, my sincere appreciation for your hard work on this book:

Laura Norman, my acquisitions and development editor, who helped me get the focus of the first edition of this book on track when I had gone astray and kept me in line the rest of the way. She also made sure that I kept the text flowing when we revised this tome for Mac OS X version 10.3. Laura, getting through such a big book with me as the author three times should earn you a medal of some kind!

Marta Justak of Justak Literary Services, my agent, for getting me signed up for this project. Marta was also a constant source of support for me during the process and was always ready to lend an ear to listen to whatever I needed to say. Marta, many times I needed to bounce an idea or complaint off someone—thanks for being there for me!

Don Mayer, CEO and founder; Hapy Mayer, CFO and co-owner; and especially, Dawn D'Angelillo, VP of Marketing, of Small Dog Electronics. Small Dog provided much of the hardware and software that I needed to write this book. Small Dog is a great and Mac-friendly retailer; whenever you need hardware or software, check them out at www.smalldog.com or call them at 802-496-7171. Also check out the ad at the back of this book. Many thanks to Small Dog for being such an important part of this project.

Brian Hubbard, my technical editor, who did a great job to ensure that the information in this book is both accurate and useful. Brian, I tried my best to sneak mistakes past you, but you caught me every time—thanks for a job well done!

Megan Wade, my copy editor, who corrected my many misspellings, poor grammar, and other problems. Megan, you made the text appear to have been written by someone who actually knows how to write. Thanks!

Tricia Liebig, my project editor, who skillfully managed the hundreds of files that it took to make this book. Tricia, thanks for keeping everything current and making sure that things got where they needed to be when they needed to be there.

Anne Jones, for the interior design and cover of the book. You made this book a pleasure to look at! Also, a thanks for developing the book's cover. It is too bad that you can't judge a book by its cover because, if you could, everyone would believe that this book is top-notch—thanks!

Que's production and sales team for printing the book and getting it into your hands. Thanks, everybody!

And now for a few people who weren't on the project team, but who were essential to me personally:

Amy Miser, for supporting me while I took on this mammoth project for the third time and for being understanding about my need to do it yet one more time; living with an author isn't always lots of fun, especially with a big, complex book like this one. Amy, I promise, no more big books—until the next one! ;-)

Jill, Emily, and Grace Miser, for helping me remember that there is a lot more to life than pounding the keys—even though sometimes it seemed as if that was all I was doing. Girls, you brought lots of smiles to my face in stressful times. Thanks for reminding me of what is really important. And, a special thanks to Buddy the guinea pig for his early-morning visits to cheer me up while I was working!

Rick Ehrhardt for being such a good friend to me; I especially appreciated the occasional evening out—La Hacienda and Best Buy anyone?

Larry McWhorter, head football coach of the Zionsville Eagles. Larry, you consistently demonstrate true leadership and excellence on and, more importantly, off the field. Thanks for your example and encouragement. Go Eagles!

Andy Gall, assistant coach of the Eagles, who provided game footage for me to use for screenshots in this book.

WE WANT TO HEAR FROM YOU!

As the reader of this book, *you* are our most important critic and commentator. We value your opinion and want to know what we're doing right, what we could do better, what areas you'd like to see us publish in, and any other words of wisdom you're willing to pass our way.

As an associate publisher for Que Publishing, I welcome your comments. You can email or write me directly to let me know what you did or didn't like about this book—as well as what we can do to make our books better.

Please note that I cannot help you with technical problems related to the topic of this book. We do have a User Services group, however, where I will forward specific technical questions related to the book.

When you write, please be sure to include this book's title and author as well as your name, email address, and phone number. I will carefully review your comments and share them with the author and editors who worked on the book.

Email: feedback@quepublishing.com

Mail: Greg Wiegand
          Associate Publisher
          Que Publishing
          800 East 96th Street
          Indianapolis, IN 46240 USA

For more information about this book or another Que Publishing title, visit our Web site at www.quepublishing.com. Type the ISBN (excluding hyphens) or the title of a book in the Search field to find the page you're looking for.

INTRODUCTION

In this introduction

WELCOME TO MAC OS X

Now in its third major release (version 10.3), Mac OS X has been called many things, from revolutionary to evolutionary to being so innovative that it threatens the very existence of the Mac as we have come to know and love it. And all of those descriptions are appropriate.

The first release of Mac OS X (version 10.1) was a giant leap forward for the Mac platform. Its innovations in basic architecture, the way it works, and even its user interface made Mac OS X the most significant event for Mac users since the first Mac was introduced back in the Jurassic period, circa 1984. Mac OS X version 10.1 was more stable, more powerful, and even more beautiful than any previous version. However, version 10.1 had some rough spots, not surprising at all because it was the first release of a brand-new OS (despite the version number implying it was the successor to Mac OS 9).

About a year later, version 10.2 was released. This release smoothed many of the rough edges left over from version 10.1 and added many new features. Due to some fundamental improvements in the core operating system, version 10.2 caused some ripples in the Mac universe because many applications had to be updated to run under that version.

And now, we have version 10.3 under which Mac OS X is showing the maturity of its more than two years of life. Version 10.3 continues the process of refining the OS along with adding some excellent new features, such as a totally redesigned Finder, Expose, improved applications, and so on. It also continues to improve the stability and performance of the OS. Much of the foundation work for the OS was accomplished by the previous two releases; version 10.3 is less disruptive than the previous releases while continuing to make major improvements in functionality, reliability, and performance.

Mac OS X is a very powerful and feature-rich OS. Although many of the features of the OS are intuitive, some might not be obvious to you. And because of the amazing number of powerful applications that are part of the standard Mac OS X installation, such as iMovie, iTunes, and many others, using Mac OS X effectively is much more than just manipulating the Finder and using the Dock. That is where this book comes in.

INTRODUCTION TO *SPECIAL EDITION USING MAC OS X, V10.3 PANTHER*

This book has two fundamental purposes:

- To help you make the jump to Mac OS X as efficiently as possible
- To provide a reference for you to use as you continue to grow in your Mac OS X use

To accomplish the first purpose, this book is written in a straightforward style; you won't find any fluff here. The book is designed to help you *use* Mac OS X as efficiently and as effectively as possible. Everything about the book is an attempt to make specific information accessible and applicable to your daily Mac life. You will find only the background information you need to understand how to apply specific techniques and technologies; more focus is placed on the information you need to apply what you learn to your own Mac.

To accomplish the second purpose, this book covers an extremely broad range of topics. In addition to coverage of the core functionality of the desktop, you will find extensive coverage of topics to enable you to accomplish productive work with your Mac, such as creating digital movies, surfing the Net, and creating and hosting a Web site. This book also contains substantial amounts of information to help you add devices to expand your system so you can accomplish even more. Because Mac OS X has been designed to be networked, you will learn how to use its capabilities in this area to connect with other Macs, as well as to Windows networks. You will also learn how to both prevent and solve problems along the way.

How This Book Is Organized

This book consists of several parts, each of which contains at least two chapters. The following list provides an overview of this book's contents:

- **Part I, "Mac OS X: Exploring the Core"**—This part contains the largest number of pages, and for good reason. In this part, you will learn the core operations of the OS, from getting started with Mac OS X to working with the Finder, the Dock, applications, and the Classic environment, to customizing and exploring Mac OS X in depth. You will also learn the basics of the Unix command line.

- **Part II, "Mac OS X: Connecting to the World"**—Mac OS X has been designed to facilitate your interaction with the Internet. This part of the book explains how to configure Mac OS X for the Internet and how to use the tools it provides after you are connected.

- **Part III, "Mac OS X: Living the Digital Life"**—The Mac has always been preeminent in creative activities, such as graphics, video, and imaging. Mac OS X continues this tradition and provides digital media tools that are unmatched by any other platform. From creating and editing digital images to making movies with iMovie to watching DVDs you create, this part of the book shows you how.

- **Part IV, "Mac OS X: Expanding Your System"**—No Mac is an island; this part of the book helps you understand the input and output technologies supported by Mac OS X to enable you to select and add the peripheral devices you need.

- **Part V, "Mac OS X: Living in a Networked World"**—From the Internet to a local network, your Mac is most likely connected to one or more other computers. In this part of the book, you will learn how to establish, maintain, and use a network.

- **Part VI, "Mac OS X: Protecting, Maintaining, and Repairing Your Mac"**—As great as Mac OS X is, you still need to know how to minimize problems and be able to effectively solve any problems you do experience.

- **Part VII, "Mac OS X: Appendixes"**—These appendixes will help you install and maintain the OS and use Mac OS X on mobile Macs.

SPECIAL FEATURES

This book includes the following special features:

- **Chapter roadmaps**—At the beginning of each chapter, you will find a list of the top-level topics addressed in that chapter. This list will enable you to quickly see the type of information the chapter contains.

- **Troubleshooting**—Many chapters in the book have a section dedicated to trouble-shooting specific problems related to the chapter's topic. Cross-references to the solutions to these problems are placed in the context of relevant text in the chapter as Troubleshooting Notes to make them easy to locate.

- **Mac OS X to the Max**—Many chapters end with a "Mac OS X to the Max" section. These sections contain extra information that will help you make the most of Mac OS X. For example, tables of keyboard shortcuts are included to help you work more efficiently. Other sections include summaries of information that is outside the scope of the book, but which you should be aware of.

- **Notes**—Notes provide additional commentary or explanation that doesn't fit neatly into the surrounding text. You will find detailed explanations of how something works, alternative ways of performing a task, and comparisons between Mac OS X and previous versions of the OS.

- **On the Web notes**—These notes provide you with URLs you can visit to get more information or other resources relating to the topic being discussed.

- **Tips**—Tips help you work more efficiently by providing shortcuts or hints about alternative and faster ways of accomplishing a task.

- **Cautions**—These sidebars provide warnings about situations that involve possible danger to your Mac or its data.

- **The new version icon**—This icon indicates a significant change from versions of Mac OS prior to version 10.3. This icon will be meaningful to you if you have used a previous version of Mac OS X because it points out significant new features or major changes made for version 10.3.

- **Cross-references**—Many topics are connected to other topics in various ways. Cross-references help you link related information together, no matter where that information appears in the book. When another section is related to one you are reading, a cross-reference will direct you to a specific page in the book on which you will find the related information.

CONVENTIONS

To make things as clear as possible, this book doesn't use many special conventions or formatting techniques to identify specific kinds of information. However, there are a few things you need to be aware of:

- Menu commands are referred to by starting with the menu name and moving down to the specific command while separating each layer with a comma. For example, rather than writing, "Open the Terminal menu, then select the Services command, then select the Mail command, and then select Mail Text," I use a shorthand technique. In this example, I would write, "Select Terminal, Services, Mail, Mail Text." This shorthand makes the command structure more clear and cuts back on the number of words you have to read.

- When you are working in the Terminal, the commands you enter and the output you see are in a `monospace font like this`.

- Variables that stand for text that is specific to you are usually in *`italic monospace`*. For example, if I need to refer to your username in a specific location, I write, "`Users/username`, where *`username`* is your username," to indicate that you should look for your own information in place of the italicized phrase.

Who Should Use This Book

In this book, I've made certain assumptions about your specific experience with the Mac OS and your general comfort level with technology. The biggest assumption is that you are quite comfortable with the fundamentals of using the Mac OS. For example, you won't find any explanations of how to use a mouse, how to copy and move files, the basics of drag and drop, and so on. When there are significant differences in these basic tasks under Mac OS X as compared to the previous versions of the OS, you will find those differences explained, but probably not in enough detail to teach you how to do them if you have never done them before.

If you are completely new to computers, you will still find this book very useful, but you will also need a companion book that explains the fundamentals of using a Mac in more detail than is provided in this book.

If you have used previous versions of the Mac OS, such as Mac OS 9 or earlier versions of Mac OS X, and are comfortable with basic tasks, this book will help you make the jump to Mac OS X version 10.3 in a short time. It will also serve as a comprehensive reference for you as you explore this amazing operating system.

MAC OS X: EXPLORING THE CORE

Mac OS X: Foundations

In this chapter

1

MAC OS X: THE FUTURE IS NOW

When the Mac OS was first introduced in 1984, it was a completely radical way of interacting with a computer. Rather than having to type long strings of arcane commands, a user could manipulate the system, files, documents, and data by simply pointing to icons and clicking. The success of the Mac OS drove the other PC-oriented operating systems to also adopt a graphical user interface (GUI).

NOTE

> Just to give credit where credit is due, the user interface made mainstream by the Mac was based on work done at Xerox. I guess that just goes to show that the inventor of something doesn't always get the most out of it.

Since that time, the Mac OS has undergone many improvements as it moved from early versions up to versions 8, 9, and finally 9.2 which carried it into the year 2001. These versions successfully made the transition from 68K processors to PowerPCs. They included Internet features early in the life of the Internet and then integrated the Net into the OS under 9. Each of the versions further refined the OS and added features (some of which were useful and survived, while others went by the wayside). Mac OS 9.2 was and is an excellent OS.

However, as the saying goes, all good things must come to an end.

Even as powerful and capable as Mac OS 9.2 was, by the end, it was showing the core architecture's age. It lacked modern, fundamental design features that are needed to support the demands of today's user in terms of reliability and stability. It didn't provide all the tools that today's power-hungry Mac users need. The time had definitely come for something new.

Mac OS X is all that and more. Although it is called version ten, a more appropriate name might be Mac OS: The Next Generation. Although Mac OS X shares some interface commonality with previous versions, that is where the similarities end—at the surface. Mac OS X is a completely new operating system. From its Unix core to the desktop's Dock, Mac OS X is the future of the Mac platform—and it's a very bright future indeed.

MAC OS X BENEFITS

Listing all of Mac OS X's advantages and benefits could consume this entire chapter; however, following are some of the highlights as to why Mac OS X is a very good thing:

- **Stability and reliability**—Because the operating system has been designed using modern architectural principles, it is very stable. When an application does crash or hang, only that application is affected. The system manages its resources much more effectively than previous versions of the OS did. The result is that Mac OS X keeps working without those annoying crashes that were far too common with previous versions. Mac OS X is as stable as a rock.

■ **Speed**—The OS is optimized for maximum performance on Mac hardware. It also takes advantage of other modern Mac hardware features such as faster memory, modern data buses, and so on. All operations under Mac OS X are much faster than under previous versions; these improvements in speed have continued in version 10.3. Mac OS X flies.

■ **Beauty**—Although it might seem odd to list beauty as a benefit of an operating system, if you have seen Mac OS X before, you probably understand why I listed this. Because of the advanced graphics subsystem, the images, fonts, icons, and other graphic elements of the operating system are very pleasing to look at. The new interface design uses color and other graphic effects in a visually stunning way. Mac OS X looks very, very good.

■ **Multiple user support**—Mac OS X is designed to facilitate many people using the same machine. Unlike previous versions of the Mac OS, this support is native to the OS rather than being an add-on. Mac OS X is meant to be shared.

■ **Organization**—Mac OS X features a logical organization that is user friendly—things are where you expect them to be. Mac OS X is your digital housekeeper.

■ **Security**—Mac OS X has many security features you can employ to protect your machine and its data from other people who use it, as well as from those who share the same network as you, and even from Internet attacks through its built-in firewall. Mac OS X makes the digital life a secure life.

■ **Compatibility**—With its Classic environment, Mac OS X can use most applications that are written for earlier versions of the Mac OS. This means that from the day Mac OS X was introduced, there were thousands of Mac OS X–compatible applications. Because Mac OS X is based on Unix, it is also compatible with many Unix applications. This brings hundreds of sophisticated applications to the Mac that were previously unavailable. Mac OS X can run thousands of applications.

■ **Power**—Mac OS X is a very powerful OS. Its multiple layers provide this power in many areas, such as graphics, the Internet, and so on. Its standards-based networking architecture enables you to connect to any system, anywhere. And you have much greater, direct access to system processes than ever before. You can access this power at many levels, from the GUI to using Unix text commands. Mac OS X has all the power you need.

■ **Network-readiness**—Mac OS X provides support for all sorts of networks, from those containing all Macintosh computers to those composed of Windows PCs. Mac OS X's networking system is powerful, flexible, and relatively easy to configure. With its Rendezvous technology, Mac OS X Macs can automatically seek out and configure other Rendezvous devices with which they can communicate. From LANs to WANs, Mac OS X has been built to connect.

- **High-technology support**—Mac OS X supports many advanced technologies, including Bluetooth, that enable the OS to interact with wireless devices, such as cell phones and PDAs. The Ink system provides Mac OS X with handwriting recognition so that you can provide input with graphics tablets and other devices in all your Mac OS X applications. FireWire 800 support means you can access the fastest hard drives and other peripherals. When it comes to high-tech, Mac OS X is all you need.

- **Ease of use**—Although power and ease of use are usually conflicting terms, Mac OS X provides both. Its interface features the tools and techniques that have made the Mac OS traditionally the most intuitive and easiest-to-use operating system. You don't have to be a rocket scientist to use Mac OS X (although it is a great OS for rocket scientists, too).

- **Customizability**—It wouldn't be a Mac OS if you couldn't tweak the interface to suit your preferences. Mac OS X is fully customizable, and you can adjust and tweak it to your heart's content. After all, what good is an OS if you can't make it your own?

MAC OS X ARCHITECTURE AND TERMINOLOGY

Understanding the architecture and terminology of Mac OS X is important to be able to use it effectively.

Functionally, the Mac OS X architecture consists of several *layers* that are often shown graphically as in Figure 1.1. The base level of the operating system is its Unix core, which is called Darwin. Moving "up" through the layers, the next layer is the graphics subsystem, which consists of three parts: Quartz, OpenGL, and QuickTime. Then comes the application layer, which has four components, those being Classic, Carbon, Cocoa, and Java. Finally, the top layer is the user interface, which is called Aqua.

Figure 1.1
You can think of Mac OS X being composed of four layers; the bottom layer provides the core OS services, whereas each layer toward the top provides services that are "closer" to the user.

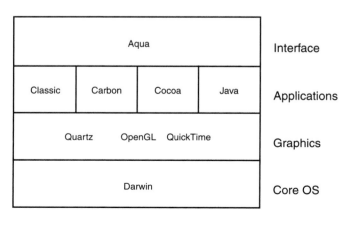

The Core OS: Darwin

Mac OS X is built on a Unix core; the Darwin core is based on the Berkeley Software Distribution (BSD) version of Unix. The heart of the Darwin core is called Mach. This part of the operating system performs the fundamental tasks, such as data flow into and from the CPU, memory use, and so on. Mach's major features include the following:

- **Protected memory**—Mach provides a separate memory area in which each application can run. It ensures that each application remains in its own memory space and so does not affect other applications. Therefore, if a running application crashes or hangs, other applications aren't affected. You can safely shut down the hung application and continue working in the others.

  In contrast, previous versions of the Mac OS did not have protected memory. When one application crashed, it usually took down others and often the OS itself, which resulted in your losing unsaved data in all the applications. Under Mac OS X, only the data in the crashing application is at risk.

- **Automatic memory management**—Mac OS X manages RAM for you; it automatically allocates RAM to applications that need it. Under Mac OS X, you don't need to think about how RAM is being used; the OS takes care of it for you (if you have ever struggled to manually allocate RAM under OS 9 and earlier, you know why not having to do this anymore is a very good thing).

- **Preemptive multitasking**—Under Mac OS X (or, more specifically, Mach), the operating system controls the processes that the processor is performing to ensure that all applications and system services have the resources they need and that the processor is used efficiently. This ensures both stability and maximum performance for both foreground and background processes.

  This is in contrast to the cooperative multitasking in previous versions of the Mac OS. Under that scheme, applications had to fight among themselves for the resources they needed. This resulted in instability when applications couldn't get the resources they needed and poor performance for those applications that were not able to "grab" the system resources they needed (this is why some processes stopped when you moved them to the background).

- **Advanced virtual memory**—The Mach core uses a virtual memory system that is always on. It manages the virtual memory use efficiently so that virtual memory is used only as necessary to ensure maximum performance.

  Under previous versions of the Mac OS, you had to control how virtual memory was used manually. Because the virtual memory system was not very efficient, you had to be careful about when you had it turned on because it would cause the performance of some applications to slow to a crawl, even if you had plenty of RAM.

NOTE

Darwin is open source. This means that the code of which Darwin is composed is freely available to anyone who wants to use it. A programmer can download the Darwin code and modify it. Thus, it is possible to provide alternative versions of the Darwin core to change and enhance Mac OS X. The Darwin code and documentation can be found at `developer.apple.com/darwin/`.

Darwin also provides the input/output services for Mac OS X and easily supports three key characteristics of modern devices: plug-and-play, hot-swapping, and power management.

Darwin, through its Virtual File System (VFS) design, supports several file systems under Mac OS X, including the following:

- **Mac OS Extended Format**—Also known as Hierarchical File System Plus (HFS+), this is the default file system under Mac OS X as it has been under the more recent versions of the Mac OS (those since Mac OS 8). This file system efficiently supports large hard drives by minimizing the smallest size used to store a single file.

NOTE

For version 10.3, Mac OS X also supports the Mac OS Extended Journaled format. This enables the OS to track changes that are made while they are being made so that the process of recovering from errors is much more reliable. You will learn more about this later.

- **Mac OS Standard Format**—Known as HFS, this was the standard for Mac OS versions prior to Mac OS 8.
- **UFS**—The standard file system for Unix systems.
- **UDF**—The Universal Disk Format, it's used for DVD volumes.
- **ISO 9660**—A standard for CD-ROMs.

Darwin supports many major network file protocols. It supports Apple File Protocol (AFP) over IP client, which is the file-sharing protocol for Macs running Mac OS 8 and Mac OS 9. Network File System (NFS) client, which is the dominant file-sharing protocol on Unix platforms, is also supported. Mac OS X also provides support for Windows-based network protocols, meaning you can interact with Windows machines as easily as you can with other Macs.

Mac OS X uses bundles; a *bundle* is a directory containing a set of files that provide services. A bundle contains executable files and all the resources associated with those executables; when they are a file package, a bundle can appear as a single file. The three types of bundles under Mac OS X are as follows:

- **Applications**—Under Mac OS X, applications are provided in bundles. Frequently, these bundles are designed as file packages so the user sees only the files with which he needs to work, such as the file to launch the application. The rest of the application resources might be hidden from the user. This makes installing such applications simple.

- **Framework**—A framework bundle is similar to an application bundle except that a framework provides services that are shared across the OS; *frameworks* are system resources. A framework contains a dynamic shared library, meaning different areas of the OS as well as applications can access the services provided by that framework. Frameworks are always available to the applications and services running in the system. For example, under Mac OS X, QuickTime is a framework; applications can access QuickTime services by accessing the QuickTime framework. Frameworks are not provided as file packages, so the user sees the individual files that make up that framework.

- **Loadable bundle**—*Loadable bundles* are executable code (just like applications) available to other applications and the system (similar to frameworks) but must be loaded into an application to provide their services. The two main types of loadable bundles are plug-ins (such as those used in Web browsers) and palettes (which are used in building application interfaces). Loadable bundles can also be presented as a package so the user sees and works with only one file.

NOTE

> Because of its Unix architecture, you will see many more filename extensions under Mac OS X than there were under previous versions of the OS. Most of the extensions for files you will deal with directly are easily understood (for example, .app is used for applications), but others the system uses are not as intuitive.

THE GRAPHICS SUBSYSTEM

Mac OS X includes an advanced graphics subsystem, which has three main components: Quartz Extreme, OpenGL, and QuickTime.

Quartz Extreme is the name of the part of the graphics subsystem that handles 2D graphics. Quartz provides the interface graphics, fonts, and other 2D elements of the system, as well as on-the-fly rendering and antialiasing of images. Under Mac OS X, the Portable Document Format (PDF) is native to the OS. This means you can create PDF versions of any document without using a third-party application, such as Adobe Acrobat (to get special features in PDF documents, such as navigation features, you still need to use an application that provides those features). You can quickly create a PDF version of any document with which you work; that document can be viewed with Acrobat Reader or Mac OS X's own Preview application. Quartz Extreme also supports TrueType, Type 1, and OpenType fonts and blends 3D and QuickTime content with the 2D content it provides directly.

NOTE

> *Antialiasing* reduces the pixelated appearance of a graphic to provide smooth edges instead of jagged ones.

Because of Quartz Extreme, you don't need to install a font-smoothing utility, such as Adobe Type Manager, to be able to view and use all sizes of PostScript fonts, as you had to do under Mac OS 9 and earlier.

NOTE

> Under version 10.3, the Preview application has been greatly improved, especially in terms of speed. The application opens and displays PDF and other documents much more quickly than it did under previous versions of Mac OS X.

The OpenGL component of the graphics subsystem provides 3D graphics support for 3D applications. OpenGL is an industry standard that is also used on Windows and Unix systems. Because of this, it is easier to create 3D applications for the Mac from those that were designed to run on those other operating systems. The Mac OS X implementation of OpenGL provides many 3D graphics functions, such as texture mapping, transparency, antialiasing, atmospheric effects, other special effects, and more.

QuickTime provides support for many types of digital media, such as digital video, and is the primary enabler of video and audio streaming under Mac OS X. QuickTime enables both viewing applications, such as the QuickTime Player, and creative applications, such as iMovie, iTunes, and many more. QuickTime is also an industry standard, and QuickTime files can be used on Windows and other computer platforms.

THE APPLICATION SUBSYSTEM

Mac OS X provides the Classic environment to enable it to run Classic applications. It also includes three application development environments: Carbon, Cocoa, and Java 2.

The Classic environment enables Mac OS X to run applications that were written for previous versions of the OS without modification. This provides access to thousands of existing applications that will run under Mac OS X. Classic applications run as they do under previous versions of the Mac OS; in other words, they do not benefit from the advanced features of Mac OS X such as protected memory (Classic applications can be affected by other Classic applications, and the Classic environment itself can be affected when a Classic application has problems).

The Carbon environment enables developers to port existing applications to use Carbon application program interfaces (APIs); the process of porting a Classic application into the Carbon environment is called *Carbonizing* it. The Carbon environment offers the benefits of Darwin for Carbonized applications, such as protected memory and preemptive

1

multitasking. Carbonizing an application is significantly less work than creating a new application from scratch, which enabled many applications to be delivered near the release of Mac OS X.

The Cocoa environment offers developers a state-of-the-art, object-oriented application development environment. Cocoa applications are designed for Mac OS X from the ground up and take the most advantage of Mac OS X services and benefits. Most of the applications included with Mac OS X are Cocoa versions; as time passes, more and more Cocoa applications will become available and will eventually be the dominant type under Mac OS X.

The Java environment enables you to run Java applications, including pure Java applications and Java applets. Java applications are widely used on the Web because they enable the same set of code to be executed on various platforms. You can also develop Java applications under Mac OS X.

THE USER INTERFACE

The Mac OS X user interface, called Aqua, provides Mac OS X's great visual experience as well as the tools you use to interact with and customize the interface to suit your preferences. From the drop shadows on open windows to the extensive use of color and texture to the extremely detailed icons, Aqua provides a user experience that is both pleasant and efficient.

MAC OS X COSTS: HARDWARE REQUIREMENTS

Mac OS X is a good thing, but as with all good things, it does come with a price. You must have a modern Mac to be able to use it. Apple states that you must have a Power Mac G5, Power Mac G4, Power Mac G3 (Blue & White), iMac, eMac, PowerBook G4, PowerBook G3 (with built-in USB), or an iBook to be able to run it. You also must have at least 128MB of RAM to run it (but I think you will have a better experience if you have at least 256MB). Also, your Mac needs to have a built-in display or one that is connected to an Apple-supplied video card. Finally, you need at least 2GB of disk space (but if you want to take advantage of Mac OS X's organization and security scheme, you should have a lot more free space than that).

→ For help moving to Mac OS X version 10.3 from previous Mac OS X versions or from Mac OS 9 or earlier, **see** Appendix A, "Installing and Maintaining Mac OS X," **p. 947**.

NOTE

Apple does not support Mac OS X running on early hardware, although you might be able to get it to run on an older machine. You might also be able to get Mac OS X to run on a machine that has an upgrade card installed in it; however, support for specific upgrade cards is a hit-or-miss proposition.

1

As with any tool as sophisticated and powerful as Mac OS X, it can take some time to learn how to use it effectively. This learning curve can also be considered one of Mac OS X's costs. This cost is one that this book can lower for you. As you read through the rest of this book, you will quickly become comfortable with all aspects of Mac OS X. And as you explore more of the OS, you can always come back to specific parts of the book to guide you on your way.

CHAPTER 2

GETTING STARTED WITH MAC OS X

In this chapter

WELCOME TO MAC OS X

After reading Chapter 1, "Mac OS X: Foundations," you understand a bit about Mac OS X, such as its features, architecture, and so on. Now it's time to start using it! The functions you'll explore in this chapter are fundamental to your use of Mac OS X.

If you have not yet installed Mac OS X, before you go any further in this chapter, read Appendix A, "Installing and Maintaining Mac OS X," to get help installing the OS and setting up an administrator user account. When you have worked through the tasks in that appendix, come back here.

If you have already installed Mac OS X, you have probably already started using it; you have created at least one user account because that is part of installing the OS. This chapter will help you get a better understanding of user accounts and learn how to customize the startup process.

STARTING UP MAC OS X

As you learned in Chapter 1, Mac OS X is truly a multiuser operating system. This offers many benefits to you, but it also means that when you use the OS, you have to log in as a particular user. When you do so, what you can see and do depends on the settings for the account you use to log in to the system.

NOTE

When you first start up Mac OS X after installing it, it uses the automatic login mode because only one user account is created for it. This means you are logged in to the administrator account automatically and so you might not even realize that you have logged in. After your Mac starts up, the desktop appears as it has under previous versions of the OS. However, the machine has gone through the login process—it just entered all the required information for you automatically.

Each user account can have its own set of preferences and system resources tailored to that user. Many preferences are stored individually for each user account, so that aspect of the OS is unique to each user. A simple example is the desktop picture, which can be different for each user account. Other customizable aspects of the desktop, such as the Dock, are also specific to user accounts. Many applications also store preferences specific to each user account.

TIP

To disable automatic login without creating additional user accounts, open the System Preferences utility, select the Accounts icon, click the Login Options button, and uncheck the "Log in automatically as" check box.

User accounts also provide system security and control which parts of the machine a particular user can access.

One of the most important aspects of a user account is its Home folder or directory.

Directory Versus Folder

Under Mac OS X, the terms *directory* and *folder* are basically synonymous. Typically, non-GUI operating systems use the term *directory*, whereas GUI operating systems use the term *folder*. Because Mac OS X has Unix as its foundation and the term *directory* is used under Unix, you will see folders referred to as *directories* in many places. The reason for this is that you can access the Unix command line; when you access your Mac's files using the command line, the concept of folder doesn't really apply (because there is no graphical element to the user interface). Practically speaking, however, the terms are equivalent and are interchangeable. You will see that I use both throughout this book.

UNDERSTANDING THE HOME FOLDER

Each user account on your Mac has a Home folder. This folder contains folders that are used to store private files, public files, and system resources (such as preferences and keychains) for that user account. With two exceptions (the Public and Site folders), only someone logged in under a user account can access the folders in that user account's Home folder.

NOTE

> The exception to the general rule about accessing the folders in another user's Home folder is the *root* account. The root user account can access everything on your Mac and is outside the normal security provided by user accounts. You should use the root account only in special situations, and you really need to understand it before you use it.

→ To learn about the root account, **see** "Logging In As Root," **p. 236**.
→ To learn more about Mac OS X directories, **see** "Understanding Mac OS X Directories," **p. 101**.

A user's Home folder contains the folders shown in Figure 2.1.

Most of these folders are easy to understand. For example, the Documents folder is the default location in which the user stores documents he creates. The Desktop folder contains items that are stored on that user's desktop (which, by the way, means that each user account has a unique desktop), and so on.

TIP

> You can quickly tell which user account is active by looking at the Home directory icon in the Finder window's Places sidebar, which is always located at the left side of Finder windows. It looks like a house for the current user's Home folder; the other Home directory icons are plain folders. The short name for a user account appears in the title bar of that user's Home folder (see Figure 2.1).

2

Figure 2.1
Every user account on your Mac has a Home folder; this folder contains folders that only that user can access (except for the Public and Sites folders).

Only someone logged in as the user can access the contents of these folders—except for the Public and Sites folders that can be accessed by anyone using your Mac. Locked folders have an icon that includes a red circle with a minus sign (see Figure 2.2); this means that the folder is locked and you can't open it to view its contents. If another user attempts to open one of these protected folders, a warning message is displayed. Unlocked folders in another user's directory have the plain folder icon, which means their contents are accessible. Unlocked folders in the current user's Home directory have the decorative Mac OS X icons (refer to Figure 2.1).

Locked folders

Figure 2.2
When you view another user's Home directory, the protected folders are marked with the minus icon to indicate that their contents are inaccessible.

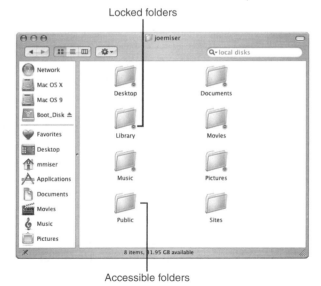

Accessible folders

The Public folder is accessible by users logged in under any account. Its purpose is to enable users to share documents and other resources. The items to be shared can be stored in this folder and other users can open the folder to get to them. The Public folder contains a Drop Box folder. This folder can be seen by other users and they can place files in it, but it can't be opened by anyone except the owner of the user account under which that drop box is stored.

The Sites folder contains files for that user's Web site.

→ To learn how to create and serve a Web site from the Sites folder, **see** "Using Mac OS X to Serve Web Pages," **p. 446**.

The Library folder is the only one in the Home directory that is not intended for document storage. It contains items related to the configuration of the user account and all the system-related files for that user account. For example, user preferences are stored here, as are font collections, addresses, keychains, and so on. Basically, any file that affects how the system works or looks that is specific to a user account is stored in the Library directory. You will learn more about the Library folder elsewhere in this book.

UNDERSTANDING THE ADMINISTRATOR ACCOUNT

When you installed Mac OS X, you created the first user account. The account you created was actually an administrator account. Administrator accounts are special because they provide wide access to the system and are one of only two accounts that can control virtually every aspect of Mac OS X (the other being the root account). A user who logs in as an administrator for your Mac can do the following:

- **Create other user accounts**—An administrator for your Mac can create additional user accounts. By default, these user accounts have more limited access to the Mac than does an administrator account, but you can allow other accounts to administer the Mac as well (in effect creating multiple administrator accounts).

- **Change global system preferences**—The administrator can change global system settings for your Mac; other user accounts can't. For example, to change the network settings on your Mac, you must be logged in as the administrator (or you must authenticate yourself as an administrator).

- **Configure access to files and folders**—An administrator can configure the security settings of files and folders to determine who can access those items and which type of access is permitted.

- **Install applications**—Applications you install under Mac OS X require that you be logged in as an administrator or that you authenticate yourself as one.

When you attempt to perform an action that requires an administrator, such as those in the previous list, you will see an Authentication dialog box. To authenticate yourself, you enter a valid administrator account username and password and click OK (if you are currently logged in as an administrator, the username is filled in automatically). This enables you to perform that action.

In areas where you need to be authenticated to perform an action, you will see the Lock icon. When the Lock is "open," you are authenticated; when the Lock is "closed," you can click it to open the Authentication dialog box.

You should control who has access to the administrator accounts for your machine. If someone who doesn't understand Mac OS X—or who wants to cause you trouble—logs in with your administrator account, you might be in for all kinds of problems. You also need to ensure either that you can remember the username and password for an administrator account you set up or that you write them down. If you forget this vital information, you could have trouble later.

NOTE

Administrator accounts are a fundamentally different concept for many Mac users. Traditionally, all areas of the operating system (such as control panels) were easily accessed by anyone who used the Mac. Unless you have used the Multiple Users feature of Mac OS 9, this is likely to be your experience. Although you can use the automatic login mode so that you don't have to log in to your Mac, the fact remains that Mac OS X is a multiuser system. To get the most out of it, you need to get comfortable with user accounts because whether you have to log in or not, you will always use user accounts under Mac OS X (unlike under previous versions of the OS in which user accounts were optional).

CREATING USER ACCOUNTS

If you share your Mac with other people, you should create a user account for each person who will be using your machine. In addition to protecting your Mac from tampering, user accounts provide specific folders for the other users in which they can store information (such as application preferences) and documents and other files that are specific to them.

You can also customize the environment of each user account in several ways; for example, you can have a different set of applications start up for each user account and each user can have her own Dock and desktop configuration.

Rather than creating a single user account for each person, you can create a user account that several people share. This can be useful if there are people who use your Mac but don't necessarily need private directories. For example, if you share your Mac with children, you might want to create a single user account for them to use.

TIP

You should create at least two administrator accounts on your Mac. Use one for your normal activities, such as configuring the machine, working with applications, and so on. Save the other for use during troubleshooting. Sometimes, preferences associated with specific user accounts can become corrupted and other problems related to a specific user account can develop. As part of the troubleshooting process, you can log in under the "clean" administrator account to recover from problems and troubleshoot and solve them. This step often tells you whether a problem is related to a specific user account or your Mac OS X installation, applications, or hardware.

NOTE

The System Preferences utility is somewhat analogous to the control panels in previous versions of the Mac OS. It enables you to make changes to various system settings. You will be using it throughout this book.

You use the System Preferences utility to create additional user accounts for your Mac with the following steps:

1. Open the System Preferences utility by clicking its icon on the Dock or by selecting Apple menu, System Preferences. The System Preferences utility window has two panes; the upper pane is the toolbar on which you can store icons you access frequently. The lower pane shows the areas of the OS for which you can set system preferences (those being Personal, Hardware, Internet & Network, and System). Within each section are the icons for each area of the OS that you can configure. When you click an icon, the lower pane is replaced by the controls for the area to which the icon is related.

2. Click the Accounts icon in the System area to open the Accounts pane of the System Preferences utility (see Figure 2.3). Along the left side of this pane is the list of user accounts on the Mac. At the top, the user account under which you are currently logged in is shown. Under the Other Accounts heading are the other user accounts that exist on the machine. Under each username, you will see the type of account it is, such as Admin, Standard, Simplified, and so on. At the bottom of the user list is the Login Options button, and just below that are the Add User (+) and Delete User buttons (-). The right part of the pane shows the tools you use to configure a user account.

Figure 2.3
You can create user accounts with the Accounts pane of the System Preferences utility; in this figure, you can see that several accounts have been created on this machine, with two being administrator accounts.

NOTE

Notice in Figure 2.3 that the lock icon in the lower-left corner of the window is open indicating that I am currently authenticated as an administrator for this machine.

3. Click the New User button, which is the plus sign located under the list of users. A new, empty user is added to the list; the tools in the right part of the pane are empty because you haven't configured them yet (see Figure 2.4).

Figure 2.4
When you create a new user account, you use the fields and tools in the right part of the Accounts pane.

Only an administrator can create new user accounts. If you aren't logged in as an administrator for your Mac, you have to authenticate yourself as being an administrator before you can create an account. To do so, click the Lock icon located in the lower-left corner of the window, enter the username and password for an administrator account, and click OK. This identifies you as an administrator temporarily so that you can make your changes.

4. Enter the Name for the user account. The name is the "full" name for the user account; it doesn't have to be a real full name—that is, one name the user can use to log in to this user account. The name can be pretty much whatever you want it to be.

5. Press Tab to move to the Short Name box. When you do, Mac OS X creates a short name for the user account. The short name is a name used for specific areas under that user account (such as the name of the user's Home folder) and for access to services provided under that account (such as the account's FTP site). The short name can be used instead of the name to cut down on the number of characters you have to type in specific situations, such as when you log in to the account (in which case the short name and name are interchangeable). However, the Home directory is always identified by the short name only.

Mac OS X automatically creates a short name for the account; it just places all the letters in the name together with no spaces. You can choose to use this one, or you can change it to something else.

The short name is used in several places, such as in the Web site address for the user account. Because of this, you should choose a meaningful short name, preferably some variation of the person's name, such as his first initial and last name.

6. Edit the short name as needed, such as by replacing it if you don't like the one Mac OS X created for you automatically.

NOTE

> Because of how they're used, short names can't include spaces. If you want to add a space to a short name, you need to use an underscore instead.

The short name can be as few as one character and can't contain any spaces, dashes, or other special characters (Mac OS X won't let you enter any characters that are unacceptable). Underscores are acceptable. You should adopt a general rule about the short name for an account, such as using the first initial of the first name and the complete last name. Keeping the short name consistent will help you deal with other user accounts more easily.

After it's created, you can't change the short name for a user account, so be deliberate when you create it.

TIP

> You can use a user account for any purpose you want. For example, because each user account has its own Web site, you might want to create a user account simply to create another Web site on your machine. For example, you might want to create a user called "Group Site" to serve a Web page to a workgroup of which you are a member.

7. Enter the password for the user account. A password is what you expect—it must be used to access the user account. For better security, use a password that is eight characters long and contains both letters and numbers (this makes the password harder to crack). Passwords are case sensitive; for example, mypassword is not the same as MyPassword.

If you leave the Password field empty, a password will not be required to log in to the account. When you choose to do this, you will see a warning dialog box when you attempt to save the account. If you ignore this warning, the account is created without a password. When the user logs in to the account, he can select it and log in without entering a password. Obviously, this is not a secure thing to do, but it can be useful nonetheless. For example, you might choose to create an account for children whom you don't want to have to use a password. When you create such "unprotected" accounts, you should use the Limitations tools to limit access to your Mac, such as by using the Simple Finder option.

TIP

> You can remove a password from an existing account even though the system tells you this can't be done. Just remove the password, save the account changes, click Ignore in the warning dialog box, and then click OK in the dialog box that tells you this change won't be accepted. It is actually accepted and the account no longer requires a password.

➜ To learn how to configure an account's capabilities, **see** "Testing and Configuring User Accounts," **p. 39**.

8. Press Tab and retype the password in the Verify box.

9. Press Tab and enter a hint to remind the user what the password is. This reminder is optional; if a user fails to log in successfully after three attempts, this hint can appear to help him remember him password.

10. Click the Picture tab. This enables you to associate an image with the user account. This image appears in the login box and is the default image associated with a user's address card in his Address Book application.

11. Select a login picture for the account.

   To choose one of the default images included with Mac OS X, click the Apple Pictures collection. The images it contains appear in the right pane of the window. To select an image, click it.

TIP

> When you are working with the current user's account and that user has an image in his Address Book card, the image from the Address Book card is used for the login image.

➜ To learn about the Address Book, **see** "Setting Up and Using an Address Book," **p. 330**.

If you want to use another image for the account, click the Edit button. The Images dialog box appears (see Figure 2.5). Drag an image onto the image well in the center of the box. Click Choose and move to and select an image, or click Take Video Snapshot to capture an image from a video camera (such as an iSight camera) attached to your Mac. When the image is shown in the image well, use the slider to crop the image to the part you want to use. Then click Set. The image is shown in the image well on the Picture tab and is used for that user account.

The image you use as the login picture can be a JPEG or TIFF. However, you can't use a GIF as a login picture.

Figure 2.5
You can use the Images dialog box to select an image for a user account.

TIP

If you have worked with other images recently, click the Recent Pictures pop-up menu at the top of the Images dialog box and select the image you want to use.

The default login pictures (those shown on the scrolling list) are stored in the directory `Mac OS X`/Library/User Pictures, where `Mac OS X` is the name of your Mac OS X startup volume. You can install additional images in this directory to make them available as part of the Apple Pictures collection.

12. Click the Security tab (see Figure 2.6).

Figure 2.6
You use the Security tab to make a user an administrator and configure the FileVault feature.

→ FileVault encrypts all of a user's files for security purposes. To learn how to use FileVault, **see** "Securing Your Mac with FileVault," **p. 897**.

13. If you want this account to be an administrator account, check the "Allow user to administer this computer" check box. If you make the account an administrator account, skip to step 14.

14. Click the Limitations tab (see Figure 2.7). You use this tab to set limits on the user account. (When working with an administrator account, this tab is grayed out because an administrator has no limitations.)

Figure 2.7
You can use the Limitations tab to define exactly which areas of the system a user will be able to access.

There are three tabs on this screen. Each implies a set of permissions for the user account you are configuring:

- **No Limits**—If you click this tab, the user has no limits except those actions that are reserved for an administrator account, such as changing certain system preferences, installing applications, and so on. If you select this option, you don't do any further configuration.

- **Some Limits**—This tab, shown in Figure 2.7, presents controls you can use to limit a user to certain actions, including opening (not changing!) all system preferences, modifying the Dock, changing a password, and burning CDs and DVDs. If the check boxes for those actions are checked, the user can perform those actions; if they are not checked, the user is prevented from performing those actions.

  The lower part of the window enables you to select specific applications to which the user has access. To do this, check the "This user can only use these applications" check box. The controls in the bottom part of the window become active. To allow all the applications stored in a specific area, such as in the Applications folder, check the box for that area. To limit a user to specific applications within an area, click the area's Expansion triangle, which causes a list of the applications in that area to be shown. Check the box next to each application you want the user to be able to use; uncheck the box for those applications you don't want the user to be able to use.

TIP

> Use the Allow All button to allow the user to use all applications. Use the Uncheck All button to uncheck all the boxes shown in the window. Use the Locate button to locate and select applications outside of those shown in the areas listed in the window.

- **Simple Finder**—This provides the most basic level of access. As you might expect from its name, the Simple Finder provides a less complex interface for a user and greatly restricts what that user can do. When a user is logged in with the Simple Finder, the Dock contains only five icons: Finder, My Applications, Documents, Shared, and Trash. These are the only areas the user can access. For example, under the Simple Finder, a user can store documents only in his Documents folder and can't open other folders. The only Finder commands the user can access are Sleep, Log Out, About Finder, the Hide/Show Finder commands, and Close Window. The Simple Finder makes your machine more secure because it limits the actions of a user so severely. Using the Simple Finder can be a good choice if the user for whom you are creating an account has minimal computer skills, such as for very young children or someone who is totally new to the Mac.

When you select this option, you will see the same application configuration tools that appear on the Some Limits tab. They work in the same way, too. Along with being limited to specific applications, when a user has the Simple Finder limitation, he has a simplified Dock, Apple menu, and other options.

NOTE

> If you have not turned off the Automatic Login mode and you create a new user account, you will see a dialog box asking whether you want that mode to be turned off. The account that is logged in automatically is also shown in this dialog box. (If you have disabled the Automatic Login mode already, you won't see this dialog box.)

Following are a few more points about setting a user account's capabilities:

- Some settings are dependent on others. For example, if you uncheck the "Open all System Preferences" check box, the "Change password" check box becomes disabled. This is because, if the user can't access the System Preferences utility, she won't be able to access the Accounts pane that contains the tools needed to change the password.

- You can use the Check All or Uncheck All button to select or deselect all applications at the same time.

- The Locate button enables you to select applications that don't appear on the list of applications by default. When you click this button, an Open dialog box appears. You can use this dialog box to move to and select an application.

- The last entry on the list of application folders is Others. If your machine can access applications that aren't stored in one of the standard Mac OS X application folders, they appear under the Others category.

> **TIP**
>
> Under Mac OS X, the default button in a dialog box is indicated by the pulsing (also called *throbbing*) action. As under previous versions of the Mac OS, you can activate the default button by pressing the Return or Enter key (as with the OK button in the authentication dialog box).

LOGGING IN, LOGGING OUT, RESTARTING, AND SHUTTING DOWN MAC OS X

As you learned earlier, you must log in to be able to use a Mac OS X–powered Mac. To log in, you simply select or enter the name of the user account, enter the password, and press Return. You then move to the desktop for that user account.

Under older versions of the Mac OS, when you were done working with the computer and wanted to "turn it off," you shut it down using the Shut Down command. Under Mac OS X, you can still do this, but most of the time you will log out instead. When you log out, all the processes currently running are stopped and the user account is "closed." To log out of the current user account, select the Apple menu, and then select Log Out (or press Shift-⌘-Q). In the resulting confirmation dialog box, press Return or click Log Out (if you don't do this within 2 minutes, the system logs you out automatically). The processes that are currently running are stopped (you are first prompted to save any open documents that have unsaved changes), and you return to the Login dialog box.

If you have enabled fast user switching, you can also select the Login Window command on the User Switching menu to protect access to your account while keeping it logged in.

> **TIP**
>
> Logging out and then logging back in is a lot faster than stopping and starting your machine. In fact, there aren't many reasons to shut down your machine, and if you use it to serve Web pages, you shouldn't shut it down. To secure your Mac when you aren't using it, just log out.

RESTARTING YOUR MAC

Although Mac OS X is much more stable than previous versions, there might be occasions when you need to restart your Mac to correct some problem that is occurring. Also, occasionally, you will need to restart your Mac after making system changes or installing new software.

Restarting Mac OS X is similar to restarting previous versions of the OS, except that after the restart, you return to the Login dialog box rather than the desktop (unless you have set the Automatic Login mode to be active, in which case you do return to the desktop). You can restart Mac OS X in a couple of ways:

- Click Restart in the Login window.
- Select the Apple menu and select Restart.

NOTE

> Some Mac-compatible keyboards (not produced by Apple) and some older Apple keyboards have a Power key, which you can use to start the machine when it is off or to bring up a dialog box that enables you to shut down, restart, or put your Mac to sleep. Newer Apple keyboards don't have this key, and some Macs running Mac OS X don't support it even if the keyboard has the Power key. If your keyboard has the Power key, press it and see whether anything happens. If the dialog box appears, you can use its controls to shut down, restart, or put your Mac to sleep. If nothing happens, you know that you never need to press the Power key again.

SHUTTING DOWN YOUR MAC

Because today's machines use very little energy, there isn't really much reason to shut them off. Most of the time, when you are done working with your computer, you should simply log out. This stops all the processes that are running and puts your Mac in a safe condition. Logging in is much faster because you don't have to wait for your computer to start up.

Still, if you are leaving your Mac for a long time, you might want to shut it down. You can do so in the following ways:

- Select the Apple menu and then select Shut Down.
- Press Shift-⌘-Q to log out, confirm the logout, and then click Shut Down in the Login window.

NOTE

> To turn on most modern Macs, you need to press the Power key located on the CPU.
>
> If you use an Apple Studio or Cinema Display, you can also turn on the Mac by pressing the Power button located on the display. If you press the Power button on the display while your Mac is on, it goes to sleep. If you press and hold down the Power button for a few seconds, your Mac is powered off without going through the shutdown process (use this only when the machine is totally locked up).
>
> Also, with certain Apple displays, you will see the Options tab on the Displays pane of the System Preferences utility. You can use this tab to configure what happens when you press the Power button on these displays. Your options are to have it control the display's power only or to control the computer's power too. This tab isn't available for newer Apple displays.

NOTE

> You can perform a hard shutdown by pressing the Power key and holding it down until the Mac turns off. You won't have a chance to save any open files so you should use this method only when all other options have failed.

CONFIGURING THE LOGIN PROCESS

You can configure the Login window and process in several ways:

- Control how user accounts appear in the window.
- Enable/disable the Automatic Login mode.
- Show/hide the Sleep, Restart, and Shut Down buttons.
- Enable fast user switching.

CONTROLLING HOW USER ACCOUNTS APPEAR IN THE LOGIN WINDOW

You can configure several aspects of how user accounts appear in the Login window:

1. Log in under an administrator account and open the Accounts pane of the System Preferences utility.
2. Click the Login Options button (see Figure 2.8). On the right side of the window, you will see the Login Options tools.

Figure 2.8
The Login Options tab enables you to configure the Login window.

3. To display empty Name and Password fields in the Login window instead of a list of the user accounts you have configured, click the "Name and password" radio button.

When this button is selected, you have to type the name or the short name and password for an account to log in to it. To display the list of user accounts, click the "List of users" radio button instead. With this option, each account (and its image) appears onscreen. To log in, the user clicks her account, enters her password, and clicks the Login button.

4. Quit the System Preferences utility. The next time the Login window appears, it will reflect the changes you made.

ENABLING AUTOMATIC LOGIN

When you started Mac OS X for the first time, you were in the Automatic Login mode. In this mode, you don't have to enter login information; Mac OS X does it for you. This means that you don't have to enter a username and password each time you start or restart your machine; by default, the first user account (created during the Mac OS X installation process) is used.

CAUTION

You should enable Automatic Login mode only if you are the only person who uses your Mac. If you enable Automatic Login mode with the administrator account, you provide access to many of your system's resources, which is an unsecure way to operate. However, if you have a Mac in a secure location and are the only person who uses it, the Automatic Login mode eliminates the need to log in every time you start or restart the machine.

TIP

If you are going to enable Automatic Login mode, create a nonadministrator account to use. That way, even if someone does get access to your Mac, he won't be able to use the administrator account. Of course, you might have to log out and then log back in as the administrator, but this strategy provides a good compromise between security and convenience.

To configure the Automatic Login mode, use the following steps:

1. Open the Accounts pane of the System Preferences utility.
2. Click the Login Options button.
3. To enable automatic login mode, check the "Automatically log in as" check box and select the user account that should automatically be logged in on the pop-up menu. The password prompt sheet appears, and the user account you selected on the pop-up menu is selected in the sheet.
4. Enter the password for the account that you want to be automatically logged in when the Mac starts up.
5. Click OK.

The next time you start or restart your Mac, the account you specified is automatically logged in and you move directly to the desktop for that account.

This setting affects only the start or restart sequence. When you log out instead of shutting down or restarting, you still see the Login window again and have to log in to resume using the Mac.

To disable automatic login, uncheck the "Automatically log in as" check box.

HIDING THE SLEEP, RESTART, AND SHUT DOWN BUTTONS

If you enable Automatic Login mode, you might run into trouble if you leave the Restart and Shut Down buttons enabled. Here's how that could happen. Say you are using your Mac and decide that you want to take a break for a while, but there are people in your area whom you don't want to be able to use the machine while you step away. You log out, and your machine is protected, right? Not necessarily. If the Restart and Shut Down buttons are enabled, someone can restart the Mac from the Login window and then it would start up in the automatic account, giving the person access to the machine. Disabling these buttons prevents someone from using them to access an account that is automatically logged into.

The previous scenario might make you pause to ask a question before you enable Automatic Login mode. If you do disable the Restart and Shut Down buttons and then log out, can someone simply press the hardware Restart or Reset button on the CPU to start up the Mac to automatically log in to the automatic login account? This would bypass the protection offered by disabling the buttons, right? Nope; when the Mac is not shut down properly (by using the Shut Down command), the automatic login feature is disabled when the machine is started or restarted the next time. So, if you have to use one of those buttons, you must log in the next time you start or restart the machine.

To disable the Sleep, Restart, and Shut Down buttons, do the following:

1. Open the System Preferences utility and then the Accounts pane, and then click the Login Options button.
2. Check the "Hide the Sleep, Restart, and Shut Down buttons" check box.
3. Quit the System Preferences utility.

When the Login window appears, these buttons are hidden and the only way to use the Mac is to log in under a valid account.

ENABLING AND USING FAST USER SWITCHING

 When a user logs out of his account, all documents are closed and all applications and processes are quit. When a user logs in again, any of these must be restarted to get back to where the user was when he logged out. Prior to Mac OS X version 10.3, this process had to be suffered every time users changed. Under Mac OS X 10.3, you can take advantage of *fast user switching*. What this means is that you can log in to another user account without logging out of the accounts that are currently logged in. This is very nice because you can leave applications and documents open in an account and log out to prevent someone from using those items. And, another user can log in and work with his account. When he is done, you can log back in to your account and everything will be as it was when you left it. This saves a lot of time and hassle reopening items, and processes you are running can continue to run while another user is logged in to the machine.

To enable this feature, do the following steps:

1. Open the Accounts pane of the System Preferences application and click the Login Options button.

2. Check the "Enable fast user switching" check box. A new menu appears in the upper-right corner of the screen, and the account name under which you are currently logged in appears as the menu name.

3. Quit the System Preferences application.

Logging in and out of accounts can be done with the User Switching menu (see Figure 2.9).

Figure 2.9
This menu enables you to log in to other accounts without logging out of the current one.

To log in under another account, select it on the menu. You will see the Login window with the account you selected (see Figure 2.10). Enter the password for the account and click the Log In button. After a cool, 3D spinning effect, that user is logged in and his desktop appears.

Figure 2.10
I wonder if he has to log in when he enters the bridge?

NOTE

Sadly, not all hadware can handle the spinning 3-D effect. If you use an older Mac, you might not get to enjoy this cool effect.

TIP

If you create a user account without a password and enable the Fast User Swtiching feature, you can log in to the account without a password immediately by choosing it on the user list. You bypass the login window altogether.

To temporarily block access to the current user account without logging out, open the User Switching menu and select Login Window. The Standard Login window appears. You can leave the machine without worries that someone will be able to access your account. When you are ready to log in—or when anyone else is, for that matter—select the user account, enter a password, and click Login (you get to see the cool 3D spin again, too).

NOTE

On the User Switching menu and in the Login window, users who are currently logged in have a check mark next to them.

If another user account is logged in and you attempt to restart or shut down the machine, a warning dialog box appears that explains that other users are logged in and the action you are taking could cause them to lose data. If you enter an administrator username and password and click Shut Down or Restart, the other users are logged out and the action you want is performed.

TESTING AND CONFIGURING USER ACCOUNTS

After you have created user accounts, you should log in under those accounts to test and configure them (some configuration can be done only while logged in under an account).

TESTING USER ACCOUNTS

After you create a new user account, you should test it by logging in under that account to make sure it works:

1. Select the Apple menu and select Log Out (or press Shift-⌘-Q).

> **TIP**
>
> If you have enabled fast user switching, you can use the User Switching menu instead.

2. When the logout confirmation dialog box appears, press Return (or click the Log Out button). You return to the Mac OS X login window. At the top of the Login window, you see the computer name. In the center part of the window, you see the login picture and name of each user account on the machine. If several user accounts appear, this will be a scrolling pane. At the bottom of the window are the Sleep, Restart, and Shut Down buttons (unless they are hidden).

> **NOTE**
>
> The system automatically logs you out 2 minutes after you select the Log Out command, even if you don't click the Log Out button.

3. If the window shows the user accounts on the machine, click the User account under which you want to log in. The dialog box contracts and you see the selected user account and an empty Password box. If the User Name and Password fields appear instead, enter the username (name or short name) for the account you want to log in to.

> **NOTE**
>
> If the user account does not have a password, you are logged in as soon as you select that account's icon.

You can return to the full login window by clicking the Back button.

4. Enter the password for the user account and click Log In (or press Return or Enter).

   If the user account information is not valid, the login dialog box "shudders" to indicate that the information you entered is invalid (remember that this information is case sensitive). After three unsuccessful attempts, the password hint appears if one has been entered for the user account.

2

When you enter correct information for the user account, the login process is completed and you see the desktop for that user account, which might look quite different from the administrator's desktop (see Figure 2.11).

Figure 2.11
Now you know why Apple calls it Simple Finder.

5. After you have logged in to the new account, you can make any changes to the configuration of the user account that you want; for example, create a startup configuration by adding items to the Login Items pane or customize the Dock.

→ To learn about customizing the Dock, **see** Chapter 5, "Using and Customizing the Dock," **p. 127**.

6. Make sure that the security of the account is correct. For example, if you meant to block access to some applications, check to ensure that you can't access those applications.

7. From the desktop, press Shift-⌘-Q and then press Return to log out of the account.

 If you are unable to log in to a user account you have created, see "I Can't Log In on a User Account" in the "Troubleshooting" section at the end of this chapter.

SETTING UP STARTUP PROCESSES

To make your Mac even more efficient, you can have applications automatically start or documents open when a user logs in to an account. And you can have a different set of applications start up for each user account; this lets you customize each user's startup experience.

NOTE

> This feature is similar to the Startup Items folder in Mac OS 9 and earlier versions.

To configure the startup items for a user account, perform the following steps:

1. Log in to the account for which you want to set the login items (because this is a personal system utility area, you don't have to be logged in as an administrator to configure login items as you do to create user accounts or configure the Login window).

2. Open the System Preferences utility.

3. Click the Accounts tab and then click the Startup Items tab. The Startup Items pane appears (see Figure 2.12). You place any items you want to open in the list window to have them opened when the current user account logs in. The order in which they are listed in the window determines the order in which they open (the topmost item opens first).

Figure 2.12
When you add applications or documents to the Startup Items list, they automatically open when you log in.

4. Click the Add button, which is the plus sign (+) at the bottom of the pane.

5. Use the Add sheet to move to the item you want to be opened at login, select it, and click Add. When the Open dialog box appears, the Applications directory is selected automatically and you can select the applications that are installed there. If you want to add documents to the login items window, use the Add sheet to move to the files you want to be opened, select them, and click Add.

→ To learn more about Mac OS X directories, **see** "Understanding Mac OS X Directories," **p. 101**.

→ To learn more about working with the Open dialog box, **see** "Opening Documents in Mac OS X," **p. 166**.

TIP

> You can also drag application or document icons directly onto the Startup Items window instead of using the Add button.

When you place an item in the window (by using the Add button or dragging it there), an alias to that item is created.

6. If you want the item to be automatically hidden when it is opened, check the Hide check box. This is useful for applications that you don't need to see right away but still want to open. For example, you might want to open your email application but leave it hidden until you receive new email.

7. When you have all the items in the window, drag them up to make them open earlier in the process or down to have them open later in the sequence.

NOTE

> Some applications might rely on others to function. In that case, you want the dependent application to open after the application on which it depends, so it should be lower on the list.

8. To remove an application or document from the list (so that it doesn't open on startup), select it and click the Remove button, which is the minus sign (–) at the bottom of the pane. This doesn't affect the item at all—it only removes it from the Startup Items list.

9. Continue adding, removing, and rearranging items until all your startup items are listed in the window in the order in which you want them to open.

10. When you are done, quit System Preferences.

The next time you log on, the login items will open automatically, in the order you specified.

TIP

> Login items are a great way to customize your Mac for other users. Simply log in to the other accounts and create a different set of login items for those users.

Editing User Accounts

You can make changes to an existing user account. To do so, use the following steps:

1. Open the Accounts pane of the System Preferences utility.

2. Select the user account you want to edit. That user's information appears in the right part of the window.

NOTE

> When the current user is editing his own account, the Address Book Card Edit button appears. If the user clicks this button, he moves to his card in the Address Book and it is ready to edit.

→ To learn about the Address Book, **see** "Setting Up and Using an Address Book," **p. 330**.

3. Make changes to the user's information (such as changing the login picture or password) as needed. If you aren't logged in as an administrator, you can change only a few items, such as the picture and startup items.

TIP

> Remember that, even if you aren't logged in under an administrator account, you can authenticate yourself as an administrator so that all the account editing tools become available to you. To do this, click the closed lock icon in the lower-left corner of the pane, enter an administrator username and password, and click OK. The lock icon opens and you can do all the actions that are allowed while logged in as an administrator.

NOTE

> Because it is used as the Home directory name for the account as well as for other items (such as in the Web site address for the user account), you can't make any changes to the short name. Once created, the short name can never be changed.

4. Use the controls on each tab to make changes to the account. These work just like they do when you create a user account.

→ To learn how to create a user account, **see** "Creating User Accounts," **p. 24**.

NOTE

> Even if you are logged in as an administrator and are changing your own name, password, or password hint, you have to confirm your password by entering it at the prompt before you can make those changes.
>
> If the current user account has permission to change the password, it can be changed by selecting the current password and trying to change it. When this is done, a sheet prompts the user for the current password. If the user enters the current password successfully, the Name, Password, Verify, and Password Hint fields become editable and the user can change the data in these fields as needed (the short name still can't be changed).

5. Test the account to make sure it works with the changes you have made.

You don't have to quit the System Preferences utility to save the changes you make. They are saved as you make them. Sometimes, you have to apply changes you make by clicking the Apply button.

 If you are unable to use the buttons in the Accounts pane of the System Preferences utility, see "The Buttons in the Accounts Pane Are Inactive" in the "Troubleshooting" section at the end of this chapter.

NOTE

After you have entered a password, you won't be able to see it, even when you edit the user account. The only way to recover from someone forgetting his password is to reset it to a new one by editing the user account.

NOTE

After you have tested and verified users accounts, provide the names and passwords for the user accounts you created to the people who need them. You should explain the limitations of the accounts to the users as well.

DELETING USER ACCOUNTS

You can also delete user accounts that you no longer need by doing the following:

1. Open the Accounts pane of the System Preferences utility.
2. Select the account you want to delete.
3. Click the Delete User button, which is the minus sign at the bottom of the user list. You will see the delete user confirmation dialog box. When you delete a user, you have two options for the contents of that user's Home folder: You can choose to save the user's Home folder so the files it contains can be accessed, or you can choose to delete the folder immediately. If you choose to save the user's Home folder, the deleted user account's Home directory is moved to the Deleted Users folder. Within this folder, you will see a disk image for the deleted user's Home folder. You can open this disk image to work with its contents.
4. If you want to delete the user's Home folder immediately, click the Delete Immediately button. If you want to preserve the user's Home folder, click OK.

The user account you deleted is no longer available in the Login window and can no longer be used.

If you elected to preserve the user's Home folder, the Home directory for that account is converted into a disk image file that is stored in the location `Mac OS X/Users/Deleted Users`, where `Mac OS X` is the name of your Mac OS X volume (see Figure 2.13).

Figure 2.13
Joe's account might be gone, but his Home folder has not been forgotten.

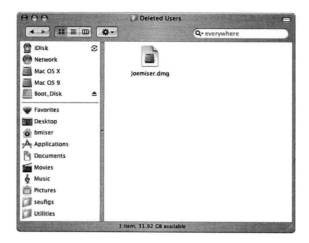

The name of the disk image is *shortusername*.dmg, where *shortusername* is the short user-name of the account that was deleted. To access the files that were in the account's Home directory, open its disk image file. The Home directory for that account will then be a mounted volume on your machine, which you can use just like another volume you mount.

The Deleted Users folder is accessible only to those accounts that have administrative privileges on your Mac. If you want other users to be able to access files that were in the deleted account's Home directory, you must change the permissions associated with the disk image.

→ To learn how to configure permissions, **see** "Securing Your Mac with Privileges," **p. 896**w.

TROUBLESHOOTING

I CAN'T LOG IN ON A USER ACCOUNT

When I try to log in under a particular user account, the login window shudders and I can't log in.

The most likely cause of this error is that you are entering the user account information incorrectly. If you are selecting a user account from the list, you must be entering the password incorrectly. If you are entering both the account name and password, you have to ensure that you use the correct combination. Try entering the information again. Remember that both name and password are case sensitive.

If you are logging in using the short name, try using the full name instead.

If you are still not able to log in under that account, log in as the administrator and open the Users pane of the System Preferences utility to check the account or edit it. You can also delete the account and start over.

If you can't log in to an administrator account because you have forgotten the password, do the following steps:

1. Restart the Mac using the Mac OS X Install CD 1.

2. When the installer opens, select Installer, Reset Password.

3. Follow the onscreen instructions to reset the administrator password.

THE BUTTONS IN THE ACCOUNTS PANE ARE INACTIVE

When I open the Accounts pane of the System Preferences utility, the buttons are all inactive.

The Lock icon in the lower-left corner of the window enables you to lock or unlock the ability to make global system changes. If this icon is in the "locked" mode, you need to authenticate yourself as the administrator (even if you are logged in under that account). Click the Lock icon, enter the Administrator User Name and Password in the Authentication dialog box, and press Return. If you enter valid information, the buttons become active and you are able to make changes to the account configurations.

CHAPTER 3

VIEWING AND NAVIGATING MAC OS X FINDER WINDOWS

In this chapter

THE MAC OS X FINDER

The basic purpose of the Finder under Mac OS X is the same as it has always been; the Finder is the Mac application that provides the desktop, enables you to work with folders and files, and provides the basic interface for interacting with the system. The Finder does look quite a bit different than it did under previous versions of the OS, and it offers many more features, but most of the basic tasks work in the same or very similar ways. These tasks include those that you use to view and navigate Finder windows. In addition to its new appearance, the Mac OS X Finder also offers better views, more customization options, and more tools.

WORKING WITH FINDER WINDOWS

When it comes to viewing Mac OS X Finder windows, there is definitely good news and bad news—assuming that you have used a previous version of the Mac OS, of course (if you haven't, there is only good news). The good news is that Mac OS X windows offer the same functionality that windows in previous Mac OSes did plus many improvements. The bad news is that under Mac OS X, windows look quite a bit different and you might have to adjust some of your normal working habits a bit (see Figure 3.1).

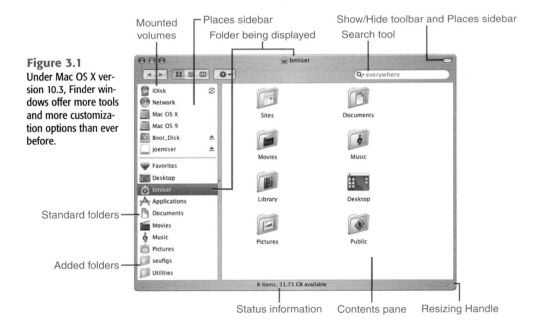

Mounted volumes — Places sidebar — Folder being displayed — Show/Hide toolbar and Places sidebar — Search tool

Figure 3.1
Under Mac OS X version 10.3, Finder windows offer more tools and more customization options than ever before.

Standard folders

Added folders

Status information — Contents pane — Resizing Handle

The fundamental purpose of Finder windows is the same as it has always been—Finder windows enable you to view and manipulate the contents of disks, CD-ROMs, DVDs, folders, and so on.

OPENING FINDER WINDOWS

You can open Finder windows in several ways. If you click the Finder icon on the Dock (which is the Mac OS icon), one of two things can happen. If no Finder windows are currently open, a new Finder window appears showing the contents of the default location you selected (initially, this is your Home folder, but you can select any folder you'd like). If at least one Finder window is already open, you will move to the Finder window in which you most recently worked.

TIP

> If you hold down the Control key while you click the Finder icon, click it and linger a moment, or right-click the icon on the Dock, a menu showing all open Finder windows appears. Select a window to jump into it.

You can also open a new Finder window by selecting File, New Finder Window (⌘-N). When you open a new Finder window, the result is always the same—the contents of your default location are displayed (this is initially set to be your Home folder, but you can change it to be any location you prefer).

The Mac OS X Finder uses a Web-like model in that each new Finder window you open starts a "chain" of windows (thus, the Back and Forward buttons in the Finder window toolbar). The first window in every new chain you start is always the directory you define as the default. You can have many window chains open at the same time, again being similar to Web windows. (You can quickly jump into specific directories using the toolbar, the Places sidebar, the Go menu, and keyboard shortcuts.)

→ To learn how to navigate Finder windows, **see** "Navigating Finder Windows," **p. 61**.

By default, when you open an item (such as a folder), its contents replace the contents of the previous item that were shown in the Finder window. You can change this behavior globally with a preference setting. You can also override this behavior so the new Finder window is separate from the first one by holding down the ⌘ key while you double-click an icon.

TIP

> This default behavior assumes that the toolbar and Places sidebar are shown in a Finder window. If not, opening a folder always opens a new, separate Finder window.

After you have one Finder window open, other Finder windows open in the same way that they did under previous versions of the OS. To open a window, double-click the icon for the item you want to open. Or select an item and select File, Open. The Open keyboard shortcut works, too—just select an item and press ⌘-O to open it. You can also open an item's contextual menu and select Open. If you select an item while a Finder window is in the Columns view, its contents are displayed in a new column. If those aren't enough options for you, here is one more; select an item and choose Open on the Action menu.

3

When you open a new Finder window, it always assumes the view you selected the last time you viewed that item in a Finder window. You'll learn more about Mac OS X Finder window views later in this chapter.

NOTE

> To reiterate this sometimes confusing behavior of Mac OS X windows, the view in which a new window opens is determined by the view you used for that window the last time you viewed it. In other words, windows retain their view settings, even if the window from which you opened a separate Finder window is different. For example, if you viewed the Applications directory in List view, it appears in List view whenever you open it in a new Finder window until you change the view in which it appears.

Mac OS X version 10.3 adds a new and very useful feature to Finder windows, which is the Places sidebar. This area is located along the left side of Finder windows (when the toolbar is displayed) and consists of two panes. In the upper pane are all the volumes mounted on your Mac, including hard disk volumes, disk image volumes, your iDisk, CDs, DVDs, and so on. In the lower pane are some of the folders in your Home folder and the Applications folder. You can add any folders, applications, documents, or other files to or remove them from this area as you'd like so that you can customize it. The purpose of the Places sidebar is to enable you to quickly get to any item shown in it.

When you select a volume or folder in the Places sidebar, its contents are shown in the Finder window. The currently selected item is highlighted so you can easily tell what is selected. (The name of the currently selected item appears at the top of the window as well.) If you select a document or application, that item opens just like when you double-click it.

TIP

> If you hold down the ⌘ key while you click an item in the Places sidebar, that item opens in a new Finder window. If you hold down the Option key when you click an item in the Places sidebar, that item opens in a new Finder window and the previous window closes.

CONFIGURING HOW NEW FINDER WINDOWS OPEN

You can also set two other Finder window preferences related to how new windows open.

To configure how Finder windows open, perform the following steps:

1. Select Finder, Preferences or press ⌘-+; then click the General tab if it isn't selected already. You will see the Finder Preferences dialog box (see Figure 3.2).

Figure 3.2
Use the General pane of the Finder Preferences dialog box to configure how new Finder windows open.

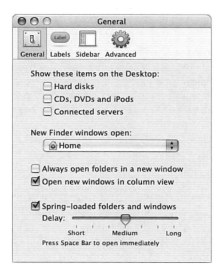

2. On the "New Finder windows open" pop-up menu, select the location you want to view each time you open a new Finder window.

   You can use that pop-up menu to select a folder you want to view in new Finder windows by default. On the pop-up menu, you will also see each volume mounted on your Mac. Select a volume to see its contents in new Finder windows by default. If you choose Other, you can select any folder on your Mac.

   NOTE

   > One of the nice features of Mac OS X is that most preference changes are made in real-time—you don't have to close the Preferences window to see the results of your changes. For example, when you make the change in the previous steps, the window-opening behavior becomes active as soon as you change the check box. A good habit is to leave preference windows open as you make changes and close the windows only when you are happy with all the changes you have made.

3. If you prefer that when you move to a new folder, the folder's contents appear in a new Finder window, check the "Always open folders in a new window" check box. Because this option can lead to a proliferation of Finder windows, I recommend that you leave this option off. You can always open a new Finder window by holding down the ⌘ key when you double-click an item. A better way to view content is to use the Columns view, which enables you to quickly move to any location.

4. If you want all new windows to open in the Columns view, check "Open new windows in column view." I recommend that you select this option because the Columns view is the most efficient for moving among the items on your Mac.

5. Close the Finder Preferences window.

→ To learn more about Mac OS X directories, **see** "Understanding Mac OS X Directories," **p. 101**.

NOTE

As you can see, you can choose a number of options for working with new Finder windows. Because my preferences are to have my Home folder open, open new items in the current Finder window, and always have new windows open in the Columns view, that is what this chapter assumes. I point out differences along the way when you choose other preferences.

WORKING WITH SPRING-LOADED FOLDERS

Mac OS X Finder windows can be *spring-loaded* (this feature is turned on by default), meaning that they pop open when you drag an item onto a closed folder. This enables you to quickly place an item within nested folders without having to open each folder individually. Simply drag an item onto a closed folder so the folder is highlighted. After the delay time has passed, the highlighted folder opens in a separate Finder window (unless you are viewing the window in Columns view, in which case a new column appears for the item onto which you are dragging the item). You can then drag the item onto the next folder and continue the process until you have placed it in its final destination. When you release the mouse button, all the folders that have "sprung" open are closed again.

TIP

You can cause a folder to spring open immediately by pressing the spacebar when you drag an item onto a closed folder.

You can configure this behavior by using the following steps:

1. Click the General tab in the Finder Preferences dialog box.
2. Check the "Spring-loaded folders and windows" check box to turn this feature back on if you have turned it off (it is on by default).
3. Use the Delay slider to set the amount of delay time (the time between when you drag an item onto a folder and when that folder springs open).
4. Experiment to see whether the delay time is set correctly for you; if not, change it.
5. Close the Finder Preferences window when you have set the delay time.

SCROLLING FINDER WINDOWS

You scroll Mac OS X windows in basically the same way you always have. By default, the scrollbars are Mac OS X blue; you can change this to graphite with the Appearance pane of the System Preferences utility. As with previous versions of the OS, you can set the scroll arrows to both be located in the lower-right corner of windows or have an arrow located at each end of the scrollbar.

Mac OS X scrolling controls work as you expect them to. You have the following options:

■ Drag the scrollbars.

NOTE

> As with previous versions of the OS, the length of the scrollbar is proportional to the amount of the window you can see in the view.

■ Click above or below or to the left or right of the bar to scroll one screen's worth at a time.

■ Click the scroll arrows.

■ Press the Page Up and Page Down keys to scroll vertically.

■ Press the Home key to jump to the top of the window or the End key to jump to the bottom.

■ Use the arrow keys or Tab (and Shift-Tab) to move among the items in the window (which also scrolls the window when you move outside the current view).

■ When using the Icon or List views, hold down the ⌘ and Option keys and drag (when you can drag to scroll, the pointer changes to the gloved hand icon).

You can modify several aspects of scrolling behavior. You can change the location of the scroll arrows. And, rather than moving an entire page each time you click above, below, to the left, or to the right of a scrollbar, you can set the scrolling such that you move to the relative location you click instead. You can also turn on smooth scrolling, which smoothes out the appearance of a window when you scroll in it. Follow these steps to modify these scrolling features:

1. Open the System Preferences utility.

2. In the Personal section, click Appearance (see Figure 3.3).

3. To change the locations of the scroll arrows, click the Together radio button to have the scroll arrows in the lower-right corner of windows or the "At top and bottom" radio button to place an arrow at each end of the scrollbars.

4. To change how scrolling works when you click in the scrollbar, click the "Jump to the next page" radio button to scroll a screen at a time or the "Scroll to here" radio button to move to a position in the window that is relative to where you click in the scrollbar.

5. Check the "Use smooth scrolling" check box to turn on smooth scrolling.

6. Quit the System Preferences utility.

Figure 3.3
The Appearance pane of the System Preferences utility enables you to modify the behavior of window scrolling.

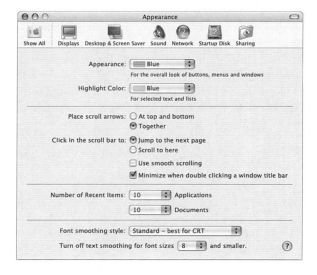

TIP

This is a good chance to practice Mac OS X preference setting techniques. Make your changes to the Appearance pane, but leave the System Preferences utility open. Click in a Finder window; your changes immediately become active. If you are satisfied, jump back to the System Preferences utility and close it. If not, jump back into the Appearance pane and continue making changes until you are.

RESIZING WINDOWS

Resizing windows also works as you might expect. To change the size of a window, drag its resizing handle until the window is the size you want it to be.

You can also use the Maximize button to make a window large enough to display all the items it contains or until it fills the screen, whichever comes first. Click the button and the window jumps to the size it needs to be to show all the items it contains. Click the button again to return it to its previous size.

You can also use this button to quickly swap between two sizes for a window. Make the window a size you like. When you click the Maximize button, it expands to its maximum size. Click the button again and it returns to the previous size. Each time you click the Maximize button, the window returns to the size it was previously (either the maximum size or the size you set).

TIP

> If you are like me and have lots of Finder windows open on the Desktop, you can use this resizing behavior to make working between multiple windows more convenient. Select an open window and make it the size you want it to be so it is out of the way and you can store many windows of this size on your desktop; make it just large enough so you can see the window's title. You can click the Maximize button to open the window to work in it. Then, click the Maximize button again to return the window to its small size. Use the button to toggle between the two sizes. When you need to work in the window, make it large by clicking the Maximize button. When you are done, click the button again to make it small. You might find this even more convenient than minimizing windows.

RESIZING THE PANES OF FINDER WINDOWS

As you learned earlier, Finder windows have two panes. The left pane is the Places sidebar, whereas the right pane is the Contents pane that displays the contents of the item selected on the Places sidebar. You can change the relative size of the Places sidebar by dragging the resize handle that is located in the center of the border between the two panes (the handle is the familiar "dot"). Drag this to the left and the Places sidebar takes up less room in the window. Drag it to the right and the Places sidebar takes up more window space.

When you resize the Places sidebar, the text and icons within the sidebar become smaller so you can still see as much of them as possible within the allocated space. When the pane becomes too narrow to display all of an item's name, the first part of the name is shown followed by an ellipsis.

You can collapse the sidebar so that just the icons show. You can also collapse it all the way so that it doesn't show at all. To reveal it again, drag the resize handle to the right.

You can also collapse or expand it by double-clicking its resize handle.

CLOSING, MINIMIZING, AND MAXIMIZING FINDER WINDOWS

Among the most distinctive features of Mac OS X are the three stoplight-type controls located in the upper-left corner of windows (refer to Figure 3.1). The red button (on the far left) closes the window. The gold button (in the middle) minimizes the window, which shrinks it and moves it to the right side of the Dock. The green button maximizes the window, which makes it as large as it needs to be to display all the items in the window until that window fills the screen (and returns it to the previous size, as you learned in the previous section).

→ To learn how to use the Dock, **see** Chapter 5, "Using and Customizing the Dock," **p. 127**.

By default, you can also minimize a window (thus moving it onto the Dock) by double-clicking its title bar.

TIP

> If you don't want to be able to minimize a window by double-clicking in its title bar, open the Appearance pane of the System Preferences application and uncheck the "Minimize when double clicking a window title bar" check box.

The Close, Minimize, and Maximize buttons work even if the window on which they appear is not active. For example, you can close a window that is in the background by clicking its Close button without making the window active first. (When you point to a button on an inactive window, the button becomes colored so that you know it is active, even though the window is not.)

TIP

> As under previous versions of the Mac OS, you can close all open Finder windows by holding down the Option key while you click the Close button in one of the windows.

MOVING FINDER WINDOWS

You can move a Finder window around the desktop by dragging its title bar, borders, or anywhere else the metallic look is.

NOTE

> If you used previous versions of Mac OS X, you'll notice that moving windows around is considerably faster under version 10.3, as are other window tasks such as changing size.

USING THE ICON, LIST, OR COLUMNS VIEWS FOR A FINDER WINDOW

You can view Finder windows in three different views: Icon, List, and Columns.

VIEWING A FINDER WINDOW IN ICON VIEW

You can easily argue that icons made the Mac. Using friendly pictures to represent files and folders made the computer much friendlier and more approachable than any command line could ever hope to be. Mac OS X continues the use of icons to represent objects, and with their improved appearance under OS X, icons have never looked so good.

You can view Finder windows in the Icon view by opening a window and then selecting View, As Icons; by pressing ⌘-1; or by clicking the Icon view button in the toolbar (see Figure 3.4). The objects in the window become icons, and if you have never seen OS X icons before, prepare to be impressed.

→ You can customize the Icon view for Finder windows. **See** "Customizing Finder Windows," **p. 68**.

Figure 3.4
The familiar Icon view of the Mac OS is now even more visually appealing. Other operating systems might have copied the Mac's icons, but none can compare to this snazzy look.

Icon View button

If you find that a window in the Icon view is messy, you can use the Clean Up command (View, Clean Up) to straighten up the window for you. This command neatly arranges icons so they line up in an orderly fashion.

To arrange icons by a specific criterion, select View, Arrange, and then select the criterion by which you want the window's icons ordered. Your options are the following: by Name, by Date Modified, by Date Created, by Size, by Kind, or by Label.

Although the Icon view is clearly the most pleasing view to look at, it is one of the least useful in terms of the information you see.

VIEWING A FINDER WINDOW IN LIST VIEW

The List view presents more information than does the Icon view (see Figure 3.5). To switch to the List view, click the List view button; select View, As List; or press ⌘-2.

The information in the List view is organized into columns, with a header at the top of the column indicating the information in it. The information in the List view is always sorted—you can select the column that is used to sort the contents of the window. You can also determine the order in which the columns appear, change the width of columns, and expand or collapse the contents of folders. The information for each item you see in the default List view is the following:

- **Name**—This is the filename for files, the folder name for folders, the volume name for volumes, and so on.

- **Date Modified**—The most recent date on which the object was changed. If the date is the current date, the time at which the object was changed is shown.

- **Size**—The size of the item, in kilobytes (KB), megabytes (MB), or gigabytes (GB).

- **Kind**—The type of object it is, such as folder, document, application, volume, and so on.

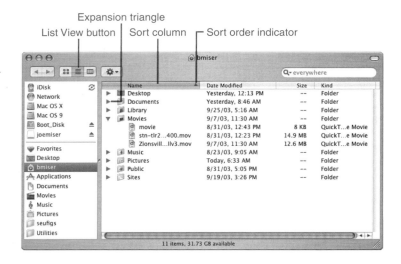

Figure 3.5
At the top of the window are the same controls that are visible in the Icon view. However, the lower part of the window contains more information than is available in the Icon view.

Expansion triangle
List View button | Sort column ┌ Sort order indicator

→ You can customize the List view for a single window or for all windows. **See** "Customizing Finder Windows," **p. 68**.

The column by which the window is sorted is highlighted with the highlight color (blue or graphite). To change the sort column, click the Column heading of the column by which you want the list to be sorted. That heading is highlighted and the list is re-sorted by that criterion. At the right edge of the column heading for the column by which the window is sorted, you see the Sort order indicator. This shows you in which direction the list is sorted. For example, if the list is sorted by the Name column, an up arrow indicates that the list is sorted alphabetically and a down arrow indicates that the list is sorted in reverse alphabetical order. To change the direction of the sort, click the Column heading—the list is sorted in the opposite order (from ascending to descending or from descending to ascending).

You can resize a column by moving the pointer to the right edge of the column heading. When you do, the cursor changes from the pointer to a vertical line with outward-facing arrows on each side of it. When you see this cursor, drag the column border to resize the column.

You can change the order in which columns appear by dragging the column heading of the column you want to move and dropping it in the new location. The columns reshuffle and then appear in the order you have indicated.

NOTE

You can't change the location of the Name column; it is always the first column in a window in List view.

One of the other benefits of the List view is that you can expand the contents of a folder so you can view them without having to open the folder's window first. To do this, click the right-facing Expansion triangle next to the folder's name. The folder expands, and its contents are listed in the window. Click the triangle again to collapse the folder down to its icon.

TIP

> When you Option-click the Expansion triangle for a collapsed folder, the folder and all the folders it contains are expanded. When you Option-click the Expansion triangle for an expanded folder, the folder and all its contents are collapsed again.

VIEWING A FINDER WINDOW IN COLUMNS VIEW

The Columns view was introduced for Mac OS X, and its benefit is that you can use it to quickly see and navigate levels of the hierarchy (see Figure 3.6). To switch to the Columns view, click the Columns view button on the toolbar; press ⌘-2; or select View, as Columns.

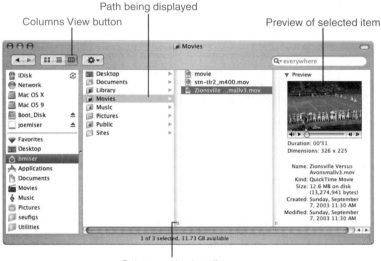

Figure 3.6
The Columns view is a great way to see the hierarchical organization of directories and folders.

Path being displayed

Columns View button

Preview of selected item

Column resize handle

NOTE

> One reason the Columns view is so important is that you use this view to navigate within Open, Save, and other dialog boxes. When you are using the Columns view in dialog boxes, it works just as it does in Finder windows.

As you might suspect, in the Columns view, the window is organized into columns, with each column representing a level of the file organization hierarchy. The leftmost column shows the highest level you can see, each column to its right shows the next level down the structure, and the column on the far right shows the lowest level you can see. When you select a file, the rightmost column shows a preview of the selected file. The "path" at which you are looking is indicated by the highlighted items in each column.

Folder icons have a right-facing arrow at the right edge of the column to indicate that when you select them, their contents appear in the column to the immediate right.

For example, put a Finder window in the Columns view and click your Home folder on the Places sidebar to see its contents. The Home folder's contents are shown in the first column in the window. If you click one of the folders, it becomes highlighted and its contents appear in one of the middle columns. As you select folders within folders, their contents appear in the column to their right. This continues all the way down into a folder until it contains no more folders.

You can move down into the hierarchy by clicking the item about which you want more detail. The column to the right of the item on which you click shows the contents of what you click. If you click something in the right column and the window is not large enough to display the contents of all the columns, the view shifts and the columns appear to move to the left. You can use this approach to quickly see the contents of any folder on your Mac, no matter how far down in the hierarchy it is stored.

TIP

> One of the best reasons to use the Columns view is that you can move inside a window with the arrow keys on the keyboard. This is the fastest way to move among the folders and files on your Mac.

When there are more columns than can be displayed in the window, you can use the scrollbars to view all the columns. Scrolling to the left moves up the hierarchy, whereas scrolling to the right moves down the hierarchy. You can also make the window larger to view more columns at the same time.

 You can resize the width of the columns in a window by dragging the resize handle located in the lower-right corner of each column. Unlike in previous versions of Mac OS X, each column in a window can have a different width.

When you click a file to select it, the far-right column shows a large icon or a preview of the file and information about that file is displayed (refer to Figure 3.6).

If you click document files for which Mac OS X can create a preview, you see the preview in the column. If the file you select has dynamic content, you can play that content in the preview that you see in the Columns view. For example, if you select a QuickTime movie, you can use the QuickTime Player controls to watch the movie without opening the file. Certain types of text files are also displayed so you can read them (scrollbars appear in the column to enable you to read the entire document). You can also see large thumbnail views of graphics stored in certain formats. For those items that Mac OS X cannot create previews of (an application is one example), you see a large icon instead of a preview.

NOTE

If you switch from the Columns view to one of the other views, the contents of the folder you most recently selected are shown in the window.

If you prefer not to see the preview, there are two ways to hide it. You can hide it in individual windows or you can hide it by using the View Options.

To hide the preview in specific windows, click the Expansion triangle next to the word Preview that appears just above the preview of a selected file in the Preview pane. This hides all previews for the current window.

You will learn about the View Options later in this chapter.

NAVIGATING FINDER WINDOWS

Mac OS X includes many features that enable you to navigate Finder windows. The two basic navigation tasks you do are moving around inside Finder windows (to select items for example) and changing the contents of Finder windows to view other volumes or folders.

USING THE KEYBOARD TO SELECT ITEMS IN A FINDER WINDOW

Although you can use the mouse to point to and click items to select them (or double-click to open them), moving to items and selecting them using the keyboard can be faster. There are two basic ways to navigate inside a window using the keyboard.

You can type an item's name to move to and select it. The OS matches item names as you type, so most of the time you don't need to type the item's whole name to move to it (for example, typing "mp3" moves you to the first item whose name begins with mp3). The more of the name you type, the more specific your movement becomes.

You can also move among items using the Tab and arrow keys. How this works depends on the view you are using for the windows.

USING THE KEYBOARD TO SELECT ITEMS IN THE ICON VIEW

When you are in the Icon view, pressing the Tab key selects the next item according to alphabetical order. Holding down the Shift key while you press Tab moves you among the items in reverse alphabetical order.

You can also use the arrow keys to move to and select items. The keys work just as you might expect. The up-arrow key moves you up the window, the right-arrow key moves you right, and so on.

The window scrolls automatically to keep the items you select in view.

USING THE KEYBOARD TO SELECT ITEMS IN THE LIST VIEW

When a window is shown in List view, you can use the up- and down-arrow keys to move up and down the list of items in the window.

When you select an item, you can use the right-arrow key to expand it and the left-arrow key to collapse it.

TIP

> The Option key works with the arrow keys as well. If you hold down the Option key and press the right-arrow key, all the folders within the selected folder are expanded as well.

USING THE KEYBOARD TO SELECT ITEMS IN THE COLUMNS VIEW

In the Columns view, the right-arrow key moves you down the hierarchy, whereas the left-arrow key moves you up the hierarchy. The up- and down-arrow keys enable you to move up and down within a selected folder.

Using these keys, you can move around your directories rapidly. As you move through the structure using these keys, the window scrolls so that you always see the currently selected item. It maintains your view at all times so you can quickly jump into different areas without scrolling manually.

TIP

> When you get used to it, using the keyboard in combination with the Columns view is the fastest way to navigate Mac OS X Finder windows.

USING THE FINDER WINDOW'S SEARCH TOOL TO SELECT ITEMS

 The Finder window toolbar includes a Search tool you can use to find and move to items within a folder. For version 10.3, this tool works better than it did previously and allows greater control over a search:

1. Open a Finder window.
2. Click the magnifying glass icon in the Search tool. A pop-up menu appears that you can use to select an area in which to search. The options are Local Disks, which searches the local disks installed on your machine; Home, which searches only in your Home folder; Selection, which searches in the selected item; and Everywhere, which searches in all volumes to which your Mac has access (see Figure 3.7).
3. Select the area in which you want to search. The area you select is then shown in the text field.

Figure 3.7
You can choose the scope of your search on the pop-up menu in the Finder window Search tool.

NOTE

The search area you choose becomes the default for searches until you choose a different search area.

4. Enter the text for which you want to search. When you start typing, the Finder window is transformed into the search results window. This window has two panes. The upper pane shows the items that match your search text, and the lower pane shows the location of any item you select in the upper pane. As you type, this window shows the items whose names contain the text you type. The more specific you make the text, the fewer items appear in the window as you perform the search.

TIP

You can change the relative size of the two panes by dragging the resize handle located in the center of the bar that separates the two panes.

5. When you find an item in which you are interested, click in the search results pane and use the up- and down-arrow keys to select the item in the upper pane. Its location is shown in the lower pane (see Figure 3.8).

6. If you want :to clear the search and return to the previous Finder window, click the Clear Search button, which is the "x" located in the right end of the Search tool.

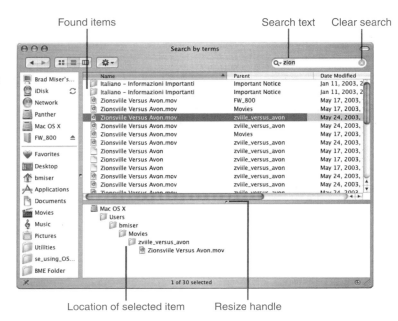

Figure 3.8
You can use the Finder window Search tool to search various areas of your Mac for files and folders that include specific text in their names.

NAVIGATING UP AND DOWN THE DIRECTORY STRUCTURE

There are several ways to move up and down the directory structure within Finder windows. You can use the keyboard as discussed in the previous section. You can also use the icons in the Places sidebar as well as the Path pop-up menu. The Go menu also enables you to jump to specific directories quickly.

CHANGING DIRECTORIES WITH THE PLACES SIDEBAR

 The Finder's Places Sidebar is a fast way to change the directory displayed in the current Finder window. The sidebar contains icons that take you to specific directories. As you read earlier, the sidebar contains two panes. The upper pane shows all the mounted volumes, including your hard disks, network drives, iDisk, CDs, DVDs, and so on. The lower pane shows several folders in your Home folder; your Favorites folder; the Applications folder; and any folders, documents, or applications you have added manually. You can customize the items that appear on the sidebar to suit your preferences.

→ To learn how to customize the sidebar, **see** "Customizing the Places Sidebar," **p. 69**.

To view the contents of an item shown in the sidebar, simply click its icon. The right pane of the Finder window shows the contents of the selected item.

USING THE BACK AND FORWARD BUTTONS TO MOVE AMONG FINDER WINDOWS

Click the Back button on the toolbar to move back to the previous Finder window. You can continue to click the Back button as many times as you want until you reach the first window you viewed using the current Finder window; at that point, the Back button is grayed out. Similarly, the Forward button moves you forward in a chain of Finder windows.

> **TIP**
>
> You can press ⌘-[to move back and ⌘-] to move forward.

→ To learn how to customize the Toolbar, **see** "Customizing the Toolbar," **p. 71**.

> **NOTE**
>
> If you open a new Finder window, the Back and Forward buttons are grayed out because there is no window to move back or forward to. Opening a new Finder window starts a new sequence of windows, so both buttons are disabled. As soon as you open a second window within the same Finder window, the Back button becomes active. If you move back along that chain of windows, the Forward button becomes active.

CHANGING DIRECTORIES WITH THE PATH POP-UP MENU

The Path pop-up menu enables you to quickly move up and down the directory structure of your Mac. To change directories, hold down the ⌘ key and click the window name in the title bar of a Finder window. When you do so, you see all the directories from the one currently displayed in the window up to the Computer directory (which is the highest level on your Mac). Select a directory from the menu and the Finder window displays the directory you chose.

> **TIP**
>
> You can add the Path button to your toolbar so you can select a directory without using the ⌘ key. You'll learn how later in this chapter.

CHANGING DIRECTORIES WITH THE GO MENU

The Finder's Go menu enables you to move into many areas of your Mac. The menu is divided into several areas that contain various kinds of options (see Figure 3.9).

At the top of the menu are the Back and Forward commands, which do the same thing as the Back and Forward buttons on the toolbar.

Just under these commands is the Enclosing Folder command. When you are displaying an item in a Finder window and press ⌘-up arrow or select Go, Enclosing Folder, the folder that contains the currently selected item is shown in the Finder window.

You can also use the Finder's Go menu to open specific directories. To do so, open the Go menu and select the directory you want to view. Its contents replace those shown in the active Finder window (if no Finder windows are active, the directory's contents appear in a new Finder window). For example, to display your Home folder, select Go, Home.

Figure 3.9
The Go menu provides quick access to various folders on your Mac.

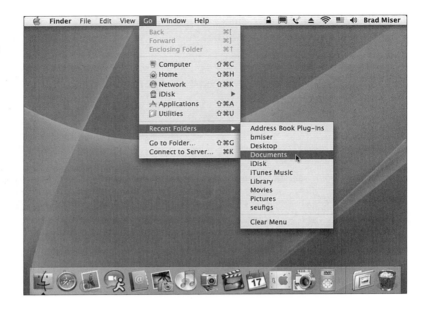

TIP

Keyboard shortcuts are available for the specific directories on the Go menu. See the "Mac OS X to the Max" section at the end of this chapter for a list of these shortcuts.

If you select, Go, Recent Folders, you can quickly move back to one of the folders you have recently viewed (you can set the number of recent folders on this list using the Appearance pane of the System Preferences utility).

You can also move to a folder using the Go to Folder command. Select Go, Go to Folder to see the Go to Folder dialog box (see Figure 3.10). You can type a pathname in this dialog box and click Go to open a Finder window for that directory. Following are some tips on how to type pathnames:

- Pathnames are case sensitive.
- A slash (/) separates each level in the path.
- Almost all paths should begin and end with the slash (/).
- The exception to the previous rule is when you want to move to a specific user's Home directory, in which case you can just type *~username/*, where *username* is the short name for the user's account.
- If the path begins with the directory on which Mac OS X is stored, you can skip that directory name and start the path beginning with the next level. If it is on another volume, you can include that volume's name at the beginning of the path.

Figure 3.10
This Go to Folder directory shows the path to the Movies folder within my Home folder.

NOTE

Although you should be careful to use the proper case in pathnames, sometimes it doesn't make a difference. For example, the path to the Mac OS X System directory can be /SYSTEM/, /system/, or /System/. Sometimes, however, the case of the path you type must match exactly, so it is good practice to always match the case of the directory names you type.

Table 3.1 provides some examples of paths you would enter in the Go to Folder dialog box to move to specific directories.

TABLE 3.1   PATHS TO SPECIFIC DIRECTORIES

Location	Path
Directory called Documents on a volume named Mac OS 9	/Mac OS 9/Documents/
The Documents folder in the Home directory for the user account with the short name bmiser	~bmiser/Documents/
The Mac OS X System Folder	/System/
A folder called Ch_02_figs located in the Documents directory in my User folder	~bmiser/Documents/Ch_02_figs

Following are some additional tips for the Go to Folder command:

■ You can open the Go to Folder dialog box by pressing ⌘-Shift-G. Type the path and press Return to move there.

- If you are patient when you type, Mac OS X will try to match the path you are typing and complete it for you. This usually takes more time than to type it yourself, but if the path is filled in for you, press Return to accept that path entered for you to move there.

- The most recent path you have typed remains in the Go to Folder dialog box; you can modify this path to move to a different directory.

TIP

> Although pathnames should end in /, you don't really have to type the last /. If it is needed, Mac OS X adds it for you. If not, the path works without it.

NOTE

> You can use the Connect to Server command to move to directories located on your network.

→ To learn how to connect to servers, **see** "Accessing Shared Files from a Mac OS X Computer," **p. 834**.

CHANGING DIRECTORIES WITH THE KEYBOARD

One of the cool navigation features of Mac OS X is the ability to move up and down the directory structure using only the keyboard. Use the previous tips to select an item and then press ⌘-down arrow to move into the item, such as a folder, an application, a document, and so on. For example, if you use the Tab key to select an application icon and then press ⌘-down arrow, that application opens. Similarly, if you press this key combination when you have a folder selected, the contents of that folder are shown in its previous view state.

NOTE

> This technique also works in the Columns view to open applications or documents. When you are viewing folders and volumes, you don't need to hold down the ⌘ key because, in the Columns view, the contents of a folder or volume are displayed when you select it.

To move up the directory structure, press ⌘-up arrow.

CUSTOMIZING FINDER WINDOWS

Mac OS X enables you to customize many aspects of Finder windows, including the Places Sidebar, the toolbar, the status bar, and the views you use.

CUSTOMIZING THE PLACES SIDEBAR

The Places Sidebar provides a convenient way to access the mounted volumes on your Mac along with specific folders, documents, and applications (see Figure 3.11). As you read earlier, the upper pane of the sidebar shows all the mounted volumes on your Mac and the lower pane shows folders, documents, and applications. By default, you will see several of the folders within your Home folder, the Applications folder, and your Favorites folder, but you can add or remove folders, documents, or applications to this area to customize it.

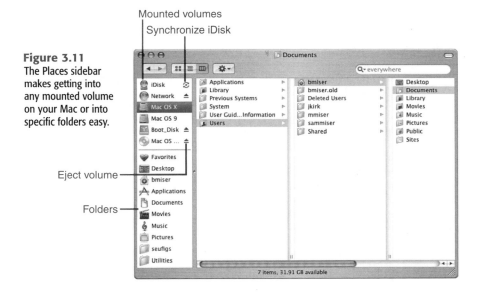

Figure 3.11
The Places sidebar makes getting into any mounted volume on your Mac or into specific folders easy.

> **TIP**
>
> You can also store files in the lower pane of the Places sidebar.

To view the contents of a volume or folder, click it; its contents are shown in the Contents pane of the Finder window. For volumes, a button enables you to perform an action. For example, when you have an ejectable volume, such as a disk image or CD, you can click an Eject button. When you are working with an iDisk, you can click the Synchronize button. When you have inserted a blank CD or DVD, you can click the Burn button.

DETERMINING THE DEFAULT ITEMS IN THE PLACES SIDEBAR

Finder preferences determine which items appear in the Places Sidebar. To set them, do the following steps:

1. Select Finder, Preferences or press ⌘-,.
2. Click the Sidebar tab (see Figure 3.12).

Figure 3.12
Use the Sidebar pane of the Finder Preferences dialog box to configure the default items in the Places sidebar.

3. Check the box next to each item you want to appear in the Places sidebar.

4. Uncheck the box next to each item you don't want to appear in the sidebar.

5. Close the Preferences dialog box.

The next time you view a Finder window, its sidebar will contain the items you specified.

Accessing and Organizing Your Folders and Files in the Places Sidebar

You can further organize the Places sidebar by doing the following tasks:

■ You can add any folder or file to the Places sidebar by dragging it onto the lower pane of the sidebar.

■ You can also add a folder or file to the sidebar by either selecting it and selecting File, Add To Sidebar or pressing ⌘-T.

■ You can remove folders from the sidebar by dragging them out of the sidebar. When you do, they disappear in a puff of smoke. Of course, the original item isn't affected.

> **NOTE**
>
> If you remove an item whose check box is checked on the Sidebar pane of the Finder Preferences dialog box, that folder is removed and its check box becomes unchecked in the Preferences dialog box.

■ Drag folders up and down within the lower pane of the sidebar to reorganize them.

As you add, remove, or reorganize the sidebar, it is resized automatically.

CUSTOMIZING THE TOOLBAR

Along the top of Finder windows, you see the toolbar. This toolbar contains the Back and Forward buttons, the View buttons, the Action menu (covered in a later section), and the Search tool. As with the sidebar, you can customize many aspects of this toolbar. You can show or hide it and customize the tools it contains.

> **NOTE**
>
> Many applications also provide a Mac OS X toolbar in their windows. You can use these same techniques to work with those toolbars.

SHOWING OR HIDING THE TOOLBAR

You can hide or show the toolbar in a Finder window in any of the following ways:

- Click the Show/Hide Toolbar button in the upper-right corner of the Finder window.
- Select View, Hide Toolbar or View, Show Toolbar.
- Press Option-⌘-T.

The state of the toolbar controls how new Finder windows open when they are viewed in the Icon or List view. If the toolbar is displayed, new Finder windows open according to the preferences you set using the Finder Preferences dialog box. If the toolbar is hidden, new Finder windows always open in a separate window.

When you open a new Finder window from a window in which the toolbar is hidden (for example, by holding down the Option key when you open a new Finder window), the toolbar is hidden in the new window. When you open a Finder window from a window in which the toolbar is shown, the toolbar is shown in the new window as well.

The toolbar state in currently open Finder windows is independent. For example, you can show the toolbar in one Finder window while it is hidden in another. In fact, if you have two Finder windows for the same directory open at the same time, you can hide the toolbar in one window while it is shown in the other.

CHANGING THE TOOLS ON THE TOOLBAR

The default toolbar contains various useful buttons, but you can customize its content by adding tools to it or removing tools from it:

1. Open a Finder window.
2. Select View, Customize Toolbar. The contents of the Finder window are replaced by the Toolbar customization window (see Figure 3.13).

3

Figure 3.13
You can add buttons to or remove them from the toolbar using the Customize Toolbar command.

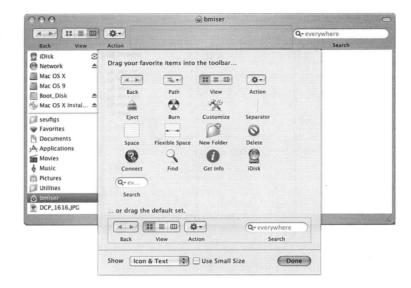

3. To add a button to the toolbar, drag it from the window to the toolbar, placing it in the location where you want it. (Table 3.2 lists the available buttons and what they do.)

When you move a button between two current buttons on the toolbar, existing buttons slide apart to make room for the new button.

NOTE

> If you place more buttons on the toolbar than can be shown in the current window's width, a set of double arrows appears at the right edge of the toolbar. Click this to pop up a menu showing the additional buttons.

4. Remove a button from the toolbar by dragging it off the toolbar.

5. Change the location of the icons by dragging them. You can move buttons and menus that you add as well as those that are installed by default.

6. Use the Show pop-up menu to determine whether the buttons have text and an icon, text only, or an icon only.

7. To use the small icon size, check the Use Small Size check box.

8. Click Done.

The toolbar now reflects the changes you made (see Figure 3.14).

Figure 3.14
This is the same window, but with a customized toolbar.

TIP

> You can rotate the toolbar among it views, such as Icon & Text, Icon Only, and so on by holding down ⌘ while you click the Show/Hide Toolbar button.

TABLE 3.2   USEFUL TOOLBAR BUTTONS

Button Name	What It Does
Back/Forward	Moves you back or forward in a chain of Finder windows.
Path	Pops up a menu that shows the path to the current directory. You can select a directory on the pop-up menu to move there.
View	Changes the view for the current window.
Action	Provides a pop-up menu with access to various context-sensitive commands.
Eject	Enables you to eject items, such as mounted volumes, CD-ROM discs, and so on, from the desktop.
Burn	Enables you to burn a CD-R, CD-RW, or DVD-R.
Customize	Enables you to open the Customize Toolbar window.
Separator	A graphic element you can use to organize your toolbar.
Space	Adds a block of space to the toolbar.
Flexible Space	Adds a block of flexible space to the toolbar.
New Folder	Creates a new folder.
Delete	Deletes the selected item.
Connect	Opens the Connect to Server dialog box.
Find	Opens the Finder's Find tool.

TABLE 3.2 CONTINUED

Button Name	What It Does
Get Info	Opens the Get Info window for a selected item.
iDisk	Accesses your iDisk.
Search	Enables you to search Finder windows.

TIP

> You can return to the default toolbar by dragging the default toolbar set onto the toolbar in the Customize Toolbar window.

TIP

> If you add more buttons than can be displayed and then want to remove some of the buttons you can't see (you see the double arrows instead), you have to make the window wider so that you can see the button on the toolbar to remove it; you can't remove a button from the pop-up menu. You can also temporarily remove other buttons until you can see the one you want to remove.

CUSTOMIZING THE STATUS BAR

The status bar provides status information for the current directory, volume, or whatever else is being displayed in the Finder window. Mostly, the status bar provides information about the number of items in the window and the amount of free space on the current volume.

Where the status bar is displayed depends on whether the toolbar is shown.

If the toolbar is shown, the status bar information is displayed at the bottom of the window.

If the toolbar is hidden, the status bar appears immediately under the title bar (see Figure 3.15). As with the toolbar, you can hide or show the status bar using the View menu. Unlike the toolbar, however, you can't change the contents of the status bar.

CUSTOMIZING FINDER WINDOW VIEWS

For each view type of Finder window view, you can set Global view preferences that affect all windows you open using that view type. You can then set the Window options for individual windows to override the global settings for that view type. For example, one of the customization options for the List view is the data you see in the window. You can choose to display the Comments column for a window in List view. If you set this as a Global preference, each time you open a new window in List view, you see the Comments column. If there is a window in which you don't want to see the Comments column, you can change the Window preferences for that window so the Comments column is not displayed.

Figure 3.15
When the toolbar is hidden, the status bar appears immediately under the title bar. (Finder windows look a bit pitiful without the toolbar and Places sidebar, don't they?)

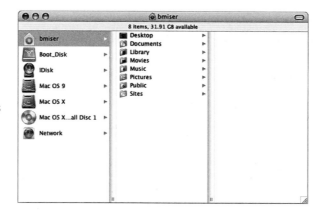

When you change a Global preference, which is called the "All windows" option, it affects all windows shown in that view. When you change a window's preference, it affects only the current window.

CUSTOMIZING THE ICON VIEW

The Icon view has the following view options:

- **Icon size**—You can set the relative size of the icons you see.

- **Text size**—You can set the size of text displayed next to the icons you see.

- **Label position**—You can set the location of the text next to icons. Your choices are on the bottom or to the right of the icon.

- **Snap to grid**—With this option enabled, icons align themselves to an invisible grid.

- **Show item info**—With this option enabled, you see information for the items in a window. The information you see depends on the items being displayed. For example, when the window shows volumes, you see the total space on the volume and the free space on each volume. When you view folders, you see the number of items in that folder. When you see files, information about the file is shown, such as the sizes of image files.

- **Show icon preview**—By default, file icons contain a preview of the file's content within the icon. At press time, this preference does not seem to affect anything. Presumably, when this feature is activated in a later update of OS X, it will cause the icon preview to be hidden if the check box is unchecked.

- **Keep arranged by**—You can choose to keep icons grouped by a criterion you select, including Name, Date Modified, Date Created, Size, Kind, and Label.

- **Background**—You can choose the background used for a Finder window. Your choices are White, a color of your choice, or a picture of your choice. If you select Color or Picture, tools appear to enable you to select the color or picture you want to use.

Set your Global preferences for the Icon view using the following steps:

1. Open a Finder window so you can preview the preferences you will set.

2. Select View, Show View Options or press ⌘-J. The View Options window appears (see Figure 3.16). You use this window to set both Global and window settings. At the top of the window is the name of the folder you are currently viewing.

Figure 3.16
The View Options window enables you to customize Finder window views.

3. Click the "All windows" radio button.

4. Use the Icon size slider to set the relative size of the icons you see. As you move the slider, the icons in the open window reflect the size you set. When you are happy with the size of the icons, release the slider.

5. Use the Text size pop-up menu to set the size of the icon labels.

6. Use the radio buttons in the "Label position" area to select the location of icon labels.

7. Use the four check boxes to enable or disable the options described in the previous bulleted list.

8. If you enabled "Keep arranged by," select the criterion by which you want icons grouped using the pop-up menu (Name is selected by default).

9. Select the folder background option by selecting one of the radio buttons under Background.

10. If you chose Color, use the Color button to open the Color Picker to select the background color you want to use.

11. If you chose Picture, click the Select button and then use the Select a Picture dialog box to select a background image.

NOTE

> Supported image formats include PICT, TIFF, and JPEG. The background image you choose appears in folders you view using the Global icon settings. This does not affect any image you are using as a background image on your desktop.

12. Close the View Options window when you have finished setting the global options.

After you have made these settings, any window you view in Icon view will be displayed using your global preferences unless you override the Global settings by setting a window's preference.

To change the preferences for an individual window, do the following:

1. Open the window you want to view and put it in the Icon view.
2. Open the View Options window by selecting View, Show View Options (or press ⌘-J).
3. Click the "This window only" radio button.
4. Use the controls to set the Icon view preferences for the window you opened in step 1 (see the previous steps for help).
5. Close the View Options window when you are done.

TIP

> You can also modify the view of the desktop, which is always in Icon view. Click anywhere on the desktop and open the View Options window. You can then set the icon size, text size, and other options just like a folder window (except for the folder background that is set using the Desktop pane of the System Preferences Utility).

This window uses the preferences you set for it until you change them.

You can reapply the global preferences at any time by returning to the View Options dialog box and clicking the "All windows" radio button. The window returns to your global view settings. Click "This window only" to return the window to its previous set of view options.

TIP

> You can leave the View Options dialog box open while you select other windows. If you do so, the name shown at the top of the dialog box changes, as do the controls you see if the window you select is in a view different from the current one.

CUSTOMIZING THE LIST VIEW

Customizing List view works pretty much the same way as Icon view, except that you have different options.

Set your global List view preferences using the following steps:

1. Open a Finder window in List view.

2. Open the View Options window (⌘-J).

3. Click the "All windows" radio button.

4. Check the radio button for the icon size you want to use.

5. Select the text size on the "Text size" pop-up menu.

6. Check the boxes next to the data columns you want to be displayed in List view. The default data are Date Modified, Size, and Kind. The other data available are Date Created, Version, Comments, and Label. Data for which you check the boxes is displayed in columns in the List view.

7. Check the Use Relative Dates check box if you want to use relative dates. When you use the relative dates option, you see relative date information (such as yesterday) for some dates rather than the full date for all dates.

8. Check the "Calculate all sizes" check box if you want the size of folders to be displayed in the Size column. This option uses a lot of extra computing power, especially for those folders that contain many folders and files. You should usually leave this box unchecked unless folder size information is critical to you.

9. Close the View Options window.

Every window you see in List view uses these options, unless you override the Global settings for a particular window.

Overriding the Global options for a specific window is analogous to what you do for the Icon view. Open the window, open the View Options window, click the "This window only" radio button, and use the controls to set the view options for the current window.

To reapply the global List view preferences to a window, click the "All windows" radio button in the View Options window.

TIP

> The Window settings for a window are retained (although not used) even after you reapply the global settings to it. You can easily switch back to them by clicking the "This window only" radio button again. The window returns to the most recent window settings you applied to it.

CUSTOMIZING THE COLUMNS VIEW

The Columns view has fewer customization options than do the other views. The Columns view preferences you set apply to all windows in the Columns view. Do the following:

1. Open a Finder window in Columns view.

2. Open the View Options window (⌘-J).

3. Uncheck the "Show icons" check box to hide the icons in the window.

4. Uncheck the "Show preview column" check box if you prefer not to see the preview of a file you have selected in the window.

5. Close the View Options window.

NOTE

> As far as I can tell, there isn't a way to select the List view or the Icon view for every window you open (you can set the Columns view for every new window you open by using the Finder Preferences dialog box). The Finder remembers the view you used the last time you opened a specific window and maintains that view each time you open that window—until you change that window's view. Unfortunately, you can't set the view to be List or Icon on a systemwide basis.
>
> Similarly, you can't tell the Finder to apply the global view preferences to all windows at the same time. If you have changed the view preferences for individual windows, you have to reapply the global view preferences to that window if you want to use them (by using the View Options dialog box).

WORKING WITH THE FINDER WINDOW'S ACTION POP-UP MENU

 One of the new default icons on the Finder window toolbar is the Action pop-up menu (see Figure 3.17). This menu provides access to context-sensitive commands, which means that commands on the menu depend on the item you have selected on the desktop. For example, when you select a folder and open the menu, you see commands including New Folder, Get Info, Color Label, Duplicate, Make Alias, Create Archive, Copy, and Show View Options. If you select a file and open the menu, you see New Folder, Open, Open With, Get Info, Color Label, Move to Trash, Duplicate, Create Alias, Create Archive, and Copy.

Figure 3.17
The commands on the Action pop-up menu change depending on the items you have selected.

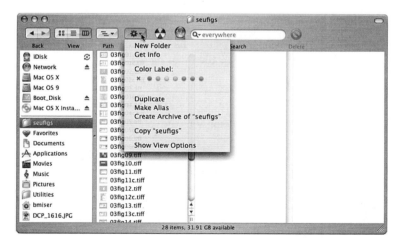

NOTE

As you probably suspect, the commands on the Action pop-up menu are the same as the commands on an item's contextual menu, which you can open by pointing to an item, holding down the Control key, and clicking the item (or right-clicking the item if you use a two-button mouse).

To use a command on the menu, select the item on which you want to use the command, open the menu, and select the command you want to use.

WORKING WITH LABELS

 Although this section is marked with the new version icon, labels aren't really a new feature, but one that has returned to the Mac OS from Mac OS 9. Labels enable you to color code and text code files and folders as a means of identifying and organizing them. For example, you can assign all the folders for a specific project using the same label. In addition to making the relationship between these folders clearer, you can choose to group items within a window by label, which keeps them near one another as well.

SETTING UP LABELS

You can assign text to the color labels by using the following steps:

1. Open the Finder Preferences dialog box.
2. Click the Labels button to open the Labels pane, which contains the seven label colors. Underneath each color is its text label, which by default is the name of the color.
3. Edit the text labels for each color to match your label needs.
4. Close the Preferences dialog box.

APPLYING LABELS

You can apply labels to a folder or file by using the following steps:

1. Select the items to which you want to apply a label.
2. Open the Action pop-up menu or the contextual menu.
3. Select the label you want to apply to the selected labels.

When an item has a label applied to it, its name is highlighted in the label's color. When you view a window in the Columns or List view, a bar filled with the label color covers the row in which the item is located. If you view a window in the List view and select to show the Label column, the label text appears in the Label column for the item.

TIP

> If you view a window in Icon view, you can choose to keep items grouped by label. This keeps all the files with which you have associated a specific location together in the window.

MAC OS X TO THE MAX: FINDER WINDOW KEYBOARD SHORTCUTS

Table 3.3 lists keyboard shortcuts for working with Finder windows.

TABLE 3.3   KEYBOARD SHORTCUTS FOR FINDER WINDOWS

Menu	Action	Keyboard Shortcut
None	Opens an item on the Places sidebar and closes the current window	Option-click
None	Opens an item on the Places sidebar in a new Finder window	⌘-click
None	Closes all open Finder windows	Option-click the Close button
None	Opens an item in a new Finder window	⌘-double-click (a folder
Finder	Preferences	⌘-,
File	New Finder Window	⌘-N
File	New Folder	Shift-⌘-N
File	Open Window	⌘-O
File	Close Window	⌘-W
File	Get Info	⌘-I
File	Show Original	⌘-R
File	Add to Sidebar	⌘-T
View	as Icons	⌘-1
View	as List	⌘-2
View	as Columns	⌘-3
View	Show/Hide Toolbar	Option-⌘-T
View	Show/Hide View Options	⌘-J
Go	Back	⌘-[
Go	Back	⌘-]
Go	Enclosing Folder	⌘-up arrow

3

TABLE 3.3 CONTINUED

Menu	Action	Keyboard Shortcut
Go	Computer	Shift-⌘-C
Go	Home	Shift-⌘-H
Go	Network	Shift-⌘-K
Go	iDisk, My iDisk	Shift-⌘-I
Go	Applications	Shift-⌘-A
Go	Utilities	Shift-⌘-U
Go	Go to Folder	Shift-⌘-G
Go	Connect to Server	⌘-K
Window	Minimize Window	⌘-M

3

CHAPTER 4

WORKING ON THE MAC OS X DESKTOP

In this chapter

THE MAC OS X DESKTOP

The Mac's desktop has always been the place from which you work with files, folders, system configuration, and so on. This setup continues in Mac OS X; the desktop enables you to manipulate the files and folders on your Mac. You also can access commands that appear nowhere else and can control many aspects of how your system performs. And, of course, you can use the Finder to find folders and files stored on your machine.

Although the basic purpose of the Mac OS X version 10.3 desktop is the same as previous versions, its appearance and functionality are quite different (see Figure 4.1). More important than the improved appearance of the desktop, which is pretty amazing in itself, are the numerous functional improvements Mac OS X version 10.3 desktop offers. These include new menus, more contextual menu commands, and so on.

Figure 4.1
The most obvious aspects of the Mac OS X's desktop are the beautiful appearance of its icons, the controls provided in Finder windows, and the Dock.

→ For information on viewing and using Finder windows, **see** Chapter 3, "Viewing and Navigating Mac OS X Finder Windows," **p. 47**.

→ Because the Dock is such an important part of Mac OS X, it has a chapter dedicated to it; **see** Chapter 5, "Using and Customizing the Dock," **p. 127**.

WORKING WITH MAC OS X MENUS

One of the strengths of the Mac OS is that it has always featured certain menus that are very similar in all applications.

THE MAC OS X APPLE MENU

The Apple menu has long been one of the staples of the Mac desktop. Its main purpose has always been to provide access to certain items while you are working on the desktop as well as from within any application.

NOTE

As hard as it is to believe now, the Apple menu was not part of early versions of Mac OS X. Rather than being a menu, the Apple icon appeared in the center of the menu bar and did not have a menu associated with it. Because many longtime Mac users were unhappy about this, Apple added the Apple menu back, although certainly not with the same form or substance as the Apple menu in previous versions.

The Mac OS X Apple menu contains the commands listed in Table 4.1.

TABLE 4.1   COMMANDS ON THE MAC OS X APPLE MENU

Command	What It Does
About This Mac	Opens a. window showing the version of Mac OS X installed, the physical RAM installed, and the number and type of processors. You can also open Software Update to get the latest versions of Apple software and the System Profiler from this window to get more information about your Mac.
Software Update	Opens the Software. Update tool, which you can use to get the latest versions of the Apple software installed on your Mac.
Mac OS X Software	Opens the default Web browser and moves to the Mac OS X software downloads Web page.
System Preferences	Opens the System Preferences application.
Dock	Provides control over the Dock's magnification, hiding, and position settings and enables you to open the Dock Preferences pane of the System Preferences application.
Location	Enables you to select a location for your Mac, which changes the network settings you are using.
Recent Items	Provides a menu of applications and documents you have recently accessed; you can select an item to move back to it. The menu is organized into separate sections for applications and documents. It also has the Clear Menu command, which clears the menu.
Force Quit	Opens the Force Quit Applications window that enables you to kill open applications (for example, when they are hung).
Sleep	Puts the Mac to sleep.
Restart	Restarts the Mac.

4

TABLE 4.1	CONTINUED
Command	**What It Does**
Shut Down	Shuts down the Mac.
Log Out *Acctname*	Logs the current user (whose account name is *Acctname*) off the Mac and opens the Login window.

→ To learn more about working with locations, **see** "Configuring and Using Locations," **p. 989**.

→ To learn more about Mac OS X's Force Quit command, **see** "Controlling Open Applications," **p. 225**.

TIP

> If you use an Apple Cinema Display, you can put your Mac to sleep by pressing the Power button on the display.

MAC OS X APPLICATION MENUS

Under Mac OS X, every application has its own Application menu. The Application menu provides the commands you use to control the application in which you are working. A certain set of commands is consistent among all Mac OS X applications. Specific applications can have more commands on their Application menu, but they must support certain basic commands on that menu. The name of the Application menu is the name of the application itself. For example, the Finder's Application menu is Finder.

NOTE

> If you used Mac OS 9 or earlier versions, don't confuse the Application menu in those versions with Application menus under Mac OS X. In previous Mac OS versions, the Application menu was a single menu that showed you all the applications running on the computer; this menu was always located in the upper-right corner of the desktop. You used the Application menu to hide or show applications as well as switch between running applications. Under Mac OS X, this functionality is provided by the Dock and the Application menus. You still see the Mac OS 9 Application menu when you use the Classic environment.

The following commands appear on all Application menus:

- **About *Application***—The About *Application* command, where *Application* is the name of the active application, displays version information about the application. Some About windows also provide links to support sites, the publisher's Web site, and so on. The About Finder command displays the version of the Finder you are using.

- **Preferences**—You use the Preferences command to set the preferences for an application. For example, you can use Finder Preferences to control specific properties of the desktop.

→ To learn about Finder Preferences, see "Changing the Desktop's Appearance," **p. 122**.

TIP

NEW

The keyboard shortcut for the Preferences command has been standardized (for Apple applications at least) to be ⌘-,. This enables you to open the Preferences dialog box for any application with the same keys. This is a good thing.

- **Hide and Show commands**—The Hide and Show commands enable you to control which running applications are visible. There are three of these commands on the Application menu. The Hide *CurrentApplication* command (where *CurrentApplication* is the name of the running application) hides the current application. The Hide Others command hides all the running applications except the current one, and the Show All command shows all open applications.

NOTE

Hiding an application causes all its windows and its menu bar to disappear. The application continues to run and any processes that are being completed continue. You can also minimize application windows, which places the window on the Dock; the application's menu bar continues to appear while the application is active, even if its windows are minimized.

All Application menus, except the Finder menu, also contain the following commands:

- **Quit**—The Quit command does the same thing as it always has—it stops the running application.
- **Services**—The Services command provides commands to enable you to work with other applications from within the current application. For example, if you are using the TextEdit word processing application, you see the Grab command on its Services menu. Selecting this command activates the Grab application that enables you to capture something on the screen. After you capture the image, it is automatically pasted into the current TextEdit document. Many other commands appear on this menu; the commands available depend on the applications installed on your Mac and how those applications support the Services menu.

→ To learn more about using the Services command with Mac OS X applications, **see** "Working with Mac OS X Application Menus," **p. 152**.

TIP

The keyboard shortcut for the Quit command hasn't changed. It is still ⌘-Q. When you are working on the desktop, ⌘-Q doesn't do anything because you can't quit the Finder. However, you can relaunch the Finder using the Force Quit command.

NEW The Finder's Application menu (the Finder menu) also has the Empty Trash and Secure Empty Trash commands, which are unique to its Application menu. The Empty Trash command does what it always has, which is to delete any files located in the Trash. The new

Secure Empty Trash deletes files located in the Trash and overwrites the disk space on which those files were stored so they can't be recovered. Because the Secure Empty Trash command overwrites the disk space on which the files where written, it takes much longer to execute than does the Empty Trash command (of course, because it works in the background, it shouldn't really be noticeable).

MAC OS X FILE MENUS

The Mac has always had a File menu; under Mac OS X, this menu is purer than it was in previous versions of the OS. For example, in previous versions, the File menu contained commands for working with files as well as controlling the application. Under Mac OS X, the File menu contains only commands for working with files or folders.

The specific commands you see on an application's File menu depend on the application. Most applications' File menus have the New, Open, Save, Save As, Print, and Page Setup commands. Many other commands might appear on the File menu as well.

The Finder's File menu contains the commands listed in Table 4.2.

TABLE 4.2 COMMANDS ON THE FINDER'S FILE MENU

Command	What It Does
New Finder Window	Opens a new Finder window
New Folder	Creates a new folder
Open	Opens the selected item
Open With	Enables you to open a selected file with a specific application
Close Window	Closes the active window
Get Info	Opens the Info window
Duplicate	Creates a duplicate of the selected item
Make Alias	Creates an alias of the selected item
Show Original	Exposes the original item for which an alias was created
Add to Sidebar	Adds an alias of the selected item to the Places Sidebar
Create Archive	Compresses the selected folders and files into a ZIP file
Move to Trash	Moves the selected item to the Trash
Eject	Ejects the selected item (disc, disk image, server volume, and so on)
Burn Disc	Burns the selected CD or DVD
Find	Opens the Finder's Find tool so you can locate files and folders
Color Label	Applies the label you choose to the selected items

NOTE

The Mac OS X version 10.3 Archive command is one of the most useful Finder commands. This command enables you to create compressed files from any folders and files on your Mac. Even better, Mac OS X now supports the ZIP compression format, which is the standard, native compression format on Windows computers. You no longer need a separate application to compress files. You can also expand any ZIP file from the desktop by opening it.

Mac OS X Edit Menus

Under Mac OS X, the Edit menu is much as it has always been. The Edit menu contains commands for editing data. The commands that always appear on the Edit menu are Cut, Copy, and Paste. Applications can provide many more commands on this menu, such as Undo, Redo, Select All, and so on.

In addition to the standard Edit commands, the Finder's Edit menu also has the Select All command, which selects everything in the active window; the Show Clipboard command, which shows what has been copied to the Clipboard; and the Special Characters command, which opens the Character palette.

The Finder View Menu

The Finder's View menu contains the commands you use to view Finder windows.

→ To learn about using the Finder's View commands, **see** Chapter 3, "Viewing and Navigating Mac OS X Finder Windows," **p. 47**.

The Finder Go Menu

The Finder's Go menu, as you might guess from its name, contains commands you use to go places. The Go menu enables you to move to the following locations:

- **Back or Forward**—You can move among the windows in a chain of open Finder windows by using the Back and Forward commands.
- **Enclosing Folder**—You can move into the folder that contains the currently selected item by choosing this command.
- **Directories**—You can move to any of the directories listed on the Go menu by selecting the directory into which you want to move.
- **Recent Folders**—This command lists the most recent folders you have used; select a folder to return to it. You can clear the Recent Folders menu by selecting Clear Menu.
- **Folders**—Use the Go To Folder command to enter the path to a specific folder to open it.
- **Servers**—Use the Connect To Server command to open a server on your network.

→ To learn how to use the Go menu to navigate directories, **see** "Changing Directories with the Go Menu," **p. 65**.
→ To learn how to connect to servers, **see** "Accessing Shared Files from a Mac OS X Computer," **p. 834**.

4

MAC OS X WINDOW MENUS

Another standard Mac OS X menu is the Window menu. This menu provides commands you use to work with windows that are currently open. Common choices on the Window menu include the following:

- **Minimize Window**—This does the same thing as clicking the Minimize button in a window—it moves the window onto the Dock.

- **Bring All to Front**—This command brings all open windows to the front. For example, if you have a lot of open Finder windows and then switch to an application and then back to the Finder, you might not see all your open Finder windows. If you use this command, they all come to the foreground so you can see them.

- **List of Open Windows**—The Window menu always displays a list of the windows open for the application providing that menu. You can switch to an open window by selecting it on the menu.

- **Close Window**—This closes the active window. (You won't see this command on the Finder's Window menu.)

- **Zoom Window**—This does the same thing as the Maximize button. (You won't see this command on the Finder's Window menu either.)

TIP

A great way to manage all open windows (not just those open in the current application) is by using the Exposé feature. More on that later in this chapter.

NOTE

The Window menu is not really new; many Mac applications have always used a Window menu to enable you to switch between open documents. However, the menu was new to the Finder for Mac OS X, and because it is now a system function, it should appear in all applications.

On the Window menu, the active window in the application you are currently using is marked with some sort of icon. The active Finder window is marked with a check mark; other applications might use a different indicator (for example, a diamond). Be aware that a window can be both active and minimized, in which case the active icon on the Window menu can help you identify the active window even if you can't see that window (because it is on the Dock).

You might see more or fewer commands on the Window menu when you are working in specific applications.

NOTE

> Note that the Window menu provided by Classic applications is not the same as the Window menu provided by Carbonized or Cocoa applications. For example, if you are running the Classic version of Word 2001, you see its Window menu rather than one provided by Mac OS X (so you won't see the Minimize or other commands you would expect to see on an OS X Window menu).

MAC OS X HELP MENUS

Most applications provide a Help menu that enables you to open their help system.

The Finder's Help menu contains one command—Mac Help. This command opens the Mac Help application, which provides extensive help for many areas of the OS (see Figure 4.2). Even better, many applications you install integrate their help systems into the OS help system. This enables you to access plenty of help using the same tool.

Figure 4.2
You can get a lot of Mac OS help by using the Help application.

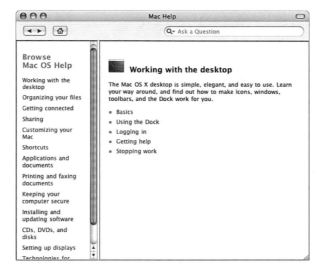

The Help application is based on HTML, so it works the same way Web pages do. You can search for help and click links and buttons to access information and move around. Fortunately, the Help engine works much more quickly in Mac OS X version 10.3 than it did under previous versions.

The Home button in the Help Center's toolbar takes you back to the current help's home page. Like other Mac OS X applications, you can customize the Help application's toolbar by using the View, Customize Toolbar command.

TIP

> When you search for help, you frequently see the Tell Me More link. This link opens other pages that contain topics related to the one for which you searched.

You can search the Help application using the Search tool located in the toolbar. This tool works just like the Search tool in other areas. Select the help area you want to search using the Magnifying Glass icon and then type the text for which you want to search. Press Return to perform the search; the results appear in the Search Results window (see Figure 4.3). This window lists each help topic that matches your search. By default, this window is sorted by the Relevance column, which is the Help system's judgment of how well a topic addresses your search criterion. The Location column shows you in which help system the topic is included.

Figure 4.3
You can search the Help application to find specific topics.

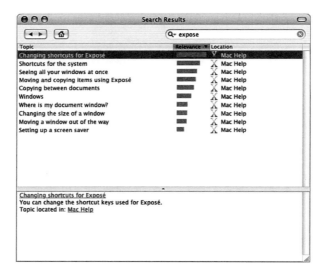

TIP

> You can also browse most help systems from their home pages. This is often an even better way to find a specific topic because you don't have to be concerned about using specific words as you do when you search for help.

You can open a topic by double-clicking it. The topic appears in the window for viewing. If you select a topic by single-clicking it, a summary of the topic appears in the bottom pane of the Help window.

The Help system's Go menu tracks the recent topics you have visited; you can return to a topic by selecting it on the menu. You can use the Library menu to view a list of all help resources served through the Mac OS X Help application; to move into another help resource such as iMovie Help, click it in the list.

NOTE

> Need help with Help? Select Help, Help Viewer Help. (Try to use the word *help* more times in the same sentence than that!)

Some help topics assist you in performing the action about which you are asking by providing hyperlinks that open the related application or resource.

MAC OS X CONTEXTUAL MENUS

As with previous versions of the OS, Mac OS X supports contextual menus. *Contextual menus* are pop-up menus that appear in various locations and contain commands specifically related to the context in which you are working. You can access contextual menus by pointing to an object that provides a contextual menu, holding down the Control key, and clicking the mouse button. The contextual menu appears and you can select a command on it.

TIP

NEW

> Mac OS X version 10.3 (finally!) supports a two-button mouse by default. You can open an item's contextual menu by right-clicking it. You can also program most multibutton input devices to perform a right-click. This is one area where Windows has been ahead of the Mac for some time; all Windows mouse devices have at least two buttons. I strongly recommend that you use a mouse or trackball that has at least two buttons, if for no other reason than the convenience or opening contextual menus with one hand.

The desktop and Finder provide contextual menus, as do many applications, including those not provided by Apple. For example, the Microsoft Office application provides excellent support for contextual menus.

NOTE

> Most Mac OS 9 applications still provide their contextual menus when you run them under the Mac OS X Classic environment.

In Finder windows or on the desktop, you can tell when a contextual menu is provided by pointing to something and pressing the Control key. If a contextual menu is available, you see the contextual menu pointer, which is a small rectangle containing horizontal lines. When you see this pointer, click the mouse button to see the menu.

A summary of some of the more useful Finder contextual menu commands is provided in Table 4.3.

4

TABLE 4.3   USEFUL FINDER CONTEXTUAL MENU COMMANDS

Object	Command	What It Does
Desktop	Change Desktop Background	Opens the Desktop & Screen Saver pane of the System Preferences application.
Folder, file	Color Label	Applies a label to the selected items.
Folder, file	Copy	Copies selected items.
Folder, file	Create Archive	Creates a Zip file containing the selected items.
Mac OS X window toolbars	Customize Toolbar	Enables you to customize the current toolbar.
Folder, file	Duplicate	Duplicates the selected items.
Desktop, Finder window, folder, file	Folder Action commands	Folder actions are AppleScripts you can attach to folders so those actions are performed automatically. You use the Attach a Folder Action command to select the actions associated with the selected item. You use the Configure Folder Actions command to configure how actions for an item work. You use the Disable Folder Actions command to disable an item's folder actions.
Desktop, Finder window, folder, file	Get Info	Opens the Info window (this is covered in more detail later in this chapter).
Folder, file	Make Alias	Creates an alias of the selected items.
Folder, file	Move to Trash	Moves the selected items to the Trash.
Desktop, Finder window	New Folder	Creates a new folder.
Folder, file	Open	Opens the selected item.
File	Open With	Enables you to choose the application to use to open the selected file.
Folder	Paste item	Pastes the previously created copy of files or folders in the current location.
Mac OS X window toolbars	Toolbar Format commands	Use these to change the format of the toolbar, such as Text Only to hide the icons and display only text.

THE FINDER ACTION POP-UP MENU

New to Mac OS X is the Action pop-up menu on the Finder window's toolbar. This pop-up menu provides contextual commands that work just like those on contextual menus. When you select an item or view a folder, the appropriate commands appear on the menu (see Figure 4.4).

Figure 4.4
The new Action pop-up menu provides contextual commands.

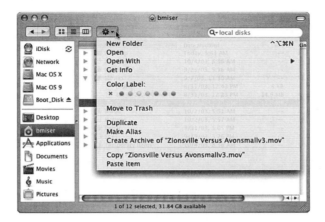

The commands that appear on this menu are the same as those that appear on contextual menus (refer to Table 4.3). The one exception is that, when you are viewing the contents of a folder with no items selected, the Show View Options command appears on the Action pop-up menu.

WORKING WITH THE SYSTEM PREFERENCES APPLICATION

The System Preferences application enables you to set preferences for many areas of Mac OS X. If you read through the previous chapters, you already have some experience with this application. However, because you will use the System Preferences application so frequently, it is worthy of a more detailed look.

You can open the System Preferences utility in various ways, including the following:

- Select Apple, System Preferences.
- Click the System Preferences icon on the Dock.
- Open the Applications folder and then open System Preferences using its icon.

NOTE

Because the System Preferences application is used so frequently, Apple should have provided a keyboard shortcut to open it but didn't. If you use a macro utility, such as QuicKeys, you should set and use a keyboard shortcut to open this application. Or you can add it to your Startup Items (use the Hide option so it is hidden on startup) so it opens each time you log in to Mac OS X.

The System Preferences application provides a window with a toolbar at the top and a series of icons or buttons in the bottom part (see Figure 4.5). To access the controls for a specific area, you click its icon. The System Preferences window changes to show the pane for that area (see Figure 4.6).

Figure 4.5
The System Preferences application enables you to configure and customize Mac OS X to suit your needs and personal preferences.

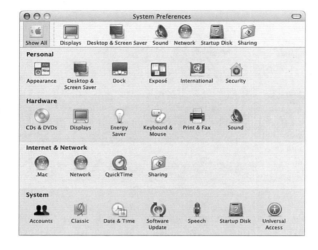

Figure 4.6
The Sound pane of the System Preferences application enables you to change your system's sound settings (notice that you can customize the application's toolbar as I have done here).

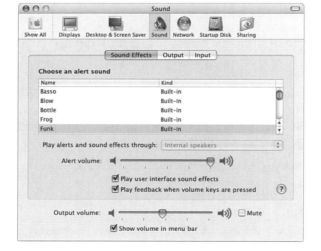

The default panes contained in the System Preferences utility (listed in alphabetical order) are the following:

- .Mac
- Accounts
- Appearance

- CDs & DVDs
- Classic
- Date & Time
- Desktop & Screen Saver
- Displays
- Dock
- Energy Saver
- Exposé
- International
- Keyboard & Mouse
- Network
- Print & Fax
- QuickTime
- Security
- Sharing
- Software Update
- Sound
- Speech
- Startup Disk
- Universal Access

By default, these buttons are organized into the following categories: Personal, Hardware, Internet & Network, and System. The Personal panes configure aspects of the user account that is currently logged in. The panes in the other three categories make systemwide changes (and so require that you are logged in under or authenticate yourself as an administrator account).

You can choose to list the icons in alphabetical order if you prefer. Just select View, Organize Alphabetically. The categories disappear and the icons are listed in alphabetical order (from left to right, top to bottom).

You can also open a pane by clicking its button in the toolbar at the top of the System Preferences window. Similar to other Mac OS X toolbars, you can add buttons to this toolbar by dragging them to it and remove buttons by dragging them out of the toolbar. (Unlike other Mac OS X toolbars, you don't have to use the Customize Toolbar command to make changes to the System Preferences' toolbar.)

If you prefer to use a menu to open a pane, select the pane you want to open on the View menu.

4

After you have selected a pane, you can show all the panes of the window again by clicking the Show All button or by selecting Pane, Show All Preferences (⌘-L).

NOTE

> Specific panes are covered in the parts of this book that explain the features they are related to. For example, the Accounts pane is explained in the section "Creating User Accounts," in Chapter 2, "Getting Started with Mac OS X."

When you add hardware or software to your system, additional panes can appear to enable you to configure the device or software you added. Common examples of this are the Bluetooth pane, which appears when your Mac supports Bluetooth, or Ink, which appears when you attach a handwriting recognition device (such as a tablet) to your Mac. For example, compare Figure 4.7 with Figure 4.5.

Figure 4.7
Compare this figure to Figure 4.5 and you will see that several panes have been added to the System Preferences application.

Panes added by Apple-produced tools, such as the Bluetooth pane, appear within the related categories, such as Hardware. Panes added by third-party tools, such as keyboard customization panes, are contained in the Other category.

MANAGING OPEN WINDOWS WITH EXPOSÉ

 Because it is so useful to have multiple applications and multiple documents within each application open at the same time, you might have dozens of windows open at the same time with those windows layered one on another. Getting to the specific window in which you are interested can be difficult. That is where Exposé comes in. It is designed to help you quickly manage all the open windows on your desktop.

TIP

> You can customize the controls used to activate Exposé functions, as you will learn in the next section.

USING EXPOSÉ

Exposé offers a number of useful functions, which are the following:

- **See all open windows at the same time**—If you press the F9 key, all open windows are reduced in size and tiled such that they can all be displayed on the desktop at the same time (see Figure 4.8). When you point to a window, its title appears so you can definitely identify it if you couldn't just by its appearance. You can click a window to move into that window; the other windows return to their previous sizes and locations. You can also move into a window in which the cursor is located by pressing F9 again.

Figure 4.8
Using Exposé, you can show all open windows on your desktop at the same time.

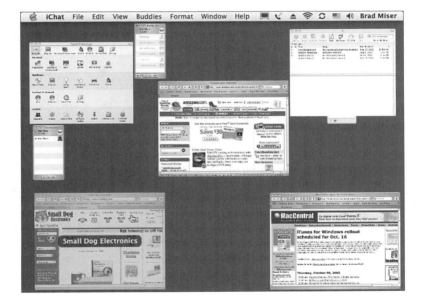

4

NOTE

> If you use multiple monitors and activate Exposé, the windows on all monitors shrink and remain on the monitor they were on.

■ **See all the windows in the current application at the same time**—If you press the F10 key, all the windows in the current application are shown. Just like the previous command, you can point to a window to see its title, click it to move into it, and so on.

TIP

> If you hold down the Shift key while you activate Exposé, you see its effects in slow motion.

■ **Hide all open windows and show the desktop**—If you press F11, all open windows are hidden and you see your desktop. This is useful if you have a bad case of desktop clutter and want to work on the desktop without closing or moving the current windows. You can return all windows to their previous locations by pressing F11 again. You can also open an item on the desktop by double-clicking it; when you do, the other windows return to their previous locations. Another option is to click one of the window borders that will be visible along the edges of your screen to return windows to their previous states.

■ **Cycle through the Open windows in each application**—If you activate Exposé by pressing F9 or F10, you can cycle through the set of open windows in each application by pressing the Tab or Shift-Tab keys (to move in the opposite direction). Each time you do, the next application becomes active and you see all its open windows. Windows open in other applications remain at their current sizes and are unselectable.

CONFIGURING EXPOSÉ

You can customize the following aspects of Exposé using the Exposé pane of the System Preferences application (see Figure 4.9):

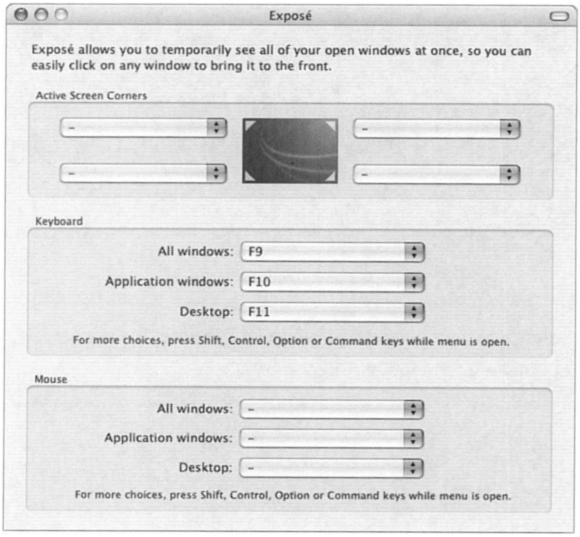

Figure 4.9
The Exposé pane of the System Preferences application enables you to customize various aspects of Exposé.

- **Active Screen Corners**—Use the pop-up menu located at each corner of the preview monitor to set an action that happens when you move the cursor to that corner. The actions you can set are All Windows (the default F9 key), Application Windows (the default F10 key), Desktop (the default F11 key), Start Screen Saver, Disable Screen Saver, and No Action (-). To set an action for a corner, select the action on the related pop-up menu. When you point to that corner of the screen, that action occurs.

- **Keyboard**—Use the Keyboard pop-up menus to set the keys to activate each Exposé action. In addition to the keys on the menus, you can see other combinations by holding down a modifier key, such as ⌘, while you open a pop-up menu.

- **Mouse**—Use the mouse pop-up menus to set Exposé actions for specific mouse buttons when you use a multi-button mouse.

UNDERSTANDING MAC OS X DIRECTORIES

Mac OS X includes many standard folders, often called *directories* in Mac OS X lingo. You have seen several of these as you learned about using the Go menu, working with Finder windows, and so on.

Some directories, such as the Mac OS X System directory, are critical to your Mac's operation, whereas others are merely organizational devices, such as the Documents directory within each user's Home directory.

There are two general groups of directories you will work with: those for the system and those for users.

MAC OS X SYSTEM DIRECTORIES

Two main directories provide access to Mac OS X system-level files and folders.

THE COMPUTER DIRECTORY

The Computer directory is the highest-level folder on your Mac. It shows the volumes mounted on your machine, including hard drives, drive partitions, disk images, DVDs, CD-ROMs, and so on (see Figure 4.10). The name of the Computer directory is the name of your Mac.

Most of the contents of the Computer directory should be familiar to you, such as volumes, CD-ROMs, and so on.

One exception to this is the Network folder, which contains the resources you can access via a network.

→ To learn more about the Network volume, **see** Chapter 26, "Building and Using a Network," **p. 821**.

Figure 4.10
The Mac OS X Computer directory represents all the contents of your machine as well as the network resources you can access.

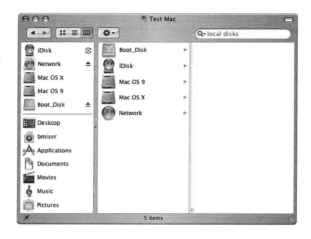

THE MAC OS X STARTUP VOLUME

One of the directories in the Computer directory is the one on which you installed Mac OS X. The name of this directory depends on what you named the volume (for example, I called mine Mac OS X).

By default, your startup volume directory contains the following four directories that are part of the Mac OS X installation:

- **Applications**—Under Mac OS X, all Carbon and Cocoa applications are stored in this directory.

→ To learn how to install applications, **see** Chapter 6, "Installing and Using Mac OS X Applications," **p. 143**.

- **Library**—The Library folder contains many subfolders that provide resources to support applications, hardware devices, and other items you add to your Mac. This library directory contains the system folders that can be modified.

- **System**—This folder contains the Library folder that provides the core operating system software for Mac OS X. The items in this folder can't be modified except by installation applications, system updaters, or using the root account.

→ To learn more about the Library and System directories, **see** "Mac OS X to the Max: Exploring Mac OS X," **p. 238**.

- **Users**—The Users directory contains the Home directory for each user for whom an account has been created. The Home directory of the user currently logged in has the Home icon; the Home directories for the rest of the users have plain folder icons. If you have deleted user accounts, it also contains folder called "Deleted Users" that contains a disk image for each deleted user account (if you elected to keep the user's resources when you deleted his folder).

The Users directory also contains the Shared folder. Items placed in this folder can be accessed by any user who logs in to the Mac.

NOTE

If you installed Mac OS X version 10.3 using the Archive and Install option, the startup volume also includes the Previous Systems folder, which contains the folders from the previous Mac OS X installations.

MAC OS X USER DIRECTORIES

As you learned in Chapter 2, each user account includes a Home folder. By default, this folder contains eight directories in which the logged-in user can store folders and files.

→ To learn about the specific directories in a user's Home directory, **see** "Understanding the Home Folder," **p. 21**.

Although the Home folder contains the eight default directories, you can add directories within these folders as well as create new folders within the Home folder itself.

The benefit to using the standard directories is that they are integrated into the OS so you can access them quickly and in many ways. For example, you can select the Documents directory in Mac OS X Save and Open dialog boxes. This makes keeping your documents organized easier than if you create your own directories outside your Home folder.

TIP

You can add any folder to the Places sidebar, which is visible in all Open and Save dialog boxes along with Finder windows (when the sidebar is displayed). Adding a folder to the sidebar makes that folder accessible from many locations.

Another benefit of using the standard Mac OS X directories is that they take advantage of the default security settings that go with the user account. When you use directories outside a user account's Home folder, you should check and set the security of the folders you are using if you want to limit the access to those resources by other people who use your Mac.

→ To learn how to configure an item's security, **see** "Understanding and Setting Permissions," **p. 843**.

Most of the user directories are self-explanatory, such as Documents, Movies, and Music. A few of them are worthy of more detailed attention, though.

THE DESKTOP DIRECTORY

The user's Desktop folder contains the items the user has placed on his desktop. Each user can have as much or as little on his desktop as he likes. When another user logs in, she sees only the contents of her desktop folder on the desktop.

THE LIBRARY DIRECTORY

In the Library directory are system files specifically related to the user account. The Library directory includes a number of subdirectories (see Figure 4.11).

Figure 4.11
Each user has a Library directory in which files that relate to that user's system resources, such as preferences, are stored.

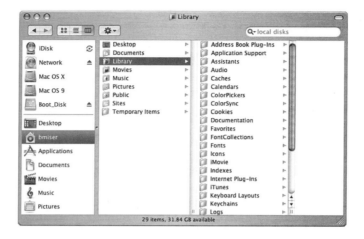

The particular folders you see depend on the applications you have used and what you have done. For instance, if you have installed iMovie, iPhoto, and iTunes, you'll find folders and files related to each of these applications. In the Fonts folder are fonts that only you can access. Your Internet plug-ins are stored in the Internet Plug-Ins folder, and the Preferences directory is where applications store your personal preferences.

THE PUBLIC DIRECTORY

A user's Public directory is available to all users who log in to a particular Mac. This directory lets users conveniently share or transfer files because placing files or folders within the Public directory makes them available to all the other users on a particular machine.

To access the files and folders in another user's Public folder, perform the following steps:

1. Open the Users directory.
2. Open the Home directory for the user who has a file you want to share.
3. Open the Public directory and use the files contained within it.

TIP

> You can open a file or folder within another user's Public directory, or you can drag the file to your own directory to make a copy of it.

Within the Public directory, you also see a Drop Box folder. Other users can place items into this folder, but no one else can open the folder. This is useful when you want others to transfer items to you but don't want all the other users to be able to see what has been shared.

THE SITES DIRECTORY

The Sites directory contains the files and folders that make up the Web site for each user account.

→ For more information on sharing a Web site under Mac OS X, **see** "Using Mac OS X to Serve Web Pages," **p. 446**.

WORKING WITH FILES AND FOLDERS

Working with files and folders under Mac OS X is quite similar to working with them under previous versions.

Under Mac OS X, you can move and copy files and folders as in previous versions of the OS. Just drag the folders or files to where you want them to reside.

To place a copy of an item in a different folder, hold down the Option key while you drag the item. To duplicate an item (make a copy of it in its current location), select it and select File, Duplicate (or press ⌘-D).

> **NOTE**
>
> The Columns view is one of the more useful for moving files and folders around because it gives you a good view of the entire hierarchy of the volume you are working with.

You can also create copies of files and folders using the contextual menu commands and the commands on the Edit menu. You can place a copy of the items in a new location by pasting them there.

> **NOTE**
> **NEW**
>
> One improvement included in version 10.3 is that folders become highlighted so you can easily see in which folder the item you are moving will be placed. This is especially useful when you are viewing Finder windows in the Columns view.

Creating and naming folders is another area in which Mac OS X uses the same model as previous versions. One thing that is new under Mac OS X is the allowable length for folder names, which is now 256 characters. Of course, you aren't likely to ever use a folder name that long because it would be very difficult to read, but at least you have more flexibility with folder names than you did previously.

To name a folder or edit its current name, select the folder and press Return. The folder's name becomes highlighted and you can create a new name.

Other tasks you do with Mac OS X are similar to previous versions as well, including those discussed in the following three sections.

4

NAMING FILES

Naming files is very similar to naming folders, with one exception. Because the underlying architecture of the Mac OS has changed, many document names now include *filename extensions*—for example, .doc at the end of a Word document filename.

Long known in the PC world, file extensions are a code that helps identify a file's type and thus the application used to view or edit that file. Many Mac OS X applications also use filename extensions; the OS uses these extensions to launch the appropriate application for that document when you open the file.

→ To understand more about filename extensions under Mac OS X, **see** "Saving Documents in Mac OS X," **p. 174**.

When you name a document from within an application that uses filename extensions, the correct extension is appended automatically to the filename you enter. However, when you rename files on the desktop or in a Finder window, you need to be aware of a filename's extension if it has one (not all applications use an extension).

A complication in this is that you can choose to show or hide filename extensions on a file-by-file basis or at the system level. However, filename extensions are almost always in use, whether you can see them or not. Hiding them simply hides them from your view.

I wrote "almost always in use" because all Mac OS X applications add filename extensions to files with which they work. And most Classic applications do not use filename extensions. Fortunately, you can use the Info tool to associate applications with specific files so the lack of a proper filename extension is not a significant problem.

→ To learn how to associate files with specific applications, **see** "Opening Documents in Mac OS X," **p. 166**.

If you want to rename a file that has an extension, you should leave the extension as it is. If you change or remove the extension, the application you use to open the file might not be launched automatically when you try to open the file.

The filename extensions you see under Mac OS X include some of the three- or four-letter filename extensions with which you are no doubt familiar, such as .doc, .xls, .html, .jpg, .tiff, and so on. However, there are many, many more filename extensions you will encounter. Some are relatively short, whereas others (particularly those in the system) can be quite long. There isn't really any apparent rhyme or reason to these filename extensions so you just have to learn them as you go. Because you will mostly deal with filename extensions that are appended by an application when you save a document, this isn't a critical task. However, as you delve deeper into the system, you will become more familiar with many of the sometimes bizarre-looking filename extensions Mac OS X uses.

NOTE

> Depending on the file type, some files open properly even if you do remove or change the file's extension. But it is better to be safe than sorry, so you should usually leave the file extension as you find it.

You can choose to hide or show filename extensions globally or on an item-by-item basis. To configure filename extensions globally, use the following steps:

1. Select Finder, Preferences to open the Finder Preferences window.
2. Click the Advanced tab.
3. To globally show filename extensions, check the "Show all file extensions" check box.
4. To allow filename extensions to be shown or hidden for specific items, uncheck the "Show all file extensions" check box.
5. Close the Preferences window.

→ To learn how to show or hide filename extensions for specific items, **see** "Working with Name and Extension Information," **p. 110**.

CREATING AND USING ALIASES

As with previous versions of the Mac OS, an alias is a pointer to a file, folder, or volume. Open an alias and the original item opens. The main benefits to aliases are that you can place them anywhere on your Mac and that they are very small, so you can use them with little storage penalty.

There are several ways to create an alias, including

- Select an item and select File, Make Alias.
- Select an item and press ⌘-L.
- Hold down the Option and ⌘ keys while you drag an item.
- Open the Action menu for an item and select Make Alias.
- Open the contextual menu for an item and select Make Alias.

You might need to find the original from which an alias was created. For example, if you create an alias to an application, you might want to be able to move to that application in the Finder. Do the following:

1. Select the alias.
2. Select File, Show Original (or press ⌘-R). A Finder window containing the original item opens.

Occasionally, an alias *breaks*, meaning your Mac loses track of the original to which the alias points. The most common situation is that you have deleted the original, but it can happen for other reasons as well. When you attempt to open a broken alias, you will see a warning dialog box that provides the following three options:

- **Delete Alias**—If you click this button, the alias is deleted.
- **Fix Alias**—If you click this one, you can use the Fix Alias dialog box to select another file to which you want the alias to point.
- **OK**—If you click OK, the dialog box disappears and no changes are made to the alias.

4

TRASHING FILES AND FOLDERS

Under Mac OS X, the Trash is located at the right end of the Dock. Other than that, the Trash mostly works the same way it always has.

To move something to the Trash, use one of the following methods:

- Drag the item to the Trash on the Dock.
- Select an item, open its contextual menu, and select Move to Trash.
- Select an item and select File, Move to Trash.
- Select an item and press ⌘-Delete.

After you have placed an item in the Trash, you can access it again by clicking the Trash icon on the Dock. A Finder window displaying the Trash directory opens, and you can work with the items it contains.

When you want to delete the items in the Trash, do so in one of the following ways:

- Select Finder, Empty Trash. In the confirmation dialog box, click either OK (or press Return) to empty the Trash or Cancel to stop the process. You can skip the confirmation dialog box by holding down the Option key while you select Empty Trash.
- Open the Trash's Dock contextual menu and select Empty Trash on the resulting pop-up.
- Press Shift-⌘-Delete. In the confirmation dialog box, click either OK (or press Return) to empty the Trash or Cancel to stop the process. You can skip the confirmation dialog box by pressing Option-Shift-⌘-Delete instead.

To permanently disable the warning dialog box when you empty the Trash, perform the following steps:

1. Select Finder, Preferences to open the Finder Preferences window.
2. Click the Advanced tab.
3. Uncheck the "Show warning before emptying the Trash" check box.
4. Close the Preferences dialog box. The warning no longer appears, no matter how you empty the Trash.

NEW Under Mac OS X version 10.3, you can securely delete items from the Trash. When you do, the data that makes up those items is overwritten so it can't be recovered. To perform a secure delete, place items in the Trash and select Finder, Secure Empty Trash.

GETTING INFORMATION ON ITEMS

The Info window is a tool you use to learn about various items on your desktop and in Finder windows. For some items, you can also control specific aspects of how those items work and how they can be used.

You can access all the tools in the Info window from a single pane by using its Expansion triangles. The window is organized into sections; you expose a section by clicking its Expansion triangle. You can have multiple information windows open at the same time (which is helpful when you want to compare items).

The Info window has slightly different features and information for each of the following groups:

- Folders and volumes
- Applications
- Documents

The sections you see for each type of item are described in Table 4.4.

TABLE 4.4   SECTIONS OF THE GET INFO WINDOW

Section	Applicable Items	Information/Tools It Provides
General	Folders and volumes; applications; documents	Provides identification information about the item, such as its name, type, and significant dates.
Name & Extension	Folders and volumes; applications; documents	Gives the full item name, including its filename extension if applicable.
Content Index	Folders and volumes	Provides information about the most recent index created for that item (an index is required to search for items by content). You can also index an item from this section and delete an item's current index.
Preview	Folders and volumes; applications; documents	Shows the icon of everything except documents. For documents, a preview of the document's content is provided (this is the same preview the Columns view provides).
Languages	Applications	Displays and enables you to choose the languages that should be available in the application.
Plug-ins	Applications	Enables you to configure plug-ins for the application. You can enable or disable plug-ins and can add or remove them.
Open with	Documents	Enables you to select an application with which to open a document. You can also set the application used for all documents of the same type.

4

Table 4.4   Continued

Section	Applicable Items	Information/Tools It Provides
Ownership & Permissions	Folders and volumes; applications; documents	Enables you to configure the access permissions for an item.
Comments	Folders and volumes; applications; documents	Enables you to add comments to an item.

Examples of how to use each of these sections for various items are provided in the following sections.

Working with General Information

The General section of the Info window is used mostly to provide detailed information about an item. However, for specific items, you can also use the controls it provides:

1. Select the item you are interested in and press ⌘-I. The Info window appears.
2. Expand the General section if it isn't expanded by default.
3. View the information provided at the top of the window.
4. Use any tools that appear to configure the item.

Depending on the item you select, you have the following choices:

- You can select the Locked check box that appears when the selected item is a document, a folder, or an application to prevent the item from being changed.
- You can use the Stationery Pad check box to convert a selected document into a template.

Working with Name and Extension Information

The Name & Extension section enables you to view and change the name of the selected item:

1. Select the item you are interested in and press ⌘-I. The Info window appears.
2. Expand the Name & Extension section.
3. Edit the item name in the Name & Extension field that appears. Remember to add or edit filename extensions as appropriate (volumes and folders don't have filename extensions).

NOTE

Applications have the filename extension .app.

When you are displaying Name & Extension information for a document, you also see the "Hide extension" check box. When this is checked, the filename extension for the file is hidden in Finder windows. This check box is overridden by the Finder's file extension preference. If the "Show all file extensions" check box in the Finder Preferences window is checked, filename extensions are shown regardless of the "Hide extension" check box for an individual file. The Finder preference must be unchecked for this box to hide or show a file's filename extension.

WORKING WITH CONTENT INDEX INFORMATION

This information relates to the index that must be created for any volume or folder to be searchable by content. This feature is discussed in the section "Finding Files by Content," later in this chapter.

WORKING WITH PREVIEW INFORMATION

The Preview section provides a preview of the selected item. For everything except documents, this preview is simply the item's icon. However, when you use this feature on a document, you get a preview of the item's content, just as you do when you view a Finder window in Columns view. If the content is dynamic, such as a QuickTime movie, you can view or hear that content from the Preview section:

1. Select the item you are interested in and press ⌘-I. The Info window appears.
2. Expand the Preview section.
3. Use the Preview section to preview the item's content. For example, use the controls to view the item if it is a QuickTime movie.

For documents for which Mac OS X can't generate a preview, you see the appropriate icon instead.

WORKING WITH LANGUAGES INFORMATION

Mac OS X applications can support various languages. The Languages section of the Information window enables you to choose the languages you want to be available in an application. Do the following steps:

1. Select the application you are interested in and press ⌘-I. The Info window appears.
2. Expand the Languages section.
3. Remove the check box next to any language you want to disable for that application.
4. Check the check box next to any language you want to enable in the application.
5. To remove a language from the application, select the language and click Remove. After you confirm what you are doing, that language's support files are removed from the application's files and are no longer available.
6. To add language support to the application, click the Add button and select the language file you want to add.

4

TIP

> You can have more than one section expanded at the same time. In fact, you can have as few as none expanded, or you can have all of them expanded.

WORKING WITH PLUG-IN INFORMATION

Mac OS X applications can use plug-ins to provide additional capabilities and functionality. You can enable or disable plug-ins for an application and remove or add plug-ins using the following steps:

1. Select the application for which you want to configure plug-ins and press ⌘-I. The Info window appears.

2. Expand the Plug-ins section (see Figure 4.12).

Figure 4.12
You can use the Plug-ins section of the Info window to configure the plug-ins for an application, such as iMovie's plug-ins that provide additional special effects.

3. Uncheck the box next to any plug-in you want to disable for that application.

4. Check the box next to any plug-in you want to enable in the application.

5. To remove a plug-in from the application, select the plug-in and click Remove. After you confirm what you are doing, that plug-in is removed from the application and is no longer available.

6. To add a plug-in to the application, click the Add button and select the plug-in file you want to add.

WORKING WITH OPEN WITH INFORMATION

You can use the "Open with" section to determine which application is used to open a file:

1. Select the document you are interested in and press ⌘-I. The Info window appears.

2. Expand the "Open with" section.

3. Select the application with which you want the file to be opened on the pop-up menu. The application currently associated with the document is shown in the pop-up menu. The "suggested" applications appear on the menu by default. If you want to select an application that is not shown on the pop-up menu, click Other and select the application you want to be used.

4. If you want all files of the same type to be opened with the application you selected, click the Change All button.

WORKING WITH OWNERSHIP AND PERMISSIONS INFORMATION

The Ownership & Permissions section is used to configure access to the item (see Figure 4.13). This area enables you to control who has access to an item, as well as defining the type of access provided.

Figure 4.13
The Ownership & Permissions section of the Information window is an important security tool whether you share your Mac directly or across a network.

→ To learn how to configure access to an item, **see** "Understanding and Setting Permissions," **p. 843**.

WORKING WITH COMMENTS INFORMATION

The Comments section enables you to add comments to the selected item:

1. Select the document you are interested in and press ⌘-I. The Info window appears.

2. Expand the Comments section.

3. Enter your comments in the field. The comments you enter remain with the item, and you can read them by either expanding the Comments section or adding the Comments column to the List view and viewing a Finder window in that view.

FINDING FILES AND FOLDERS ON YOUR MAC

Under Mac OS X version 10.3, there are several ways to search for files or folders.

SEARCHING FOR FILES AND FOLDERS FROM FINDER WINDOWS

You can search for folders and files from within any Finder window using the Search tool on the Finder toolbar. To do so, use the following steps:

1. Open a new Finder window.

2. Click the Magnifying Glass icon in the Search tool (see Figure 4.14). You see the Search location pop-up menu.

Figure 4.14
You can use the Finder window's Search tool to search in different locations on your Mac.

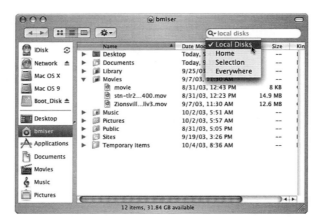

3. Select the area on your Mac that you want to search. Your options are Local Disks, which searches all the disks physically installed in or connected to your Mac; Home, which searches in your Home folder; Selection, which searches in the selected folder; or Everywhere, which searches everywhere you can access (such as network volumes).

> **NOTE**
> The currently selected area is shown in faint text in the Search field after a search area has been selected.

4. Start typing in the Search tool. As you type, the items that include your search text are shown in the Search Results window, which appears in List view. The search continues

as you type. The more specific you make the text, the more specific your results will be. The status of the search is shown at the bottom of the window.

> **NOTE**
>
> The Search Results window always appears in List view. You can configure the view using the View Options tool.

For each found item, you see its name and the object that contains the found item.

5. To see where an item is located, select it in the upper pane. The path to it is shown in the lower pane (see Figure 4.15).

Figure 4.15
Selecting an item in the search results pane presents the path to it in the lower pane.

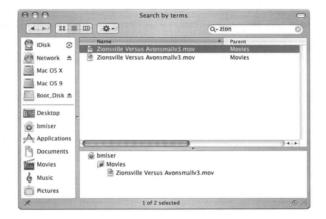

6. To clear the search and return the Finder window to its previous state, click the Clear button (the *x* located on the right side of the Search text field).

> **NOTE**
>
> You can open folders and files in either pane of the window. You can also open an item's contextual menu in the upper pane of the window.

SEARCHING FOR FILES AND FOLDERS USING THE FIND COMMAND

There are two ways to use the Find command to search for files and folders on your Mac. The first is to search by attribute, such as name, creation date, or size. The second is to search by content. You can now mix and match search types as necessary.

Finding folders and files by attribute is useful when you know an item exists but just can't remember where it is, what it is called, and so on.

Finding files by content is a great help when you know that a file exists on a machine that contains a word, phrase, sentence, or topic, but you can't quite remember what the name of the file is or even when it was created. You can also use the Find by Content feature to locate all the files you can access that relate to a specific topic or concept.

FINDING FOLDERS AND FILES BY ATTRIBUTE

The most common type of search you are likely to do is search by attribute, such as name or creation date. You can search by one or more attributes at the same time.

NOTE

In the context of searching by attribute, *filename* is synonymous with *folder name*.

To search by attribute, use the following steps:

1. From the Finder, select File, Find (or press ⌘-F). You see the Find window (see Figure 4.16).

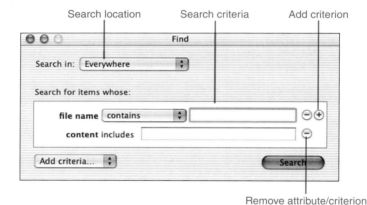

Figure 4.16
The Mac OS X Find function is both powerful and flexible.

2. Select the location in which you want to search on the Search in pop-up menu. You have the following options:
    - **Everywhere**—This option searches in all the volumes mounted on your Mac, including its internal drives and removable discs and volumes on your network.
    - **Local disks**—This option searches only those volumes physically installed on your Mac (including removable discs).
    - **Home**—This option searches only in your Home directory.
    - **Specific places**—This option enables you to select the volumes you want to search; when you select this, an additional pane appears. Check the check boxes for the volumes you want to search. Click the Add button and select individual folders to search specific folders (the volume on which those folders are located does not have to be selected).

3. The filename criterion is included in the search by default. If you don't want to search by filename, click the Remove attribute/criterion button next to the filename field and skip to step 10.

> **NOTE**
>
> You can't remove a criterion if it is the only one contained in the search.

4. Select the operand for the filename on the pop-up menu. By default, this is "contains," but you can change it to "starts with," "ends with," or "is." The meaning of these operands is self-explanatory.

5. Enter the text or numbers for which you want to search in the field. The more information you enter, the more specific your search will be, no matter which operand you select.

6. If you want to add more criteria for the filename, click the Add button. An additional pop-up menu and field appear.

> **NOTE**
>
> A limitation of the Find tool is that all criteria for an attribute are connected with an "and." This means that all criteria for that attribute must be met for an item to be found. Unfortunately, no easy way exists to do "or" searches, such as this filename or that one. You'll learn a workaround later in this section.

4

7. Use the pop-up menu to select the operand for the second filename.

8. Enter the second filename for which you want to search in the field.

9. Repeat steps 6–8 for each filename for which you want to search.

10. Select the next attribute by which you want to search on the Add criteria pop-up menu. Your options are "date modified," "date created," "kind," "label," "size," "extension," "visibility," "type," and "creator." You see only those attributes that aren't already included in the search on the pop-up menu. The attribute you select appears in the window along with any tools you use to define its search criteria.

11. If applicable, use the pop-up menu to select the operand for the attribute you selected. For example, if you chose "date modified," the available operands are "is today," "is within," "is before," "is after," or "is exactly."

12. Use the attribute's field, if one appears, to enter the value for which you want to search. For example, if you selected the "date modified" attribute and the "is after" operand, enter that date for which you want to search.

13. If you want to add more criteria for the attribute, click the Add button. An additional pop-up menu and appropriate fields appear.

14. Use the pop-up menu to select the operand for the criterion you added.

15. Enter the value for which you want to search in the field if applicable.

16. Repeat steps 13–15 for each criterion you want to add for the attribute.

17. Repeat steps 10–16 for each attribute you want to include in your search.

18. Click the Remove attribute/criterion button for any attributes you are going to search on. For example, remove the content attribute if you are not including it in your search.

19. Review the Find window to ensure that the search is configured properly (see Figure 4.17).

Figure 4.17
This search finds all files for this book (the filename contains 2904) that were modified after 8/1/02 and that are less than 1MB.

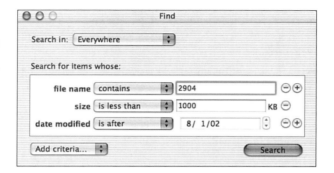

20. Click Search (or press Return). A separate Search Results window appears. The top of the window shows the number of places being searched and the progress of the search. You can cancel the search by clicking the "x" button that appears in the window's status bar. When the search is complete, the "x" becomes the Refresh Search button and the items that met your search criterion appear (see Figure 4.18). The results window contains two panes. The upper pane lists all the files that meet your criteria, whereas the lower pane shows the location of items selected in the upper pane. To resize the panes, drag the resize handle in the middle of the separating line between the panes.

Figure 4.18
A number of files that met my search parameters were found.

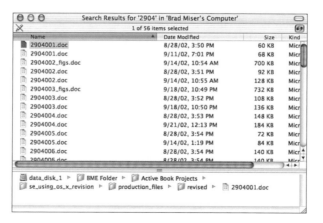

The Search results window works just like a Finder window in List view. For example, you can sort it, open items from within in, and so on.

You can view the location of any found item by selecting it. The path to that item appears in the lower pane.

Following are some additional tidbits about searching with the Finder:

- The Find window and the results window produced are independent. You can move the windows around so you can see both of them at the same time.

- Each time you click the Search button, a new results window appears. You can run the same search as many times as you want. For example, you can refine a search by running it, viewing the search results, moving back to the Find window and modifying the search, and then rerunning it.

  This also enables you to perform pseudo-or searches. Perform the first search. Then move back to the Find window, revise the search (such as by changing the filename), and run it again. The two results windows show you the files that meet both sets of criteria.

- You can rerun a search by clicking the Refresh Search button (the double-arrow icon) in the status bar of the results window.

- Unfortunately, you can't save your searches. If you want to run the same search again, leave the results or Find window open. If you close both of these windows, the search is lost and you must re-create it to run it again.

FINDING FILES BY CONTENT

Performing content searches is similar to performing attribute searches. The only significant difference is that any sources you are going to search by content must be indexed first. When a volume is indexed, all the files it contains are searched and a list of keywords is built.

CAUTION

> To index a server or folder that is shared, you must be the server's administrator or the folder's owner. If these conditions aren't true, the Index Status column shows Not indexable. This indicates that you can't index the volume, so you won't be able to search it for files by content.

To index sources you want to search, carry out the following steps:

1. Select the source you want to index and press ⌘-I to open the Info window.

2. Expand the Content index section (see Figure 4.19). The current index status is shown.

3. Click Index Now.

Figure 4.19
You can index a source using the Content index section of the Info window.

The progress of the indexing process is shown in the window. If there are many items to be indexed, this process can take a while. You can abort the process by clicking the Stop Indexing button. When the process is complete, the status information is updated accordingly. The source is then ready for content searches.

Indexes are created when you execute the Index Now command. As files change, the index becomes out of date. If you search by content regularly, you should reindex your sources periodically to keep the indexes current.

NOTE

> Unfortunately, you can't schedule indexes to be run periodically as you could when Sherlock was used to search for files and folders. To automate the indexing process, you need to use AppleScript or another automation tool.

After you have created an index, performing content searches is not difficult:

1. Create a search as explained in the preceding section.
2. Add the Content attribute to the search. (You can search for only a single content criterion at a time.)
3. Enter the content for which you want to search in the field.
4. Configure other attributes for the search.
5. Execute the search. Items that include the content you specified and meet the other search criteria are listed in the results window.

CUSTOMIZING THE MAC OS X DESKTOP

Although the default Mac OS X desktop is very nice to look at, you will probably want to customize it to suit your preferences. You can customize the appearance of your desktop in many ways, including the following:

- Change the clock
- Change the mounted disk behavior
- Change the desktop icon size
- Change the desktop icon arrangement
- Set desktop pictures

NOTE

You can also change the menu bar by adding icons to it, such as the Displays icon, the Volume icon, the AirPort icon, and others. These icons are discussed in the related sections of this book. For example, you will learn about the Displays menu bar icon in the section on configuring monitors using the Displays pane of the System Preferences application.

CHANGING THE CLOCK DISPLAY

By default, Mac OS X provides a clock in the upper-right corner of the desktop. You can also configure the clock to be shown in a window that floats on the desktop if you prefer. You can control the appearance of the clock by using the System Preferences application:

1. Open the System Preferences application.
2. Click the Date & Time icon.
3. In the Date & Time pane, click the Clock tab (see Figure 4.20).

Figure 4.20
The Clock tab of the Date & Time pane of the System Preferences application enables you to customize the clock on the desktop.

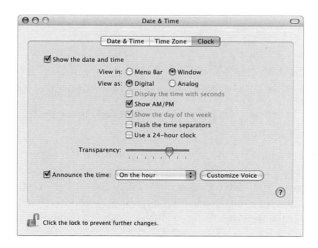

4. To hide the clock, uncheck the "Show the date and time" check box. The clock is removed and all the clock options are disabled.

5. If you want the clock to be displayed on the right end of the menu bar, click the Menu Bar radio button. If you want the clock to appear in a floating window, click the Window radio button.

6. If you prefer the time to be displayed in digital format, click the Digital radio button; to see it as an analog clock, click the Analog radio button.

7. If you chose the menu bar clock, check the "Display the time with seconds" check box to include the seconds in the display.

8. If you want the AM/PM indicator to be shown, check the Show AM/PM check box.

9. If you have selected the menu bar clock, click the "Show the day of the week" check box to include the day in the clock display.

10. If you want the colon between the hour and minutes to be displayed, check the "Flash the time separators" check box.

11. If you want to use a 24-hour clock, check the "Use a 24-hour clock" check box.

12. If you chose the window display, use the Transparency slider to set the transparency of the window. Because the window floats on top of all the others, making it less transparent can block the view of underlying windows.

13. If you want the time to be announced, check the "Announce the time" check box. Then select the time interval on the pop-up menu. Finally, click the Customize Voice button to select the voice used to announce the time.

14. Quit the System Preferences application.

TIP

As in previous versions of the OS, you can click the menu bar clock to briefly display the date. The menu on which the date appears also enables you to change the view option (analog or digital) and open the Date & Time pane of the System Preferences application.

CHANGING THE DESKTOP'S APPEARANCE

You can customize other aspects of the appearance of the desktop using the following steps:

1. Select Finder, Preferences or press ⌘-, to open the Finder Preferences window.

2. Click the General tab.

3. Check the check boxes for the mounted items you want to appear on the desktop. Your choices are "Hard disks," "CDs, DVDs, and iPods," and "Connected servers." If you uncheck the boxes, you don't see the items on your desktop; you can access these items through the Computer folder or within any Finder window. If you check the boxes, the items appear on the desktop.

4. Close the Finder Preferences window.

5. Click on the desktop.

6. Press ⌘-J to open the View Options window for the desktop.

7. Use the View Options controls to configure how icons on the desktop appear, such as size and grouping.

→ To learn about the details of these options, **see** "Customizing Finder Window Views," **p. 74**.

8. Close the View Options window.

9. Open the Desktop & Screen Saver pane of the System Preferences application. This pane has two tabs. The Desktop tab enables you to set your desktop picture, whereas the Screen Saver tab enables you to configure the screen saver.

10. Click the Desktop tab (see Figure 4.21). The Image well shows the desktop picture currently being used. In the left pane of the window, the Source pane shows the available image collections. The right pane shows the images contained in the selected source.

Figure 4.21
While writing a book, I use the ever exciting Sold Grey Light desktop picture.

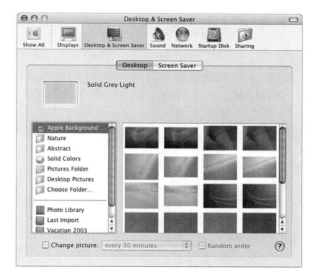

TIP

> If you just want to replace the current image with another one, drag the image you want to use onto the well. It replaces the image currently shown there and appears on the desktop immediately.

11. Select the source containing the image you want to apply to the desktop. You have the following options:

   • By default, Mac OS X includes three image collections (Apple Background Images, Nature, and Abstract); these appear at the top of the Source pane.

   • You can select the Solid Colors source to apply a solid color to the desktop.

   • The Pictures folder is the Pictures folder in your Home directory.

- Desktop Pictures is the Desktop Pictures folder included in the Library folder (basically, all the default Apple background images, but you can add images to this folder to be able to select them).

- Select Folder enables you to select any other folder to use as a source of images.

- The lower part of the pane contains iPhoto collections. You can select your Photo Library to choose any image in your iPhoto Library or select any photo album to use its images.

- Except for the Choose Folder option, when you select an option, the images contained in the location appear in the preview pane in the right part of the window.

  If you select the Choose Folder option, you can use the resulting sheet to move to and select a folder. When you do so, the images contained in that folder are shown in the preview pane.

- When you select a folder, including the predefined ones, only the images at the root level of that folder are available on the preview pane. For example, if you select your Pictures folder, only the images that are loose in that folder are available. Any images contained within folders that are inside the Pictures folder are not available.

12. Apply the image to the desktop by clicking it on the preview pane. It appears in the Image well and on your desktop.

13. If you want to change desktop pictures automatically, check the "Change picture" check box. The image in the well becomes the "recycle" icon to show that you have selected to have the system change images periodically.

14. Use the pop-up menu to select the time at which you want the images to be changed. The options include "when logging in," "when waking from sleep," and a time interval from every 5 seconds to once per day.

15. To have the images selected at random, check the "Random order" check box. If you uncheck this, the images appear in the same order as they appear in the selected source (for example, alphabetically).

16. Quit the System Preferences application when you are done making changes.

You can use just about any graphic file as a desktop image, such as JPEG, TIFF, and PICT files.

If you want to install images in the Mac OS X Desktop Pictures folder so they appear by default, just place them in the location *macosx*/Library/Desktop Pictures/, where *macosx* is the name of your Mac OS X startup volume.

This folder contains the collections of images that appear on the Collection pane. You can add your images to the default folders, and they will appear in those collections. Unfortunately, you can't add collections to the menu by creating folders within the Desktop Pictures folder.

NOTE

> If you use more than one monitor, each monitor has its own desktop picture. A Desktop Picture pane appears on each desktop. You use that pane to configure the desktop images on each monitor.

TIP

> If you want to change the image that is shown when the login window is displayed, name an image file "Aqua Blue.jpg" and copy it to the following location *Mac OS X/Library/Desktop Pictures/* where *Mac OS X* is the name of your startup volume. You will be prompted to replace the existing file. Do so. The next time the background image is displayed, such as when you log out, the new image will be shown. (If you will want to use the default image, save a copy of the file before you replace it.)

MAC OS X TO THE MAX: DESKTOP KEYBOARD SHORTCUTS

Table 4.5 lists keyboard shortcuts for working with the Finder.

TABLE 4.5   KEYBOARD SHORTCUTS FOR THE FINDER

Action	Keyboard Shortcut
Add to Sidebar	⌘-T
Close Window	⌘-W
Connect to Server	⌘-K
Duplicate	⌘-D
Eject	⌘-E
Empty Trash	Shift-⌘-Delete
Find	⌘-F
Force Quit	Option-⌘-Power
Get Info	⌘-I
Go Back	⌘-[
Go Forward	⌘-]
Go to Enclosing Folder	⌘-up arrow
Go to Computer Folder	Shift-⌘-C
Go to Home Folder	Shift-⌘-H
Go to Network Folder	Shift-⌘-K
Go to iDisk Folder	Shift-⌘-I

4

TABLE 4.5   CONTINUED

Action	Keyboard Shortcut
Go to Applications Folder	Shift-⌘-A
Go to Utilities Folder	Shift-⌘-U
Go to Folder	Shift-⌘-G
Hide Finder	⌘-H
Hide Toolbar	⌘-B
Log Out	Shift-⌘-Q
Mac Help	⌘-?
Make Alias	⌘-L
Minimize Window	⌘-M
Move to Trash	⌘-Delete
New Finder Window	⌘-N
New Folder	Shift-⌘-N
Open	⌘-O
Paste item	⌘-V
Preferences	⌘-,
Select All	⌘-A
Show Original	⌘- R
Show View Options	⌘-J
View as Icons	⌘-1
View as List	⌘-2
View as Columns	⌘-3

4

CHAPTER 5

USING AND CUSTOMIZING THE DOCK

In this chapter

UNDERSTANDING THE DOCK

The Dock was one of the most revolutionary parts of the original Mac OS X desktop, and it remains one of the most noticeable aspects of the OS under version 10.3. If you want to master Mac OS X, you should learn to take full advantage of the Dock's capabilities.

The Dock provides you with information about, control over, and customization of Mac OS X and the applications and documents with which you work (see Figure 5.1). By default, the Dock appears at the bottom of the desktop, but you can control many aspects of its appearance and where it is located. You can also control how it works to a great degree.

Figure 5.1
The Dock is an essential part of Mac OS X; as you learn to use it, you will probably wonder how you ever got along without it.

Applications

Running application markers

Application/document separation line

Documents and folders

Minimized Finder window

NOTE

The Dock was (and is) one of the most controversial parts of Mac OS X. Some Mac users love it, some hate it, and some just don't get it. I fall into the "love it" camp myself. Although the Dock takes a bit of getting used to, doing so will pay off for you in a big way.

The Dock is organized into two general sections; the application/document separation line, as shown in Figure 5.1, divides them. On the left side of this line, you see application icons. On the right side of the line, you see icons for documents, folders, minimized Finder or application windows, and the Trash/Eject icon.

NOTE

> In addition to applications or documents and folders, you might encounter another type of Dock icon. This type is called a *dockling*. Docklings are modules you can use to control applications or provide additional functionality on the Dock. Many docklings are available; some applications include docklings, whereas other applications consist entirely of a dockling. Docklings can be placed on either side of the Dock's dividing line. You will see an example of docklings later in the chapter.

The Dock performs the following functions:

- **Shows running applications**—Whenever an application is running, you see its icon on the Dock. A small triangle is located at the bottom of every running application's icon (see Figure 5.1). The Dock also provides information about what is happening in open applications. For example, when you receive email, the Mail application's icon changes to indicate the number of messages you have received since you last read messages.

- **Enables you to open applications, folders, minimized windows, and documents quickly**—You can open any item on the Dock by clicking its icon.

- **Enables you to quickly switch among open applications and windows**—You can click an application's or window's icon on the Dock to move into it. You can also use the Tab key and Shift+Tab keyboard shortcuts to move among open applications.

- **Enables you to control an application and switch to any windows open in an application**—When you hold down the Control key and click the icon of an open application, a pop-up menu appears. This menu lists commands as well as all the open windows related to that application; you can choose an item by selecting it from this menu.

- **Enables you to customize its appearance and function**—You can store the icon for any item (applications, folders, and documents) on the Dock. You can also control how the Dock looks, including its size, whether it is always visible, where it is located, and so on.

5

NOTE

> The Dock menu for Classic applications does not list the windows open in that application. However, the other commands do appear on the menu.

TIP

> When you open an application whose icon is not installed on the Dock, its Dock menu includes the Keep in Dock command. If you choose this, the icon is added to the Dock.

If you have used pre-Mac OS X versions of the Mac OS, you will see that the Dock is sort of a combination of the Apple menu, Application menu (and Application Switcher), and Control Strip. The Dock can be always available; you can customize its contents; and you can use it to quickly access any item on your Mac—these are all features that are similar to the Apple menu under Mac OS 9 and earlier. You can manage running applications using the Dock; this is similar to the Application menu. You can also open items with a single click from the Dock, just as you can with the Control Strip in previous versions of the Mac OS. Docklings, which are miniapplications stored on the Dock, are also similar to some items that appeared on the Control Strip in previous versions of the Mac OS.

When the Trash Is Not the Trash

Here is a question for you, "When is the Trash not the Trash?" If you have worked with Mac OS X before, you know the answer to this one! When you select an ejectable item, such as a CD or a mounted network volume, the Trash icon on the Dock becomes the Eject icon. When you drag an ejectable item onto this icon, it is ejected from your Mac. This makes more sense than dragging something onto the Trash to eject it. If you have ever seen a new user freak when you tell him to remove something by dragging it to the Trash under Mac OS 9 or earlier, you understand why this is a good thing. Dragging something onto the Trash to eject it was always one of the most counterintuitive aspects of the Mac OS.

USING ITEMS ON THE DOCK

By default, the Dock is preconfigured with various icons you can begin using immediately. When you point to an item on the Dock, a ToolTip appears above the icon that provides the name of the item.

The default items on the Dock can include the following:

- **Finder**—The Finder icon opens a new Finder window that shows your default new Finder window location (which can be to your Computer, Home folder, Documents folder, or just about any other location you choose) if no Finder windows are visible on the desktop. If at least one Finder window is open on the desktop, clicking the Finder icon doesn't do anything. If you hold down the Control key while you click this icon, you will see a list of all Finder windows that are open; choose a window from the list to move into it.

→ To learn how to set your default new Finder window location, **see** "Configuring How New Finder Windows Open," **p. 50**.

TIP

> There are at least two other ways to open a Dock icon's menu. One is to just click the Dock icon and hold down the mouse button. After a second or two, the Dock item's menu appears. Even better, if you use a two-button mouse (which I strongly recommend), you can right-click a Dock item to open its menu.

→ To learn about two-button mice, **see** "Finding, Installing, and Configuring a Mouse," **p. 728**.

■ **Safari**—This is Mac OS X's excellent Web browser. Under Mac OS X version 10.3, Safari has replaced Internet Explorer as the default Mac OS X Web browser. That is a good thing because Safari offers many improvements over Internet Explorer. Among other things, when you open the Safari Dock icon's menu, you can quickly jump to any Web page that is open.

■ **Mail**—Mail is Mac OS X's email application. When you receive email, an attention icon showing how many new messages you have received appears. If you open the Mail icon menu, you can choose from several commands, such as Get New Mail and Compose New Message.

■ **iChat AV**—This is Apple's instant messaging application, which you can use to communicate with others on your local network or over the Internet (it is compatible with AOL Instant Messenger).

> **N O T E**
>
> The *AV* part of iChat is new for version 10.3. The *V* is definitely cool because it allows you to add video to your online chats.

■ **Address Book**—Address Book is Mac OS X's contact manager application. You can store all sorts of information for everyone with whom you communicate, such as email addresses and phone numbers.

■ **iTunes**—iTunes is the Mac's excellent digital music application. Its Dock menu offers selections you can use to control music playback.

■ **iPhoto**—iPhoto is Mac OS X's awesome image cataloging, editing, and sharing application.

■ **iMovie**—iMovie is as powerful and easy to use as applications get; you can use it to create and edit your own digital video masterpieces.

■ **iCal**—You can use iCal to manage your calendar; it offers other cool features such as the ability to publish your calendar to the Web so other people can access it.

■ **System preferences**—The System Preferences utility enables you to configure and customize various aspects of Mac OS X. You will be using it frequently, which is why its icon is included on the Dock by default.

■ **Readme documents**—On the right end of the Dock, to the left of the Trash, you might see some readme and help documents Apple has included to provide late-breaking news about Mac OS X.

■ **Apple – Mac OS X**—Clicking this icon takes you to Apple's Mac OS X Web page.

■ **Trash/Eject**—Some things never change; under Mac OS X, the Trash does what it always has. It is always located on the right end of the Dock. One difference between the Mac OS X Trash and previous versions is that when you select an ejectable item, the Trash icon changes to the Eject symbol.

5

Using items on the Dock is easy: Simply click an icon to open whatever the item is. If the icon is for an application, that application opens (or moves to the front if it is already open). If the item is a document, the document opens, and if the item is a folder, the folder opens in a new Finder window. If the item is a dockling, a pop-up menu containing commands appears, and if the icon is a minimized Finder window, that window becomes active and moves onto the desktop. I'm sure you get the idea.

NOTE

> When you click a non-running application's icon, you might notice that it "bounces" as the application opens. This provides feedback to you that your selection was registered with the OS and it is working on opening your application. You can turn off this feature, as you will learn later in this chapter.

Unless the application is permanently installed on the Dock (in which case the icon remains in the same position), the icon for each application you open appears on the right edge of the application area of the Dock. As you open more applications, the existing application icons shift to the left and each icon becomes slightly smaller.

NOTE

> The Dock is very insistent about getting your attention, even when it is hidden. If the Dock is hidden and an application needs to present information to you, such as an error dialog box, its icon appears to bounce up out of nowhere and continues to bounce up and down until you switch to that application to see what it has to say.

To move among the open applications you see on the Dock, you can press ⌘-Tab. As long as you hold down the ⌘ key, a menu appears across the center of the screen (see Figure 5.2). On this menu, you will see the icon for each open application (which, by no mere coincidence, are the icons that have the open application marker under them on the Dock). The icons are listed in the order in which you have most recently used the applications, with the current application being on the left side of the menu. Each time you press ⌘-Tab, the icon for the open application you are selecting becomes highlighted and you see the application's name below its icon. When you release the ⌘-Tab keys, the application you select becomes active (and visible, if it is hidden). You can move backward through the open applications on the menu by continuing to hold down the ⌘ key and pressing Shift-Tab.

If you don't hold down the ⌘ key and instead just press ⌘-Tab, the menu won't appear; instead you will move immediately into the next application on the list of open applications. Again, this list is organized according to the applications you have most recently used. For example, suppose you checked your email in Mail and then began working in Word. If you pressed ⌘-Tab once, you would jump back into Mail. If you pressed ⌘-Tab again, you would move back to Word because that was the application you were most recently using. Likewise, if you pressed ⌘-Tab twice in a row, you would move back to the application you were using before the most recent one. Although this might be a bit hard for me to describe, this technique enables you to easily switch among open applications by using only the keyboard.

Figure 5.2
This list of open applications appears when you hold down the ⌘ and press the Tab key.

NOTE

If an application is open but the window in which you want to work is minimized, when you select that application with the ⌘-Tab shortcut, you will move into the application but any windows that are minimized will not appear. You have to click a minimized window's icon on the Dock for it to move back onto the desktop.

Unlike open applications, open documents don't automatically appear on the Dock. Document icons appear on the Dock only when you add them to the Dock manually or when you have minimized the document's window. Remember that, when you open an application's menu in the Dock, you will see a list of all the documents open in that application. You can then choose a listed document to move into it.

NOTE

Just like all icons on the Dock, the names of folders, minimized windows, and documents are shown above their icons when you point to them.

When you minimize a window, by default, the window moves into the Dock using the Genie Effect, during which it is pulled down into the Dock and becomes an icon that is a thumbnail view of the window. The icon for a minimized window behaves just like icons for

5

other items do. To open (or maximize) a minimized window, click its icon on the Dock and it is pulled back onto the desktop. You can change this so that the Scale Effect is used instead. This looks like the window is being quickly scaled down while it is placed on the Dock. Functionally, these effects do the same thing, but the Scale Effect is a bit faster, although not as impressive looking.

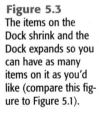 Minimized windows are marked with the related application's icon in the lower-right corner of the Dock icon so you can easily tell from which application the windows come. For example, minimized Finder windows have the Finder icon in the lower-right corner, mini-mized Safari icons have the Safari icon, and so on.

> **TIP**
>
> You can quickly minimize an open window by pressing ⌘-M.

When you minimize an application window, it is moved onto the Dock, just like any other window. However, when you hide an application, its windows do not appear on the Dock. The hidden application's icon continues to be marked with the arrow so you know that the application is running. You can open its Dock menu to jump into one of its open docu-ments.

As you add items to the Dock, the icons on the Dock continue to get smaller and the Dock expands so it shows all open items as well as the icons that are permanently installed on the Dock (see Figure 5.3).

Figure 5.3
The items on the Dock shrink and the Dock expands so you can have as many items on it as you'd like (compare this fig-ure to Figure 5.1).

Just as with an application's icon, if you point to a folder, an application, or a dockling icon on the Dock and press the Control key while you click, a pop-up menu appears. What is on this menu depends on what you click.

TIP

> Remember that if you don't want to press the Control key while you click, just click an icon and hold down the mouse button. The menu will appear after a second or two. Or, right-click a Dock icon if you use a two-button mouse.

When you use Dock icons, the following outcomes are possible:

- If you open the menu for the Finder Dock icon, the pop-up menu shows a list of all the open Finder windows whether the windows are minimized or are on the desktop. Select a window on the menu to make it active. You can also select Hide to hide all open Finder windows.

- If you open the Dock menu for a closed application, folder, or document, you will see the Show In Finder command, which opens a Finder window containing the item on which you clicked; the item is selected when the Finder window containing it appears. This can be a quick way to find out where something is located.

- If you open the Dock menu for a folder, the menu becomes a hierarchical menu showing the contents of that folder. You can display the contents of any folder within that folder, and you can select any item on the menu to open it (see Figure 5.4).

Figure 5.4
Adding the Applications folder to the Dock enables you to choose any of your applications from the Dock.

5

- If you open the Dock menu for a dockling, the commands provided by that dockling appear.

- If you open the Dock menu for a URL reference or other item (such as a minimized document window), an identification bubble appears above the icon to explain what the item is. If the icon is for an open document, you can close the document by selecting Close.

- If you open the Dock menu for an open application, you will see some basic commands, including Quit. You will also see a list of open windows; you can quickly jump to an open window by selecting it. Some applications also enable you to control what is happening from the Dock menu. For example, when iTunes is open, you can control music playback by using its Dock menu.

When you quit an open application, its icon disappears from the Dock—unless you have added that application to the Dock so that it always appears there. Minimized windows disappear from the Dock when you maximize them or when you close the application from which the document window comes.

TIP

> If you fill the Dock with many open applications, documents, and folders, it can be a nuisance to switch to each item and close it. Instead, log out (either select Apple menu, Log Out, or press Shift-⌘-Q). When you log out, all open applications are shut down, all documents are closed, and all minimized folder windows are removed from the Dock. When you log back in, the Dock is back to normal. All Finder windows that were on the Dock are gone from there, but they remain open on the desktop. Hold down the Option key and click the Close box of one of the open windows to close them all.

Organizing the Dock

The default Dock is powerful, but it gets even more useful when you include the items in it that you use often and organize the Dock to suit your preferences. You can move icons around the Dock, add more applications to it, remove applications that are currently on it, and add your own folders and documents to it so they are easily accessible.

Moving Icons on the Dock

You can change the location of any installed item on the Dock by dragging it. When you move one icon between two others, they slide apart to make room for the icon you are moving. However, you can't move most icons across the dividing line; for example, you can't move an application icon to the right side of the Dock.

NOTE

> You can't move most icons across the dividing line on the dock; however, exceptions to this are dockling icons, which can be placed on either side of the line.

If you move the icon of an open application that isn't installed on the Dock, that icon moves to the location to which you drag it and becomes installed on the Dock.

The Dock has two icons you can't move at all: Finder and Trash/Eject. The Finder icon always appears on the left end of the Dock, and the Trash is always on the right end. Other than these two end points, you can change all the other icons on the Dock as much as you like.

ADDING ICONS TO THE DOCK

You can add applications, folders, and files to the Dock so it contains the items you want. Drag the item you want to add down to the Dock and drop it where you want it to be installed. Application icons must be placed on the left side of the dividing line, and all others (folders and files) are placed on the right side (the exception is docklings, which can be placed on either side). Just as when you move icons on the Dock, when you add items between other icons already installed on it, the other icons slide apart to make room for them. When you add an item to the Dock, an alias to that item is created and you see its icon on the Dock.

> **TIP**
>
> You can add multiple items to the Dock at the same time by holding down the ⌘ key while you select each item you want to add to the Dock and then drag them there.

REMOVING ITEMS FROM THE DOCK

You can remove an icon from the Dock by dragging it up onto the desktop. When you do this, the icon disappears in a puff of digital smoke and no longer appears on the Dock.

Because the icons on the Dock are aliases, removing them doesn't affect the applications or files that those aliases represent.

If you drag a minimized window from the Dock, it snaps back to the Dock when you release the mouse button. You remove minimized windows from the Dock by maximizing or closing them.

ADDING FOLDERS TO THE DOCK

You can also add any folder to the Dock; when you click a folder icon on the Dock, the folder opens in a Finder window.

When you place a folder on the Dock, you can open its Dock menu that shows the contents of that folder (refer to Figure 5.4). All the subfolders also appear in hierarchical menus.

This feature is one of the most useful the Dock offers. You can use it to create custom menus containing anything on your Mac (literally). The uses for this feature are almost unlimited. Some ideas include the following:

5

- Add your Home directory to the Dock so you can easily move to an item within it.

- Add your project folders to the Dock so you can easily get to the files you need for the project on which you are working.

- Add the Applications folder to the Dock. This gives you quick access to all the applications on your Mac that are installed in the default Applications folder.

NOTE

NEW

Although adding folders to the Dock is useful, it can be easier and just as useful to add folders to the Places sidebar in Finder windows. The benefit to adding folders to the Dock is that you can access them without bringing the Finder to the front.

You might find that adding folders to the Dock is even more useful than adding application or file icons. Remember that you can make more room on the Dock by removing items from it. For example, you might choose to remove most or all of the application icons from the Dock and instead add the Applications folder to it. This works well, although you do lose the indicator features of an application's icon (such as Mail's new mail alert) if its icon is not installed on the Dock directly.

CUSTOMIZING THE APPEARANCE AND BEHAVIOR OF THE DOCK

The Dock offers several behaviors you can change to suit your preferences. You can also change various aspects of its appearance, as follows:

- **Size**—You can change the default or current size of the Dock.

- **Magnification**—The magnification effect causes items on the Dock to be magnified when you point to them. This can make identifying items easier, especially when many items are on the Dock or when it is small (see Figure 5.5). You can set the amount of magnification that is used.

- **Hide/Show**—The Dock does consume some screen space. Because it is always topmost, it can get in the way when you are working near its location on the screen. You can set the Dock so that it is hidden except when you point to it. When this behavior is enabled and you point to the Dock's location, it pops onto the desktop and you can use it. When you move off the Dock, it is hidden again.

  If the Dock is hidden, you need to hover a moment in the area of the screen in which it is located before it will appear. This prevents the Dock from popping up when you are working in a document near the edge of the screen and pass the mouse over the Dock's location.

- **Dock location**—The Dock can appear at its default location on the bottom of the screen, or you can move it to the left or right side of the desktop.

- **Minimize Effect**—You can choose either the Genie Effect or the Scale Effect.
- **Icon animation**—You already know about this one because it is on by default. When you click an application's icon to open that application, the icon bounces to show you that the application is opening.

Figure 5.5
The magnification effect makes identifying items easier, although the magnification level of this particular Dock would be a bit much for most Mac users.

> **NOTE**
>
> The amount of magnification is not relative to the size of the Dock. For example, the magnified icons are the same size whether the Dock is large or small. Of course, because the Dock size is different, the magnified icons do make more contrast with a smaller Dock, but that is only because of the comparison your eye makes.

You can control these settings using the Dock pane of the System Preferences utility. Do the following:

1. Open the System Preferences utility by clicking its icon on the Dock.
2. Click Dock to open the Dock pane of the utility (see Figure 5.6).

> **TIP**
>
> You can also open the Dock preferences pane by selecting Apple menu, Dock, Dock Preferences. The Dock command on the Apple menu also enables you to quickly turn Dock magnification and hiding on or off; you can also change its location by selecting the location in which you want it to be.

Figure 5.6
Use the Dock pane of the System Preferences utility to configure the appearance and behavior of the Dock.

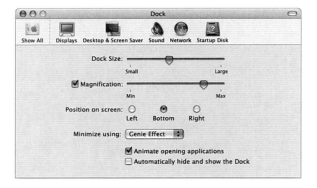

3. Use the Dock Size slider to set the default size of the Dock.

   Using the Dock Size slider changes the size of the Dock as well as the items on it. The best practice is to configure the Dock with the items you will want it to contain. Then, use this slider to set its size when it contains those items. As you add items to it, it gets larger until it fills the screen. After the Dock has expanded to the width of the screen, the items on it get smaller as you add more items to the Dock.

   TIP

   You can also change the size of the Dock by pointing to the line that divides the application side of the Dock from the document and folder side. When you do so, the cursor becomes a horizontal line with vertical arrows pointing from the top and bottom sides. Drag this cursor up to make the Dock larger or down to make it smaller.

4. Check the Magnification check box to have the Dock use that behavior, and then use the Magnification slider to set the amount of magnification.

   NOTE

   Changes you make in the Dock pane of the System Preferences utility are live, and you see their effects on the Dock immediately. Of course, to see the magnification effect, you must point to an item on the Dock.

5. Click the Left, Bottom, or Right radio button to set the Dock's location on the desktop.

6. Use the "Minimize using" pop-up menu to choose the minimize/maximize effect; the options are Genie Effect or Scale Effect.

7. If you prefer that application icons not bounce when the application opens, uncheck the "Animate opening applications" check box.

8. Check the "Automatically hide and show the Dock" check box if you want the Dock to be visible only when you linger at its location on the screen.

9. Quit System Preferences.

TIP

> You can also control the Dock by using its pop-up menu. Point to the application/folder dividing line. When you see the size-change pointer (the horizontal line with vertical arrows coming from it), hold down the Control key and click. You will see a pop-up menu that enables you to control the magnification, hiding, position, and minimization effects. You can also open the Dock pane of the System Preferences utility.

All Dock settings are specific to each user account, meaning that each user can have her own items installed on her Dock, configure the Dock to be hidden, and so on. One user's Dock does not affect any other user's Dock.

WORKING WITH DOCKLINGS

Some applications provide a dockling you can use to work that application (as more applications are created for Mac OS X, you can expect that more applications will take advantage of this feature). Some applications are provided as a dockling that you install on the Dock to take advantage of its features (see Figure 5.7).

Figure 5.7
This dockling, called Calindock, provides a calendar on the Dock; the dockling's controls enable you to set which month is being displayed. *(Calindock is a freeware dockling written by Mike McNamara.)*

5

Using docklings is similar to other items on the Dock. Open the dockling's Dock menu to choose from among its list of commands or options. If the dockling is for an application, you can open the application (if it is closed) or use its controls (if the application is open). For example, when iTunes is open, you can Ctrl+click its icon to pop up its Dock menu, from which you can control music playback. If the dockling provides control over your system, open the menu and choose the settings you want.

The docklings installed on a Dock are also specific to each user account. However, the same docklings can be installed on the Dock for each user or each user can install only those docklings that he wants to be able to use.

To install a dockling, drag it to the Dock. (As mentioned earlier, docklings can be placed anywhere on the Dock.)

NOTE

> When you install a dockling, the dockling is installed only on the Dock of the administrator who installed that dockling on the machine. However, any user can drag the dockling to the Dock for that user account.
>
> For this reason, you should always store docklings you want other users to be able to add to their Docks in a Public folder so that every user can access them (to install them on their Docks).

MAC OS X TO THE MAX: USING DOCK KEYBOARD SHORTCUTS

Dock-related keyboard shortcuts are listed in Table 5.1.

TABLE 5.1   KEYBOARD SHORTCUTS FOR THE DOCK

Action	Keyboard Shortcut
Turn hiding off or on	Option-⌘-D
Move to the next open application	⌘-Tab
Move to the previous open application	Shift-⌘-Tab
Minimize a window	⌘-M

INSTALLING AND USING MAC OS X APPLICATIONS

In this chapter

UNDERSTANDING APPLICATIONS YOU CAN RUN UNDER MAC OS X

You can run the following types of applications under Mac OS X:

- **Classic applications**—Classic applications are those designed to run under previous versions of the Mac OS; however, because of Mac OS X's Classic environment, you can also run these applications under Mac OS X.

- **Unix applications**—Because Mac OS X is based on Unix, you can run many Unix applications on your Mac. Some of these applications have to be recompiled to run on the Mac, but most will work as they are. Of course, you will need to run them from the command line (unless you find and install a graphical user interface for the Unix subsystem). Because Unix is such a prevalent OS, thousands of Unix applications are available for you to use.

- **Java applications**—You can run applications written in the Java and Java 2 programming languages. Because Java is a platform-independent programming language, the same applications work on Windows, Macintosh, and other platforms. You mostly encounter Java applications on the Web, but you will find some standalone Java applications as well.

- **Carbon applications**—These applications are written using the Carbon programming environment, which is designed to take advantage of the Mac OS X architecture. Many are Classic applications that have been ported over to Mac OS X—in Mac OS X-lingo, they have been *carbonized*. Because carbonizing an application requires considerably fewer resources than does creating a Cocoa application, most Mac OS X applications were carbonized Mac OS 9 applications early in Mac OS X's life. As Mac OS X continues to mature, this will change and the majority of applications will be written specifically for Mac OS X (using Carbon or Cocoa).

- **Cocoa applications**—These applications are written using the Cocoa programming architecture, which means they take full advantage of all the advanced features Mac OS X provides. Cocoa applications have to be written from the ground up in the new environment rather than being ported over as carbonized applications can be. Eventually, most new Mac OS X applications will be based on Cocoa.

→ To learn about installing and using Classic applications, **see** Chapter 7, "Working with Mac OS 9, the Classic Environment, and Classic Applications," **p. 183**.

By the time version 10.3 was released, most major Mac applications were available in Carbon or Cocoa versions. Some are still in the carbonized state.

Because many carbonized applications are applications that were created for earlier versions of the OS and ported over to Mac OS X, some do not meet certain standard Mac OS X interface conventions. For example, some of the Mac OS X standard menus you see in Cocoa applications are not present in carbonized applications.

INSTALLING MAC OS X APPLICATIONS

Although carbonized and Cocoa applications behave somewhat differently, their similarities are at least as great as their differences. This is especially true when it comes to installing them.

Under Mac OS X, the two basic strategies by which applications are installed are

- **Drag and drop**—Under this method, you simply drag the application files (usually just one file or folder) from one location to the location in which you want to install them (usually the Applications folder).

- **Installer**—Some applications use an installation program to install the application and related files for you. Most applications use the standard Mac OS X Installation application as their installation mechanism. These applications are provided as package files, which have the file extension .pkg.

Because Mac OS X is designed as a multiuser OS, where you install Mac OS X applications is an important consideration. The two locations in which you should install Mac OS X applications are

- **The Applications folder**—If you want the application to be accessible to everyone who uses your Mac, you should install it in the Applications folder. To do this, you must be logged in as an administrator. Most applications that use an installer are installed in the Applications folder, and you usually don't have the option to install them elsewhere.

- **The Home folder**—You can sometimes install applications in a user's Home directory (primarily applications that have drag-and-drop installation). You should install applications in a user's Home directory only if you don't want everyone who uses your Mac to be able to use that application. Because users can access only areas to which they have been granted permission through their security settings, you need to ensure that everyone who needs to use the application can access the location in which it is stored.

NOTE

> Accessing an application installed in a Home folder is dependent on the permissions you assign to that application's folder. Modifying the permissions of the application's folder so that all users have access allows everyone to use the application, even if they are not logged in as the user who owns that application.

6

These installation locations are appropriate only for Mac OS X (carbonized or Cocoa) applications. You install Classic or Unix applications in locations that are appropriate for those types of applications.

CAUTION

> If you have trouble installing an application, make sure you are logged in as an administrator. Many application installations can be done only while using an administrator account.

INSTALLING MAC OS X APPLICATIONS WITH DRAG AND DROP

Under Mac OS X, applications can be provided as *bundles*. A bundle is a collection of the executable files and other resources required for an application. An application bundle can be presented to you as a single icon, which makes the drag-and-drop installation technique possible. Instead of having to deal with an installer application or a bunch of individual files, you can easily act on an entire application bundle by acting on its single icon.

Installing applications that use the drag-and-drop method is especially simple. Most of these applications are provided as self mounting image (.smi) or disk image (.dmg) files. This means that the file behaves just as if it were a volume you mount on your desktop.

Many Mac OS X applications use this method, making installation of these applications almost trivially easy.

> **NOTE**
>
> The only difference between the behavior of .smi and .dmg files is that .smi files automatically mount on your desktop when you launch them. Disk image files use Apple's Disk Utility software to mount—because this application is installed on your Mac by default, these files behave quite similarly and you probably won't notice any difference between them. However, you could use a .smi file even if Disk Utility wasn't installed on your machine, whereas you can't use a .dmg file without the Disk Copy application.

The general process to install an application provided in a .smi or .dmg file is the following:

1. Download and uncompress the .smi or .dmg file.
2. If the file isn't mounted on your Mac automatically, double-click the file (which is likely a .dmg file). Its volume is mounted on your desktop, just like any other volumes, such as a CD, DVD, or volume on a hard drive.
3. Open the resulting volume and drag the application's folder or file to the appropriate directory on your Mac.
4. Unmount the mounted volume by selecting it and pressing ⌘-E (or select File, Eject).
5. Discard the .smi or .dmg files if you won't need to install the application again. However, in most cases, I recommend that you keep the original file in the event you need to reinstall the application (for example, you can copy it to a CD or DVD).

→ To learn how to download files from the Web and prepare them for use, **see** "Downloading and Preparing Files," **p. 411**.

> **NOTE**
>
> Some applications don't even provide a .smi or .dmg file. After you download and uncompress the file, you will have the application's folder immediately. Drag this folder to where you want the application to be installed.

Many Mac OS X applications that you can download from the Web are provided in the .smi format. As an example, download and install Snapz Pro X, which is the best tool to use to capture screenshots or desktop movies:

1. Log in as an administrator for your Mac.

2. Go to http://www.ambrosiasw.com/utilities/snapzprox/.

TIP

> If you need to take screen shots or simply want to take them, there is no better way to do so than Ambrosia Software's Snapz Pro X. This application offers many more features than Mac OS X's built-in screen shot function. I have used this application for many years for all my books and find it one of the handful of indispensable third-party applications for Mac OS X (almost all the screen shots in this book were captured with Snapz Pro X). You can use a demo version of the application for 30 days without charge. The license fee is very reasonable.

3. Download Snapz Pro X. After the file is downloaded, it is uncompressed and decoded automatically. When the process is complete, you see the SnapzProX .dmg file. The disk image is mounted automatically and you see the Snapz Pro X volume on your desktop.

→ To learn how to download files from the Web and prepare them for use, **see** "Downloading and Preparing Files," **p. 411**.

4. Open another Finder window and display the Applications folder.

TIP

> The fastest way to open the Applications folder is to press ⌘-N to open a new Finder window and then press Shift-⌘-A.

5. Drag the Snapz Pro X folder icon into the Applications directory to copy it there (see Figure 6.1).

6. Close and unmount the Snapz Pro X volume and store the original .dmg file in a safe location.

7. Launch Snapz Pro X to start capturing screen shots.

TIP

> If you want to save a little disk space, save the original .sit files that you download instead of the .dmg files. When you want to access the .dmg files again, you can uncompress the .sit files. You don't need to save both versions. The .dmg file is slightly more convenient than the .sit file, but it also requires slightly more disk space.

6

Figure 6.1
Installing the excellent
Snapz Pro X is a sim-
ple matter of drag
and drop.

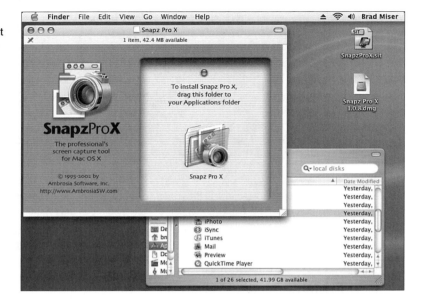

CAUTION

Some companies remove the installers for one version from their Web site when the next
version is released. In such cases, you might not be able to download and install the
application again without paying an upgrade fee to get the new version. Although this is
not a very good practice in my opinion, some companies do have this policy. The only
way to ensure that you will be able to reinstall the same version of an application you
downloaded and licensed is to keep the original installer files. You should also keep any
updates you download and install for that version.

 *If you aren't able to place the application in the appropriate directory, see "I Can't Install an
Application Because I Don't Have Sufficient Privileges" in the "Troubleshooting" section at the end
of this chapter.*

Installing Mac OS X Applications Using an Installer

All Mac OS X applications that use the standard Mac OS X installer application install in a
similar fashion; however, minor variations can exist.

Under Mac OS X, applications that use the Installer application come in package files,
which have the extension .pkg. For example, when you installed Mac OS X on your
machine, you used this installer.

NOTE

When you download an application that comes in a .pkg file, it often is included in a
.dmg or .smi file. This usually is done when there are files outside the application to be
installed that the developer wants to include with the application but that should not be
installed as part of it (readme files, for example).

The general process to install and use .pkg files is the following:

1. Download and prepare the file containing the application you want to install.
2. Mount the disk image and open it.
3. Double-click the .pkg file.
4. Work through the steps in the installer application.

An example of an application that uses this technique is the software that supports the excellent wireless keyboards and mouse devices from Logitech. This software enables you to customize many aspects of these excellent devices:

1. Log in as an administrator for your Mac.
2. Go to www.logitech.com and move to the support/download page for the keyboard/mouse model you have.
3. Download and uncompress the file you downloaded. The .dmg file is opened automatically; then the volume containing the software is mounted and appears on the desktop.
4. Look at the contents of the volume and read any readme files you see.

NOTE

> Some installer packages also come with an uninstaller application; you should definitely keep the original files so you can run the uninstaller to easily remove the application later should you need to. This is especially important for those applications that install resources in the system, such as software that supports peripheral devices.

5. Open the package file, which has the .pkg file extension, such as Logitech Control Center.pkg. You will see the Installer window (see Figure 6.2). Just as when you installed Mac OS X, the left pane shows you the steps you will work through using the installer. The right pane provides information about each step. You use the Continue and Go Back buttons to move through the installation process.
6. If prompted, verify that you are an administrator by entering your administrator password (and username if you aren't logged in under an administrator account).

NOTE

> Some installations require that you authenticate yourself as an administrator before you can begin the installation—even if you are already logged in as the administrator.

7. Continue working through the steps in the installer until you get to the screen that tells you that the software was successfully installed.
8. Quit the Installer application.

Figure 6.2
Here, you can see the Logitech installer in the foreground, while the disk image containing the .pkg file is in the background.

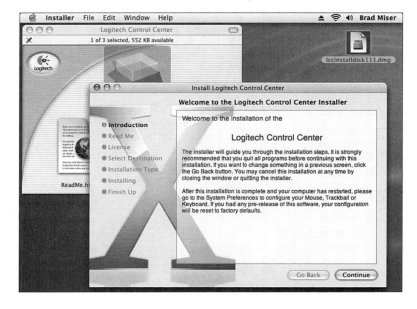

TIP

To unmount a disk image, click the Eject button next to it in the Places sidebar; select it and select File, Eject; or select it and press ⌘-E.

 If Classic launches when you run an application's installer application but the installer has problems, see "I Can't Install an Application Because I Am Having Problems with Classic" in the "Troubleshooting" section at the end of this chapter.

LAUNCHING MAC OS X APPLICATIONS

There are many ways to launch Mac OS X applications, including the following:

- Select the application in a Finder window and select the Finder's Open command (⌘-O).
- Double-click the application's icon.
- Single-click an application's icon on the Dock.
- Open an alias to the application, such as one stored in your Favorites directory.
- Open a document of the file type that the application is set to open.
- Drag and drop a document onto an application's icon (or an alias's icon).
- Select an application's icon or alias and press ⌘-down arrow.
- Launch the application from within another application. (For example, you can launch a Web browser by clicking a URL in an email program.)

- Add the application to the Login Items window so it is launched automatically when you log in.
- Launch the application from a script created by AppleScript or another scripting utility.

If you have used a Mac before, you have probably used many of these methods to open applications. Most of them are very straightforward and require no discussion. A couple of them, though less often used, can be effective techniques for quickly opening an application.

One of the most powerful methods—although it's underused by many Mac users—is to launch an application by drag and drop. Macintosh drag and drop is a function of the OS whereby you move information from one location to another by simply selecting it, dragging it to where you want it to go, and then dropping it.

The drag-and-drop approach is especially efficient when you want to open a document with an application that wasn't used to create it initially. For example, if you receive a plain-text file and double-click it, it opens in TextEdit. If you want to open it in Word instead, you can simply drag and drop the document onto Word's icon and Word is used to open the file. Otherwise, you would have to first open Word, use the Open command, maneuver to the text file, and then open it.

If the file type is compatible with the application on which you drag it, the application icon becomes highlighted to indicate that it is a compatible file.

TIP

> You can force an application to attempt to open a document with which it is not compatible by holding down the Option and ⌘ keys while you drag the document onto the application's icon. If the application is capable of opening files of that type, the file is opened. If not, either the application still launches but no document window appears or the document window appears and is filled with garbage.

You can also use drag and drop to open documents using applications installed on the Dock. Simply drag the file you want to open onto the icon on the Dock for the application you want to use to open it. If the application is capable of opening the document, its icon becomes highlighted. When you release the mouse button, the application launches and the document is opened.

If the drag-and-drop technique doesn't work, see "I Can't Drag a Document on an Icon to Open It" in the "Troubleshooting" section at the end of this chapter.

If a file opens, but its contents are "munged," see "When I Open an Application, What I See Is Incomprehensible" in the "Troubleshooting" section at the end of this chapter.

6

UNDERSTANDING AND USING STANDARD MAC OS X APPLICATION MENUS

Just like under all versions of the Mac OS, Mac OS X applications designed to work on the Mac follow certain conventions when it comes to the menus they provide. Although applications can provide more menus than the core set of standard menus, they are not supposed to provide fewer.

CAUTION

The information in this section is based on standard Mac OS X menus for Cocoa applications. Classic applications provide Mac OS 9 menus, whereas carbonized applications provide a mixture of the two sets of menus. For example, all carbonized applications provide an Application menu, but not all provide Cocoa's Format menu.

If you have used a Mac before, which I have assumed you have, some application menus under Mac OS X aren't much different from those under previous versions of the OS, such as the File and Edit menus. In the following sections, you will learn about some standard application menus that are new or revised for Mac OS X.

WORKING WITH MAC OS X APPLICATION MENUS

All Mac OS X applications have an application menu, which provides the commands you use to control the application itself as well as to interact with the OS (see Figure 6.3).

Figure 6.3
This TextEdit menu is typical of the application menu provided by Mac OS X applications.

Typical commands on an application's application menu are the following:

- About
- Preferences
- Services
- Hide/Show
- Quit

One of the more interesting commands on the application menu is the Mac OS X Services command. This command enables you to access functions provided by other applications to add information or perform functions while you are using the current application. Although it is not supported in all applications, when it is supported, it can be quite useful.

NOTE

> Game applications are the most likely to not provide standard menus, and that is okay. After all, who needs a Format menu when you are shooting bad guys?

There are various uses for the Services command, but as an example, suppose you are having trouble understanding an error message you are getting in a certain application and you want to send an email to the technical support organization to get some help. That email might be a lot more meaningful if you can include an image of the actual error dialog box that you see with your explanation. Using the Services commands from within the Mail email application, you can do just that:

1. Move to the dialog box you want to capture; perhaps it is an error message that suddenly pops up on your screen.

2. Without doing anything in the dialog box (for example, don't click its OK button), launch the Mail application by clicking its icon on the Dock.

3. Create a new email message and move into its body.

4. From the Mail menu, select Services, Grab, Timed Selection.

5. Bring the dialog box you want to capture to the front by clicking its window.

6. Wait for Grab's timer to go off.

7. Move back into the Mail application. The screen that Grab captured is pasted into the new email message.

8. Finish your message and send it.

The specific services offered on the Services menu depend on the application you are using and the data with which you are working. You should explore Services options that you have with the applications you use most often. Most Apple applications do provide some services, but even with those, support for Services can be spotty. The only way to know is to explore the Services menu for the applications you use.

Even though Apple's basic Mac OS X text editing application, TextEdit, isn't all that great for word processing, it does provide a great example of how many Services commands can be supported. For a list of the Services commands available in TextEdit and what they do, see Table 6.1.

6

TABLE 6.1   COMMANDS ON THE TEXTEDIT SERVICES MENU

Services Command	What It Does
Finder	Activates various Finder commands, such as Open, Reveal, and Show Info, on the selected item
Grab	Enables you to capture screen shots and paste them into the current document
Import Image	Enables you to import images from an imaging device, such as a digital camera, connected to your Mac
Mail	Emails selected text or the entire document via the Mail application
Make New Sticky Note	Creates a new sticky note from the selected text
Open URL	Opens a selected URL in the default Web browser
Script Editor	Enables you to work with AppleScript, such as creating a new AppleScript or running an existing one
Search with Google	Searches for the selected text on www.google.com
Send File To Bluetooth Device	Sends a file to a Bluetooth device, such as a PDA
Speech	Enables you to have your Mac speak selected text
Summarize	Launches Mac OS X's Summary Service application that creates a summary of selected text
TextEdit	Opens a selected file in TextEdit or creates a new TextEdit file from selected text

NOTE

Some third-party applications can add their own commands to the Services menu. For example, QuicKeys, which enables you to create and run macros, adds a command to the Services menu that enables you to create a macro from within any application.

WORKING WITH MAC OS X FORMAT MENUS

As you might expect from its name, the Format menu provides commands that enable you to format the file with which you are working. The specific commands on the Format menu depend on the particular application you are using.

NOTE

The Mac OS X Format menu, including the Fonts panel, is available only in Cocoa applications that are designed to use it. Many Mac OS X applications provide format and font commands that are specific to those applications.

One of the most useful commands on most applications' Format menus is the Font command. This command enables you to work with the fonts you use in a document (see Figure 6.4). In addition to the commands you expect to see, such as Bold, Italic, and so on, you also will see the Show Fonts command, which opens the Font panel.

Figure 6.4
TextEdit's Font command is typical of this command on many applications' Format menus.

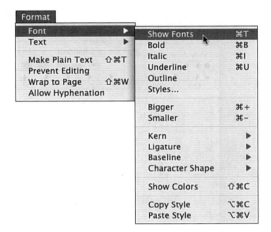

The Mac with OS X Font panel enables you to choose and work with the fonts installed on your Mac. The Font panel provides control over the particular font used in your documents as well as enables you to manage the fonts installed on your Mac (see Figure 6.5).

Figure 6.5
The Mac OS X Font panel provides much more control over your fonts than was possible under previous versions of the Mac OS.

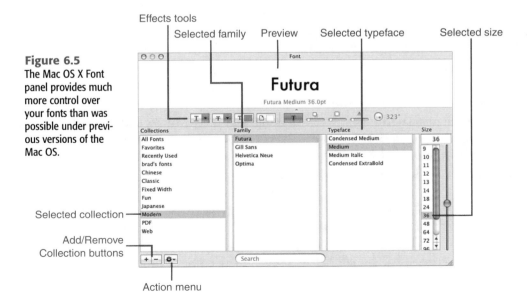

TIP

> In most applications, you can open the Font panel by pressing ⌘-T.

CAUTION

> Not all applications support Mac OS X's Font system. If an application doesn't use this system, it provides its own set of formatting tools that you use to format a document. For example, Microsoft Word X for Mac, service release 1 does not support Mac OS X's font system so you can't access the Font panel from within the application. You have to use its own font tools instead.

The Font panel has a number of panes, and you can choose to display some panes while others are always visible. The various panes of the Font panel are the following:

- **Collections (always displayed)**—Under Mac OS X, the ability to group fonts together in collections is built in to the operating system and into the Font panel. Font collections make selecting fonts easier because you can group fonts into collections, so you can select a set of fonts by choosing the collection in which those fonts are contained. You can use the default font collections and create your own, and you use the Collections pane to select the collection with which you want to work. The collections you see in the Collections pane of the Font panel include all those fonts and collections that are installed and enabled via the Font Book application. Applications can also provide distinct collections. For example, in TextEdit, you see the Favorites collection, which contains a set of fonts, typefaces, and sizes you have added via the Add to Favorites action, and the Recently Used collection, which contains the fonts, typefaces, and sizes of text formatting you have recently applied in the current document.

→ To learn about installing and maintaining fonts on your Mac using the Font Book application, **see** "Installing and Using Mac OS X Fonts," **p. 230**.

- **Family (always displayed)**—The Family pane lists all the font families that are part of the selected collection. You select the family you want to work with on the list of available families in the selected collection.

- **Typeface (displayed except when working with the Favorites and Recently Used collection)**—In the Typeface pane, you choose the typeface for the selected font family, such as Regular, Bold, and so on.

- **Size (always displayed)**—You choose the size of the font you are applying in the Size pane.

- **Preview (displayed when you select Show Preview on the Action menu)**—This pane, which appears at the top of the Font panel, provides a preview of the font you have configured.

- **Effects (displayed when you select Show Effects on the Action menu)**—This pane provides buttons you use to configure underline, strikethrough, text color, background color, and text shadow effects.

6

A couple of the default collections are worth some additional detail. The PDF collection contains font families that are suited to the creation of PDF documents (PDF is a native file format under Mac OS X). The Favorites collection is empty by default and is a collection designed for you to be able to create a customized set of your favorite font families, typefaces, and sizes so you can reapply specific text formats by selecting the Favorites collection and clicking the text formatting you want to apply (this is similar to styles in some applications). The Recently Used collection automatically gathers the families, typefaces, and sizes you have recently used so you can reapply them easily. The Web collection contains fonts that are designed to be used on the Web.

The Action menu at the bottom-left corner of the panel provides access to the following commands:

- **Add to Favorites**—This command adds the current font, typeface, and size to the Favorites collection.
- **Show/Hide Preview**—This choice opens or hides the Preview pane.
- **Show/Hide Effects**—This command opens or hides the Effects pane.
- **Color**—Choosing this causes the Color Picker to open.
- **Characters**—This command opens the Characters palette.
- **Typography**—This command opens the Typography panel that you can use to choose ligatures, adjust the space before and after characters, and shift the text baseline.
- **Edit Sizes**—Using this command, you can customize the sizes that appear in the Size pane.
- **Manage Fonts**—This command opens the Font Book that enables you to manage the fonts installed on your Mac.

PREVIEWING FONTS

If you select Show Preview on the Action menu, a new pane appears at the top of the panel. This pane provides a preview of the currently selected family, typeface, and size. You can use this preview to help you make better selections more quickly. To hide the Preview pane, select Hide Preview on the Action menu.

USING FONT FAVORITES

When you select a font family, typeface, and size and then use the Add to Favorites command on the Action menu, that font is added to your Favorites collection. When you select the Favorites collection in the Font panel, you can quickly choose one of your favorite fonts to use; this saves you a couple of steps (see Figure 6.6).

6

Figure 6.6
When you add a font, typeface, and size to your Favorites collection, you can easily apply that formatting to selected text in a document.

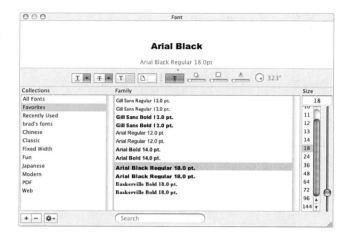

CREATING OR REMOVING FONT COLLECTIONS

You can add or remove font collections from the Font panel. When you do so, the font collection is also added or removed to the Collections available in the Font Book application (which contains all the fonts installed on your Mac).

→ To learn about the Font Book application, **see** "Installing and Using Mac OS X Fonts," **p. 230**.

From the Font panel, you can make the following changes to the collections shown in the Collections list:

- Add new font collections.
- Remove font collections.
- Add fonts to collections.

Although you can manage font collections from within the Font panel, you should generally use the Font Book application, which was added to Mac OS X in version 10.3. This is because font collections are really a system-level resource, so it is better practice to manage them using a system tool—that being the Font Book.

→ To learn about the Font Book application, **see** "Installing and Using Mac OS X Fonts," **p. 230**.

CAUTION

If you select a collection and click the – button to delete it, the collection is removed from the Font Book, which means the included fonts are deleted from your Mac. Using the Font Book, you can disable both font collections and individual fonts from within collections. This is the best technique because you can prevent collections and fonts from being available within an application but maintain those collections and fonts on your Mac.

APPLYING EFFECTS TO FONTS

Using the Effects tools, you can apply the following effects to selected text:

- Apply underline effects
- Apply strikethrough effects
- Apply color to text
- Apply color to a document's background
- Apply text shadow effects

NOTE

You can also apply color effects by selecting Color on the Action menu.

To apply effects to text, do the following steps:

1. Select the text to which you want to apply the effects.
2. Open the Font panel.
3. Open the action menu and select Show Effects. The Effects pane appears (see Figure 6.7).

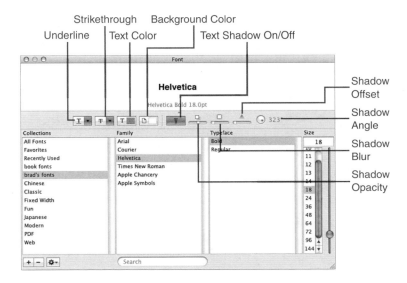

Figure 6.7
You can use the Effects pane to apply various effects to selected text.

4. Select from the underline effects on the Underline pop-up menu. The options are None, Single, Double, or Color. If you select Color, use the Color Picker to choose the color of the underline.

→ To learn how to use the Color Picker, **see** "Choosing Colors," **p. 160**.

5. Select the strikethrough effects on the Strikethrough pop-up menu. The options are None, Single, Double, or Color. If you select Color, use the Color Picker to choose the color of the strikethrough.

6. Click the Text Color button and use the Color Picker to choose the text color.

7. Click the Background Color button and use the Color Picker to select the background color of the document on which you are working.

8. To apply a shadow to the text, click the Text Shadow button; when a shadow is applied, the button is blue.

9. Use the Shadow Opacity, Show Blur, and Shadow Offset sliders to configure those properties of the shadow.

10. Use the Shadow Angle wheel to set the angle of the shadow.

NOTE

Unfortunately, you won't see the effects you apply in the Preview pane. You need to be able to see the document on which you are working to see the results of the text effects you apply.

CHOOSING COLORS

When you choose to apply color from the Font panel, you use the Color Picker (see Figure 6.8). As with the other versions of the Mac OS, you use the Color Picker to define and choose the color to apply to specific items—in this case, text effects.

Figure 6.8
You can control the color applied to fonts using the text effects tools using the Color Picker.

TIP

You can open the Color Picker directly by pressing Shift-⌘-C or by selecting Format, Font, Show Colors. You don't need to have the Font panel open to use the Color Picker.

6

As an example of how the Color Picker works, the following steps show you how to use the Color Picker to choose the color of underline:

1. Select the item to which you want to apply color (such as text).

2. Open the Color Picker by clicking the Text Color button or selecting Color on the Underline pop-up menu.

3. At the top of the Color Picker window, select the color tools with which you want to work. For example, click the Color Wheel to use the standard color wheel as shown in Figure 6.8.

4. Use the color tools to select the color you want to apply. The color you select is applied to the selected item.

TIP

> You can drag the color you select to the palette at the bottom of the Color Picker so you can easily apply it again later. This palette serves as a place in which you can store your favorite colors so you can apply them again easily.

EDITING THE SIZES AVAILABLE ON THE SIZE PANE

If you select Edit Sizes on the Action menu on the Fonts panel, you will see the Font Size sheet, which you can use to change the sizes that appear in the Size pane of the Font panel (see Figure 6.9).

Figure 6.9
You can control the specific sizes of font that appear in the Fonts panel using the Font Size sheet.

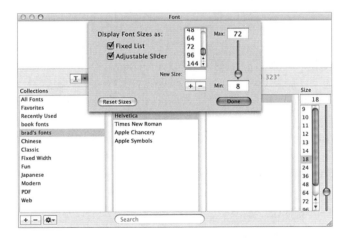

Using the Font Size sheet, you can perform the following tasks:

■ To add a size to the Size pane, enter the size you want to add in the New Size box and click + (the plus sign).

■ To remove a size from the Size pane, select it on the size list and click – (the minus sign).

- To remove the list of fixed sizes from the Size pane, uncheck the Fixed List check box. Check that box again to display the list of fixed sizes again.

- To add a size slider to the Size pane, check the Adjustable Slider check box. Then, enter the minimum font size and maximum size to be included on the slider in the Min Size and Max Size text boxes.

- To reset the sizes to the default values, click the Reset Sizes button.

Save your changes by clicking the Done button. The sheet disappears and the changes you made are reflected in the Size pane.

APPLYING TYPOGRAPHY EFFECTS TO FONTS

The Font panel enables you to apply some basic typography effects to text. To do so, use the following steps:

1. Select Action, Typography. The Typography window appears (see Figure 6.10).

Figure 6.10
You can use the Typography tools to apply some basic typography to text.

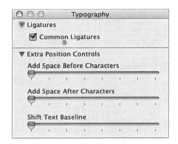

2. Check the Common Ligatures check box to apply common ligatures to the selected text.

3. Use the Add Space Before Characters slider to add space before characters in the selected text.

4. Use the Add Space After Characters slider to add space after characters in the selected text.

5. Use the Shift Text Baseline slider to change the text baseline of the selected text.

WORKING WITH THE CHARACTER PALETTE

Special characters can be a pain to enter because remembering which font family the character you need is part of is often difficult. The Character Palette is designed to help find special characters in various languages and quickly apply those characters to your documents. You can also add characters you use frequently for even easier access.

NOTE

If you are a longtime Mac user, you probably remember the Key Caps application you could use to locate and use special characters. The Mac OS X Character Palette is like that application, but it is much more powerful.

You can open the Character Palette from within applications that use the Mac OS X Font panel, or you can install the Character Palette menu on the Mac OS X menu bar.

To open the Character Palette from the Mac OS X Font panel, select Characters on the Action menu. The Character Palette opens (see Figure 6.11).

Figure 6.11
The Mac OS X Character Palette enables you to efficiently work with special characters.

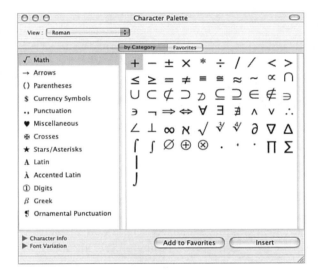

INSTALLING THE CHARACTER PALETTE

You can also install the Character Palette on the Input menu on the Mac OS X menu bar so it is available in all applications, whether they use the Mac OS X Font panel or not. To install the palette, perform the following steps:

1. Open the System Preferences Utility.
2. Click the International icon. The International pane opens. Click the Input Menu tab.
3. Check the box next to Character Palette.
4. Check the boxes next to any languages you want to install on the Input menu.
5. Check the "Show input menu in menu bar" check box. This enables the Input menu that will appear on the right end of any application's menu bar, including the Finder (see Figure 6.12).

6

Figure 6.12
The Input menu enables you to access the Character Palette from any application.

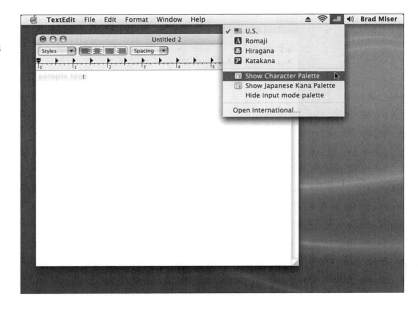

After you have installed the Character Palette on the Input menu, you can open it by selecting Input menu, Show Character Palette.

USING THE CHARACTER PALETTE

The Character Palette has two tabs. The "by Category" tab enables you to select and insert characters you need. When you find a character you use regularly, you can add it to the other tab, which is the Favorites tab, so you can grab it easily and quickly.

To find and use a character, carry out the following steps:

1. Open the Character Palette (either through the Font panel or from the Input menu).
2. On the Character Palette, select the language sets you want to view on the View pop-up menu. For example, to see Roman characters, select Roman.
3. Click the "by Category" tab and choose the category of character you want to view in the left pane. For example, select Math to view mathematical symbols.
4. To apply different fonts to the character, click the Expansion triangle next to the Font Variation tab. Select the font collection you want to use on the Collections pop-up menu. Then, click the font you want to apply to the character you selected.

TIP

> To limit the fonts shown in the Font Variation pane to only those that contain the character you are working with, select "Containing selected character" on the Collections pop-up menu. The character is shown with the fonts that contain it.

5. Click the Expansion triangle next to the `Font Variation` text; a preview pane appears, showing a preview of the character you have selected along with its name. You also see characters related to the one you are working with and the name and Unicode number of the character.

6. Continue adjusting the character until it is the way you want it.

7. Click Insert with Font. The character is pasted into the active document at the insertion point.

NOTE

If you don't apply a font to the character, the Insert with Font button is just the Insert button.

If the symbol you selected doesn't appear correctly in the document you inserted it in, see "The Special Character I Inserted Doesn't Look Correct" in the "Troubleshooting" section at the end of this chapter.

SETTING UP CHARACTER FAVORITES

You can create a set of favorite characters on the Character Palette to let you quickly choose a character to insert into a document. This is especially useful when you have applied specific fonts to a character.

To create favorite characters, take the following steps:

1. Open the Character Palette.

2. Create the character just as you would to insert it into a document.

3. Click Add to Favorites. This copies the character onto the Favorites tab (see Figure 6.13).

Figure 6.13
The characters shown on the Favorites tab can be inserted into a document quickly and easily.

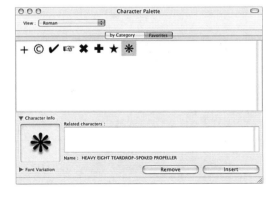

To insert a favorite character from the Favorites tab into a document, perform the following steps:

1. Open the Character Palette.
2. Click the Favorites tab.
3. Select the character you want to insert.
4. Click Insert.

You can remove a character from the Favorites tab by selecting it and clicking Remove.

WORKING WITH MAC OS X APPLICATION WINDOW MENUS

Although some previous applications running in Mac OS provided a Window menu, it was not the standard Window menu as it is now under Mac OS X. When applications can have more than one window open at the same time, you can use the Window menu to manage those open windows. You can do the following:

- Zoom the current window.
- Minimize the current window.
- Bring all windows to the front.
- Choose a window to bring it to the front.

Using the Window menu is simple. To bring an open window to the front, select it on the menu. To use one of the Window commands, select it.

NOTE

Some applications mark the frontmost window with a check mark or diamond symbol; however, this behavior is not consistent. In many cases, the frontmost window is marked with some sort of character.

Windows that are open and minimized also appear on the Window menu. If you use the Bring All to Front command, minimized windows remain on the Dock (windows on the Dock are always at the front).

OPENING DOCUMENTS IN MAC OS X

Using most applications involves opening documents, and although opening documents using Mac OS X applications is similar to opening documents in applications under previous versions of the OS, some substantial differences exist. Mac OS X offers several features that applications can use to make opening documents faster and easier.

As with previous versions of the Mac OS, there are several ways in which you can open documents:

- Select the document's icon in a Finder window and select the Finder's Open command (press ⌘-O).
- Double-click a document's icon in the Finder.

- Single-click a document's icon on the Dock.
- Drag a document icon or alias onto an application's icon or alias (on the desktop, in a Finder window, or on the Dock).
- Select the document's icon or alias and press ⌘-down arrow.
- Open the document using an AppleScript or other macro.
- Open a compatible application and use its Open command to open a document.

> **NOTE**
>
> If you see the document's icon on the Dock, an alias to that document has been placed there. If you see a thumbnail of the document's window on the Dock, that document is open and its window has been minimized. In either case, single-clicking the icon causes the document to open so you can work on it.

Most of these techniques are simple. However, because the Open dialog box has improved dramatically for Mac OS X version 10.3, it is worthy of some attention. Also, you need to understand how you can associate documents with specific applications so you can determine which application opens when you open a document.

Using the Mac OS X Open Dialog Box

 Finally, under Mac OS X version 10.3, Open dialog boxes have been harmonized with Finder windows so behavior of these windows, which serve a similar purpose (that being to enable you to access files and folders), is similar. And because Finder windows have been greatly improved for version 10.3, Open dialog boxes are also greatly improved.

As under previous versions, different applications can add features to the Open dialog box for specific purposes, but most Open dialog boxes offer a similar set of features.

> **NOTE**
>
> Many dialog boxes, although not called Open, are actually the Open dialog box with the name modified to suit the specific purpose at hand. These dialog boxes have names such as Choose a Picture, Choose a File, and so on. However, they all work in basically the same way and offer similar features as the Open dialog box.

6

A typical Open dialog box is shown in Figure 6.14.

If you read through earlier chapters in this book, you are quite knowledgeable of Finder windows, and Open dialog boxes work like Finder windows in many ways. The Places sidebar enables you to choose the location from which you want to open a file. When you select a place, its contents appear in the center pane of the window. You can choose to view this pane in the List view or the Columns view; again, these views are the same as when you are viewing Finder windows. You can use the List View or Columns view button to change the view used in the dialog box. You can use the Forward and Back buttons to move back to locations you viewed previously.

Forward/Back   Location pop-up menu
List view   Columns view

Figure 6.14
This Open dialog box, from Microsoft Word, is typical of those offered by Mac OS X applications. The similarity to Finder windows is more than skin deep.

Places sidebar —

Application tools pane —

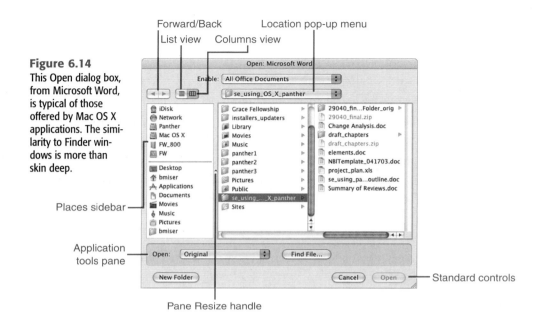

Standard controls

Pane Resize handle

→ To learn how to work with Finder windows, **see** Chapter 3, "Viewing and Navigating Mac OS X Finder Windows," **p. 47**.

The location shown in the Location pop-up menu is the currently selected folder whose contents are displayed in the pane. For example, if Documents is shown in the Location pop-up menu, the Documents folder is selected and its contents are displayed. If you have selected the Columns view, the contents of the location selection on the Location pop-up menu appears in the leftmost column.

You can also use the Location pop-up menu to quickly access many areas of your Mac, from your current location up to the volume on which Mac OS X is installed and the folders you have most recently opened (see Figure 6.15).

If you use the List view, to open a file or folder, simply move to it, select it, and click Open or double-click the file or folder you want to open. If you use the Columns view and select a folder, that folder becomes selected and you see its contents in the pane to the right of the folder. You can then select a folder or document it contains. In either view, you can select a document and double-click it or click Open.

You can change the Open dialog box in several ways, including the following:

- Use the Pane Resize handle to make the Places sidebar wider or narrower.
- Use the resize handle to make the dialog box larger or smaller.
- Click the Maximize button to make the dialog box its maximum size.

Figure 6.15
The Location pop-up menu in the Open dialog box has two sections; the upper section enables you to move "up" from your current location and the lower pane enables you to choose a place you have been recently.

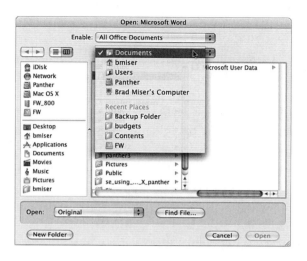

NOTE

The Maximize button is not included in the Open dialog box under all applications—typically, only Cocoa applications include this feature.

- Drag the dialog box around the screen. Because the Open dialog box is an independent window, you can move it around on the screen.

The Open dialog box might contain application-specific controls. For example, in Figure 6.15, you saw the Enable pop-up menu that lets you choose the type of Office documents you want to open. In the Application Tools pane, you will also see different tools depending on the application in which you are working. As you locate and open files or documents, you should be aware of these additional options and apply them as needed.

DETERMINING THE APPLICATION THAT OPENS WHEN YOU OPEN A DOCUMENT

As with previous versions of the Mac OS, the system determines which application should be used when you try to open a file (other than when you open a document from within an application using its Open command, of course). Typically, the document's creator opens if it is installed on your Mac, such as Microsoft Word opening a .doc file.

Several factors determine which application opens when you open a document, including the document's file type and creator information, as well as the file's filename extension. Mac OS X does a good job evaluating these properties to ensure that the correct application opens.

However, there might be times when you want to use a different application than the one the system selects, or you might not have the application that was used to create the document. In such cases, you can choose the application in which a document opens.

6

You can also change the association for all files of a specific type to determine which application opens when you open any file of that type.

There are two ways to associate document types with the applications used to open them. One is by using the Get Info window; the other is by using a document's contextual menu.

USING THE GET INFO WINDOW TO ASSOCIATE DOCUMENTS WITH AN APPLICATION

You can use the Open with section of the Info window to determine which application is used to open a file:

1. Select the document you are interested in and press ⌘-I. The Info window appears.
2. Expand the Open with section. The application with which the document is currently associated is shown on the pop-up menu. The associated application is called the default application—the text (default) appears after the application name.
3. Open the pop-up menu. You will see all the applications the system recognizes as being able to open the document, along with the Other selection (see Figure 6.16).

Figure 6.16
This menu lists all the applications Mac OS X thinks you can use on the document.

4. If one of the listed applications is the one you want to associate with the document, choose it on the menu. The document is opened with that application the next time you open it.
5. If you want to select an application that is not shown on the pop-up menu, select Other. You will see the Choose Other Application dialog box (see Figure 6.17).

Figure 6.17
You can use the
Choose Other
Application dialog box
to select applications
to open a document,
even if Mac OS X
doesn't recommend
them.

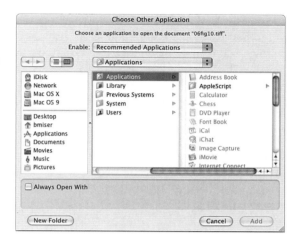

The Choose Other Application dialog box moves to the Applications directory auto-matically, and by default, it shows you only the recommended applications, which are those that Mac OS X recognizes as being compatible with the document. This set of applications might or might not be the same as you saw on the pop-up menu in the Info window. Mac OS X recognizes that some applications that can open files of that type might not really be intended to work with files of that type and so doesn't show them in the pop-up menu. However, they might be active in the Choose Other Application dia-log box. Applications Mac OS X doesn't think can be used at all are grayed out.

6. To make all applications active, select All Applications from the Enable pop-up menu.

7. Use the dialog box's controls to move to the application you want to select, select it, and click Add. After you click Add, you return to the Info window and the application you selected appears in the window. That application is used the next time you open the file.

TIP

If you want to permanently change the application used to open the document, check the Always Open With box.

CAUTION

Just because you told Mac OS X to use a specific application, even if it is the one that Mac OS X recommended, that doesn't mean you will actually be able to open the docu-ment with the application you select. If you try to open the document and generate error messages, you need to go back and select an application that can handle the type of file you are working with.

6

If you choose an application that Mac OS X isn't sure can open files of the selected type, you see a warning saying so in the dialog box after you select the application. You can proceed even when you see the warning, but you might get unexpected results.

TIP

> Even though Mac OS X tries to recommend applications that are appropriate for the selected document, it doesn't always do a great job. For example, it doesn't usually list a Classic application even when that application is the best choice for the selected document. In those situations, use the All Applications command on the Enable pop-up menu to add the application you want to use for the document.

You can also use the Info window to associate all files of a specific type with an application. Here's how:

1. Use the previous steps to associate a file of the type you want to associate with an application. After you have changed the application association, the Change All button becomes active.

2. Click the Change All button. You will see a warning dialog box that explains what you are about to do; for example, it lists the document types you are changing and the application with which you will associate documents of that type (see Figure 6.18).

Figure 6.18
This warning dialog box provides the information you need to ensure that the file association you are creating is the correct one.

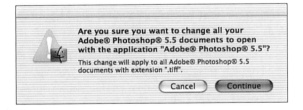

3. If you are sure that you want to make the change, click Continue. All files of the selected type become associated with the application you selected. The application you selected becomes the default application for all documents of that type.

USING A CONTEXTUAL MENU TO OPEN A DOCUMENT WITH A SPECIFIC APPLICATION

You can also use a file's contextual menu to determine which application is used to open it by doing the following:

1. Select a document that you want to open with a specific application.

2. Hold down the Control key and click the file to open its contextual menu.

3. Select Open With. Another menu appears that lists all the applications the system recognizes as being compatible with the document you are trying to open. The application currently associated with the document is marked as the default (see Figure 6.19).

Figure 6.19
This menu provides the same controls as the Open with section of a document's Info window.

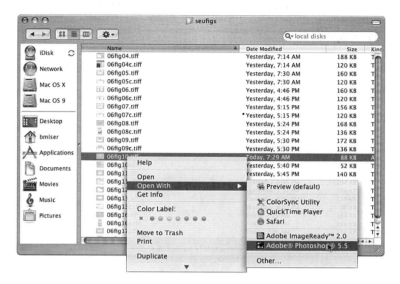

4. Select the application with which you want to open the document from the list. If you want to use an application that is not on the list, select Other and use the Choose Other Application dialog box to move to and select the application you want to use. (See the preceding section for detailed information on how this dialog box works.) The document opens in the application you selected.

When you use this technique, the document is associated with the application only if you save the document from within that application. If you simply open it and view it, the previous application continues to be associated with the document.

If you want the file to always be opened with a different application, even if you don't make any changes to it, open the contextual menu and then press the Option key. The Open With command becomes the Always Open With command. After you choose an application, the file is associated with that application and always opens in it.

NOTE

> Note that setting an application for all files with a specific type and creator combination does not override any documents for which you have set a specific application. For example, suppose you set the application to use for a specific document. Then, using another document, you change the application used for documents of that type and creator to be a different application. The first document would still open with the specific application you selected previously.

6

USING FILENAME EXTENSIONS TO ASSOCIATE DOCUMENTS WITH APPLICATIONS

You can also try to change the application associated with a specific document by changing the document's filename extension. For example, to associate QuickTime Player with a document, you would change its extension to .mov. When you do so, the file's icon might change to reflect that extension and the document opens with the application that extension is associated with. But this doesn't always happen. Do the following:

1. Edit the filename extension of the file you want to associate with an application so the extension is unique to that application. For example, you can change .rtf to .doc to associate a file with Microsoft Word.

   The filename extension you use must be specific to an application for this to work. For example, some filename extensions, such as .tiff, can be associated with many applications. You must use the Info window or contextual menu to change the association for such files.

   A warning dialog box appears (see Figure 6.20). In this dialog box, you see two buttons: One keeps the file's current filename extension, and other causes the new one to be used.

Figure 6.20
When you change a filename extension, you have to confirm the change by clicking the Use button in a dialog box like this one.

2. Click the Use button; the filename extension is changed. The file is associated with the application currently associated with files that have the filename extension you chose to use. (If you click the Keep button, nothing is changed.)

Changing the filename extension does not override a selection you have made with the Info window. If you associate an application with a document by using the Info window tools and then subsequently change the filename extension, the choice you made with the Info window overrides the filename extension and determines the application used to open that document.

SAVING DOCUMENTS IN MAC OS X

 When you use applications, you will also be saving documents frequently. Fortunately, Save sheets under Mac OS X version 10.3, like Open dialog boxes, have been redesigned to be more consistent with Finder windows.

The specific Save sheet or dialog box you see depends on the application you are using. Cocoa and some carbonized applications use the Save sheet that is described in this section. Some carbonized and all Classic applications use the older Save dialog boxes from Mac OS 9.

A typical Mac OS X Save sheet is shown in Figure 6.21.

Expand/Collapse Sheet button

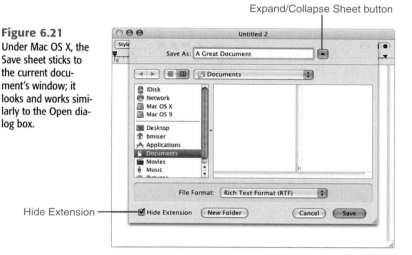

Figure 6.21
Under Mac OS X, the Save sheet sticks to the current document's window; it looks and works similarly to the Open dialog box.

Hide Extension

Mac OS X Save sheets are a good example of the dialog type called *sheets*. A sheet drops down from the top of the document window you are saving. Unlike the Open dialog box, the Save dialog box is attached to the top of the window and therefore moves when you move the document window.

NOTE

> The size of a sheet is fixed, but you can still resize the document to which it is attached. In fact, you can make the document so small that it is completely hidden behind the sheet, but I wouldn't recommend it.

6

The sheet contains the Save As text box in which you enter the filename. If you click the Expand/Collapse button, the sheet expands so you see a window that is very similar to the Open dialog box you learned about in the previous section. If you click this button again, you see the collapsed version of the sheet.

NOTE

One of the benefits of a sheet is that an open sheet will not prevent you from working with other documents, even within the same application. The sheet stays with the document to which it is attached. You can open, work with, and save other documents without closing the sheet.

Save sheets and Open dialog boxes look and work very similarly, but a couple of items on Save sheets aren't on Open dialog boxes so you need to pay attention to them.

One is the Format pop-up menu, which is sometimes called File Format depending on the application in which you are working. You use this pop-up menu to choose the format of the file you are saving.

The other is the Hide Extension check box. If you check this box, the filename extension is hidden. If you uncheck this box, which I recommend that you do, the filename extension is shown in the Save As box. Because filename extensions are important clues about how a document will open, you should generally choose to display them.

Some applications (such as Microsoft Office X) work in an opposite way: Instead of the Hide Extension check box, their Save sheets include the "Append file extension" check box. When this box is checked, the filename extension is added to the file's name.

TIP

Creating a new folder in the Save As sheet can be a bit confusing. The new folder is created in the currently selected directory, which is shown in the Location pop-up menu. Because viewing multiple levels of the hierarchy using the Columns view controls is easy, you might be creating a new folder in a location you didn't realize you had selected. Before using that command, double-check the Location pop-up menu to ensure that you have selected the correct location in which to create the new folder.

In some applications' Save As sheet, you will see additional controls, such as an Options button that enables you to configure options for the file format you have selected.

UNDERSTANDING FILENAMES AND FILENAME EXTENSIONS

An important aspect of saving documents under Mac OS X is that it uses filename extensions. Filename extensions consist of a period and three or more characters that are added to the end of the filename. When you save a document, most Cocoa and carbonized applications automatically append the correct filename extension for the type of file you are saving. Mac OS X uses the filename extension to associate the file with a particular application.

The addition of filename extensions to Mac filenames can be confusing because one of the Mac's strengths has traditionally been the lack of such extensions. However, because most applications tack the appropriate filename extension onto the filename you enter automatically, you generally don't have to worry about them.

NOTE

> In fact, if an extension is left off a filename, the Mac still uses the file creator and type information to open the file in a compatible application. However, you should include filename extensions for all documents you save.

Most Mac OS X files have a filename extension, including documents, system resources, and so on. In fact, a bewildering number of filename extensions exist under Mac OS X, and because it is based on the Unix operating system, Mac filename extensions are not limited to a certain number of characters. However, most document filename extensions consist of three or four characters. Some examples are shown in Table 6.2.

TABLE 6.2 EXAMPLES OF MAC DOCUMENT FILENAME EXTENSIONS

Filename Extension	What It Stands For	Default Application Associated with It
.mov	Movie	QuickTime Player
.tiff	Tagged Interchange File Format	Preview
.rtfd	Rich Text Formatted Document	TextEdit
.rtf	Rich Text Format	TextEdit
.jpg or .jpeg	Joint Photographic Experts Group	Preview
.pdf	Portable Document Format	Preview
.html	Hypertext Markup Language	Default Web browser (such as Safari)
.doc	Microsoft Word Document	Word
.xls	Microsoft Excel Spreadsheet	Excel
.mp3	Motion Picture Experts Group, Audio Layer 3	iTunes

System Filename Extensions

Although dealing with document filename extensions is fairly straightforward, dealing with system filename extensions can get really ugly. Some are straightforward, such as .app for applications and .dock for dock-lings, but many seem to be gibberish. Usually, you can just take system filename extensions as they are (because you can't change them), and sometimes you can even figure out what they stand for. For example, the .kext filename extension stands for kernel extension, which is an extension to the operating system software.

One system filename extension that is useful to know is .plist. It indicates a preference file, as in loginwindow.plist, which is the preferences for the Login window.

At the top of the Save sheet, you enter the filename you want to use. Under Mac OS X, you can use long filenames—up to 255 characters, including the filename extension and the period between the filename extension and the filename itself (so be sure to allow room for the filename extension when you enter a filename). When you save a document in many applications, the appropriate filename extension is added to the filename automatically (you won't see it if the Hide Extension check box is checked). As mentioned previously, in some applications, you have to check a box to add the filename extension to the filename.

If you intend to share your files with people who use Mac OS 9.1 or earlier, you need to keep the name under 31 characters, including the filename extension the application will add to the name you enter.

If you want to share your files with Windows computer users, you need to ensure that the filename extension used is comprehensible to Windows PCs.

NOTE

> Some applications provide a File Format pop-up menu in the Save As sheet that you can use to choose the file format in which you want to save the document. Sometimes, the options on it are disabled. In such cases, look for the Save To command. This command enables you to save one file type to another type. The Save To dialog box looks and works exactly as the Save As sheet does, except that the options on the File Format pop-up menu are enabled.

VIEWING OR HIDING FILENAME EXTENSIONS

Under Mac OS X, you have the option to view or hide filename extensions. However, filename extensions are usually used whether you can see them or not. Generally, I recommend that you always view them because they provide valuable information.

You can choose to hide filename extensions for specific files, or you can set the Finder to always display filename extensions for all files (regardless of the filename extension setting for a specific file).

You can show or hide the filename extensions for specific files by using the following steps:

1. In a Finder window, select the file for which you want to hide the filename extension.
2. Open the Info window.
3. Expand the Name & Extension section.
4. Check the "Hide extension" check box. (To show the extension for a file, uncheck this box.)
5. Close the Info window.

TIP

> You can edit a file's name and filename extension in the box in the Name & Extension pane of the Info window.

To override the filename extension display setting for every file, use the following steps:

1. Open the Finder Preferences window.
2. Click the Advanced button to make the Advanced pane appear.
3. Check the "Show all file extensions" check box.
4. Close the Finder Preferences window.

Filename extensions will always be shown, regardless of the "Hide extension" check box in the Info window.

Under most applications, the filename extension status (hidden or not) for specific files is saved, even when you use the Finder preferences to always display filename extensions. If you turn off "Show all file extensions" again, the filename extensions for any files you have hidden become hidden again.

Some applications, especially carbonized applications such as Office X, don't automatically add filename extensions unless the appropriate check box is checked in the Save sheet.

SAVING DOCUMENTS AS PDFS

One of the many benefits of Mac OS X is that the Portable Document Format (PDF) is a native format. This means you can create a PDF from *any* application without using Adobe's Acrobat or Distiller (although those tools offer some special features that are not available to Mac OS X natively).

PDF documents are useful for two primary reasons. First, they retain their appearance regardless of the fonts and applications installed on the viewing computer. Second, PDF documents can be viewed natively in Mac OS X (using the Preview application) or by Adobe's free Acrobat Reader application (which is available for all platforms). These reasons make PDF the ideal format for distributing and viewing documents electronically.

PDFs also retain their formatting when they are printed. This makes PDF a good way to distribute documents that you know the recipient will want in hard copy. You can email a PDF and the receiver can print it. Unlike faxing, in which the document format degrades significantly, when the recipient prints the PDF, it will look as good as it does when you send it.

An additional benefit to PDFs is that they can't be easily modified. When you send a PDF to someone, he will have a difficult time changing it (it can't be changed at all without special tools). So, PDFs are also a good way to secure documents you provide to others.

→ To learn more about working with PDFs, **see** "Working with PDFs," **p. 774**.

To create a PDF version of a document, you use the Print command to "print" the document to a PDF file:

1. Create your document using the appropriate application.
2. Save the document.
3. Select File, Print to open the Print sheet.

> **NOTE**
>
> You probably noticed that the Print dialog box is also a sheet. This means you can leave it open and work with other documents in the same or different applications.

4. Click Save As PDF.
5. Use the Save to File sheet to name the file and choose a location.
6. Click Print.

A PDF file is created in the location you specify. This document can be viewed using the Preview application or with Adobe's free Acrobat Reader.

→ To learn more about printing documents, **see** "Finding, Installing, and Using Printers," **p. 759**.

> **NOTE**
>
> You can also choose to print documents in the PostScript file format. To do this, open the Print sheet and select Output Options on the Options pop-up menu. Click the Save as File check box and choose the format in which you want to save the file on the Format pop-up menu. The other option on this menu is PDF, which does the same thing as the Save As PDF button.

FAXING DOCUMENTS

NEW Under Mac OS X version 10.3, you can fax documents from within the application you use to edit those documents:

1. Prepare the document you want to fax.
2. Select File, Print to open the Print sheet.
3. Click Fax, and the Fax sheet appears (see Figure 6.22).

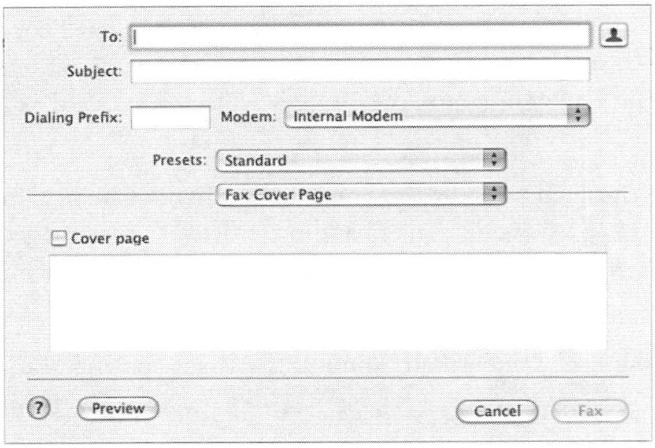

Figure 6.22
Using the Fax sheet, you can fax any document you can open.

6

4. Enter the fax number in the To box or click the Address Book button to choose a fax number from your Address Book.

→ To learn how to use the Address Book, **see** "Setting Up and Using an Address Book," **p. 330**.

5. Type the subject in the Subject box.

6. If you need to dial a prefix to connect to the fax number you entered in step 2, enter it in the Dialing Prefix box.

7. Choose the modem by which you want to send the fax on the Modem pop-up menu. In most cases, you will use the Internal Modem option, but you can use any fax device that is configured on your Mac.

8. With Fax Cover Page selected on the Options pop-up menu, check the Cover page check box if you want to include a cover page on the fax.

9. If you elected to use a cover page, enter its text in the box.

10. Use the other choices on the Options pop-up menu as needed. For example, to config-ure the modem, select Modem.

11. To preview your fax, click the Preview button. The fax opens in the Preview applica-tion.

12. Click Fax to fax the document to the recipients you selected.

TROUBLESHOOTING

I CAN'T INSTALL AN APPLICATION BECAUSE I DON'T HAVE SUFFICIENT PRIVILEGES

When I try to install an application, I see an error message stating that I do not have sufficient privileges.

To install an application in the Applications folder, you must be logged in as an administra-tor. If you can't log in as an administrator, try installing the application in your Home folder instead.

If this doesn't work, you might have to log in as root to install the application.

→ To get additional help, **see** "Logging In As Root," **p. 236**.

I CAN'T INSTALL AN APPLICATION BECAUSE I AM HAVING PROBLEMS WITH CLASSIC

When I try to run an application's installer, Classic starts up but is unable to install the application.

If a Classic application won't install under Mac OS X, reboot in OS 9.2 and run the installer from there. If you use a Mac that can't reboot under Mac OS 9, you are pretty much out of luck. You will have to get an OS X version of the application.

I CAN'T DRAG A DOCUMENT ON AN ICON TO OPEN IT

When I try to open a document by dragging its icon on top of an application's icon, the icon doesn't highlight so that it will open.

This happens when you try to open a document for which the application is not recommended. You can force it to open by holding down the Option-⌘ keys while you drag the document's icon onto the application's icon.

You can also associate an application with a document using the document's Info window.

WHEN I OPEN AN APPLICATION, WHAT I SEE IS INCOMPREHENSIBLE

I opened a document, but what appears onscreen is a bunch of gobbledy-gook.

This happens when you open a file that contains data the application can't interpret. Use the Info window for the document to associate a different application with the document; using an application that Mac OS X lists as a recommended application makes it more likely to open successfully. You can also try opening the document from within an application rather than from the Finder.

THE SPECIAL CHARACTER I INSERTED DOESN'T LOOK CORRECT

I inserted a special character from the Character Palette into a document, but the character that appeared wasn't the one I selected.

This can happen if the application you are working with does not support the Mac OS X font and formatting tools. The most likely case is that the format information you associated with the character, such as the font, was not translated into the application properly.

To solve the problem, use the application's formatting tools to apply the same font to the character as is selected in the Character Palette. The symbol should then appear just as it does in the Character Palette.

CHAPTER 7

WORKING WITH MAC OS 9, THE CLASSIC ENVIRONMENT, AND CLASSIC APPLICATIONS

In this chapter

UNDERSTANDING MAC OS 9.2, THE CLASSIC ENVIRONMENT, AND CLASSIC APPLICATIONS

As you have learned throughout this book, Mac OS X was an entirely new operating system rather than an evolution of Mac OS 9. As such, applications created for previous versions of the Mac OS won't work under Mac OS X—well, not directly anyway. Rather than forcing you to either obtain a Mac OS X–compatible version of all the applications you use (which might or might not be available) or to go without, Apple includes the Classic environment in Mac OS X. As you learned in Chapter 1, "Mac OS X: Foundations," and Chapter 6, "Installing and Using Mac OS X Applications," the Classic environment enables you to run Classic versions of applications.

NOTE

> A *Classic* application is one that was created for Mac OS 9.2 or earlier versions of the Mac OS.

The Classic environment is provided solely to enable you to run applications that were created for earlier versions of the Mac OS. After you have obtained Mac OS X versions of all the applications you use, you will no longer have any reason to use the Classic versions and thus, the Classic environment. Classic is really a bridge between the past (previous versions of the Mac OS) and the present and future (Mac OS X).

The Classic environment is actually a Mac OS X application that emulates Mac OS 9.2; you run Classic applications from within this emulated environment. The configuration of the Classic environment is the configuration of the Mac OS 9.2 installation you choose to use. The Classic environment provides all the system resources of Mac OS 9.2, such as extensions and control panels, and you can customize the Classic environment just as you can Mac OS 9.2 itself.

Although you will use the Classic environment to run Classic applications most of the time, you might also run into situations in which you want to start up under Mac OS 9.2 directly (for example, to use applications that access a hardware device that doesn't work under Mac OS X). The ability to boot up under OS 9.2 depends on the specific Mac model you have. Many modern Mac models can't start under Mac OS 9, but if you have an older model or one specifically designed to boot under OS 9.2 it might be possible.

Classic, a Bridge to the Past

The Classic environment is analogous to the transition from 68K processors to the PowerPC processor. Applications written for the 68K processor could not run on PowerPC machines, and vice versa. For a period of time, most applications were provided in *fat* versions, which meant the application came in both a 68K and a PowerPC version. You could use the application installer to choose which version was installed (sometimes both were installed or only the one appropriate for the processor you were using). After a period of time, the 68K versions of applications were dropped because most people who were purchasing new software were also using a PowerPC machine.

You can expect a similar transition for Classic applications as Mac OS X versions are released. For a time, both versions will be available, but as more Mac users make the switch to Mac OS X, the development and distribution of applications compatible with Mac OS 9 or earlier versions of the OS will cease. Because Mac OS X has been around for a couple of years, this transition period is coming to an end as most major Mac applications have now been ported to or rewritten for Mac OS X.

The Classic environment mostly does its job well and will enable you to use applications that were designed for Mac OS 9. However, it does have limitations, some of which are the following:

- **No memory protection**—Because the Classic environment is an emulation of Mac OS 9.2, Classic applications do not have protected memory. When one Classic application has a problem, it can (and usually does) affect other Classic applications you are running. In this respect, running applications under the Classic environment is just like running them under Mac OS 9.2 or earlier. When a Classic application crashes, it can take down the rest of the open Classic applications as well as the Classic environment itself.

NOTE

> The Classic application itself is a Mac OS X application and does benefit from Mac OS X's protected memory architecture. If the Classic environment crashes, it doesn't affect the Mac OS X Finder, Carbonized applications, or Cocoa applications that are running.

- **Emulated performance**—When you run a Classic application, you are using three layers of software, which are Mac OS X, the Classic environment, and the Classic application. Because of this, the performance of a Classic application can be considerably slower than when running it under Mac OS 9.2. This speed differential is most noticeable on slower Mac hardware and while using processor-intensive applications (such as advanced graphics or video applications).

- **Spotty hardware support**—Because they run in an emulated environment, Classic applications can sometimes have trouble accessing hardware with which they are supposed to work. When you are unable to access a hardware device through the Classic environment, your only options are to restart under Mac OS 9.2 (if you can) or to get Mac OS X–compatible software for the hardware you want to run.

NOTE

> All user accounts on your Mac share the same Classic environment. However, each user account can access the Classic pane of the System Preferences utility and so can change the Classic environment to suit his purposes. (The Classic pane does not require Administrator authentication.)

7

INSTALLING, CONFIGURING, AND RUNNING THE CLASSIC ENVIRONMENT

To use the Classic environment (and thus Classic applications), you need to install and configure the Classic environment you want to use. After these tasks are accomplished, you can run the environment to run Classic applications.

When you installed Mac OS X, you should have also installed Mac OS 9.2, preferably on a different partition than Mac OS X is installed on (although they can be installed on the same partition). You can also have more than one volume containing Mac OS 9.2 on a single machine. Each instance of Mac OS 9.2 can be used to provide a different Classic environment. If you intend to run Classic applications a significant amount of time, the ideal scenario is to have two partitions on your machine: one for Mac OS X and one for the Mac OS 9 environment you will use. For a number of reasons, it is less desirable to have only one partition on your machine (with both Mac OS X and Mac OS 9 installed on it).

INSTALLING A CLASSIC ENVIRONMENT

The good news is that if you have installed Mac OS X, you already have installed a Classic environment.

→ For help installing Mac OS 9.2 and Mac OS X, **see** Appendix A, "Installing and Maintaining Mac OS X," **p. 947**.

If you installed Mac OS X on a machine that already had a previous version of the OS on it, you had two fundamental choices as to where to install it. You could install it on the same volume as the one on which you installed Mac OS 9.2, or you could choose a different volume.

Hopefully, you chose to install Mac OS X on a separate volume from Mac OS 9.2. This configuration is a bit cleaner to work with because Mac OS 9.2 and Mac OS X resources are clearly separated and working with them is somewhat easier. It also makes repairing either version of the OS easier because you can choose to erase one volume without affecting the other volumes you use. If both operating systems are installed on the same volume, making changes to one operating system can affect the other.

However, installing Mac OS X on the same volume as Mac OS 9.2 also works; the organization of each system's resources is just a bit more complex. The primary drawback is that if you have problems with the single-volume configuration, it can be more difficult to troubleshoot and repair.

NOTE

> Installing Mac OS X on the same volume as Mac OS 9.2 is called installing Mac OS X *over* Mac OS 9.2. This terminology can be confusing because it implies that the Mac OS 9.2 software was erased, but that isn't the case.

7

Whichever way you installed it, somewhere on your Mac is a folder containing the Mac OS 9.2 resources (see Figure 7.1).

Figure 7.1
Here you see a Finder window showing the contents of a volume called Mac OS 9 that has Mac OS 9 installed on it.

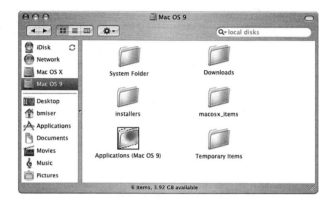

If you open a separate volume on which Mac OS 9.2 is installed, the items you might see include the following:

- **System Folder**—The Mac OS 9.2 System Folder contains all the software needed to run Mac OS 9.2.

- **Desktop Folder**—The Desktop Folder on your Mac OS 9.2 volume is the desktop folder for Mac OS 9.2 only. This is the desktop you will see when you restart your Mac in Mac OS 9.2.

- **Applications (Mac OS 9)**—This folder is the default location for Classic applications that are installed as part of the Mac OS 9.2 installation. You can install Mac OS 9.2 applications anywhere on your Mac OS 9.2 volume. However, it is helpful to keep your Mac OS 9 applications as well organized as the Mac OS X applications are; this is a lot easier if you use the Applications (Mac OS 9) folder for Classic applications and the OS X Applications folder for Carbon and Cocoa applications.

- **Documents**—This folder contains the default document folders for Mac OS 9.2, such as Installer Logs, Web pages, and so on. Many Classic applications, such as iTunes and Microsoft Office, store user-specific data here as well.

NOTE

If you installed Mac OS 9.2 on a separate volume from that on which you installed Mac OS X, you might see the Desktop (Mac OS 9) folder on your Mac OS X desktop. You can open this folder to access the items installed on your Mac OS 9.2 desktop. If you installed Mac OS X over Mac OS 9.2, you won't see this folder on your desktop. To access the Mac OS 9.2 Desktop Folder, you must open your Mac OS 9.2 volume.

7

CONFIGURING THE CLASSIC ENVIRONMENT

You control the configuration and behavior of the Classic environment using the Classic pane of the System Preferences utility (see Figure 7.2).

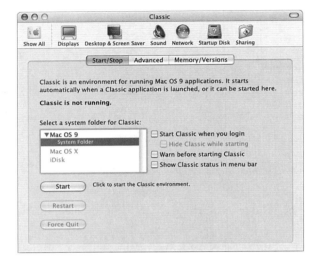

Figure 7.2
You control various aspects of the Classic environment, such as which Mac OS 9.2 System Folder is used, with the Classic pane of the System Preferences utility.

This pane has three tabs: Start/Stop, Advanced, and Memory/Versions. As you might expect, the first deals with starting and stopping the environment. The Advanced pane enables you to configure various aspects of the Classic environment, and the Memory/Versions tab enables you to monitor the processes running in the Classic environment, including how much of the Classic environment's memory allocation each Classic application is using.

Under the Start/Stop tab, you will see a window in which you can select the startup volume for Classic. You can have more than one version of Mac OS 9.2 installed on the same machine. You might want to do this to keep one "clean" version that contains only default Mac OS 9.2 system software. This can be your test environment; other environments can include third-party software you use. You use the startup volume list to control which of the installed Mac OS 9.2 installations Classic uses.

When Classic starts, you have two options that relate to the extensions that are part of the Mac OS 9.2 system when it starts up. These options are configured on the Advanced tab and configure the OS to have all extensions turned off or to use Extensions Manager to choose the startup set of extensions used for the Classic environment. You configure the startup extension options on the Advanced tab of the Classic pane (see Figure 7.3).

If you choose to open Classic with no extensions, you move directly into the Classic environment.

7

Figure 7.3
Using the Advanced tab of the Classic pane, you can control the configuration of the System Folder for the Classic environment.

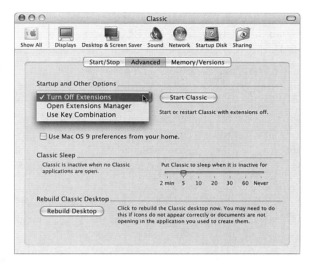

If you choose to use the Extensions Manager to control the extensions used in the Classic environment, Extensions Manager opens the next time you restart Classic. You can then configure the extension set you want to use.

NOTE

If you use a Mac that was produced before January 2003 or one of the select models produced after that date, you can also boot under Mac OS 9.2 and use Extensions Manager to create custom startup sets for your Mac OS 9.2 environment. Then, you can choose the extension set you want to use when you start the Classic environment. The details of using Extensions Manager are beyond the scope of this book. For help with the Mac OS 9 Extensions Manager, see my book *The Mac OS 9 Guide*.

TIP

A third option on the Startup Options pop-up menu is Use Key Combination. If you choose this, you can set a keyboard shortcut to use to start or restart the Classic environment. To do so, select the Use Key Combination option on the Startup and Other Options pop-up menu and then press up to five keys that you want to be the shortcut. (You can click Clear Keys to remove the keyboard shortcut you created.) When you use the keyboard shortcut, the other startup option you chose (for example, Turn Off Extensions) will be used when you start or restart Classic.

To configure your Classic environment, use the following steps:

1. Open the Classic pane of the System Preferences utility (it is in the System section) and click the Start/Stop tab. The application searches all the volumes mounted on your Mac and displays those that contain a valid Mac OS 9 startup volume (refer to Figure 7.2).

7

2. Choose the specific Mac OS 9.2 System Folder the Classic environment should use in the "Select a system folder for" Classic list. (If only one installation of Mac OS 9.2 is on your Mac, it will be the only choice you have and will be selected automatically.)

3. If you want Classic to start each time you log in to your Mac, check the "Start Classic when you login" check box. This option is useful if you regularly use Classic applications because you don't have to wait for Classic to start the first time you launch a Classic application. If you are like me and use Classic applications only rarely, don't select this option. The Classic environment does use system resources, so you shouldn't have it open if you aren't using Classic applications. Because Classic opens so quickly under 10.3, it isn't painful to wait for it to open when you open a Classic application.

4. If you choose to have Classic start when you log in, you can check the "Hide Classic while starting" check box. This causes Classic to be hidden while it is starting.

5. If you want to see a warning dialog box before Classic starts, check the "Warn before starting Classic" check box.

6. If you want to install the Classic menu on the Finder menu bar, check the "Show Classic status in menu bar" check box. In addition to showing the current status of the Classic environment, this menu enables you to control the Classic environment, open Classic preferences, and access Apple menu items.

7. Click the Advanced tab.

8. Choose the startup option you want from the Startup and Other Options pop-up menu; in most cases, Open Extensions Manager is the best choice. If you don't want any extensions to load, select Turn Off Extensions instead.

9. If you want to have Classic preferences that are specific to your user account, check the "Use Mac OS 9 preferences from your home" check box. This causes your extensions, startup, Apple menu, and other Mac OS 9 preferences to be stored in your Home folder. Then, should another user reconfigure the Classic environment, your setup will not be affected.

10. Set the amount of inactive time before Classic goes to sleep by using the slider. To preserve the resources it uses, Classic goes to sleep when no Classic applications are running or when the amount of inactive time set on the slider passes. Because Classic is an application, having it become inactive is useful because it then requires fewer system resources. The amount of inactive time you should set depends on the resources your Mac has. If you have a lot of RAM and a fast processor, you can set a longer sleep time and avoid the time lag that occurs when Classic wakes up when you move in and out of the Classic environment. If you have limited resources, use a shorter inactive time so more resources are available to other applications when you aren't actively using a Classic application.

11. Quit the System Preferences utility.

RUNNING THE CLASSIC ENVIRONMENT

Because the Classic environment is an application, you must open it when you want to use it. There are several ways to launch the Classic environment:

- Launch a Classic application.

- Open the Start/Stop tab of the Classic pane of the System Preferences utility and click Start.

- Open the Advanced tab of the Classic pane of the System Preferences utility, select the startup option you want, and click Start Classic if Classic is not running or Restart Classic if it is already running.

- Press the keyboard combination you set using the pop-up menu on the Advanced tab of the Classic pane.

- Open the Classic menu on the Finder menu bar and select Start Classic.

- Use the Classic pane of the System Preferences utility to have Classic start on login and then log in to the computer.

When the Classic environment starts, you can view the Classic Environment window by switching to the Classic icon on the Dock (Classic startup is hidden by default). This window contains a progress bar to show you how the startup process is proceeding. At the top of the window, you see the Mac OS 9.2 volume you are using. You will also see the Stop button that you can use to abort the startup process. By default, the window is collapsed, so these elements are all you see. If you click the Expansion triangle on the left side of the Classic window, you will see a larger window that shows the traditional Mac OS 9 startup screen, complete with the "marching" icons as the Classic environment starts (it almost makes me nostalgic for OS 9, but just almost).

If you chose to have extensions off or if you started Classic in any way except from the buttons on the Advanced tab, the Classic window disappears when the environment is running.

If you started Classic from the Advanced tab and selected the Extensions Manager startup option, you will see the Extensions Manager window (see Figure 7.4).

 If you see a dialog box asking you to update your Classic-specific resources, see "I Have to Update My Classic Resources" in the "Troubleshooting" section at the end of this chapter.

Use Extensions Manager to configure the Mac OS 9.2 system you want to use—for example, turn off extensions you don't need. You can also create sets of extensions so you can quickly configure the Classic environment for specific tasks (such as enabling the extensions associated with specific hardware devices). After you have configured Extensions Manager, click Continue.

7

Figure 7.4
When you start the Classic environment using the Open Extensions Manager option, you can use Extensions Manager to configure the Mac OS 9.2 system Classic uses.

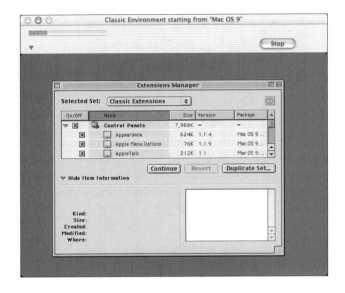

NOTE

If you have used previous versions of the Mac OS, you are probably familiar with extensions, control panels, and the Extensions Manager utility. If not, refer to a Mac OS 9 resource, such as my book *The Mac OS 9 Guide*.

After you have clicked Continue in Extensions Manager or if you have chosen to start Classic using another option, you will see the familiar Mac OS 9.2 startup screen. The first time you start the Classic environment from a specific Mac OS 9.2 volume, you will enter the Mac OS Setup Assistant utility. Use this utility to configure the Mac OS 9.2 installation.

NOTE

The first time you start Classic with a specific Mac OS 9 environment, you will see a dialog box asking whether it is okay for Mac OS X to install some Classic-specific resources into the Mac OS 9 System Folder you have selected as your Classic environment. You must click OK to be able to use the selected environment for Classic. This is one reason it can be better to install a Mac OS 9 volume that is dedicated to running Classic. You can then maintain another Mac OS 9 volume that has no Mac OS X resources installed in it for starting under Mac OS 9.

 If you see a warning dialog box about AirPort, see "Classic Doesn't Support What I Am Doing" in the "Troubleshooting" section at the end of this chapter.

After you have completed the Mac Setup Assistant, you have the option of running the Internet Setup Assistant to configure your Classic environment for the Internet. Most of the time, you will use Mac OS X to connect to the Net because it includes Mac OS X applications to do so; however, you can also access the Internet under Classic. If you do need to connect to the Net from within Classic, it should work without running the Internet Setup Assistant because the Classic Environment picks up your network settings from Mac OS X. So, you can safely quit the Internet Setup Assistant without making any changes in it.

→ To learn how to configure your Mac for the Internet, **see** Chapter 10, "Connecting Your Mac to the Internet," **p. 263**.

> **NOTE**
>
> Configuring various Mac OS 9.2 options is beyond the scope of this chapter. For help working with Mac OS 9.2, see my book *The Mac OS 9 Guide*.

After the Classic environment launches, what you see depends on how you started it. If you launched Classic by launching a Classic application, you see the application. If you launched the Classic environment without opening a Classic application, you return to the Mac OS X desktop. If you used the Classic pane of the System Preferences utility to start Classic, you return there.

> **TIP**
>
> To see whether Classic is running, open the Classic pane of the System Preferences utility. Just above the startup volume selection window, you will see a message about the status of the Classic environment (such as Classic is running) when the Classic environment is running. If you installed the Classic menu on the Finder menu bar, you can open that menu to see the current status of the Classic environment.

The Classic environment continues to run until one of the following events happens:

- You manually stop it.
- You log out of Mac OS X.

> **NOTE**
>
> Remember that the Classic environment sleeps after the amount of inactive time you specify in the Classic pane of the System Preferences utility.

CONTROLLING THE CLASSIC ENVIRONMENT

You can control the Classic environment in the following ways:

- Log out to close it.
- Click the Stop button on the Start/Stop tab of the Classic pane in the System Preferences utility.
- Open the Classic menu on the Finder menu bar and select Stop Classic.

7

- Click Restart on the Start/Stop tab of the Classic pane in the System Preferences utility to restart it.

- Click Force Quit on the Start/Stop tab of the Classic pane in the System Preferences utility to force it to quit.

- Press Option-⌘-Esc to open the Mac OS X Force Quit Applications window; then select Classic Environment, click Force Quit, and click Force Quit a second time to force it to quit.

- Click Restart Classic on the Advanced tab of the Classic pane in the System Preferences utility to restart it.

CAUTION

> When you stop the Classic environment, all Classic applications are stopped as well. During a normal shutdown, this is not a problem because you are prompted to save any unsaved changes to open documents. However, when you force the Classic environment to quit, all unsaved changes are lost. You should force Classic to quit only when you have no other option.

 If your Classic environment locks up and seems to have stopped responding, see "My Classic Environment Is Hung Up" in the "Troubleshooting" section at the end of this chapter.

To keep things running efficiently, stop the Classic environment when you are done using Classic applications if your Mac has limited RAM or other resources.

When you want to restart your Classic environment using a different set of extensions, open the Advanced tab of the Classic pane of the System Preferences utility. Select the Open Extensions Manager startup option and click the Restart Classic button.

When you have Classic startup at login or when you use the controls on the Start/Stop tab of the Classic pane, the environment starts up using the set of extensions that were most recently used. To change the configuration used without using the Extensions Manager, you must configure the environment manually.

CONFIGURING THE CLASSIC ENVIRONMENT MANUALLY

You can manually configure the Classic environment by manipulating the files in its System Folder. For example, you can add or remove startup or shutdown items.

NOTE

> If your Mac can be started from the Mac OS 9 volume you use for the Classic environment, you can also make configuration changes using the Extensions Manager while running under Mac OS 9.2.

The general steps to manually configure the Classic environment are as follows:

1. Open a Finder window for the Mac OS 9.2 System Folder you use for the Classic environment.

2. Open the Extensions folder and move any extensions you want to disable to the Extensions (Disabled) folder.

> **NOTE**
>
> If you have never used the Extensions Manager option, you might have to create the (Disabled) folders yourself. If you have used Extensions Manager, the folders are created for you.

3. Open the Control Panels folder and move control panels you want to disable to the Control Panels (Disabled) folder.

4. Place aliases of any items you want to launch when Classic starts in the Startup Items folder.

5. Place aliases of any items you want to launch when Classic stops in the Shutdown Items folder.

6. Place aliases of documents or Classic applications in the Apple Menu Items folder.

7. Close the Finder window.

The next time you start the Classic environment, it will reflect the changes you made.

> **TIP**
>
> If you have a "Mac OS 9 bootable" Mac, another way to configure your Classic environment is to boot in Mac OS 9 and configure the system there. Then, when you start the Classic environment, it uses that configuration. To create Extensions Manager sets from which to choose when you use the Extensions Manager startup option, you can restart under Mac OS 9, run Extensions Manager, and create the startup sets you want to have available. Then, start in Mac OS X again and restart the Classic environment using the Extensions Manager option. You can choose the startup sets you create when Classic starts.

MONITORING RESOURCES BEING USED BY THE CLASSIC ENVIRONMENT

The Memory/Versions tab of the Classic pane enables you to monitor the performance and resource use of the Classic environment. This can be helpful when troubleshooting Classic or just to see how many system resources the Classic environment is consuming. Follow these steps:

1. Open the Classic pane of the System Preferences utility.

7

2. Click the Memory/Versions tab. You will see a list of the Classic applications currently running, along with the memory usage. The memory usage is shown as *X/Y*, where *X* is the amount currently being used and *Y* is the total memory allocation for that process or application within the Classic environment.

3. To see all the processes running under Classic, check the "Show background applications" check box. All system and application processes are shown in the window (see Figure 7.5).

Figure 7.5
Here, you can see that I am running the Classic version of Photoshop. You also see the Classic applications that are running.

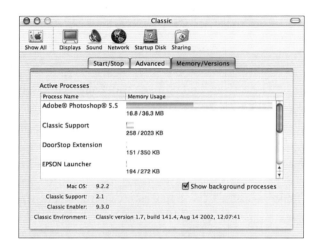

4. View the details of your Classic environment (such as the version number) in the lower-left corner of the pane.

INSTALLING AND USING CLASSIC APPLICATIONS

Because the only purpose of the Classic environment is to run Classic applications, you need to know how to install and work with those applications.

Using Classic applications is similar to using an application under previous versions of the Mac OS. Installing Classic applications can be a bit trickier, however.

INSTALLING CLASSIC APPLICATIONS

You have two general options when installing a Classic application on your Mac OS X machine: You can install the application under Mac OS X, or you can restart in Mac OS 9.2 and install the application as you normally would.

Installing Classic applications under Mac OS X is easier because you don't have to restart the machine in Mac OS 9.2, install the application, and then restart the machine in Mac OS X. However, not all installers run properly under Mac OS X, so this is a bit of a crapshoot.

Installing Classic applications while you are running Mac OS 9.2 is the safer choice, although it does require a bit more work on your part.

INSTALLING CLASSIC APPLICATIONS UNDER MAC OS X

Installing Classic applications under Mac OS X is similar to installing them under previous versions of the OS. You locate the installer application and run it, or just drag the application's folder to the appropriate location on your hard drive.

Installation involves two main issues. The first is where you will install the application. The second is whether the application's installer will run correctly under Mac OS X.

Generally, you can install Classic applications in any folder for which you have permissions to write. However, for organizational and functional purposes, you should install Classic applications in the Applications (Mac OS 9) folder on your Mac OS 9 startup volume.

CAUTION

> If you are logged in as an administrator, you can install Classic applications in the Mac OS X Applications folder. However, this is generally not a good idea. Some applications need to write information on the volume on which they are installed. Mac OS X's security system might prevent this and the application might not work properly. For example, if you install a Classic email application in the Applications directory, other users won't be able to use it unless you configure the account information and email to be stored where other users can write to it. (Because other users won't be able to write information to the Applications folder, their email can't be stored there.)

If you have more than one Mac OS 9.2 instance on your system, the installer might give you a choice about which Mac OS 9.2 volume you want to install the software on. In those cases, select the same Mac OS 9.2 volume the Classic environment uses.

Determining whether a Classic application's installer will work under Mac OS X is mostly a matter of trial and error. Launch the installer. If it runs successfully (if the Classic environment is not running already, the installer launches the Classic environment because the installer is a Classic application in itself), you are probably in good shape. Test the application to make sure it works as it should.

NOTE

> The Classic applications with which you are most likely to have problems are those that have many extensions or control panels or those that interface with a specific piece of hardware. These installers have to make changes to the System Folder of the Classic environment and can sometimes get confused by the way Mac OS X has organized the system.

7

If the Classic application doesn't install or work properly, install it under Mac OS 9.2 instead.

INSTALLING CLASSIC APPLICATIONS UNDER MAC OS 9.2

CAUTION

Not all modern Macs can start under Mac OS 9. If your Mac was produced before January 2003, it can. If, however, you have a Mac that is newer than that, check the documentation that came with the machine to see whether it can be booted up under Mac OS 9.

To install a Classic application in Mac OS 9.2, restart your Mac using the Mac OS 9.2 startup volume as the startup disk. Then, install the application as you normally would, such as with the installer or by dragging the application onto one of your disks.

→ To learn how to start your Mac in Mac OS 9.2, **see** "Running Mac OS 9.2," **p. 200**.

USING CLASSIC APPLICATIONS

Working with Classic applications under Mac OS X is similar to working with the same applications under Mac OS 9.2 (see Figure 7.6). When you open a Classic application, the Classic environment opens if it isn't already running and you see the application's normal startup screen. When the application is running and frontmost, its menu bar appears and the Mac OS X Apple menu has been replaced by the Mac OS 9 Apple menu. This indicates that you are running in the Classic environment.

Figure 7.6
Here the Classic version of PageMaker 6.5 is running. Notice the Mac OS 9.2 Apple menu, the Classic style scrollbars (no Aqua look and feel), and the Mac OS X Dock. (Check out the Classic Calculator icon on the Dock; it is running, too.)

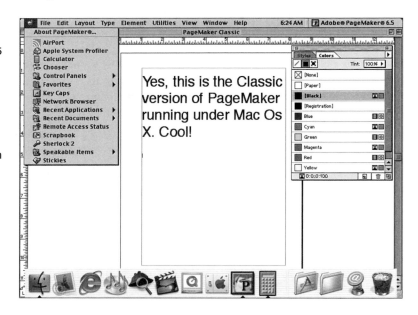

Other than this, running Classic applications is mostly just like running applications under Mac OS X. While using a Classic application, you have access to all Mac OS 9 resources, such as items installed on the Mac OS 9 Apple menu. The Classic applications you are running appear on the Dock, again just like Mac OS X applications (you won't see any indication on the Dock that the Classic environment itself is running).

 If a document you created with a Classic application won't open, see "My Classic Document Won't Open" in the "Troubleshooting" section at the end of this chapter.

Several issues when running Classic applications under Mac OS X will be slightly different from when you run them under Mac OS 9. These include where you store your documents, how you go about printing your documents, and how control panels and extensions work.

If you want to store the documents you create using a Classic application on the same volume as the Mac OS 9.2 software or on another non–Mac OS X volume, the process is the same as under Mac OS 9.2. If you want to store documents under the Mac OS X volume, such as in your Documents folder, you need to be logged in to Mac OS X with the permissions necessary to access that folder. Although you might be able to see other Mac OS X folders within Classic applications' Save dialog box and even open them, you won't be able to save files within them.

Also, although you can see secured folders (such as another user's Documents folder) from within Classic application's Open dialog boxes, you won't be able to see or open items within them unless you have the appropriate privileges.

NOTE

> When you use the Open or Save dialog box from within the Classic environment, you will see all sorts of Mac OS X files and folders that are normally hidden from view when using the Mac OS X Save or Open dialog boxes. You can safely ignore these (and you should ignore them unless you want to cause problems for yourself).

Printing documents under Classic is a bit different, too. To print from a Classic application, you must have the Mac OS 9.2 printer driver software installed on your Mac, even if you have added the printer in the Mac OS X Printer Setup Utility. The Classic environment uses Mac OS 9.2 system software to manage printing. Therefore, you must select a printer using the Mac OS 9.2 Chooser as you would if you had started under Mac OS 9.2.

 If you have installed the Mac OS 9.2 printer driver, but still can't print, see "I Can't Print Under Classic" in the "Troubleshooting" section at the end of this chapter.

When you are using a Classic application, you will see the traditional Apple menu in the upper-left corner of the screen. Although this menu looks the same as it does when you start under Mac OS 9, it doesn't work the same. Many of the items on the Apple menu are disabled because what they control is managed by Mac OS X instead. For example, if you try to use a control panel to make a system setting change, you simply move back into Mac OS X. This is because Mac OS X controls the configuration of the Classic environment. To make changes to Mac OS 9 control panels, you need to restart under Mac OS 9, make the change, and then move back into Mac OS X. If the setting you changed is controlled by Mac OS X, it is reset again, so this doesn't always work.

7

The applications on the Classic Apple menu will work as will the Chooser. Any document or folder aliases you place there will also work (you have to move them to the Apple Menu Items folder on your Classic startup volume manually). Any Classic Internet applications should also work normally, assuming you have configured Mac OS X to connect to the Internet successfully. The Network Browser doesn't work because Mac OS X manages all your network connections.

USING CLASSIC APPLICATIONS WITH HARDWARE DEVICES

The most problematic Classic applications you will deal with are those that interface with hardware devices. Some devices will work fine under Classic, but others won't. The only way to tell for sure is to install the software for the device and try to run it. When you launch it and attempt to access the hardware device, it might or might not be capable of communicating with it successfully. It depends on how the device's software is written. For example, in my case, an HP PSC 750 printer/scanner/copier device worked just fine in Classic, but I could not access my Nikon CoolPix 990 digital camera (the application could see the device but could not communicate with it).

NOTE

> You should regularly check for Mac OS X updates for all your Classic applications, but especially for those that interface with hardware. Accessing hardware using the Classic versions of applications can be cumbersome if you have to restart your Mac in Mac OS 9.2 every time you want to do so (to access hardware, for example).

 If you run a Classic disk utility and it keeps reporting problems, see "My Mac OS 9.2 Disk Utility Keeps Saying That I Have Disk Problems" in the "Troubleshooting" section at the end of this chapter.

If plug-ins or other resources for your Classic application are missing, see "My Application Can't Access the Plug-ins It Needs" in the "Troubleshooting" section at the end of this chapter.

CAUTION

> Don't use Classic disk utilities on your Mac OS X disks. Doing so can cause problems for the Mac OS X installation.

RUNNING MAC OS 9.2

On several occasions, you might want to restart your Mac in Mac OS 9.2. The most common one is when a Classic application can't do what you want it to do when running in the Classic environment.

However, this might or might not be possible for you. Apple announced that as of January 2003, Macs will no longer be capable of booting up in Mac OS 9. The company later revised this policy and still produces a few Macs that can be started under Mac OS 9. Macs that are incapable of starting under Mac OS 9 are limited to the Classic environment only. This might be the only time in Mac history that having a new Mac is not totally a good thing. Of course, because Mac OS X has been around for a while now, most applications and hardware are compatible with Mac OS X itself or with the Classic environment. Hopefully, being unable to start in Mac OS 9 will not be a problem for you.

If you use a Mac that can be started under Mac OS 9, you can restart in Mac OS 9.2. Following are the two ways you can restart your Mac in Mac OS 9.2:

- Open the Startup Disk pane in the System areas of the System Preferences utility, select the volume containing the Mac OS 9 system you want to start in, and click Restart.

NOTE

You must be authenticated as an administrator to access the Startup Disk pane of the System Preferences utility.

- Restart your Mac and hold down the Option key. As the machine restarts, icons appear for each of the startup volumes on your Mac. Click the startup volume, such as a Mac OS 9.2 startup volume, that you want to use and press Return. That startup disk is used to start up your Mac.

NOTE

When you restart in Mac OS 9.2, it is normal for the Disk First Aid utility to check for disk errors. Just let it run as you normally would.

When your Mac restarts, you will feel as if you have moved back in time (see Figure 7.7).

CAUTION

When your Mac is started under Mac OS 9.2, you lose all security features of Mac OS X. For example, you can open any folders in the user accounts folders, muck around with the system, and so on. This is one reason that when you are not using Mac OS X you should log out, especially if you are using an administrator account, when you leave your machine. If you don't, someone can restart the Mac in Mac OS 9.2 and all the files on the machine become vulnerable.

To restart in Mac OS X, select Apple menu, Control Panels, Startup Disk. Then, select your Mac OS X startup volume and click Restart.

7

Figure 7.7
Restarting in Mac OS 9.2 takes you back to the old days.

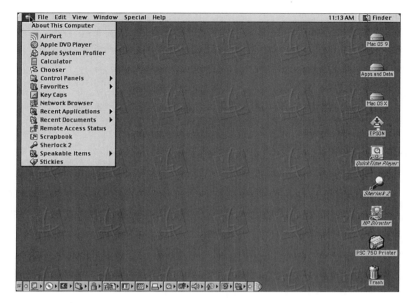

TROUBLESHOOTING

I HAVE TO UPDATE MY CLASSIC RESOURCES

The first time I launched the Classic environment, I saw a dialog box asking whether I wanted to add or update Classic-specific resources to the System Folder that I was using. Is this normal?

The first time you start Classic using a specific Mac OS 9.2 System Folder, Mac OS X needs to install some resources in that System Folder. This is normal operation. Just click OK in the dialog box to install the resources. You won't see this dialog box again until you choose a different System Folder to use for the Classic environment.

CLASSIC DOESN'T SUPPORT WHAT I AM DOING

When I started the Classic environment for the first time, I got a warning dialog box that a particular service was not supported. Am I out of luck?

Classic doesn't support *every* feature of Mac OS 9.2. When there are specific features that it doesn't support, you see an alert telling you exactly which service is not supported. To use these features, you have to restart under Mac OS 9.2.

MY CLASSIC ENVIRONMENT IS HUNG UP

I was working with a Classic application, but it stopped responding. I thought Mac OS X was designed to avoid this type of crashing. Is this just a Classic problem?

When an application crashes in the Classic environment, it can take down all the other applications you have open (the Classic environment does not provide protected memory for each application—all applications run in the Classic's memory space).

All you can do in this situation is try to force the hung application to quit. Hold down the Control key and click the application's icon on the Dock; then select Quit.

If the quit is successful, immediately save all the documents you have open in other Classic applications. Then restart Classic.

If you are unable to force the hung application to quit or if other applications start to hang, you must force the Classic environment itself to quit. Open the Classic pane of the System Preferences utility, click the Start/Stop tab, and click Force Quit. Or you can press Option-⌘-Esc; then in the Force Quit Applications dialog box, select the Classic Environment and click Force Quit. You will lose any unsaved changes in documents that are open in Classic applications, but those are lost anyway if the applications are hung.

MY CLASSIC DOCUMENT WON'T OPEN

When I try to open a document that was created with a Classic application, nothing happens.

This can happen when the Classic environment can't find a suitable application to open for the document because something has happened to the Classic's desktop database. Rebuild the Classic desktop by opening the Classic pane of the System Preferences utility, clicking Advanced, and then clicking Rebuild Desktop.

If the document still fails to open, try restarting in Mac OS 9.2 and opening and saving the document from there. If that is successful, you should be able to open the document under Mac OS X again.

I CAN'T PRINT UNDER CLASSIC

I have installed the Mac OS 9.2 printer software for my printer, but I get errors when I try to print.

Some printer driver software that has been designed to work under Mac OS 9.2 cannot access that printer even though you can select it in the Chooser. The solution is to either work on the document in a Mac OS X application and print it from there or restart your Mac under Mac OS 9.2 and print the document from there.

MY MAC OS 9.2 DISK UTILITY KEEPS SAYING THAT I HAVE DISK PROBLEMS

Each time I run a Classic disk utility, it reports that I have disk problems, even when I'm sure there aren't any.

Many Classic disk utilities can't properly analyze and repair Mac OS X disks. You should use Mac OS X's Disk Utility or a Carbonized or Cocoa version of a third-party disk utility only when you are running under Mac OS X.

You can use a Classic disk utility on the Mac OS 9.2 partition when you are running under Mac OS 9.2.

MY APPLICATION CAN'T ACCESS THE PLUG-INS IT NEEDS

When I attempt to run an application, some of its resources, such as plug-ins, aren't available to it.

Ensure that the application's resources are actually installed correctly. For example, open the application's Plug-ins folder to make sure that the plug-in you need is installed.

This situation can also occur when an application's bundle contains both Mac OS X and Classic versions of the application. Sometimes, the Mac OS X version is incapable of accessing specific application resources, such as plug-ins. In such cases, you should run the Classic version of the application so you have access to the resources you want to use.

To have such an application always open in Classic, open the application's Info window and check the "Open in Classic" check box.

You can also restart the Mac in Mac OS 9.2 and use the application from there.

CHAPTER 8

CONFIGURING, CUSTOMIZING, AND EXPLORING MAC OS X

In this chapter

8

SETTING YOUR PREFERENCES

The System Preferences application is an important tool you use to control how your Mac OS X system works and looks. If you have read through other parts of this book, you have already used some of the panes it contains to work with various parts of the system. Table 8.1 provides a summary of each pane and tells you where in this book you can learn more about it.

TABLE 8.1 SYSTEM PREFERENCES APPLICATION PANES

Category	Pane	What It Does	Where You Can Learn More About It
Personal	Appearance	Sets interface colors, scrollbar behavior, the number of recent items, and font smoothing	"Setting Appearance Preferences," p. 209
Personal	Desktop & Screen Saver	Sets the background image of the desktop and configures the screen saver you use	"Customizing the Mac OS X Desktop," p. 121; "Using the Mac OS X Screen Saver," p. 212
Personal	Dock	Controls how the Dock looks and works	"Customizing the Appearance and Behavior of the Dock," p. 138
Personal	Exposé	Configures Exposé	"Managing Open Windows with Exposé," p. 98
Personal	International	Controls the language and formats used depending on the language you are working with	"Setting International Preferences," p. 210
Personal	Security	Configures FileVault and other security settings	"Securing Your Mac with the Security Pane," p. 897
Hardware	Bluetooth	Configures Bluetooth services on your Mac	"Finding, Installing, and Using Bluetooth Devices," p. 735
Hardware	CDs & DVDs	Configures the actions that occur when you insert CDs or DVDs	Chapter 24, "Understanding and Using Data Storage Devices," p. 781; "Using Disks and Discs," p. 227

Category	Pane	What It Does	Where You Can Learn More About It
Hardware	Displays	Controls the display properties you use	"Finding, Installing, and Using a Monitor," p. 744
Hardware	Energy Saver	Controls how your Mac sleeps	"Managing Your Mobile Mac's Power," p. 982
Hardware	Ink	Configures handwriting recognition	"Installing and Using an Ink Device," p. 731
Hardware	Keyboard & Mouse	Sets keyboard and mouse preferences	"Finding, Installing, and Configuring a Keyboard," p. 722; "Finding, Installing, and Configuring a Mouse," p. 728; "Using and Configuring the Trackpad," p. 988
Hardware	Print & Fax	Configures printer settings and fax services	"Finding, Installing, and Using Printers," p. 759; "Working with Mac OS X's Built-in Fax Capability," p. 772
Hardware	Sound	Manages your system sound and alert sounds	"Controlling Your System's Sound," p. 217
Internet & Network	.Mac	Configures your .Mac account and enables you to work with your iDisk	"Using a .Mac iDisk and HomePage to Create and Serve Your Web Pages," p. 426; "Working with Your iDisk," p. 228
Internet & Network	Network	Configures your network settings for both Internet access and your LAN	Chapter 10, "Connecting Your Mac to the Internet," p. 263; Chapter 26, "Building and Using a Network," p. 821

8

TABLE 8.1 CONTINUED

Category	Pane	What It Does	Where You Can Learn More About It
Internet & Network	QuickTime	Enables you to configure QuickTime for your Mac	"Configuring QuickTime," p. 648
Internet & Network	Sharing	Controls access to your computer's services from the network and the Internet and enables you to configure Mac OS X's built-in firewall and set up Internet account sharing	"Using Mac OS X to Serve Web Pages," p. 446; Chapter 26, "Building and Using a Network," p. 821; "Defending Your Mac Against Net Hackers," p. 911; "Using a Mac Running OS X to Share an Internet Account," p. 857
System	Accounts	Creates, configures, and manages user accounts	"Creating User Accounts," p. 24
System	Classic	Controls your Classic environment	"Installing, Configuring, and Running the Classic Environment," p. 186
System	Date & Time	Manages the time and date settings and the clock for your system	"Changing the Clock Display," p. 121; "Working with the Date and Time," p. 221
System	Software Update	Maintains your system software	"Using Software Update to Maintain Your Software," p. 874
System	Speech	Manages speech recognition and Text-to-Speech	"Controlling Your Mac's Speech," p. 223
System	Startup Disk	Selects the startup volume that is used the next time you start your Mac	"Choosing a Startup Volume with System Preferences," p. 228
System	Universal Access	Controls options to improve access for physically or mentally challenged users	"Using the Universal Access Pane to Make Your Mac More Accessible," p. 216

NOTE

> You might see more or fewer panes in the System Preferences application than are listed in Table 8.1 depending on the hardware and software you have installed. For example, if your Mac doesn't support Bluetooth hardware, you won't see the Bluetooth pane. If you have installed additional hardware or software that is configurable, such as a keyboard, you might see additional panes in the Other category.

TIP

> Remember that you can customize the System Preferences application's toolbar by dragging icons from the lower pane of the window to the toolbar. You can remove icons from the toolbar by dragging them off the toolbar.

SETTING APPEARANCE PREFERENCES

Use the Appearance pane of the System Preferences application to control several basic settings for your system.

Use the Appearance pop-up menu to select Blue if you want color in the buttons, menus, and windows. Select Graphite if you want to mute the color so the color elements are gray instead. Use the Highlight pop-up menu to select the highlight color.

Use the radio buttons to set scrolling behavior. You can place the scroll arrows together or choose to have a scroll arrow placed at each end of the scrollbar. You can select "Scroll to here" to cause a window to jump to the relative position on which you click or "Jump to next page" to scroll a page at a time when you click above or below the scroll box.

Set the number of recent items tracked on the Apple menu for applications and documents using the Number of Recent Items pop-up menus. You can track as few as none or as many as 50 recent items.

The lower part of the pane provides the controls you use to configure how font smoothing is enabled on your Mac. *Font smoothing* (known as antialiasing for graphics) reduces the jaggies that occur when you view certain fonts onscreen; this is most noticeable when you use larger sizes or thick fonts or when you apply bold or other formatting. Font smoothing is always turned on, but you can configure it specifically for your system:

1. Open the Appearance pane of the System Preferences application.

2. At the bottom of the pane, select the smoothing style you want to use on the "Font smoothing style" pop-up menu. Your options are Standard – Best for CRT, Light, Medium – best for Flat Panel, or Strong. You will probably be satisfied with the option appropriate for the display type you use, but you can experiment with the other options to see whether one of them matches your needs better.

3. Select the font size at or below which text smoothing is disabled on the "Turn off text smoothing for font sizes" pop-up menu. Because the effect of smoothing is less noticeable at small font sizes, your system can save some wasted processing power by not

smoothing fonts displayed at small sizes. The default value is 8 points, but you might not even notice if you increase this value slightly.

SETTING INTERNATIONAL PREFERENCES

Mac OS X includes support for a large number of languages; language behaviors; and date, time, and number formats. You control these properties through the International pane of the System Preferences application (see Figure 8.1).

Figure 8.1
You can use the International pane of the System Preferences application to control various language and format properties based on a language and the conventions of particular nations.

Use the Language tab to configure the languages you want to use. The Languages list shows the languages that are currently active. You can drag these languages up and down in the list to set the preferred order in which you want to use them on menus and in dialog boxes. If you click the Edit button, you can choose the languages that appear in the Languages list by unchecking the check boxes for the languages you don't want to use. If you click the Customize Sorting button, you can choose the set of behaviors for each script. For example, to configure the Roman script for English, select it on the list of scripts and select the English option on the Behaviors pop-up menu. You can configure behaviors for other languages using similar steps to match the language you use.

Use the Formats tab to configure the format of the dates, times, and numbers used on your Mac. When you open this tab, you see a section for each of these areas along with the Region pop-up menu (see Figure 8.2).

Select the region setting for your Mac on the Region pop-up menu. By default, you see region choices that relate to the languages you have installed. If you want to see all possible region options, check the "Show all regions" check box. When you make a selection, default formats for the region you selected are applied to each setting area (dates, times, and numbers).

Figure 8.2
Use the Formats tab of the International pane to set the format of dates, times, and numbers for your system.

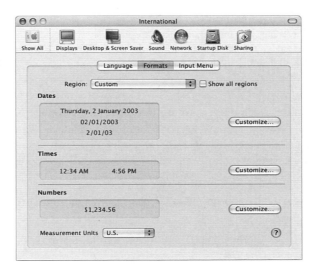

After you have set general format preferences via the Region pop-up menu, you can customize the format in each area.

NOTE

> The options described in the following paragraphs are for the United States region. If you choose a different region, different options might be available to you, but they can be set using similar steps.

In the Dates section, click the Customize button. The Customize Dates sheet appears. Use these controls to set the date formats displayed in Finder windows and other locations. There are two general date formats: Long Date and Short Date. Use the pop-up menus, check boxes, and text fields to set the format for each type of date. For the Long Date format, you choose a prefix as well as separators for the day of the week, month, day, and year. If you want to use a leading zero for single digit dates, check the "Leading zero for day" check box. For the Short Date format, you select the format option you want on the pop-up menu, input a separator, choose to use a leading zero for day or month, and choose to show the century. At the bottom of the sheet is an example of dates as you have configured them. Click OK to close the sheet.

In the Times section, click the Customize button. The Customize Times sheet appears. Use the radio buttons to select a 12- or 24-hour clock and whether noon and midnight are shown as 0:00 or 12:00. Use the Before Noon and After Noon boxes to select how your Mac indicates these relative times, such as AM or PM. Use the Separator box to input the separator you want to use. Finally, use the check box to determine whether a leading zero is used for the hour. Click OK when you are done making changes.

8

NOTE

> The settings you make in the Dates and Times sheets affect the format of these values in the Finder and other locations. They do not affect the clock display; you control the format of the clock using the Time & Date pane.

In the Numbers section, click the Customize button. The Customize Numbers sheet appears, which you can use to set the format for numbers displayed on your Mac. You can use the pop-up menus to select the separators in numbers (for the decimal and thousands), and you can select a currency symbol and where that currency symbol is located (before or after the amount). Click OK when you are done.

Use the Measurement Units pop-up menu to select the default measurement units used (U.S. [aka English] or Metric).

Use the Input Menu tab to control and configure the Input menu that appears on the menu bar.

→ To learn how to configure a keyboard for different languages, **see** "Configuring a Keyboard," **p. 723**.

→ To learn how to configure the Character Palette, **see** "Working with the Character Palette," **p. 162**.

USING THE MAC OS X SCREEN SAVER

Mac OS X was the first version of the Mac OS that included a built-in screen saver. Many Mac users enjoy having a screen saver, and Mac OS X's version provides the features you would expect. However, the quality and style with which the screen saver displays images are quite nice, especially when you use your own images.

Display Sleep Time

If you really want to protect your screen, use the Energy Saver pane to set a display sleep time. Display sleep actually turns off the display mechanism, which saves the screen. Of course, a blank screen isn't nearly as interesting as the screen saver. Using a screen saver with modern CRT displays isn't really necessary because they do not suffer the screen burn-in that earlier generations of such displays did.

Although LCD flat-panel monitors haven't been around long enough to be sure, some theorize that using display sleep is very important to maximize the working life of such displays. To be safe rather than sorry, you should keep the display sleep setting at a relatively low value if you use an LCD flat-panel display so it sleeps when you aren't actively using your Mac.

You use the Screen Saver tab of the Desktop & Screen Saver pane of the System Preferences application to configure a screen saver for your machine (see Figure 8.3).

You have three general choices: Use one of Mac OS X's default modules, use a module from images you have created or downloaded, or use a module that someone else has created and published via his .Mac account.

Figure 8.3
You can use one of Mac OS X's built-in screen saver modules, create your own screen saver, or add a screen saver that someone else created (such as by using one that has been posted to a user's .Mac account).

USING A BUILT-IN SCREEN SAVER MODULE

Using one of Mac OS X's built-in modules is straightforward. The general steps are the following:

1. Open the Screen Saver tab of the Desktop & Screen Saver pane.

2. If you want your Mac to randomly select and use a screen saver, check the "Use random screen saver" check box and skip to step 6.

3. Select the screen saver module you want to use from the Screen Savers list; you see a preview in the Preview window.

4. Use the Options button to set various parameters for the screen saver you select, such as whether a cross-fade is used between slides and whether slides are kept centered on the screen (not all modules have configuration options). The available display options are the following:

   - **Cross-fade between slides**—When enabled, one image fades into the next. If disabled, one image disappears before the next image appears.

   - **Zoom back and forth**—When enabled, the screen saver zooms in and out of each image.

   - **Crop slides to fit screen**—When enabled, images are sized so they fit onto the display by cropping the parts that don't fit.

   - **Keep slides centered**—When enabled, images are always centered on the screen.

   - **Present slides in random order**—When enabled, images appear in a random order rather than the order in which they are listed in the folder that contains them.

8

5. Test the screen saver by clicking the Test button. The images that are part of the screen saver are rendered and displayed with the configuration options you selected.

> **NOTE**
>
> If you use multiple displays, a different image from the screen saver is shown on each display.

6. Use the "Start screen saver" slider to set the idle time that must pass before the screen saver is activated.

7. Click the Hot Corners button.

8. On the resulting sheet, select the corners to which you can move the mouse to manually start or disable the screen saver by selecting the action you want to occur on the pop-up menu located at the corner you want to configure. The default is to have no action occur at any corner.

9. Click OK

> **NOTE**
>
> If the display sleep time set on the Energy Saver pane is less than the time you set in step 6, you will never see the screen saver because the display will sleep before the screen saver is activated. If this is the case, a warning appears on the Energy Saver pane and a button enables you to jump to the Screen Saver tab. However, you don't see any warning on the Screen Saver tab. If you want to see a screen saver, check the display sleep setting on the Energy Saver pane to ensure that the display sleep time is greater than the screen saver activation time.

CREATING A CUSTOM SCREEN SAVER MODULE

Some of the built-in modules are pretty cool (I especially like Cosmos), but you can have even more fun by creating or using a custom module. There are several ways to do this:

- Gather the images you want to use for a screen saver in a folder and use the Choose Folder module to select that folder.

- Create a screen saver from a collection of your own images by creating a photo album for that purpose in iPhoto. You can access any images in your iPhoto Photo Library as well as any of its photo albums on the Screen Savers list.

- Use a screen saver that someone has made available through .Mac.

- Use a screen saver you download from the Internet.

To create a screen saver from your own images, use the following steps:

1. Create a folder containing the images you want to use. The images can be in the standard image formats, such as JPG or TIFF.

→ To learn about creating images, **see** Chapter 15, "Creating and Editing Digital Images," **p. 457**.

8

2. Open the Screen Saver tab and select the Choose Folder module.

3. Use the Choose Folder sheet to move to and select the folder containing the images you want to use; then click Choose.

4. Use the other controls on the tab to configure the screen saver. You have the same display options as for the built-in screen savers.

You can choose to use the images within your Pictures folder by selecting it on the list of Screen Savers. Only the images located in the root folder (not within folders that are inside the Pictures folder) are used. You configure the screen saver using the same steps you use for other options.

Similarly, you can choose any images with your iPhoto Photo Library as a screen saver by selecting Photo Library. You can also select a photo album you have created in iPhoto as a screen saver by selecting it on the list that appears under the Photo Library on the screen saver list.

→ To learn how use iPhoto, **see** "Using iPhoto to Master Digital Images," **p. 470**.

USING .MAC SCREEN SAVER MODULES

Using the .Mac service, people can make their screen savers available to you and you can make your screen savers available to other people.

→ To learn how to use .Mac services, **see** "Using a .Mac iDisk and HomePage to Create and Serve Your Web Pages," **p. 426**.

To use a module available via .Mac, perform the following steps:

1. Open the Screen Saver tab and select the .Mac module. (A default .Mac module is available and is selected automatically.)

2. Click Options to see the Configuration sheet. The top of the sheet contains a list of .Mac screen savers to which you are subscribed. If the Selected check box is checked, the images in the screen saver are used. If not, they aren't used. You can see that you are already subscribed to the .Mac public slideshow.

3. Enter the .Mac member name of someone whose slideshow you would like to use as your screen saver in the .Mac Membership name field and press Return. The sheet closes.

4. Click Options again. The Configuration sheet appears. Now, the person whose .Mac name you entered in step 3 appears on the list of slideshows to which you are subscribed.

5. Repeat steps 3 and 4 to add more public slideshows to the list.

6. Check the Selected check box for each slideshow you want to be used in your screen saver. If the check box is unchecked, the slideshow is still available to you, but it isn't displayed. Because the .Mac screen saver displays all the images to which you are subscribed in the same screen saver, uncheck any screen savers whose images you don't want to be included.

TIP

> To unsubscribe from a public slideshow, select the slideshow and press Delete. Of course, you can always just uncheck the box to prevent the images in that screen saver from being included. The difference is that if you unsubscribe, the images will no longer be downloaded to your Mac.

7. Use the Display Options check boxes to configure the screen saver. You have the same display options as for the built-in modules.

8. Click OK.

9. Configure and test the screen saver just like one of Mac OS X's built-in screen savers.

TIP

> If you have people who are interested in you (such as relatives), you can create a .Mac public slideshow and inform those people who are interested that it is available. As you update your slideshow, people who subscribe to and use it see the images you add to the collection.

→ To learn how to publish a .Mac screen saver, **see** "Publishing Images As .Mac Slides," **p. 508**.

USING SCREEN SAVERS ACQUIRED FROM THE INTERNET AND OTHER SOURCES

You can also download and use other screen savers from the Internet or other sources. Screen saver modules have the .saver filename extension. To do this, follow these steps:

1. Download the screen saver you want to use and prepare it for use.

→ For help with downloading and preparing files, **see** "Downloading and Preparing Files," **p. 411**.

2. Place the .saver file in the directory Mac OS X/Library/Screen Savers, where Mac OS X is the name of the startup volume.

3. Use the Screen Saver tab to choose and configure the screen saver you added.

USING THE UNIVERSAL ACCESS PANE TO MAKE YOUR MAC MORE ACCESSIBLE

You can use the Universal Access pane to make your Mac more accessible to those with various physical or mental challenges.

You configure special access to the system by using the Universal Access pane of the System Preferences application. This pane includes the following four tabs:

■ **Seeing**—Using the Seeing tab, you can configure the visual aspects of the system. You can use zoom to increase the size of items on the screen. You can also change the display to be white on a black background or grayscale. Use the "Enhance contrast" slider to increase the display contrast.

- **Hearing**—The Hearing tab enables you to set the screen to flash when the alert sound plays.

- **Keyboard**—Using the Keyboard tab, you can configure Sticky Keys that enable users to choose key combinations by typing only one key at a time. Click the Keyboard tab, and then use the radio button and check boxes to configure Sticky Keys. When Sticky Keys is on, each modifier keystroke is shown on the screen. For example, if you press the ⌘ key, the ⌘ key symbol appears onscreen. You can turn off this feature by unchecking the "Display pressed keys on screen" check box. You can also turn off the audible feedback by unchecking the "Beep when a modifier key is set" check box. You can enable Sticky Keys to be turned on or off from the keyboard by checking or unchecking the "Press the Shift key five times to turn Sticky Keys on or off" check box.

  For people who have difficulty pressing and releasing keys, you can use the Slow Keys feature to set a delay for the time between when a key is pressed and when the input is accepted by the system. Use the Slow Keys radio button to enable or disable this feature. If enabled, use the slider and check box to configure it.

- **Mouse**—The Mouse tab enables you to control the mouse by using the numeric pad on the keyboard. Click the Mouse tab of the Universal Access pane, and then click the On radio button to turn on Mouse Keys. Use the Initial Delay and Maximum Speed sliders to control how the pointer moves in relation to keystrokes. You can enable Mouse Keys to be turned on or off from the keyboard by checking or unchecking the "Press the option key five times to turn Sticky Keys on or off" check box.

The two check boxes at the bottom of the Universal Access pane enable you to configure general aspects of the universal access functionality. If you check the "Enable access for assistive devices" check box, you can control the system with specific assisting devices. If the "Enable text-to-speech for Universal Access preferences" check box is selected, the Mac speaks various options as you move the pointer over them.

TIP

> You can click the ? button that appears on some panes to jump to specific topics in the Help system relating to the controls you are viewing.

CONTROLLING YOUR SYSTEM'S SOUND

You use the Sound pane of the System Preferences application to control the volume, sound effects, and input sources for your system (see Figure 8.4). The Sound pane has three tabs: Sound Effects, Output, and Input. You use the Sound Effects tab to configure your system alert sounds and various audio feedback. You use the Output tab to control the sound output of your Mac and use the Input tab to configure sound input devices attached to your Mac, such as USB microphones.

8

Figure 8.4
You use the sliders, list, pop-up menu, and check boxes on the Sound pane of the System Preferences application to control various sound properties of your system.

You can control your system's volume using the "Output volume" slider at the bottom of the pane. Use the Mute check box to mute all system sound. Check the "Show volume in menu bar" check box to show the Volume menu in the menu bar. You can control your main system volume by clicking this icon and using the pop-up slider to set the volume level.

TIP

> If you use an Apple Pro keyboard, an iBook, or a PowerBook, you can also control the volume level using the mute and volume keys located just above the numeric keypad. When you press one of these keys, a sound level indicator appears onscreen so you can visually tell what the relative volume level is. (This also appears when you use another device to control the volume, such as a keyboard with a volume wheel.) You also hear the alert sound each time you press one of the volume keys. You can disable this audio feedback by unchecking the "Play feedback when volume keys are pressed" check box.

To configure your system alert sound, carry out the following steps:

1. Open the Sound pane of the System Preferences application.
2. Click the Sound Effects tab.
3. Select the alert sound you want to use on the list—you will hear a preview of the sound you select.
4. Select the output device through which you want the alert sound to be played on the "Play alerts and sound effects through" pop-up menu. If you have USB speakers installed, such as SoundSticks, you can choose to play alerts through them, or if you want to use your Mac's internal speaker, select Internal speakers.
5. Use the "Alert volume" slider to control the relative volume level of the alert sound.

8

TIP

If you have external USB speakers, it is usually a good idea to play the alert sound through the Mac's built-in speakers, especially if you like to listen to music or watch movies with high sound volume. This prevents the alert sound from knocking you out of your chair (if this has ever happened to you, you know exactly what I mean). If you set things this way, you probably need to set the alert volume high because the Mac's built-in speaker will be overwhelmed by your external speakers.

If you have analog speakers plugged in to the Mac's speaker jack, you won't be able to do this because the Mac's built-in audio controller controls the output to those speakers. You must be using USB speakers or those connected to another interface such as the digital audio port on a Power Mac G5.

Mac OS X can play various sound effects when you perform specific actions or when something specific happens (such as when you send an item to the Trash). This feature is enabled by default. To disable it, uncheck the "Play user interface sound effects" check box.

To configure the sound output for your system, use the following steps:

1. Open the Sound pane and click the Output tab. A list of all sound output devices attached to your machine appears; at the least, you see the Internal speakers option, which is your Mac built-in speaker or speakers, depending on which type of Mac you use.

2. Select the output device you want to configure. If output options are available for the selected output device, controls appear just under the list of available devices (see Figure 8.5).

Figure 8.5
If you use external USB speakers, such as these SoundSticks, you can configure them using the controls on the Output tab.

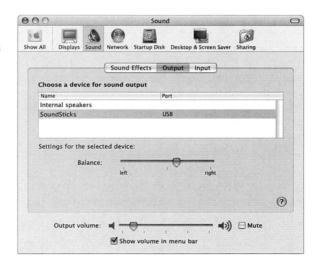

3. Use the controls to configure the selected output sound source. For example, if you use a two-speaker system, use the Balance slider to set the relative volume balance between the speakers.

NEW To configure sound input devices attached to your Mac, perform the following steps:

1. Attach the sound device you want to use. For example, to use a USB headset microphone, attach it to an available USB port.

2. Open the Sound pane of the System Preferences application and click the Input tab. You see a list of all input devices your Mac recognizes.

3. Select the device you want to configure.

4. Use the Input volume slider to configure the device's sensitivity. Dragging the slider to the right increases the level of sound through the device.

5. Test the device by speaking into it or making some other noise. The relative sound level appears on the Input level indicator.

6. Continue adjusting the device until you achieve the proper level of input.

Although these sound options satisfy most Mac users, there are more sound options you can choose to implement.

INSTALLING ADDITIONAL ALERT SOUNDS

Under Mac OS X, system alert sounds are in the Audio Interchange File Format (AIFF). This is a good thing because you can use many sounds as your alert sound, and using QuickTime Pro, you can convert almost any sound into the AIFF format.

→ To learn how to convert sounds into the AIFF format using QuickTime Pro, **see** "Using QuickTime Pro to Convert Files into Other Formats," **p. 672**.

> NOTE
>
> Under Mac OS X, AIFF files have the `.aiff` filename extension. By default, QuickTime Player Pro appends the `.aif` filename extension to files when you export them in the AIFF format. Be sure to add the second *f* to the filename extension for the sound you want to add as an alert sound. If you don't, the file will not be recognized as a valid alert sound.

There are two basic ways in which you can add alert sounds. You can add them to specific user accounts or to the system so they are accessible to everyone who uses your Mac.

To add an alert sound to a specific user account, perform the following steps:

1. Create or download the AIFF files you want to add to your available alert sounds.

2. Log in to the user account under which you want to make the alert sounds available.

3. Drag the new alert sounds to the following directory: /*shortusername*/Library/Sounds. The new alert sound is available to that user account on the Alert Sounds list in the Sound pane of the System Preferences application.

NOTE

> If the System Preferences application is open when you install a new alert sound, you must quit and restart it to see the new sound on the list.
>
> When you install your own system alert sounds in the alert sound list, the type for the sounds you add is Custom instead of Built-in. Built-in sounds are stored in the Sound folder in the System Library folder instead of the user's Library folder.

You can also add alert sounds to the system so they are available to all the user accounts on your machine. However, to do this, you must log in under the root account.

CAUTION

> You can't modify files or directories that are within the Mac OS X system directory without being logged in under the root account. Be careful when you are logged in under the root account because you can change anything on your system, including changing vital system files in such a way that your Mac fails to work. You can also delete any files on the machine while you are logged in as root.

→ To learn how to enable and log in under the root account, **see** "Logging In As Root," **p. 236**.

To add alert sounds to your system, do these steps:

1. Create or download the AIFF files you want to add to your alert sounds.
2. Log in under the root account.
3. Drag the AIFF file into the directory *Mac OS X*/System/Library/Sounds, where *Mac OS X* is the name of your Mac OS X startup volume.
4. Log out of the root account and then log back in under another account. The new sounds are available on the Alert Sounds list on the Sound pane of the System Preferences application.

NOTE

> The kind of alert sounds you add to the system are Built-in, just as the alert sounds that are preinstalled.

WORKING WITH THE DATE AND TIME

The Date & Time pane of the System Preferences application enables you to set and maintain your system's time and date (see Figure 8.6). You can set the time and date manually, or you can use a network timeserver to set and maintain your system's time and date for you.

Figure 8.6
Mac OS X's time and date features are similar to those in previous versions of the OS.

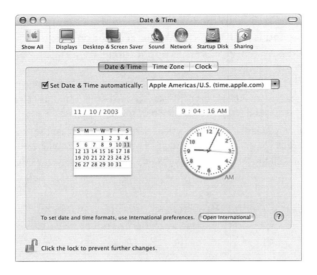

To set your system's date and time, do the following:

1. Open the Date & Time pane of the System Preferences application.

2. Click the Time Zone tab and use the map to set your time zone. Drag the highlight bar over your location to select the correct time zone. Then, use the Closest City pop-up menu to select the specific time for the area in which you are located.

3. Click the Date & Time tab.

4. If you are going to use a network timeserver to maintain the time and date for your machine, check the "Set Date & Time automatically" check box and select the timeserver you want to use on the drop-down list. The options you see depend on where you are. There are three primary timeservers, one for the Americas, one for Asia, and one for Europe. Select the server that is appropriate for your location.

5. If you want to set the time and date manually, uncheck the "Set Date & Time automatically" check box. Use the straightforward controls to set the date and time.

6. Quit the System Preferences application.

→ To learn how to use the Clock tab to configure the desktop clock, **see** "Changing the Clock Display," **p. 121**.

NOTE

You can find the official time for any time zone in the United States at www.time.gov. Of course, this is useful only if you live in the United States and can handle the time being off by as much as 0.3 seconds.

CONTROLLING YOUR MAC'S SPEECH

You can use the Speech pane of the System Preferences application to control two aspects of how your Mac uses speech (see Figure 8.7). Speech Recognition enables you to speak commands to your Mac; Spoken User Interface controls how your Mac reads the text in windows and dialog boxes or in documents from applications that speak text.

Figure 8.7
The Speech pane of the System Preferences application enables you to communicate with your Mac by speaking and listening.

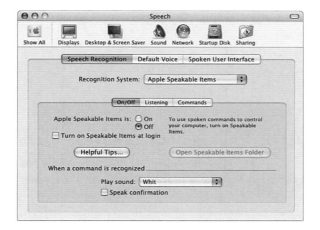

To configure speech recognition on your Mac, click the Speech Recognition tab and use the controls to configure how speech recognition works. On the On/Off tab, turn on speech recognition and then use the Listening tab to configure how your Mac listens to commands. Use the Commands tab to select the commands that are available when Speakable Items is turned on. Additional information about this feature is beyond the scope of this chapter. However, you might want to explore it to see whether it is useful to you.

TIP

> To see which commands you can speak, turn on Speech Recognition. The feedback window appears after speech recognition is on. Click the arrow at the bottom of that window and select Open Speech Commands window. In the Speech Commands window is the list of commands you can speak. When you open an application that supports speech recognition, that application appears in the Speech Commands window and the list of spoken commands it supports is shown.
>
> If you double-click the feedback window, it moves to the Dock.

If you use applications that support Text-to-Speech, those applications can read text to you. To configure the voice they use, open the Default Voice tab of the Speech pane of the System Preferences application. Select the voice from the Voice list and then set the rate at which the voice speaks using the slider. You can click the Play button to hear a sample.

Use the Spoken User Interface tab to configure spoken feedback from the system. You can use the Talking Alerts controls to configure specific phrases spoken to you and the voice used to speak those phrases. You can also choose to have a voice speak to you when any of the following events occurs:

- **An application requires your attention**—With this feature enabled, when an application needs your attention, you hear an audible warning.

- **There is text under the mouse**—You must be using an assistive device configured on the Universal Access pane to use this feature. When it's enabled, you hear the text under your pointer.

- **Text is selected and the key is pressed**—When you enable this feature and press the key combination you select, your Mac reads to you any text you have selected.

Using the Color Picker to Choose Colors

There are many areas in which you will choose to use colors for certain things, such as when you apply colors to text or apply a color to the background of a Finder window. To apply colors, you use the Color Picker (see Figure 8.8). Within applications, you use the Colors panel to apply colors to text and images.

TIP

> How you open the Colors panel depends on the application you are using. However, in some applications, such as TextEdit, you can open it by pressing Shift-⌘-C.

Figure 8.8
The Color Picker enables you to create and apply custom colors to selected elements, such as to the background of a Finder window.

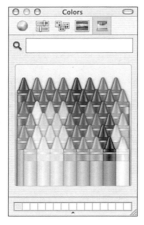

The five modes in the Color Picker are represented by the five buttons along the top of the window. From left to right they are the Color Wheel, Color sliders (including Cyan Magenta Yellow Black [CMYK], Crayon, Hue Saturation Balance [HSB], Gray Scale, and

Red Green Blue [RGB]), Palette colors, Spectrum colors, and the Crayon Picker. Each of these modes works similarly. Select the mode you want to use, and the controls in the Color Picker window change to reflect the mode you are in. Use the mode's controls to select or configure a color to apply (you can use the Original and New areas to compare the new color to the current one). When you want to apply the color to the selected object, click it.

TIP

> You can add the configured color to the list of favorite colors at the bottom of the window so you can easily apply the color again in the future.
>
> If you click the Magnifying Glass icon, the pointer turns into a magnifying glass. If you move this over an area and click, the color in that area appears in the current color box of the Color Picker.

NOTE

> The Colors panel you see within particular applications might have the same or slightly different modes.

CONTROLLING OPEN APPLICATIONS

Mac OS X provides many ways to control open applications, including these:

- You can switch among open applications by clicking the icon of the open application to which you want to switch on the Dock.

- You can also move among open applications using the ⌘-Tab or Shift-⌘-Tab keys. When you press these keys, a list of the currently open applications appears (see Figure 8.9). The active application has a box around it and its name appears under the box. You can move into a different application by pressing the ⌘-Tab or Shift-⌘-Tab keys until the application you want is selected, or you can click an application to move into it.

- Use Exposé to show all open windows and click a window in the application to which you want to switch.

- Hide applications quickly by either pressing ⌘-H or choosing *Application*, Hide where *Application* is the name of the active application .

- Quit an open application by holding down the Control key while clicking the application's icon on the Dock. From the pop-up menu, select Quit.

- There are several ways to force a hung application to quit. Press Option-Command-Esc to open the Force Quit Applications window, select the application you want to quit, and click Force Quit (see Figure 8.10). (If an application is hung, its name appears in red in the Force Quit Applications window.) Open the Activity Monitor application (Applications/Utilities); select the application (process) you want to quit; and select Process, Quit (or press Option-⌘-Q). You can also use the Unix kill command in the

Terminal application along with the process number of the application you want to force to quit. Yet another way is to choose the Apple menu and then Force Quit.

Figure 8.9
This list appears when you press the ⌘-Tab or Shift-⌘-Tab keys.

Figure 8.10
You can force an application to quit by opening the Force Quit Applications window, selecting the application you want to quit, and clicking Force Quit.

TIP

When you select the Finder in the Force Quit Applications window, the Force Quit button becomes Relaunch—the Finder must always be running when you are using Mac OS X. If the Finder hangs, force it to relaunch.

→ To learn more about the Activity Monitor, **see** "Using the Activity Monitor to Understand and Manage Processes," **p. 925**.

→ To learn more about using Unix commands, **see** Chapter 9, "Unix: Working with the Command Line," **p. 243**.

8

> You can use the Force Quit Applications window to quickly move into open applications. Just open the window by pressing Option-⌘-Esc and then double-click an application shown on the list. That application moves to the front. You can leave the window open all the time if you want to; because it is always on top, it makes a convenient application palette. Of course, if you don't have a lot of screen real estate, this window can get in the way.

USING DISKS AND DISCS

Working with hard drives, CDs, DVDs, and other similar types of storage devices is an important part of using Mac OS X. The following bullets provide information about some useful disk-related tasks:

- You can control whether mounted disk and volume icons are automatically shown on the desktop using the Finder Preferences window (select Finder, Preferences and click the General tab). Check the "Show these items on the Desktop" check boxes to show icons on the desktop, or uncheck them to keep those icons from appearing on the desktop. (If you chose not to have disk icons mounted on the desktop, you can access the mounted disks and volumes using the Computer folder and the Places sidebar.)

- You can eject removable disks by dragging them to the Trash; selecting them and selecting File, Eject; pressing ⌘-E; using the contextual menu Eject command; or using the Eject icon that you can place on the Finder toolbar. You can also eject any ejectable item by clicking the Eject button that appears next to that item in the Places sidebar.

TIP

> When you select a mounted volume (such as a CD), the Trash icon on the Dock becomes an eject symbol to indicate you are unmounting a volume rather than deleting it.

- To configure the action that happens when you insert CDs or DVDs, use the CDs & DVDs pane of the System Preferences application. You can configure what happens when you insert blank media or when you insert "full" discs. When you configure what occurs when you insert "full" discs, your options are to have a selected application open (such as DVD Player when you insert a video DVD), to cause an AppleScript to run, or to do nothing (which Mac OS X calls Ignore).

- To erase a disk under Mac OS X, you use the Disk Utility application (Applications/Utilities). Open the application, select the disk you want to erase, click the Erase tab, select the format on the Volume Format pop-up menu, enter the volume name, and click Erase.

- Disk Images is a file type that mimics the behavior of a disk. When you open a disk image, it acts just as if it were a real disk. Disk images are most commonly used to distribute applications. When a disk image is mounted, you can open it as you would a physical disk, eject it, and so on.

→ To learn how to configure the action when you insert blank media, **see** Chapter 24, "Understanding and Using Data Storage Devices," **p. 781**.

→ To learn how to use the Disk Utility to format and partition a disk, **see** "Initializing and Partitioning a Hard Drive," **p. 786**.

→ To learn more about disk images, **see** "Installing Mac OS X Applications," **p. 145**.

WORKING WITH YOUR iDISK

Adding .Mac services to your system provides a lot of great benefits such as an email address, Web page, and so on. The most useful of the .Mac services is the iDisk. This is space allotted to you on servers that Apple maintains so you can store files there. There are many uses for an iDisk, such as creating Web pages, providing FTP sites, synchronizing files across machines, making your files available from different locations, performing online backups, and so on. Except for delays you might experience because of a slow Internet connection, an iDisk acts much like a disk physically connected to your system.

To use an iDisk, you must obtain a .Mac account. After you have done so, you can configure and use your iDisk.

→ To learn how configure and use an iDisk, **see** "Using a .Mac iDisk and HomePage to Create and Serve Your Web Pages," **p. 426**.

CONTROLLING SYSTEM STARTUP

Under Mac OS X, there are several ways to configure and control the startup process. The most straightforward way is to use the Startup Disk pane of the System Preferences application to select a startup volume. There are other ways you can control system startup as well, such as selecting a startup volume during the startup process, starting up in the single-user mode, and starting up in the verbose mode.

CHOOSING A STARTUP VOLUME WITH SYSTEM PREFERENCES

The Startup Disk pane of the System Preferences application enables you to select a startup volume. Open the pane to see a list of the valid startup volumes on your machine. Select the volume from which you want to start up and click Restart. You are prompted to confirm this action by clicking the Restart button. Your selection is saved and your Mac restarts from that volume.

CHOOSING A STARTUP VOLUME DURING STARTUP

Under Mac OS X, you can select the startup volume by holding down the Option key while the machine is starting up. When you do, you see a window that displays each of the valid startup volumes on your machine. The currently selected startup volume is highlighted. You can select a startup volume by clicking it and pressing Return (you can also click the right-facing arrow icon to select the startup volume).

TIP

> You can refresh the list of valid startup volumes by clicking the circular arrow button.

STARTING UP IN CONSOLE MODE

The Console mode starts up your Mac in a Unix-like environment. In this environment, you can run Unix commands outside of Mac OS X. This can be useful in a couple of situations, mostly related to troubleshooting problems.

NOTE

> Console mode is also called *single-user mode*.

To start up in Console mode, hold down ⌘-S while the machine is starting up. Many system messages appear and report on how the startup process is proceeding. When the startup is complete, you see a date and time message, and near that you see the localhost Unix prompt.

NOTE

> During the startup process, you are likely to see some information that doesn't make a lot of sense to you unless you are fluent in Unix and the arcane system messages you see. You will also probably see some odd error messages, but typically I wouldn't worry about them too much. However, if you have particular problems you are trying to solve, some of these messages might provide valuable clues for you.

One of the more useful things you can do is to run the Unix disk-repair function, which is fsck. At the prompt, type

`/sbin/fsck -y`

and press Return. The utility checks the disk on which Mac OS X is installed. Any problems it finds is reported and repaired (if possible).

NOTE

> If the startup disk is Journaled, type `/sbin/fsck -yf` to force the utility to run.

You can use many other Unix commands at this prompt, just as if you were using the Terminal application from inside Mac OS X.

→ To learn more about using Unix commands, **see** Chapter 9, "Unix: Working with the Command Line," **p. 243**.

To resume the startup process in Mac OS X, type the command **reboot** and press Return. Additional, even more arcane Unix messages appear and then the normal Mac OS X startup process continues. When that process is complete, you end up at the Login window or directly in the Mac OS X desktop, depending on how your Login preferences are configured.

STARTING UP IN VERBOSE MODE

If you hold down ⌘-V while your Mac is starting up, you start up in the verbose mode. In this mode, you see all sorts of system messages while the machine starts up. The difference between verbose mode and single-user mode is that the verbose mode is not interactive. All you can do is view the system messages; you can't control what happens. Many of the messages you see will probably be incomprehensible, but some are not (particularly messages about specific system processes starting up). This mode is likely to be useful to you only in troubleshooting. And even then, the single-user mode is probably more useful because it gives you some control over what is happening.

USING OTHER STARTUP OPTIONS

Table 8.2 lists various startup options and their keyboard shortcuts.

TABLE 8.2   MAC OS X STARTUP OPTIONS

Startup Option	How to Select It
Prevent automatic login	Hold the left Shift key and mouse button down when you see the progress bar during the startup process.
Close open Finder windows	Hold down the Shift key.
Start up from a computer connected via FireWire in Target Disk Mode	Press T during startup.
Eject a CD during the startup process	Hold down the mouse button.
Prevent startup items from opening	Hold down the Shift key.

INSTALLING AND USING MAC OS X FONTS

Mac OS X offers improved fonts and font support as compared to previous versions of the Mac OS. The Quartz Extreme graphics layer renders Mac OS X fonts clearly at any size and makes using special font features such as kerning controls, ligatures, and so on easy. You control fonts within applications using the new Font panel. The Font panel offers several useful features such as the ability to create and use sets of your favorite fonts.

→ To learn how to work with fonts using the Fonts panel, **see** "Working with Mac OS X Format Menus," **p. 154**.

Mac OS X includes a large number of high-quality fonts in the default installation. You can install additional fonts you want to use.

You use the new Font Book application to manage the fonts on your Mac.

UNDERSTANDING MAC OS X FONTS

One difference between Mac OS X fonts and Mac OS 9 fonts is that in Mac OS 9, fonts contain both a resource and data fork, but in Mac OS X, fonts contain only a data fork. Fonts with the file extension .dfont are single-fork files, meaning all the data for that font is stored in the single fork of its file. This is the native Mac OS X font format. However, under Mac OS X, you can also install and use any of the following types of fonts:

- TrueType fonts (.ttf)
- TrueType collections (.ttc)
- OpenType fonts (.otf)
- Fonts and font suitcases used by Mac OS 9 and earlier versions of the Mac OS (these might or might not have a filename extension)

NOTE

> One advantage of Mac OS X font files being able to provide all their information in a single fork is that these fonts can be shared with operating systems that do not recognize files with resource forks (Windows, Unix, and so on).

There are two locations in which fonts are installed under Mac OS X. To make a font available to everyone who uses your Mac, it is installed in the directory Mac OS X/Library/ Fonts, where Mac OS X is the name of the your Mac OS X startup volume. Within this directory are at least two types of font files. Those with the filename extension .dfont are the single-fork font files. You will also see fonts whose names do not have a filename extension.

NOTE

> Under Mac OS X, you can install or remove fonts while applications are open; fonts you install instantly become available to the system and any applications you are running.

To make a font available only to specific users, it is installed in the following directory: users/shortusername/Library/Fonts. A user's Library directory also contains the FontCollections folder. The FontCollections directory contains the set of font collections available to the user in the Font Book application and the Font pane.

NOTE

> Any user can install fonts into the Fonts folder in the Library folder in her Home directory.

If you have fonts installed on a Mac OS 9.2 volume that you want to be able to use with Mac OS X applications, you can use the Font Book to install those fonts so they are available under Mac OS X as well.

8

To make a font available to a Mac OS X application, it must be installed in one of the Mac OS X Font directories; similarly, for a font to be available to Classic applications, it must be installed in the Fonts folder in the Classic startup volume you are using.

CONFIGURING FONTS WITH THE FONT BOOK

The Font Book application is new to Mac OS X with version 10.3. This application enables you to manage all the fonts installed on your Mac. You can organize fonts into collections and enable and disable individual fonts or font collections.

When you open the Font Book application, you see three panes by default (see Figure 8.11). The Collection pane shows you the font collections on your Mac; collections are a means to gather fonts into groups to make them easier to select and apply. When you work with the Mac OS X Font panel, its fonts are organized by collection. You can use these collections to group fonts into smaller, focused groups to make font selection easier and faster. Many collections are installed by default, and you can create your own collections. The center pane is the Font pane, which shows the fonts that are part of the collection selected in the Collection pane. The right pane of the window is the Preview pane, which shows a preview of the font selected in the Font pane.

Figure 8.11
The Font Book application enables you to manage the fonts on your Mac.

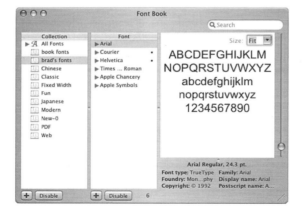

→ To learn how to access fonts you manage with Font Book from within applications, **see** "Working with Mac OS X Format Menus," **p. 154**.

WORKING WITH FONT COLLECTIONS

You can use the default font collections included with Font Book and create your own collections.

To view the fonts that are currently part of a collection, select that collection on the Collection list. The fonts it contains are listed on the Fonts pane. You can expand font families shown on the Fonts pane by clicking the Expansion triangle next to that font (see Figure 8.12).

Figure 8.12
Here, you can see that I have created a collection called `brad's fonts` and placed the fonts I use most frequently in it.

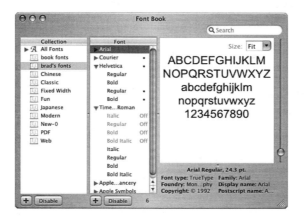

TIP

If a bullet appears next to a font's name, multiple versions of that font are installed. To remove the multiple versions, select the font and select Edit, Resolve Duplicates. This causes Font Book to turn off the duplicate fonts (see Figure 8.12).

If you select and expand the All Fonts collection, you see the following three sub-collections:

- **User**—This collection contains fonts accessible only to the current user.
- **Computer**—This is the collection of fonts available to all users.
- **Classic Mac OS**—These are the fonts available in the Classic environment if you have one installed on your Mac.

If you select the All Fonts collection itself, you see all the fonts installed on your Mac, regardless of the sub-collection in which they are stored.

ADDING A FONT COLLECTION

To add a font collection, do the following steps:

1. Click the New Collection button (the plus sign) below the bottom of the Collection list. Select File, New Collection, or press ⌘-N. A new collection appears on the list; its name is selected and ready for you to edit.
2. Type the name of the collection and press Return. The collection is created.
3. View other collections, such as the All Fonts collection, to see all the fonts installed on your computer.

TIP

To locate a specific font, select the All Fonts collection and type the font name in the Search tool on the Font Book toolbar

4. Drag a font you want to install in the new collection from the Fonts pane and drop it on the collection in which you want to place it.

5. Repeat steps 3 and 4 to add more fonts to the collection.

EDITING FONT COLLECTIONS

After you have created a collection, you can change it in the following ways:

- Double-click the collection name and edit it.

- Select the collection; select a font you want to remove from the collection; and select File, Remove Font. Click OK in the Confirmation dialog box; the font is removed from the collection (the font remains installed on your Mac).

- Select a font within a collection and click the Disable button below the bottom of the Font pane or select Edit, Disable Font. Click Disable in the Warning dialog box. The font is no longer able to be selected from within applications. The word Off appears next to the font to indicate it has been disabled.

- Select a font that has been disabled and click the Enable button or select Edit, Enable Font. The font is again available within that collection from within applications.

- Select a collection and click the Disable button below the bottom of the Collection pane. Click the Disable button in the warning dialog box. The collection is no longer selectable within applications. The word Off appears next to the collection to indicate it has been disabled.

- Select a collection that has been disabled and click the Enable button below the bottom of the Font pane or select Edit, Enable Collection. The collection is again available within applications.

> **TIP**
>
> If you use specific sets of fonts in specific applications, consider creating a font collection for each application and placing the fonts you use within it. Then, you can easily choose fonts from this group by selecting the application's font collection.

CONFIGURING THE FONT BOOK USING PREFERENCES

Using its Preferences dialog box, you can configure the following Font Book preferences:

- **Install options**—You can use the Installing fonts radio buttons to select which location is the default for fonts you install. (You can make a different choice for specific fonts you install.)

- **Disable options**—You can disable collections to hide them from within applications. If you click the "just the collection" radio button, only the collection itself is hidden. If you click the "all fonts in the collection" radio button, the collection is hidden along with all the fonts included in it (so those fonts can't be used even if they are also part of other collections).

- **Copy option**—If you check the "Always copy font files when installing" check box, a copy of the font's file is installed and the original file is left where it was. If you don't check this check box, the font file is moved to the appropriate location.

CONFIGURING THE FONT BOOK WINDOW

You can also configure the Font Book window itself in the following ways:

- Select Preview, Show Font Info. When you do, information about the selected font appears underneath the Preview pane.

- Change the size of the font preview in the Preview pane by either selecting a size on the Size pop-up menu or dragging the vertical slider along the right side of the pane. If you select Fit on the pop-up menu, the preview size is adjusted so you can see all of the preview within the pane.

- Change the relative size of the panes by dragging their resize handles.

> **TIP**
>
> The panes are limited to certain relative sizes. If you try to make a pane larger but are unable to do so, increase the size of the Font Book window itself and then make the other panes larger. You should then be able to resize the first pane.

- Change the size of the Font Book window by dragging its resize handle.

- Change the configuration of the preview shown in the Preview pane by selecting one of the options on the Preview pane. The Sample option shows each letter and number in the selected font, whereas the Repertoire option shows all the characters included in the selected font. The Custom option enables you to type characters in the Preview pane to preview them.

INSTALLING FONTS WITH THE FONT BOOK

You can use the Font Book to install fonts by performing the following steps:

1. Select File, Add Fonts (⌘-O). The Choose File sheet appears.

2. Move to and select the font you want to install.

3. Select the installation option for the font. If you want the font to be available only to you, click the "for me only" radio button. To make it available to everyone who uses your Mac, click the "for all users of this computer" radio button. To make the font available to Classic applications, click the "Classic Mac OS" radio button.

4. Click Open. The font is added to the All Fonts collection within the sub-collection related to the choice you made in the previous step. You can add it to other collections and work with that font with Font Book and from within applications.

8

TIP

> To see where a font is installed, select it and select File, Show Font File (⌘-R). A Finder window opens that shows the file in each location in which it has been installed.

LOGGING IN AS ROOT

Because Mac OS X is based on Unix, a user account called root exists on every Mac OS X machine. The root account has permission to do everything that is possible; the root account permissions go way beyond even the administrator account permissions. Because of this, logging in under this root account is very powerful, and it is also dangerous because it isn't that hard to mess up your system, delete directories (whether you intend to or not), and so on. However, because you sometimes need to log in under the root account to accomplish specific tasks, you should understand and become comfortable with it.

You should be logged in under the root account only for the minimum time necessary to accomplish specific tasks. Log in, do what you need to, and then log out of root again. This minimizes the chance of doing something you didn't intend to do because you forgot you were logged in under root.

CAUTION

> Be careful when you are working in your Mac under the root account. You can cause serious damage to the system as well as to data you have stored on your machine.

The root account is a very special user account, but it is still a user account. The full name of the root account is System Administrator, and its short name is root. One difference between the root account and other accounts is that the root account exists without having to create it. However, you have to activate the account and assign a password to it before you can begin using it.

You can activate the root account and create a password for it by following these steps:

1. Log in to the Mac.
2. Open the NetInfo Manager application found in the Applications/Utilities folder (see Figure 8.13).

→ NetInfo Manager is a very powerful system administration application; to learn more about it, **see** "Using the NetInfo Manager to Administer Your Network," **p. 848**.

3. Authenticate yourself as an administrator by clicking the Lock icon and entering user account information for an administrator account. (You have to do this even if you are logged in under an administrator account.)
4. Select Security, Enable Root User to see an alert explaining that the root password is currently blank; this is not a good thing.
5. Click OK to close the warning. The Set Root Password dialog box opens.

Figure 8.13
NetInfo Manager is a very powerful administrative application.

6. Type the new password for the root account.

7. Type the new password a second time in the "Retype new root password" box.

8. Click OK or press Return.

9. Enter your admin password in the resulting Authenticate dialog box and click OK.

10. Quit the NetInfo Manager application. Save you changes if prompted to do so.

After you have activated the root account and created the root password, you can log in under the root account by performing the following steps:

1. Log out of the current account.

2. Log in under the root account. If the login window is configured to show user accounts, select Other on the list and then enter **root**, type the root password, and click Login. If the Login window just shows the User Name and Password fields, enter the root account username and password and click Login.

3. Confirm that you are logged in as root by opening the Home directory; root appears as the username and as the label of the Home folder in the Places sidebar (see Figure 8.14).

NOTE

If you enable Fast User Switching, the root account isn't listed on the Fast User Switching menu. To log in to the root account, you must bring up the Login window by choosing Login Window on the Fast User Swtiching menu each time you want to log in as root.

Figure 8.14
When you can see the Home directory for the root user, you are logged in as root.

Because the root account has unlimited permissions, you can add or remove files to any directory on your Mac while you are logged in under the root account, including those for other user accounts. You can also make changes to any system file, which is where the root account's power and danger come from.

Use the root account only when you really need to. Make sure that other people who use your Mac do not know the root password; otherwise, you might find yourself with all sorts of problems.

TIP

> You can also log in to the root account directly in the Terminal window to enter Unix commands using the command line. This can be a faster way to enter a few commands if you are comfortable with the command-line interface.

MAC OS X TO THE MAX: EXPLORING MAC OS X

If you have read most of this book to this point, you have already explored quite a bit of Mac OS X and have seen how its structure and organization differ from previous versions of the Mac OS. The purpose of this section is to give you an overview of the Mac OS X system so you are familiar with its most important parts from a holistic perspective.

Starting from the top level or root of the machine is the Computer folder. As you learned earlier, this directory contains each of the volumes mounted on your machine as well as the Network folder.

In this section, I refer to the Mac OS X startup volume as the Mac OS X volume (a clever feat on my part, eh?). If you have named your Mac OS X startup volume something different from this, you need to swap your name for mine to understand my references to system items.

If you open the Mac OS X volume, you see the following four system directories: Applications, Library, System, and Users.

THE APPLICATIONS DIRECTORY

As you know from Chapter 6, "Installing and Using Mac OS X Applications," and other chapters, the Applications directory is the default installation directory for all Mac OS X applications. This directory contains application package files as well as application folders and folders that contain other applications (such as the Utilities directory). Mac OS X includes a large number of applications in this directory by default, and you generally install all other Carbon or Cocoa applications in this directory as well.

THE LIBRARY DIRECTORY

The Library directory contains system-level Library resources that are modifiable when you are using an administrator account. As you saw earlier in this chapter, one of the directories in this directory is the Fonts folder in which you store the fonts available to all user accounts. However, this directory contains many more directories than just this one, such as the Sounds directory that you also learned to change earlier in the chapter. Basically, any system-level resources that can be changed (without logging as root) are stored in this Library directory. Some examples are the following:

- **Application Support**—This directory contains files that provide various types of support to specific applications. For example, the StuffIt Engine that provides services to several StuffIt applications (such as StuffIt Expander) resides here.

- **Desktop Pictures**—These graphics files are available for you to use as desktop pictures, which you configure using the Desktop pane of the System Preferences application.

- **Documentation**—This is an interesting directory; it contains documentation and support files for various services that are part of Mac OS X. For example, you can find files for the Mac OS X help system here as well as information about Unix services such as Apache. Applications can also add documentation here. You should explore this folder to see what documentation is available.

- **Internet Plug-ins**—This directory contains plug-ins accessible to Internet applications you have installed on your system.

- **Preferences**—System-level preferences (as opposed to user-level preferences) are stored here. Examples are Software Update preferences (`com.apple.SoftwareUpdate.plist`) and login window preferences (`com.apple.loginwindow.plist`).

■ **Printers**—This directory contains the printer drivers. Mac OS X includes native support for many printers, and the drivers for any printers you add to the system are also stored here. Within the directory, the drivers are organized into folders, one for each brand of printer installed.

■ **Receipts**—This is another interesting directory you should explore. It contains various packages for applications and software updates you have installed on your machine, such as OS updates you install using the Software Update feature of the OS. You can view information about these updates or applications by opening one of the packages you find here.

TIP

When you download a system update using the Software Update, you can run its package to read about what was installed. Launch the update's installer and move to the readme page to read about that update.

The System Directory

The System directory contains the basic software that makes the system work. It contains one directory, which is the Library directory (not to be confused with the Library directory on the root level of the Mac OS X volume).

NOTE

The System directory is the most analogous to the System Folder in previous versions of the Mac OS. However, the System Folder was really more a combination of the System and Library directories under Mac OS X.

This Library directory contains the fundamental operating system files that provide the services needed to make Mac OS X work. It contains many directories, which you can't modify without being logged in as root. And there aren't really many times when you will need to access the files and directories stored here.

NOTE

The Mac OS X directory has many other files and subdirectories that are invisible to you when you are logged in under the Mac OS X interface, even if you are logged in under the root account. You can see all the files installed on your Mac using the Terminal application and Unix commands.

Examples of the directories contained in the System's Library are the following:

■ **ColorPickers**—These files provide the Color Picker services you learned about earlier in this chapter.

8

- **Components**—Component files (filename extension `.component`) provide various system services such as AppleScript support and the Sound Manager.

- **CoreServices**—As its name implies, this directory contains files that provide core services to the operating system, such as the Dock, Finder, Help Viewer, Login window, and so on. Several of the items in this directory are applications, including the Finder and Dock.

- **Extensions**—Although extensions in the traditional Mac OS sense are not part of Mac OS X, there are Mac OS X extensions. These files provide support to various hardware devices and hardware-related services. Mac OS X extension files have `.kext` as their filename extension (which stands for Kernel extension).

- **Fonts**—This Fonts directory provides the fonts that are fundamental to the system, such as those used in the menu bar.

- **Frameworks**—As you learned in Chapter 1, "Mac OS X: Foundations," Mac OS X frameworks are the subsystems within the OS that provide various services. The files related to these frameworks are stored in the Frameworks directory. Examples of frameworks installed in this directory are AppleShare, Cocoa, Java, QuickTime, and Security.

- **OpenSSL**—Secure Sockets Layer (SSL) is the most common encoding scheme used to securely transmit data over the Internet. This directory contains information related to SSL on your machine, such as the various SSL certificates you have installed.

- **PreferencePanes**—This directory contains the panes in the System Preferences application such as for the date and time (`DateAndTime.prefPane`), Dock (`Dock.prefPane`), keyboard (`Keyboard.prefPane`), and QuickTime (`QuickTime.prefPane`). Interestingly, third-party preference panes aren't added to this directory when they are installed on the System Preferences application. This folder contains all possible Apple System Preferences application panes, even if they don't appear to you (such as the Ink pane that doesn't appear unless you have a tablet installed).

- **Sounds**—As you learned earlier in this chapter, this directory contains the alert sounds available to all the users on your machine.

- **StartupItems**—This directory contains additional system services that become active when the system starts up. Examples include AppleShare, Network services, and so on. Many startup items are listed in this directory, such as the Apache Web server, AppleTalk, Network services, and so on.

THE USERS DIRECTORY

The Users directory contains the Home directory for each user account configured on your machine. Within this directory are a directory for each active user account, a directory for the user accounts you have deleted (if you chose to save the user's Home folder), and the Shared directory for items that can be shared.

8

NOTE

The one user directory you won't see is the root directory. That is hidden except when you are logged in as root.

→ To learn more about the contents of a user's Home directory, **see** "Understanding the Home Folder," **p. 21**.

CHAPTER **9**

UNIX: WORKING WITH THE COMMAND LINE

In this chapter

A COMMAND LINE WITH THE MAC OS?

As you learned earlier in the book, Mac OS X is running on top of a version of the Unix operating system. This means that Mac OS X can use many of the Unix applications. It also means you can enter Unix commands directly in the command-line interface to manipulate your system. In fact, in some situations, using a Unix command might be the only way you can accomplish a task (such as deleting a rogue file that you can't delete by dragging it to the Trash).

Unix is a very powerful language/operating system; however, it is also enigmatic and many of its commands require you to use complicated syntax to get them to work properly. Unix commands are incomprehensible to most people by just looking at them, so don't expect to be able to figure out how a particular command works without some help. Mostly, you will learn about commands you want to use from various Unix resources (such as this chapter, other books, Web sites, and Unix manual pages). You might find using the command line to be so counter to the traditional Mac interface experience that you don't want to use it; if so, that is fine because few situations exist in which it is required in everyday Mac use. However, if you want to master Mac OS X, you should become familiar with the command line and learn some basic Unix commands. You might find that Unix provides ways of doing things that are both powerful and efficient.

There is so much you can do with Unix that there is no way you can learn how to work proficiently with it in the few pages of this chapter. To become even remotely fluent in Unix, you will need to do some additional learning outside of this book. What you can learn here is generally how the command-line interface works, and you can also learn how to use some basic Unix commands as examples. In the "Mac OS X to the Max" section at the end of the chapter, I provide references for you so you can learn more about using Unix if you choose to.

TERMINAL

You use the Terminal application (Applications/Utilities) to enter Unix commands in the command-line interface (see Figure 9.1). The Terminal window is simple; all you see are your last login date and time, a Welcome message, the hostname, the user account under which you are logged in, and the command prompt.

NOTE

> Hostname is the name of the machine that is hosting your Unix session. When you are running a Unix session from your local machine, this will be localhost for most default configurations. If you are providing services over the network, the computer's network name is used.

SHELLS

In Unix, the *shell* is the user interface you use to interact with Unix. You can use different shells for the same set of Unix tools; each shell will have slightly different features, but they all work somewhat similarly (although the specific commands you use can differ). You can change the specific shell you use if you find one that offers features in which you are interested.

Figure 9.1
The command-line interface in Terminal isn't much to look at, but it is very powerful.

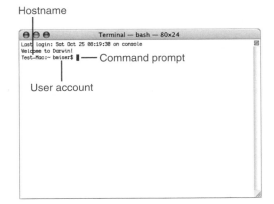

The default shell for working with Unix under Mac OS X is called bash. Other shells are available, but bash is a good place to start.

NOTE

You can install other shells on your Mac to work with them. After you download and install the shell, you use the Terminal's Preferences to set the shell you want to use. The details of using different shells are beyond the scope of this chapter. See some of the references listed at the end of this chapter for help.

UNIX COMMAND STRUCTURE

To enter commands, you type them at the prompt. All Unix commands use a specific syntax and consist of the following three parts:

- Command
- Options
- Argument

The *command* is the specific action you want to take, such as listing the contents of a directory using the ls command.

You can enter *options* for that command to make the command work in a specific way. To add an option to a command, you type a hyphen followed by a letter. The options you can use are specific to each command. For example, when used with the ls (list) command, the -l option tells Unix to list the contents of the directory in the long format.

The *argument* is the "thing" on which the command will be executed, such as a file or directory. For example, to list the contents of a directory called `mydirectory`, the argument would be that directory name and the path to that directory.

When you enter specific commands, you might not use options or arguments; in some cases, you won't use either and will simply enter the command by itself.

NOTE

> Unix is case sensitive, so you must always follow the case conventions for specific commands. Most of the time, you will type everything in lowercase letters for commands and options, but paths can include both uppercase and lowercase letters.

You can run several commands in sequential order by separating the commands with a semicolon, as in `command1; command2`. Each command will be activated in the order in which you list it.

You can send the output of one command to be the input of another command by separating them with the pipe symbol (¦), as in `command1 ¦ command2`. This is called *piping*.

When entering commands, you will frequently need to use the path to a directory or file you want to manipulate. The path is the means by which you locate yourself in the hierarchy; levels of the hierarchy are indicated by the slash (/). Also, Unix uses relative pathnames. When you refer to something within or below the current directory, you need to enter only the portion of the path from the current directory to the subdirectories and files rather than the full path from the top level of the hierarchy. For example, to refer to a directory called `mac_files` within a directory called `user_docs` when you are currently in the `user_docs` directory, you would enter the path `mac_files`. When you want to move above or outside the current directory, you must type the full path. In Unix, full paths always start with /.

NOTE

> The full path to your Home directory is `/macosx/Users/shortusername/`, where `macosx` is the name of your Mac OS X startup volume and `shortusername` is the short username for your account. However, because you can use relative paths, you can leave out the first / and the name of your Mac OS X startup volume to get to this directory. You need to add only the volume name when you are working outside the current volume.

Unlike GUIs, Unix does not like spaces in filenames, volume names, or paths. To enter a space in one of these, use the backslash (\) followed by the space. For example, to refer to the volume called Mac OS X, you would enter `/Mac\ OS\ X`.

To get to the root of the startup volume, the path is simply /. However, unless you are logged on under the root account, you won't be able to do anything with the files and directories you see using a command line because of the system security.

One of the best ways to become familiar with entering pathnames is to drag items from a Finder window onto the Terminal window. When you do so, the pathname to that item is entered in the Terminal. You can use this trick to make entering paths easier because you can drag the item onto the prompt after you have entered a command and option to quickly add the argument to complete the command. And, after you drag several onto the window, you will get a good idea of how to type pathnames at the prompt manually. Follow these steps:

1. In a Finder window, open the Home directory for your user account.

2. Open a new Terminal window from within the Terminal application by selecting File, New Shell. A new Terminal window appears.

9

> **TIP**
>
> When using the Terminal, you can have multiple windows open at the same time. Each window is independent, so you can have multiple sessions running independently. You can save each session separately too, which you will learn about later in this chapter.

3. Drag the Documents directory from the Finder window onto the new Terminal window. The path to the directory is shown at the prompt (see Figure 9.2). (Note that you can't drag the folder from the Places sidebar; you must drag it from a Finder window.)

Figure 9.2
You can quickly enter a path at the prompt by dragging an item from a Finder window onto the Terminal; in this case, I dragged the Documents folder from my Home directory onto the Terminal window.

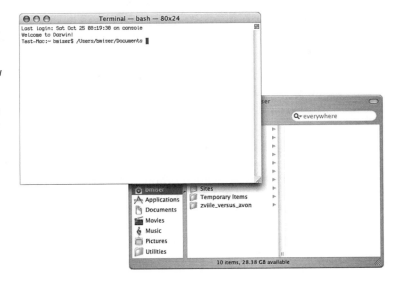

> **NOTE**
>
> If you deal with Unix systems outside of Mac OS X, you will notice that paths almost never include spaces. Unix can have trouble properly interpreting spaces, so you can run into problems if the path you want to use includes spaces. Generally, if you plan to use Unix frequently, you should include underscores when you name your files and

directories instead of spaces. Or, you can simply drag the object into the Terminal window and let the Mac enter the path for you. Spaces will be replaced by a backslash and a space (\ ).

→ To see examples of specific Unix commands, **see** "Learning Unix by Example," **p. 248**.

Unix Applications

Because Unix has been around so long, thousands and thousands of Unix applications are available. You can run many of these under Mac OS X, and the OS includes several of these applications as part of the standard installation. For example, the Apache Web server application enables you to host your own Web pages. Mac OS X comes with a couple of Unix text editors, which are vi (Visual Editor) and emacs (an abbreviation of editing macros).

→ To get some examples of running these Unix applications, **see** "Working with Basic Unix Applications," **p. 257**.

Shell Scripts

You can invoke a series of commands using a Shell script; you can save the script and run it at any time to save yourself from having to retype the commands over and over. You create a script using the same syntax as in regular Unix commands. The difference is that you save those commands to a text file. When you want to run the commands, you execute the file instead. You can also run scripts that others have written just as easily.

The details of writing and running scripts are beyond the scope of this book. See the references listed at the end of this chapter for information about creating and using Shell scripts.

Unix Flavors

Finally, you should be aware that various versions of Unix are available. And, different releases of different versions exist as well. When it was released, Mac OS X included version 4.4 of the Berkeley Software Distribution (BSD) version of Unix. As this version is updated, the version that is part of Mac OS X will be updated as well.

Learning Unix by Example

Many Unix commands are available, and there is no way you can do more than scratch the surface in this small chapter. However, you can learn how Unix commands work in general by trying some specific examples of useful Unix commands.

→ For references in which you can learn more Unix commands, **see** "Learning Unix," **p. 260**.

Each of the following sections provides information about specific commands. For each command, you will see four areas of information about that command. First, you will read a general description of what the command does. Second, you will see the command's syntax and some of the useful options for that command. Third, you will see a more specific description of the command's effect. Fourth, you will see the steps you can take to use the command.

NOTE

For the commands in this section, you won't see all or even many of the options that are possible for each command. You will need to access a more detailed reference for that type of information, such as the command's manual pages.

9

LEARNING ABOUT THE ENVIRONMENT

When you are troubleshooting, it can be helpful to understand the environment in which you are running Unix. You can use the uname command to get information about the computer on which you execute the command. Or, you might need to check this information to make sure some software or hardware is compatible with your system:

Command: uname

Options: -a provides all the information about your machine; -s shows the operating system name; -n lists the machine name

What it does: Provides information about various aspects of the machine on which you are running Unix

1. Launch the Terminal application and at the command prompt, type **uname -a**; then press Return. You will see various items of information about your machine, such as the core operating system (Darwin), hostname (localhost), version of the kernel you are running, and so on (see Figure 9.3).

Figure 9.3
The uname command provides information about the machine on which you are running Unix.

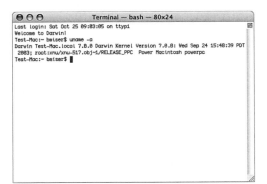

2. Type **uname -s** and press Return. You will see only the core operating system (Darwin).

3. Type **uname -n** and press Return. You will see the name of the machine hosting the Unix session.

   Command: env

   What it does: Provides extensive information about your Unix session (your Unix environment)

Type **env** and press Return. You will see information including your Home directory, the shell you are running, the username you are using, the language being used, the application you are using to enter Unix commands, and so on. This information can get pretty extensive; scroll up the window to just below where you entered the command to see the more meaningful parts.

TIP

> At the top of the scrollbar in the Terminal window is a broken square. If you click this, the Terminal window splits into two panes, and you can work within each pane independently. This is useful when you want to view two areas of the window at the same time but can't expand the window large enough to be able to do so.

VIEWING THE CONTENTS OF DIRECTORIES

You will frequently need to move up and down the directory structure to work with specific files or other directories. Unix has many commands that enable you to do so, including

   Command: pwd

   What it does: Shows you the full path to your current location

Use the pwd command when you aren't sure about the directory in which you are currently located. When you use the command, you will see the full path in which you are working. This can be helpful if you become confused about where you are as you move around the directories.

   Command: cd *pathname*

   What it does: Changes your directory location to the one in the path *pathname*

NOTE

> When a specific command is listed in a step, you should ignore the period at the end of the command. For example, in the following steps, don't type the period after the command cd Music in step 1.

1. Type **cd Music**. The prompt will change to [localhost:~/Music] to indicate you are in the Music directory in your Home directory.

9

TIP

> Remember that the ~ represents your Home directory, so ~/Music means you are in the Music directory that is within your Home directory. This can help you take some shortcuts when entering paths, as you will see in the next step.
>
> Also remember that the forward slash (/) in a path indicates a change in level in the hierarchy. If you are in your Home directory and type cd /Music, you will get a message telling you that no such directory exists. When you enter the forward slash, Unix looks back to the highest level in the structure and there is not a directory called Music in that directory. Leaving the / out indicates that Unix should look in the current directory, which is where the directory is actually located.

2. Type **cd /Users/*shortusername***, where *shortusername* is the short username for your account. This moves you back into your Home directory. You include /User/ because you are moving above the Music directory and so need to include the full pathname.

NOTE

> In a pathname, the tilde character (~) indicates that you are in your Home directory. In the step 2, you could have just entered cd ~ to move back into your Home directory.

Command: ls

Options: -F differentiates between files and directories; -l shows full information for all the files in the directory

What it does: Lists the contents of a directory in various formats and with various information

NOTE

> Although most commands and options are in lowercase, they aren't always. For example, the -F option is different from the -f option (both are valid for the ls command).

1. Use the cd command to move into the directory of which you want to see the contents.

2. Type **ls**. You will see a multiple-column view of the directory; files and directories are listed by name.

3. Type **ls -F**. You will see the same list as before except that now directories are indicated by a / after their names.

4. Type **ls -l**. You will see the contents of the directory listed along with plenty of information about each file and directory within the current directory (see Figure 9.4). If there are many items, the information will scroll so quickly that you might not be able to see all of it. This is a good opportunity to see an example of piping two commands together.

9

Figure 9.4
Listing a directory using the `ls -l` command provides detailed information about each item in that directory.

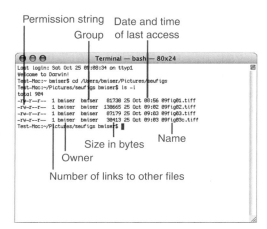

Permission string   Date and time
Group   of last access

Size in bytes   Name

Owner

Number of links to other files

5. Type **ls -l ¦ more**. This time, the same list will appear, but the display will stop when the screen is full and you will see the `more` prompt at the bottom of the window. Press the spacebar to see the next screenful of information. You can also scroll the window using the scrollbars to see all the items in the window.

TIP

If you type the command `ls -la`, you will also see the invisible files in a directory.

The permissions string you see at the start of each item in the full listing indicates how the item can be accessed. The first character indicates whether the item is a file (-) or a directory (d). The next three characters indicate what the owner of the file can do; r is for read, w is for write, and x is for execute. If any of these characters is the hyphen (-), that action can't be taken. The next three characters indicate the permission that the group has to the file. For example, if these characters are r-x, other members of the group can read, not write, and execute the file. The last three characters indicate what everyone else can do.

The execute permission applies to a directory. To access a directory, you must have both read and execute permission. If you also have w permission, you can change the contents of the directory as well.

Command: `file filename`

What it does: Indicates what type of file `filename` is

Type **file**, followed by the filename you would like information about, and press Return. Information about the file is displayed.

CHANGING THE CONTENTS OF DIRECTORIES

You can use Unix commands to change the contents of directories as well. For example, you can delete files using the `rm` command. This can sometimes be faster than using the Trash.

Once in a while, you might not be able to use the Trash to get rid of a file; you can often use the Unix commands to accomplish the task when other means fail.

Command: `rm`

Options: `-i` prompts you before deleting each file; `-r` removes the entire directory

What it does: Deletes everything that you indicate should be deleted

1. Use the `cd` and `ls` commands to find a file you want to delete.

2. Type **rm *filename***, where *filename* is the name of the file you want to delete, and press Return. The file is deleted.

3. Type **rm -i *filename*** and press Return. You are prompted about removing the file; type **Y** to remove the file or **N** to cancel.

4. Type **rm -r *directoryname***, where *directoryname* is the name of a directory you want to delete, and press Return. The directory and all its contents are deleted.

NOTE

> You can't remove the current directory unless you enter the full path to it.

TIP

> The asterisk (*) is a wildcard character. For example, to delete all the files in a directory that have the file extension `.tiff`, you can type `rm *.tiff`.

Command: `cp`

What it does: Copies a file

1. Type **cp *filename filenamecopy***, where *filename* is the name of the file you want to copy and *filenamecopy* is the name of the file to which it will be copied; then press Return. The first file is copied into a new file that has the second name you typed.

2. Type **cp *filename path***, where *filename* is the name of the file you want to copy and *path* is the location in which you want the copy to be created; then press Return. A copy of the file is placed into the location you specified.

Command: `mv`

What it does: Moves a file or directory

Type **mv *filename path*** and press Return. The file or directory *filename* is moved to the location *path*.

Command: `mkdir`

What it does: Creates a directory

1. Use the `cd` command to move into the directory in which you want to create a new directory.

2. Type **mkdir** *directoryname* and press Return. A new directory with the name *directoryname* is created in the current directory.

USING THE MANUAL

All Unix commands have a manual associated with them. This manual lists the syntax for the command and defines its options; manuals can be a good reference when you are using a specific command but can't remember an option or the command's exact syntax. Many manual pages also provide some explanation about how the command works.

Command: man

What it does: Brings up the manual pages for the command you enter

1. Type **man ls** and press Return. The manual pages for the ls command appear (see Figure 9.5).

Figure 9.5
You can get extensive information about any command by using the man command.

2. Press the spacebar to move to the next page.

3. Continue reading the manual pages until you have the information you need.

It is a good idea to take a look at the manual pages for any Unix commands you use. Pay special attention to the list of options that are available for the command.

NOTE

> Some Unix applications provide manual pages using the help argument. For example, perl --help brings up information about the Perl application.

TIP

> Pressing the spacebar moves you down the manual page one screen's worth at a time; you can move down a manual page one line at a time by pressing the Return key instead.

USING SUPERUSER COMMANDS

As you learned earlier in the book, the root account is the fundamental user account that can do *anything* under Mac OS X. The root account has more access to the system than even an administrator account does. Using this account can be hazardous to your system because, when you are under root, the OS assumes that you know what you are doing and doesn't provide any checks on your activities. You can easily delete things you don't mean to or mess up the system itself.

CAUTION

> By entering the root account, you can do damage to your system. You should use this only when you really have to, and even then, you need to be very careful about the commands you enter while you are working on the root prompt.

However, when you need to use a specific command at a specific time that you can't do under another user account, it can be helpful to enter commands as root.

Command: `sudo`

Option: `-s`, which runs the command in the default shell

What it does: Gets you into the root account so you can enter a command that you can't enter under another account

→ For help activating the root account and creating a password for it, **see** "Logging In As Root," **p. 236**.

1. Open a new shell window. The prompt shows the short name of the user account you are logged in under.

2. Type **sudo -s** and press Return. If you are using the `sudo` command for the first time in a session, you will see a warning regarding what you are about to do and will be prompted to enter your password; enter your root password and press Return. If you have logged in as root previously, you won't have to enter the password again. When the `sudo` command is successful, the prompt shows that you are logged in as root (see Figure 9.6).

TIP

> To return to the previous account, type `exit` and press Return.

KILLING A PROCESS

When a process goes wrong, it can cause problems, such as hanging, or it might start consuming tremendous amounts of processing power, thus bringing your system's performance to a crawl. You can tell that a process has gone out of control by monitoring its percentage of CPU usage. If this number gets high and stays there, the process is likely hung. Because the information in the top window is dynamic, you should open it in a Terminal window and then open another window to enter commands. Under Mac OS X, there are several ways to stop an out-of-control process. For applications, you can use the Force Quit command. At the process level, you can use the Process Viewer to force a process to quit. You can also use the powerful Unix command `kill` to stop a running process.

Command: `kill` *ProcessID*

Options: `-9` kills the process no matter what; `-3` quits the process

What it does: Stops the process with the ID number *ProcessID*

Figure 9.6
The `root#` prompt indicates that you are logged in under the root account; be careful when you see this prompt.

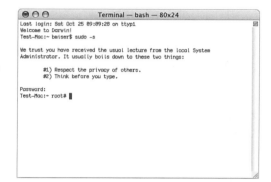

1. Launch the Terminal.

2. Type **top**. You will see a listing of all the processes currently running on your Mac (see Figure 9.7). Use the information in the table to identify the problematic process, such as one that is consuming an unreasonable amount of processing power. In this example, assume that Internet Explorer has gone out of control (although, as you can see in the figure, it is using only .9% of the CPU so it really doesn't have a problem at this point). In the figure, Internet Explorer's process ID number is 429.

Figure 9.7
This top window shows all the processes running on your Mac; you can use the process ID with the `kill` command to stop any running process.

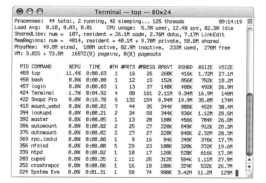

3. Open a new shell by selecting File, New Shell (⌘-N).

4. Type **kill -9 429**.

5. Switch back to the Terminal window showing top. You will no longer see Internet Explorer listed in the process list. You can use the same steps to kill any process by using the process ID of that process.

You can stop the top process by pressing Ctrl-C.

NOTE

> If the process you are trying to kill is an Administrator process, you will have to use the `sudo -s` command to get into the root account before you use the `kill` command.

WORKING WITH BASIC UNIX APPLICATIONS

You learned earlier that several Unix applications are included with Mac OS X. Although you aren't likely to use these instead of your Mac OS X applications for your everyday work, sometimes these applications can be quite useful. For example, you might want to use the vi text editor to create Shell scripts. A couple of examples will show you how such applications work.

EDITING TEXT WITH VI

The Unix application vi is a basic text editor. You can use it to create and edit text files, but it is most useful for creating Shell scripts. You are unlikely to use it to create text documents, but you can use it to create plain-text documents if you would like.

The vi program has two modes: Edit and Command. In Edit mode, you can enter and edit text. In Command mode, you issue commands to the program. Do the following:

1. Type **man vi**. Read the manual pages to get an idea of how vi works.

2. Open a new Terminal window (⌘-N) and type **vi** and the name of the text file you want to create, such as vi newtestfile.txt. The program opens, the file is created in the current directory, and you see a screen containing tilde symbols in the editing area. At the bottom of the screen, you will see the vi command line.

3. Type **i** to enter Insert mode.

4. Type your text.

5. Press Esc to move into Command mode. While you are in Command mode, you will hear an alert sound if you try to type anything that isn't a recognized vi command; you will also see a prompt at the bottom of the vi window telling you that the text you typed isn't a recognized command.

NOTE

> Determining which mode you are in can be confusing. When you enter Command mode, the cursor appears to jump back a couple of spaces and the bottom line of the window is empty. You can then type a command. If you see text on the screen when you type, you are in Edit mode.

6. Type **:w** and press Return to write the text to the file you created. At the bottom of the vi window, you will see confirmation that the text has been written to the file (see Figure 9.8).

7. To continue adding text to the file, type **a**. The command line disappears and the cursor becomes active after the last text you entered.

8. Continue adding text and writing it to the file.

9. When you are done, press Esc to enter Command mode; then type **:q** and press Return to quit vi. You will return to the command line.

Figure 9.8
The message at the bottom of this vi window indicates that one line of text has been written to the file newtest.txt.

TIP

> To save long manual pages for a command, use the man command on that command and press the spacebar to reveal the entire text of the manual pages. Select the manual text you want to save in a file and select File, Save Selected Text As. Name the text file and save it. You can then refer to that file when you need help with that command.

Because GUI text editors are available, you might not want to use Unix text editors such as vi, but for short, plain-text documents, such as a Shell script, these editors can be useful.

To edit an existing file with vi, type **vi *filename***, where *filename* is the name of the file you want to edit, and press Return. The file opens and you can begin editing it.

If you intend to use vi, make sure that you read its manual pages in detail; vi has many commands available, but they are hard to figure out without help.

COMPRESSING, UNCOMPRESSING, AND EXTRACTING FILES

Unix has some built-in programs to enable you to work with compressed files, including

- To compress a file, type **compress *filename***. The file named *filename* is compressed and a .Z is appended to its name.

- To uncompress a file, type **uncompress *filename***, where *filename* is the name of the compressed file. The file is uncompressed.

- You can also use the gzip compression application by typing gzip `filename`. Uncompress the file using the `gunzip` command. gzip offers various options; check its manual pages to see them.

Many Unix files are archived in the tar (tape archive) format before they are compressed. After you compress such files, you will see a file that has the `.tar` extension. You can extract a tar file using the command tar `xvf` `filename`, where `filename` is the name of the tar file.

NOTE

> Tar also has various options; check its manual pages for help.

MAC OS X TO THE MAX: UNIX RESOURCES

Using Unix proficiently requires some additional learning—Unix is a very complex and sophisticated tool that you should become familiar with to master Mac OS X. In this part of this chapter, you will learn the keyboard shortcuts that will help you use the Terminal application more efficiently. You will also find references to Web sites and books that can help you learn Unix in more depth.

USING TERMINAL KEYBOARD SHORTCUTS

Table 9.1 lists keyboard shortcuts for the Terminal application.

TABLE 9.1   TERMINAL KEYBOARD SHORTCUTS

Action	Shortcut
Use Selection for Find	⌘-E
Find Next	⌘-G
Find	⌘-F
Find Previous	Shift-⌘-G
Jump to Selection	⌘-J
Line Down	⌘-Down arrow
Line Up	⌘-Up arrow
New Command	Shift-⌘-N
New Shell	⌘-N
Next Page	Spacebar
Next Terminal	⌘-Right arrow
Previous Terminal	⌘-Left arrow
Save Selected Text As	Option-Shift-⌘-S
Save Text As	Option-⌘-S

Action	Shortcut
TABLE 9.1 **CONTINUED**	
Send Break	⌘-.
Set Title	Shift-⌘-T
Show Info	⌘-I

LEARNING UNIX

The following list describes Web sites for learning more about Unix:

- `www.uwsg.indiana.edu/usail/`—Site name: Unix System Administration Independent Learning. This is an online course about administering Unix.

- `www.comp.lancs.ac.uk/computing/users/eiamjw/unix/`—Site name: A Course in the Unix Operating System. This is another online Unix course.

- `www.eco.utexas.edu/Help/Unixhelp/TOP_.html`—Site name: Unixhelp for Users. This is a nicely organized and fairly extensive reference site.

- `www.comet.ucar.edu/strc/unix/index.htm`—Site name: SOO/STRC Unix Resources. This is a page containing links to other Unix learning sites.

- `http://www.rice.edu/IT/help/documents/index_platform.html#UNIX`—Site name: Rice University IT Document Index. This is an archive of various PDF docs; there are many on various aspects of Unix.

The following list describes some recommended books for learning more about Unix:

- *Sams Teach Yourself Unix in 10 Minutes*—Author: William Ray. This is a good "fast and easy" entry into the world of Unix.

- *Sams Teach Yourself Unix in 24 Hours, Second Edition*—Authors: Dave Taylor and James C. Armstrong, Jr. This contains 24 one-hour lessons to get you into Unix.

- *The Complete Idiot's Guide to Unix*—Author: Bill Wagner. This book's friendly approach to Unix is good if you prefer a less-structured approach than the *Sams Teach Yourself* books.

- *Special Edition Using Unix, Third Edition*—Author: Peter Kuo. This is a comprehensive Unix reference. This is a good resource to have when you become comfortable with Unix and want to explore it in great detail.

PART II

Mac OS X: Connecting to the World

CHAPTER 10

CONNECTING YOUR MAC TO THE INTERNET

In this chapter

CONNECTING TO THE INTERNET

The Internet is one of the most significant social and economic movements—it is a movement as much as it is technology—in human history. In just a few years, the Internet (or more simply, the Net) moved from an obscure scientific and government computer network to become a dominant means of global and local communication, commerce, entertainment, and information. Fortunately, Mac OS X has equipped you to make the most of the Net.

Finding, installing, and configuring an Internet account can be complex. You can use many technologies to connect to the Net, and you can obtain an Internet account from thousands of Internet service providers (ISPs).

The general steps to connect your Mac to the Internet are the following:

1. Determine the technology you will use to connect to the Internet.
2. Find an ISP and obtain an account.
3. Install and configure the modem or other hardware you need.
4. Configure your Mac to connect to the account you have established.
5. Test your configuration and troubleshoot any problems you find.

Depending on how you are going to connect to the Net, you might have to do most of these steps yourself or your ISP might handle them for you—at least for the initial installation and configuration. Even if your ISP handles the initial configuration for you, you will need to understand how to reconfigure your Mac when the inevitable happens and you have to reinstall the system, move your account to another Mac, and so on.

CHOOSING YOUR INTERNET CONNECTION TECHNOLOGY

There are six general technologies you can use to connect your Mac to the Internet. These technologies are summarized in Table 10.1 and explained in more detail in the following subsections.

TABLE 10.1   INTERNET CONNECTION TECHNOLOGIES

Technology	Connection Method	Advantages	Disadvantages
Dial-up	Dial-up modem via standard phone line	Available anywhere; inexpensive; simple configuration; accessible from any location; dial-up modem included in all modern Macs	Very slow; connection must be established each time services are needed; not as reliable as other connection methods; can be difficult to achieve maximum performance; makes phone line unavailable
DSL	DSL modem via standard phone line	Broadband connection speeds (both directions); always-on connection; reliable connection; consistent communication speed	Limited availability; more expensive than a dial-up account
Cable	Cable modem via fiber-optic cable	Broadband connection speeds (both directions); always-on connection; reliable connection	Limited availability; more expensive than a dial-up account; connection speed can fluctuate depending on activity of local cable trunk
ISDN	ISDN modem via one or more standard phone lines	Slow to fairly fast connection speed depending on number of lines used	Expensive; not as fast as other broadband connections; limited availability

10

TABLE 10.1 CONTINUED

Technology	Connection Method	Advantages	Disadvantages
Satellite	Satellite receiver via satellite dish	Fast download connection; widely available; always-on connection	Expensive; upload connection speed can be limited; some configurations require a dedicated upload account (such as over a dial-up connection); requires more complex installation and setup than other methods
T-1/ Fractional T-1	Direct cabling from ISP	Fastest connection; always-on connection; most reliable connection	Very expensive; requires complex and expensive installation and configuration.

TIP

> Some broadband ISPs, such as cable providers, offer dial-up accounts as part of their services (some include the cost in the basic account, whereas others charge an additional fee for the dial-up access). Typically, these dial-up services are intended for those times when you are traveling and need to access your account from locations other than those at which the service was initially installed. If you are able to use a broadband connection and will need to access it from multiple locations, check with your ISP to see whether it offers dial-up access to your account.

Generally, you will want to choose the fastest connection method that is available in your area and that you can afford. A broadband Internet connection makes the Internet even more useful when compared to a slower connection (such as a 56K dial-up connection). For example, with a broadband connection, you can download files as large as 10MB or more in just a few moments. A broadband connection makes downloading even very large files, as much as 100MB or more, practical. Just to give you a reference point about how large the files you download can be, using a cable modem, I have routinely downloaded 400MB and larger files in less than 20 minutes. Try that with a dial-up account!

In addition to making downloading files faster, a broadband connection enables you to experience online video and audio in a fashion quite similar to watching cable TV or listening to a radio. Finally, a broadband connection enables you to avoid the delays and hassles of waiting for a dial-up account to connect to the Internet each time you want to use it because it is always on. With a broadband connection, the Internet actually becomes an extension of your desktop.

NOTE

> When calculating the cost of an Internet connection, don't forget to include the cost of a phone line that might be dedicated to Internet access. For example, many people who are serious about Net access add a second phone line to dedicate to that purpose. When considering the cost of a broadband connection, such as a cable modem account, don't forget to include the cost of a dedicated phone line as part of the cost of the dial-up account. The cost of a dial-up account and dedicated phone line is usually similar to the cost of a broadband account.

10

DIAL-UP INTERNET CONNECTIONS

Even with the rapid rise of broadband connections, the dial-up Internet account is still the most widely used. Because you can access a dial-up connection over standard phone lines, dial-up accounts are available just about everywhere. And because all modern Macs include a dial-up modem by default, you don't need any additional hardware to install and configure a dial-up account. Dial-up accounts are also relatively inexpensive and easy to configure.

The primary problem with dial-up connections is that they are slow. Even in the ideal case, a true 56K connection, a dial-up connection is just not fast enough to enable some of the more interesting applications on the Internet, such as video, audio, and moving large files (such as those 3MB or larger). And most of the time, you won't be connecting at your account's maximum speed—phone-line noise and other factors often limit the speed you can achieve. Another problem is that you have to establish a connection each time you want to use an Internet service. The connection process can take anywhere from 10 seconds to a minute or more depending on the particular situation. When you frequently need to access Net services throughout the day, the time you have to wait for a connection to be established can be quite annoying, not to mention a waste of your time.

Another problem with dial-up accounts is that they can be unreliable. You can experience busy signals, and your connection is dependent on the quality of the phone lines between you and your provider. Internet sessions are occasionally disconnected in the middle of doing something, such as downloading a file. This can be a huge waste of time, as well as frustrating.

If you use the Internet as much as most Mac users do, you should use a dial-up account only if one of the broadband connection technologies is not available to you or you can't afford one of the faster connection technologies.

NOTE

> If the Internet is vital to your business or other important activities, you might consider obtaining and maintaining a dial-up account as a relatively inexpensive backup. If your primary connection, such as cable service, goes down for some reason, you can switch to the dial-up account to access the Net. Some ISPs offer low-cost, low-usage accounts that are suitable for this purpose.

DSL CONNECTION

Digital subscriber line (DSL) accounts communicate over standard phone lines through a DSL modem. DSL accounts offer broadband communication speeds and always-on access.

The primary downside to DSL is that the technology requires that you be within a maximum distance from a central office or hub for the telephone company that provides service to your location. This maximum distance is fairly short (usually about 3 miles), and this single factor makes DSL unavailable for many locations. As telephone infrastructures improve, DSL service should become more widely available.

Because it is an always-on connection and you have the same IP address for long periods of time, security is a very important consideration when you use a DSL modem to access the Net. You must also install some type of protection to keep your machine from being hacked or used in an Internet attack on other sites. Fortunately, Mac OS X includes a firewall that does this for you, and most Internet sharing hubs protect your machines as well.

If DSL is available in your location and cable isn't an option, you should consider obtaining a DSL account.

NOTE

> You might notice that I am not being specific when I mention connection speeds. This is because most of the connection speeds quoted in advertisements or even in technical information are theoretical maximums. The actual speed you experience will depend on your specific situation and how your account is configured (for example, DSL accounts can offer various speeds). Generally, you need to consider whether you are dealing with a broadband connection (such as cable or DSL) or not (dial-up).

CABLE MODEM

Cable modem access is provided through a cable modem using the same cable over which cable TV service is provided. Cable Internet accounts offer broadband speeds (in fact, the speed of cable accounts is faster than most other technologies) and always-on access.

As with DSL, cable modem service is not available in every location. However, if your area is covered by a cable TV service, there is a good chance that cable modem service is currently offered in your area or soon will be. Because the cable infrastructure is already in place, companies can offer Internet access without making major infrastructure changes.

One downside to cable Internet access is that you share the data pipeline with other users of the service and the cable TV viewers who are on the same cable trunk you are on (such as a neighborhood). This means that the speed you experience is dependent on the load on the system at any point in time (whereas DSL uses a dedicated line to provide service to you so that you always experience the same speed—bear in mind that even at peak times, cable access is still usually somewhat faster than DSL). Another downside to cable is that it tends to be relatively expensive (typically about $50 per month). And you have to deal with the local cable company; these companies are not noted for having the best service practices.

Because it is an always-on connection and you have the same IP address for long periods of time, security is a very important consideration when you use a cable modem to access the Net. You must also install some type of protection to keep your machine from being hacked or used in an Internet attack on other sites. Fortunately, Mac OS X includes a firewall that does this for you, and most Internet sharing hubs protect your machines as well.

Even with these downsides (which are relatively minor compared to the benefits), a cable modem account can offer excellent performance and is worth exploring if the service is available in your area.

ISDN

For a time, integrated service digital network (ISDN) was going to be the thing to make Internet access faster because its access is significantly faster than standard dial-up connections. Because ISDN also uses standard phone lines, it is also widely available.

However, with the rise of cable and DSL technologies, ISDN has largely gone by the wayside. This is primarily because it is a slower connection technology than cable or DSL. To obtain high speeds with ISDN, you must use more than one phone line, which makes it quite expensive just to obtain speeds that can't match those that DSL or cable provide.

Nonetheless, ISDN can be a reasonable option if you want to have faster connection speeds than are provided over a dial-up account but can't access DSL or cable service.

SATELLITE

Satellite Internet access works much like satellite TV. The data is downloaded through a small satellite dish and fed to your Mac. The speed of communication is quite fast.

However, satellite Internet access has several disadvantages. The biggest is that some satellite accounts support only downloads, so you still maintain a separate account for uploading information. Second, you have to install the satellite dish. Third, and perhaps most importantly, not all satellite providers support Macs—the majority don't.

You should consider a satellite Internet account only in those cases in which you can't obtain broadband in any other way and you really need the additional download speed the satellite account provides. Because of its limited applicability, additional information on satellite access is beyond the scope of this chapter.

10

NOTE

Satellite Internet access can be more appealing if you also use a satellite for TV. Some satellite services combine TV and Internet access.

T-1 LINE

A T-1 line is a dedicated broadband connection delivered over a line consisting of 24 channels, with each channel delivering up to 64Kb per second. T-1 connections are the fastest possible for workstations but are also expensive and are usually limited to businesses to provide access for many people through a single account. Most providers also offer fractional T-1 service, in which only a portion of the 24 channels is dedicated to the subscriber.

Finding a T-1 provider is much like finding other providers; you should typically start with local ISPs who offer this service. After you have purchased a T-1 account, the ISP handles the installation and initial configuration of the line for you. Because T-1 and fractional T-1 connections are fairly complex and their costs limit them to business use, additional information about T-1 lines is beyond the scope of this chapter.

PICKING THE TECHNOLOGY

After you have an understanding of all the possibilities, you need to determine which technology is appropriate for you. Most Mac users will be better off with a broadband connection of some type; dial-up accounts just don't cut it for the most interesting Internet resources. However, if no broadband services are available in your area or you can't afford a broadband connection, dial-up certainly beats no Internet connection.

To determine which technologies are available to you, you need to obtain information from various ISPs that offer services in your area. Following are some tips to help you find an ISP:

- **One of the best sources of information about local ISPs is the people you know—** Many people in your immediate circle probably have Internet access through a local provider. You should ask these folks if they are happy with their providers. You can also find out which services are available, whether the provider has good technical support, how much the services cost, and so on. Using your personal network is an excellent way to find ISPs to contact.

- **If you have cable TV service, check with your cable company to see whether it offers Internet access—**Most cable companies advertise their Internet service to death, but some don't—especially when they first introduce it and want to test it on a limited number of users.

- **If you have access to the Internet, use the Web to locate a provider—**Go to `http://thelist.internet.com/`, which enables you to find local access providers for just about every location in the world (see Figure 10.1).

Figure 10.1
The List Web site lives up to its claims; it truly is the definitive ISP buyer's guide.

- **Check out the local news broadcasts in your area**—Almost all local TV stations have Web sites that are maintained by a local ISP. At the end of the broadcast, you will see a credits screen saying that Internet services are provided by XYZ Company. XYZ Company might be a good choice for you to check out.

- **Check with your company's ISP**—If the company you work for has a Web site that is administered by an outside ISP or if an outside ISP provides Net access for your company, check with that ISP to see which services it offers and whether it offers a discount for employees of your company. Often, an ISP will provide inexpensive Internet access to the employees of a company to which it provides business services.

- **Watch and listen for advertisements**—Most service providers advertise in local newspapers and on the radio and TV.

You should also check with national Internet access providers such as America Online (www.aol.com) or EarthLink (www.earthlink.net) to see which services are offered in your location.

TIP

> Many ISPs provide more than one connection technology for their accounts. When you contact an ISP, make sure that you ask about all the possible ways you might connect. Sometimes, especially when introducing a new access method, an ISP might not promote all its options.

The process of determining which connection technology is available to you should be fairly simple. If you have access to cable TV service, check with the cable provider to see whether it also offers Internet access. If so, obtain cost information. Most cable TV companies have a monopoly on the areas to which they provide service, so you usually have only one source to check for cable modem access.

NOTE

If you obtain a new Internet account via the Setup Assistant that runs when you install Mac OS X, you will use EarthLink, which has been the Mac's default ISP for some time. EarthLink is an excellent company and should be on your list of possible ISPs.

Earthlink offers numerous ways to connect, including cable, DSL, and dial-up. You should check out `www.earthlink.net` to see which of its Internet services are available at your location.

Next, try to determine whether DSL service is available in your location. The best way to do this is to search the Web for DSL providers in your state (see Figure 10.2). You can use a general search site to search for information about DSL providers in your state. Also, check the national DSL providers to see whether a company in their networks provides local DSL access. Typically, you can go to the provider's site and check availability of DSL service at your location. If the service is available, obtain information about the cost and whether the Mac is supported. You can also check with your telephone service provider because they typically offer DSL if your location supports it. If DSL service from one provider is not available at your location, it is likely that it is not available from any provider because they all use the same telephone infrastructure.

Figure 10.2
The DSLindiana Web site is a good example of a Web resource you can use to determine whether DSL is available in a specific area (the state of Indiana in this case).

Beware that DSL service is one of the most over-advertised and over-hyped services around. Just because you hear or see advertisements for local DSL service does not mean that it is actually available. Some of this advertisement is for "future" service, even though your location might not be close enough to a central phone node to be capable of accessing DSL from any provider. Even worse, sometimes the checks these organizations do on your phone line to see whether you can access this service are not reliable. I have heard more than one case in which the initial contact, even up to the point of signing a contract, indicated DSL service was available, but when the installation was attempted, it failed because the service was not really available.

Check with your local phone company and local ISPs to see whether ISDN service is available. Again, get cost information and see whether the Mac is supported.

Be careful about eliminating companies that claim not to provide Mac support. Most of the time, this just means they won't be able to provide tech support if you use a Mac. The service probably will work just fine. If you are comfortable that you will be able to solve any problems you encounter, not having tech support available might not be a problem for you. I prefer not to do business with companies that don't support the Mac, but you might have to choose otherwise to get the Internet access you want.

Finally, locate ISPs in your area that provide dial-up Internet access. This should be the most commonly available option, even if it isn't the most productive.

10

Making the Connection Work for You

You should ensure that any dial-up account you consider has a phone number you can dial without paying any time-based fees if possible. If you have to pay a usage charge while you connect to the Internet, you are likely to connect less frequently than you would like, or you will end up spending a lot of money for telephone charges. Usually, you should look for a provider that offers a number you can dial without any toll charges (long distance or otherwise).

One of the other important things to look for in a dial-up connection is an account that offers you unlimited access (or at least a very large number of hours per month). This means that you pay the same amount whether you are on the Net for 1 hour or 100. If you pay on some sort of time basis (such as so many dollars per hour), you will spend all your time worrying about how much time you have spent online instead of enjoying the Net. Fortunately, it isn't hard to find an unlimited account these days, although this wasn't always the case.

After you have obtained all the available connection information, you should be able to decide which technology is appropriate for you. If possible, try to locate a cable or DSL provider because you will get the most out of a broadband account. If all else fails, locate a good provider of dial-up access.

NOTE

In some cases, such as a DSL or dial-up account, you will have several ISP options. One of the most fundamental considerations is whether you use a national provider or a local one. National providers offer several advantages. In many cases, a national provider offers more extensive resources for you, such as better access to technical support, a self-install kit, and so on. National providers can enable you to access your account in different ways (such as DSL or dial-up) from many locations; if you travel often, this should be an important consideration for you. Local providers, on the other hand, often offer more personalized service and local resources.

OBTAINING AND CONFIGURING AN ACCOUNT

After you have decided on the technology, contact the provider to obtain an account. You usually have to call to set up your account, but some ISPs enable you to request service over the Net; others provide self-install kits that enable you to obtain and configure an account without any human intervention (one example is EarthLink).

If you use a broadband account of some sort, the provider sometimes installs any needed hardware for you, such as a cable modem, and configures your machine to use it (although self-install kits are becoming more common). If you use a dial-up account, you usually receive instructions about how to configure that account; some providers, such as EarthLink, provide software that does the installation and configuration for you.

CAUTION

Be wary about any dedicated "front-end" software a provider might want to install on your machine. Most of the time, this software consists of an application that gives you a specialized interface for using the service. This software is almost never necessary and can cause problems for you. It is better to just use the configuration information the provider gives you and then use Mac OS X software to access the Net.

Even if the provider handles the initial installation and configuration for your account, you still need to understand how to configure your account yourself. You should try to understand the configuration information related to your account. You at least should ensure that you have all the information you need to configure your account for the inevitable situation in which you must reconfigure it on your machine.

TIP

If your provider offers more than one way to connect, such as via a cable modem and a backup dial-up account, be sure you get the information you need for both connection methods.

The following data is required to configure your Mac for Internet access:

- **Type of configuration**—This information tells your computer which protocol to use to connect to the Net. If you are using a dial-up account, this is the Point-to-Point Protocol (PPP). If you are using a broadband connection, several possibilities exist, which include a static IP address, Dynamic Host Configuration Protocol (DHCP), PPP over Ethernet (PPPoE), DHCP with a fixed IP address, or the Bootstrap Protocol (BootP). A static IP address means that your Mac always has the same IP address. When you use DHCP, your provider assigns your Mac an IP address along with most of the other information you need to connect. PPPoE is most often used for DSL accounts and works similarly to PPP over a dial-up account. DHCP with a fixed IP address means that your IP address is fixed, but the DHCP server provides the other information for you. BootP access is used for "diskless" machines that use a server to provide the operating system.

- **IP address, subnet mask, and router**—These addresses locate your machine on the Internet and provide it with its address. Most dial-up accounts and many broadband accounts use dynamic IP addressing, which simply means that your Mac has an IP address assigned each time it connects rather than having a static address. If you have a manual or static IP address, it never changes and is permanently assigned to your machine. When you have a static IP address, you also need the subnet mask and router; with dynamic addressing, this information is provided by the server.

- **DHCP Client ID**—If you use DHCP access, you sometimes have a client ID name for your computer. In some situations, this is optional; however, if your provider includes a DHCP Client ID with your account, you need to use it. If you are configuring an account using a local DHCP server, you probably don't have to use a client ID.

- **Domain Name Server**—A domain name server (DNS) translates the addresses the computers use into English that we humans can usually understand. The DNS enables you to use an address such as www.companyname.com rather than having to deal with a series of numbers such as 233.453.22.345. The DNS number you need from your provider will be something such as 234.45.234.563. Ideally, your provider will include several DNS addresses so you have a backup in case the primary DNS fails. (If your DNS fails, you won't be able to access Web sites unless you know their numeric IP addresses.)

- **Search domain**—This information is related to the particular part of the provider's network on which you are located. It is usually optional. You might be provided with more than one search domain.

- **Usernames and passwords**—These are the two pieces of information that uniquely identify you and enable you to access your account. You probably chose your own username when you established your account. Your password might or might not have been assigned by the ISP.

  You might have more than one username or password. Sometimes, your ISP gives you one username and password that enable you to connect to the Net and another set (or maybe just a different password or username) to let you use your email account. Make sure that you know which is which and use the right ones in the right setting fields. If you use a PPPoE account, your username is your account name.

NOTE

> In some cases, you might not need a username and password to access the Net. For example, if you have a static IP address, you don't need a username and password to connect to the Net. However, you will need a username and password to access your email accounts.

■ **Phone number**—If you use a dial-up account, you need to have the phone number that you need to dial to reach your ISP. Some ISPs offer different numbers for different modem speeds, so be sure you get the phone number for your modem's speed.

■ **Email account information**—You will be given your email address (probably something such as username@isp.net). You will also need an address for the server that receives your mail (this often has a "pop" in it, such as pop.isp.net). The third piece of information you need is the address of the server that sends your mail (this often has "smtp" in it, such as smtp.isp.net). Some broadband accounts have simpler server configuration for both sides, such as "mail."

■ **News server**—You might also be provided with a newsgroup server (this enables you to read newsgroups), although dedicated news servers are not so common these days. It might look something like news.isp.net.

■ **Web customer support address**—If your account offers additional services, such as multiple email accounts, obtain the information you need to access that site so you can manage your account.

TIP

> Make sure that you collect and organize the information you need to access your account. You will need to reconfigure your Mac at some point and, if you don't have the information handy, this will be harder than it needs to be. One way to do this is to configure your account and after you are sure it works properly, you can take screenshots (Shift-⌘-3) of the various configuration screens. This enables you to quickly re-create your specific configuration. Of course, you should also keep copies of any information your provider gives you.

NOTE

> Most broadband providers include the modem hardware (such as a cable modem) you use to connect with your account. In some cases, they also install the hardware for you. However, you can usually supply your own hardware if you prefer (this is usually less expensive over the long haul). And, many providers offer "self-install" kits at local retailers. These kits include the hardware, software, and instructions you need to install the service yourself. (One benefit to these kits is that you don't have to wait all day for the cable guy to show up!)

If you need to install the modem you will be using, do so. In the case of an Ethernet-based connection, this requires you to connect the modem to your Mac's Ethernet or USB port or the WAN port on the hub on your network and then connect the modem to the source (such as the cable modem). If you have a modern Mac and will be using a dial-up account, the modem is already installed and you just need to connect it to a phone jack using a standard phone cable.

→ For information about various connection devices, such as Ethernet hubs, **see** Chapter 25, "Installing and Configuring Connecting Devices," **p. 807**.

→ In many situations, you will be able to share a single Internet account among many machines; **see** Chapter 27, "Sharing an Internet Connection," **p. 855**.

→ When you use a broadband connection, it is vital that you protect your Macs from Internet attacks; **see** "Defending Your Mac from Net Attacks," **p. 908**.

NOTE

My bias has probably already shown through, but in my experience cable Internet access is the way to go if it is available to you. The access speed is fast and the connections tend to be reliable. (It is delivered over the same infrastructure as cable TV service, and we know that people can't be without TV!) Because cable TV reaches a significant proportion of homes (in the United States at least), cable Net access is more likely to be available to you than even DSL. Typically, cable service is provided via DHCP, which makes configuration simple.

10

CONFIGURING YOUR MAC FOR INTERNET ACCESS

The three fundamental ways to connect a Mac to the Internet are dial-up accounts over a phone line and dial-up modem, broadband connections that use Ethernet, and wireless connections using AirPort. Although configuring dial-up accounts is relatively standard, many options are available for an Ethernet-based account. And, when you use AirPort to connect, you actually connect the AirPort hub (whether it is a Mac or an AirPort Base Station) through one of the two other methods.

→ A great way to network Macs and connect them to the Internet through a single account is by using AirPort; **see** Chapter 11, "Using an AirPort Network to Connect to the Internet," **p. 297**.

Providing the details of configuring every type of Internet account is beyond the scope of this chapter, but some examples of each type of access should enable you to configure your particular account.

NOTE

When you install Mac OS X on a Mac, the Internet Setup Assistant leads you through the configuration of your Internet account. You can launch the Internet Setup Assistant at other times to walk you through the configuration process by clicking the "Assist me" button on the Network pane of the System Preferences application.

If you use a provider that includes configuration software with your account, such as AOL, you can configure your account by using that software. In this section, you learn how to configure your account manually.

CAUTION

> Here's another caution about any specific access software a provider might give you to access this Net. This software tends to be more problematic than it is worth, especially if it is Web-based. When you get an account and such software is provided, ask the provider whether it is required. Many times, this software is mostly a way for the provider to generate revenue by using it to advertise. I recommend you avoid this kind of software if you can.

You can configure multiple sets of Internet configurations for your machine so that you can switch between them easily. And, you can have multiple accounts configured and active on a machine at the same time (they will be used according to the priority you determine). This is useful when you use your Mac in different locations—for example, with a PowerBook that you use at a work location and at home or while traveling. Another case in which this is useful is if you have several ways of connecting from the same location, such as via a cable modem or dial-up account. As with previous versions of the Mac OS, you use the Location Manager to manage the Internet configurations on your machine. If you envision needing to do this, you should set up a location before configuring it. If you will need only one set of configurations, you don't need to use the Location Manager. Also, a single location can include multiple configurations, such as a dial-up account and a cable modem account.

→ To learn how to configure and use locations, **see** "Configuring and Using Locations," **p. 989**.

The Internet accounts you configure on your Mac will be available to all users who have accounts on your machine.

Connecting to the Net with a Dial-up Account

As you read earlier in the chapter, dial-up access is still the most commonly used connection method. Dial-up access is available everywhere and is simple to configure and use (although solving connection problems can be tough).

Configuring Your Modem

All modern Macs include an internal 56K modem as standard equipment; very little work is required to configure the Apple internal modem.

NOTE

> If you use an external dial-up modem for some reason, you will need to obtain a Mac OS X–compatible driver for it and then configure that modem using the instructions provided by the manufacturer. Covering external modems is beyond the scope of this chapter.

To configure a modem, use the following steps:

1. Open the System Preferences utility and in the Internet & Network section, click the Network icon. The Network pane appears.

NOTE

If you are configuring more than one location, select the location you want to configure on the Location pop-up menu (Automatic is the default). You can also choose to create a new location on that menu (see Appendix B, "Computing on the Move with PowerBooks and iBooks," for details).

2. Select Network Status on the Show pop-up menu if it isn't selected already. In the lower part of the pane, you will see all the connection options available in the selected location. For example, if your Mac is connected to an Ethernet network, an AirPort network, and has an internal modem, you will see each of these connections listed in the window. When a connection is active, it has a green circle next to it. When the connection method is available but is not configured, it has a red circle instead (see Figure 10.3). If you use AirPort but it is not currently connected to the Internet, its status light will be yellow.

Figure 10.3
This Mac has two network connections available: AirPort and the internal modem. You can see the status of each.

3. Select Internal Modem from the Show pop-up menu.

4. Click the Modem tab (see Figure 10.4).

5. Use the pop-up menu, radio buttons, and check boxes to configure your modem. In most cases, the default values will work fine. If you use something other than the Apple Internal 56K Modem, select your modem from the Modem pop-up menu. If your telephone system is not touch-tone, you must click the Pulse radio button. Also, if you have voice mail or another system that can interfere with a standard dial tone (such as beeping to indicate that you have a message waiting for you), you need to uncheck the

"Wait for dial tone before dialing" check box. Leave the sound on until you are sure that your connection works reliably; the noise made by your modem can help you troubleshoot connection problems. After you are sure that your connection works, select the Off radio button to turn off your modem sound.

Figure 10.4
Generally, you should leave the options in the Modem tab in the default state.

6. Use the Country Setting tools to configure your modem for the country in which you are using it.

7. Check the "Show modem status in menu bar" check box. This places a telephone icon on your menu bar. You can use this to control and monitor your dial-up connection.

8. Click Apply Now to save any changes you make.

TIP

> When you are working with the Network pane, you can click the "Assist me" button to open the Network Setup Assistant. The application helps you configure network connections, such as a dial-up connection to the Internet. However, mostly what this does is just ask you for the same data you can more quickly enter manually.

CONFIGURING TCP/IP AND PPP

Next, you'll need to configure your TCP/IP and PPP settings:

1. Click the TCP/IP tab.

2. Select the configuration option you want from the Configure IPv4 pop-up menu. For almost all dial-up accounts, this should be Using PPP. If you use an AOL dial-up

account, select AOL Dialup. However, if your dial-up account includes a static IP address, select Manually and enter the IP address.

NOTE

IPv4 is the current Internet protocol standard in almost all situations. However, IPv6 is a newer standard that is being used in some research institutions. If you need to configure a connection based on IPv6, you can do so by clicking the Configure IPv6 button and using the resulting sheet to configure the service. In most cases, the automatic settings should work fine, but you can also enter manual settings if you need to.

3. If your provider provided DNS and search domains for your account, enter the information in the appropriate boxes.

4. Click the PPP tab (see Figure 10.5).

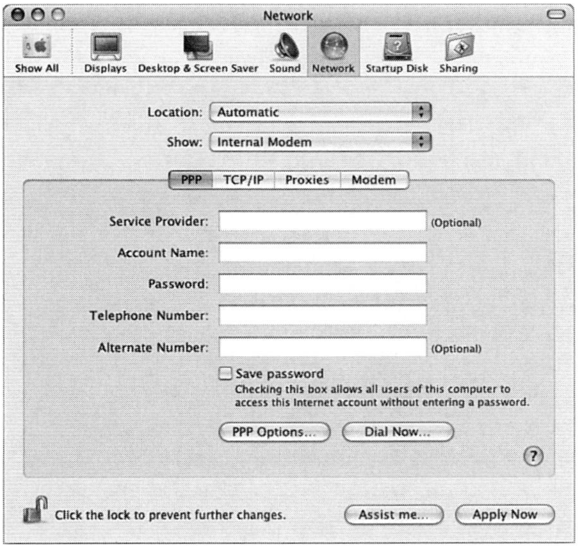

Figure 10.5
You use the PPP tab to configure your specific dial-up account.

5. Enter the name of your ISP in the Service Provider field. This is optional, but it is a good idea so that the connection is easy to identify by name.

6. Enter your access account name in the Account Name field. Make sure that you use the account name that will access your account; this might be different from your email user account name.

7. Enter your access password in the Password field and make sure that the "Save password" check box is checked. This is especially important if you share your Mac and want everyone to be able to access the Net. Again, your access password might be different from your email account password. If you prefer to have to enter your password each time you connect, leave the Password field empty.

NOTE

When you enter a password, the "Save password" check box is checked by default; if you uncheck it, your password will be deleted from the field.

8. Enter the telephone number you need to dial to connect to the provider in the Telephone Number field. Make sure that you enter the number *exactly* as you would dial it to make a standard phone call to this number. For example, if you need to dial an access code to reach an outside line, enter that code followed by a comma before the number (as in 9, 555-5555). If you need to dial a 1 or the area code to reach that number, enter those numbers as well.

If you have call waiting, you also need to enter the code to disable it, such as *70. If a call comes in while you are connected to the Net, the call waiting signal might disrupt or cancel your Net connection. Check with your telephone provider to find out the specific code you need to use to turn off call waiting. Remember to turn it back on when you are done with your Internet session.

9. If your provider offers more than one access number, enter the second one in the Alternate Number field. If you receive a busy signal when your Mac dials the first number, it will try the alternate number.

10. Click the PPP Options button to open the PPP Options sheet (see Figure 10.6). Use the controls on this sheet to configure your dial-up access.

Figure 10.6
The Session Options enable you to control how your dial-up account works.

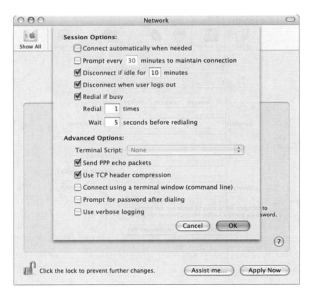

11. In most cases, you should check the "Connect automatically when needed" check box. This enables your Mac to automatically connect to the Net when it needs to. If you

have to pay for access by the minute or have to pay toll charges, you might want to leave this unchecked.

12. Use the next three check boxes to control how your Mac disconnects your connection:

- If you want to be prompted when your Mac is connected but is not actively using the connection, check the "Prompt every XX minutes to maintain connection" check box and enter the time after which you want to be prompted.

- If you want your Mac to automatically disconnect after a specific period of time, check the "Disconnect if idle for XX minutes" check box and enter the idle time. These options are beneficial primarily if you have to pay for access on a time basis or if you share a phone line for Internet access and voice conversations.

- Most users should check the "Disconnect when user logs out" check box so that the connection is broken when the current user logs out of the machine.

13. Use the redial controls to set the number of times you want your Mac to redial in the event of a busy signal and how long you want it to wait between tries.

NOTE

> Only in rare cases will you need to use the controls in the Advanced Options area. The options can be useful when troubleshooting a dial-up connection.

14. Click OK to close the PPP Options sheet, and then click Apply Now to save your changes.

NOTE

> A *proxy server* is a server that sits between your machine and the Internet and actually downloads and serves Internet resources to your machine. It is highly unlikely that you will use proxy servers with a dial-up account, although it is possible.

→ To learn how to configure proxies, **see** "Configuring TCP/IP Using a DHCP Server," **p. 286**.

CONFIGURING THE .MAC PANE OF THE SYSTEM PREFERENCES UTILITY

If you use a .Mac account, the last step is to configure the .Mac pane of the System Preferences utility for your account. This enables your Mac to automatically access your .Mac account when it needs to.

NOTE

> If you configured your .Mac account when you installed Mac OS X version 10.3 or chose to install it using an existing installation for which you had configured a .Mac account, you can skip these steps.

To configure the .Mac pane for the current account, do the following:

1. Open the .Mac pane of the System Preferences utility.
2. Click the .Mac tab if it isn't selected already.
3. Enter your .Mac member name.
4. Enter your .Mac password.
5. Click the iDisk tab.
6. Configure your iDisk. If you are using a dial-up connection, you probably don't want to synchronize your iDisk, so make sure that the "Create a local copy of your iDisk" check box is unchecked.

→ To learn more about configuring and using an iDisk, **see** Chapter 14, "Putting Yourself on the Web," **p. 423**.

7. Quit the System Preferences utility.

TESTING YOUR CONFIGURATION

You can test your account by opening an Internet application, such as a Web browser (assuming you enabled your Mac to connect automatically). If you are able to access Internet resources, your configuration is complete. Or, you can use the application that you use to manually connect and disconnect from your account, which is Internet Connect.

> **TIP**
>
> You can check your connection from the Network pane by clicking the Dial Now button on the PPP pane.

Test your configuration using these steps:

1. Open the Internet Connect application (Applications directory) and click the Internal Modem button on the toolbar. You will see the account information you configured earlier.
2. Click the Connect button. You will see the status of the connection in the window. You will also hear your modem dialing out and the delightful tones of the handshaking process. If your connection is successful, you will see the connected message and status information in the lower part of the Internet Connect window.
3. Click Disconnect to shut down the connection.
4. Quit Internet Connect.

If you are able to connect successfully, you can use Internet applications, such as your email and Web browser.

TIP

> In Internet Connect, select Window, Connection Log to see information about your connection status, such as the current IP address.

 If you are unable to connect using your dial-up account, see "My Dial-up Connection Fails to Connect" in the "Troubleshooting" section at the end of this chapter.

→ Using AirPort, you can easily set up a wireless connection to the Internet and share a single dial-up account among several machines. You can also use Mac OS X's built-in sharing capability to share a single account among several machines. **See** Chapter 27, "Sharing an Internet Connection," **p. 855**.

MANAGING A CONNECTION

If you choose to show the modem status in the menu bar, you can easily manage your connection from there. When you open the menu, you will see various options and information, depending on your modem's current status (see Figure 10.7).

Figure 10.7
The Modem status icon provides total control over your dial-up account from the desktop.

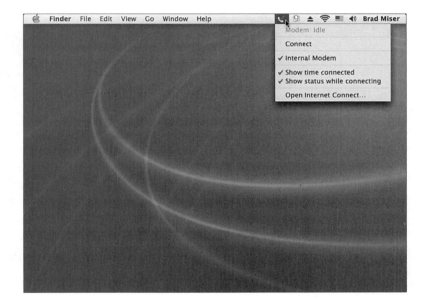

When you open the menu, you will see your modem's status. If disconnected, you can click Connect to connect and vice versa. You will also see which modem you have selected; you can open Internet Connect quickly and easily by selecting Open Internet Connect. You can also choose the status information that is displayed by selecting "Show time connected" or "Show status while connecting."

NOTE

> When you are connected to the Internet and Internet Connect is open, its icon includes a green lightning bolt. You can install Internet Connect on your Dock if you prefer to manage your connection from there rather than from the menu bar.

CONNECTING TO THE NET WITH ETHERNET

CAUTION

> As soon as you connect your Mac to the Internet with an always-on connection, especially one with a fixed IP address, your Mac becomes vulnerable to attacks from hackers. You shouldn't connect a machine to the Internet with a fixed address unless you have some type of firewall protection in place; fortunately, Mac OS X includes a built-in firewall.
>
> However, best practice is to install a hub between your Mac and the modem. Most hubs offer firewall protection and enable you to share an Internet account.

→ To learn how to install and use an AirPort Base Station as a hub, **see** Chapter 11, " Using an AirPort Network to Connect to the Internet," **p. 297**.

→ To learn how to install and use a hub to share an Internet account, **see** Chapter 27, "Sharing an Internet Connection," **p. 855**.

→ To learn how to protect your Mac from Net attacks, **see** "Defending Your Mac from Net Attacks," **p. 908**.

Configuring an Internet account for Ethernet connection is actually a bit simpler than configuring a dial-up account. The three main options you use for an Ethernet-based Internet account are Manual IP Settings, DHCP Server, and PPPoE. DHCP Server is the most likely option you will use. However, your ISP will tell you which option is appropriate for your connection.

Connect your Mac's Ethernet port to the cable modem or to the hub to which the cable or DSL modem is connected. Then, configure the OS to use that connection.

NOTE

> Some broadband modems connect to a USB port rather than an Ethernet port, but configuring the account on your Mac works in the same way.

CONFIGURING TCP/IP USING A DHCP SERVER

If your provider provides access through a DHCP server, configuring your account is straightforward.

NOTE

Many local area networks provide Internet access by installing a DHCP server on the network and connecting that server to the Internet (often with a T-1 line). In such cases, you can configure your Mac to use that DHCP server to connect to the Net just as you can when you deal directly with an ISP for an account.

To configure your account, do the following:

1. Open the Network pane of the System Preferences utility.

2. From the Show pop-up menu, select Built-In Ethernet (see Figure 10.8).

Figure 10.8
Use the Built-in Ethernet option on the Show pop-up menu to configure an Ethernet Internet connection.

10

3. Click the TCP/IP tab.

4. Select Using DHCP from the Configure IPv4 menu.

5. If you have a DHCP Client ID (your ISP will tell you if this is the case), enter it in the DHCP Client ID field. (If you are using a DHCP server on a local network, you can probably leave this field empty. In some cases, you can leave this field empty even when you are using an ISP to gain Internet access.)

6. If you have DNS and search domain information, enter it in the appropriate fields (these are optional when you use a DHCP server).

7. If you are on a network that uses a proxy server, click the Proxies tab and configure the proxies for your network.

→ For more information about proxy servers, **see** "Understanding and Configuring Proxy Servers," **p. 289**.

8. Click Apply Now to save your changes.

9. Open an Internet application, such as a Web browser. If you can access Internet resources, your configuration is complete.

10. Configure the .Mac pane of the System Preferences utility if you have a .Mac account.

→ For more information about configuring the .Mac pane, **see** "Configuring the .Mac Pane of the System Preferences Utility," **p. 283**.

 If you are unable to access Internet resources after configuring your account with a DHCP server, see "My Ethernet Connection Can't Connect" in the "Troubleshooting" section at the end of this chapter.

CONFIGURING STATIC TCP/IP SETTINGS

If your provider supplies a static or manual address for you, use the following steps to configure it:

1. Open the Network pane of the System Preferences utility.

2. From the Show pop-up menu, select Built-in Ethernet.

3. Click the TCP/IP tab.

4. Select Manually from the Configure IPv4 pop-up menu.

NOTE

> You can also use a static IP address with the router being assigned dynamically. If this is the case for you, select "Using DHCP with manual address" instead of Manually. The rest of the steps are the same, except you don't configure the router because that is done for you by the DHCP router.

5. Enter the IP Address, Subnet Mask, Router, DNS, and Search Domains information your ISP provided in the appropriate fields.

6. Click Apply Now to save your changes.

7. Open an Internet application, such as a Web browser. If you can access Internet resources, your configuration is complete.

8. Configure the .Mac pane of the System Preferences utility if you have a .Mac account.

→ For more information about configuring the .Mac pane, **see** "Configuring the .Mac Pane of the System Preferences Utility," **p. 283**.

 If you are unable to access Internet resources after configuring your account manually, see "My Ethernet Connection Can't Connect" in the "Troubleshooting" section at the end of this chapter.

NOTE

> IPv4 is the current Internet protocol standard in almost situations. However, IPv6 is a newer standard that is being used in some research institutions. If you need to configure a connection based on IPv6, you can do so by clicking the Configure IPv6 button and using the resulting sheet to configure the service. In most cases, the automatic settings should work fine, but you can also enter manual settings if you need to.

UNDERSTANDING AND CONFIGURING PROXY SERVERS

A *proxy server* is a server that sits between end-user computers on a network and the Internet. All Internet traffic of a specific type (such as HTTP for Web pages) passes through a specific proxy server. There can be separate proxy servers for each type of service (such as HTTP, FTP, and so on), or a network can use a single proxy server for all Internet services.

When a machine on the network requests a resource (such as a Web page), the proxy server downloads the resource and serves it to the machine as if the resources originated from the proxy server itself (although the user doesn't notice that the page is being served by the proxy server instead of the server hosting the requested page).

Proxy servers serve two main purposes:

- **They can improve speed in some cases**—Because the Internet resources are downloaded to the proxy server and then served to users on the local network, after the first access, subsequent accesses to that resource are much faster. This is true because the resource must be downloaded from the Internet to the proxy server only once; from there, it can be served to users on the local network rather than downloading it from the Internet each time.

- **They can be used to filter requests**—Because all information from the Internet flows through a proxy server, that server can be set to block access to specific Internet resources.

NOTE

> For more information on proxy servers, see `http://webopedia.internet.com/TERM/p/proxy_server.html`.

If you are on a network that uses proxy servers, you use the Proxies tab of the Network pane of the System Preferences utility to configure them (see Figure 10.9). You configure a proxy for a specific service by checking the check box for that service and entering the proxy address and port in the appropriate fields. Typically, you obtain the proxy server information you need from your network administrator.

Figure 10.9
If you need to configure Internet access through a proxy server, you use the Proxies tab to do so.

CONFIGURING A PPPoE ACCOUNT

Configuring a PPPoE account is more complicated than the other Ethernet options, but it still doesn't take more than a few minutes:

1. Open the Network pane of the System Preferences utility.

2. From the Show pop-up menu, select Built-In Ethernet.

3. Configure the TCP/IP settings for your PPPoE account (see the previous sections for details).

4. Click the PPPoE tab (see Figure 10.10).

5. Check the "Connect using PPPoE" check box.

6. Enter the name of your service provider in the Service Provider field. (This is optional.)

7. Enter your access account name in the Account Name field.

8. Enter your access password in the Password field; again this might be different from your email account password. If you leave this field empty, you must enter your password each time you connect. (When you enter a password, the "Save password" check box is checked by default; if you uncheck the check box, your password is deleted from the field.)

9. Enter the service name in the PPPoE Service Name field. (This is also optional.)

10. Check the "Show PPPoE status in menu bar" check box. This puts a menu on the menu bar that you can use to control your PPPoE connection.

11. Click the PPPoE Options button to open the Session Options sheet. Use the controls on this sheet to configure your Internet access.

Figure 10.10
Use the PPPoE tab to configure a PPP over Ethernet connection.

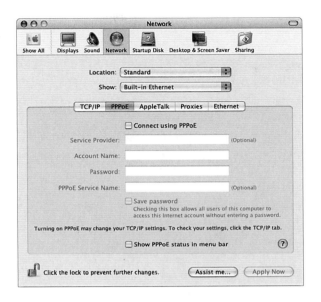

12. In most cases, you should check the "Connect automatically when needed" check box. This enables your Mac to automatically connect to the Net when it needs to.

13. Use the next three check boxes to control how your Mac monitors your connection. If you want to be prompted when your Mac is connected but is not actively using the connection, check the "Prompt every XX minutes to maintain connection" check box and enter the time after which you want to be prompted to maintain the connection. If you want your Mac to automatically disconnect after a specific period of time, check the "Disconnect if idle for" check box and enter the idle time. Most users should check the "Disconnect when user logs out" check box so that the connection is broken when the current user logs out of the machine.

> **NOTE**
>
> In only rare cases will you need to use the controls in the Advanced Options area. The options can be useful when troubleshooting a PPPoE connection.

14. Click OK to close the PPPoE Options sheet, and then click Apply Now to save your changes.

TESTING A PPPoE CONNECTION

You can test your account by opening an Internet application, such as a Web browser (assuming you enabled your Mac to connect automatically). If you are able to access Internet resources, your configuration is complete. Or, you can use the application that you use to manually connect and disconnect from your account, which is Internet Connect. Do the following:

1. Open the Internet Connect application (if you turned on the PPPoE status menu, open it and select Open Internet Connect).

2. Select Built-In Ethernet from the Configuration pop-up menu. You will see the PPPoE account information you configured earlier.

3. Click the Connect button. You will see the status of the connection in the window. If your connection is successful, you will see the connected message and status information in the lower part of the Internet Connect window.

4. Click Disconnect to shut down the connection.

5. Quit Internet Connect.

If you are able to connect successfully, you can use Internet applications, such as your email and Web browser. You can monitor and control your connection from the PPPoE status menu on the menu bar.

→ If you use a .Mac account, you need to configure it on your Mac, **see** "Configuring the .Mac Pane of the System Preferences Utility," **p. 283**.

TIP

> In Internet Connect, select Window, Connection Log to see information about your connection status, such as the current IP address.

NOTE

> You can also add Internet Connect to the Dock. When the Internet Connect icon appears in the Dock, it displays a green lightning bolt when you are connected to the Internet.

 If you aren't able to connect to the Internet, see "My Ethernet Connection Can't Connect" in the "Troubleshooting" section at the end of this chapter.

→ To learn how to share a single Internet connection among multiple Macs, **see** Chapter 27, "Sharing an Internet Connection," **p. 855**.

MANAGING MULTIPLE INTERNET ACCOUNTS

If the Internet is vital to you, such as for business purposes, you might have more than one Internet account you access in different ways. For example, you might use a cable modem as your primary access and maintain a dial-up account as a backup. You can maintain multiple Internet accounts on a single Mac.

You can manage the Internet accounts on your machine through the Network Port Configurations pane of the Network pane of the System Preferences utility (see Figure 10.11).

Figure 10.11
Use the Network Port Configurations controls to manage multiple network connections, such as Internet accounts, on a single machine.

In Figure 10.11, three Internet connections have been configured and two are active. The active ports are AirPort and Built-in Ethernet. The Internal Modem configuration is available but is not active. (You can tell which ports are active by the check marks.) The order in which the ports are listed determines which port is tried first when a connection is needed. In this example, the AirPort connection will be tried first, followed by the Built-in Ethernet port.

To configure multiple accounts, do the following:

1. Open the Network pane of the System Preferences utility.

2. Select the port you want to be your primary connection method on the Show menu.

3. Configure that port for the related account (see the previous sections in this chapter for details). For example, configure your machine to use an Ethernet network to connect to the Internet.

4. From the Show menu, select Network Port Configurations.

5. Make sure the connection you configured is turned on (its check box is checked) and that it is first in the list of port configurations.

6. From the Show menu, select the port you want to be the second connection option, such as an internal modem.

7. Repeat steps 2–4 to configure that account.

8. Make sure that the port is turned on; it should appear second in the list of port configurations.

9. Continue configuring ports you want to be active and arranging them on the list in the order in which you want them to be used.

10. Turn off any ports you don't use. Turning off active ports might provide some small performance and boot time improvements, and it might make your Mac more secure. But mostly it is a matter of keeping your configuration settings as accurate as possible.

11. Click Apply Now and then quit the System Preferences utility.

When your machine needs to connect to the Internet, it tries the accounts you specified in the order in which you specified them. Following are some other points about managing multiple connections:

- You can have more than one configuration of the same port. To create a new instance of a port, click the New button. Name the port and then select the type of port it is (Internal Modem, External Modem, Built-in Ethernet, and so on). Click OK and the new port appears on the list. You can configure it in the same way as the default ports. For example, new ports you create appear on the Show menu; select the port to configure it.

- AirPort, PPPoE, internal modem, and external modem ports appear on the Configuration pop-up menu in Internet Connect. You can use that application to manage those connections.

- The Duplicate button duplicates a port configuration. This can be useful when you are configuring more than one port of the same type.

- You can edit a port's name by double-clicking it.

TIP

Only those ports that are active appear on the Show pop-up menu.

You can also maintain multiple sets of network and Internet configurations that you create and maintain through the Location Manager. For example, if you use a PowerBook, you might have a configuration when you use the machine from home, another when you use it from work, and so on.

→ To learn how to configure and use locations, **see** "Configuring and Using Locations," **p. 989**.

TROUBLESHOOTING

MY DIAL-UP CONNECTION FAILS TO CONNECT

I've followed the steps for configuring my account, but I still can't connect via a dial-up connection. What is causing this?

Troubleshooting a dial-up connection can be difficult. However, the following list of guidelines can help you solve your connection problems:

- The most common cause of connection problems is an improperly configured machine. Run through all the steps provided to configure a dial-up connection to ensure that you have entered the correct information.

- If you don't hear the modem dialing, make sure you have the modem sound enabled. If you still don't hear the modem dialing out when you attempt to connect, check the modem configuration you learned about earlier in the chapter.

- If you hear the modem dialing but the call is never answered, your ISP might be offline for some reason or you might not have the correct phone number configured. Double-check the phone number you entered to ensure that you entered the access phone number, and make sure you entered it the same way as you would have to dial that number on the phone.

- If you hear the call being answered but you never reach the connection state, a problem exists with the communication between your modem and ISP. The most likely cause of this is an incorrect username or password; make sure you are using your access username and password rather than your email username and password.

You can sometimes get a better insight into what is happening by using the Terminal window to connect:

1. Open the Session Options sheet in the PPP tab of the Network pane of the System Preferences utility.

2. Check the "Connect using a terminal window (command line)" check box.

3. Click OK and then click Apply Now.

4. Open Internet Connect and click Connect. After your modem dials your ISP, you will see the Terminal window. If you see a login prompt, you are successfully communicating with your provider. If you don't see the login prompt, something is wrong with your configuration or your ISP is offline.

5. At the login prompt, type your access username and press Return.

6. At the password prompt, type your access password and press Return. If your login was successful, the Terminal window disappears and you are connected. If it wasn't successful, a problem probably exists with your user account. Contact your ISP for assistance.

If you have worked through these paragraphs but still can't connect, call your ISP for help.

MY ETHERNET CONNECTION CAN'T CONNECT

I've followed the steps for configuring my Ethernet connection, but I still can't get a successful connection. How do I figure out where I'm going wrong?

The most common cause of problems connecting with an Ethernet account is an incorrect configuration. Still, there can be other problems as well. The following guidelines should help you troubleshoot problems you experience when trying to connect with an Ethernet-based connection:

- If you are using a modem (such as a cable modem), make sure that the modem you are using is powered up and properly connected to your Mac. Most modems have power, PC link, and activity lights. If any of these don't indicate the proper status, check your modem installation.

- If you are using an ISP for access, make sure that the ISP services are currently available. Usually, ISPs provide a status hotline you can call to see whether problems with service have been reported in your area. If there are problems, you will have to wait for the provider to correct them before you will be able to connect (in these situations, it is nice to have a backup account, such as a dial-up account).

- Work through the configuration steps for your account again, being especially careful to check all the configuration information you enter.

- If you are using a DHCP server, see whether you can obtain static settings for your account. Sometimes, you will be able to connect to an account with static settings when the automatic (DHCP) settings fail. If you use DHCP, check the IP address listed in the Sharing pane of the System Preferences utility. If you see one that starts with 169, that means your Mac is not obtaining an IP address from the provider and so won't be able to connect to the Internet. You must either figure out why it isn't able to obtain an IP address from your ISP or use a manual IP address.

- If you use a DHCP service and something changes, your Mac's IP address can become invalid. When this happens, you lose your Internet connection. You can force the system to get a new address by opening the TCP/IP pane and clicking the Renew DHCP Lease button. This attempts to obtain a new IP address and might solve the problem.

- If you are still unable to connect, contact the service provider or network administrator from whom you obtain your service. Confirm that you are using the correct installation information for your account. If you are, ask for assistance in troubleshooting the connection from the provider's end.

> **TIP**
>
> If you are troubleshooting the connection of a machine on a network, try isolating that machine from the rest of the network while you are troubleshooting. This eliminates the potential for problems induced by other machines on the network and helps you more quickly isolate the cause of the problem you are trying to solve. For example, if you connect through a hub attached to a modem, connect your Mac directly to the modem; of course, be careful to turn on your Mac's firewall before you do this.

Getting Help

In past versions of the Mac OS, the OS itself was sometimes responsible for Ethernet connection problems. For example, under Mac OS 9.2 and earlier versions, the Mac had unreliable support for certain types of DHCP servers, and it was often necessary to switch to static settings. These issues have been eliminated under Mac OS X.

Be aware that you might get flak from your ISP's technical support when you tell them you are using a Mac. Because the Mac has a smaller number of users, the tech support person to whom you talk will probably have less experience with Macs than with Windows machines. Also, many technical support people, such as those with cable companies, are overloaded and will try to get you off the line as soon as possible. If your problem doesn't fit into a checklist, they might want to stop before your problem is solved. Try to stay positive; you might have to be assertive (not aggressive) to get the support you need. Sometimes, it is better to explore the support area of a provider's Web site (which, of course, assumes that you can connect in some fashion, perhaps from another computer) before calling for help.

CHAPTER 11

USING AN AIRPORT NETWORK TO CONNECT TO THE INTERNET

In this chapter

AirPort Wireless Networking

AirPort is an amazing technology that makes wireless communication affordable to own and relatively simple to install and configure. With AirPort, you can quickly and easily set up and manage a wireless network to do the following tasks:

- **Connect to the Net**—You can use AirPort to connect to the Internet wirelessly, and you can easily share a single Internet connection among multiple Macs.

- **Connect to a network**—You can connect an AirPort-equipped Mac to an existing Ethernet (wired) network.

- **Share a USB printer**—You can connect a USB printer directly to an AirPort base station to share that printer with AirPort devices.

- **Connect directly to other AirPort-equipped computers**—You can directly network to one or more AirPort-equipped computers. As long as all the computers are set up to use the same AirPort connection, they can communicate with each other up to 150 feet apart. This makes instant, temporary networks fast and easy.

AirPort functionality is provided through the following components:

- **AirPort-ready Macs**—If your Mac is AirPort ready, it has built-in antennas that are used to transmit and receive signals to and from the wireless network. It also has a slot in which you can install an AirPort card. The good news is that all modern Macs are AirPort compatible.

NOTE

> Power Mac G5s have an AirPort antenna port into which you plug an external antenna.

- **AirPort card**—To use AirPort, your Mac must have an AirPort card installed in it. There is more good news here too: AirPort Extreme cards cost only about $99, whereas AirPort cards are about $79. Both are simple to install. If you use a PowerMac G5, you also need an external AirPort antenna, which is provided with the Mac.

- **AirPort software**—The AirPort software is necessary for Macs to communicate through the AirPort hardware. The software to configure and use an AirPort network is part of the standard Mac OS X installation.

- **AirPort base station**—The AirPort base station transmits the signals for the AirPort network. There are two basic types of base stations. The AirPort Extreme hardware access point (HAP) is a dedicated hardware device that contains access points for a modem, USB printer, and an Ethernet network. When you use it for a dial-up connection to the Internet, for example, the AirPort base station's modem is used to connect to the Net. Your Mac communicates to the base station through the AirPort card and antenna. A single AirPort HAP can support multiple computers so you can share a n Internet connection among up to 50 computers. You can also configure any

AirPort-equipped Mac to act as a base station by using Mac OS X's built-in Internet sharing capabilities.

NOTE

> Functionally, an AirPort HAP and an AirPort-equipped Mac OS X machine sharing its Internet connection are identical. In this chapter, when I use the term *base station*, it can refer to either means of providing an AirPort network.

The general steps to configure and use an AirPort network are the following:

1. Install and configure the base station (AirPort HAP or an AirPort-equipped Mac OS X machine).
2. Install AirPort cards in the machines you want to connect to the AirPort network.
3. Configure those machines to use the AirPort network.

NOTE

> Although using AirPort to connect to the Internet and to share an Internet account is the focus of this chapter, an AirPort network provides access to all the services of a wired network. For example, computers connected to a wired network via AirPort can print to printers on that network, use file sharing, and so on. If you connect a USB printer to an AirPort Extreme base station, you can share that printer with any AirPort-equipped Mac.

11

Before getting into the meat of this chapter, there are a few AirPort tidbits you need to understand.

The two flavors of AirPort are AirPort and AirPort Extreme.

AirPort is the original incarnation and offers many wireless benefits. AirPort communicates at 11Mbps and is compatible with wireless devices based on the 802.11b standard.

AirPort Extreme is the newer standard and offers even more benefits. First, is speed. AirPort Extreme communicates at 54Mbps, which is almost five times the speed at which the original AirPort communicates. AirPort Extreme is compatible with devices using the 802.11g Wi-Fi standard. Second, AirPort Extreme can support more computers at the same time than does AirPort. Third, AirPort Extreme enables you to share a USB printer from a hub. Fourth, with AirPort Extreme, you can wirelessly link Base Stations together to expand the range of an AirPort network to cover large areas.

Mac OS X supports both flavors of AirPort, but specific Mac models support either AirPort or AirPort Extreme; in other words, some Macs can support an AirPort card, whereas others support AirPort Extreme cards. The two cards are not interchangeable. To find out which flavor your Mac supports, check its documentation. At press time, all shipping Macs support AirPort Extreme.

Fortunately, even though the hardware for the two standards is different, it is compatible. AirPort machines can connect to AirPort Extreme networks, and vice versa. The primary difference is that AirPort networks are much slower than AirPort Extreme networks are. And, AirPort Extreme base stations offer more features than AirPort base stations do.

Because it is the newer standard, this chapter focuses mostly on AirPort Extreme. I do my best to use the term *AirPort Extreme* when discussing something that is specific to AirPort Extreme technology or *AirPort Standard* when referring to the older technology. When I use the term *AirPort*, I mean to refer to something that is applicable to both technologies.

NOTE

> Because it is based on the 802.11 standards, AirPort is compatible with 802.11 networks and devices. For example, you can connect an AirPort-equipped Mac to any wireless network that supports 802.11b or 802.11g (Extreme only) devices, such as those designed for Windows computers. Similarly, Windows machines equipped with 802.11b or 802.11g devices can also access an AirPort network.

SETTING UP AN AIRPORT BASE STATION

Setting up an AirPort base station is slightly different depending on the type of base station you use: the AirPort HAP or an AirPort-equipped Mac OS X machine that provides Internet sharing.

The benefit of using an AirPort HAP is that it doesn't place any processing load on an individual Mac and is intended to run at all times, so the AirPort network is always available. It also provides the ability to share an Internet connection with devices to which it is networked using an Ethernet connection. The disadvantage of this device is its cost (currently $199 without a modem and antenna port or $249 with modem and antenna port direct from Apple). If you are going to use an AirPort network regularly to serve more than one or two machines, an AirPort HAP is a good investment.

The benefit of using an AirPort-equipped Mac OS X machine as a base station is that you don't need to purchase any additional hardware (except for the AirPort card in the Mac that will act as the base station). You get most of the functionality of the AirPort HAP but don't have to support another dedicated device. Using this method does have several disadvantages, though. One is that it places additional processing load on the machine that acts as the base station. Another is that the network can be affected by the state of that machine. For example, if the machine is shut down or crashes, the network is taken down as well. Another is that a Mac acting as a base station doesn't support all the HAP's features, such as the option to add an antenna or to wirelessly link base stations together to increase the range of a network.

NOTE

> You can have multiple base stations operating in the same area at the same time to grow your AirPort network to be quite large.

SETTING UP AN AIRPORT HARDWARE ACCESS POINT

Apple's AirPort Extreme hardware access point (also called the AirPort Extreme base station) is a relatively simple device. It contains a transmitter that broadcasts the signal over which the network is provided. It has two Ethernet ports. One is used to connect to a broadband Internet connection, such as a cable modem. The other is used to connect to a wired Ethernet network so the base station can also share its Internet connection with the machines connected to that network. Along with the power adapter port, if offers a USB port to which you can connect a USB printer to share that printer with an AirPort network.

The AirPort Extreme base station comes in two models. One offers only the ports described previously, but the other model also includes a 56K modem, enabling you to use it to connect to a dial-up Internet account, and an antenna port to which you can connect an external antenna to increase the range of a network.

The AirPort HAP also includes the software it needs to perform its functions.

NOTE

> The only reason I use the term *HAP* is to distinguish between a dedicated hardware device and using a Mac as a base station. In practice, these devices are called *base stations*.

11

Setting up an AirPort HAP consists of the following two tasks:

1. Install the AirPort HAP.
2. Configure the AirPort network, including the Internet connection the base station will use to connect to the Internet.

INSTALLING THE BASE STATION

There is not much to installing the AirPort base station.

First, you locate the device in a central area so it provides the maximum amount of coverage where you install it. In most houses, the AirPort base station provides adequate signal strength even if you locate it at one end of the house and place machines you want to network at the other end. However, the closer the machines are to the base station, the stronger the signal is.

NOTE

> AirPort Extreme signals don't offer the range that AirPort Standard signals do. If you want to provide AirPort Extreme services over a large distance (such as greater than 150 feet depending on the environment), you should get the base station model that includes an antenna port and add an antenna to it.

Of course, a major consideration for the location of the base station is where your Internet connection will come from. If you use a cable modem, you need to locate the device so that you can connect the cable modem to it. If you use a DSL modem, you need to locate the base station relatively close to the phone line port to which the DSL modem is attached.

After you have placed the base station in its location, attach its power adapter to the station and plug it in to a wall outlet. Attach the base station's modem port to a phone jack if you will be connecting to the Internet via a dial-up account. If you will be using the AirPort HAP to connect to the Internet via a cable or other broadband connection, connect the Ethernet (WAN) port on the AirPort HAP to the broadband modem.

NOTE

> The first generation of HAPs included only one Ethernet port. This meant you could use the hub as an Internet sharing hub for a wired or a wireless network, but not both. Either you had to connect the access point to the broadband connection and use only AirPort-equipped Macs to share the account, or you had to connect the hub to a wired network that already had a hub providing sharing services and have the access point share the connection as well. Fortunately, all AirPort Extreme base stations offer two ports as do newer AirPort base stations.

If you are going to use the base station to act as a sharing hub for an Ethernet network, attach an Ethernet cable to the station's network Ethernet (LAN) port. If you want to use the base station to network your Mac with a single computer, you can connect the Ethernet port on the other computer to the base station with an Ethernet crossover cable. Otherwise, attach a standard Ethernet cable to your base station and to an Ethernet hub.

NOTE

> Some modern Macs, such as the PowerBook G4, don't require the use of an Ethernet crossover cable. The port automatically senses whether it is connected to another machine or to a hub and communicates appropriately.

→ To learn more about Ethernet, **see** "Ethernet," **p. 705**.

If you want to share a USB printer with all AirPort-equipped Macs that can access the network, connect the printer's USB cable to the USB port on the base station.

CONFIGURING THE BASE STATION

After you have installed the base station, you need to configure it. You can configure it manually through the AirPort Admin Utility, or you can use the AirPort Setup Assistant to configure it for you. With either method, you configure the base station from a machine with which it can communicate either via AirPort or through an Ethernet network.

NOTE

> The machine you use to configure a base station must have an AirPort card installed in it to use the AirPort Setup Assistant. It does not need to have an AirPort card if it is connected to the access point via Ethernet.

→ To learn how to install an AirPort card, **see** "Installing an AirPort Card," **p. 318**.

CONFIGURING THE BASE STATION USING THE AIRPORT SETUP ASSISTANT

Use the following steps to configure the base station using the AirPort Setup Assistant:

1. Configure the Internet connection on the Mac from which you will be configuring the base station in the same way that the base station is going to be configured. For example, if the base station will be using a dial-up account, configure the Mac using that account.

→ To learn how to configure a Mac for the Internet, **see** Chapter 10, "Connecting Your Mac to the Internet," **p. 263**.

2. Open the AirPort Setup Assistant (Applications/Utilities) to see the first window in the Assistant (see Figure 11.1).

Figure 11.1
The AirPort Setup Assistant guides you through the steps to configure an AirPort base station or an AirPort-equipped Mac to access the AirPort network you create.

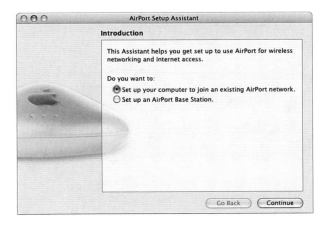

3. Click the "Set up an AirPort Base Station" radio button and click Continue. The Select an AirPort network dialog box opens.

CAUTION

If you are configuring an access point that has already been configured and is protected by a password, you have to enter that password before you can proceed.

If the base station you are configuring has outdated software installed on it, the Setup Assistant attempts to update it. To do so, you must be able to connect to the Internet, which is sort of a Catch-22 in that it assumes that it is already configured and you are reconfiguring it. You can download the update to the Mac you are going to use to configure the base station and then the base station can update its software from there.

4. Choose the base station you want to configure from the "Available AirPort networks" pop-up menu and click Continue. If you have only one base station in range, it is selected automatically.

5. Enter the password for the base station you selected in the previous step and click Continue. If you are configuring a new base station or one that has to be reset, the password is public.

NOTE

Some base stations have two passwords. One is to join the network, and the other allows you to configure the base station itself. If you are prompted to enter a second password, do so.

6. Click the "I am using another Internet Service Provider" radio button and click Continue. The Internet Access window opens (see Figure 11.2).

Figure 11.2
Configuring an AirPort base station for Internet access is similar to configuring a Mac for Internet access.

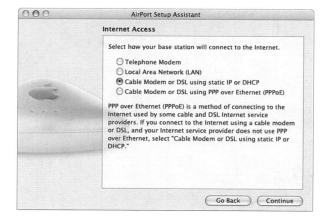

NOTE

You can also use an AirPort base station to connect to an AOL account. If so, select the "I am using America Online" radio button in the previous step and follow the onscreen instructions.

7. Choose the method by which the AirPort base station will connect to the Internet. Most of the options are the same as when you configure a Mac to access the Internet. For example, to configure the base station's dial-up modem, click Telephone Modem and then click Continue. You see the Internet configuration of the machine you are using to set up the base station. For example, if you are configuring the dial-up account, you see the Modem Access screen. The information for the dial-up account of the Mac you are using is shown. The one that is not the same as when you configure a Mac is the Local Area Network (LAN) option. You should choose this one when you are connecting the access point to a wired network that already has Internet sharing services on it; in this case, the access point uses the same DHCP services to connect to the Internet as the other machines on the wired network.

NOTE

> If you have more than one network port configured for the same type of access, you see information for the port that has the highest priority. For example, if you have two dial-up accounts configured on your machine, you see the information for the one higher on the list of network ports in the Network pane of the System Preferences utility.

8. Make any changes to the Access window that you need to. If the Mac you are using can connect to the Internet using the same settings, you shouldn't need to make many changes.

    If you are using a dial-up account, check the "Automatically dial" check box to allow the base station to connect to the Internet automatically when it needs to. In some cases, this setting is not carried over from the PPP Options area of the Network pane of the System Preferences utility.

    When you use an AirPort HAP with a dial-up account on your only phone line, it is especially important that you set the configuration to disconnect automatically after a specific amount of idle time passes. Because you don't deal directly with the AirPort HAP, it isn't easy to tell when it is connected and your phone line might be busy without your knowing about it.

→ To understand how to configure the access option you selected, **see** Chapter 10, "Connecting Your Mac to the Internet," **p. 263**.

9. When you are done configuring the access method, click Continue. The Network Name and Password dialog box opens.

10. Configure the network you are creating by entering the network's name and the network password. Users will identify the AirPort network you are creating by its name and will need to enter the password you give your network to connect to it. You have to type the password twice to verify it.

11. Use the WEP Key Length pop-up menu to choose how the base station should encrypt data over the network. The options are 40-bit and 128-bit. The larger value is more secure.

11

NOTE

Wired Equivalent Privacy (WEP) is an encryption strategy that attempts to provide wireless networks with the same level of protection that wired networks have. WEP does provide improved security compared to nonencrypted transmissions, but be aware that it does have some flaws, as do almost all security measures.

12. Click Continue to see the Base Station Password dialog box. This dialog box enables you to set a separate administration password for the access point. The network password you create should be different from the base station's network password. If you make them the same, anyone who uses the network will also be able to administer it (which might not be a problem if you are the only person using the AirPort network). If you want to use the same password for the network and the base station, click the "Use the same password" radio button and skip the next two steps.

13. Click the "Assign a separate password" radio button and click Continue.

14. Enter the base station password in the Base Station Password box and in the Retype password box; then click Continue. You see the Conclusion screen.

15. In the Conclusion dialog box, click Continue. The base station configuration is updated and the base station is reset. A dialog box stating that the configuration was successful appears (see Figure 11.3).

Figure 11.3
When you see this screen, the base station is ready to use.

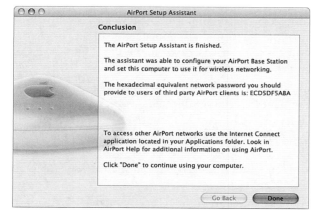

16. Click Done. The AirPort Setup Assistant quits and the AirPort network becomes available to any AirPort-equipped Mac within the access point's range.

If you see an error message stating that the required AirPort hardware was not found when you started the AirPort Setup Assistant, see "No AirPort Hardware Is Found" in the "Troubleshooting" section at the end of this chapter.

If you can't access the base station because you don't know the password, see "I Don't Know the Base Station Password" in the "Troubleshooting" section at the end of this chapter.

CONFIGURING A BASE STATION MANUALLY

You should also know how to manually configure the base station. Manual configuration can be a better and more complete way to configure it. If you want to change only one aspect of a base station's configuration, using the manual method is the way to go. And, it can also be a faster way to configure a base station. For example, you need to manually configure a base station when you want to share an Internet account with other machines on an Ethernet network or to use the AirPort base station as a bridge between the wireless network and a wired one (for example, to allow AirPort-equipped machines to use a printer connected to a wired network). You use the AirPort Admin Utility application to configure an access point manually. You can do so with the following steps:

> **NOTE**
>
> The original Graphite base station did not include a LAN port that you could use to connect the station to a wired network at the same time you connected it to a broadband modem. Because of this, its configuration is slightly different from the newer Snow and AirPort Extreme base stations. The most significant difference is that you have to configure a Graphite base station to provide services to a wired network. This is explained in the "OS X to the Max" section at the end of this chapter.

1. Open the AirPort Admin Utility (Applications/Utilities). The Select Base Station window opens (see Figure 11.4).

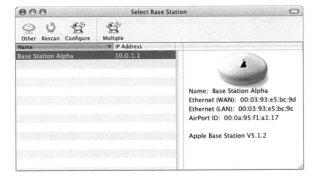

Figure 11.4
The AirPort Admin Utility enables you to configure a base station manually.

2. Select the base station you want to configure and click Configure (if there is only one base station in range, it is selected automatically).

 If you get an error message when trying to configure your base station manually, see "I Can't Configure My Base Station Manually" in the "Troubleshooting" section at the end of this chapter.

3. If the base station has been reset, you see a dialog box informing you that the base station has been reset and is not currently configured. (If the base station has not been reset, you won't have to do this step.) Click Automatic and then authenticate yourself

using an administrator name and password. The software reconfigures the base station and restarts it. When it is complete, you return to the Select Base Station window. Click Configure again.

NOTE

When you have problems with a base station, sometimes you must reset it so that it returns to its default settings (in effect, you start over).

You next see a window that has the base station name as its title (see Figure 11.5).

Figure 11.5
This window enables you to access all aspects of a base station.

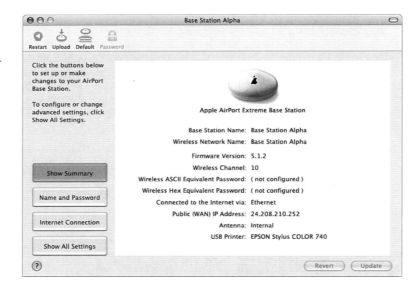

This window has the following controls:

- **Restart**—This button causes the base station to restart. You must do this occasionally if you are experiencing problems.
- **Upload**—This button enables you to upload revised software onto the base station to update it.
- **Default**—This returns the base station to its defaults.
- **Password**—Use this button to change the base station's password.
- **Show Summary**—This presents the summary window for the base station, which is the default view. This view presents information about the base station at a summary level. This includes the station's name, its firmware version, the channel it is using, and so on.
- **Name and Password**—This button enables you to change the name and password for the base station.

- **Internet Connection**—This opens the tools you use to configure the base station's Internet connection.
- **Show All Settings**—This button exposes a tabbed interface that enables you to access all the base station's configuration.

NOTE

These steps assume the base station you are configuring has been configured previously. If not, the steps might be slightly different.

4. Click the Show All Settings button. This opens all the configuration areas for the base station and presents a tabbed interface (see Figure 11.6).

Figure 11.6
You can use this view to quickly access any configuration control for a base station.

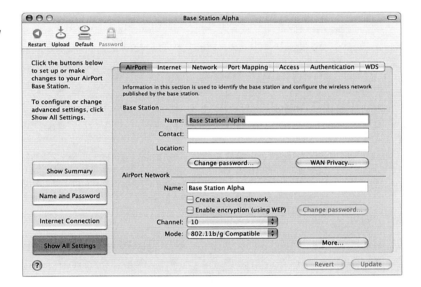

5. Select the AirPort tab if it isn't selected already. On this tab, you can change the identification information for the base station and configure how it serves its network.

6. Enter the base station name (this is the name of the hardware, not the name of the network it provides) in the Name field, the contact for the base station in the Contact field, and the station's location in the Location field (this information can help users contact you for help).

7. To change the base station's password (not the network's password), use the "Change password" button. In the resulting sheet, type and verify the new password and click OK.

8. If you want to configure various aspects of the base station's security settings, click the WAN Privacy button. Use the resulting sheet to select the security options you want to

enable or disable. Generally, the more options you select, the less secure the network will be. Check the boxes for the options you want to enable and click OK. The available options are the following:

- **SNMP Access**—The Simple Network Management Protocol network management service makes networks easier to manage, but it also makes them somewhat more vulnerable to denial-of-service attacks (where servers are overloaded because numerous, bogus requests for service are received). Generally, you should leave this option on.

- **Remote Configuration**—This setting enables a base station to be configured over its WAN port. If you uncheck this box, you can configure the base station by connecting it to a LAN or by using an AirPort network.

- **Remote Printer Access**—Use this option if you want printers to be accessible via the WAN port.

- **Default Host**—If you want to be able to play network games over AirPort, check the Enable Default Host check box and enter the IP address of the machine that will act as the host for the game.

9. Enter the name of the network that will be provided in the Name field in the AirPort Network area of the window.

NOTE

> If the base station is already providing a network and you change the name or password of the network, people who use the network need to change the network they use. The new network name appears as an available network on the client machines, but you must provide the new password to those whom you want to use the network.

10. If you want to create a closed network, check the "Create a closed network" check box. A closed network does not appear on other users' AirPort menus. To join closed networks, users have to know the name and password for that network (because they can't see the network on a menu). Using a closed network is a good way to keep your network more secure.

11. Use the "Enable encryption (using WEP)" check box to encrypt data over the network. You should usually leave this check box enabled.

NOTE

> Wired Equivalent Privacy (WEP) is an encryption strategy that attempts to provide wireless networks with the same level of protection that wired networks have. WEP does provide improved security compared to nonencrypted transmissions, but be aware that it does have some flaws as do almost all security measures. If the information that is transmitted over your network is very sensitive, you should use WEP to provide at least some protection.

12. Use the "Change password" button to change the network password. In the resulting sheet, enter the password and verify it. Then choose the level of encryption you want to use on the WEP key length pop-up menu. Click OK to return to the Base Station window.

13. Use the Channel pop-up menu to select the channel over which the base station communicates. Generally, the default channel works fine, but if you are having trouble communicating with devices, you can try different channels to improve signal transmission and reception. If you have mulitple AirPort networks in the same area, you can use the Channel pop-up menu to have each network use a different channel so that they don't interfere with one another.

14. If you are configuring an AirPort Extreme base station, use the Mode pop-up menu to choose the wireless standard used on the network. Use 802.11b/g Compatible to make the network available to both 802.11b (AirPort) and 802.11g (AirPort Extreme) devices. You can also select 802.11g only or 802.11b only. You use one of these options if you want to restrict the network to one of these protocols for some reason.

15. Click the More button to see the More sheet (see Figure 11.7). These settings control the physical properties of the base station's signal. Generally, the default settings will work fine. However, if you have problems providing a network, you can adjust these settings, such as the multicast rate, to obtain better performance.

Figure 11.7
Use this sheet to configure certain physical aspects of the signals used on an AirPort network.

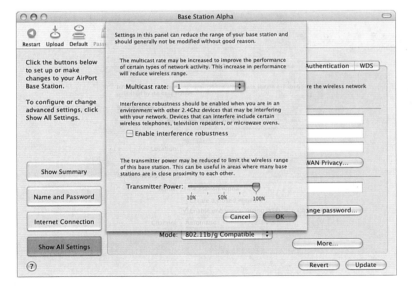

16. Use the "Multicast rate" pop-up menu to set the multicast rate. Choosing a higher value improves performance but also reduces range.

17. Use the "Enable interference robustness" check box to make the AirPort signal less sensitive to interference.

18. Use the Transmitter Power slider to change the strength of the base station's signal. If many base stations exist in the same physical area, reduce the signal strength to limit the interference of these stations with one another. You can also reduce the strength to limit the size of the AirPort network's coverage.

19. Click OK to return to the Base Station window.

20. Click the Internet tab and configure the base station for Internet access. This works similarly to configuring a Mac for Internet access. Choose the connection method from the Connect using pop-up menu and then enter the settings you want to use in the lower part of the window.

→ To learn how to configure a Mac for the Internet, **see** Chapter 10, "Connecting Your Mac to the Internet," **p. 263**.

NOTE

One additional control available for a base station's Internet access that is not present for a Mac is the WAN Ethernet Speed pop-up menu. Use this to set the speed at which the base station communicates with a wired network over its LAN port. In most cases, the Automatic (Default) value is the best choice, but you can choose a specific speed.

21. Click the Network tab to control how the base station provides services to the network (see Figure 11.8).

Figure 11.8
Use the Network tab to configure the services the base station provides to the network.

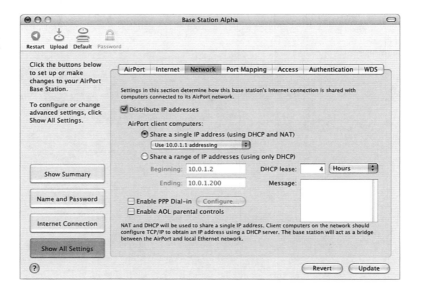

The default settings enable all the machines connecting to the AirPort network to share the base station's Internet account. By default, the base station provides IP addresses to each machine dynamically and uses NAT protection to isolate the IP addresses of each machine from the connection to the Internet. To choose this option, click the "Share a single IP address (using DHCP and NAT)" radio button. Then select the range of addresses that should be assigned to each device on the network using the pop-up menu. In most cases, the "Use 10.0.1.1 addressing" option will work, but you can choose a different range if you want to.

If you want to use a specific set of IP addresses, check the "Share a range of IP addresses (using only DHCP)" check box and enter the starting and ending IP numbers you want to assign. As machines connect to your network, these IP addresses are assigned to each machine that connects (you have to have enough addresses in the range so one is available for each machine). Use the "DHCP lease" box and pop-up menu to set the number of hours for the DHCP lease on each machine. When this time passes, a new address is assigned to each machine. You can enter a DHCP lease message in the Message box.

→ To learn how to configure a Graphite base station so that all the machines on a network, including machines connected via Ethernet, can share the same Internet account, **see** "Using a Graphite AirPort Base Station to Share an Internet Connection with a Wired Network," **p. 325**.

22. Use the Port Mapping tab to add more ports to the network for other services, such as AppleShare, Web sharing, and so on. (Covering these options is beyond the scope of this chapter.)

23. Use the Access tab if you want to limit network access to machines with specific AirPort ID numbers (you find these numbers on the client machines, as you will see in a later section). Click Add, enter the AirPort ID of the machines to which you want to allow access to your network, enter a description of the machine, and click OK. Only the machines with AirPort IDs shown in the list can then access your network. (If the list is empty, any AirPort machines can connect by using the network's password.)

24. Use the Authentication tab to configure a RADIUS server for the AirPort network. This prevents AirPort machines without valid IDs from connecting to the network. Explaining the details of this is beyond the scope of this chapter.

25. Use the WDS tab to configure multiple base stations to provide a single network to extend its range.

→ To learn how to configure WDS, **see** "Making AirPort Go Farther," **p. 326**.

26. Click Update to transfer the settings to the base station. The base station is restarted after the settings have been transferred.

27. When the process is complete, click OK; you return to the Select Base Station window.

28. Quit the AirPort Admin utility.

If you see an error message stating that the required AirPort hardware was not found when you started the AirPort Admin Utility, see "No AirPort Hardware Is Found" in the "Troubleshooting" section at the end of this chapter.

NOTE

> For more detailed information on AirPort, visit Apple's Knowledge Base at `http://kbase.info.apple.com/` and search for AirPort.

You can now access the Net from an AirPort-equipped Mac using the AirPort network. The base station also provides services to a wired network if it is connected to one.

CONFIGURING AN AIRPORT-EQUIPPED MAC TO ACT AS A BASE STATION

As you learned earlier, you can use any AirPort-equipped Mac running Mac OS X to act as a base station. When you do this, the Mac OS X machine provides services similar to those that a HAP provides, but you don't have as much control over the AirPort network.

CAUTION

> For a Mac to act as a base station, you must first disable its built-in firewall by using the Firewall tab of the Sharing pane of the System Preferences utility. If the Mac you use is connected directly to the Internet, such as through a cable modem, it is vulnerable to attack. You should use a Mac as a base station only if it is protected by some other means, such as a hardware firewall or an Internet sharing hub that offers NAT protection.

→ To learn how to enable or disable the Mac OS X firewall, **see** "Defending Your Mac Against Net Hackers," **p. 911**.

To configure a Mac as a base station, perform the following steps:

1. Install an AirPort card in the machine you are going to use as a base station.

→ To learn how to install an AirPort card, **see** "Installing an AirPort Card," **p. 318**.

2. Configure that machine so it can connect to the Internet, such as through DHCP services provided on an Ethernet network or over a dial-up account.

→ To learn how to configure a Mac for the Internet, **see** Chapter 10, "Connecting Your Mac to the Internet," **p. 263**.

3. Open the Network pane of the System Preferences utility.

4. Select AirPort on the Show menu.

5. Click the AirPort tab (see Figure 11.9).

6. Check the "Allow this computer to create networks" check box.

7. Open the Sharing pane of the System Preferences utility and click the Internet tab (see Figure 11.10).

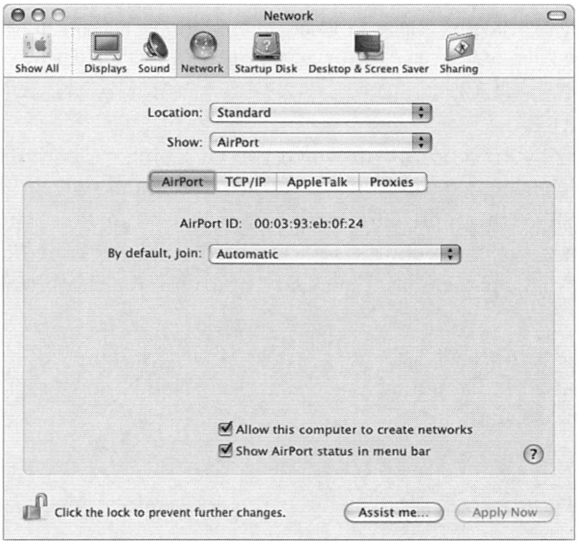

Figure 11.9
Using the AirPort tab, you can enable an AirPort-equipped Mac to provide an AirPort network.

Figure 11.10
You use the controls on the Internet tab of the Sharing pane to enable a Mac to share its Internet connection with other computers.

8. Select the Internet connection you want to share with other machines on the "Share your connection from" pop-up menu. For example, if your computer gets its Internet connection from a wired network, select Built-in Ethernet.

NOTE

You can choose to share a connection from a wired network to AirPort-equipped machines or from an AirPort-equipped machine to a wired network.

9. Select the type of connections with which you are going to share the machine's Internet connection by checking the appropriate "To computers using" check box. For example, if you want to share the connection with computers via AirPort, check AirPort, and if you want to share the connection via a wired network, check the Built-in Ethernet check box. You can choose more than one connection type with which to share the connection.

10. If you enabled AirPort sharing, select AirPort and click the AirPort Options button. The AirPort network configuration sheet appears (see Figure 11.11).

Figure 11.11
With this sheet, you configure the AirPort network your Mac provides to other machines.

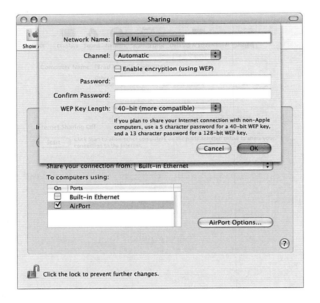

11. Edit the default name as needed. The default name is the name of your computer, but you can make it something more interesting if you want to.

12. Unless you have multiple AirPort networks active in the same area or you experience interference that prevents your network from operating properly, leave the Channel pop-up menu set to Automatic. If you want to choose a channel manually, select it on the pop-up menu.

13. For a more secure network, check the "Enable encryption (using WEP)" check box.

NOTE

> WEP is an encryption strategy that attempts to provide wireless networks with the same level of protection that wired networks have. WEP does provide improved security compared to nonencrypted transmissions, but be aware that it does have some flaws as do almost all security measures. If the information transmitted over your network is very sensitive, you should use WEP to provide at least some protection.

14. Enter the network password in the Password and Confirm Password fields. This is the password users will enter to connect to the network.

15. Select an encryption key length on the WEP Key Length pop-up menu. The options are 40-bit and 128-bit. If only newer Macs running Mac OS X will be connecting to the network, select 128-bit. If you aren't sure which level of encryption other machines can support, select 40-bit. If you don't want to use the encryption at all, uncheck the "Enable encryption (using WEP)" check box.

16. Click OK.

17. Click Start. The Internet connection is shared with other computers via AirPort or built-in Ethernet.

18. Use the Services pane to configure other services you will provide over the network, such as File and Printer Sharing. Your Mac then begins providing services over AirPort and its network becomes available to AirPort-equipped Macs.

→ To learn how to configure sharing services, **see** "Configuring the Services on a Network," **p. 827**.

TIP

> If Printer Sharing is enabled, USB printers connected to the Mac acting as a base station are also available to the AirPort network. This is a great way to share USB printers with other Macs. Also, the AirPort menu on the menu bar on a Mac acting as a base station is different than the menu on a client machine. This menu also has different options than a client menu.

Using a Mac As a Base Station

One of the disadvantages of using a Mac as a base station is that the Mac must be on for the network to be available. If that Mac is turned off or crashes, the AirPort network is lost.

Another disadvantage of using a Mac as a base station is that you can't have Mac OS X's built-in firewall turned on. This means that if the Mac you are using to provide the network is connected directly to the Internet, such as through a cable modem, it is vulnerable to attack. (If it is protected by some other device, such as a sharing hub, it is okay to have its firewall turned off.)

If the Mac that is acting as the base station goes into Sleep mode, its services are also lost. Use the Energy Saver pane of the System Preferences utility to ensure that the software base station machine never sleeps while you want the AirPort network to be available. Also, if Sleep interrupts AirPort network services, client machines might have to quit and then restart Internet applications, such as Safari, to resume using the network.

→ To learn how to control sleep, **see** "Managing Your Mobile Mac's Power," **p. 982**.

CONNECTING TO THE AIRPORT NETWORK WITH MAC OS X

After an AirPort network has been established, you can access it from any AirPort-equipped Mac (running Mac OS 9 or Mac OS X). First, install an AirPort card in each Mac you want to add to the network. Then, configure each Mac to access the AirPort network.

INSTALLING AN AIRPORT CARD

An AirPort card contains the hardware receiver, transmitter, and firmware that enables a Mac to communicate with an AirPort network (including a base station or other AirPort-equipped machines). Each machine that will access an AirPort network must have an AirPort card installed in it. When your Mac detects that an AirPort card is installed, it activates the AirPort software that is part of all Mac OS installations since Mac OS 9.

If you ordered an AirPort card to be installed when you ordered your Mac, you can skip this section. If you obtained the AirPort card separately, you need to install it in the AirPort card slot in your Mac. Generally, this involves exposing the AirPort card slot, inserting the card in the slot, connecting the antenna to the card, and then closing up the machine.

As with base stations, there are AirPort cards and AirPort Extreme cards. These cards can be used only in compatible machines—that is, you can't use an AirPort Extreme card in a machine that has an AirPort slot, and vice versa.

On Power Mac G4s and G5s, you open the case to access the AirPort card slot. On older iMacs, you open the rear panel to expose the slot (for some iMacs, the card fits into an adapter that you install into the iMac AirPort card slot). Newer iMacs have the AirPort card slot on the bottom side of the case. On PowerBooks and iBooks, the AirPort card slot is located underneath the keyboard or just above the bottom cover (on PowerBook G4s, you remove the bottom cover to access the AirPort card slot).

NOTE

> When you order an AirPort card separately from a machine, it includes an installation pamphlet that provides installation instructions for every Mac model. The owner's manual for your Mac also contains the instructions you need to install an AirPort card.

Because of the differences in the location of AirPort slots on various models, the exact steps to install the card are slightly different. However, installing a card is never particularly difficult. As an example, the following steps describe how to install the card in a Power Mac G4:

1. Shut down the machine, disconnect any cables that prevent you from opening the case, and open the case.

2. Locate the AirPort card slot; in Power Mac G4s, the slot is located on the same side as the motherboard near the front of the machine toward the bottom of the case (see Figure 11.12).

Figure 11.12
Installing an AirPort card in a Power Mac G4 takes less than 5 minutes (and most of that time is required to disconnect and reconnect cables).

AirPort card slot

3. Insert the card into the metal guide with the bar code side of the card up; push the card until the end of the card is inserted into the connector mounted on the motherboard.

4. Connect the antenna to the hole on the card (see Figure 11.13).

Figure 11.13
This Power Mac G4 has an AirPort card installed and is now ready to connect via AirPort.

5. Close up the case, reconnect any cables you disconnected, and restart the machine.

11

NOTE

Power Mac G5s use an external AirPort antenna. Connect the antenna that is provided with the machine or with the AirPort card to the external antenna port.

CONFIGURING MAC OS X TO JOIN AN AIRPORT NETWORK

To access an AirPort network, you must configure a Mac OS X machine to connect to it.

You can do this in several ways. First, use the AirPort tab of the Network pane of the System Preferences utility to determine which AirPort networks your Mac uses by default when it restarts or wakes up from sleep.

Configure your default, or preferred, AirPort network with the following steps:

1. Open the System Preferences utility and click the Network icon to open the Network pane. Select AirPort from the Show pop-up menu.

2. Click the AirPort tab (see Figure 11.14).

Figure 11.14
This Mac has been configured to use the Base Station Alpha network by default.

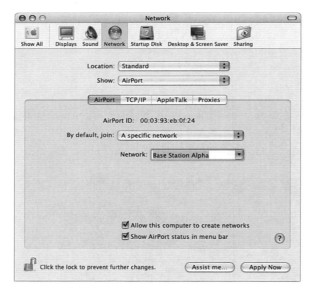

3. To have your Mac join the AirPort network with the strongest signal, select Automatic on the "By default, join" pop-up menu. This causes your Mac to scan all the available networks and log on to the one that has the best signal. If you haven't saved the password for the network your Mac selects, you must enter the password manually.

4. To join a specific network, select "A specific network" on the "By default, join" pop-up menu, select the network you want to join on the drop-down list, and enter the password if the network requires one.

5. Check the "Show AirPort status in menu bar" check box to put the AirPort menu on your menu bar. You can use this icon to quickly select and control your AirPort connection.

6. Click Apply Now and quit the System Preferences utility.

NOTE

As your Mac connects to the network, the name of the network to which you are connecting briefly appears next to the AirPort icon in the menu bar.

If you want to use an AirPort network other than your preferred one, select the network you want to use on the AirPort menu on the menu bar and select the AirPort network to which you want to connect (see Figure 11.15). If its password is not already stored on your keychain, you are prompted to enter it. Do so and you are logged on to the AirPort network.

Figure 11.15
The AirPort icon on the menu bar provides control over AirPort under Mac OS X (the current AirPort network is marked with a check mark).

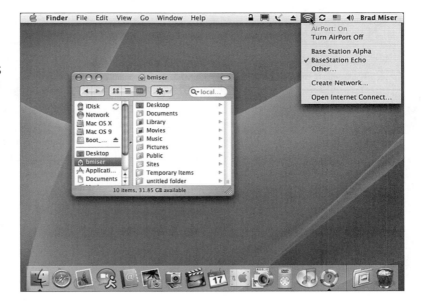

TIP

When prompted to enter your password, check the Add to Keychain check box to have Mac OS X remember the password so you don't have to enter it again.

 If you can access an AirPort network but can't access the Internet, see "I Can't Access the Internet Through AirPort Even Though I Can Connect to the AirPort Network" in the "Troubleshooting" section at the end of this chapter.

You can use the AirPort menu on the menu bar to control AirPort in several ways, including the following:

- **Measure the signal strength of the connection**—The "waves" emanating from the AirPort icon show the relative strength of the signal your Mac is receiving. As long as you see two or more waves, the signal you are receiving is plenty strong.

- **Turn AirPort on or off**—You can disconnect your Mac from the AirPort network and disable AirPort services by selecting Turn AirPort Off.

- **Choose a different AirPort network from the list of available networks**—When you do so, you are prompted to enter the password for that network—unless you have saved the password to your keychain. Do so and you change to the network you select.

NOTE

> Some AirPort networks are hidden and do not broadcast their identities. To join such a network, you must know the name and password of the network you want to join. To join a hidden network, select Other on the AirPort menu on the menu bar, enter the name and password for the network, and click OK.

- **Create a computer-to-computer network**—When you select Create Network, you can create a network between two or more AirPort-equipped Macs. In the Computer to Computer dialog box, enter the name and password of the network you are creating, select the channel you want to use, and then click OK. Other users can select the network on their AirPort menus (of course, you need to provide the password for your network to those users if you require one). When your Mac is hosting a computer-to-computer network, the AirPort icon changes to a Mac "inside" a quarter circle to show that you are in the computer-to-computer mode. To switch to another AirPort network, select it on the AirPort menu.

The Channel you choose for a network controls the frequency of the signal used to create an AirPort network. If you have trouble connecting to other machines over the network you create, try a different channel.

When you create and use a computer-to-computer network, other AirPort connections, such as the one you use to connect to the Internet, are deselected and therefore can't be used.

To require and configure a password for the network, click Show Options in the Computer to Computer dialog box.

TIP

> Computer-to-computer networks are a great way to play network games. You can create an AirPort network and host a game. Other users can connect to the network and join the game by selecting your network using their AirPort controls.

■ **Open Internet Connect to control the Internet connection**—You can select Open Internet Connect to open the Internet Connect application to control the connection you are using via AirPort. You can turn AirPort on or off, select the network you want to use, see the strength of the signal your machine is receiving, and so on (see Figure 11.16). For example, if your base station connects to the Internet over a dial-up connection, click the Disconnect button to disconnect the base station from the Internet. To connect again manually, click the Connect button.

Figure 11.16
You can also control an AirPort connection to the Net by using the Internet Connect application.

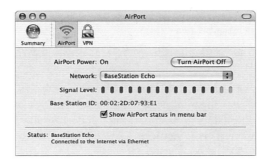

NOTE

To use Internet Connect to control an AirPort network, click the AirPort button on the Internet Connect toolbar. Internet Connect works for an AirPort connection very similarly to how it works for a dial-up connection.

 If you are getting no signal or a weak signal from the AirPort network you want to join, see "Weak Signal" in the "Troubleshooting" section at the end of this chapter.

Using AirPort is a great way to quickly create and use wireless networks. After you have connected to the Net without wires (especially when roaming with a PowerBook or iBook), you won't want to settle for anything else.

Although this chapter has focused on using AirPort to access the Internet, an AirPort connection works just like any other network connection (such as an Ethernet connection). For example, you can access the files on another machine over an AirPort network just as you can with an Ethernet network.

→ For more information about configuring other network services; **see** Chapter 26, "Building and Using a Network," **p. 821**.

TROUBLESHOOTING

NO AIRPORT HARDWARE IS FOUND

When I launch the AirPort Setup Assistant, I see an error message stating that the required AirPort hardware can't be found.

The AirPort software requires that you have an AirPort card installed on the machine you use to configure a HAP base station. If an AirPort card is not found, the software won't run.

If you don't have an AirPort card installed in your Mac, you need to do so before running the AirPort Setup Assistant.

If you do have an AirPort card installed, it is not properly installed. Repeat the installation steps to ensure that the card is properly installed.

→ To learn how to install an AirPort card, **see** "Installing an AirPort Card," **p. 318**.

I CAN'T CONFIGURE MY BASE STATION MANUALLY

When I try to configure a base station manually, I get an error stating that the base station can't be configured.

This problem can occur for various reasons. First, try resetting the base station (see the next section). If that doesn't work, try opening the AirPort Setup Assistant and configuring the base station using the assistant. Then, go back into the AirPort Admin Utility and try to configure the base station again. This sometimes clears the error.

I DON'T KNOW THE BASE STATION PASSWORD

I can't access the base station because I don't know its password.

When you have trouble with an AirPort HAP, you can reset it to its factory defaults by inserting a paper clip into the reset button hole on the bottom or back of the unit. Hold down the button for 5 seconds and the base station is reset—all settings are returned to the default and the password becomes public.

WEAK SIGNAL

My AirPort signal strength is low. Or, I can't find the network to which I want to connect.

Two primary factors affect the strength of the AirPort signal your Mac receives from a base station (hardware or software) or from Macs providing a computer-to-computer network. One is the distance from the base station to your Mac; the other is the amount of interference in the area.

If your Mac is within 150 feet of the base station you want to use, there should be no trouble getting a strong enough signal. If you are at the edge of or beyond that range, move your Mac closer to the base station or move the base station closer to you. You can also try repositioning the base station because it can sometimes be affected by materials or other fields between it and your Mac.

If you are close to the base station but can't get a strong signal, try changing the frequency of the network in the event that it is being interfered with by another signal of some type.

→ To learn how to change an AirPort network's frequency, **see** "Configuring a Base Station Manually," **p. 307**.

If you use an AirPort Extreme base station with an antenna port, you can add an antenna to extend its range. You can also daisy-chain base stations together.

→ To learn how to use WDS, **see** "Making AirPort Go Farther," **p. 326**.

I CAN'T ACCESS THE INTERNET THROUGH AIRPORT EVEN THOUGH I CAN CONNECT TO THE AIRPORT NETWORK

My Mac is connected to an AirPort network, but I can't access the Internet.

If you are connecting to the Internet through a HAP, the most likely cause is that the access point has lost its Internet connection. Use some means to confirm that Internet services are available to the base station, such as by using a machine connected independently or calling your service provider. If services are available, use the AirPort Admin Utility to check its configuration to ensure that it is correct. If all else fails, reset the access point.

If you are connecting through a network provided by a Mac acting as a base station, make sure that the Mac is still running and that its firewall is *not* turned on. The Mac OS X firewall blocks access to the Internet from machines attempting to use it in that way.

It is also possible that the base station Mac went into Sleep mode. If so, wake it; then quit any Internet applications on the machine with which you are trying to connect to the Internet and restart them.

If that doesn't work, restart the machine itself and try again.

If none of these steps works and you have a broadband modem connected to the base station that provides DHCP services, use the following steps to attempt to reset the connection:

1. Unplug the modem for at least 20 seconds, and then plug it back in again. This forces the modem to get a new address.
2. Reset the base station by pressing its reset button for 5 seconds.
3. Open the AirPort Setup Assistance and select the Join an Existing Network option.
4. Follow the onscreen instructions to update the base station.

MAC OS X TO THE MAX: MAKING THE MOST OF AIRPORT

AirPort is an amazingly powerful yet easy-to-use technology. In the section, you learn a couple of tricks to make the most of it.

USING A GRAPHITE AIRPORT BASE STATION TO SHARE AN INTERNET CONNECTION WITH A WIRED NETWORK

AirPort enables you to easily share an Internet connection among AirPort-equipped machines. However, you can also use an AirPort base station to share an Internet account among machines that are connected to it via a wired network, such as an Ethernet network. You can do this because the base station is actually a DHCP server.

→ To learn more about DHCP servers, **see** Chapter 27, "Sharing an Internet Connection," **p. 855**.

Snow and AirPort Extreme base stations include a LAN port to which you can attached a wired network. These base stations provide services to the wired network automatically and no further configuration is required.

However, the original Graphite base station did not have this additional port and therefore has to be configured to act as a bridge between an Ethernet and AirPort network.

To configure an original Graphite AirPort HAP as a DHCP server, use steps similar to those you used to manually configure the AirPort HAP earlier in this chapter. On the Network tab, check the following boxes: "Ethernet client computers also share a single IP address (using NAT)" and "Enable DHCP server on Ethernet." Update the base station settings by clicking the Update button. Any machines set to use a DHCP server can then access the Internet through the AirPort HAP whether they connect to it via AirPort or Ethernet.

If you want AirPort-connected machines to be capable of accessing devices on an Ethernet network, such as printers, check the Enable AirPort to Ethernet Bridging check box.

→ To configure an AirPort HAP, **see** "Configuring a Base Station Manually," **p. 307**.

MAKING AIRPORT GO FARTHER

AirPort provides large range in most circumstances, and a single base station can usually provide coverage for an entire house easily.

NOTE

> The original PowerBook G4s have a very poor internal antenna and often have trouble connecting in the same location as other machines, such as iMacs.

However, there are a couple of ways you can extend the range of an AirPort network to make it cover an even larger area.

If you use an AirPort Extreme base station with an Antenna Port, you can plug an external antenna into this port to increase the base station's range by a significant amount. There are several third-party antennas available; check out www.smalldog.com to get more information about them.

You can also link AirPort Extreme base stations together wirelessly so that the signal is rebroadcast from one base station to the next. You can continue this chain of base stations to extend a network over a very large area. This is called a *wireless distribution system (WDS)*. Following are the general steps to create a WDS:

1. Configure one base station to connect to the Internet.
2. Open the AirPort Admin Utility, select that base station, and click Configure.
3. Click Show All Settings and then click the WDS tab (see Figure 11.17).

Figure 11.17
Using WDS, you can dramatically extend the range of an AirPort network.

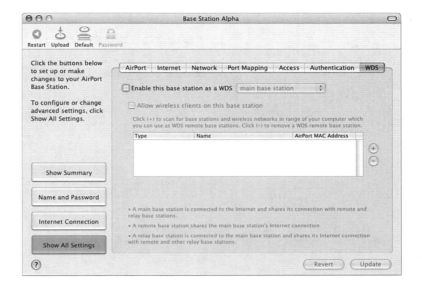

4. Check the "Enable this base station as a WDS" check box and select "main base station" on the pop-up menu.

NOTE

A *remote* base station shares the Internet connection of the main base station. A *relay* base station shares the main base station's Internet connection and can also share its connection with additional base stations.

5. Check the "Allow wireless clients on this base station" check box.

6. Click the Add Base Station button, which is the plus sign next to the list of base stations. The Base Station Selection sheet appears (see Figure 11.18).

7. Choose the base station you want to add to the WDS. Its ID should be configured automatically; if not, enter it (this ID is located on the base station).

8. Check the "Auto configure as a WDS remove base station" check box.

9. Click OK to return to the Base Station window; the base station you added is shown on the list.

10. Repeat steps 6–9 to add other base stations to the WDS.

11. Click Update. The Admin Utility selects and connects to each base station. As it does, you must enter the appropriate passwords. When the process is complete, you see a sheet that provides a status for each base station. If the WDS setup was successful, you can use that base station as part of the WDS.

11

Figure 11.18
Use this sheet to
select a base station
to add to the WDS
you are creating.

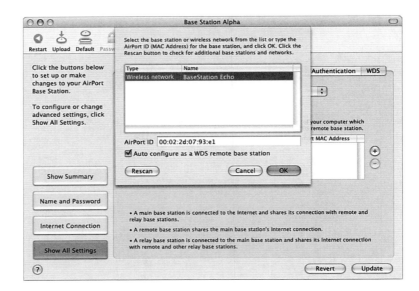

After you have configured the WDS, you can place the base stations on it in various locations throughout an area to increase the coverage. You can then set machines to use the base station that is closest to their locations.

11

CHAPTER 12

USING EMAIL

In this chapter

INTRODUCING THE ADDRESS BOOK AND MAIL

In today's world, email is an essential form of communication for just about everyone. Mac OS X includes two powerful applications that enable you to send, receive, and manage your email: Address Book and Mail. As its name implies, Address Book enables you to manage all sorts of contact information. Mail is a Cocoa email application that provides many powerful features rivaling any other email application.

SETTING UP AND USING AN ADDRESS BOOK

Mac OS X includes the Address Book application, in which you can store all your contact information. The most obvious use for this information is within Mail, but other applications can access the Address Book as well. This is useful because it enables you to use a single contact database for other applications that use information about your contacts, such as iChat.

For Mac OS X version 10.3, the Address Book provides its services to a wider range of applications and offers more functionality itself. You can store as much information as you want, and you can customize each entry in the Address Book as much as you like. You can also print Address Book information in more ways under version 10.3 than you could under previous versions.

TIP

> If you enter a Web site address for a contact, you can access that Web site from within Safari's Address Book tab. You'll learn more about this in Chapter 13, "Surfing the Web."

Address Book is based on *virtual cards*, or *vcards*. A vcard is an electronic information card that you can drag and drop between applications to transfer the information contained on that card. You can also share vcards with other users to exchange information. For example, you can drag someone else's vcard onto your Address Book to quickly add that person's information to your list of contacts.

TIP

> Address Book is not the only application that can work with vcards. Many other applications can use vcards. For example, Microsoft Entourage can read vcards, so you can provide your vcard to someone who uses that application and that person can easily add your contact information to her contact database. Microsoft Outlook, the dominant email, calendar, and contact information application on Windows computers, also uses vcards.

USING THE ADDRESS BOOK

When you open the Address Book, you will see that its window consists of three columns. The first two columns are Group and Name. The Group column shows the groups you have created, and the Name column lists each card in your Address Book. The third column is the Card column, which shows the card that is selected in the Name column (see Figure 12.1). Before you add any contact information, your Address Book includes a card for you and one for Apple. You can build your Address Book over time so that it includes all your contacts.

NOTE

The contact information entered for you is whatever you provided when you registered your copy of Mac OS X.

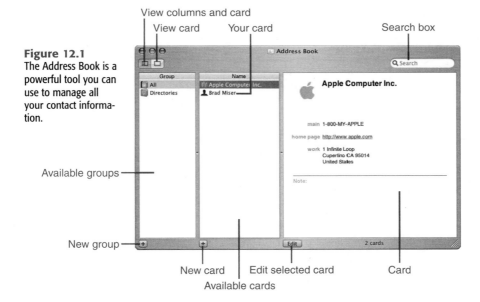

Figure 12.1
The Address Book is a powerful tool you can use to manage all your contact information.

View columns and card
View card   Your card   Search box

Available groups

New group

New card | Edit selected card | Card
Available cards

NOTE

If you use a Bluetooth-equipped Mac, a third button is shown to the right of the View Card button. This button enables you to pair your Address Book with a Bluetooth-capable cell phone. This lets you keep contact information on your phone synchronized with that stored in your Address Book.

In the upper-left corner of each card is an image well that you can use to place an image for your contact, such as a photo of the person for whom you created the card or the logo for a company (such as the apple for Apple). You can add a photo to a card by dragging a photo onto this well. The photo you use can be a JPEG, GIF, TIFF, or PDF file and should be 64×64 pixels.

The card marked with a silhouette is your card. This is important because your card can be used to add your contact information in various locations automatically.

NOTE

> When you send email to or receive email using Mail from a contact who has an image in the related card, that image appears in the email.

WORKING WITH ADDRESS BOOK CONTACT INFORMATION

Although Address Book provides the standard functions you expect, such as email addresses and phone numbers, the information in Address Book is dynamic. For example, when a contact's card includes an email address, you can click the address to send the contact email. When you include a home page for a contact, you can click it to visit that home page, and when the contact has a .Mac account, you can open the contact's iDisk. You can also use the contact's card to chat with the person using iChat and visit the contact's Web site from within Safari. Address Book information is also accessible in many other places, such as when you are faxing documents using Mac OS X's built-in fax capability.

To locate information within Address Book itself, you can browse your contacts or search for specific contacts.

To browse your contacts, perform the following steps:

1. Open the Address Book by clicking the Address Book icon on the Dock or by opening the Applications folder and double-clicking the Address Book icon.
2. Scroll in the Name column to find the contact you are interested in.
3. Select the contact whose information you want to view. The contact's card is displayed, and you can see the person's information.

The information in Address Book is extremely flexible. The fields displayed for each contact can be configured individually. When you display a card, only the fields that contain information are displayed. For example, compare Figure 12.1 and Figure 12.2 to see how Address Book has reconfigured the card display for cards with different amounts of information.

You can also search to locate a contact's information:

1. Open the Address Book by clicking the Address Book icon on the Dock or by opening the Applications folder and double-clicking the Address Book icon.
2. Enter text in the Search field. You can enter text found in any of the contact's information, including name, address, home page, and so on. As you type, the list of names shown in the Name column is narrowed so it includes only those contacts whose data contains the text you enter.
3. Select the contact whose information you want to view. The contact's card is displayed, and you can see the contact's information.

Figure 12.2
Come now, you didn't really expect me to include my real phone number and address in this book did you? (The email address is real.)

To view all your contacts again, click the X button that appears in the Search field when you perform a search.

When working with the Address Book, you can easily do the following tasks:

NOTE

> When you click a data label, such as an email or address, the pop-up menu that results has different commands for different items. For example, when you open an email address's pop-up menu, one of the options is Send Email. However, if you click a physical address, you see different options including Map Of, which enables you to retrieve a map for the address.

- **Send an email**—To send an email to one of your contacts, view the contact to which you want to send an email. Then click the label next to the email address to which you want to send an email. A pop-up menu appears. Select Send Email (see Figure 12.3). Your default email application opens and a new message addressed to the contact is created.

- **Visit the contact's Web site or home page**—Click the label next to a Web site you want to visit. From the resulting pop-up menu, select Go to Web Site. Or, click a URL shown on the card. Your default Web browser opens and you move to the Web site.

- **View a map to an address**—Click the label next to an address and select Map Of from the resulting pop-up menu. Your default Web browser opens and moves to the Map Quest Web site. A map to the selected address is then displayed.

- **Chat**—Select iChat to use the iChat AV application to text, audio, or video chat with the contact.

- **Open an iDisk**—If the contact has a .Mac account and you have configured his .Mac email address, you can open the person's iDisk by clicking the label next to the .Mac email address and selecting Open iDisk. The contact's iDisk opens in a new Finder window.

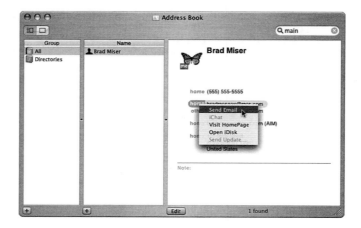

Figure 12.3
Sending an email from Address Book can be done with the Send Email command.

- **Scroll through your contacts**—Select Card, Next Card (or press ⌘-]) or select Card, Previous Card (or press ⌘-[) to browse through your contacts.

- **Edit your contacts**—Click the Edit button to move into the Edit mode (more on this later).

You can change the view of the Address Book to show only cards by clicking the View Card Only button; selecting View, Card Only; or pressing ⌘-2. The window collapses down to the card only. You can add cards, edit cards, or browse cards from the collapsed window.

Show the other columns again by selecting View, Card and Columns or by pressing ⌘-1.

CONFIGURING YOUR ADDRESS BOOK

You can configure several aspects of the Address Book by using its Preferences dialog box (see Figure 12.4). To open this dialog box, select Address Book, Preferences or press ⌘-,.

Figure 12.4
Maximize the benefits of your Address Book by customizing it using the Preferences dialog box.

CONFIGURING ADDRESS BOOK GENERAL PREFERENCES

Using the General tab of the Preferences dialog box, you can configure the following preferences:

- **Display Order**—Click the "First name Last name" radio button to have Address Book display contact information in the first name, last name format. Click the "Last name First name" radio button to display contacts in the last name, first name format.

- **Sort criterion**—Select First Name or Last Name on the Sort By pop-up menu to have Address Book sort the Cards column by that criteria.

- **Address Format**—Use the Address Format pop-up menu to select the address format you want to use by country.

- **Font Size**—Use the Font Size pop-up menu to select the Regular, Large, or Extra Large font size for the information shown in the Address Book window.

- **Notifications about changes to your card**—If you want contacts to be notified when your contact information changes and want to send them your revised information, create at least one group containing the contacts whom you want to be notified (you'll learn how to do this later in this chapter) and check the "Notify people when my card changes" check box. Whenever you change something on your own vcard, you can notify people in the group by selecting File, Send Updates. In the resulting Send Updates dialog box, select the groups to which you want to send the update by checking their check boxes; then enter a subject and text for the message and click Send. The message you send includes your updated vcard that the recipients can use to replace the outdated version of your card in their own contact lists.

- **Synchronization with Exchange**—Many organizations use an Exchange server to provide email and contact information services to the network.

You can synchronize your Address Book with the information stored on an Exchange server by doing the following:

1. Check the Synchronize with Exchange check box.

2. Click Configure. In the resulting dialog box, enter your username, password, and the Outlook Web Access server address with which you want to synchronize your Address Book.

3. If you want to synchronize this information every hour, check the "Synchronize every hour" check box.

4. Click OK; information from the Exchange server is added to your Address Book and your Address Book information is added to the Exchange server.

12

CAUTION

For synchronization to work, you must enter the address for Outlook Web Access server rather than the Exchange server address itself. Address Book uses the Web access address to retrieve your information. If you don't know what this address is, contact the administrator for the Exchange server you are trying to access. To confirm that you are using the right server address, access the address through Safari or Internet Explorer. If you can access your email this way, you should be able to synchronize Address Book with your Exchange information.

CUSTOMIZING YOUR ADDRESS BOOK CARD TEMPLATE

You can customize the information and layout of the cards in your Address Book.

Open the Address Book Preferences window and click the Template button to open the Template preferences pane (see Figure 12.5).

Figure 12.5
You can use Address Book's Template preferences to design the cards in your Address Book.

TIP

You can also edit the card template by selecting Card, Add Field, Edit Template.

To change the layout of and the information contained on the cards in your Address Book, you can do any of the following:

- **Add or remove fields**—Use the Add Field pop-up menu at the top of the dialog box to add or remove fields from the cards in your Address Book. To add a field, select it on the menu. The field is added and a check mark is placed next to the field on the pop-up menu. To remove a field, select that field (which is marked with a check mark) on the pop-up menu; it is removed from the card.

> **TIP**
>
> The fields that are grayed out on the menu are already on the card. To remove them, you use the minus sign next to the field as explained in the next bullet.

- **Remove fields**—Click the minus sign next to a field to remove it from the card.
- **Add more fields of the same kind**—Click the plus sign next to a field to add another field of the same type to the card.
- **Change a field's label**—Use the pop-up menu next to a field's label to change that label. You can select one of the labels on the menu or select Custom and create a custom menu.

Using these tools, you can customize the contents of cards and the specific fields they contain as much as you like. Because Address Book displays only those fields that contain data (when you view a card), you don't need to be concerned about having too many fields on your cards.

CONFIGURING ADDRESS BOOK'S PHONE NUMBER FORMAT

You can change the phone number format used in Address Book by using the following steps:

1. Open the Phone pane of the Address Book Preferences dialog box.
2. To have Address Book format phone numbers automatically, check the "Automatically format phone numbers" check box.
3. If you do check the check box mentioned in the previous step, use the Formats pop-up menu to select the format that should be used.

> **TIP**
>
> You can create custom phone number formats by clicking the down arrow next to the Formats pop-up menu, which opens a pane showing the configured formats. Select one and click Edit to change it. To add a format, click the plus sign. To remove a format, select it and click the minus sign.

CHOOSING VCARD PREFERENCES

On the vCard pane of the Address Book Preferences dialog box, you can set the following preferences:

- **vCard Format**—Click the 3.0 radio button to use the newer vcard format. Click the 2.1 radio button and select a format on the pop-up menu to use a version of the previous vcard standard.

- **Private 'Me' Card**—You can use this option to hide information on your vcard so that information won't be exported when you provide your vcard to someone else. To do so, check the Enable Private 'Me' Card check box. Edit your card and uncheck the check boxes for the data that you don't want to include on your vcard when you share it.

- **Export Notes with Vcards**—If you check the Export Notes in vCards check box, when you export vcards, any notes you have entered for a card are exported with the card. If you put information in the notes on cards, be careful with this one!

NOTE

> Address Book can also work with Lightweight Directory Access Protocol (LDAP) directories that can provide address information over a network. Such directories appear when you select the Directories icon in the Group column. You can add directories to your Address Book by using the LDAP tab of the Address Book Preferences dialog box. Explaining how to use such directories is beyond the scope of this chapter. If you need help, see the administrator of the network that is providing one or more LDAP directories to you.

ADDING ADDRESSES TO YOUR ADDRESS BOOK

Obviously, before an address book is of much value, it has to have some information in it. There are several ways to get information into your Address Book:

- Edit your own address card.
- Add cards manually.
- Add a card from an email message you have received.
- Import a contact's vcard.
- Import address information from an email application.

CREATING AND EDITING YOUR OWN ADDRESS CARD

The first time you open Address Book, a card is created for you automatically based on the information you entered when you installed Mac OS X. If you entered one or more email addresses when you installed Mac OS X, those addresses are included in your address card automatically. You should edit this card, mostly so that you can easily send your contact information to other people simply by sending them your vcard.

NOTE

> Another place your card's information is used is for Safari's AutoFill feature. When you complete a form on the Web, your card's information is used if you choose to enable Safari's AutoFill feature.

Your card's icon has a silhouette next to your name. When you select your name in the Name column, your card appears; its image well is marked with the text me.

If you want to create a different card for yourself for some reason, you can create a new card and enter your contact information in it. After you have created your new card, select it and select Card, Make This My Card (this is disabled if you have already selected your card).

You can edit your own card using the same steps you use to edit any other cards (editing cards is explained shortly).

ADDING ADDRESSES MANUALLY

As you might expect, you can add people to your Address Book by inputting their information manually.

To manually add an address, do the following:

1. Click the Plus button in the Name column; select File, New Card; or press ⌘-N to see a new, empty address card. The fist name is highlighted by default so you can edit it immediately (see Figure 12.6).

Figure 12.6
This is a new card, ready for the contact's information.

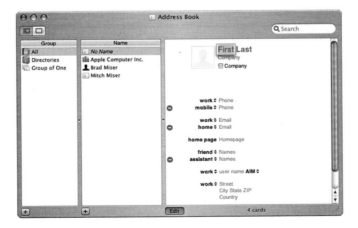

2. Input the first name.
3. Press Tab to move to and select the Last field, and then enter the contact's last name.

4. Press Tab to move to and select the Company field, and then enter the person's company information if applicable.

5. If you want the company to be listed above the name, check the Company check box.

6. Press Tab to move to and select the first contact information, which is work by default.

7. Click the menu icon to reveal the label pop-up menu (see Figure 12.7).

Figure 12.7
You use this pop-up menu to label contact information.

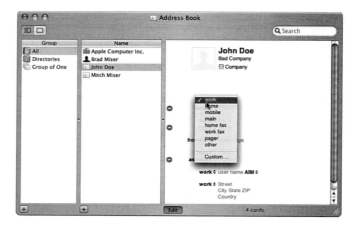

8. Select the label for the contact information, such as home.

NOTE

Two entries on the label pop-up menu require some explanation. The selection called other inserts the label `other`. If you select Custom, you can create a custom label for a field.

9. Enter the contact information, such as a work phone number if you chose the label work.

10. Continue tabbing to each field on the card, selecting the label for that field and editing the information to fill in the rest of the card.

11. If the contact has a home page, select the home page field and enter the URL of the home page with which you want to associate the contact.

12. If you want to remove fields from the card, click the Remove Field button (the minus sign) next to the field you want to remove. The field is removed from the current card only.

13. If you want to add more fields of the same type to the card, click the Add Field button (+) next to one of the existing fields. After you have added a field, you can edit it in the same way as the default fields. Similar to removing a card, when you add a field to the card, it is added on the current card only.

→ To learn how to add a field to all cards in the Address Book, **see** "Customizing Your Address Book Card Template," **p. 336**.

14. If you have an image you want to associate with the contact, drag the image onto the contact's image well. (You can add images in the usual graphics formats, such as JPEG or TIFF.) When you are over the image well, the cursor changes to a green circle with a plus sign in it. Release the mouse button and you see the image in a new window (see Figure 12.8).

Figure 12.8
Okay, I don't really look like Mel Gibson, so sue me.

15. Use the slider at the bottom of the window to crop the image.

16. When the image appears as you want it, click the Set button.

TIP

When you are editing a card, you can double-click an image or the image well to open the image editing window. You can also select Card, Choose Custom Image to open the same window. In that window, click the Choose button to move to and select an image to display in the window. If you have a camera, such as an iSight camera, connected to your Mac, click the Take Video Snapshot button to capture the image being taken by the camera.

17. Add notes for the card by clicking next to the Note label and typing the note.

18. Click the Edit button to move out of the Edit mode. Your new card is now ready to use (see Figure 12.9).

NOTE

When you edit your own card and have the "Notify people when my card changes" preference selected, you are prompted to send a message notifying others that your card has changed.

Figure 12.9
You can create an address card for anyone you know (or even for those you don't know!).

ADDING AN ADDRESS FROM AN EMAIL MESSAGE

You can create a contact in your Address Book by adding the sender's information from an email message to it. To add a contact from an email that you receive in the Mail application, do the following:

1. Use Mail to open an email message from the person whom you want to add to your Address Book.

2. Select Message, Add Sender to Address Book (or press ⌘-Y). The person's name and email address are entered on a new address card.

USING VCARDS TO ADD INFORMATION TO YOUR ADDRESS BOOK

The benefit to using a vcard is that you can add a lot of information about a contact with very little work on your part. When you receive a vcard from someone, use the following steps to add that person's address card to your Address Book:

1. Drag the vcard onto the Name column in Address Book.

2. Click OK when prompted. The vcard is added to your Address Book.

3. Select the card and click the Edit button.

4. Edit the information as needed (you learn how to edit cards later in this chapter).

NOTE

> When you import vcards to your Address Book, the group called Last Import always contains the cards you most recently added.

NOTE

> Vcard files have the filename extension `.vcf` (virtual card file).

IMPORTING ADDRESSES FROM ANOTHER APPLICATION

If you have used another email application in the past, you probably have an Address Book or Contact database in that application. If that application supports vcards, you can easily export vcards from the application and then add them to the Address Book.

As an example of how this works, the following steps show you how to export contacts from Microsoft's Entourage email application and then add those contacts to the Address Book. Because Entourage supports vcards, you can create vcards for your Entourage contacts and then import those contacts into the Address Book:

1. Create a folder to temporarily store the vcards you export from Entourage.
2. Open Entourage.
3. Click the Address Book button to move into the Address Book mode.
4. Drag the contacts for whom you want to create vcards from the Entourage window onto the folder you created in step 1, and drop them in that folder. A vcard is created for each of your Entourage contacts.

NOTE

> If you drag an Entourage group to create a vcard, a text clipping file is created instead. You need to re-create your groups within Address Book.

5. Open the Address Book.
6. Drag the vcards from the folder in which you stored them onto the Name column. The contacts you added are now available for you to use and edit.

NOTE

> Unfortunately, if the application you have used for your contact information does not support vcards, there isn't a way to import its information into Address Book.

It is unlikely that all the information in your current address book or contact list will make it into the Address Book application. For example, if you have added Category information for your Entourage contact list, that information is not imported into the Address Book. After you have imported contacts into the Address Book, you should check them over so you know exactly what information made it in, and what didn't. If you lost any important information, you might have to spend some time re-creating it within Address Book.

12

NOTE

> When you import addresses into your Address Book and it finds duplicates, you have the opportunity to review the addresses you are adding so you can remove the duplicated entries.

EDITING ADDRESSES IN YOUR ADDRESS BOOK

To edit an address in your Address Book, use the following steps:

1. In Address Book, view the card containing the information you want to edit.
2. Click the Edit button. Address Book moves into the Edit mode. The first name is selected and is ready to edit.
3. Use the same steps to change the information on the card that you do to create a card (see the earlier section on creating cards for the details).

TIP

> You can use the Add Field button on the Template pane of the Address Book Preferences dialog box to add fields to the card. You can also add fields by using the Card, Add Field command. On the Add Field menu, you can select the type of field you want to add.

Many of the data fields have pop-up menus containing the data field's label. You can open these menus and select a new label for that field. The changes you make by doing this affect only the current address card; this means you can configure the information for a specific card independent of other cards. For example, if you know someone who has three mobile phones, you can select Mobile Phone as the label for three of the fields on that person's address card. You can also select Custom to create custom field labels for existing or new fields.

You can quickly swap the last name with the first name for the card by viewing the card and selecting Card, Swap First/Last Name.

To remove an image from a card, view the card and select Card, Clear Custom Image.

If you don't want a field's data to appear on a card, select the data and delete it. The data is replaced with the type of data it is, such as Email for an email address. The data does not appear on the card when it is viewed.

NOTE

> After you add a field, you can't remove it. You can only delete its data so that it doesn't appear on the card any more.

To delete a card from the Address Book, select it and press Delete. Click Yes in the resulting prompt and the card is deleted.

TIP

> You can view a card in an independent window by viewing it and selecting Card, Open in Separate Window (or by pressing ⌘-I).

WORKING WITH ADDRESS GROUPS

Address groups (just called *groups* in Address Book) enable you to email multiple people using a single address. Working with an address group is similar to working with other address cards in your Address Book. Creating an address group is simple, as you can see in the following steps:

1. Click the New Group button, which is the plus sign in the Group column; select File, New Group; or press Shift-⌘-N. You see a new group in the Group column, and the name of the group is selected and ready to edit.

2. Change the group's name to something meaningful and press Return.

3. Click All in the Group column to view all the cards in the Address Book.

4. Search or browse for the cards you want to add to your Address Book.

5. Drag the cards you want to be included in the group onto the group's icon in the Group column. Those cards become part of the group.

TIP

> You can create a new group and add selected address cards to it by first selecting the cards you want to place in the new group and selecting File, New Group From Selection. A new group is created and includes the cards you selected.

You can view a group by selecting it on the Group column. The Name column shows only those cards that are included in the group. You work with the cards in a group just as you do individual cards. For example, you can edit the card, use it to send email to that individual, and so on.

To remove a card from a group, view the group, select the card you want to remove, and press Delete. After you confirm the action, the card is removed from the group. However, the card still exists in the Address Book.

You can also export a group as a vcard. Select the group, hold down the Control key, click the mouse button, and select Export Group vCard. Select a location, name the card, and click Save. You can use the group's vcard just like vcards for individuals.

If any of the cards you add to a group includes more than one email address, you can edit the mailing list for the group to set the specific addresses that are used:

1. Select the group for which you want to configure the mailing list.

2. Select Edit, Edit Distribution List. The Edit Distribution List sheet appears.

3. Select the email address you want to use for an individual by clicking it. The address that will be used appears in bold; other addresses are grayed out to show that they won't be used.

TIP

> You can change all the email addresses used for the group to be of the same kind by selecting a type on the Change All Labels pop-up menu. For example, to use only home email addresses, select home.

4. Click OK. When you send a message to the group, the addresses you selected is used.

TIP

> You can back up your Address Book by selecting File, Backup Database. If you want to return to the version of the database you have backed up, select File, Revert to Database Backup.

ADDRESSING EMAIL

There are several ways in which you can address email to people in your Address Book:

- View the contact to whom you want to send a message and Control-click the label for the email address you want to use. Select Send Email on the pop-up menu.
- Drag the contact's vcard to the To, Cc, or Bcc box of a Mail email message.
- Control-click a group and select "Send email to *groupname*," where *groupname* is the name of the group you clicked.
- Drag a group's vcard to the To, Cc, or Bcc box of a Mail email message.

NOTE

> When you send email from the Address Book, the email application used is your default email application.

PRINTING YOUR ADDRESS BOOK

As you work with your Address Book, you might want to print it to take it with you, to print address labels, and so on. When you print from the Address Book, you have the following two layout options:

- **Lists**—This option prints the cards you select in a list. You can select the attributes that are included on the list for each card.
- **Mailing Labels**—This prints the cards as mailing labels.

To print the Address Book as a list, use the following steps:

1. Select the cards you want to print. To print the entire Address Book, select All in the Groups column.
2. Select File, Print or press ⌘-P. The Print dialog box opens.
3. On the Style pop-up menu, select Lists.
4. Configure the printer, presets, paper size, and orientation just as you do with any print job.
5. Select the attributes you want included for each card by checking their boxes. You see a preview of the list in the left side of the dialog box.
6. Select the font size on the Font Size pop-up menu.
7. Print the list.

> **TIP**
>
> To access the standard print options from the Address Book Print dialog box, click the Advanced Options button.

To print mailing labels, use the following steps:

1. Select the cards you want to print. To print the entire Address Book, select All in the Groups column.
2. Select File, Print or press ⌘-P. The Print dialog box opens.
3. On the Style pop-up menu, select Mailing Labels.
4. Click the Layout tab.
5. If you are printing on standard Avery or DYMO labels, select the label type on the Page pop-up menu. If you are creating a custom label, select Define Custom instead; in the Layout Name sheet that appears, enter the name of the label you are creating and click OK. As you make choices, a preview of the labels appears in the left pane of the dialog box.
6. If you selected a standard label, select the specific label number you are printing on the label number drop-down list that appears next to the Page pop-up menu. If you selected Define Custom in the previous step, use the controls under the Layout tab to design the label, such as by defining the margins, number of rows and columns, and the gutters.
7. Click the Label tab.
8. Select the group for which you want to print labels on the Addresses pop-up menu. If you want to print labels for all addresses, select All.
9. On the Sorting pop-up menu, select how you want the labels to be sorted. The options are Last Name and Postal Code.

12

10. If you want country to be included on the labels, check the "Print country" check box. If you don't want your own country to be included, check the "Except my country" check box.

11. Click the Color box and use the Color Picker to select the color of the text on the labels.

12. Drag an image into the image well to include that image on the labels.

13. Click the Set button to open the Font panel and select the font you want to use on the labels.

14. Check the labels in the preview pane.

15. Print the labels.

CONFIGURING MAIL

Before you can start using Mail to work with your email, you need to configure the accounts it uses. If you entered account information in the Setup Assistant when you installed Mac OS X, those accounts are configured for you already. For example, if you set up or entered the information for your .Mac account in the Setup Assistant, your .Mac email account is configured in Mail.

If you are like most Mac users, you probably have more than one email address; you can use Mail to access any or all of them.

There are also several other areas that you don't necessarily have to configure before you begin using Mail, but I have included them in the section so that all the configuration information is together for your reference.

CONFIGURING GENERAL MAIL PREFERENCES

Using the General pane of the Mail preferences dialog box, you can configure the following preferences:

- **Default email application**—Use the Default Email Reader pop-up menu to select the email application you will use by default. If you want to use Mail, you don't need to make a selection on this menu. If you want to use another application, choose Select and use the resulting sheet to select the application you want to use instead of Mail.

- **Frequency of mail checking**—Use the "Check for new mail" pop-up menu to determine how often Mail checks for new mail. Select Manually to disable automatic checking or the frequency at which you want Mail to check for new email automatically, such as "Every 5 minutes" to have Mail check every 5 minutes.

- **Mail sounds**—Mail can play sounds for the following events: new mail received, mail error, and mail sent. You can choose the sound that is played when new mail is received by choosing the sound for that event on the "New mail sound" pop-up menu. To turn this sound off, choose None. To disable the sound for other events, uncheck the "Play sounds for other mail actions" check box.

TIP

You can use custom mail sounds by selecting Add/Remove on the pop-up menu and selecting the custom sound you want to use. Mail will place the sound file your select in the `Library/Sounds` folder in your Home folder. You can then choose it on the pop-up menu in Mail and other applications, such as iChat.

- **Sounds for other events**—If you want Mail to play sounds for all events, check the "Play sounds for other mail actions" check box. If you uncheck this check box, Mail plays a sound only when new email sound is received.
- **Indexing decrypted messages**—Using properly configured certificates, Mail can work with encrypted messages. If you configure Mail to do so, check the "Index decrypted messages for searching" check box to enable Mail to search these messages.

CONFIGURING EMAIL ACCOUNTS

The most basic configuration for Mail is the email accounts you are going to access it with. Before you get started, gather the following information for each mail account you want to configure in Mail:

- **Account type**—There are four types of email accounts with which Mail can work. A .Mac account is one provided by Apple's .Mac servers. A Post Office Protocol (POP) account is provided by most ISPs. An Internet Message Access Protocol (IMAP) is similar to a POP account but offers additional features, and an Exchange account is provided by an Exchange server, which is used on many business networks.

NOTE

When you use a .Mac email account with Mail, it is configured as an IMAP account. In Mail, it is treated as its own category because it is part of your .Mac account.

12

- **Your email address**—This should be self-explanatory.
- **Incoming mail server**— This is the address of the server that handles retrieving your email. For POP accounts, it often looks something like `pop.isp.net`.
- **Your email username**—This is your username for your email account, which might or might not be the same as your username for your Internet account. Typically, this is everything before the @ in your email address.
- **Your email password**—This is the password for your email account, which might or might not be the same as that of your Internet access account.
- **Outgoing email server or Simple Mail Transfer Protocol (SMTP) host**—This is the address of the server that handles sending your email.
- **Authentication**—You need to know whether your SMTP server uses authentication.

- **SMTP username**—This is the username for your SMTP server; it is usually the same as your email username, but it isn't always.

- **SMTP password**—Again, this is usually the same as your email password.

To add email accounts to Mail, do the following:

1. Launch Mail.

2. Select Mail, Preferences (or press ⌘-]-,).

3. Click the Accounts button to see the Accounts pane of the Preferences window (see Figure 12.10). This pane has three tabs: Account Information, Special Mailboxes, and Advanced. In the left part of the pane is the list of email accounts that are currently configured.

Figure 12.10
If you configured a .Mac account when you installed Mac OS X, your .Mac email account is configured in Mail automatically.

4. Click the Add Account button, which is the plus sign at the bottom of the list of accounts. A new account, called New Account, is created on the list of accounts.

5. Click the Account Information tab. You use this tab to configure the basic settings for the email account.

6. On the Account Information tab, select the account type from the Account Type pop-up menu.

NOTE

Mail helpfully fills in many fields with examples of how the data you should enter probably looks.

7. Enter a description of the account in the Description field. As you enter this, the name of the account on the list of accounts changes to the text you type.

8. Enter the rest of the information for the account including the email address (except for .Mac accounts), your full name, the incoming mail server address, your email username, and incoming mail server password.

NOTE

What you enter in the Full Name field is what appears next to your return email address shown in the Email Address data field. If a recipient uses Mail, he sees your full name instead of your email address.

9. Open the Outgoing Mail Server (SMTP) pop-up menu and select the outgoing mail server on the list; then skip to step 14. If the server you want to use is not on the list, select Add Server. The SMTP Server Options dialog box opens.

10. Enter the outgoing mail server address in the Outgoing Mail Server field.

11. If you need to change the server port for the SMTP server, enter the port number in the Server port box. You need to change this only in rare situations.

12. If the SMTP server uses Secure Sockets Layer, check the Use Secure Sockets Layer (SSL) check box.

13. If the account uses authentication, select the type of authentication it uses on the Authentication pop-up menu and configure the User Name and Password fields in the dialog box accordingly; the username and password might or might not be the same as those for the incoming mail server. Click OK when you are finished configuring the outgoing mail server.

TIP

If you need to edit the settings for an account's SMTP server, click the Server Settings button. Use the resulting SMTP Server Options dialog box to make changes to the SMTP server settings.

14. Click the Special Mailboxes tab. This tab provides several controls you can use to control how the account you are configuring behaves. The options you see depend on the type of account you are creating. For example, you see fewer options for a POP account than you do for the other three types. Because .Mac accounts are popular with many Mac users, you see the options you can configure for .Mac accounts in the following list (see Figure 12.11). You can configure the options on this tab for other account types in a similar way, although the specific options you have might be different:

- Use the check box in the Drafts area to determine whether messages are stored on the .Mac server when you are writing them. This causes email that you are writing saves on the .Mac server as you are writing it. If you write email offline, you don't want to select this. If you use a broadband connection to the Net, you can check the "Store draft messages on the server" check box to have your drafts stored online as you write them.

- Use the controls in the Sent area to determine whether sent messages are stored on the server and when sent messages are deleted. Usually, you don't want to save sent messages on the server because those messages count against your total storage allowance for your account. If you do want sent messages to be stored on the server, check the "Store sent messages on the server" check box. Then use the "Delete sent messages when" pop-up menu to select how often the sent messages will be deleted. The options are Never, One day old, One week old, One month old, or Quitting Mail.

- Use the Junk controls to configure how Mail handles messages that are classified as junk. Similar to the first two options, you can select to have junk mail stored on the server; if you select to allow this, use the pop-up menu to determine when junk mail is deleted from the server.

- Use the Trash controls to configure how trash is handled. If you want deleted messages to be moved to the Trash mail box, check the "Move deleted messages to the Trash mailbox" check box. If you want deleted messages to be stored on the server, check the "Store deleted messages on the server" check box, and to determine when deleted messages are actually erased, use the "Permanently erase deleted message when" pop-up menu. The options are Never, One day old, One week old, One month old, or Quitting Mail.

Figure 12.11
You can configure these special mailbox actions when using a .Mac mail account.

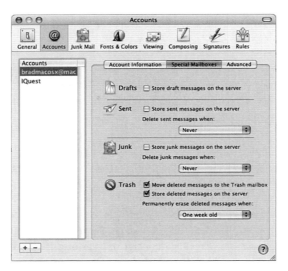

15. Click the Advanced tab. Just like the Special Mailboxes tab, the specific controls you see depend on the type of account you are configuring (see Figure 12.12). The rest of these steps assume a .Mac account, but you can configure other account types similarly.

Figure 12.12
These are the
Advanced controls for
a .Mac email account.

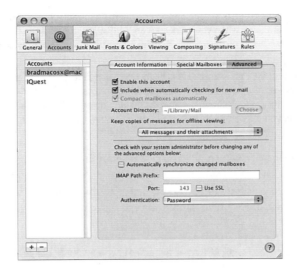

16. Use the "Enable this account"" check box to enable or disable the account. If you disable an account, it won't be used.

17. Check the ""Include when automatically checking for new mail"" check box if you want this account always included when Mail automatically checks for mail. If you uncheck this check box, you must manually check for mail in the account.

18. Use the "Keep copies of messages for offline viewing" pop-up menu to determine what Mail does with the messages it receives when you are not connected to the Internet. For example, if you select "All messages and their attachments," all your messages and any attachments they contain are downloaded to your Mac so you can view them even if you aren't connected to the Net. If you select "Only message I've read," only the messages you have read are downloaded to your Mac.

NOTE

> Other options are available at the bottom of the pane, but you aren't likely to use them unless you are specifically directed to do so by the administrator of the email system you are using.

19. Close the Preferences dialog box. You are prompted to save the account you just created.

IMAP Accounts

One area in which an IMAP account (such as a .Mac account) is significantly different from a POP account is in how email is stored. Under an IMAP account (such as a .Mac email account), mail is always left on the server until you delete it manually. The benefit of this is that you can access that mail from different machines without forwarding it to each machine or having duplicate copies (on the server and in the inbox in your email applications). As you will learn later, when you work with an IMAP account that has a limited amount of storage for email messages, you have to be aware of how full your email storage is and make sure that you keep it under its limit.

When you use a POP account, the mail you read is actually downloaded to your Mac. So, a copy exists in both places. With POP accounts, you should check the "Remove copy from server after retrieving a message" check box and select a timeframe for messages to be deleted on the pop-up menu. Otherwise, the email you read remains on the server, and you might download it again the next time you check your email.

Using steps similar to these, you can add the rest of your email accounts to Mail to work with them all from the Mail application. As you read previously, the steps for a specific account depend on the type of email account you are adding. Just use the specific configuration information provided for each account and repeat the previous steps.

NOTE

> Mail can't access an AOL email account. However, you should be able to add just about any other email account to it.

SETTING OTHER MAIL PREFERENCES

There are various other Mail preferences you might want to set. The general steps you use to set these preferences are shown here:

1. Select Mail, Preferences to open the Mail Preferences window.
2. Click the button for the area of preferences you want to set.
3. Set the preferences.
4. Set more preferences or close the Preferences window.

In the following sections, you will get an overview of each preference area and a description of some of the more useful preferences you can set.

SETTING JUNK MAIL PREFERENCES

You use the Junk Mail pane to configure Mail's Junk Mail feature.

→ To learn how to configure and use Mail's junk mail feature, **see** "Handling Junk Mail," **p. 375**.

SETTING FONTS & COLORS PREFERENCES

Use the Fonts & Colors pane of the Mail preferences window to control how text appears in Mail windows:

■ Use the font and size pop-up menus to select the font and size for the Message list font (the pane in which all the messages in a mailbox are listed) and the message font (which is the font used for messages you read).

- If you prefer a fixed-width font for plain-text messages, check the "Use fixed-width font for plain text messages" check box and use the pop-up menus to select the font and size to be used for plain-text email.

- If you want different levels of quoted text to use different colors, check the "Color quoted text" check box and select the colors for each level.

Email Formats

Mail enables you to send and read email in two formats: plain text and Rich Text Format (RTF). Plain-text messages contain no formatting, but RTF messages can be formatted. Whether the formatting you apply in an RTF message will be seen or not depends on the email application the recipient of your email uses. Most can interpret RTF messages correctly, but others cannot.

Email purists prefer plain-text format because any email application can handle them and plain-text messages are quicker to compose and read (which is part of the point of email in the first place). Also, proper quoting is much easier with a plain-text message. I prefer plain text myself for these very reasons.

Many mailing lists enable you to select the format in which you receive messages. You often can select between the plain-text or HTML format. Selecting the plain-text format results in much faster performance, although you won't see all the bells and whistles that can be contained in an HTML email message. However, plain-text messages usually contain links to that content on the Web so you can easily view the specific content you want to see.

SETTING VIEWING PREFERENCES

Using the Viewing pane of the Mail Preferences window, you can control the following viewing options:

- Use the ""Show header detail"" pop-up menu to determine how much information is shown in the header of email messages you receive. Your choices are Default, None, All, and Custom. If you select Custom, you can select the specific data you want to see in the header of your messages.

NOTE

Note that the "Show header detail" pop-up menu affects mail you have already downloaded. For example, you can select an email message to read and then select a level of header detail from the "Show header detail" pop-up menu to change the header information for the mail you are reading.

TIP

You can show all header information in messages by selecting View, Message, Long Headers or by pressing Shift-⌘-H.

- Check the "Show online buddy status" check box if you want the status of people whom you have designated as being online buddies to be displayed. This helps you know when these people are online so you can chat with them.

- Uncheck the "Display images and embedded objects in HTML messages" check box if you want only the text portion of HTML messages that you receive to be displayed.

> **NOTE**
> **NEW**
>
> Mail now uses the Safari HTML rendering engine to display HTML messages. This improves the formatting you see when you view HTML messages and makes HTML messages fully interactive.

- Check the "Highlight related messages using color" check box, and select a color by using the color button. *Threads* (a series of messages connected by replies to an original message) in your mailbox are highlighted with the color you select so you can spot them more easily.

SETTING COMPOSING PREFERENCES

The Composing pane of the Preferences window controls various composing options, which are the following:

- Use the "Format" pop-up menu to set the default format for new messages you can create. Your options are Plain Text and Rich Text. You can override your default choice for specific messages.

> **TIP**
>
> For example, if you select Plain Text as your default format, you can create a message in the Rich Text format by creating the message and selecting Format, Make Rich Text (Shift-⌘-T). If you select Rich Text, you can select Format, Make Plain Text (Shift-⌘-T) to create a plain-text message.

- Check the "Check spelling as I type" check box to have Mail check your spelling as you type messages.
- Check the "Always Cc: myself" check box to include yourself in the Cc block of every message you send. If you prefer to include yourself on the address list for a message but hide your address from the other recipients, select Bcc: on the pop-up menu.
- Check the "Automatically complete addresses" check box to have Mail look up addresses in your Address Book or on specific LDAP servers. Then click the Configure LDAP button and use the resulting sheet to configure the servers on which you want Mail to look up addresses.
- Check the "When sending to a group, show all member addresses" check box to list members of a group by their names in an email that you send to a group (rather than listing just the group name).

- If you want to highlight email addresses when you are sending them outside of "safe" domains, check the "Mark addresses not in this domain" check box and enter the domain you want Mail to consider safe in the box. For example, you might want to be careful about sending messages outside your work domain. In that case, you would check the box and enter your company's domain (such as company.com) in the box. Whenever you address messages to someplace other than that domain, the address is highlighted in red.

- Use the controls in the Responding area to configure how Mail handles reply messages. To use the same mail format as the original message (such as plain text), check the "Use the same message format as the original" check box. If you don't check this, your reply uses your default format. To include the original message's text in your reply (which is a good idea so you can use quoting), check the "Quote the text of the original message" check box. Check the "Increase quote level" box to have Mail indent each message's text by one level; this makes an email conversation clearer because you can more easily see the flow of the mail threads. If you select to use quoting (which you should), use the radio buttons to determine whether the entire message is quoted or only the selected part. The second option is preferable because, if you don't select any text in the original message when you reply to it, the entire text is quoted, which is the same thing the "Include all" option does anyway. However, if you want to reply only to a specific part of a message, you can select it and only that part is included in the message. This provides better context for your reply.

SETTING SIGNATURE PREFERENCES

You can configure signatures to be attached to your email messages. You can have as many signatures as you would like, and you can select a default signature or select one each time you compose a new message:

1. Click the Signatures icon to open the Signatures pane of the Mail Preferences window.
2. Click Add Signature.
3. Name the signature in the Description field of the resulting Signature sheet.
4. Enter the signature in the sheet.
5. Click OK to return to the Signatures pane which shows the signature you just created.
6. Create other signatures you want to use.
7. Use the Automatically Insert Signature pop-up menu to select the signature that is used by default on email messages you create and send. You can select any of the signatures you have created or use the same signature for all your messages—select None to never add a signature to messages you write, In Random Order to select a random signature from those you have created, or In Sequential Order to select a signature in the order they are listed on the pane.
8. If you want to select a signature each time you compose mail, check the "Show signature menu on compose window" check box. When you compose a message, you can select the signature you want to use on the Signature pop-up menu.

9. Check the "Place signature above quoted text" check box, and your signature is placed above any text that is quoted when you reply to a message. Signatures appear at the bottom of a message by default. When you use quoting, this can be odd because your signature appears after the quoted text instead of after the part you wrote. Use this check box to ensure that your signature appears after what you write and above the quoted text.

Here are a few more signature tips:

- **Change signatures**—To change a signature, select it and click Edit. Use the resulting sheet to make changes to the signature.

- **Copy a signature**—You can make a copy of a signature by selecting it and clicking Duplicate. This is useful if you want to base a new signature on one you have previously created.

- **Delete a signature**—You can delete a signature by selecting it and clicking Remove.

SETTING RULES

You use the Rules pane to set up automated mail rules.

→ To learn how to create rules for your email, **see** "Configuring and Using Rules for Email," **p. 373**.

CONFIGURING THE MAIL TOOLBAR

As with the Finder toolbar and other Mac OS X toolbars, you can configure Mail's toolbar to be more compatible with the way you work:

- Use the Hide Toolbar or the Show Toolbar command on the View menu to hide or show Mail's toolbar. You can use the Show/Hide toolbar button in the Mail title bar as well.

- Select View, Customize Toolbar to add buttons to, remove buttons from, and reorganize the toolbar. Just like other toolbars, you can drag icons onto the toolbar to add them to it or drag them off it to remove them. You can also select how the buttons are displayed and their size.

- Select View, Hide Status Bar to hide the status bar that appears just below the toolbar. If you want to show the status bar again, select View, Show Status Bar. You can toggle the status bar by pressing Option-⌘-S.

> **TIP**
>
> Hold down the ⌘ key and click the Hide/Show Toolbar button to cycle through various views, such as large icons, text only, and so on.

SENDING, RECEIVING, AND REPLYING TO EMAIL

If you have used an email application before, such as Outlook Express, Entourage, or Eudora, using Mail to send, receive, and reply to email will be familiar to you after you learn about the Mail interface.

The main Mail window has three panes. The top pane contains the Mail Toolbar and the Status Bar. The second pane from the top is the Message List, in which you see the list of items in the selected mailbox. The lower pane of the Mail window is the reading pane in which you read a mail item that is selected in Message List. All your mailboxes are in the Mail Drawer, which is a window that pops out of either side of the main Mail window (see Figure 12.13).

Figure 12.13
The Mail application uses three panes to enable you to browse, view, and organize your email.

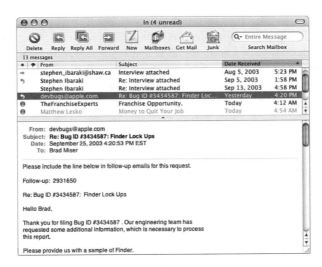

The Message pane of the Mail window behaves much like a Finder in List view. For example, you can change the width of the columns, sort the window, and so on. The columns in the default Mail window are the following (from left to right in Figure 12.13):

- Message status
- Buddy availability
- From
- Subject
- Date Received

The Mailbox Drawer shows all your mailboxes. You can open the Mailbox Drawer by selecting View, Show Mailboxes (Shift-⌘-M). You can close the Drawer by either selecting View, Hide Mailboxes (Shift-⌘-M) or dragging the Drawer by its outside edge. You can control the width of the Drawer by dragging the handle located in the center of its outside edge so it is the width you want it to be (if you try to make the drawer narrower than its minimum width, it closes instead).

TIP

> The Mailbox Drawer can appear on either side of the Mail window. To change the side on which the Drawer appears, hide the Mailbox Drawer and then drag a message from the Message List pane to the side on which you want the Drawer to be located. The Mailbox Drawer pops open on that side. Until you change its location again, it remains on that side.

You can expand or collapse the contents of a mailbox by using its expansion triangle. The Drawer contains several mailboxes and folders by default. The Inbox is used to store all your received mail; within the main Inbox is a mailbox for each of your email accounts. You also see Out, Drafts, Sent, and Trash mailboxes; the purpose of each of these should be self-evident. You might also see Drafts and Sent Messages folders for specific types of email accounts.

NOTE

> If you use a .Mac, IMAP, or Exchange email account, the Drafts, Junk, and Sent Messages mailboxes appear and have folder icons. These are folders stored on your Mac, whereas the other mailboxes are stored online. If you configured a .Mac email account to store messages online, they are stored in the online folders rather than those stored on your Mac.

RETRIEVING AND READING EMAIL

There are several ways to retrieve email from your accounts, including

- Setting Mail to retrieve your mail automatically using the General pane of the Mail Preferences window
- Clicking the Get Mail button on the Mail toolbar
- Pressing Shift-⌘-N to get new mail in all your accounts
- Selecting Mailbox, Get New Mail in *accountname*, where *accountname* is the account from which you want to retrieve your mail

NOTE

> The first three methods listed retrieve mail for all the email accounts you have config-ured in Mail (for those accounts that are enabled and that you set to be included in the retrieve all action using that account's settings).

TIP

You can temporarily hide the Reading pane by double-clicking the border between the Message List and the Reading pane. The Reading pane disappears and the Message list consumes the entire Mail window. Double-click the bottom of the Mail window to reopen the Reading pane. You can change the relative height of the two panes by dragging the resize handle located in the center of the bar between the two panes.

When you get mail, it is placed in the In mailbox, with the account's mailbox.

When you receive email, Mail's Dock icon indicates that you have new email and shows you the total number of new messages you have received. If you chose to have Mail play a sound when new mail is received, you hear that sound when mail is recieved. When you open the Mail icon on the Dock, a list pops up that shows you all the windows open in Mail, as well as some useful commands (see Figure 12.14).

Figure 12.14
When you receive new mail, Mail lets you know how many messages you have received (five in this case); you can quickly access the mailboxes containing the new messages by opening the Mail icon on the Dock and selecting your In mailbox.

When you select In on the Dock menu, you move into Mail to read your email; each unread message has a blue dot in the Status column to indicate that it is a new message. The number of new messages is also indicated next to the In mailbox.

TIP

You can also create a new message or check for new email from the Mail Dock menu.

If you have more than one email account, each account has its own Inbox. To see all your inboxes, click the expansion arrow next to the In folder (see Figure 12.15). The Inbox for each of your accounts appears. Select an Inbox to see the messages for that account only, or select the In folder to see all your messages at the same time.

Figure 12.15
Each of my email accounts has its own Inbox, as you can see listed under the In folder.

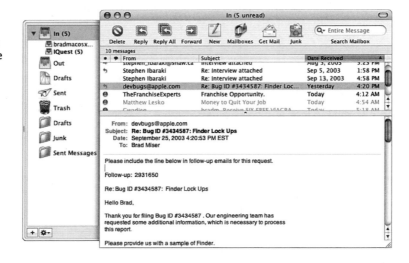

TIP

In Mail, you can display the contents of more than one mailbox at a time. To do so, select File, New Viewer Window (Option-⌘-N). In the new Viewer window, select the mailbox whose contents you want to view. You can have as many Viewer windows open as you want. For example, you might select to have a Viewer window open for each of your mail accounts.

If you are unable to retrieve your mail, see "My Mail Can't Be Retrieved" in the "Troubleshooting" section at the end of this chapter.

NOTE

You can see the activity of Mail as it downloads messages using its Activity Viewer. To see the Activity Viewer, select Window, Show Activity Viewer (or press ⌘-0).

The Status bar just above the Message List pane tells you the number of messages in the currently selected mailbox. When Mail is doing something, such as retrieving email, you see information about that activity at the left edge of the Status bar.

READING INDIVIDUAL MESSAGES

To view the contents of a mailbox, select it in the Drawer. The Message list shows the messages contained in that mailbox. To read a message, select it in the Message list and read it in the Reading pane.

> **TIP**
>
> If the sender of a message is included in your Address Book, the name on that person's card is shown in the From box instead of the person's email address. If you click the From name or email address, a pop-up menu appears. This menu shows the email address that the message is from and enables you to reply to the message, create a new message, or add the contact to your Address Book.

To read your mail, use the following shortcuts:

- Scroll down in a message by pressing the spacebar.
- Move up and down the messages in the Message List using the up- and down-arrow keys.
- Double-click a message to read it in its own window.

> **TIP**
>
> If the mailbox you are viewing has several messages in it, select those that are interesting to you; then hold down the Shift key to select contiguous messages or hold down the ⌘ key to select messages that are not contiguous. Select View, Display Selected Messages Only. The other messages in the mailbox are hidden and you can quickly read the messages you selected (using the shortcuts mentioned in the previous list). To see all the messages in the mailbox again, select View, Display All Messages.

12

WORKING WITH EMAIL THREADS

 As you read and reply to messages, each message and its replies become a thread, as in a thread of conversation about a topic (or at least started from a topic). If the "Highlight related messages using color" preference is set, Mail highlights all the messages in a thread with the color you select (it is light blue by default). You can also select to organize a mailbox by threads so that all the mails that form a conversation are grouped together.

To organize messages in the Message List pane by threads, select View, Organize by Thread. Messages that are part of a thread are highlighted in the selected color and are grouped together (see Figure 12.16). Select View, Organize by Thread again to return the Message pane to its previous organization. The messages in a thread are sorted just like other messages in the Message List pane.

Figure 12.16
While all the messages at the bottom of the Message List pane are from me, they are part of a thread.

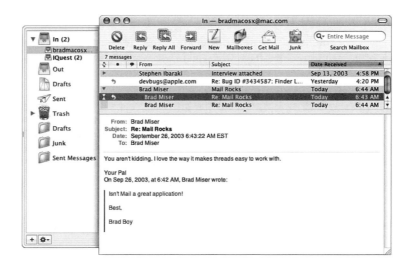

NOTE

If you don't organize by threads, messages in threads are still highlighted with the color indicated in Mail's preferences settings.

Following are some thread tips:

■ The first message in the thread is a summary of the other messages. Select that message to see each sender, title, and date of each message in the thread. At the top of the summary message is the name of the first message in the thread, who started it, and when the first message was sent.

■ You can collapse a thread by clicking the expansion triangle next to the summary message. The thread collapses so you see only that message. You can also collapse a thread by clicking the up and down arrow icon in the Status column for a message in the thread.

■ Click the Reply icon (which is the curved arrow) in the Status column to open a message in a separate window.

■ Select View, Expand All Threads to expand all the threads in a selected mailbox, or select View, Collapse All Threads to collapse all the threads in a selected mailbox.

TIP

Mail defines the messages that make up a thread by a special header element. This means you can change the subject of a reply in a thread and Mail will still recognize that the message is part of the thread. However, not all applications can do this and sometimes header information is removed from a message; therefore, it is usually better to leave the subject as it was when the thread was started.

If the person who sent you a message is in your Address Book and has an image on her card, that image appears in the upper-right corner of the email message (see Figure 12.17).

Figure 12.17
The image contained in a person's address card appears in the upper-right corner of a message you receive from that person.

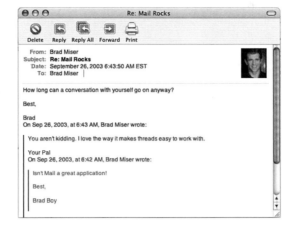

WRITING AND SENDING EMAIL

Writing email in Mail is also quite similar to other email applications. You can create a new mail message in several ways, including the following:

- Click the New button on the toolbar.
- Select File, New Message.
- Press ⌘-N.
- Point to a name in the To, From, or Cc block for a message you have received; click it; and select New Message on the resulting pop-up menu. A message is created and is addressed to the person whose name you clicked.
- Open the Mail's menu on the Dock and select Compose New Message.

> **TIP**
>
> If you point to the From block on an email message and click, a pop-up menu appears. On this menu, you can see the email address of the person, chat with the recipient, create a new message, open the related address card (if the recipient has a card, that is), or create an address card.

When you create a new message, you see the New Message window (see Figure 12.18). Creating the message is straightforward. If the message is not already addressed, type the email address(es) in the To and Cc fields. Mail attempts to match what you type to the addresses in your Address Book or on the list of previous recipients that Mail maintains automatically. The addresses that match what you type appear on a drop-down list. You can move up and down this list with the up- and down-arrow keys. To select an address on the list, highlight it and it is entered in the message's address box. (If there is only one address for the name you type, it is selected by default.) You can enter multiple addresses in an address field by typing a comma and then repeating the previous steps to add more addresses. When you have added all the addresses in the To field, press Tab to move to the next field.

Figure 12.18
If you have used other email applications, Mail's New Message window will no doubt look familiar.

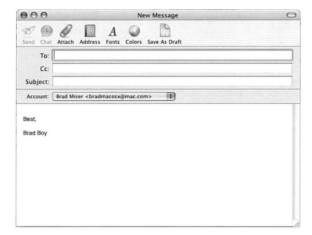

TIP

Mail automatically tracks a list of people to whom you have sent email. This list is called the Previous Recipients list. When you enter an email address in the To field, Mail attempts to match what you are entering to the recipients on this list. If it finds a match, it fills in the rest of the address for you. You can view the list by selecting Window, Previous Recipients. On this list, you can view addresses to or delete addresses from the list, or add addresses to your Address Book.

TIP

When an address is selected on the drop-down list that appears when Mail attempts to match the address you are typing, you can add it to the message and be ready to enter the next address by pressing comma.

To use your Address Book to address a message, open the Address Book by clicking the Address icon on the New Message window's toolbar or by pressing Option-⌘-A. An Addresses window appears that contains the contacts in your Address Book. Browse or search the window to find the people or groups to which you want to send the message. Select the person or group to whom you want to send mail, and click To or Cc to send those addresses to the respective fields in the New Message window.

TIP

> You can add a Bcc (blind carbon copy) address line by selecting View, Bcc Header or by pressing Option-⌘-B. You can add a Reply To address line by selecting View, Reply-To Header (or by pressing Option-⌘-R). You can also use the Reply To header to enter an address to which people should reply if it is different from the return address associated with the account selected on the Account pop-up menu.

Enter the subject of the message in the Subject field.

Select the account from which you want to send the mail using the Account pop-up menu (your default account is listed automatically).

Mail uses the following two rules to determine the account that is used to send a new message:

- If you have selected a mailbox associated with an account (such as the Inbox for an account), that account is the default for a new message.
- If you don't have a mailbox with which an account is associated selected, the account shown at the top of the Accounts list on the Accounts pane of the Mail Preferences dialog box and as the first mailbox under the Inbox is the default account.

You can determine which account is the default account by the order in which your accounts are listed on the Accounts pane of the Preferences window or by the order in which the account inboxes are listed under the Inbox in the Mailbox drawer. The account that is highest in the Preferences window or is first under the Inbox listed in the Account pop-up menu automatically. To change the order of the accounts, drag them up or down in either location.

TIP

> The New Message window has its own toolbar; you can customize its toolbar just as you can other Mail and Mac OS X toolbars (View, Customize Toolbar).

If you have configured Mail to show it, select the signature you want to use from the Signature pop-up menu.

Move into the body and type your message. As you type, Mail checks your spelling. When it identifies a misspelled word, it underlines the word in red. You can Control-click or right-click a misspelled word to pop up a menu that enables you to change the word to the correct spelling, ignore the spelling, or learn the word that Mail thinks is misspelled.

TIP

> You can also control Mail's spell checker using the Spelling commands on the Edit menu. You can open the Spelling window by selecting Edit, Spelling, and then Spelling again. You can check the spelling in a message by selecting Edit, Spelling, Check Spelling. You can turn off Check Spelling As You Type by selecting Edit, Spelling, Check Spelling As You Type.

12

NOTE

Because I encourage the use of plain-text email rather than formatted email, I won't be addressing formatting email in this chapter. However, if you select to create RTF messages, use the commands on the Format menu to format them. You can change the format of a new message (plain text or rich text) by moving the pointer into the body of a new message and opening the contextual menu (Control-click or right-click). Use the resulting pop-up menu to change the message's format.

As you work with a new message, open its contextual menu to gain quick access to various commands, such as formatting commands for an RTF message, Spell Checker controls, and quoting commands.

To send a message, do one of the following:

- Click the Send button on the toolbar.
- Select Message, Send Message.
- Press Shift-⌘-D.

TIP

While you're composing a message, you can save it in the Draft mailbox by either selecting File, Save As Draft (⌘-S) or clicking the Save As Draft button on the New Message toolbar. You can leave a message you are working on in your Draft folder as long as you'd like. If you close it, you can open it to work on it again by selecting the Draft folder and double-clicking the message. As you work, Mail saves your messages as drafts periodically, but you can use the command to save them manually.

 If your mail can't be sent, see "My Mail Can't Be Sent" in the "Troubleshooting" section at the end of this chapter.

REPLYING TO EMAIL

Replying to messages you receive in Mail is also similar to other applications. By default, Mail marks the different levels of quoting with different colors along with a change bar. As with other applications, you can select the message to which you want to reply and click Reply on the toolbar; select Message, Reply; or press ⌘-R, which replies to only the sender of the message. You can also click Reply All; select Message, Reply All; or press Shift-⌘-R to reply to everyone to whom the original message was sent.

You can use the same tools to reply to a message as you use to write a new message.

NOTE

You should always quote carefully in your replies. Quoting makes email much more effective because it gives the reader a good context for the information you are providing. Quoting is one reason I prefer plain-text messages. Quoting in a plain-text message is much easier; formatting often gets in the way of clear quoting.

You can also perform the following actions on mail you have received:

- **Replay with iChat**—Select Message, Reply with iChat or press Shift-⌘-I if the sender of the message is available via iChat.

- **Forward**—Select Message, Forward or press Shift-⌘-F to forward a message to other recipients.

- **Redirect**—Select Message, Redirect or press Shift-⌘-E to redirect the message to someone else. The difference between redirecting and forwarding a message is that when you redirect a message, the message's original sender's email address still appears in the From field so the person to whom you redirect the message can reply to the message to send email to the person who sent the message. If you forward a message and the recipient replies to it, the reply comes to you because your address becomes the From address on a forwarded message.

- **Bounce**—Select Message, Bounce or press Shift-⌘-B to bounce a message back to the sender. When you do so, the bounce message that is sent makes it appear as if your email address is not valid.

TIP

You can open a message's contextual menu to access many useful commands, such as Reply, Reply All, Forward, and so on.

NOTE

You might be tempted to bounce spam email that you receive. However, this usually doesn't do any good because most spam includes a bogus return address so your bounced message has no legitimate place to go. You can use the Bounce command to respond to email from legitimate organizations that have sent unwanted email to you. Hopefully, the bounce results in your address being removed from the related mailing list. Use Mail's Junk Mail feature to deal with spam.

12

DELETING EMAIL

You can delete messages by selecting the messages you want to delete and doing one of the following:

- Click the Delete button on the toolbar.
- Select Edit, Delete.
- Drag a message from the Message List pane or mailbox onto the Trash in the Mail Drawer.
- Press Delete.

Deleted messages are stored in the Trash folder in the Drawer. You can open this folder just like other folders you have. Messages aren't actually removed until the Trash folder is emptied.

When you use an IMAP account, such as a .Mac email account, you have to empty the Trash folder to actually remove the messages from the server. If you don't, those messages continue to count against the total storage space you have on the server. Typically, you are limited to a certain storage space for *all* your messages (under an IMAP or a .Mac account, all your messages remain on the server). Because messages in the Trash folder count against this limit, you should empty this folder more frequently under an IMAP account than you do with POP accounts.

Because they are actually IMAP accounts, .Mac email accounts are limited to a certain amount of storage. If the messages stored in your .Mac email account approach or exceed this limit, you receive email messages warning you that you are exceeding your allotted storage space. To move messages off the server, you need to move them from the Inbox for that account to one of your personal mailboxes stored on your Mac or to the Trash and then empty it.

You can determine whether deleted messages are stored on the server by using the Special Mailboxes tab of the Accounts pane of the Mail Preferences window. Open this tab and uncheck the "Store deleted messages on the server" check box. This causes the messages you delete to be downloaded to your Mac, so they won't count against your storage limit.

You can also use the "Permanently erase deleted message when" pop-up menu to select a time period for your deleted messages to be permanently erased.

NOTE

> Just like the Inbox, each email account has its own Trash.

To empty Mail's Trash, do one of the following:

- Select Mailbox, Erase Deleted Messages, In All Accounts or press ⌘-K.
- Select Mailbox, Erase Deleted Messages, *accountname*, where *accountname* is the name of the account whose Trash you want to empty.
- Select Mailbox, Erase Junk Mail or press Option-⌘-J to erase the messages stored in the Junk folder (more on that later).
- Open the Trash's contextual menu and select Erase Deleted Messages.
- Use Mail's preferences to set an automatic deletion point, such as a time period or when you quit Mail.

CUSTOMIZING YOUR EMAIL

Mail provides many tools you can use to customize various aspects of your mail. These include customizing the Mail window, organizing your email, sorting your email, and automating your mail with rules.

CUSTOMIZING THE VIEWER WINDOW

You can customize the Viewer window by using the commands shown in Table 12.1.

TABLE 12.1 WAYS TO CUSTOMIZE THE VIEWER WINDOW	
Command	**What It Does**
View, Columns	Enables you to select the columns displayed in the Viewer window. In addition to the columns shown by default, you can select from many columns, including Attachments, Date Sent, and so on.
View, Sort By	Sorts the Message List pane by the column you select.
View, Hide/Show Mailboxes	Hides/shows the Drawer.
View, Use Small Mailbox Icons	Changes the size of the mailbox icons displayed in the Drawer.
View, Hide/Show Toolbar	Hides/shows the Mail toolbar.
View, Hide/Show Status Bar	Hides/shows the Status bar.

NOTE

Remember that you can also customize the Message List window by moving the columns to change the order in which they appear, resizing them, changing the column by which the pane is sorted, and so on, just as you can in Finder windows in the List view.

ORGANIZING YOUR EMAIL

You can create your own mailboxes to organize your messages. The mailboxes you create are shown under the On My Mac folder in the Drawer. You can also create nested mailboxes to create a hierarchy of mailboxes in which you store your messages.

1. Select Mailbox, New to see the New Mailbox dialog box (see Figure 12.19).

Figure 12.19
You use the New Mailbox dialog box to create a new mailbox either on your Mac or on a server.

2. On the Location pop-up menu, select the location of the mailbox you are creating. If you select On My Mac, the folder is created on your computer and appears under the

On My Mac folder in the Drawer. If you use an IMAP or .Mac account, you can select that account to create a folder on that account's server; to access the folder, you expand the icon for that account in the Drawer.

Remember that if you store the folder on a server, the contents of that folder count against your storage quota.

3. In the New Mailbox dialog box, enter the name of the mailbox you want to create. To create a nested mailbox, enter the name of each mailbox separated by a slash (/). For example, to create a mailbox called "Receipts" within a mailbox called "Mail to Keep," you would enter **Mail to Keep/Receipts**.

4. Click OK.

The mailbox is created. If you have created a mailbox that contains other mailboxes, you can use its expansion triangle to expand or collapse it. In Figure 12.20, you can see that I have created a folder called Receipts that is nested within a folder called Mail To Keep. Because these folders are stored on my computer, they are listed under the On My Mac mailbox. You can also see that I have a .Mac account and its folders are shown under the .Mac mailbox, which is next to my .Mac email address. Messages you place in folders stored on a server count against your storage limit on that server, so it is generally a better idea to create folders on your Mac instead.

Figure 12.20
Folders under the On My Mac icon are stored on your computer; folders under a server's icon, such as the .Mac mail account in this figure, are stored on that server.

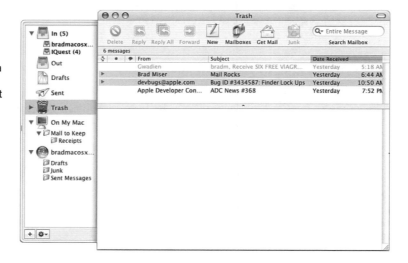

You can move messages from one mailbox to another in the following ways:

■ Drag and drop a message from the Message List pane to a mailbox.

NOTE

> If the Drawer is hidden and you drag a message "out" either side of the Mail window, the Drawer pops open so you can place the message in a mailbox.

- Drag messages from the Message List pane in one Viewer to the Message List pane in another Viewer; this copies the messages in the mailbox shown in the second Viewer window.

- Select messages and select Message, Move To; then select the mailbox to which you want to transfer the messages.

- Select messages and select Message, Copy To; then select the mailbox to which you want to create a copy of the selected messages.

- Select messages and select Message, Move Again to move the selected messages into the same mailbox into which you most recently transferred mail (Option-⌘-T).

- Open a message's contextual menu and select the Move To, Copy To, Move Again, or Apply Rules command.

- Select messages and select Message, Apply Rules (Option-⌘-L); then select a rule that transfers the messages.

CONFIGURING AND USING RULES FOR EMAIL

You can automate the handling of your email by configuring and using rules. For example, you might want to create a mailbox for the mail related from a certain person and have that mail automatically transferred into that mailbox. Or, you might have the messages from a mailing list to which you are subscribed placed in a specific mailbox for later reading.

To create and implement rules, you use the Rules pane of the Mail Preferences window:

1. Open the Mail Preferences window and click the Rules icon to open the Rules pane. Some rules are installed by default.

2. Click Add Rule to open a Rule sheet to define the rule you are creating.

3. Name the rule by entering a description.

4. Use the If pop-up menu to determine whether at least one criterion (select any) or all the criteria (select all) in the rule must be met for the actions in the rule to be taken.

5. Use the first condition pop-up menu to select the first criterion on which the rule will act. You can select any of the fields in a mail message. You can also select from various criteria, such as whether the sender is in your Address Book.

6. Use the Contains pop-up menu to select how the criteria will relate to the value you enter (such as Contains, "Is equal to," and so on).

7. Enter the value for which the rule will be implemented, if applicable, or use a pop-up menu to select a value. (Some conditions, such as "Sender is in my Address Book," don't require any values.)

12

8. To add more criteria, click the Add button (+) and repeat steps 5 and 6 to create additional conditions for the rule.

9. Use the Action area to select the actions that will be performed by the rule by making a choice from the first pop-up menu and making other choices from the other pop-up menus or fields related to that choice.

   The actions you can select are Move Message, Copy Message, Set Color of Message, Play Sound, Bounce Icon in Dock, Reply to Message, Forward Message, Redirect Message, Delete Message, Mark as Read, Mark as Flagged, Run AppleScript, or Stop evaluating rules. You can include multiple actions in the same rule.

10. Click the Add button next to the action and repeat step 9 to create and configure additional actions. When you are done, review the rule you have created. For example, the rule shown in Figure 12.21 checks to see whether a message is from me, the subject contains Special Edition Using Mac OS X, or is from my email address; if any of these conditions is true, the message is moved to the Trash and the Frog sound plays.

Figure 12.21
Hopefully, you won't want to create a rule like this one!

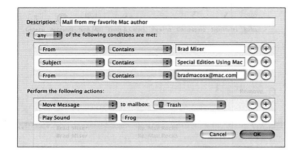

> **T I P**
>
> You can remove conditions or actions by clicking the Remove button (–).

11. Click OK to see the rule you created in the Rules pane.

12. Create more rules or close the Preferences window.

> **N O T E**
>
> If you apply a color in a rule, that rule appears in that color in the Rules pane. Messages already in a mailbox that meet the rule's criteria are also shown in the color applied by the rule.

You can use the Edit and Duplicate buttons to edit or duplicate rules and the Remove button to delete rules.

Any future messages you receive that meet the criteria for a rule are acted upon by that rule. You can also manually apply rules to messages by selecting messages and selecting Message, Apply Rules (Option-⌘-L).

TIP

> Manually applying rules is a good way to test your rules to ensure that they do what you intended.

HANDLING JUNK MAIL

Unfortunately, no matter how careful you are with your email address, it might eventually get on a junk mail list. And after it gets on one such list, it will get on many, and your inbox will overflow with junk mail. Fortunately, Mail includes some built-in tools for dealing with junk mail.

TIP

> Although Mail's Junk mail feature is a good way to deal with spam, it doesn't eliminate spam. See the sidebar at the end of this section for recommendations about how to deal with spam more effectively.

You can configure Mail's Junk feature via the Junk Mail pane of the Mail preferences dialog box (see Figure 12.22).

Figure 12.22
Use the Junk Mail pane to configure Mail's junk feature.

The Junk feature has three modes.

In the Disabled mode, the Junk Feature is inactive and doesn't do anything. You can disable this feature by unchecking the "Enable Junk Mail filtering" check box on the Junk Mail pane of the preferences dialog box.

In the Training mode (which is the default mode), Mail applies its Junk rules to your messages. This causes Mail to color the message brown or gold (depending on your color perception), indicating that Mail thinks the message is junk. You use this mode to fine-tune the Junk Mail feature so it correctly filters your messages to identify the junk. When you view a message that has been correctly identified as junk, don't do anything. When a message has been identified as junk but it isn't, click the Not Junk button. If you find a message that is junk, but Mail has not identified it as such, click the Junk button on the toolbar. You can place the Junk Mail feature in the Training mode by clicking the "Leave it in my inbox, but indicate it is junk mail (Training)" radio button.

After some time has passed and you are confident that Mail's Junk filter is working properly, you can move into Junk Mail's Automatic mode. When you do so, Mail creates a Junk folder in the Drawer and prompts you to ask whether it should move all the identified junk mail to this folder. Click Yes. You move into the Automatic mode by clicking the "Move it to the Junk mailbox (Automatic)" radio button.

When the Junk feature is in the Automatic mode, it moves all the messages it identifies as junk into the Junk folder. You should review the contents of this folder periodically to ensure that no messages you want are in this folder by mistake. If there are messages you want to keep, move them to a different folder. Then delete all the messages in the Junk folder.

By checking the related check box on the Junk Mail pane of the preferences dialog box, you can exempt email messages from the Junk Mail filter in the following situations:

- The sender of a message is in your Address Book.
- The sender of a message is on the list of previous recipients.
- The message is addressed to your full name (most spam uses an email address).

If your Internet service provider (ISP) provides junk mail headers that attempt to identify junk mail by its own rules and you want Mail to recognize and use those headers, check the "Trust Junk Mail headers set by your Internet Service Provider" check box.

If you click the Advanced button, you move to a Rules sheet and the default Junk rules are ready to edit. (Mail's Junk Mail feature is actually just a special mail rule.) You can change this mail rule just like any rule you create on the Rule pane to change how Mail handles junk mail. If you open the Junk rule, you see that this is simply a rule that acts on any messages that are from people who are not in your Address Book, are not on your Previous Recipient list, are not addressed to your full name, or are marked as Junk. If the Training mode, this rule changes only the color of the messages. In the Automatic mode, it moves the messages to the Junk folder.

If you click the Reset button, the Junk Mail feature is returned to its default state. This also removes any learning the filter has done so you have to repeat the training process.

THE END OF SPAM

With all due respect to Mail's Junk feature, there are certain circumstances in which providing your email address is likely to result in your address being obtained by a spammer. And after it gets into one spammer's hands, it will get into lots of spammers' hands and you will start receiving dozens or even hundreds of spam messages every day. The only real way to stop spam is to stop using the email address that has been spammed. Junk mail filters, such as Mail's Junk feature, are really only a way to make dealing with spam easier; they don't eliminate the spam from your life.

Several situations should be considered to have high risk of your address being spammed. One is public discussion forums, such as on Web sites, in newsgroups, in chat rooms, and so on; in fact, getting spammed from these locations is guaranteed. Another is when you are shopping online; many online retailers have valid privacy policies that allow you to opt out of your address being provided to others, but some don't have such policies. Another is any time you are asked for an email address, such as when you are taking a survey, registering for a "free" prize, and so on. Providing an email address in any of the situations will likely get you spammed.

If that happens and you use an email address for work or to keep in touch with people, you aren't likely to want to change the address you use.

There is a solution to this dilemma: You can create "disposable" email accounts for use in the situations that are more likely to result in an addressed getting spammed. If that happens, you can simply stop using the spammed email account and create another disposable account to use in the high spam risk situations.

Meanwhile, you can keep your permanent email address close the vest by providing it only to people you know or to companies that you are sure are legit and won't sell your address to spammers.

There are many sources of good disposable email accounts, including the following:

- Yahoo Mail (`mail.yahoo.com`).
- MSN Hotmail (`www.hotmail.com`).
- Other similar sites that enable you to create and use email accounts at no cost.
- Your own Internet access account. Many ISP accounts provide multiple email accounts under your access account. Even better, most of the time you can create and delete your own sub-accounts, which is the ideal situation. Keep your base email account private; never use it in any circumstance. Then create an email account as your permanent address and provide that to the people with whom you really want to communicate. Finally, create your disposable address and use that in high spam risk situations. If that address gets spammed, just delete it and create another one.

NOTE

> You might have noticed that I provide my email address in this book, which is bradmacosx@mac.com. I like to receive email from readers, and spammers aren't likely to read a book to get a single address. So, even exposing an email address in a public place like a book isn't all that risky. However, I use the practice described in the last bullet in the previous list to manage my own email. For example, I have an email address for personal email and another disposable address I use when shopping online (mostly Mac stuff and DVDs). If that address ever gets spammed, I can just delete it and create a replacement.

SENDING AND RECEIVING FILES WITH EMAIL

One of the most valuable uses of email is to send and receive attachments. Again, Mail handles file attachments similarly to other email applications you might be accustomed to.

ATTACHING FILES TO YOUR EMAIL

Attaching files to messages you send can be done in the following ways:

- In the message to which you want to attach files, select File, Attach File (Shift-⌘-A). Then, use the Choose File sheet to select the files you want to attach.

- Click the Attach button on the New Message window's toolbar. The Choose File sheet appears; use it to select the files you want to attach to a message.

TIP

> In the Choose File sheet, check the Send Windows Friendly Attachments if you are sending files to Windows users. This makes these users more likely to be able to use the files you send. You can turn on this feature so it applies to all attachments by selecting, Edit, Attachments, Always Send Windows Friendly Attachments.

- Drag the files onto the New Message window.

When you place a file in a new message window, you see a thumbnail preview of the file with its icon, the filename, and its size in parentheses. If the file type is one that can be displayed in the message, such as a TIFF image or a PDF file, you actually see the contents of the file in the body of the message.

By default, Mail displays the contents of files you attach if it can. If the contents of the file are being displayed and you would rather see just an icon, open the file's contextual menu and select View as icon. The file is displayed as an icon instead. To view the file's content again, open the menu and select View in Place.

File attachments must be *encoded* before they can be sent. When a file is encoded, it is translated into a string of text. The application that receives the message must then decode that message so the files become usable. Encoding and decoding is handled automatically, and you can't select the encoding method used.

If recipients of your file attachments have trouble with them, see "Recipients of My Attachments Are Seeing Odd Things" in the "Troubleshooting" section at the end of this chapter.

You should also compress files you attach to email messages. Under Mac OS X version 10.3, you can compress any file in the Zip format using the Finder's Archive command. Simply select the files you want to attach to an email message, open the contextual menu, and select Archive. The files you selected are placed in a Zip file. You can then rename the file (don't change the .zip file extenstion) and attach the Zip file to the message you are sending.

Sending file attachments is simple except for one thing—the Windows versus Mac situation, which raises its ugly head in the area of file attachments, too. Basically, Mac and Windows operating systems use different file format structures. Mac files have two "forks," whereas Windows files have only one. This is a problem when you send files to Windows users because they end up with two files. One is the usable file and one is unusable to them (the names of the files is *filename* and *_filename*). Recipients can use the first one and safely ignore the second one. However, it is still confusing for them.

Mail includes a solution for this problem, which is called sending Window Friendly Attachments. This causes Mail to strip the second file away, so the Windows recipient receives only one file for each attachment. That is a good thing.

However, Mac users who receive Windows-friendly attachments might lose some features, such as thumbnail preview or information about the file. In the worst case, the file might be unusable.

You can select to attach files as Windows friendly by checking the box in the Attach File dialog box. If you always want to send files in the Windows-friendly format, select Edit, Attachments, Send Windows Friendly Attachments.

Unless you always send files to other Mac users or only to Windows users, you have to decide whether to use the Windows-friendly option each time you attach files. You should either use this option when you send files to Windows users (if you don't know which type of computer the recipient uses) or not use it if you are certain the recipient uses a Mac.

USING FILES ATTACHED TO EMAIL YOU RECEIVE

When you receive a message that has files attached to it, you see the files in the body of the message. As when you send files in a message, you see the file's icon, name, and size. If the file can be displayed in the body, such as a TIFF or PDF, the contents of the file are displayed in the message. You can use the file attachments in the following ways:

- Select File, Save Attachments. Use the resulting sheet to move to a location and save the attachments.

- Click the Save All button at the top of the message. Use the resulting sheet to move to a location and save the attachments.

- If multiple files are attached, click the expansion triangle next to the attachment line in the message's header and work with each file individually.

12

- Double-click a file's icon to open it; drag a file's icon from the message onto a folder on the desktop to save it there.

- You can open the attachment's contextual menu and select one of the listed actions, such as Open Attachment, which opens it in its native application; Open With, which enables you to select the application in which you want the file to open; Save Attachment; or Save to Downloads folder, which saves the attachment in your designated Downloads folder.

> **TIP**
>
> If the contents of the file are being displayed and you would rather see just an icon, open the file's contextual menu and select View as icon. The file is displayed as an icon instead. To view the file's content again, open the menu and select View in Place.

> **TIP**
>
> If you have trouble viewing a message and the folder into which you want to store the file attachments, double-click the message to open it in its own window. Then you can resize the window so you can more easily see the folder into which you want to drag it.

If the files you receive are compressed, you must uncompress them before you can open them.

→ To learn more about uncompressing files, **see** "Downloading and Preparing Files," **p. 411**.

SEARCHING EMAIL

As you collect email, you will probably need to search it. You can quickly search for messages, or you can search for specific text in a message.

You can search for messages using the following steps:

1. If you want to search only in a single mailbox, select that mailbox.

2. Click the triangle next to the magnifying-glass icon in the Search tool on the toolbar. A pop-up menu appears. You can use this menu to select the fields you want to search (Entire Message is the default) and the mailboxes in which you want to search (the selected mailbox is the default).

3. If you want to search in the selected mailbox, select the field you want to search in the upper section of the menu to search in the selected mailbox. If you want to search in all mailboxes, select the field you want to search on the lower section of the menu.

4. Type the text you want to search for. As you type, the messages shown in the Message List pane is reduced to those that meet your criteria.

You can also search for text within a specific message using the Find Panel.

1. Select Edit, Find, Find (⌘-F). The Find Panel appears (see Figure 12.23).

Figure 12.23
You can search for text and replace it using the Find Panel.

2. Enter the text you want to search for.

3. Click Next to search for the text.

You can use the Replace with box in the Find panel to replace the text you find with different text.

TROUBLESHOOTING

MY MAIL CAN'T BE RETRIEVED

When I check my mail, I get a "Fetch Error," saying that Mail couldn't connect to my mail server.

This can happen for various reasons, such as a problem with your Internet connection, a misconfigured email account, and so on. Use the following information to correct the problem.

Open and use another Internet application, such as a Web browser.

If it works properly, there is a problem with Mail or your mail account configuration.

If it doesn't work properly, you are having trouble with your Internet access, which is why your mail account can't be accessed. You need to troubleshoot your Net connection.

→ For help troubleshooting your Net connection, **see** "Troubleshooting," **p. 294**.

If you have more than one email account, try all your accounts. If you have problems with all your accounts, something might have happened to the Mail application.

→ For help with troubleshooting applications, **see** Chapter 29, "Solving Mac Problems," **p. 915**.

If your other accounts work, the problem is related to the specific account. If you have successfully retrieved email under this account before, the problem is likely a temporary one with the server from which you retrieve email or a temporary interruption in your communication with that server. In this case, wait awhile and try again later. If you continue to have problems or you have never been able to retrieve email from this account, try the following:

1. In Mail, select Mail, Preferences.

2. Click the Accounts button.

3. Select the account with which you are having trouble.

4. Click Edit. Check the account information for that account—especially the Host Name, User Name, and Password fields—and correct any errors you find. If no errors exist in these fields, the account is configured properly.

5. Allow some time to pass and try the account again. If you are still unable to retrieve your mail, the problem might reside with the provider of the mail account.

6. Contact the technical support for the organization providing your mail service for further help.

MY MAIL CAN'T BE SENT

When I try to send mail, I get an error message stating that my mail can't be sent.

Troubleshooting this problem is similar to troubleshooting a problem retrieving mail. The only difference is in step 4. You should carefully check the SMTP Host, SMTP User, and SMTP password boxes. If authentication is used for your SMTP account, make sure the Authentication check box is checked.

 For help troubleshooting a problem with sending mail, refer to "My Mail Can't Be Retrieved," earlier in this section.

RECIPIENTS OF MY ATTACHMENTS ARE SEEING ODD THINGS

People to whom I send attachments see duplicate files, missing file attachment messages, and other odd things.

This happens when the recipient's email application does not fully support the encoding scheme Mail uses to encode files you attach to your messages. Most email applications decode files well enough for the files to be used, although some strange things can happen on the recipient's end. A few email applications can't decode the Mail file attachments at all. Problems with can be experienced with very old Mac email applications, some Windows email applications, and some Unix email applications.

In some cases, Windows recipients receive two files for each file you attach. Mail sends two files; one contains the file data and other contains the resource information. Most of the time, the recipient can use one of the duplicate files normally, safely ignore the resource file, and work with the data file. Tell the recipients who are having problems to try opening the files to determine which one is the correct file. The recipients can discard the unused resource files.

The missing file attachment message can usually be ignored, or you can try to resend the attachments using the Windows-friendly setting.

If the recipient's email application is incapable of decoding the files at all, you must find another means to transmit the files to her, such as an email application that enables you to select a different encoding scheme. Or, you can create a .Mac Web site to share the files.

→ To learn how to use .Mac to share files, **see** "Using a .Mac iDisk and HomePage to Create and Serve Your Web Pages," **p. 426**.

MAX OS X TO THE MAX: EMAIL AWAY

In this section, you learn where Mail and Address Book information is stored and find keyboard shortcuts for the Address Book and Mail.

UNDERSTANDING WHERE YOUR MAIL AND ADDRESS BOOK INFORMATION IS STORED

Mail stores all your email in the location *username*/`Library`/`Mail`, where *username* is your short username. In this folder, you will find the following:

- A folder for each of the accounts you have configured in Mail. Within each accounts folder are the Inbox, a Drafts folder, and support files for that account.
- The Mailboxes folder that contains each mailbox you have created. If you have nested mailboxes, the inclusive mailbox appears as a folder.
- Your mailing sort, signature, and other preferences files.

> **NOTE**
>
> The filename extension for a mailbox is `.mbox`. The filename extension for preference files is `.plist`.

Your Address Book is stored in the location *username*/`Library`/`Application Support`/ `AddressBook`/`AddressBook.data`, where *username* is your short username.

USING ADDRESS BOOK KEYBOARD SHORTCUTS

Table 12.2 shows keyboard shortcuts for the Address Book application.

TABLE 12.2   KEYBOARD SHORTCUTS FOR THE ADDRESS BOOK

Action	Keyboard Shortcut
Address Book Help	⌘-?
Edit Card	⌘-L
Hide Address Book	⌘-H
Import vCards	⌘-O
Merge Cards	⌘-|
Minimize Address Book Window	⌘-M
Move Between Fields on an Address Card	Tab and Shift-Tab
New Card	⌘-N
New Group	Shift-⌘-N
Next Card	⌘-]

12

TABLE 12.2 CONTINUED	
Action	**Keyboard Shortcut**
Open in Separate Window	⌘-I
Preferences	⌘-,
Previous Card	⌘-[
This is a Company	⌘-\
View Card and Columns	⌘-1
View Card Only	⌘-2
View Directories	⌘-3

USING MAIL KEYBOARD SHORTCUTS

Table 12.3 shows keyboard shortcuts for the Mail application.

TABLE 12.3 KEYBOARD SHORTCUTS FOR MAIL	
Action	**Keyboard Shortcut**
Add Reply-To Header	Option-⌘-R
Add Sender to Address Book	⌘-Y
Address Panel	Option-⌘-A
Append Selected Messages	Option-⌘-I
Apply Bcc Header	Shift-⌘-B
Apply Rules	Option-⌘-L
Attach File	Shift-⌘-A
Bigger	⌘--
Bounce	Option-⌘-B
Check Spelling	⌘-;
Copy Style	Option-⌘-C
Decrease Quote Level	Option-⌘-'
Delete	Delete
Erase Deleted Messages In All Accounts	⌘-K
Erase Junk Mail	Option-⌘-J
Find Messages	Option-⌘-F
Find Next	⌘-G
Find Previous	⌘-D

Action	Keyboard Shortcut
Find Text	⌘-F
Forward	Shift-⌘-F
Get New Mail In All Accounts	Shift-⌘-N
Go To In	⌘-1
Go To Out	⌘-2
Go To Drafts	⌘-3
Go To Sent	⌘-4
Go To Trash	⌘-5
Go To Junk	⌘-6
Hide Deleted Messages	⌘-L
Hide/Show Mailboxes	Shift-⌘-M
Hide/Show Status bar	Option-⌘-S
Increase Quote Level	⌘-'
Jump to Selection	⌘-J
Message Long Headers	Shift-⌘-H
Make Plain Text	Shift-⌘-T
Mark As Flagged	Shift-⌘-L
Mark As Junk Mail	Shift-⌘-J
Mark As Unread/Mark As Read	Shift-⌘-U
Move Again	Option-⌘-T
New Message	⌘-N
New Viewer Window	Option-⌘-N
Next Alternative	⌘-]
Paste as Quotation	Shift-⌘-V
Paste With Current Style	Option-Shift-⌘-V
Plain Text Alternative	Option-⌘-P
Preferences	Option-,
Previous Alternative	⌘-[
Raw Source	Option-⌘-U
Redirect	Shift-⌘-E
Reply All	Shift-⌘-R
Reply	⌘-R

12

TABLE 12.3   CONTINUED

Action	Keyboard Shortcut
Reply With iChat	Shift-⌘-I
Save As	Shift-⌘-S
Save As Draft	⌘-S
Select All Highlighted Messages	Shift-⌘-K
Send Again	Shift-⌘-D
Show Activity Viewer	⌘-0
Show Colors	Shift-⌘-C
Show Fonts	⌘-T
Show Long Headers	Shift-⌘-H
Smaller	⌘--
Spelling	⌘-:
Use Selection for Find	⌘-E

CHAPTER 13

SURFING THE WEB

In this chapter

BROWSING THE WEB WITH SAFARI

Apple's Safari is a Mac OS X-only Web browser that has become the default Mac browser with Mac OS X version 10.3. Safari offers many great features and excellent performance (see Figure 13.1).

Figure 13.1
Safari works as good as it looks.

Introducing the new PowerBook G4 family.

An all-new 15-inch PowerBook G4 – plus new ultracompact 12-inch and ultrawide 17-inch models. All feature the DVD-burning SuperDrive, ultrafast wireless networking and breathtaking graphics.

Because you are reading this book (indicating that you know your way around a Mac), I assume that you are quite comfortable with the basics of using Safari, such as using its buttons, navigating the Web by entering URLs in the Address bar, and so on. In this section, you will learn about some of Safari's great features that might not be quite so obvious.

CONFIGURING SAFARI

Like other browsers, there are a number of ways in which you can configure Safari to match your browsing preferences.

CONFIGURING SAFARI'S WINDOW

By default, Safari's window is pretty standard looking (refer to Figure 13.1). However, using the options on the View menu, you can customize the Safari browser experience to suit your likes (see Figure 13.2). On that menu, you have the following options:

- **Address Bar**—This command shows or hides the Safari Address bar. At its most basic, the Address bar displays the URL of the page currently being shown. You can also add more tools and buttons to the Address bar by using the eight view options listed underneath the Address Bar option on the menu. If you hide the Address bar, the other eight options are hidden as well. You show or hide the Address bar by pressing ⌘-| (which is actually Shift-⌘-\ on the keyboard).

- **Back/Forward**—This option shows or hides the Back and Forward buttons.
- **Home**—If you select this option, the Home button is displayed. You can configure your home page using the General preferences.
- **AutoFill**—If you click the AutoFill button, a form is completed with information from your card in your Address Book (more on this feature later).
- **Text Size**—These buttons enable you to increase or decrease the size of text being displayed on a page (if you have ever squinted while trying to read a page designed on Windows, you know why increasing the size of text on a page can be necessary!).
- **Stop/Reload**—This button can be used to stop a page that is currently being loaded or to reload a page currently being displayed.
- **Add Bookmark**—Use this option to show or hide the Add Bookmark button.
- **Google Search**—The Google Search tool is a great way to search for information, as you will learn in a later section.
- **Bug**—When you click this button, you can send a bug report about Safari to Apple.
- **Bookmarks Bar**—The Bookmarks bar provides easy access to your favorite bookmarks. It appears under the Address bar if it is being displayed or at the top of the window if it is hidden.
- **Status Bar**—The Status bar provides useful information about what Safari is doing at any point in time or information about a link to which you are pointing, such as its URL.

Figure 13.2
Using the View menu, you can configure the Safari window to match your browsing needs.

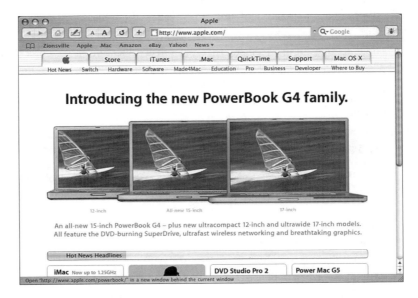

13

You might want to show most of these options until you have used Safari enough to know which you don't need or until you are comfortable using keyboard shortcuts and don't need to display the buttons or controls in the Address bar.

CONFIGURING SAFARI'S GENERAL PREFERENCES

Press ⌘-, to open the Safari Preferences dialog box, and click the General button to open its General pane (see Figure 13.3). The general preferences are explained in the following list:

- **Default Web Browser**—Use the Default Web Browser pop-up menu to choose your default Web browser, which is the browser Mac OS X will use to view Web pages and to open Web links. Intitally, Safari is the option selected on the pop-up menu. However, you can select Internet Explorer to choose that browser or choose Select and then pick another browser. This sets your browser preference for all areas of the OS, not just within Safari.

- **New Window Behavior**—Use the "New windows open with" pop-up menu to choose what happens when you open a new Safari window. The options are Home Page, Empty Page, Same Page, or Bookmarks. In most cases, Empty Page is the best choice because it doesn't cause Safari to download a page that you probably don't want to view anyway. However, if you frequently use bookmarks to move to a new page, that can be a useful option as well.

- **Home Page**—Type a URL in the Home page field to set it as your home page. Alternatively, you can move to the page you want to be your home page, open the General pane, and click Set to Current Page. The home page is displayed when you use the Home button or if you have it set to be displayed when you open a new Safari window. If you leave the field empty, moving to the home page opens a new empty page.

- **Download Behavior**—You will frequently use Safari to download files. Use the "Save downloaded files to" pop-up menu to select a location in which you want those files to be placed by default. The choices are Desktop or Other. I recommend that you select Other, create a folder called Downloaded Files or something similar, and set that folder as your download location. That way, you will always know where files you download are located.

NOTE

Setting a file download location, similar to choosing a default Web browser, affects the OS—not just Safari. For example, if you use a download tool that uses your download location preference, that application uses the preference you set within Safari.

Use the "Remove download list items" pop-up menu to choose when items are removed from the Downloads window (you'll learn about that later).

If you want "safe" files to be opened as soon as you download them, check the "Open 'safe' files after downloading" check box (it is checked by default). When Safari downloads image, movie, text, sound, and other content files, they are opened automatically. For those files that might cause damage to your system, such as applications, macros, and other suspicious files, you must open them manually after you download them.

- **Link behavior**—When documents, such as email messages, contain URL links, the two radio buttons determine how those links open when you click them. If you click the "in a new window" radio button, a new Safari window opens and displays the page at which the link points. If you click "in the current window," the content at which the link points replaces that shown in the current window.

Figure 13.3
Although simple in appearance, the General pane enables you to configure important Safari behaviors.

Configuring Safari's Appearance Preferences

Click the Appearance button in the Safari Preferences dialog box to move to the Appearance tab. Here you can set the standard font, fixed-width font, and default encoding that is used when pages are displayed. (If a page uses a built-in style sheet, your options might be overridden by the style sheet, but most of the time, your preferences will be used.) To select a font, click the related Select button and use the Font panel to configure the font. To choose an encoding method, use the pop-up menu.

If you want images to be displayed when a page is opened, check the "Display images when the page opens" check box (it is checked by default). If you use a slow connection, you might want to uncheck this check box so you don't waste time downloading images you aren't interested in.

Configuring Safari's Security Preferences

Safari has a number of good security features, some of which you can configure on the Security pane of the Safari Preferences dialog box (see Figure 13.4).

13

Figure 13.4
Use the Security pane to set how Safari manages the security of your Mac; the best part is the ability to block pop-up windows.

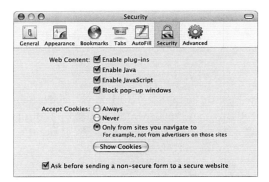

The Web Content controls determine whether certain types of content is enabled. These controls include

- **"Enable plug-ins"**—Determines whether any Safari plug-ins, such as those for QuickTime, Flash, and so on, are enabled. If you disable the plug-ins, content that requires them is not displayed. I recommend you leave this check box checked because most content that requires such plug-ins is safe. And, except for the plug-ins installed by default, you will choose the plug-ins you want to install.

- **Enable Java and Enable JavaScript**—Java and JavaScript are two programming languages that can be used to execute complex operations within the Safari browser. For example, if you use a bank service, it likely uses JavaScript to deliver its functionality. Again, you should typically allow these types of content.

- **"Block pop-up windows"**—If you have ever been annoyed by the numerous and obnoxious pop-up windows that appear when you visit some Web sites, you might think that this is the single best feature of Safari. If this option is checked, Safari does not allow a Web page to open additional windows. This means that all pop-up windows that point to different URLs are blocked and you never have to see them.

  Although blocking pop-up windows is mostly a good thing, some pop-up windows actually provide useful information and are necessary to get the most out of a Web site. If you block them, a site might not work well, or at all.

TIP

> If you block pop-up windows and a site that needs them doesn't work properly, you can enable them again by selecting Safari, Block Pop-Up Windows or by pressing ⌘-K. This toggles the pop-up window setting, so you can also use it to quickly prevent pop-ups if you generally allow them.

You use the Cookies radio buttons to determine how Safari deals with cookies it encounters. Typically, the "Only from sites you navigate to" is the best setting because cookies often provide a useful service for the sites you intentionally visit, such as shopping sites. If you want to block all cookies, click Never. I don't recommend that you ever use the Always option.

To see the cookies that have been accepted, click the Show Cookies button. A sheet appears that shows you all the cookies that have been downloaded to your Mac (prepare to be astounded at their number!). In addition to the information you see about the cookies, you can select cookies and either click Remove to delete them or click Remove All to delete all the cookies on your Mac. It's not a bad idea to review this list from time to time and delete any cookies you can't recognize (or at least recognize where they came from). If a site needs a cookie to function, it creates it again.

Cookies

On the Web, *cookies* are small text files Web sites use to track information about you. When you visit a site that uses cookies, the site can check the cookies it previously installed on your machine to serve you or capture more information about you. For example, a cookie can contain areas of interest so you are automatically taken to spots on the site that are more likely to generate a purchase from you.

Most cookies are relatively harmless and some even serve a good purpose, but you do need to be aware that a lot of information about you and what you do on the Web is captured whether you know it or not. If this thought bothers you, select the Never radio button so cookies are never accepted. If you do this, be aware that some sites might not work for you.

If you want Safari to warn you when you send nonsecure information to a secure site or vice versa, check the "Ask before sending a non-secure form to a secure website" check box. You'll learn more about Web security later in this chapter.

The Greatest Browser Feature Ever

That might be a bit of an overstatement, but if you frequently access secured services over the Web using usernames and passwords, such as banking or shopping sites, you might find the following feature to be the best thing about Safari. Safari is fully integrated with Mac OS X's keychain feature. Basically, this means you can store usernames and passwords from within Safari and use the AutoFill feature to have Safari enter that information for you. All you then have to do is move to the URL for the service, and the username and password are entered for you automatically. Click Login, Enter, or a similar button or link and you are in.

To enable this, Safari creates the Safari Forms AutoFill keychain item and stores usernames and passwords there.

→ To learn how to configure and use AutoFill for usernames and passwords, **see** "Using Safari AutoFill," **p. 402**.

→ To learn more about keychains, **see** "Securing Your Mac with Keychains," **p. 900**.

Configuring Safari's Advanced Preferences

To see Safari's Advanced preferences, click the Advanced button on the Safari Preferences dialog box. The Advanced preferences consist of style sheet options and proxy settings.

13

If you have a style sheet you want Safari to use, you can add it by selecting Other on the Style Sheet pop-up menu and then selecting the sheet you want to install. If you add more than one sheet, you can select that sheet you want to use on the Style Sheet pop-up menu.

NOTE

Cascading style sheets can be used to determine the formatting for Web pages. Many pages use these sheets. If not, a page is presented based on Safari's own interpretation of the HTML and the other code of which the page is composed.

You can use the Proxies button to access the Proxies tab of the Network pane of the System Preferences application.

→ To learn about proxy servers; **see** Chapter 26, "Building and Using a Network," **p. 821**.

SEARCHING WITH SAFARI

Of course, you can use Safari to access the many Web search engines available, such as Yahoo, Lycos, and so on. You do this by visiting that search engine's site.

However, you can access one of the best search engines, Google, directly from the Safari Address bar. This enables some great features, most notably the SnapBack button.

NOTE

If you don't see the Google Search tool, make sure the Address bar is displayed and that the Google Search option is selected.

To search the Web using the built-in Google search field, do the following:

1. Type the text for which you want to search in the Search box and press Return. You jump to Google and the results of your search are displayed (see Figure 13.5).
2. Use a link on the results page to move to a page that looks promising (see Figure 13.6).
3. To return to the results page so you can try other links, click the SnapBack button; select History, Search Results SnapBack; or press Option-⌘-S.

Performing a Google search from within Safari is fast and easy. Here are few tips:

- To repeat a previous search, click the magnifying glass icon in the search tool; then on the pop-up menu, select the search you want to repeat.
- To clear the searches you have performed, click the magnifying glass icon in the search tool; then on the pop-up menu, select Clear Entries.
- To clear the current search (when the Google page is being displayed), click the x button inside the search field.

Figure 13.5
Safari's built-in search tool enables you to quickly search on Google.

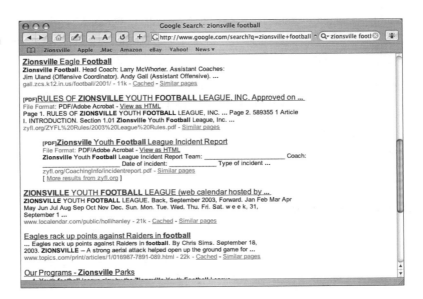

SnapBack

Figure 13.6
The SnapBack button enables you to return to the Google search results page.

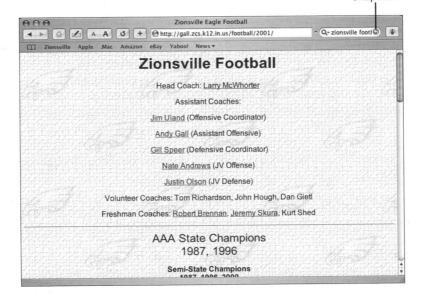

USING SAFARI SNAPBACK

Using the SnapBack button when you search with the Google search tool is great, but you can also use this feature when you are browsing. Safari marks the first page you visit on any site as the SnapBack page. As you move to other pages on the site, you can return to the

SnapBack page by clicking the SnapBack button shown at the end of the URL of the page you are currently viewing. You then move back to the SnapBack page for that site.

Here are a couple more SnapBack tips:

- You can mark a page to be the SnapBack page for a site by either selecting History, Mark Page for SnapBack or pressing Option-⌘-K. Whenever you click the SnapBack button, you return to this page. (If you don't set a SnapBack page, you return to the first page on the site.)

- You can also return to the SnapBack page by selecting History, Page SnapBack or pressing Option-⌘-P.

USING SAFARI BOOKMARKS

Like all other browsers, Safari enables you to bookmark Web pages so you can easily return to them. And, also similar to other browsers, Safari provides tools you can use to organize your bookmarks. However, Safari's bookmark tools are more refined and powerful than most of the browsers I've used.

CONFIGURING SAFARI BOOKMARKS PREFERENCES

Open the Bookmarks pane of the Safari Preferences dialog box to configure your bookmark preferences. On this pane, you have the following options:

- **Bookmarks Bar**—The two Include check boxes determine whether Address Book and Rendezvous sites are accessible from the Bookmarks bar.

  If you make your Address Book available from the Bookmarks bar, you can access any Web sites associated with cards in your Address Book by selecting the site you want to visit on the Address Book menu (see Figure 13.7). This is a very cool way to quickly access the Web site for anyone or any company in your Address Book.

  Similarly, you can make all the Rendezvous computers that provide services Safari can access available via the Rendezvous menu. This enables you to quickly move to Web, FTP, or other resources on your local network.

- **Bookmarks Menu**—This area enables you to add your Address Book and Rendezvous sites to the Bookmarks menu. Additionally, you can include all the Bookmarks bar's bookmarks on the Bookmarks menu by checking the Include Bookmarks Bar box.

- **Collections**—Safari uses the term *collections* for groups of bookmarks. You can use collections to organize bookmarks; a number of collections are included by default. You use the Bookmarks window to work with these (this is covered later in this section).

- **Synchronize**—If you use machines in different locations, you might find yourself adding bookmarks on one machine and not being able to use those bookmarks when you are working on another machine. If you have a .Mac account, you can synchronize your bookmarks across many machines so they all have the same set. To do this, click the Configure button. iSync opens and you can use it to register and synchronize each machine. When you have done this, check the "Synchronize my bookmarks using .Mac" check box. This causes the bookmarks on the Mac to be synced with those on your .Mac account. You can then sync the same set with other machines so you have a consistent set of bookmarks on all your machines.

→ To learn how to use iSync, **see** "Synchronizing with iSync," **p. 689**.

Figure 13.7
You can access the Web site for any person or company in your Address Book from the Address Book menu.

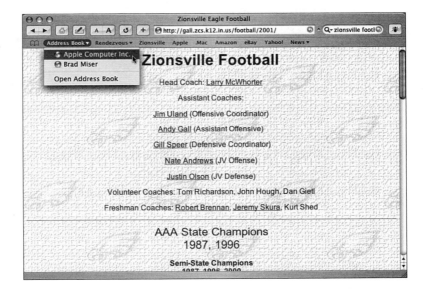

ACCESSING SAFARI BOOKMARKS

You can use bookmarks in the following ways:

- Click a bookmark on the Bookmarks bar.
- Select a bookmark on the Bookmarks menu.
- Press ⌘-1 to move to the first bookmark on the Bookmarks bar, ⌘-2 to move to the second one, and so on up to ⌘-5 to move to the fifth one listed on the Bookmarks bar.
- Open the Bookmarks window and double-click a bookmark.
- Open the Address Book or Rendezvous menu on the Bookmarks bar and select a site to visit.
- Open a bookmark's contextual menu and select either Open, Open in New Window or Open in New Tab.

SETTING SAFARI BOOKMARKS

You can bookmark Web pages with the following steps:

1. Move to the page you want to bookmark.

13

2. Select Bookmarks, Add Bookmark or press ⌘-D. The Add Bookmark sheet opens (see Figure 13.8).

Figure 13.8
Adding a bookmark is a simple task.

3. Edit the name of the bookmark. You can use the default name, change it, or replace it with one of your choosing.

4. On the pop-up menu, select the location in which you want the bookmark to be stored. You can select Bookmarks Bar to add the bookmark to the Bookmarks bar, any folder to place the bookmark in that folder, or Bookmarks Menu to place the bookmark on the Bookmarks menu.

5. Click Add or press Return. The bookmark is added in the location you selected.

TIP

You can add a bookmark to the Bookmarks bar by dragging across the URL in the Address bar and dropping it on the Bookmarks bar. In the resulting name sheet, edit the name of the bookmark and click OK. The bookmark is added to the Bookmarks bar.

ORGANIZING SAFARI BOOKMARKS

Use Safari's Bookmark tools to organize your bookmarks. You can determine the location of bookmarks, place them in folders to create hierarchical bookmark menus, rename them, and so on. To do these tasks, open the Bookmarks window by clicking the Bookmarks button at the left end of the Bookmarks bar, by selecting Bookmarks, Show All Bookmarks, or by pressing ⌘-B. The Bookmarks window opens (see Figure 13.9).

Figure 13.9
You can also open the
Bookmarks window
by selecting
Bookmarks, Show All
Bookmarks.

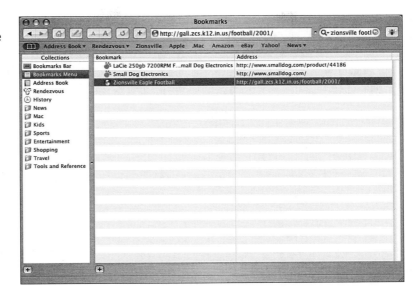

In the left pane of the window is the list of collections (groups of bookmarks). At the top of the list are the Bookmarks Bar and Bookmarks Menu collections that contain the bookmarks in those areas. Under those are the Address Book and Rendezvous collections, and under those is the History collection that contains a list of sites you have visited. Under that are the rest of the bookmark folders; Safari includes several folders with many bookmarks by default. You can add your own folders and bookmarks, as well as adding your bookmarks to existing collections.

To view the contents of a collection, select it. The bookmarks it contains are shown in the right pane. For each bookmark, its name and address are shown.

Organizing bookmarks is straightforward:

- Move bookmarks from one collection to another by dragging them to and dropping them on the collection in which you want to place them. For example, to move a bookmark from the Bookmarks bar to the Bookmarks menu, drag it from the Bookmarks Bar collection to the Bookmarks Menu collection.

- Create new collections by clicking the New Collection button at the bottom of the Collections pane.

- Create a new folder in a collection by clicking the New Folder button at the bottom of the right pane.

- Rename a collection, folder, or bookmark by selecting it, opening the contextual menu, and selecting Edit Name.

- Change the URL for a bookmark by selecting it, opening the contextual menu, and selecting Edit Address.

13

■ Add a folder to the Bookmarks Bar or Bookmarks Menu collections. Then place bookmarks in the folder you created. When you select the folder in either location, a pop-up menu appears to enable you to quickly select any bookmarks in the folder.

■ Delete a collection, folder, or bookmark by selecting it and pressing Delete. If you delete a folder or collection, you delete any bookmarks contained in those items.

TIP

Put the bookmarks you use most often on the Bookmarks bar or Bookmarks menu because you can get to them most quickly there (if you have so many that these become cluttered, use folders to keep them organized). In the next section, you learn a technique that enables you to open an entire folder of bookmarks with a single click.

USING SAFARI TABS

If you have spent any time on the Web, you have no doubt seen the benefits of having many Web browser windows open at the same time. Of course, you can do this with Safari by selecting File, New Window or pressing ⌘-N. If you have done this, you also know that after opening more than a couple of windows, moving back to specific windows can be cumbersome. That is where Safari's Tabs feature comes in. You can open many pages within the same window; each window appears as a tab. You then select the tab to view that page. After you have used this, you will wonder why every Web browser doesn't have this feature.

CONFIGURING TABS

First, enable and configure the Tab feature by opening the Tabs pane of the Safari preferences dialog box (see Figure 13.10).

Figure 13.10
Configure tabs to open many windows on the Web in only one Safari window.

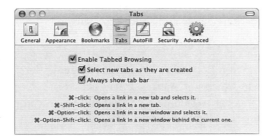

To enable and configure tabbed browsing, follow these steps:

1. Click the Enable Tabbed Browsing check box to turn on Safari's Tab feature.

2. If you want new tabs to be selected, so the page on the tab is displayed, as soon as they are created, check the "Select new tabs as they are created" check box.

TIP

> The previously mentioned preference affects what the tab keyboard shortcuts do. If you don't enable this preference, you have to physically select a tab after you create it to view it. I have assumed that this preference is enabled for the rest of this section.

3. If you want the Tab bar to be shown, check the "Always show tab bar" check box. If don't check this, the Tab bar is shown only if at least one page is being displayed.

4. Close the Preferences dialog box.

TIP

> Notice the keyboard shortcuts at the bottom of the Tabs pane. These are important tips that help you effectively work with tabs. If you can't remember them, they are listed in the next section and in Table 13.4 at the end of this chapter.

USING COOL SAFARI TAB TRICKS

After you have enabled tabs, the Safari window contains a tab for each Web page you have opened. To open a new tab and display it, hold down the ⌘ key while you click a link or bookmark. The page opens and appears in a new tab. You can open as many tabs as you like (see Figure 13.11).

Figure 13.11
Each tab is a separate and independent Web page; very cool!

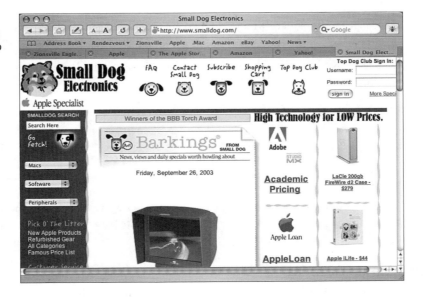

Following is a list of tab tricks:

- Click a tab to view its Web page.
- To close a page, click the x button in its tab. The tab and page close.

- To open a page in a new tab and move to it, ⌘-click a link or bookmark.
- To open a new tab without moving to it, ⌘-Shift-click a link or bookmark.
- To open a link or a bookmark in a new window and view it, ⌘-Option-click it.
- To open a link or a bookmark in a new window but not view it, ⌘-Option-Shift-click it.

NOTE

The previous four actions are reversed if you uncheck the "Select new tabs as they are created" preference. For example, you would ⌘-Shift-click a link or bookmark to open it in a tab and view it.

- To move into the next tab, choose Window, Select Next Tab or press Shift-⌘-right-arrow key.
- To move into the previous tab, choose Window, Select Next Tab or press Shift-⌘-left-arrow key.

Okay, I have saved the coolest thing about Safari for this moment: Safari enables you to open as many pages as you want by clicking a single bookmark. Each page included in the group opens in a new tab. If you frequently open the same set of pages, you can click a single folder to open them all at the same.

First, create the group of bookmarks you want to open:

1. Open the Bookmark window and create a folder in the Bookmarks Bar collection.
2. Check the Auto-Tab box for the folder you just created.
3. Place bookmarks for all the sites you want to open simultaneously in the folder you created in step 1.

TIP

To make moving bookmarks into folders within collections easier, open a second Safari window and view the Bookmarks window. You can drag bookmarks from the first window onto the second to move them among collections.

Close the Bookmarks window and click the button on the Bookmarks bar for the folder you created in the previous steps. Every page opens in its own tab. Working with a set of Web pages has never been so easy.

USING SAFARI AUTOFILL

If you access services on the Web, such as travel planning, shopping, banking, and so on, you no doubt have a lot of experience filling out the same information time and time again. Completing a Web form is fun the first time, but after completing your address, phone number, username, and password a few dozen times, it gets old. This is where Safari's AutoFill feature comes in. It enables you to complete various kinds of information automatically or at the click of the AutoFill button.

Using AutoFill, Safari can enter the following types of information for you:

- **Your Address Book information**—Safari can access the information stored on your card in your Address Book. This can include your address, phone number, Web site, and so on.

→ To learn how to configure the information on your card in your Address Book, **see** "Creating and Editing Your Own Address Card," **p. 338**.

- **Usernames and passwords**—Safari can capture your username and password at many Web sites. When you return to those sites, your username and password are entered for you automatically.

- **Information entered on various Web sites**—As you provide information in other types of Web sites, Safari can gather this data and remember it so that the next time you visit a site, you can complete any information by clicking the AutoFill button.

CONFIGURING AUTOFILL

First, you need to tell Safari which AutoFill features you want to use by configuring your AutoFill preferences:

1. Press ⌘-, to open the Preferences dialog box.
2. Click the AutoFill button to the AutoFill pane (see Figure 13.12).

Figure 13.12
Using Safari's AutoFill feature saves you a lot of typing.

3. If you want Safari to be able to enter the information from your Address Book card, check the "Using info from my Address Book card" check box.

TIP

If you click the top Edit button, the Address Book application opens and you jump to your Address Book card in the edit mode so you can make changes to it.

4. If you want Safari to capture usernames and passwords at various Web sites you use, check the "User names and passwords" check box.

13

5. If you want Safari to capture other types of information you enter on the Web, check the "Other forms" check box.

6. Close the Preferences dialog box.

USING AUTOFILL

Using AutoFill is straightforward.

To enter your personal information from your Address Book card, use the following steps:

1. Move to a Web page that requires your personal information, such as name, address, and so on.

2. Click the AutoFill button on the Address Bar; select Edit, AutoFill Form; or press Shift-⌘-A. Safari transfers the information from your card in your Address Book and places it in the appropriate fields on the Web form.

3. Review the information that was entered to ensure that it is correct. AutoFill isn't perfect and sometimes Web forms use slightly different terms for data.

> **TIP**
>
> If you find AutoFill consistently not entering specific information, add that information to your card in your Address Book.

To use the username and password feature, do the following steps:

1. Move to a Web site that requires a username and password.

2. Enter your username and password on the page.

3. Click Login. You are prompted about whether you want Safari to capture the username and password for this site.

4. In the prompt, make one of the following choices:

   - Click Yes if you want the information to be added to AutoFill.
   - Click Not Now if you don't want the information to be captured at this time but want to be prompted the next time you access the site.
   - Click "Never for this Website" if you don't want the information captured and never want to be prompted again.

If you click Yes, the next time you visit the Web site, your username and password will be filled in automatically. All you have to do to log in to the site is click the Login button or link.

13

CAUTION

> The username and password feature is convenient, but you shouldn't use it unless you are the only one who uses your Mac OS X user account or the people who share your Mac OS X user account are very trustworthy. Because the usernames and passwords for your accounts are entered automatically, anyone who uses your Mac OS X user account and moves to the related Web sites can log in to your account on that Web site.

If you decide you don't want to provide automatic access to a specific Web site, you can remove that site's username and password:

1. Open the AutoFill pane of the Safari Preferences dialog box.
2. Click the Edit button next to the text "User names and passwords." A sheet appears that lists each Web site and username you have captured in Safari.
3. Select the Web site you want to remove.

TIP

> Click Remove All to delete all the Web sites for which you have captured usernames and passwords.

4. Click Remove. Continue removing Web sites until you have removed all the sites you no longer need.
5. Click Done and close the Preferences dialog box.

NOTE

> If you don't turn off the username and password feature by unchecking the "Use names and passwords" check box, you will be prompted by AutoFill the next time you visit any Web sites you deleted from the list.

Using the AutoFill feature for other kinds of forms is similar to the first two. When you enable the "Other forms" feature and enter information in Web sites, that information is captured. When you return to those sites in the future, you can enter the information again by clicking the AutoFill button; selecting Edit, AutoFill Form; or pressing Shift-⌘-A. You can edit the list of Web sites for which information is remembered by clicking the Edit button next to the text "Other forms" on the AutoFill pane of the Safari Preferences dialog box.

13

USING SAFARI'S ACTIVITY VIEWER

As you move around the Web, Safari tracks the sites you have visited. You can view this information on the Activity window. To do so, select Window, Activity or press Option-⌘-A. The Activity window appears, showing the sites you have visited. You can expand each site to see the individual pages you have visited and double-click any of these to return to that page.

USING SHERLOCK TO SEARCH THE WEB

The Mac's Web searching application, called Sherlock, can help you search for various types of content from various providers on the Web. Sherlock is very powerful and enables you to find certain kinds of information on the Web quickly and easily.

Sherlock uses channels to categorize the information you search for. When you use a channel, the tools you search with are specific to that channel. For example, one of Sherlock's included channels is the Movies channel, which enables you to search for movie information in your area (see Figure 13.13). To use a channel, click its button on the Sherlock toolbar.

Figure 13.13
Sherlock's Movies channel enables you to locate information and show times for movies you are interested in; you can even view the trailer in the Sherlock window!

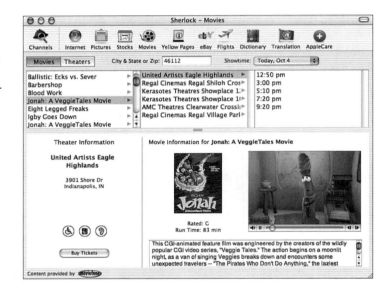

When you select a channel, such as the Internet channel that you can use for general Web searches, Sherlock's window provides a set of tools you can use to perform your Web content search (see Figure 13.14).

By default, Sherlock includes a number of Apple-supplied channels, which you see on the Sherlock toolbar. These include the following:

- **Internet**—Use this channel for your general Internet searches.
- **Pictures**—With this channel, you can find images related to specific topics.
- **Stocks**—Use this channel to track your favorite stocks.
- **Movies**—This is one of the coolest channels. You can use it to find show times and location information for movies you are interested in. You can also view a movie's trailer in the Sherlock window.
- **Yellow Pages**—Use this channel to find addresses, phone numbers, and even driving directions for businesses.

- **eBay**—If you are an eBay fan, this channel is for you.
- **Flights**—This enables you to find flight information and purchase tickets.
- **Dictionary**—Use this channel to find correct spellings of specific words or synonyms.
- **Translation**—This channel enables you to translate words and phrases among various languages.
- **AppleCare**—Use this channel to search for information from Apple, such as to get help with problems you are having.

Figure 13.14
Sherlock provides a powerful set of tools you can use to find all sorts of information on the Web.

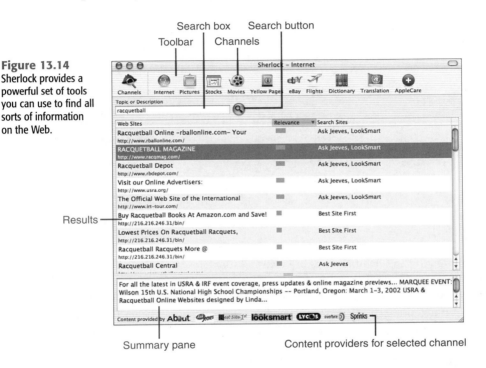

Search box   Search button
Toolbar   Channels
Results
Summary pane   Content providers for selected channel

There are also a number of other channels you can use; these are visible when you click the Channels button on the toolbar and select the collection of channels in which you are interested (see Figure 13.15). For each channel, you see its name and icon, the countries in which it can be used, and a description.

Figure 13.15
When you select the Other Channels collection, you see a large number of other channels you can use to search the Web.

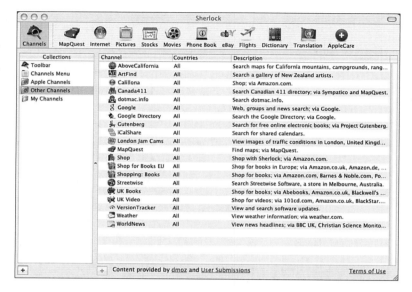

You can organize the channels in Sherlock using tools similar to those you use in other locations. For example, to add a channel to the Sherlock toolbar, drag it from the list of channels onto the toolbar (for example, in Figure 13.15, you can see that I placed the MapQuest channel on my toolbar). You can also add channels to and access them from the Channel menu; to add them there, simply place the channel in the Channels Menu collection.

PERFORMING SEARCHES WITH SHERLOCK

Now you that you understand the basics of Sherlock, you can use it to search:

1. Open Sherlock.

2. Click the channel you want to use for your search. The Sherlock window is updated to reflect the channel you selected (see Figure 13.16). Each channel has its own search tools, but they are all simple to use.

3. In the Search box at the top of the window, type the text you want to search for. You can enter individual words or phrases in the Search box. The more information you enter, the more specific your search will be.

4. Configure the channel's other tools. For example, when you search the Movies channel, you select Movies to search by movie, or Theaters to search by theater; then enter your ZIP Code and select the date you want information for.

Figure 13.16
Don't know how to spell "menagerie"? I didn't either, but with Sherlock, it doesn't take long to find out.

5. Click the Search button. If you aren't already connected to the Internet, your Mac connects itself. Then, Sherlock moves onto the Net and performs your search. The results of your search appear in the Results area.

6. Browse through the results of your search; when you find a site that looks interesting, double-click it. If the result is a Web site, it opens in your default Web browser.

TIP

You can show or hide the toolbar by clicking the Show/Hide toolbar button; selecting View, Show/Hide Toolbar; or pressing Option-⌘-T.

13

The Sherlock Results pane looks quite different depending on the channel you are using. When you use the Internet channel, the results are Web sites that meet your search criteria. When you use the Pictures channel, the results are individual images. Although the channels provide different types of results, they are all easy to work with, and after you've used one channel, you won't have any trouble using the others.

In some channels, such as the AppleCare channel, the content that Sherlock finds appears in the lower pane of the window. You can view such content directly in the Sherlock window.

TIP

> You can change the relative sizes of the panes in the Sherlock window by dragging the resize handle located in the center of the separating bar.

CUSTOMIZING THE SHERLOCK TOOLBAR

You can customize the Sherlock toolbar just as you can the toolbar in Finder windows:

1. Open Sherlock.
2. Select View, Customize Toolbar. The Customize toolbar sheet appears.
3. Drag channels off the toolbar to remove them. (You can add them again by dragging them back onto the toolbar.)
4. Drag the space, flexible space, and separator icons onto the toolbar to organize it.
5. Drag channel icons around on the toolbar to rearrange them.
6. Use the Show pop-up menu to select how you want the toolbar to look, such as including both icons and text or text only.
7. Check the Use Small Size check box to use small icons on the toolbar.
8. Click Done.

TIP

> You can restore the default Sherlock toolbar by dragging the default set onto the toolbar.

ADDING OTHER SHERLOCK CHANNELS

The default installation of Sherlock includes a number of Apple and third-party channels, but you can also add your own using the following general steps:

1. Locate the channel you want to add, such as by visiting a Web site.
2. Download the channel.
3. Select Channel, Add Channel.
4. Select the channel you want to add.

TIP

> You can create shortcuts to channels so you can open a channel from the Finder by opening its shortcut. To do so, select the channel for which you want to create a shortcut. Then select Channel, Make a Shortcut ($\mathcal{H}$-L). In the resulting sheet, name the shortcut, select a location, and click Make. When you want to use that channel, open its shortcut. A new Sherlock window opens and the channel is ready for your search.

13

DOWNLOADING AND PREPARING FILES

One of the best things about the Web is that you can download files from it. These files can be applications, graphics, MP3 files, text files, updaters, or any other file you can think of. Downloading files is simple; the only two areas that might give you some trouble are finding the files you download and preparing them for use.

The general process for downloading and preparing files is the following:

1. Locate the file you want to download.
2. Download the file to your Mac.
3. Prepare the file for use by decoding and uncompressing it.

NOTE

> Because of Mac OS X's Unix underpinnings, this step can be a little more complicated than it has been in past versions of the OS. Fortunately, most of the time, this process is relatively automatic. You have to intervene manually only infrequently.

There are two basic ways to download files. You can use a Web browser to download files, or you can use an FTP client (or the Finder) to download files from FTP and other sites. Using a Web browser to download files is simpler, but it is also slower. A dedicated FTP client can dramatically speed up file downloading.

→ For information on using the Finder to download files from an FTP site, **see** "Downloading Files Via FTP in the Finder," **p. 420**.

→ For information about configuring and using the Interarchy FTP application, **see** "Downloading Files Better with Interarchy," **p. 420**.

CONFIGURING A DOWNLOADS FOLDER

By default, your Web browser stores files you download in the Desktop folder in your Home directory (and thus, they appear on your desktop). If this isn't where you want downloaded files to be stored, you should create a folder into which your Web browser will always download files. That way, you will always know where to find the files you download and they won't clutter your desktop.

NOTE

> Because a directory is modified when you store files in it, you must use a directory that you have permissions to write to. On your Mac OS X startup volume, you are limited to downloading files to a directory within your Home directory. However, you can choose a location outside your Mac OS X startup volume if you want.
>
> If you want other users of your machine to be able to access the files you download, you can use your Public folder as your downloads folder.

13

After you have created your downloads folder, open the General pane of the Safari Preferences dialog box and use the "Save downloaded files to" pop-up menu to choose that folder.

DOWNLOADING FILES USING SAFARI

Downloading files is as simple as anything gets on the Mac. Safari uses its Downloads window to show you information about the files you are downloading. To start the download process, just click the download link for the file you want to download.

TIP

> You can download multiple files at the same time. Start one; then, move back to a Web window, move to the next, and start it downloading.
>
> You can also continue to browse the Web while your files are downloading. The speed decreases a bit (or a lot if you are using a dial-up Internet account), but at least you can do something while the file is downloading.

Some sites simply provide the file's name as its link, whereas others provide a Download button. Whichever way it is done, finding the link to click to begin the download process is usually simple.

After you click the link to begin the download, the Downloads window opens showing the progress of the file you are downloading (see Figure 13.17). As a file is downloaded, you see its name, the download progress, and the file size. During the download process, you see the stop button for the file you are downloading; you can stop the process by clicking this button.

Figure 13.17
The Downloads window provides the information and tools you need to manage your downloads.

TIP

> A quick way to switch windows is by pressing ⌘-~. This is a good way to jump between the Downloads window and your other Web windows. You can also move directly into the Downloads window by pressing Option-⌘-L.

When the download is complete, you see the file's icon. Also, the Stop button becomes the Find in Finder button, which contains a magnifying glass. Click this button to open the file you downloaded in the Finder.

TIP

> If the download process is interrupted for some reason (such as a connection problem or if you clicked the Stop button), the Stop button becomes the Retry button, which contains a circular arrow. Click this button to try to download the file again.

As you download files, Safari continues to add them to the list in the Downloads window. You can clear them manually by clicking the Clear button. You can have Safari remove them automatically by selecting either When Safari Quits or Upon Successful Download on the "Remove download list items" pop-up menu on the General pane of the Safari Preferences dialog box.

After the download is complete, Safari tries to prepare the file that downloaded so you can use it. Most of the time, this works automatically, but in some situations, you must perform this task manually. This process can be somewhat complicated depending on the file you download.

PREPARING FILES FOR USE

Most files you download are encoded and compressed. *Encoding* is the process of translating an application or other file into a plain-text file so it can be transferred across the Internet. *Compressing* a file is a process that makes the file's size smaller so it can be transferred across the Internet more quickly.

Before you can use a file you have downloaded, it must be decoded and it might also need to be uncompressed. Depending on the type of file it is, these two actions might be done at the same time or might have to be handled separately. An application is required for both tasks; a single application can usually handle them, but occasionally the file might need to be uncompressed with one application and decoded with another.

UNDERSTANDING FILE EXTENSIONS FOR COMPRESSED FILES

Knowing what will happen in any situation requires that you understand the types of files you are likely to download. You can determine this by the filename extension. The most common extensions with which you will have to deal are listed in Table 13.1.

13

TABLE 13.1 COMMON FILE EXTENSIONS FOR COMPRESSED OR ENCODED MAC FILES

File Extension	What It Means	Comments
.bin	Binary file format	A common encoding format for the Mac.
.gz	Unix compression format	The dominant compression format for Unix files.
.hqx	Binhex encoding	Another very common encoding format for the Mac.
.img	Disk Image file format	A file that is a disk image and must be mounted with the Disk Utility application before it can be used.
.pkg	The package format	Package files are installed with the application installer.
.sea	StuffIt compression format that can be uncompressed by double-clicking the file	Useful because the recipient of the file doesn't have to have a decompression tool. He simply double-clicks the file to decompress it.
.sit	StuffIt compression	The standard compression for Mac files.
.tar	Tape Archive format	An archiving format for Unix computers that is used for some files you might want for Mac OS X.
.zip	Zip compression format	The dominant compression format for Windows PCs.

Aladdin's StuffIt application is the dominant application for compressing, uncompressing, decoding, and encoding Mac files. The freeware application StuffIt Expander is included with Mac OS X to enable you to deal with compressed and encoded files you download. StuffIt Expander can handle almost all the file formats listed in Table 13.1. So, most of the time, you will use StuffIt Expander to prepare the files you download for use. Safari or other tools with which you download files typically handle this process for you automatically.

Because Mac OS X is based on Unix, you can use files that use the .tar and .gz formats as well. Preparing these files can be a bit more complicated (if StuffIt Expander doesn't work) because you have to use Unix commands to prepare them.

→ To learn how to use Unix commands to prepare a file you have downloaded, **see** Chapter 9, "Unix: Working with the Command Line," **p. 243**.

MANUALLY PREPARING A FILE FOR USE

Although you can rely on Safari's preconfigured helper applications to handle most of the files you download, it is useful to know how to manually decode and uncompress files you download so you can handle them yourself and better understand how to configure a helper application to do it for you.

By default, Safari attempts to launch the appropriate helper application to handle files you download. If a file you download can be handled successfully by the helper application, it is prepared and a usable version of it is placed in the same folder into which it was downloaded.

To manually prepare a file, use the following steps:

1. Locate the file you want to uncompress or decode.

2. Access the StuffIt Expander application by opening the following path:
   `Applications/Utilities`.

3. Drag and drop the file you want to prepare onto the StuffIt Expander icon. The StuffIt Expander application launches, showing a progress bar for the processing of the file.

CAUTION

> If the StuffIt Expander icon doesn't become highlighted when you drag a file onto it, that file type cannot be handled with the free version of the StuffIt application. If the file is a Unix file, use the Unix tools to prepare it. Otherwise, you will probably have to upgrade to StuffIt Deluxe to be able to work with the file.

When the process is complete, you see a new item in the same folder as the file you downloaded. If the original file contained more than one item, you see a new folder containing the decoded and uncompressed items instead of a file.

You can work with the uncompressed/decoded items just like any other items on your Mac. For example, if a file expands into a folder, you can open that folder to work with the files in it. If the file expands into a `.img` file, you can double-click that file to mount the disk image on your Mac; often, these files are mounted automatically after they are processed.

TIP

> You can also prepare a file by launching StuffIt Expander and selecting Expand from its File menu.

For almost all the files you download, even the manual process is just that simple. Occasionally, you might run into a file on which this process doesn't work. In such a case, you have to try another tool (such as a Unix command or the StuffIt Deluxe application).

13

Configuring StuffIt Expander

A bit of configuration of StuffIt Expander will make this process even less difficult:

1. Open the StuffIt Expander application.

2. On the StuffIt Expander menu, select Preferences (⌘-,) to open the Preferences window. This window has a toolbar in which you select the panes you want to view in the lower part of the window. Some of the options you might want to configure are listed in Table 13.2.

3. After you configure your preferences, click OK.

TABLE 13.2	Useful StuffIt Expander Preferences
Group of Options	**Useful Settings**
Expanding	Check the "Delete after expanding" check boxes if you want the application to delete files it has expanded. This can prevent your downloads folder from being cluttered with files you don't need (not to mention saving your disk space). Use the Scan for viruses using pop-up menu to set an application that StuffIt Expander will use to check files you expand for viruses.
Disk Images	Use these controls to have the application automatically mount disk image files.
Destination	Use the Destination controls to set a folder into which expanded files should be placed. For example, you can set files to expand into a specific folder or have the application prompt you for a folder location each time it expands a file.
Watch Folder	Use these controls to identify a folder StuffIt Expander should watch. When it finds a compressed or encoded file in this folder, it automatically expands the file. For example, you can set your downloads folder to be the watch folder so files there are handled automatically.
Internet	Use these controls to determine which file types StuffIt Expander handles. Click the "Use StuffIt Expander for all available file types" button so the application will work with as many file types as possible.

Working with Plug-Ins and Helper Applications

Many file types are available on the Internet. In addition to HTML, JSP, GIF, JPEG, and other files that are used to present a Web page, there are graphics, movies, sounds, PDFs, and many other file types you can open and view. Safari can't work with all these file types directly, and fortunately, it doesn't have to. Safari and other Web browsers use plug-ins and helper applications to expand their capabilities so they can work with files they don't natively support.

Working with Plug-Ins

Plug-ins are software that can be incorporated into a Web browser when it opens (thus, the term *plug-in*). Internet plug-ins enable applications to display files that are of the specific types handled by those plug-ins. For example, the QuickTime plug-in enables Web browsers to display QuickTime movies.

INSTALLING INTERNET PLUG-INS

As you travel around the Web, you might encounter file types for which you do not have the required plug-in. In that case, you must find and install the plug-in you need. Usually, sites have links to places from which you can download the plug-ins needed for the file types on the site. There are a couple of places in the system where plug-ins can be stored.

Plug-ins that are available to all user accounts are stored in the folder `Mac OS X/Library/Internet Plug-Ins/`, where `Mac OS X` is the name of your startup volume.

You must be logged in under an Administrator account to store a plug-in in this directory.

Internet plug-ins can also be stored in a specific user account, in which case they are available only to that user. A user's specific plug-ins are in the location `shortusername/Library/Internet Plug-Ins/`, where `shortusername` is the short name for the user account.

To install a plug-in, simply place it in the directory that is appropriate for that plug-in (to be available either to all users or to only a specific user). Quit the Web browser and then launch it again to make the plug-in active.

NOTE

Some plug-ins are installed using an installer application, in which case you don't need to install the plug-in manually.

If you open the Internet Plug-Ins directories, you will see the plug-ins currently installed. Any plug-in installed in these folders can be used by a supported Web browser.

Many plug-ins are available for Web browsers. The QuickTime plug-in is installed by default so you can view QuickTime movies in Web browsers. Additionally, the Shockwave Flash plug-in is installed by default, as is the Java Applet plug-in. There are many other plug-ins you might want to download and install.

You can see the plug-ins installed for Safari by selecting Help, Install Plug-ins. A new window opens showing all the installed plug-ins (see Figure 13.18).

When you attempt to view a file for which you do not have the appropriate plug-in, you see a warning dialog box that tells you what to do. Usually, you see instructions to help you find, download, and install the plug-in as well.

USING INTERNET PLUG-INS

After a plug-in is installed in the appropriate folder, it works with a Web browser to provide its capabilities. When you click a file that requires the plug-in to be used, the appropriate plug-in activates and enables you to do whatever it is designed to do. For example, when you open a QuickTime movie, you see the controls that enable you to watch that movie within the Web browser.

13

Figure 13.18
Safari's Installed
Plug-ins window
shows you all the
plug-ins to which
Safari has access.

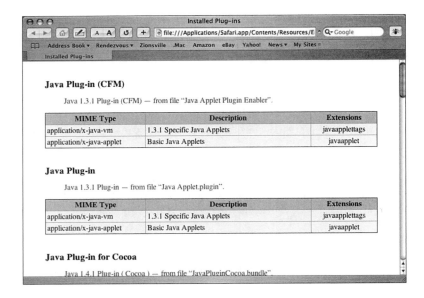

WORKING WITH HELPER APPLICATIONS

Although plug-ins provide additional capability by "plugging in" to a Web browser, *helper applications* are standalone applications Web browsers can use to work with files of specific types. Any application on your Mac can be used as a helper application.

Safari determines the helper applications it uses to open files based on the file type and file-name extensions with which specific applications are associated via the Finder. For example, if PDFs are set to open in Preview, Safari launches Preview when you download a PDF file (assuming that the "Open 'safe' files after downloading" preference is enabled).

→ To learn how to associate files with applications, **see** "Determining the Application That Opens When You Open a Document," **p. 169**.

For example, in the previous section, you learned how StuffIt Expander can decode and uncompress files you download from the Internet. StuffIt Expander is a helper application; as you saw earlier, you can also use the application independently of a browser. When a browser opens a file type for which StuffIt Expander is the designated helper application, the browser opens StuffIt Expander and passes the file to it for processing.

MAC OS X TO THE MAX: GOING FURTHER ON THE WEB

There is a lot you can do to take your browsing on the Web to the max, including using keyboard shortcuts and exploring useful Mac and other Web sites.

USING SAFARI KEYBOARD SHORTCUTS

Table 13.3 lists keyboard shortcuts for Safari.

NOTE

Table 13.3 assumes you have enabled Safari's Tab feature.

TABLE 13.3   KEYBOARD SHORTCUTS IN SAFARI

Menu	Command	Keyboard Shortcut
Safari	Preferences	⌘-,
Safari	Block Pop-Up Windows	⌘-K
Safari	Empty Cache	Option-⌘-E
File	New Window	⌘-N
File	New Tab	⌘-T
File	Open File	⌘-O
File	Open Location	⌘-L
File	Close Window	Shift-⌘-W
File	Close Tab	⌘-W
File	Save As	⌘-S
Edit	AutoFill Form	Shift-⌘-A
View	Address Bar	⌘-Shift-\
View	Bookmarks Bar	⌘-B
View	Status Bar	⌘-/
View	Stop	⌘-.
View	Reload Page	⌘-R
View	Make Text Bigger	⌘--
View	Make Text Smaller	⌘--
View	View Source	Option-⌘-V
History	Back	⌘-[
History	Forward	⌘-]
History	Home	Shift-⌘-H
History	Mark Page for SnapBack	Option-⌘-K
History	Page SnapBack	Option-⌘-P
History	Search Results SnapBack	Option-⌘-S
Bookmarks	Show All Bookmarks	Option -⌘-B
Bookmarks	Add Bookmark	⌘-D
Bookmarks	Add Bookmark Folder	Shift-⌘-N

13

TABLE 13.3   CONTINUED

Menu	Command	Keyboard Shortcut
Bookmarks	Go to first bookmark	⌘-1
Bookmarks	Go to second bookmark	⌘-2
Bookmarks	Go to third bookmark	⌘-3
Bookmarks	Go to fourth bookmark	⌘-4
Bookmarks	Go to fifth bookmark	⌘-5
Window	Select Next Tab	Shift-⌘-right arrow
Window	Select Previous Tab	Shift-⌘-left arrow
Window	Downloads	Option-⌘-L
Window	Activity	Option-⌘-A
Help	Safari Help	⌘-?
	Cycle Through Open Windows	⌘-~
	Open link or bookmark in a new tab and view it	⌘-click
	Open link or bookmark in a new tab	Shift-⌘-click
	Open link or bookmark in a new window and view it	Option-⌘-click
	Open link or bookmark in a new window behind the current one	Option-Shift-⌘-click

DOWNLOADING FILES VIA FTP IN THE FINDER

Using the Finder, you can download files directly from an FTP site to your Mac:

1. Use Safari to open the FTP site from which you want to download files. The FTP site is mounted on your desktop (see Figure 13.19).

2. Drag the files you want to download from the FTP site volume onto your Mac. The files are downloaded, and the Copy progress window shows you the progress of the download process.

3. Prepare the files for use.

DOWNLOADING FILES BETTER WITH INTERARCHY

Many sites from which you can download files use the File Transfer Protocol (FTP) to provide files to you. Your Web browser or the Finder can handle FTP downloads, but a dedicated FTP application handles FTP downloads much better than a Web browser. The speed at which FTP applications can download files is many times greater than a Web browser can achieve—for this reason alone, you should use an FTP client whenever possible. When it comes to FTP on the Mac, several excellent FTP applications are available. My favorite is Interarchy.

Figure 13.19
The selected volume is an FTP site; you can download its files by dragging them to a folder on your Mac.

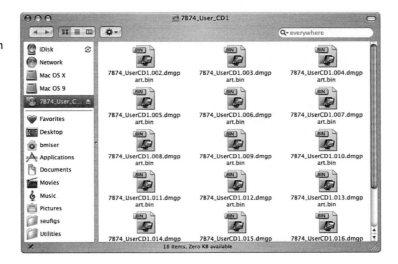

You can download, install, and configure Interarchy so it is used to download files via FTP automatically. For example, you can configure it so that, when Safari attempts to download a file using FTP, it launches Interarchy and uses it to download the files instead. The result is much faster and more reliable downloading.

First, download, install, and configure Interarchy:

1. Go to www.interarchy.com.

2. Download the latest version of Interarchy. When the file has been downloaded, its disk image is mounted on your machine.

   NOTE
   You can download a free evaluation version of the application. At press time, the Interarchy license costs about $45. If you don't like to wait while files download, this might be one of the better investments you can make.

3. Open the mounted Interarchy disk image.

4. Drag the Interarchy folder to the Applications folder or another location.

5. Launch Interarchy.

6. Select Interarchy, Preferences to see the Preferences window. In the Protocol Handlers area, the Use Interarchy for FTP check box is checked by default.

13

7. Check the "Internet Explorer uses Interarchy for FTP" check box.

8. Confirm the switch by clicking Switch in the resulting dialog box.

9. Repeat the process for Netscape if you use that Web browser.

10. Click Save and quit Interarchy.

Depending on the application for which you have configured Interarchy to be used, you might have to do some additional configuration in the application so Interarchy will always be used for FTP, or you can configure the application to use Interarchy manually.

NOTE

> Interarchy can do more than just download files for a Web browser. You can also interact with FTP sites directly. For example, in Interarchy, select Home, List Bookmarks. You can open any of the folders you see to work with those FTP sites.

CHAPTER 14

PUTTING YOURSELF ON THE WEB

DEVELOPING YOUR PRESENCE ON THE WEB

If you spend much time on the Internet, you probably will want to develop your own presence there. With Mac OS X, some additional tools, and a bit of creativity, you can develop your own Web pages and serve them to the world.

UNDERSTANDING WEB SITES

Two fundamental "parts" are required to provide Web pages to the Internet or an intranet. First is the content and format of the information that is presented. As you probably know, *Web pages* are a collection of Hypertext Markup Language (HTML), Java Server Pages (JSP), and other files (JPGs, GIFs, and so on). In turn, a *Web site* is a collection of Web pages organized in some fashion (sometimes, this organization appears to be quite random!). Typically, a site's *home page* (often called the *index* of the site) provides the top-level structure for the site and includes the links that connect the home page to other pages.

The second part of the system needed to get Web pages "out there" is the *Web server application* that actually hosts the pages on the Internet (or on an intranet). The Web server is responsible for ensuring that the files on the site can be accessed properly. A Web server also provides the tools to monitor and manage the Web site.

NOTE

> A Web server usually runs concurrently with servers providing other services, such as File Transfer Protocol (FTP) and email.

CREATING YOUR WEB SITE

Many tools are available that you can use to create a Web site. These range from using text editors to hand-code the HTML on each page to using "what you see is what you get" (WYSIWYG) Web page editors, which automate the coding process and enable you to see what you are creating as you create it. WYSIWYG tools can also enable you to develop, organize, and manage an entire Web site. For example, you can visually map the entire site so you can see where each link takes you.

Explaining how to create a Web site is beyond the scope of this book. However, you can use many easily accessible resources to help you decide how you want to create your site and to explain the details of doing so. For example, for an explanation of HTML codes, visit `www.willcam.com/cmat/html/tags.html`. In addition, numerous books are available that describe how Web sites can be created and managed, such as the following:

- *Special Edition Using HTML and XHTML*
- *The Art and Science of Web Design*
- *Easy Web Pages, Second Edition*

14

SERVING A WEB SITE

After a Web site has been created, it must be *served* by a Web server application; this process is also known as *Web hosting*. There are two ways that a site can be hosted. One is to use a hosting service, and the other is to host the site yourself from your own Mac.

USING A HOSTING SERVICE

A *Web hosting service* takes content you provide (your Web site) and serves it to the Internet. At their most basic level, Web hosting services simply offer you space on the server on which you can store your site; you are usually assigned a specific address based on the account you have on that service. Some Web hosting services go beyond these basic services, though. Many hosting services also provide domain name registration for you so you can choose the URL for your site. Other hosting services provide tools you can use to create the site as well. These tools can be standalone tools you use, or the service might provide pre-formatted pages you complete by adding your own content. Many hosting services charge a fee for their services, but many serve your pages free (usually with limitations on the size of your site or the amount of data that can be served from it; many also require that they be able to place ads on your site).

With Mac OS 9, Apple introduced its own Web hosting service as part of the iTools service. For Mac OS X, version 10.2, iTools became .Mac and continued to be integrated into the OS so that it is a natural extension of your system. Mac OS X version 10.3 continues this trend; for example, a local copy of your iDisk can now be created and synchronized from your desktop automatically. Using .Mac, you can quickly create your own Web site—you get a mac.com email address and have access to other services, such as the use of storage space on the .Mac servers (iDisk). When you use .Mac to host a Web site, you upload the files for your site to your iDisk. Then, the .Mac server handles serving your site to the Internet. This approach is beneficial because you don't use your Mac's resources or your Internet connection to host the site.

→ To learn how to create a Web site with .Mac, **see** "Using a .Mac iDisk and HomePage to Create and Serve Your Web Pages," **p. 426**.

USING MAC OS X TO HOST A SITE FROM YOUR MAC

You can also use Mac OS X to host a Web site for the Internet or for a local intranet because the Web server software you need is already built in to Mac OS X. Serving a Web site to the Internet is a fairly complex task, and there are many nuances you need to consider. However, serving a Web site to a local network is fairly straightforward. In either case, you can use Mac OS X to get your site online.

→ To learn how to host a Web site on your Mac, **see** "Using a .Mac iDisk and HomePage to Create and Serve Your Web Pages," **p. 426**.

14

USING A .MAC iDISK AND HOMEPAGE TO CREATE AND SERVE YOUR WEB PAGES

Apple's .Mac is a suite of services you can access. These services include the following:

- **Email**—Using .Mac provides you with an email account you can use to send and receive email. Your .Mac email address ends in @mac.com, so using it is a good way to identify yourself as a Mac user. Using the Webmail service, you can also access your .Mac email account from a Web browser.

→ To learn how to configure the Mail application to use your .Mac email account, **see** "Configuring Email Accounts," **p. 349**.

- **iCards**—These are electronic greeting cards you can send to others via email. There are numerous card combinations you can send—these are great for the artistically challenged because you can create a customized greeting card by selecting from the available images and styles.

- **Software**—The .Mac service enables you to download and use software for free, such as Apple's Backup, Virex Anti-virus, and games. You can also access a lot of other software, such as demos, updates, and more.

- **Online resources**—You can store your Address Book and bookmarks online so you can access them from anywhere you can access the Web. You can share your iCal calendar online as well.

- **Online chat**—Take advantage of iChat AV to chat online via text, audio, and video.

 - **iDisk**—The iDisk is a virtual disk space you can use to store files. A number of folders exist on an iDisk by default. For example, you can place items in your Public folder, and any Mac users who know your .Mac member name can access the files in that folder (which is an excellent way to share files with other Mac users around the world). And, you can create a Web site to share the files in your Public folder with anyone. You also store the data that forms your .Mac Web page on your iDisk. Under Mac OS X version 10.3, you can configure your Mac to create a local copy of your iDisk and keep it automatically synchronized with the online version.

- **HomePage**—The HomePage service enables you to create and serve a Web site.

The only requirement to use .Mac is that you are using Mac OS 9 or later. Because you are using Mac OS X, this certainly isn't a problem.

CREATING A .MAC ACCOUNT

Before you can access .Mac services, you need to obtain a .Mac account.

At press time, the cost of a .Mac account was $99.95 per year. However, you can obtain and use a trial .Mac account that provides access to most of the .Mac services free for 60 days. Obtaining a .Mac account is pretty straightforward.

When you installed Mac OS X, you were prompted to enter your existing .Mac account information or to create a .Mac account. If you entered your .Mac account information or created a .Mac account at that time, you are all set and can skip to the next section.

NOTE

> If you created or configured an existing .Mac account when you installed Mac OS X, your .Mac email account was configured in the Mail application for you automatically.

To create a .Mac account outside of the Mac OS X installer, do the following:

1. Open the System Preferences utility and click the .Mac icon to open the .Mac pane.

NOTE

> The .Mac pane replaces the Internet pane that was part of previous versions of Mac OS X.

2. Click the Sign Up button (see Figure 14.1). Your default Web browser opens and you move to the .Mac Signup Web site.

Figure 14.1
Clicking the Sign Up button takes you to the .Mac Account Setup Web site.

3. Follow the onscreen instructions to create your .Mac account. You will have to provide personal information and accept a license agreement. As part of the process, you create a member name and password for your account. You can choose to create a free trial account, or you can pay for a full account. If you create a full account, you must provide payment information, such as a credit card.

14

4. Create your member name by typing it in the .Mac Member Name text box. You should put some thought into this step. The member name you choose will be part of your .Mac email address (which will be *membername*@mac.com), and it will also be part of the URL to your .Mac Web site. Typically, you should choose some variation of your name so that people can remember your email address and URL and can easily associate both with you. Your member name has to be at least 3 characters long and must be fewer than 20 characters. Again, you should keep your member name fairly short to make it easier for other people to work with.

5. Create your password and password hint question. Your password has to be between 6 and 32 characters long, and you can use special characters if you want. The password hint question is a means that you can use to identify yourself if you forget your password (and if you have a memory as poor as mine is, you will!). Try to use a question you can answer only one way, such as your birth city or your mother's last name. Don't use something that can change (such as the name of your favorite movie), because by the time you need to use the hint, it might have changed and you won't be able to answer your own question.

6. When you have successfully created an account, you see a page that provides your member name, password, email address, and email server information. You might consider printing this page so you will have the information if you need to retrieve it at a later time.

> **TIP**
>
> You can also save the page using your browser's Save As command. You can also save it as a PDF via the Print command.

7. Move back to the .Mac pane of the System Preferences utility. Enter your .Mac member name and password in the pane.

8. Quit the System Preferences utility.

ACCESSING YOUR .MAC ACCOUNT

To use .Mac services, you need to log in to your .Mac account. When you enter your member name and password in the .Mac pane, your Mac handles the login process for you automatically if you access .Mac from your desktop, such as when you work with your iDisk.

For other services, such as HomePage, you need to log in to your .Mac account on the .Mac Web page. Open a Web browser, move to www.apple.com, and click the .Mac tab. When the .Mac page appears, log in using your member name and password. Your member name will be entered for you automatically; all you have to do is input your password and click Log in. You will move to the .Mac services page; click an icon to begin working with that service (such as HomePage).

After you have logged in once, you can sometimes return to your .Mac services page without having to log in again. If you can move directly to one of the services pages, such as the HomePage page, you are already logged in to your account. If you see the Login page instead, you have to log back in to your account before you can use a service. (At the time of writing, this behavior seemed to be a bit inconsistent, so you just have to try it for yourself.)

To log out from your current .Mac account, click the Logout link on the .Mac Web page. If you click the "Log out completely" link, your member name won't be remembered on the .Mac login screen.

NOTE

> Each user account on your Mac can have its own .Mac account. The settings in the .Mac pane of the System Preferences utility of one account do not affect the other accounts. The steps to work with other accounts are exactly the same as those to work with the first one you create.

TIP

> You can log in to your .Mac account from any computer running Mac OS 9 or later by visiting the .Mac Web page and logging in.

 If the Member sign-in area doesn't appear, see "No Member Sign-In Area Appears" in the "Troubleshooting" section at the end of this chapter.

USING YOUR IDISK

Your iDisk is a vital element of the creation of your Web site because you store all the files you use on your Web page in the appropriate folders on your iDisk. And, you can use your iDisk to store any files you choose online. You can make these files available to others, or you might use the space to back up important files. You can also store files on your iDisk and access them from another Mac. Under version 10.3, you can configure a Mac to create a local copy of your iDisk and keep it synchronized with your online iDisk. This is especially useful when you work with the same set of files from multiple locations, such as a work Mac and your home Mac.

→ To learn more about iSync, **see** "Synchronizing with iSync," **p. 689**.

When you purchase a .Mac account, your default iDisk can store up to 100MB of data. You can increase this up to 1GB, but you'll have to pay a fee for additional storage.

14

CAUTION

Using an iDisk over a slow Internet connection can be an exercise in futility. When you use an iDisk, you are usually moving a large amount of data from your machine to the iDisk. When using a dial-up account or other slow connection, this can be quite frustrating—even simple tasks such as opening the iDisk can seem to take forever. If you use a dial-up account to connect to the Internet, try to use the iDisk at less popular times of the day (such as early in the morning) so that the performance will be as good as it gets. The speed might still annoy you, but at least you stand a better chance of being able to tolerate it. A good choice for dial-up users is to create a copy of your iDisk on your Mac and choose the manual synchronization option. Then, you can move files to and from the local copy of your iDisk. When you are ready to put those files on the Net, you can perform synchronization. This might take a long time to do, but you don't have to be at your Mac during the process (unlike if you work with your online iDisk to move files).

The good news is that using the iDisk is faster under Mac OS X than it was using previous versions of the Mac OS.

CONFIGURING YOUR IDISK

You can configure your iDisk for your Mac OS X user account by opening the iDisk tab of the .Mac pane of the System Preferences utility (see Figure 14.2).

Figure 14.2
Using the iDisk tab of the .Mac pane, you can configure your iDisk; here, you can see that I have 100MB of space available, but I am currently using only 14MB.

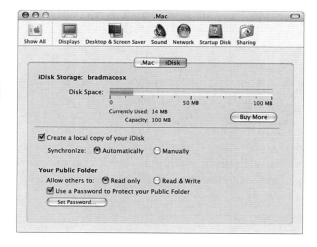

To configure your iDisk, perform the following steps:

1. Open the System Preferences utility and click the .Mac button to open the .Mac pane.

2. Click the iDisk tab.

3. Use the Disk Space bar to assess the status of your disk space. You can upgrade the amount of space you have by clicking the Buy More button (more on that later).

14

4. To create a copy of your iDisk on your Mac, check the "Create a local copy of your iDisk" check box. This causes your Mac to download a copy of your iDisk so you can access it from your desktop. If you want your Mac to keep the local copy and the online iDisk synchronized at all times, click the Automatically button (this option should be selected only if you have a broadband connection to the Net). If you prefer to manually synchronize your local and online iDisks, click the Manually button (this option should be used if you use a dial-up account).

5. To control whether others can input information to the Public folder on your iDisk, use the radio buttons. Click the Read-Only button if you want users to only be able to read files in the Public folder on your iDisk. Click the Read & Write button if you want them to also be able to place files there. If you chose the latter option, you should protect your iDisk with a password.

6. To protect your iDisk with a password, check the "Use a Password to Protect your Public Folder" check box and click the Set Password button.

7. In the resulting sheet, enter the password you want to use, confirm it, and click OK.

8. Quit the System Preferences utility.

WORKING WITH A LOCAL COPY OF YOUR iDISK

If you chose to create a local copy of your iDisk, you can open it from the Finder by clicking its icon in the Places sidebar (see Figure 14.3). In the resulting Finder window, you will see the folders on your iDisk. At the bottom of the window, you can see the current space being used along with information about the last synchronization that was performed.

Figure 14.3
You can access your local copy of your iDisk by clicking its icon in the Places sidebar of a Finder window.

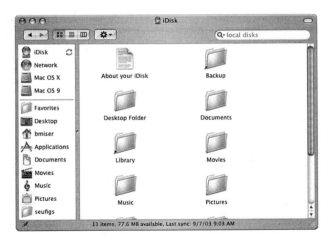

NOTE

The local iDisk is actually a disk image file called `Previous local iDisk for username.dmg`, where `username` is your member name.

If you set the local copy of your iDisk for manual synchronization, you can perform synchronization by clicking the Synchronize now button located to the right of the iDisk icon in the Places sidebar (see Figure 14.4). The two versions of the iDisk are synchronized; a progress bar at the bottom of the Finder window informs you about the status of the process.

Click here to synchronize your iDisk

Figure 14.4
You can click the Synchronize button to synchronize the online and local versions of your iDisk.

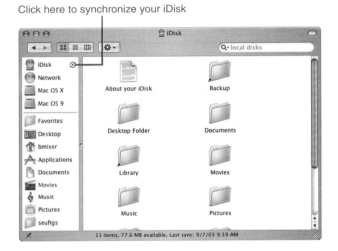

TIP

If you open the Action button or the contextual menu for a Finder window showing your iDisk, you can select the Sync Now command to perform synchronization or the Automatic Syncing command to set your iDisk to be synchronized automatically.

WORKING WITH YOUR ONLINE IDISK

If you choose not to create a local copy of your iDisk, you can still work with your iDisk from the Finder. However, when you move files to and from the iDisk, you will actually be moving those files across the Net rather just between locations on your hard drive. In most cases, you should use a local copy instead. However, you can access your online iDisk directly to work with it.

To do so, select Go, iDisk, My iDisk or press Shift-⌘-I. The contents of your iDisk are shown in a Finder window.

If you have set your desktop preferences such that mounted disks appear on your desktop, you will see a disk with your member name as its name and an icon of a hard disk in front of a globe—this is your online iDisk. If your mounted disks don't appear on your desktop, open the Computer directory and you will see your iDisk there.

14

→To learn how to set the preference for disks being shown on the desktop, **see** "Customizing the Mac OS X Desktop," **p. 121**.

> **TIP**
>
> Look for the Synchronize symbol to the right of the iDisk volume in the Places sidebar of the Finder window to tell the difference between the online iDisk and a local copy of your iDisk. If you don't see any symbol, you are working with the online iDisk. If you do see a symbol, you are working with a local copy. Telling the difference on the desktop is easier. The online version has your member name as its name, whereas the local copy is just called iDisk.

> **TIP**
>
> If you use more than one .Mac account, you can download and use the iDisk Utility application to make working with multiple .Mac accounts more convenient. You can download this application from the .Mac Web site.

WORKING WITH YOUR iDISK

After your iDisk is mounted on your Mac (whether it is a local copy or the online version), you can work with it just like the other volumes and disks on your machine. Open your iDisk and you will see the following folders:

- Documents
- Library
- Movies
- Music
- Pictures
- Public
- Sites
- Backup
- Software

The Documents, Movies, Music, and Pictures folders contain elements for Web pages you might want to add to your .Mac Web site. For example, if you want to include a Pictures page on your site, you can store the images you want to include on the page in the Pictures folder.

The Public folder is where you can store files you want other .Mac users to be able to access.

The Sites folder is where you store your own HTML pages to be served from the .Mac Web site (rather than using the page templates that are provided for you).

14

The Software folder contains software you can download to your Mac. Apple stores system and application software updates here so you can easily access and download them. To see what software is available, simply open the Software folder. To download any of the files you see to your Mac, drag the file from the Software folder to a folder on your machine. For example, a folder called Mac OS X Software contains applications you can download to your Mac by simply dragging them from the folder to your hard drive. The contents of the Software folder do not count against the 100MB size limit (or other size if you have increased it) of your iDisk.

The Backup folder is where your data is stored if you use the Apple Backup application to back up your Mac.

The Library folder contains files that support use of the iDisk, such as application support files.

TIP

> When working with an early version of Mac OS X version 10.3, I couldn't delete files on my local copy of my iDisk by selecting them and pressing ⌘-Delete or by selecting File, Move To Trash as I do with files on other local volumes. I had to actually drag the files to the Trash icon on the Dock to delete them. I could remove files from the online iDisk using the usual techniques. This might be related to the early version of 10.3 I was using, but if you ,are unable to remove files from your local copy of your iDisk, try the good old drag method.

ACCESSING IDISKS FROM THE GO MENU

The iDisk commands on the Finder's Go menu are the following:

- **My iDisk**—The command opens your own iDisk.
- **Other User's iDisk**—When you select this command, you see the Connect To iDisk dialog box. Enter the member name and password of the user's iDisk that you want to access and click Connect. That iDisk is mounted on your Mac and you can work with it just like the iDisk that is configured as part of your Mac OS X user account. For example, if you have two .Mac accounts, you can configure one iDisk as part of your Mac OS X user account and use this command to access the iDisk that is part of another .Mac account.
- **Other User's Public Folder**—When you select this command, the Connect To iDisk Public Folder dialog box appears. Enter the member name of the user whose Public folder you want to access and click Connect. If the user has not selected the option to protect the Public folder with a password, that user's Public folder on her iDisk is shown in a Finder window. If the folder is protected with a password, enter the password and click Connect when prompted to do so.

TIP

> When you need to enter a password to access someone else's Public folder, your user-name is Public, which is entered for you. If you add the password to your keychain, you don't have to enter it again. The Public folder is unlocked for you automatically when you access it.

SHARING INFORMATION ON YOUR IDISK WITH OTHERS

One of the most useful things about an iDisk is that you can place files in the Public folder and then share them with other .Mac users.

To share your Public folder, you can publish it so that others can access it using a Web interface. You don't have to do this for others who use .Mac because they can mount your Public folder directly (as you saw in the previous section). However, publishing a File Sharing Web page can be helpful to users who don't or can't use .Mac. To create your File Sharing Web page, follow these steps:

1. Move to the .Mac page and click the HomePage icon to open HomePage (if you aren't logged in already, you will be prompted to do so). You move to the HomePage window. Toward the bottom of the window are tabs that enable you to create various types of Web pages.

TIP

> If you have more than one site, click the site on which you want to place the file-sharing page before doing step 2.

2. Click the File Sharing tab. You will see the format options for a file-sharing Web page (see Figure 14.5).

Figure 14.5
When you create a file-sharing Web page, you can choose the format of that page.

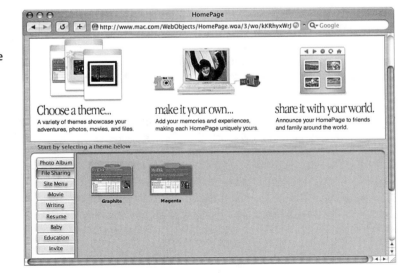

14

3. Choose the look of your Public folder page by clicking one of the Appearance choices (such as Graphite or Magenta). You will move to the My iDisk page.

4. Click the Edit button. Three fields become editable: the name of the page, the member name displayed, and the page description.

5. Change the text as needed.

6. Click Publish.

You'll see a screen confirming that you have successfully published the page, and you also see its URL (see Figure 14.6).

Figure 14.6
The contents of my Public folder have been published to the File Sharing page located at the URL shown in this window.

NOTE

> When HomePage creates a page for you, the URL ends in the name of the template you selected to create the page followed by a sequential number (in Figure 14.7, you can see the URL ends in `FileSharing27.html`). These URLs aren't likely to be easy for others to type. However, you can create site menu navigation pages on your site and link to each page (you'll learn how later in this section). People can access your site menu at `http://homepage.mac.com/membername/`, where *membername* is your member name.

To make files available from your iDisk Web page, drag them into the Public folder on your iDisk. When you do so, they will appear on the iDisk Web page (see Figure 14.7).

NOTE

> If you work with a local copy of your iDisk, it must be synchronized before the files will be available on the Web. If you use the manual synchronization option, click the Synchronize button after you put the files in the Public folder.

Other people can download these files by moving to the Web page and clicking the Download link for the files they want to download.

Figure 14.8
Anyone who accesses the files on this Web page can download them from my iDisk's Public folder.

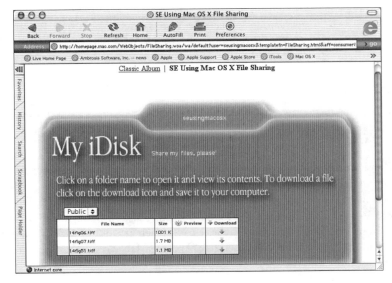

TIP

Anyone who can access the Web can use the files you share. This includes Windows PC users as well as users of Macs running Mac OS 9 or earlier. Using a .Mac Web site is a great way to share files because it is easy to upload files and others can also access the files easily. Using a Web site is better than emailing large files because the recipient can choose when he wants to deal with the files (especially for those people using a dial-up connection to the Internet). And you don't have to worry about an email application properly decoding the files.

NOTE

For some file types, you can preview the file before you download it. When this is possible, the Preview icon appears in the Preview column.

UPGRADING YOUR iDISK

You might need to have more space available than the 100MB that is provided as part of a standard .Mac account. In fact, if you want to create a Web site with lots of movies, music, and photos on it, 100MB might not be enough for you. If you will be using the .Mac backup application to back up your data, you will definitely want to obtain more iDisk space. You can purchase additional storage space for your iDisk. At the moment, you can choose to have 200MB for $60/year, 300MB for $100/year, 500MB for $180/year, or 1GB for $350/year.

To add more space to your iDisk, go to the iDisk tab of the .Mac pane and click the Buy More button. Follow the onscreen instructions to add more space to your iDisk.

14

NOTE

> You can also upgrade other aspects of your .Mac account. You can add email accounts or increase the amount of email storage space you have for your .Mac email account.

CREATING A .MAC WEB SITE

As you saw in the previous section, you can easily create a Web page using .Mac. However, you can just as easily create an entire Web site using the HomePage tools. Your site can include multiple sites, with each having multiple pages.

There are two basic ways to use .Mac to publish your Web site. The first is to use the HomePage templates to build your Web pages. You add content to these pages by placing files in the related folders on your iDisk. The second, and more flexible, way is to add your own Web site files to the Sites folder on your iDisk to publish it. For example, you can create your Web site using your favorite tools, such as Adobe's GoLive, and then post those files in the Sites folder on your iDisk. Apple's .Mac server takes care of serving the site you upload to the Internet.

CREATING YOUR WEB SITE USING THE HOMEPAGE TEMPLATES

When you build a Web site using the HomePage templates, you actually can create a set of sites and place different pages on each site. People can access each site directly, or you can provide a site menu to help them navigate your sites.

To build a Web site using the HomePage templates, you first create some pages. Then you can add sites and add each page to each site, one page at time. When you choose a page to add to your site, you choose a template (called a *theme*) for that page. Then, you select the contents for the page, edit it as needed, and publish it. You can also choose the start page for your site, which is the first page a visitor to your site sees (more commonly called the *home page*).

You can use templates to add any of the following pages to your site:

- **Photo Album**—I bet you can guess what you store on these pages. Use these pages to share your photos with friends and family.

- **File Sharing**—As you have already seen, this page presents the files in your Public folder for easy downloading.

- **Site Menu**—These pages help you create a menu so visitors can explore your site by clicking links.

- **iMovie**—You can serve iMovies you create so others can watch them over the Web.

- **Writing**—These pages are formatted as personal newsletters.

- **Résumé**—You can create a résumé to land that next big job.

- **Baby**—Use these pages to make a grandparent's day.

- **Education**—These pages are designed for those involved in education. The template pages include pages for school events, a school album, teacher information, and so on.

- **Invite**—You can use these pages to create custom Web invitations.

→ To learn how to create photos to share over the Web, **see** Chapter 15, "Creating and Editing Digital Images," **p. 457**.

→ To learn how to create movies to share over the Web, **see** Chapter 17, "Making Digital Movie Magic with iMovie," **p. 571**.

Before you get started adding pages to your site, decide what kinds of pages you want to have on your site or what types of sites you want to include. Add the files for each page to the appropriate folder on your iDisk. For example, if you are going to have an iMovie page, add your movie files to the Movies folder. Add photos you want to post by placing the files in the Pictures folder, and so on, until you have added the content you want to have on your site to the appropriate folder on your iDisk.

The process to add each type of page is quite similar. You can create pages based on any of the available templates by following these steps:

1. Move to the .Mac Web page.

2. Click the HomePage icon. You will see the HomePage page (see Figure 14.8). This page contains the tools you need to build and edit your site. In the upper part of the window, you see all the sites and pages that are currently part of your site. You will also see the URL to your site. In the lower part of the page, you will see the tools you use to create pages.

Figure 14.8
The HomePage Web page enables you to build your own Web site quickly and easily; so far, my Web site contains only one set of pages (called a site), and that set contains only one page (called Sharing Files).

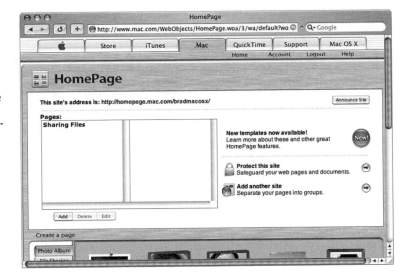

14

The page shown in bold is the Start Page—your home page—which is the first page people see when they access your Web site.

3. In the Create A Page area, click the button for the type of page you want to create (for example, iMovies to create a movie page). You will see the various themes (templates) available for the type of page you selected.

4. Click the template you want to use. You will move to the default page that is based on the template you selected. Here, you edit the text associated with the page (usually, this means the title of the page and a description of its contents) and add the content to it.

5. Click the Edit button and the text fields become editable.

6. Edit the text that will appear on your page (see Figure 14.9).

Figure 14.9
Here I have changed the default text to be more appropriate to the movie I am posting on the page.

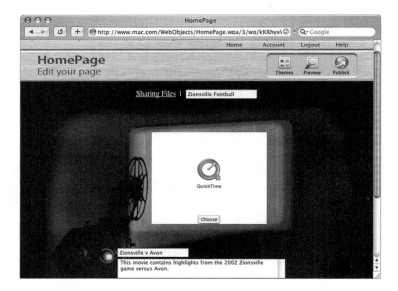

7. Click the Choose button. You will see the Select Files screen.

8. Select the files you want to appear on the page. For example, if you are creating a movie page, click Choose, select a movie from your Movies folder, and then click Choose to add the movie to the page. Other templates present these controls in slightly different formats, but they all work similarly—for example, for a Photo Album page, you choose the folder in which the images that will be stored on it are located.

9. Scroll to the bottom of the window. Check the check boxes for any special features you want to add. Most pages provide for a counter that shows the number of people who have visited the page (the check box next to the zero) and a "Send me a message" link that enables visitors to send email to you.

10. Click the Preview button to see how your page will look.

11. If you need to make changes, click the Edit button.

12. When you are done with the page, click Publish. The Web page you created is added to your site and you see its URL.

13. Click the URL to visit your new page (see Figure 14.10).

Continue adding pages to your site until it contains all you want it to. When you are done, you will see all the pages on your site in the upper-left corner of the HomePage window.

You can also create additional sites and then add pages to those sites using the same process. In .Mac lingo, these additional sites are called *groups*, meaning you can collect a set of pages and place them into groups.

Figure 14.10
An example of a Web page that offers some movie entertainment; using .Mac, I was able to create this page in just a few minutes (and most of that was the time required to upload the movie file into the Movies folder on my iDisk).

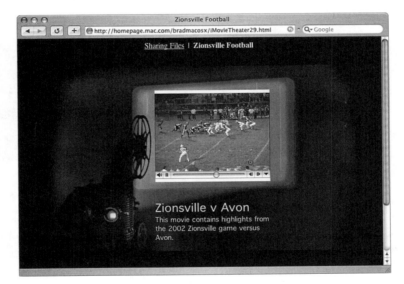

To create another group on your site, carry out the following steps:

1. On the HomePage page, click the arrow button next to "Add another site." You will move to the "Create a site" page.

2. Enter the name of the site you are creating in the Site Name field.

3. If you want a password to be required for someone to be able to view your site, check the On check box and enter the password in the Password field.

4. Click Create Site. You will return to the HomePage page and will see the new site you have created. The HomePage page now contains boxes for your sites and the pages on those sites.

14

5. To see the pages included in a group, select the group on the Sites pane; its pages appear in the Pages pane. Select a page and a preview appears in the third column on the screen (see Figure 14.11).

Figure 14.11
My Web site now includes two groups of pages: One is called Photos, and the other is the default group that is called bradmacosx.

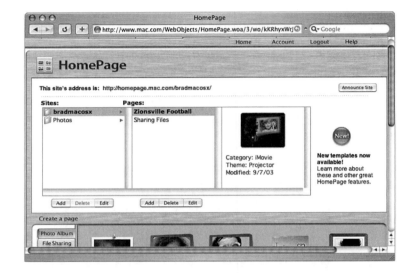

The URL for the Web site you create is http://homepage.mac.com/yourmembername/. (Don't include the period shown in this URL—that is only to please my editors!)

When someone visits this URL, she sees the page you designated as the Start Page. She can use the links on this page to move to the other pages on your Web site.

You can move directly to a specific page using the URL for that page. For example, if you create an iMovie page, the URL for that page will be http://homepage.mac.com/yourmembername/iMovieTheater.html, where *yourmembername* is your member name. As you add more pages of each type, the names are differentiated by sequential numbers, as in iMovieTheater1, iMovieTheater2, and so on.

Creating Web sites using HomePage is easy and powerful. Following are some additional tips for your consideration:

- Set the home page for each group (called the *start page* in .Mac lingo) for your Web site by dragging the page you want to use to the top of the Pages list.

- You can see the URL for any group by selecting it. Its URL appears at the top of the HomePage screen.

- The Home site is always the one with your member name as its URL. Any other sites you create have URLs based on this one. For example, if you create a site called Book_Information, its URL is http://homepage.mac.com/yourmembername/Book_Information, where *yourmembername* is your member name.

14

- To add more pages to a site, select that site on the Sites list and click the Add button under the Pages list.

- To add more sites, click the Add button under the Sites list.

- You can delete sites or pages by selecting what you want to delete and clicking Delete. Then click Yes on the resulting confirmation screen.

- Password-protect any sites that contain information you want to limit access to.

- Use site menu pages to organize your site and enable visitors to move around using links. You can also place images on site menu pages as a preview of the pages that are linked to the site menu page.

- To place a counter on a page, use the Show check box next to the counter icon (a box with a zero in it) that becomes available when you edit the page. This counter counts the number of visits to that page.

- Use the "Send me a message" check box next to the Send me a message icon to place an email link on a page. Visitors can click this link to send email to your .Mac email address.

CREATING YOUR WEB SITE BY ADDING YOUR OWN PAGES TO THE SITES FOLDER

Although you can quickly and easily create a basic Web site using the .Mac templates and tools, you are somewhat limited in what you can do. The available templates might or might not be suitable for the site you want to create. Even if you want to do more than you can with the .Mac Web page templates, .Mac is still valuable because you can use .Mac to host *any* Web site you create using any other Web site editing tools, such as Adobe's GoLive or Macromedia's Dreamweaver. In this scenario, .Mac acts just like any other Web hosting service you might use.

The general process to get your customized Web site on the .Mac is the following:

1. Create your Web site using the tools you prefer.

> **NOTE**
>
> Name the home page of your site `index.html`. This ensures that a viewer is taken to the right start page for your site when he moves to its URL.

2. Test the site by accessing it while it is stored on your Mac. You can test a Web site by opening it from within a Web browser. For example, open your site using Safari by selecting File, Open File. Then, maneuver to the home page for your site and open it. The site will work just as it will after you post it on your .Mac Web site (except that it will be a lot faster, of course). You should test your site in various browsers and operating systems to ensure that it can be viewed properly.

3. Fix any problems you find.

14

4. When your site is ready to post, copy all its files and folders into the Sites folder on your iDisk.

5. Test your site again by accessing it over the Net.

To access the Web site in your Sites folder, use the following URL: `http://homepage.mac.com/yourmembername/`. (For this to work, you must have named the home page for the site `index.html`.)

When you move to the site, you see the page you named `index.html` (see Figure 14.12).

Figure 14.12
I created this site on my Mac and uploaded it to the Sites folder on my iDisk.

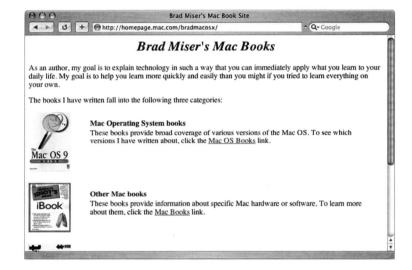

The Web site you store in the Sites folder is not integrated into a .Mac Web site you create using the .Mac template. In fact, any pages you create using the .Mac templates are not accessible after you copy your own site into the Sites folder because your custom site replaces any HomePage sites you have created.

USING OTHER HOSTING SERVICES TO PUBLISH A WEB SITE

Thousands of Web hosting services are available for you to use. All of them work similarly to .Mac; you first create your Web site and then upload all the files onto the hosting service's servers. As with the .Mac, the hosting service maintains all the hardware and software needed to serve your site to the Web.

Unlike .Mac, however, many hosting sites are free or charge only a minimal fee. Some hosting services offer more than just Web serving, including domain name registration, email, FTP, and other services. Hosting services that offer these additional services are usually fee-based. Such fees usually depend on the size of your site and how much traffic it will be generating.

→ To learn about domain name registration, **see** "Registering Your Domain," **p. 448**.

NOTE

> You might wonder why companies would offer hosting services free. Most free hosting services generate income by including advertising on the sites they host. When someone views your Web site, he also sees whatever advertising the hosting service has been able to sell. You usually don't get any say in the sorts of ads that appear on the sites, so you should investigate this before you start using a free site. Sometimes these ads can be more than just annoying for people visiting your site. Often, they can be offensive.

If you want to explore the hosting services that are available, develop answers to the following questions:

- **How large is your site?** Many hosting services limit the amount of storage space you have (such as the .Mac 100MB limit) or charge you additional fees for larger sites (again, like .Mac).

- **Do you want a more specific URL for your site?** If you want your site to have a more specific URL, such as `www.yourname.com`, you need to register a domain name for that site. Many hosting services will take care of this for you. Most free sites provide the same domain and your page is accessed via a path or document name (such as a .Mac Web address that looks like `homepage.mac.com/yourmembername`).

- **How much traffic do you expect to generate?** Many hosting services limit the total amount of data transferred across your site. Some for-fee companies might allow you to have as much traffic as you can generate, whereas with others, you might have to pay additional fees if the traffic goes over the maximum allowed in your service agreement.

- **What is the purpose of your site?** Some hosting sites, especially the free ones, do not permit you to conduct business using their free sites. However, many hosting services specialize in commercial sites and offer many tools to help you transact business across the Net.

- **What is the nature of the information on your site?** Many hosting services have specific guidelines about what is allowed on a site they host. Make sure that the material you intend to post on your site does not violate these guidelines.

- **What software do you use to create your site?** Different Web-creation software offers different tools and creates pages in slightly different ways. Some hosting services are optimized for particular Web-creation applications.

- **How much information about your site will you want?** Some services offer information about the traffic that comes across your site (such as the number of hits on it), whereas others (mostly the free services) offer little to no feedback.

After you have answered these questions for yourself, you can find many hosting services by doing a quick search on the Web. After you find a hosting service, you can create an account with it (you might also need to pay for it and provide additional information depending on the services you are getting). When you have an account, most hosting services work similarly to .Mac.

14

NOTE

One of the nice things about .Mac is that posting the files for your site to your iDisk is so easy. Many services require that you use FTP software to post your files, and sometimes they even require specific FTP applications to be used. Typically, the required applications are shareware or freeware, so it usually isn't a big deal. However, if you try to use the wrong FTP application, you can have problems.

USING MAC OS X TO SERVE WEB PAGES

For most Mac users, a hosting service is the way to go. Hosting services handle the hard work of maintaining the hardware and software that is needed to serve your site to the Web. A hosting service must also deal with all the hacking to which most Web sites are subjected. A hosting service enables you to concentrate on your Web site rather than the Web server that provides it to the Web. Additionally, you can get many other services that make your Web site even more powerful (such as domain name registration).

However, there might be situations in which you want to be your own hosting service. If you have a site that will be accessed in a limited fashion by people outside your local network, hosting your own site can be an easy and effective way to share information. Also, you can easily host a site that will be accessed through your local intranet.

One of the great things about Mac OS X being based on Unix is that many of the tools available for Unix work with it as well. And when it comes to the Internet, most of the back end runs on Unix, so many useful tools are available.

Even better news is that Mac OS X includes very powerful and sophisticated Web server software—Apache. This software is widely used across the Internet to serve Web pages, and Mac OS X users can take full advantage of it out of the box. Although Apache is a Unix application, you can perform the basic tasks of serving a Web site without messing around with text commands. Of course, to really customize and master Apache, you do need to get your hands into the command line. However, you can get a site up and running without ever interacting directly with Apache.

Establishing and maintaining a Web server is a complex and challenging task, and explaining all the details associated with hosting a Web site is beyond the scope of this book. However, in this section, you will learn the basics of hosting a Web site on your Mac and see how easily you can get started doing so. From there, you'll see pointers to more information so you can take your Web hosting to the next level.

CAUTION

If you plan to have a very active Web site with heavy traffic, you will need a dedicated machine to act as a Web server. In fact, if you want to be serious about hosting a Web site, you are foolish to use your "production" Mac. Bad things can happen to Web servers, so you should never host a Web site from a machine that you also use to do work. (However, this is feasible if your Web site will be accessed by only a few people and will have little traffic.) The biggest threat to a Web server is the hackers who love to break into such servers and wreak havoc. Because your Mac should be directly connected to the Internet to be capable of serving a site, it will be vulnerable to attack. If you use your production machine to host Web pages, you are opening yourself up for trouble. This is a prime advantage of using a hosting service because that service has to deal with the security of its hardware and software. There is no direct link between your Web site and your production Mac.

The general process for using for your Mac to host a Web site is the following:

1. Create your Web site using any tools you prefer.
2. Test it to make sure that it works.
3. Register your domain.
4. Move the files for your Web site to the appropriate location on your Mac.
5. Start the Web server.
6. Monitor your site to ensure that it has adequate performance and is available 24/7.

To host a Web site, you need to have the following:

- **A powerful Mac with a large amount of RAM**—Preferably, it should be a dedicated machine that is used for no other purpose. A busy Web site will generate a great deal of activity on the Web server. Don't try to skimp by using a low-end machine; otherwise, your Web site might be a big flop.

- **A Web server application**—Because you are using Mac OS X, you have this one (Apache is built in).

- **A registered domain name**—To make it easier for people to find and use your site, you need to register its domain name.

NOTE

If you are hosting a site only for a local intranet, you don't have to register a domain name. You can use the IP address of the machine just as well.

- **A direct, high-bandwidth Internet connection**—Because the point of having a Web site is so that people can access it, you need to have an always-on connection to the Internet. You also need to have high bandwidth to handle all the data that will be moving among many users at the same time. You need to have a fast cable modem for a site on which you don't expect that much activity, and you need a T-1 or fractional T-1 line for a site on which you expect to have a fair amount of activity.

14

NOTE

> Again, you don't need this if you are hosting a site on an intranet. You just need the network connection and an IP address for your machine.

- **A permanent IP for the machine from which you will be hosting the site**—This goes hand in hand with the previous point. (After all, how can people find your site if its address changes?) If you can use a static IP address, it will be provided by your access provider when you obtain your Net access, such as when you use a T-1 or fractional T-1 connection.

→ To learn about connecting your Mac to the Net with a high-bandwidth connection, **see** Chapter 10, "Connecting Your Mac to the Internet," **p. 263**.

- **A security system that will protect the Web server**—Hackers will try to crack your site so you need to install and use tools to protect it.

Hosting a serious Web site is resource- and labor-intensive, as you can see from this list. (A hosting service looks better and better, doesn't it?)

NOTE

> If you try to host a site from a "consumer" ISP, make sure that your license agreement does not prohibit such activity. For example, many cable modem service providers explicitly prohibit you from hosting a Web site through your Internet access account.

REGISTERING YOUR DOMAIN

Web sites are designed for people, and people don't like to deal with IP addresses. They much prefer working in letters and, even better, words that make some sort of sense to them. Because IP addresses are actually four series of numbers separated by periods, the two have a hard time getting together. That is where the *domain name service (DNS)* comes in. Basically, the DNS relates text that people use to the numbers that computers use. When someone enters a URL, the DNS server he uses translates the text he types into the literal IP address so he can move to that address.

For this to happen for your site, you must enter the domain you want to use and the IP address it is associated with. This process is called *registering* the domain name.

There are various ways to register your domain name (the easiest is to use a hosting service that also offers domain name registration). You can search the Web to find sites at which you can register a domain name. The fees you will pay vary depending on the length of time for which you register the name and the other services that are included.

NOTE

> Although many companies will register your name free, you usually have to pay the fee associated with the registration. (A fee is charged for each domain name so someone has to pay that fee.) Some companies charge you to register the name and require you to also pay the name fee. And some companies subsidize the fees if you use other services. Does this sound confusing to you? If so, join the club. There are as many fee structures as there are companies doing this, so you just have to make sure you know what you are signing up for.

When you search for domain name registration sites, you will find many of them. And most offer similar deals. For example, I could register a name for about $10/year. Some even include additional services in this agreement, such as email forwarding.

NOTE

> Email forwarding enables email to your domain name to come to your current email address. For example, if I registered the domain `mymacrocks.com`, I could have email addressed to `brad@mymacrocks.com` delivered to any address I prefer.

CAUTION

> Be sure you carefully read all domain name registration agreements before you finalize them. You need to be absolutely clear on what you are getting into.

Put some thought into the domain you register because that is how people will find your site. Avoid really long names, no matter how clever you think they are. Simple names are better.

CONFIGURING YOUR MAC TO SERVE A WEB SITE

Each user account on your Mac can serve its own Web site; this means you can serve many Web sites from your Mac at the same time. To provide a Web site for a user's account, you place the files for that site in the Sites folder that is contained in that user's Home directory.

NOTE

> Each user's Sites folder contains an `index.html` file that provides a default home page for that user's Web site. You replace this file with your own `index.html` file to serve your specific site (you can also modify the default index page if you want). The default `index.html` page contains information about how Web sharing works and is worth reading if you are new to the topic.

There is also an overall Web site for the Mac itself. You should also ensure that you add a Web site for the Mac so that when people move to the home page for your machine, they will see a meaningful site. (You will learn about that shortly.)

14

After you have created your site, registered a domain name, and configured your Mac for the connection you are using, the steps to get it online are pretty simple:

1. Place the files for the site you want to post in the Sites folder of the user account you want to use. For example, if the username under which you want to post a site is bmiser, open the Home directory for that user and then copy the Web site into the Sites folder (see Figure 14.13).

   As with the .Mac site, make sure that the name of your home page is index.html. You can organize the other files and folders according to the scheme used by your Web-creation application.

Figure 14.13
When a Web page is stored in a user's Sites folder, it can be served to an intranet or the Internet.

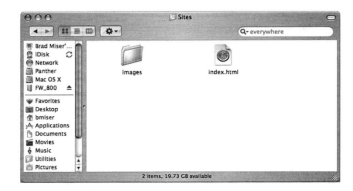

TIP

> You can test any user's Web site without actually adding Web pages to the Sites folder. Because the index.html page is part of each Sites folder, that page is served up for every account. So, if you move to the URL for a user account on your machine, you should see the Mac OS X Personal Web Sharing page. If you do, that means Web sharing is working. All you need to do is replace the default content with your content.

2. Open the System Preferences utility, open the Sharing pane, and then click the Sharing tab.

3. On the Services tab, check the "Personal Web Sharing" check box. This starts the Web server on your Mac. Just below the list of sharing services, you will see the URL of the Mac along with the URL for the user's Web site. You build the URL for your site based on either of these. For example, if your IP address is 12.34.567.89, the basic URL for your site is http://12.34.567.89/. Similarly, if the registered domain name for your Mac is agreatmac.com, the URL to your machine is also http://www.agreatmac.com/. If you use the IP address to access the site, it is resolved to the hostname and that is what appears in the address bar of the browser.

   The URL to a specific user's Web site on your Mac is the URL for the Mac itself with a ~ (tilde character) followed by the short version of the username appended to it. For example, if the short name for my user account is `bmiser`, the URL to my Web site would be `http://12.34.567.89/~bmiser/` or `http://www.agreatmac.com/~bmiser/` (if I had registered a domain name appropriately of course).

NOTE

> The tilde (~) character in the URL indicates that the address points to that user's Home directory, in which the Sites folder is stored. If you leave this out of the URL, the user's site won't be found.
>
> You also need to include the end slash (/) in the URL.

4. Close System Preferences.
5. Use another machine to access the URL for your Web site.

If you see the site, everything is in great shape and your pages are "out there."

When you attempt to move to a user's Web site, but it can't be found even though the root-level site can be displayed, see "You Can Access Your Root-Level or Other Web Sites, but Not the Site for a Particular User" in the "Troubleshooting" section at the end of this chapter.

TIP

> The concept that each user who has an account on your Mac can have a unique Web site opens many possibilities for you. You can create user accounts for the sole purpose of providing specific Web sites. For example, if I wanted to host a Web site for this book, I could create a user account called `SEUsing MacOSX` with the short name `usingosx`. I could then place the Web site in the Sites folder for this account and the site would be published.

If your site isn't found at all, see "Your Web Site Can't Be Found" in the "Troubleshooting" section at the end of this chapter.

If, instead of your Web site, you see an Apache page that says the Web server is working, see "The Web Server Is Working, but You Don't See Your Site" in the "Troubleshooting" section at the end of this chapter.

If you are going to be hosting any Web pages on your Mac, you should also configure the root-level Web site for your Mac. This site will appear if someone accesses the Web site on your Mac without including a specific user's account in the URL. For example, if someone enters only `http://12.34.567.89/`, he would see the root-level Web page.

TIP

> Consider creating a Web page that provides URL links to all the Web sites that are hosted on your Mac and posting that at the root level. This would make it easy for a visitor to get to any of the sites on your machine.

14

NOTE

If you open the directory located at Mac OS X/Library/WebServer/Documents/, where Mac OS X is the name of your Mac OS X startup volume, you will see many index pages. Each of these has an abbreviation for the language for which that page is applicable at the end of its filename (for example, the file index.html.en is the English version of the page). The version that Apache serves depends on how your machine is configured.

To post a root-level Web page, do the following:

1. Create the Web site that you want to be at the root level of your machine.

2. Name the home page for this site; again, the name of the home page for the site should be index.html.

3. Place the files and folders for the site in the following location: Mac OS X/Library/WebServer/Documents/, where Mac OS X is the name of your Mac OS X startup volume. Make sure that the index file is in this directory.

By default, a test page is placed at this location so that when you move to your root level, you can tell that the Web server is working (see Figure 14.14). This page also contains links to information about Apache.

Figure 14.14
This page lets you know that Apache is up and working on your Mac.

NOTE

The Web server continues to run as long as your Mac is turned on and the Web site for each user account is served continuously, even if no one is logged in to the system. You can stop the server by shutting down the Mac or by turning off Web sharing using the Sharing pane of the System Preferences utility.

GOING FURTHER WITH APACHE

The information in this section has barely scratched the surface of Apache specifically and Web serving in general. However, a great deal of information on both topics is available within Mac OS X as well as on the Net.

To access the Apache documentation included with Mac OS X, open the manual alias that is within the Documents folder (contained in the WebServer folder). The Apache folder will open. Open the `index.html` file and the Apache User Guide will open.

To find information on the Web about Apache, visit `www.apache.org`. There is plenty of information on this site, including some nice tutorials.

CAUTION

> Before you leave this section, I must give you two more warnings.
>
> First, make sure you protect your Mac from attack if you intend to publish and publicize Web pages you host from it.
>
> Second, some ISPs have limitations on what you can do from particular types of accounts. For example, the license agreement you signed with your ISP might preclude you from hosting Web sites using that account. Make sure you understand any such limitations on your ISP account before you use it to host a Web site.

→ For information about protecting a Mac from Net attacks, **see** "Defending Your Mac from Net Attacks," **p. 908**.

TIP

> You can also serve an FTP site from your Mac. On the Sharing pane, check the FTP Access check box. When you use `ftp` instead of `http` in the URLs for your machine, you move to the FTP site instead of the Web site.

TROUBLESHOOTING

NO MEMBER SIGN-IN AREA APPEARS

When I log on to the .Mac Web site, the Member Sign-In area does not appear; instead I see a message saying that the .Mac installer software must be downloaded and installed.

This situation occurs under Mac OS X when the .Mac software cannot be found on your Mac. This can happen when you update the System folder or when some other system change prevents .Mac from being able to find your information. When this happens, you will automatically be moved to the .Mac Installer download page. Follow the onscreen instructions to download the installer. Run the installer. When the installation is complete, move back to the .Mac Web site and you will see the Member sign-in area in which you can log in to your .Mac account.

MY WEB SITE CAN'T BE FOUND

When I try to move to my Web site's URL, I see a message stating that the site can't be found.

For some reason, your site isn't even making it onto the Net. There are many possible reasons for this, and figuring out which ones are causing your problems can be tough. Start with the most basic and work from there. First, check that Web Sharing is turned on. Second, double-check that the URL you are entering is the correct one. Third, check the Net connection of the Web server (make sure that it can access the Net). Fourth, ensure that you don't have any firewall or security software or hardware that prevents other computers from connecting to the Web server. If all these seem to be right, you will have to explore more functions of Apache to make sure that it is working properly. Use the online information that comes with Mac OS X to do so.

THE WEB SERVER IS WORKING, BUT I DON'T SEE MY SITE

When I move to my Web site's URL, I see a page that says that the Web server is working, but I don't see the Web site I created.

This happens when the index site for your site can't be found. The Apache installation includes a test page so that something will appear when the Web server is operating properly. Your challenge is to figure out why your site is not being served. First, check to make sure that your site's files are in the proper location. Second, make sure that the home page for your site is named `index.html`. Third, make sure that the index file is a valid HTML file. When the Web server is working and these conditions are correct, you will see the appropriate Web page.

I CAN ACCESS MY ROOT-LEVEL OR OTHER WEB SITES, BUT NOT THE SITE FOR A PARTICULAR USER

When I attempt to move to a specific user's Web site, I get a site not found error even though I can access the root-level Web site for my Mac.

Whenever you get a `site not found` error, check the root-level Web site for the machine as well as other Web sites on your Mac. To check the root-level site for your Mac, leave out the portion of the URL related to a specific user account (for example, use `http://12.34.567.89/` without the username appended to it). If this works, you know that the problem is related to the specific user's site. Make sure that the tilde character (~) appears before the user's short name and the slash (/) appears after it. If the site is being served (you can access the root-level page) and the URL is correct (for example, `http://12.34.567.89/~bmiser/`), there might be a problem with the user's account configuration. Sometimes, the short version of the username can cause problems for the Web server. Change the short version of the user's username and then try again. (Use the Accounts pane of the System Preferences utility.)

Mac OS X: Living the Digital Life

CREATING AND EDITING DIGITAL IMAGES

In this chapter

15

Capturing Images for the Digital Lifestyle

Images are a huge part of the digital lifestyle. From the snapshots you took on your last vacation to that "killer" graphic extolling the virtues of your product for your Web site, digital images are an important part of what you do on your Mac.

The Mac has long been known as the computer platform of choice for many digital artists. With Mac OS X, the place of the Mac in the hearts and minds of digital artists is ensured. And, just as important, Mac OS X makes it possible for those of us who might not be quite so artistic to create and use excellent digital images.

The situations in which you might create digital images are literally endless. To give you a few ideas, consider the following list:

- Digital photo albums that make organizing and accessing all your photos easy (unlike all the hard copy photos stacked around your house)
- Sophisticated slideshows that include music and special effects
- Images of all kinds to enhance your Web site
- Images to include in the movies you create
- Desktop images to enhance your working environment
- Images to include in work projects (proposals, reports, and so on)

→ To learn how to quickly create a Web page to display your digital photos, **see** "Creating a .Mac Web Site," **p. 438**.

→ To learn how to use digital images in your digital movies, **see** "Creating and Editing a Movie with QuickTime Pro," **p. 660**, and "Building a Basic Video Track," **p. 573**.

→ To learn how to use QuickTime to create slideshows with your images, **see** "Creating a QuickTime Slideshow," **p. 665**.

→ To learn how to use your favorite images on your desktop, **see** "Customizing the Mac OS X Desktop," **p. 121**.

With Mac OS X, there are several ways to create or obtain digital images for your use. These include the following:

- Use a graphics application to create an image.
- Use a digital camera to capture an image.
- Use a scanner to create a digital image from a hard-copy version.
- Capture a still image from a digital movie.
- Take a screenshot of your desktop to use in documents or when you are trying to get help with your Mac.
- Download an image from the Web.
- Purchase an image from a stock photo CD collection or Web site.

→ To learn how to capture images with a digital camera, **see** "Capturing Images Using a Digital Camera," **p. 459**.

→ To learn how to capture a screenshot, **see** "Capturing Screen Images with Grab," **p. 469**.

The best thing about Mac OS X and digital images is Apple's iPhoto application. iPhoto is simply amazing; you can use it to capture, organize, view, print, and be creative with all types of digital images. In fact, iPhoto is so amazing, people have switched to Mac OS X just because of iPhoto! (iPhoto is available only for Mac OS X.) iPhoto empowers you to make the most of digital images for all kinds of purposes, from your own personal snapshots to images for your projects. It might be the only digital imaging application you ever need.

CAPTURING IMAGES USING A DIGITAL CAMERA

The age of digital photography is upon us. The increase in the quality of the images that digital cameras capture along with an equally impressive drop in their cost has made digital photography available to almost everyone. Digital cameras offer many benefits over film-based cameras.

If your camera supports the Picture Transfer Protocol (PTP), you can use it with Mac OS X even if its software is not Mac OS X–compatible. You can use iPhoto or Mac OS X's Image Capture application to download images from any camera that uses PTP.

Because iPhoto is an ideal application to use for all aspects of working with images you capture with a digital camera (as you will learn later in this chapter), you are very likely to want to use it. To make the most of its capabilities, you should use a camera that is iPhoto-compatible. Fortunately, many brands and models are. To see whether a camera is compatible with iPhoto, visit `www.apple.com/iphoto/compatibility/`.

After your images are captured, the real power of a digital camera comes into play. Unlike film-based cameras in which you have to have the film processed, you can immediately download images to your Mac and begin working with them.

NOTE

> Some cameras include other software you can use to download and work with images from the camera. This chapter assumes that a camera supports PTP and thus Image Capture or iPhoto. Explaining how to use software specific to cameras is beyond the scope of this chapter.

DOWNLOADING IMAGES TO YOUR MAC

There are several ways in which you can transfer the images you capture from the camera to the Mac. These are covered in the following sections.

USING IPHOTO TO DOWNLOAD IMAGES

iPhoto is the best and easiest way to download and manage your images.

→ To learn how to use iPhoto to download images from your camera, **see** "Downloading Images from a Digital Camera into iPhoto," **p. 475**.

15

USING IMAGE CAPTURE TO DOWNLOAD IMAGES

Mac OS X was designed to work with digital cameras; it includes the basic Image Capture application that provides a consistent interface for various models of digital cameras. Its single purpose is to download images from digital devices to your Mac. Because iPhoto is also included with Mac OS X, there isn't a whole lot of reason to use Image Capture, but because Image Capture remains part of the standard Mac OS X applications, you should understand its capabilities.

Image Capture works with cameras that support the Picture Transfer Protocol (PTP). If you aren't sure whether your camera supports this protocol, check the manufacturer's Web site and product specifications to see whether your particular model supports PTP.

N O T E

> The more technical name for PTP is ISO 15740.

Image Capture can be used to download images from some scanners, and that is the more likely circumstance in which you will use it. But it works similarly whether your image source is a camera or a scanner.

Image Capture can be configured so it automatically downloads images when you plug your camera or scanner into your Mac. By default, Mac OS X is configured to open iPhoto when it detects a camera. You can change this behavior with the Image Capture Preferences command.

Working with Image Capture is straightforward. Use the following steps to get images from your camera to your Mac:

1. Connect your camera to your Mac using its USB cable.

N O T E

> By default, your Mac opens iPhoto when you connect a camera to it. You can allow that to happen and then open Image Capture. Both applications can be running at the same time.

2. Power up your camera (if it has a mode selector to communicate with a computer, choose that mode—most cameras switch to this mode automatically). If you haven't configured Image Capture to open automatically, open the application (Applications folder). If you have configured Image Capture to open automatically, it will do so when your Mac detects the camera. You will see the Image Capture window (see Figure 15.1). The application communicates with the camera to determine how many images need to be downloaded. When the camera is ready to begin downloading images, the Download Some and Download All buttons become active.

Figure 15.1
When you connect a supported camera to your Mac, Image Capture displays the number of images that are ready to be downloaded (and you might even see an image of the camera, as is the case for this Kodak DC4800).

NOTE

If your camera is not recognized by Image Capture, it probably does not support PTP. In that case, you have to use the camera's software to download images from it.

3. Select the folder into which you want the images to be downloaded on the Download To pop-up menu. By default, Image Capture selects the Pictures, Movies, and Music folders option. You can select Other on the menu to choose a different folder.

4. To download all the images on the camera, click Download All. The images you download are downloaded into the appropriate directories in your Home folder or in the folder you selected on the Download To pop-up menu. For example, photos are downloaded to the Pictures directory. As the images are downloaded, you see a progress dialog box that shows you a preview of the images being downloaded (see Figure 15.2). When the application is done downloading images, it moves to the background and the directories into which it downloaded images are opened.

Figure 15.2
As Image Capture downloads your photos, you see a preview of each image it is downloading.

5. Move to the appropriate folder to work with the files you have downloaded.

NOTE

Notice that the default download folders are Pictures, Movies, and Music. Some cameras can capture movies and sound. If your camera has QuickTime movies on it, those are placed in the Movies directory in your Home directory. Likewise, sounds are placed in the Music directory.

If Image Capture does not recognize your camera, see "The Digital Camera Is Not Recognized by Image Capture or iPhoto" in the "Troubleshooting" section at the end of this chapter.

TIP

When you connect a camera, the Options button in the Image Capture window becomes active. You can use this feature to configure various aspects of how your camera interacts with your Mac. For example, you can set the camera's time and date, cause images to be automatically deleted after they are downloaded, and so on.

To download only selected images, use the following steps:

1. Connect your camera and open Image Capture.

2. After the application is ready to begin downloading images, click Download Some. You will see a window that shows a preview of each image stored in the camera (see Figure 15.3). By default, the window appears in the Icon view.

Figure 15.3
You can use the preview window to select images to download; you can also rotate images or delete them.

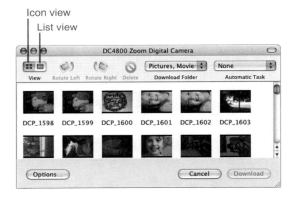

3. Click the List View button or select View, as List to see the images in the List view. In this view, you see the images in a Finder-like window. You see a lot of information for each image, including its name, file size, date and time of capture, width and height in pixels, and so on.

NOTE

You can change the width of the columns in the List view; however, you can't change the sort order—the window is always sorted by image number.

4. Return the window to the Icon view by clicking the Icon view button or by selecting View, as Icons.

5. If you need to rotate images, select the images you want to rotate and click the Rotate Left or Rotate Right button.

6. Select the folders into which you want to download the images on the Download folder pop-up menu. The default is the same as when you download all images, but you can change it to be any folder you'd like to use.

7. Select the images you want to download (use the Shift key or ⌘ key to select multiple images) and click Download. The images are downloaded into the selected directory.

TIP

You can connect multiple cameras to your Mac at the same time. To choose the one with which you want to work, use the Camera pop-up menu.

USING IMAGE CAPTURE OPTIONS

Image Capture has other options that are useful:

- **Automatic Task**—You can attach AppleScripts to Image Capture so it performs an action you select from the Automatic Task pop-up menu when you download images. A number of actions are on the menu by default, including Build Web Page, Build Slide Show, Crop to 3×5, and so on. You can use any of these tasks or add your own. To add a task to the menu, place it in the `Mac OS X/System/Library/Image Capture/ Automatic Tasks` directory, where `Mac OS X` is the name of your Mac OS X startup volume.

- **Options dialog box**—If you click the Options button in the Image Capture window, you will see a sheet that contains three tabs. The Download Options tab enables you to configure how downloads are handled, such as whether all images are downloaded automatically or whether images are deleted from the camera after they are downloaded. The View Options tab enables you to configure the two views in the Download Some window; for example, you can select the size of the icons in the Icon view or determine which columns are displayed in the List view. The Device Options tab displays information about the device you are using, such as the type of camera and the application your Mac is using to interface with it. If you use Image Capture regularly, you should explore these options.

NOTE

Image Capture downloads only those images that aren't already in the selected directory. So, you won't get duplicate files if you have previously downloaded images on the camera and then perform another download with new images.

SETTING IMAGE CAPTURE PREFERENCES

If you use Image Capture to download images from a camera or a scanner, you should configure it to suit your preferences.

15

NOTE

> Although the Image Capture Preferences is accessed via the Image Capture application, what you choose here affects other applications. For example, you must use this preference to set the application that opens automatically when you connect a camera to your Mac. This is because Image Capture provides the basic framework your Mac uses to interact with cameras and scanners regardless of the specific application you use.

To set your preferences, perform the following steps:

1. Select Image Capture, Preferences. The Image Capture Preferences dialog box appears.
2. On the Camera tab, and select Image Capture (iPhoto is selected by default) on the pop-up menu.

TIP

> If you want an application other than Image Capture or iPhoto to open when you connect a digital camera, select Other and select the application you want to open automatically.

3. Click the Scanner tab.
4. If you want to use TWAIN software to capture images from a scanner, check the "Use TWAIN software whenever possible" check box.
5. If you want the scanner window not to be opened when Image Capture is launched, uncheck the lower check box.
6. Close the Preferences window.

CAPTURING DIGITAL IMAGES USING A SCANNER

A scanner enables you to create a digital image from a hard-copy image. The uses for a scanner are almost limitless; these include scanning photographs, business cards, slides and film, 3D objects, and so on. Having and using a scanner enables you to bring items from the analog age into the digital lifestyle.

You can use Image Capture to download images to your Mac. For this purpose, it works very much like it does when you download images from a camera.

SHARING IMAGING DEVICES ON A NETWORK OR VIA THE WEB

 With Mac OS X version 10.3, you can share image devices on a network or over the Web. This enables others to access devices connected to your Mac and you to access devices others are sharing.

→ To learn how to configure Web sharing, **see** "Using Mac OS X to Serve Web Pages," **p. 446**.

→ To configure a local network, **see** Chapter 26, "Building and Using a Network," **p. 821**.

SHARING A CAMERA OVER A NETWORK OR THE WEB

To share a device connected to your Mac with a network, use the following steps:

1. Open Image Capture; then select Image Capture, Preferences.

2. In the Preferences dialog box, click the Sharing tab (see Figure 15.4).

Figure 15.4
Using the Image Capture Preferences Sharing tab, you can share a digital camera or other device with those on your network or via the Web.

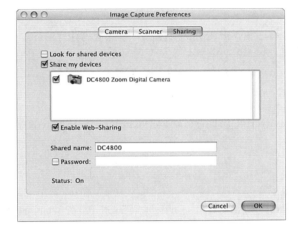

3. Check the "Share my devices" check box. In the pane just below that, you will see all the devices that are available for sharing, such as a digital camera or scanner.

4. Check the check box next to each device you want to share.

5. If you want to enable devices to be shared over the Web, check the Enable Web-Sharing check box.

6. Provide a name for the device in the Shared name box. This is the name people who access the device will see.

7. If you want to require a password to be entered to access the device, check the Password check box and enter a password in the Password field.

8. Click OK. The device will be shared.

CAUTION

For a device to be shared over a network, the computer to which it is connected must be on the same subnet as the computer trying to access it. For small networks, this is not an issue. However, if you are using a large network, make sure the machines are on the same subnet because sharing will not work otherwise.

ACCESSING A SHARED CAMERA

There are two basic ways to access devices that have been shared: via a local network or over the Web. The method you use depends on how the device has been shared with you.

To access a device that has been shared with you over a network, use the following steps:

1. Open Image Capture; then select Image Capture, Preferences.
2. In the Preferences dialog box, click the Sharing tab.
3. Check the "Look for shared devices" check box.
4. Click OK.
5. Select Devices, Browse shared devices. The Browsing dialog box appears showing each device that has been shared with you.
6. Select the device you want to access and click OK.
7. Access images on the device.

You can also access a device that has been shared with you over the Web by doing the following:

1. Launch Safari.

> **NOTE**
>
> For Rendezvous devices to be available in Safari, you must turn on that preference in the Bookmarks pane of the Safari Preferences dialog box.

2. Select Bookmarks, Rendezvous, *devicename*, where *devicename* is the name of the device you want to access. Your Mac connects to the device and you see its contents in a Web page called "Digital Cameras on *machinename*", where *machinename* is the name of the Mac sharing the camera, assuming the device is a camera of course (see Figure 15.5).

→ To learn how to configure Safari to access Rendezvous services, **see** "Browsing the Web with Safari," **p. 388**.

> **TIP**
>
> If more than one device is being shared with you, select the device you want to work with on the Camera pop-up menu.

3. Use the Browse arrows to view each page of content being provided by the device.
4. To download images to your Mac, select them and click Download.

Figure 15.5
This Web page shows the contents of a camera being shared over the Web.

Accessing a camera over the Web offers many cool features, including the following:

- Click the List View button to view the page as a list instead of with icons.
- To select all the images on the device, click Select All.
- You can delete images from the shared device by selecting them and clicking Delete.
- To take picture with the shared device, click Take Picture. The camera takes a picture. To see the new picture, refresh the Web page by selecting View, Reload Page (or by pressing ⌘-R).
- You can view a larger version of an image by double-clicking it. To return to the thumbnail views, click the Return button (it is an upward-pointing, curved arrow). You can browse through all the images at the large size by using the Browse arrows.

USING DEVICE SHARING TO MONITOR AN AREA

If you want to feel like Big Brother, you can use a shared device to monitor an area remotely. You can set the remote device to capture an image periodically and display that image on a Web site. Here's how:

1. Set up the camera so it captures the image you want to be able to monitor, such as a doorway into a room or some other part of a room.
2. Share the camera over the Web.
3. Access the shared camera (see the previous section for details).
4. Click the Remote Monitor tab. The camera takes a picture and transfers it to the Web page; to see the results immediately, reload the page. Just below the tab is the time at which the image was last updated and the time at which it will be updated again.

NOTE

> Images capture via Remote Monitoring are not stored on the camera; they are only displayed. You can capture an image and store it on a camera by clicking the Take Picture button.

The camera keeps taking pictures at the set interval and displaying them on the Web page. This enables you to see what is happening in an area over time.

TIP

> By default, a new image is captured every 60 seconds. To change this, click the Preferences button located just under the Remote Monitor tab. Enter the interval at which you want images to be captured and click Set. Setting a shorter interval provides more active monitoring.

Capturing Screen Images

In many instances, capturing an image of what is happening on your Mac's screen is useful. One example is if you are writing instructions about how to do a particular task, such as when you are writing your own book about Mac OS X. Another is when you want to capture an error message or some other anomaly you want to be able to explain to someone (for example, you might want to capture the image of an error dialog box so you can email it when you try to get technical support).

With Mac OS X, you have two built-in ways to capture screen images. One is to use keyboard commands. The other is to use the Grab application.

Capturing Screen Images with Keyboard Shortcuts

Mac OS X includes keyboard commands you can use to capture desktop images. After you capture an image, it is stored on your desktop as a PDF and is called Picture X, where X is a sequential number. You have the following three options:

- Shift-⌘-3 captures the entire desktop.
- Shift-⌘-4 changes the pointer to a plus sign. Drag this pointer to select the part of the screen you want to capture. When you release the mouse button, an image of the selected area is captured.
- Shift-⌘-4-spacebar enables you to capture a window, menu bar, Dock, or other area of the screen. First, open the area you want to capture, such as a window or menu. When you press the key combination, a large camera pointer icon appears. Move this icon over the area that you want to capture, which becomes highlighted. Click the mouse button to capture the image.

TIP

> To choose not to capture an image after you have pressed these key combinations, press Escape. If you want to save an image to the Clipboard so you can easily paste it into a document, hold down Control while you press the keys for the kind of screenshot you want to take.

CAPTURING SCREEN IMAGES WITH GRAB

Mac OS X includes the Grab application. As its name implies, using Grab, you can "grab" an image of your Mac's desktop. There are several options you can use to capture a specific image. To capture a desktop image follow these steps:

1. Open Grab (Applications/Utilities).

2. Select the Capture mode you want for your screenshot using the Capture menu. Your options are as follows:

    - Selection captures an area of the screen you select.

    - Window captures the active window.

    - Screen captures the entire screen.

    - Timed Screen provides a timer so you can set up a screen before it is captured (so you have time to switch to a window and open a menu before the image is captured, for example).

3. Follow the instructions you see. For example, if you select Timed Screen, the Timed Screen Grab dialog box appears. Then open the area you want to capture, such as a document window with a menu open. When you are ready to take the shot, click Start Timer in the Timed Screen Grab dialog box and get the window as you want it to be captured. After 10 seconds have passed, Capture captures the image.

    When the capture is complete, you see a new window containing the image you captured.

4. To see the size of the image you captured and its color depth, select Inspector from the Edit menu or press ⌘-1. The Inspector window appears and you see information about the image.

5. Save the image. Grab's default file format is TIFF.

The images you capture with Grab are just like images you create in other ways. You can open them in image-editing applications, preview them in Preview, print them, and so on.

T I P

Grab's capturing capabilities are provided to the OS so that other applications can use them. For example, if you are working in a Carbon or Cocoa application, you can easily grab an image of its screen by selecting the Services command from that application's menu. Then, select Grab and select the type of grab from the menu. When you release the mouse button, the image you captured is displayed. How it is displayed depends on the application from which you captured it. For example, if you grab an image while you are using TextEdit, a Rich Text Format (RTF) file is created. If you grab an image while using Preview, that image appears in the Pasteboard window.

N O T E

If you are at all serious about capturing screen images, there is a much better solution than that which Mac OS X provides natively. The best screen capture utility for Mac OS X is Ambrosia Software's Snapz Pro X. This application provides numerous options for your screen captures and even enables you to capture QuickTime movies of movement on your desktop. Check it out at www.ambrosiasw.com. (All the screen captures in this book were taken with Snapz Pro X.)

USING iPHOTO TO MASTER DIGITAL IMAGES

Mac OS X includes one of the most amazing image applications ever produced: Apple's iPhoto. iPhoto enables you to work with digital photos you have captured using a digital camera or from any other source. With iPhoto, you can organize, edit, print, email, and export your photos. You can also do all sorts of other cool things with your images, such as creating books, Web pages, and screensavers.

When you open iPhoto, you see its three panes (see Figure 15.6). The Source pane enables you to select a source to work with. The Content pane shows either the contents of the selected source or the image you are working with, depending on the mode you are in. The Tool pane of the window contains various tools you use for the mode you are working in. Between the Tool pane and the other two panes are iPhoto controls, the mode buttons, and the Size slider.

iPhoto has four modes of operation

- **Import**—You use: the Import mode to import images from a camera.
- **Organize**—You use this: mode to create photo albums, apply keywords to your images, and perform other tasks to keep your images organized.
- **Edit**—In the Edit: mode, you can edit your images by cropping, changing brightness and contrast, removing red-eye, and so on.
- **Book**—Using :Book mode, you can create custom books to display your images.

Between the Source and Content panes and the Tool pane, iPhoto controls are available in whichever mode you are in (see Figure 15.7).

15

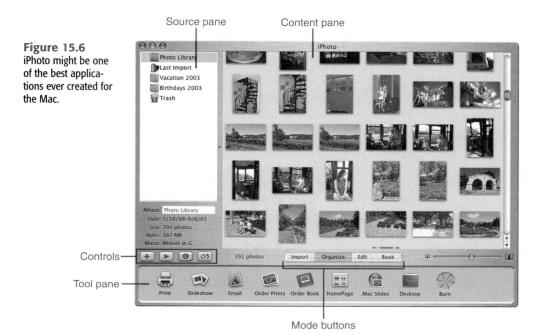

Figure 15.6
iPhoto might be one of the best applications ever created for the Mac.

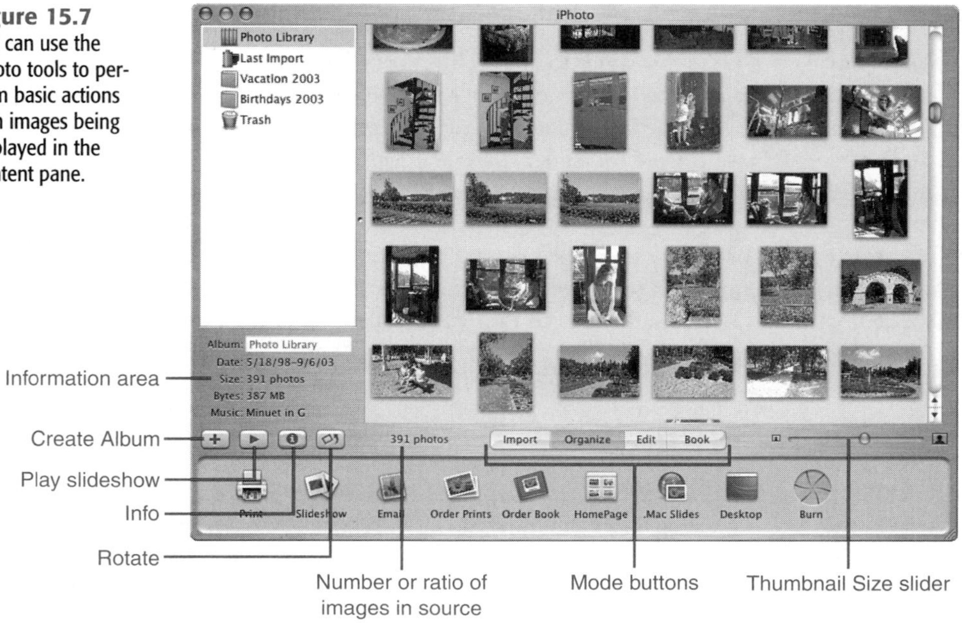

Source pane

Content pane

Controls

Tool pane

Mode buttons

Figure 15.7
You can use the iPhoto tools to perform basic actions with images being displayed in the Content pane.

Information area

Create Album

Play slideshow

Info

Rotate

Number or ratio of images in source

Mode buttons

Thumbnail Size slider

You have the following controls available to you at all times:

- **Create Album**—Click this button to create a new album. You will learn more about creating albums later in this chapter.

- **Play Slideshow**—Click this button and a nice slideshow displaying the images in the selected album plays (accompanied by a music soundtrack).

- **Info**—Click this to open or expand the Information area of the Source pane. If the Info area is not displayed, clicking this button once opens it. If it is displayed, clicking this button expands it, and if it is expanded, clicking this button closes it.

- **Rotate**—Use this button to rotate a selected image by 90° increments in the counter-clockwise direction. When you select an image and then click this button, the image is rotated in the Content pane; the image assumes the orientation you choose from that point forward (meaning the image itself is changed to be the orientation you select). You can change the direction of rotation in the Preferences window. You can also rotate in the opposite direction by holding down the Option key when you click the button.

- **Number or ratio of images in source**—If you have a source selected, this shows the number of images in that source. If you have one or more images selected, it shows the number of images you have selected compared to the total number of images in the selected album.

- **Mode buttons**—Use these buttons to change the mode in which iPhoto is working. When you click a mode button, the Content and Tool panes change to reflect the mode you select.

- **Display Size**—Drag this slider to change the size of the thumbnails of the images you see in the Content pane. Moving the slider to the right makes the thumbnails larger, whereas moving it to the left makes them appear smaller and shows more images at the same time. The setting of this slider doesn't actually change the image in any way; it only determines how large the images appear onscreen.

To get started in iPhoto, you should set several of its preferences. The first time you open iPhoto, you are prompted to set some of these preferences, but you can make changes to them at any time by opening the iPhoto Preferences dialog box.

The iPhoto preferences you can set are described in Table 15.1.

TABLE 15.1   IPHOTO PREFERENCES

Preference	Options	What It Does
Appearance	Drop Shadow	The Shadow option puts a drop shadow behind the thumbnail images in the Content pane when you are in the Organize mode.
	Border	When you select this option, each thumbnail appears inside a border.

15

Preference	Options	What It Does
	No Border	With this preference, thumbnails don't have any border or drop shadow.
	Background	You use this slider to set the color of the background of the Contents pane. Dragging the slider to the right makes the background white; moving it all the way to the left makes it black. Placing it in the middle results in a shade of gray.
	Align to grid	With this option checked, your images remain aligned to the iPhoto grid.
	Place most recent photos at the top	When this check box is checked, the photos you imported most recently appear at the top of the Content pane.
Double-click Action	Opens in Edit view	With the Edit view option, when you double-click an image, it opens in the Edit mode.
	Opens in separate window	With the separate window option, when you double-click an image, it opens in a separate window in which you can view and edit the image. This is very useful, especially because you can customize the toolbar that appears at the top of the window.
	Opens in other/Select button	When you select this preference and then use the Select button to choose an image editing application, the images open in the editing application you selected. For example, you might choose to edit your images with a more powerful image editing application, such as Adobe Photoshop.
Rotate	Clockwise button	With this button selected, the Rotate button rotates images in the clockwise direction by default (you can hold down the Option key while you click the Rotate button to rotate images in the opposite direction).

TABLE 15.1   CONTINUED

Preference	Options	What It Does
	Counterclockwise button	With this button selected, the Rotate button rotates images in the counterclockwise direction by default (you can hold down the Option key while you click the Rotate button to rotate images in the opposite direction).
Mail	Email application	Use this pop-up menu to choose the email application you want to use to email images from within iPhoto. For example, if you use Apple's Mail application, select Mail on the pop-up menu.

NOTE

> The first time you open iPhoto, you are prompted to have iPhoto open automatically when you connect a camera to your Mac. If you do this, you don't need to use Image Capture to set that preference.

Finally, set iPhoto to open automatically when you connect a camera to your Mac:

1. Open the Image Capture application.
2. Select Image Capture, Preferences and click the Camera tab.
3. On the Camera Preferences pop-up menu, select iPhoto.
4. Click OK and quit Image Capture.

IMPORTING IMAGES

The first step in working with images in iPhoto is to import the images you want to work with into the iPhoto Photo Library. You can import images from the following two sources:

- A digital camera
- Image files outside of iPhoto

To import images into iPhoto, you use its Import mode. In this mode, the Tool pane contains the following elements (left to right in Figure 15.8):

- **Camera information**—When iPhoto is communicating with a camera, you see that camera's information, such as its model name. You also see how many images are available to be downloaded into iPhoto. When a camera is not connected, you see the "No camera connected" message.

- **Preview window**—When you import images, a preview of each image is shown in the Preview window.

- **Progress bar**—The progress bar displays the progress of the import process.

- **Files remaining**—Just below the progress bar, the number of files remaining to import from the selected source is shown.

- **Import/Stop button**—This button is Import when you aren't importing images. When you click the Import button, the import process starts and the button becomes Stop (the Stop button does just what you think it does).

- **"Erase camera contents after transfer" check box**—If you check this box, the images on your digital camera are erased after they have been imported into iPhoto.

Figure 15.8
When you connect a camera to your Mac, iPhoto moves into the Import mode automatically.

Erasing Images

Here are two comments for you on the Erase check box. First, if you don't have a camera connected to your Mac, it is inactive. Second, even when it is active, I recommend that you don't use it. I suggest that you leave images on your camera until you are sure they have been imported correctly. If something happens to the image you import and it is erased from your camera, it is gone forever. After you have verified that your images have been imported successfully, you can delete them by using your camera's controls.

DOWNLOADING IMAGES FROM A DIGITAL CAMERA INTO IPHOTO

To download images from your camera into your iPhoto Photo Library, perform the following steps:

1. Connect your camera to your Mac with its USB cable.

2. Power up your camera. iPhoto opens if it isn't already open and moves into the Import mode. Your camera is recognized in the lower-left corner of the Import Tool pane, and you see how many photos are ready to be downloaded.

3. Click Import; the application begins moving the images from the camera's memory into your Photo Library. As the process proceeds, you can see its progress in the Progress bar.

4. Click the Last Import album in the Source pane. iPhoto moves into the Organize mode, and you see the photos you just imported.

5. Work with the Organization mode tools to organize and identify the images you just imported.

→ To learn how to use iPhoto's Organize mode, **see** "Labeling, Finding, and Organizing Images," **p. 477**.

After you have organized the images you have imported, use your camera's tools to empty its memory card so you will be ready for your next shooting session.

To remove: images you imported but don't want to keep, select the images and press the Delete key. Click OK in the warning dialog box, and the image is deleted from iPhoto. Obviously, you should do this only with images you are sure you will never want again.

IMPORTING OTHER IMAGES INTO IPHOTO

You can also add: images from other sources to your iPhoto Photo Library. For example, if your digital camera is incompatible with iPhoto, you have to download images from that camera (such as by using a USB memory card reader) and then import them into iPhoto. Or you might want to add previously scanned photos to iPhoto so you can use iPhoto's great tools to work with them.

You can import a wide variety of image file formats into iPhoto, including JPEGs, Photoshop files, and other formats you are likely to encounter when dealing with digital images. Here's how:

1. Prepare the images you want to import (for example, scan the photos or download them from a USB memory card reader to your Mac).

2. Select File, Import or press Shift-⌘-I. The Import Photos dialog box opens.

3. Move to the files you want to import and select them. You can select multiple images at the same time by holding down the ⌘ key while you click each image.

4. Click Import (or press Return). The images are imported into your Photo Library. You can monitor the process by watching the Progress bar—importing images from files is much faster than importing them from a camera, so the process moves along pretty quickly.

5. Click the Last Import album in the Source pane. iPhoto moves into the Organize mode, and you see the images you just imported.

6. Work with the Organization mode tools to organize and identify the images you just imported.

→ To learn how to use iPhoto's Organize mode, **see** "Organizing Your Images with Photo Albums," **p. 487**.

15

NOTE

> The Last Import album contains the most recent set of images you imported or downloaded from a camera. The images remain in this album until the next import, at which point they are replaced by the next set. Of course, because it is an album, it doesn't actually contain the images themselves, just pointers to them. The imported images are always stored in your Photo Library.

TIP

> When you are done importing images, you should immediately label them and attach the appropriate keywords to them. These tasks are essential to enable you to find images in your Photo Library after you have built it up with hundreds or thousands of images. If you wait until you have hundreds or thousands of images before labeling them, the job will be much harder. Labeling them as you go makes the process much easier.

LABELING, FINDING, AND ORGANIZING IMAGES

Images in iPhoto can be organized into albums; iPhoto albums are analogous to analog photo albums that contain the images in your collection. The iPhoto Source pane shows all the albums contained in your collection. iPhoto includes three albums that are always present: Photo Library, Last Import, and Trash. The Photo Library album contains all the images you have imported into iPhoto (regardless of how you imported them). The Last Import album contains the images you downloaded during the last time you imported images. Just like the Trash on the Dock, iPhoto's Trash contains images you have deleted.

To work with an album, select it in the Source pane and the images its contains are shown in the Content pane. (iPhoto moves into the Organize mode automatically.) When in the Organize mode, the Tool pane contains tools that enable you to perform many actions with your images (see Figure 15.9).

TIP

> You can resize the Source pane by dragging the Resize handle to the left or right.

Because you are likely to accumulate a large number of images, it is imperative that you keep them organized and that you use iPhoto's information tools to help you identify your photos so that you can find them when you need them. To help you keep your images organized, you can attach the following information to them:

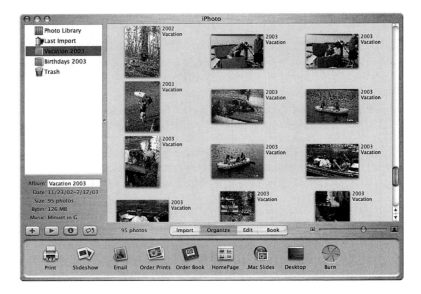

Figure 15.9
In the Organize mode, you can organize the images in your Photo Library.

- **Title**—Each image in your Photo Library has a title. When you import images, the title that iPhoto assigns to them is the same as the filename that iPhoto assigns to that image. But you can change this to give an image a more meaningful title.

- **Date**—iPhoto labels each image with the date and time on which it was captured (if the image came from a digital camera) or with a file's date if the image is imported from a hard disk. You can also change this information if you want to.

- **Comments**—iPhoto enables you to add comments to each image. For example, you can provide the context for the image so that when you look at it later, you will understand it better or if you have a poor memory like I do, you can explain where the information was captured. Comments are especially useful when you create books because they can include interesting things you've said about those images.

- **Film roll**—As you import images, iPhoto labels each image session as a *film roll* and attaches that film roll number to the image. (A film roll number is a sequential value.) You can use this information to find images based on the group in which you imported them. You can't change the film roll number. Film roll is only visible when you are working with the Photo Library as the source.

- **Keywords**—Keywords are short phrases you can assign to images so you can find them again by searching for the keywords attached to them. The benefit of keywords is that you can define a set of keywords and apply them consistently over time. For example, suppose you like to take photos of your vacations. You can create a keyword "Vacation" and assign that to the images you take. Because you use the same phrase, you can find the images again easily because you don't have to remember how you labeled particular images; instead, you can find them by doing a keyword search. You can also combine keywords. For example, you can create and use keywords for each year. If you wanted to find the images you captured during a specific year's vacation, you could search for the keyword "Vacation" and the year in which you are interested.

ADDING TITLES AND COMMENTS TO YOUR IMAGES

You can label images with a title or add comments to the images in your Photo Library to make them easier to find or to document something about those images. Titles and comments can also be useful when you are creating some projects, such as when you create a book or a Web site for a group of images. Do the following:

1. Move into the Organize mode by clicking the Organize button on the iPhoto Tool pane.

2. Find the images you want to label.

TIP

> One reason I suggested earlier that you should label images immediately after you import them is because finding the images that you most recently imported is easy by clicking the Last Import album in the Source pane. The images in that album are displayed in the Content pane.

3. Click the Information button located just underneath the Source pane until you can see the Comments box (see Figure 15.10). Depending on your starting point, you might have to click the button once, twice, or not at all if the Comments box is already displayed.

Figure 15.10
Using the fields in the Information area, you can attach titles, a date, and comments to images.

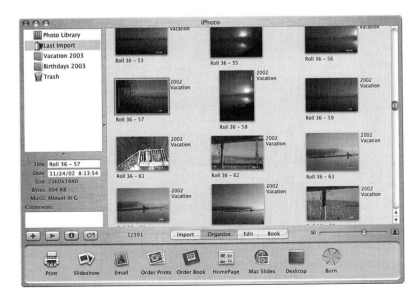

4. Click an image's thumbnail to select the image to which you want to attach information. The image is enclosed in a blue box to show that it is selected. In the Information area, you see iPhoto's default title for the image (the filename the image was assigned when you imported it), the date and time on which the image was captured (assuming that iPhoto was able to retrieve this information from the source), the size (the resolution at which the image was captured and file size), the music associated with the image when it is displayed in a slideshow, and the Comments for the image.

TIP

You can adjust the height of the Information area by dragging its resize handle (the dot between the Source pane and the Information area).

5. If you want to use something other than the iPhoto file name as the image's title, click in the Title field, select the default title, and replace it with a title of your choosing.

6. If you want to change the date iPhoto has associated with an image, click the in Date field, select the current information, and change it. In most cases, this isn't necessary.

7. Click in the Comments box and enter comments about the image. Comments can be anything you desire, such as a description of the location where the image was captured, something amusing that happened at the same time, and so on.

8. Repeat steps 2–7 for each image you want to label.

CREATING KEYWORDS FOR IMAGES

iPhoto includes a number of keywords by default. However, you can create your own keywords, and you can change any keywords that are available (whether you added them or they came with iPhoto). After you have set the keywords you want to use, you can associate them with your images and use them to search for specific images.

First, make a list of keywords you want to use to identify images. Some examples are the following:

- Holidays
- Birthday (this a default keyword)
- Scenic
- Vacation (this a default keyword)
- Sports
- Specific years (2003, 2004, and so on)
- People's names

Adding each year and specific people's names as keywords is useful because you can combine keywords to quickly find individual images. For example, suppose you have defined "2003"

15

as a keyword. If you also use "Birthday" and a person's name as keywords, you can find images associated with that person's birthday in 2003 by searching on the person's name, "2003", and "Birthday". Combing keywords is a powerful way to search for specific images.

To add keywords, use the following steps:

1. Select Edit, Keywords (or press ⌘-K). The Keywords/Search dialog box appears.
2. On the Keywords pop-up menu at the top of the dialog box, select New. You see a new keyword called "untitled".
3. Type the keyword you want to add (see Figure 15.11).

Figure 15.11
I have added the keyword "2003".

4. Press the Return key to add the keyword to the application. It is then available for you to assign to images and then use to search for images.
5. Repeat steps 2–4 for each keyword you want to add.

Following are a couple of keyword tips:

■ You can remove a keyword from the list by selecting it and selecting Delete on the Keywords pop-up menu at the top of the Keywords/Search dialog box.

■ You can change a keyword by selecting it, selecting Rename on the Keywords pop-up menu, typing the new name, and pressing Return. This action changes the keyword on the list as well as on any images with which it is associated.

15

NOTE

> One of iPhoto's default keywords is a check mark. This is the one keyword you can't change. The check mark is intended to be assigned to images temporarily so you can perform a specific task for those images. For example, you might want to order prints from only a few photos in an album. You can apply the check mark keyword to each image you want a print of and then find those images by searching for the check mark keyword. (The check mark actually appears in the lower-right corner of the image itself instead of next to it, which is where other keywords appear.) After you order the prints, you can remove the check mark keyword from the images.

ASSIGNING KEYWORDS TO IMAGES

To use your newly created keywords (or the default ones) to find images, you need to associate keywords with those images.

Before you start working with keywords, make sure they are displayed by selecting View, Keywords or pressing Shift-⌘-K. Keywords are shown on the right of the image thumbnails in the Content pane.

Now, assign keywords to images with these steps:

1. Select the images to which you want to apply one or more keywords. You can assign the same keywords to multiple images at the same time.
2. Select Edit, Keywords or press ⌘-K. The Keywords/Search dialog box opens.
3. Click the first keyword you want to assign to select it. That keyword becomes highlighted.
4. Click Assign. The keyword you selected is assigned to the images you selected in step 1.
5. Click the next keyword you want to assign to the selected images.
6. Click Assign. The keyword you selected is assigned to all the images you selected in step 1.
7. Repeat steps 5 and 6 for each keyword you want to assign to the selected images. The keywords you have assigned to the selected images are highlighted (see Figure 15.12).
8. Click the Keywords/Search dialog box's Close button. When you return to the iPhoto window, the keywords you assigned appear next to the images you selected.

The Keywords/Search dialog box is independent of the iPhoto window, which means you can leave it open and switch between it and the iPhoto window. This saves you the steps of opening and closing the dialog box each time you want to assign keywords or search for images.

Figure 15.12
I have attached the keywords "2002" and "Vacation" to the images selected in the Content pane.

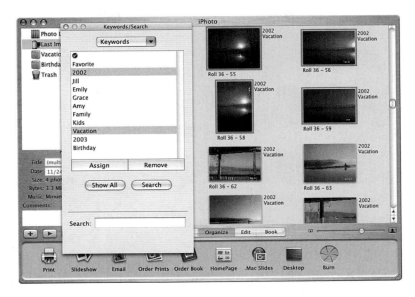

To remove a keyword from an image, do the following steps:

1. Select the images containing the keyword you want to remove.

2. Select Edit, Keywords or press ⌘-K. The Keywords/Search dialog box opens.

3. Select the keywords you want to remove from the images. (Only the keywords that are currently applied to the selected images are highlighted.)

4. Click Remove. The keyword you selected is no longer associated with the selected images.

CONFIGURING THE INFORMATION DISPLAYED IN THE CONTENT PANE

There are a number of ways in which you can configure the Content pane when you are working in the Organize mode, including those described in the following paragraphs.

Use the Thumbnail Size slider to set the size of the thumbnails you see. Making the thumbnails larger makes identifying images easier. The trade-off is that you see fewer of them in the pane.

Select View, Titles or press Shift-⌘-T to show image titles if they are hidden or to hide them if they are shown. When you show titles, they appear just below the lower-left corner of the images.

Select View, Keywords or press Shift-⌘-K to show keywords if they are hidden or to hide them if they are shown. When you show keywords, the keywords you have assigned to images appear just to the right of the upper-right corner of the images.

If you have selected the Photo Library, select View, Film Rolls or press Shift-⌘-F to show film roll information if it is hidden or to hide it if it is shown. (You can display or hide film roll information only when you are working with the Photo Library. If you are working with a photo album, this option is disabled.)

Select View, Arrange Photos to see the Arrange Photos menu. On this menu, you can choose how you want images in the Content pane arranged. The choices are by Film Roll, by Date, by Title, or Manually. (Manually is disabled when you are viewing the Photo Library.)

When you select one of these attributes, the images in the selected source are sorted by the attribute you select, such as by their dates to list the images in the Content pane chronologically.

When you select the Photo Library and select by Film Roll, the images are grouped by film roll. Next to the film roll title, you can click the Expansion triangle to show or hide the images within that film roll.

When you select a photo album, you can select Manually. This choice enables you to manually organize the images in a photo album, which is essential when you are creating projects because the order in which images appear in the Content pane is the order in which they appear in a project, such as a Web site.

You can choose to view each source differently. For example, you can choose to view one photo album by date and another manually. The view settings you choose are specific to each source. However, the Thumbnail Size slider setting applies to all sources.

VIEWING DETAILED INFORMATION FOR IMAGES

iPhoto keeps very detailed information on each image in the Photo Library. You can view this information by using the following steps:

1. Select the image about which you want to get detailed information.

2. Select File, Show Photo Info or press ⌘-I. The Photo Info window appears.

3. Click the Photo tab. Information about the image is shown, such as its size, date, filename, file size, and the camera with which it was captured.

4. Click the Exposure tab. This tab contains technical information about the settings with which the image was captured, such as shutter speed, aperture, and so on.

5. Click another image to view its information. Because the Info window is independent of the iPhoto window, you can leave it open and select the images in which you are interested.

6. Click the window's Close button when you are done using it.

The information captured for each image depends on the device used to capture it and how the image was imported into iPhoto. Some cameras can communicate more information to iPhoto and some can communicate less. Likewise, if you import images from a disk instead of a camera, they are likely to have less information.

FINDING IMAGES

After you have added hundreds or thousands of images to your Photo Library, finding specific images with which you want to work can be a challenge. Fortunately, iPhoto includes powerful search tools that can help you locate individual images so you can work with them.

There are two basic ways to search for images: by keyword or by title or comments.

To find images by keywords, do the following:

1. Select the source you want to search by clicking it in the Source pane. Select a photo album to search it, or select the Photo Library to search all your images.

2. Select Edit, Keywords or press ⌘-K. The Keywords/Search dialog box opens.

3. Click a keyword for which you want to search. It becomes highlighted to show that it is selected.

4. Hold down the ⌘ key and click the other keywords for which you want to search. When you select more than one keyword for a search, all those keywords must be associated with an image for it to be found.

5. Click Search. Only the images associated with the selected keywords are shown in the Contents pane (see Figure 15.13).

Figure 15.13
By selecting the keywords "2002" and "Vacation," the images shown in the Content pane (in the background) are only those with which those keywords are associated.

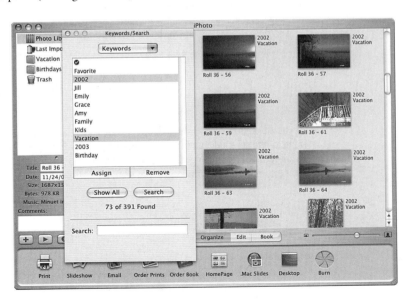

6. Click the iPhoto window to see the images you found in the Contents pane.

CAUTION

> If you close the Keywords/Search dialog box, your search is lost and you see the contents of the selected source instead. Leave the dialog box open as long as you want to work with your search results. Because the dialog box is independent of the iPhoto window, you can move it out of the way if you want to.

7. When you are done with your search, close the Keywords/Search dialog box.

TIP

> You can show all the images in the selected source again by clicking the Show All button in the Keywords dialog box.

You can also search for images by title or comments in a similar way:

1. Select the source you want to search by clicking it in the Source pane. Select a photo album to search it, or select the Photo Library to search all your images.

2. Select Edit, Keywords or press ⌘-K. The Keywords/Search dialog box opens.

3. Type the text for which you want to search in the Search box. As you type, the selected source is searched for the images that contain the text you typed (in their Title or Comments fields), and they are shown in the Contents pane.

NOTE

> Because the search is performed each time you type a letter or a number, typing might be sluggish if you are searching in a source that has a lot of images. After these are narrowed down, the speed at which you can type will increase.

4. Click the iPhoto window to see the images you found in the Contents pane.

CAUTION

> If you close the Keywords/Search dialog box, your search is lost and you see the contents of the selected source instead. Leave the dialog box open as long as you want to work with your search results. The dialog box is independent of the iPhoto window, so you can move it out of the way if you want to.

5. When you are done with your search, close the Keywords/Search dialog box.

ORGANIZING YOUR IMAGES WITH PHOTO ALBUMS

Photo albums are the tool you use to create collections of images for specific purposes, such as to view specific images or create slideshows, books, Web sites, and other projects. You can create albums containing the images you are interested in and then work with those images by selecting an album in the Source pane.

NOTE

> If you have used iTunes' playlists, the concept of albums should be easy to grasp because playlists and albums are analogous.

You can choose any criteria for the photos you include in an album, and you can include any number of photos in any album you create. Here's how:

1. Click the New Album button located just below the Source pane; select File, New Album; or press ⌘-N. You see the New Album dialog box.

2. Name your album and click OK. The album you create appears in the Source pane.

3. Select the Photo Library source and find the images you want to include in the new album; use the keyword searching technique you learned in the preceding sections to do so.

4. Select the images you want to include in the album (select multiple images by holding down the ⌘ key), and drag them onto the new album in the Source pane. As you drag the images onto the album, a red circle containing a number appears—the number is the number of images you have selected.

5. Continue finding images and dragging them onto the album.

6. When you are done, select the album in the Source pane to see the images it contains in the Content pane.

Following are points to consider when you work with albums:

- Placing images in an album does not remove them from the Photo Library; the Photo Library always contains all the images you have imported into iPhoto (unless you have deleted some images from the Library). When you drag an image onto an album, a pointer from the original image to the album is created.

- You can create an album by dragging images from the Photo Library or from other albums onto the Source pane. An album called Album-# is created; you can edit the album name by selecting it and, when it is highlighted, changing the name to what you want it to be.

- You can place the same image in as many albums as you'd like.

- When you select an album, you can select and then drag the images around in the Content pane to change their order. The order in which images appear in an album affects projects you create from that album. For example, if you create a book, the

15

images appear in the book in the same order in which they appear in the album. The first image in an album is the one in the upper-left corner of the Content pane, the second image is the one to the right, and so on to the end of the row. The first image in the next row is the next image and so on right to left, top to bottom.

- To remove an image from an album, select it and press the Delete key. The image is removed from the album, but not from the Photo Library.

- Changes you make to an image in an album, such as associating keywords with it, editing it, or rotating it, *do* affect the image in all its locations, including in the Photo Library.

ROTATING IMAGES

Images can have one of two orientations: landscape or portrait. When you capture images, you are likely to change the camera's orientation to capture the best image possible. For example, landscape shots are often best captured in the Landscape orientation, which is wider than it is tall (hmmm, I wonder how they named that one?). When you are capturing images or people, the Portrait orientation, which is taller than it is wide, is frequently a good choice (another naming coincidence, do you suppose?).

Because you are likely to rotate your camera as you take pictures, the pictures you import will probably be of mixed orientation. For most uses, including simple browsing, slideshows, books, and so on, this is usually not a good thing. iPhoto's Rotation tool comes in handy at this point and enables you to rotate images so that the bottom of all your images is toward the bottom of the screen. Do the following:

1. Select the photo album containing the images you want to rotate.
2. Select the images you want to rotate.
3. Click the Rotate button. The images you selected are rotated in a 90° increment in the default direction you have configured for the button.

Rotating images is simple, as you can see. Still, here are some tips to make you an expert in the art of rotation:

- Images are rotated in a 90° increment each time you click the Rotate button.

- To rotate images in the direction opposite to what's set as the default rotation direction, hold down the Option key while you click the Rotate button.

- You can change the default direction of rotation when you click the Rotate button by using the iPhoto Preferences dialog box.

- You can rotate images in the clockwise direction by selecting them and selecting Edit, Rotate, Clockwise or by pressing Shift-⌘-R.

- You can rotate images in the counterclockwise direction by selecting them and selecting Edit, Rotate, Counter Clockwise or by pressing ⌘-R.

Editing Your Images

You can use iPhoto's Edit mode to make changes to your images. Although iPhoto is not a full-featured image editing application such as Adobe Photoshop, its tools enable you to make common changes that most people want to make to their images. For example, you can remove red-eye, crop, and so on.

Editing a Copy or the Original

When you edit an image, your changes affect *all* instances of that image in all your photo albums, in the Photo Library, and wherever else that image is used within the application. (Fortunately, iPhoto maintains the original image should you ever want to go back to it. You'll learn more about this later.)

This is a problem if you want to have multiple versions of an image, say one cropped and one not cropped or one in black-and-white for a book and another in color for a slideshow. Fortunately, you can create duplicates of images. Each copy becomes a new, independent image just as if you had imported it again. You can create one copy for each version of the image you want to use in your projects.

You can create as many copies of an image as you'd like, but remember that each image consumes disk storage space. If you are going to use only one version, you don't need to duplicate it because iPhoto maintains the original version for you. But, if you do want to use multiple versions of the same image, select the images you want to duplicate and select File, Duplicate or press ⌘-D. You move into the Import mode temporarily and a copy of the image is created.

The copies have all the same information associated with them as the originals, such as keywords, dates, and so on. The only difference is that the word copy is appended to the images' titles.

Choosing Editing Options

When you edit images within iPhoto, there are two basic ways the Edit window can be configured. Slight differences exist between the two ways, but they each work similarly.

One way is to edit images within the iPhoto window itself—this is the default configuration. When you use this configuration and double-click an image (or select it and click the Edit mode button), the image fills the Contents pane and the edit tools appear in the Tool pane (see Figure 15.14).

The other way is to have the images you edit appear in a separate Edit window. To enable this method, set the Double-click preference to "Opens in separate window." With this preference set, when you double-click an image, a new, separate Edit window appears (see Figure 15.15). You can use the editing tools that appear in the window's toolbar to edit the image.

Figure 15.14
You can edit images within the main iPhoto window.

Figure 15.15
You can also configure iPhoto so you can edit images in the Edit window.

One of the nice things about the second method is that you can customize the tools in the Editing window's toolbar so it contains only the tools you use most frequently:

1. Open the Edit window.
2. Click the Customize button to open the Customize sheet.
3. To add tools to the toolbar, drag them from the sheet onto the toolbar.
4. To remove tools from the toolbar, drag them off the toolbar.

5. Use the Show pop-up menu to choose how you want the tool icons to appear. Your choices are Icon & Text, Icon Only, and Text Only.

6. To use small icons (which take up less space on the toolbar), check the Use Small Icons check box.

7. Click Done. The toolbar now contains the tools you selected in the format you chose.

> **TIP**
>
> Another advantage of using the separate Edit window is that you can have multiple Edit windows at the same time.

The method you use to edit images depends on your personal preference. The "edit in the same window" option is especially useful if you want to edit a series of images, such as those in a photo album. You can use the Prev and Next buttons to quickly move to and edit each image in the selected source. The "edit in a separate window" option is useful because you can develop and use a custom set of tools to make editing easier and faster. Plus, you can move the Edit window around, which is especially helpful if you use multiple monitors. And you can minimize the Edit window to move it out of your way temporarily.

> **TIP**
>
> You can resize the Edit window, just like other Mac windows. To fit an image so it fills the Edit window, click the Fit button on the toolbar.

Both methods are easy to use. I recommend that you configure the application to use the Edit window (by setting the "Opens in separate window" preference). When you want to use the Edit window, double-click the image you want to edit; it opens in the Edit window. When you want to edit an image within the iPhoto window, select the image and click the Edit mode button; the image fills the iPhoto window and you can edit it there.

> **NOTE**
>
> A third editing option is to use a different application to edit images, such as Photoshop. Use the Double-click preference to choose the application you want to use. When you double-click an image, the editing application you selected opens and you can edit your image. When you save your changes, the edited image is stored in the Photo Library.

SELECTING PARTS OF AN IMAGE YOU WANT TO EDIT

The Crop and Red-Eye editing tools require that you select the part of the image to which you want to apply the editing tool. When you select parts of an image, you have two basic choices: unconstrained or constrained. When you use the unconstrained option, you can select any part of the image. When you select the constrained option, you can only choose part of the image with a specific proportion.

You typically should use the constrained option when you crop images and the unconstrained when you are applying the Red-Eye tool. To select part of an image using the unconstrained technique, do the following steps:

1. Open the image in the Edit window or select the image and click the Edit mode button.
2. Move the pointer over the image. The cursor becomes a plus sign.
3. Drag in the image. As you drag, the pointer becomes the arrow again, a selection box appears, and the part of the image you have selected remains clear while the part that is not selected becomes shaded.
4. When the part of the image you want is selected, release the mouse button. The cursor becomes a plus sign again.
5. To move the selection box around in the image, move the pointer inside the selection box. The pointer becomes a hand icon. Drag the selection box to the location that contains the part of the image you want to select.
6. To resize the selection box, drag one of its borders.

When you want to ensure that the part of the image you select has a specific proportion, you use the constrained option:

1. Open the image in the Edit window or select the image and click the Edit mode button.
2. On the Constrain pop-up menu, select the option you want, such as 4 x 3 (Book,DVD).

> **TIP**
>
> If you use the "separate window" editing option, you can add buttons for the constraints you use most frequently to the toolbar.

3. Use steps 2–6 in the previous list to select part of the image. The only difference is that the selection box remains in the proportion you selected on the Constrain pop-up menu.

ZOOMING ON IMAGES FOR EDITING

As you edit images, you need to zoom in and out to see the results of your changes. How you do this depends on the editing mode you are in.

When you use the "same window" editing mode, use the Thumbnail Size slider to zoom in or zoom out.

> **TIP**
>
> If you select part of the image before you zoom, iPhoto attempts to keep that part of the image centered on the screen as you zoom.

If you use the "separate window" option, click the Up arrow in the toolbar to zoom in. As you zoom, the current percentage of zoom is shown in the window's title bar. Click the Down arrow to zoom out.

TIP

> Each click of the Zoom arrows zooms you in or out by a percentage increment, such as from 75% to 100%.

CROPPING IMAGES

Images often contain extra stuff that doesn't help the image and might distract the viewer from the image's intended subject. You can crop images so they contain only the material you want to be included. Or you might choose to crop an image to increase the focus on the central subject captured in the image. When you crop an image, you select the part of the image you want to keep and get rid of everything else. In addition to removing part of the image, the remainder of the image appears to be larger because a smaller image fills the same space on the screen during a slideshow. Do the following:

1. Select the image you want to crop and then double-click it or click the Edit mode button. The image appears in the Edit window or fills the Content pane.

2. If you are going to use a constrained selection, select the constraint on the Constrain pop-up menu.

3. Use the selection techniques covered in the previous sections to select the part of the image you want to keep.

4. Click the Crop button. All the image outside of the selection box is removed.

5. Press the Control key. While you are holding down the Control key, iPhoto displays the uncropped version again.

6. Compare the two versions to make sure the cropped version is the one you want to keep.

ENHANCING IMAGES

When an image doesn't look quite right, you can use the Enhance tool to enhance the image. This tool attempts to adjust colors and contrast so they look better. You will be amazed at how well this tool works. It can do wonders with even not-so-good photos. Do these steps:

1. Select the image you want to enhance and then double-click it or click the Edit mode button. The image appears in the Edit window or fills the Content pane.

2. Click the Enhance button; iPhoto adjusts the photo's colors and contrast.

3. Hold down the Ctrl key and iPhoto removes the enhancements you have applied and shows you the original image.

15

4. Release the Ctrl key. The enhancements you have applied are shown again, enabling you to quickly compare the enhanced and unenhanced versions of an image.

5. Continue clicking the Enhance button until you are satisfied with the image's appearance. Don't be afraid to click this button too often. Eventually, you will click once too often, and the image will become worse instead of better. When that happens, select Edit, Undo Enhance Photo to undo the last enhancement you applied.

REMOVING RED-EYE

If you take photos of anything with eyes (for example, people or animals) in conditions where you use a flash, you have no doubt seen the dreaded demon eye effect that can sometimes occur. This red-eye can ruin an otherwise good photo. Fortunately, you can use iPhoto's editing tools to get the red out:

1. Select the image you want to change and then double-click it or click the Edit mode button. The image appears in the Edit window or fills the Content pane.

2. Use the zoom tools covered in the previous section to zoom in on the eyes that have gone over to the dark side.

3. Use the selection techniques to select the eyes from which you want to remove red-eye. Because the Red-Eye tool removes all the red in the area that you select, you should select as small an area as possible. Your goal should be to select only the red part of the eye.

4. Click the Red-Eye button. The red in the area you selected is removed, and the selection area is cleared.

5. Hold down the Control key to see the red back in again.

6. Keep selecting areas and using the Red-Eye button until you have returned all eyes to their normal condition.

RETOUCHING IMAGES

The Retouch tool enables you to blend in scratches and other unwanted marks from a photo by blending the mark into the surrounding image. You have to use this one carefully because too much retouching becomes very obvious and has a detrimental effect on the image.

1. Select the image you want to retouch and then double-click it or click on the Edit mode button. The image will appear in the Edit window, or it will fill the Content pane.

2. Use the zooming techniques covered previously, zoom in on the area that you want to retouch.

3. Click on the Retouch button.

4. Move the cursor—which will now be a crosshair—to the area that you want to retouch.

5. Press the mouse button down and move the pointer over the area you want to retouch. As you move the pointer, the area will be smudged so that the blemish is blended in with the surrounding area of the image.

6. Hold the Control key down to see the image without the retouch effect.

7. Keep selecting areas and using the Retouch tool until you have removed the blemishes from the image.

CONVERTING IMAGES TO BLACK AND WHITE

For some images, you might like the artistic look and feel of black-and-white. iPhoto enables you to convert any image into black-and-white.

1. Select the image you want to convert into black-and-white and then double-click it or click on the Edit mode button. The image will appear in the Edit window, or it will fill the Content pane

2. Click on the B & W button. iPhoto will process the image and when this is complete, the image will be in black-and-white.

3. Hold the Control key down to see the image in color again.

ADJUSTING BRIGHTNESS AND CONTRAST

Contrast is the relative brightness of the darker areas of an image as compared to the lighter areas of an image. *Brightness* is the overall light level of the entire image. These two controls are lumped together because they tend to work in tandem. When you change the contrast, you lighten the lights or darken the darks, which can make the overall brightness of the image look wrong. Similarly, when you change an image's brightness, you can make the dark areas too dark or the light areas too light. You can use the Brightness/Contrast sliders to make substantial changes in the way an image appears.

1. Select the image you want to adjust and then double-click it or click the Edit mode button. The image appears in the Edit window or fills the Content pane.

2. Drag the Brightness slider to the right to make the light level of the entire image brighter or to the left to darken the image. As you move the slider, the brightness level of the image changes so you can see the results of your changes as you make them.

3. Drag the Contrast slider to the right to increase the contrast between light and dark areas or to the left to decrease the contrast between the light and dark areas.

4. Hold down the Control key to to see the image as it was.

5. Continue using the sliders to get the image to look the way you want it. You will often find that changing one slider causes you to need to change the other. You might need to spend some time in this balancing act to get the image to look its best.

RESTORING AN IMAGE

One of the great things about iPhoto is that it maintains an original version of all the images you edit. If you make several kinds of edits, such as a crop followed by an enhancement and retouch, and then decide you really want the image back to the way it was before you improved it, you can easily recover the original version of the image.

CAUTION

> Just as when you edit an image, when you restore an image, that image is changed everywhere the image is used, such as in photo albums, books, and so on. Restoring an image to its original condition, just like editing an image, can have unintended results.

1. Select an edited image you want to restore to original. You can select it in a photo album, in the Photo Library, or display it in the Edit mode.

2. Select File, Revert to Original to see the Revert confirmation dialog box.

3. Click OK. The image is restored to the state it was in when you first imported it into iPhoto.

BUILDING PHOTO BOOKS

In Book mode, you can create very nice books of your photos in various formats and styles. You can also choose to display a variety of information next to the photos in the book. After you have created a book, you can print it yourself or order a printed copy.

In Book mode, the Content pane contains a preview of the selected book page above thumbnails of each page in the book. The Tool pane contains the tools you use to build your book (see Figure 15.16).

Creating books is a relatively simple process. First, select the album for which you want to create a book. Second, place the images in the order in which you want them to appear in the book. For example, the first image in the album will be on the cover of the book. Then, use the following tools to create the book:

Figure 15.16
You can create custom photo albums in various formats and then print them or order copies from Apple.

- **Theme pop-up menu**—Each book you create can be on one of six themes. The theme determines how images are displayed on each page of the book. For example, if you select Story Book, images appear at different sizes and orientations on the pages for a more casual look. If you select the Year Book theme, thumbnail images appear on each page of the book. Each theme style also has corresponding text boxes in which you can enter commentary of other information for the book.

- **Show Guides check box**—When this box is checked, you see blue guidelines around the various text boxes on a page.

- **Show check boxes**—These check boxes determine which elements of an image's information appear next to the image in the book. If a check box is checked, that information appears on the book page. However, some themes don't show certain information, even if the check box is checked. For example, the Story Book theme doesn't display any of the image's information regardless of the check box settings. Instead, that theme provides a separate text box for each page in which you can use text to narrate the book you create.

- **Page Design pop-up menu**—Use this pop-up menu to select a page's design, such as making it the Cover or Introduction or to choose how many images will appear on that page. If pages are selected when you make a choice on this menu, only the selected pages are affected. If you don't select pages, all the pages are affected. You can select different designs for each page in the book.

- **Lock Page check box**—When this box is checked, you can't change a page's design. Use this to prevent accidental changes to a page. This is useful because as you work through the pages in a book, you can lock them so changes you make to other pages don't affect a page you are done with.

15

■ **Preview button**—When you click the Preview button, a separate preview window opens and you can page through your book as it will be when it is printed. You can also make changes to the book in this window, such as adding text to pages.

■ **Order Book button**—Click this to order a professionally printed version of the book you have created.

TIP

Remember to use the Display Size slider in each mode. For example, when you are editing an image, you can make the image appear larger so you can make more refined selections. In the Book mode, use the slider to change the size at which the pages you work with appear in the Content pane.

As you select each page on the thumbnail view, it appears in the upper part of the Content pane and you can edit it there. Use the tools in the previous list to make changes to it, such as setting the number of images on the page. Then, add any text called for on the page. When you are done with the page, lock it and move on to the next page. Keep working through each page until you have designed the whole book.

After you have created a book, preview it to see it in a PDF.

When you have fixed any mistakes, you can print it. You can also order a professionally printed book from Apple.

TIP

You can create a PDF of a book by using Mac OS X's print to PDF option.

PRINTING IMAGES

Even using an inexpensive inkjet printer, you can print photos that are of pretty good quality. Printing photos from iPhoto is similar to printing documents from other applications (although the specific settings you use are more important because of their effect on the quality of the printed images). Do the following steps:

1. Select the images you want to print.

TIP

When you are printing images that have the portrait orientation in sizes that will fit more than one image per page, you should rotate them to have the landscape orientation before you print them. This aligns the long axis of the image with the long side of the paper (which is the width). After you have printed the image, you can rotate it back to normal.

2. Click the Print button to see the Print dialog box (see Figure 15.17). On the left side of the dialog box is the first page of images you selected. In the right side of the dialog

box are controls you use to configure the print job. At the bottom of the dialog box are various buttons you can use to perform specific actions.

Figure 15.17
The Print dialog box in iPhoto contains more options than it does in most applications.

3. Select the printer on which you want to print the images from the Printer pop-up menu.

4. Use the Presets pop-up menu to select preset settings for the selected printer. For example, most printers have special settings for printing on photo paper.

5. Use the Style pop-up menu to select the style in which you want to print the images:

- Select Full Page to print a single image per page; when you select this, you can use the Margins slider to set the margins around the image.

- Select Greeting Card to print the images in a format designed to be folded into a greeting card; use the Style radio buttons to select the style of card you want to print.

- Select Standard Prints to print images in standard sizes; then select the size of the prints on the Size pop-up menu (check the "One photo per page" check box if you want only one image to be printed on each sheet).

TIP

Some printers support printing on specialized photo paper that is segmented in the standard print sizes, such as 5"×7". You should select one of these papers if you are printing standard size prints.

6. Use the other controls in the dialog box to adjust how your image will be printed. For example, click the Advanced Options button to open the full Print dialog box for your printer.

7. When you are done setting options, click Preview. The images are converted into a PDF document and open in the application you use to view documents of that type.

8. If the images appear as you want to print them, print the images. If not, move back into iPhoto and make changes to the print settings.

TIP

Each printer has its own set of print options. You should explore the user manual included with your printer so you understand its options and how they impact the quality of images you print.

VIEWING A SLIDESHOW FROM YOUR IMAGES

iPhoto slideshows are a great way to view images on your Mac. When you display your images in a slideshow, you can select music to accompany the images and configure various other aspects of the slideshow, such as how long the images appear on the screen. You can also save your settings so you can easily use them on other slideshows.

CONFIGURING AND VIEWING A SLIDESHOW

Use the following steps to configure a slideshow:

1. Select a group of images you want to see in a slideshow. The easiest way to do this is to select a photo album in the Source pane. (If you have a lot of time or not many photos, you can select your Photo Library to see all your photos in the same slideshow.)

2. Click the Slideshow button in the Tool pane to see the Slideshow Settings dialog box (see Figure 15.18).

3. Use the "Play each slide for __ seconds" box and arrows to set the number of seconds that each image will appear on the screen. The default is 2 seconds, which seems about right for most photos. If you like to linger over your photos longer, increase this number. If you are relatively impatient, change this to 1 second. You can change this value by clicking the up or down arrow or by typing a number in the box.

Figure 15.18
Use this dialog box to configure a slideshow.

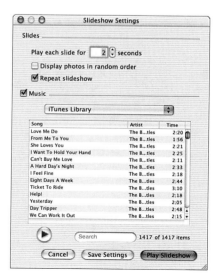

15

4. If you want the images to be shown in a random order, check the "Display photos in random order" check box. If you leave this check box unchecked, the images are displayed in the order that they are shown in the selected source, such as the photo album.

5. If you want the slideshow to play through once and then stop, uncheck the "Repeat slideshow" check box.

6. If you want music to play while the slideshow is displayed, check the Music check box and do steps 7–9 to select the music you want to hear. If you don't want to hear music, uncheck the Music check box and skip to step 10.

7. Select the source of the music you want to hear on the pop-up menu. You have two fundamental choices: Sample Music contains music that came with iPhoto, whereas iTunes Library enables you to access all the music you have in your iTunes Library. Within the iTunes Library, you can select any of the simple playlists you have created (you can't choose a smart playlist to accompany a slideshow). When you make a choice on the pop-up menu, you see the songs in the source you select in the bottom part of the dialog box.

8. Select the song you want to play during the slideshow by clicking it.

TIP

> You can preview a song by selecting a song and clicking the Play button (click the Stop button to stop the preview). You can search for a song by typing the song's information in the Search box. As you type, the list of songs is reduced to include only those that match your search.

9. If you want to permanently associate the selected song with the source when you view it in a slideshow, click the Save Settings button. If you click this button, the dialog box closes and you return to the iPhoto window. You can skip the rest of the steps in this section. (In the iPhoto window, you can view the slideshow by clicking the Play Slideshow button located under the Source pane.)

10. Click Play Slideshow or press Return. Prepare to be impressed as your screen fills with your images and they transition smoothly from one to the next.

11. To stop the slideshow before it finishes or if it repeats, click the mouse button or press the Esc key.

VIEWING A SLIDESHOW WITH SAVED SETTINGS

You can also view a slideshow without configuring it first from any mode (such as the Organize or Edit mode). When you view a slideshow in this way, it is displayed with the default settings, such as the default music, or with the settings you have saved by using the Slideshow Settings dialog box:

1. Select the source you want to view in a slideshow. The music configured for that source appears in the Information area below the Source pane.

15

2. Click the Play Slideshow button located above the Tool pane. The slideshow plays.

3. To stop the slideshow before it finishes or if it repeats, click the mouse button or press the Esc key.

EMAILING YOUR IMAGES

Sending images to others via email is a great way to share your photos with others. First, you need to set the email application you want to use to send photos. Then you can send images with a single mouse click.

Use the iPhoto Preferences window to select the email application you want to use to send your images. By default, Mail is selected, but you can choose any email application.

TIP

> When you send images, consider the connection the recipient uses to retrieve email. If the recipient uses a dial-up connection, be careful not to overload her connection with high-resolution images or even with a lot of low-resolution images. Even if the recipient uses a broadband connection, her email account might have a file size limit for attachments to email messages. If you want to transfer many images, consider posting them to a .Mac Web site instead.

After you have configured an email application, you can send images with the following steps:

1. Select the images you want to email to someone.

2. Click the Email button in the Tool pane to see the Mail Photo dialog box.

3. Select the resolution of the images you email on the Size pop-up menu. The higher the resolution you choose, the better the quality of the images, but the file sizes will be larger as well. The choices on the pop-up menu range from Small to Full Size (which is the resolution with which the images were captured). Use the Estimated Size value to assess whether the size of the files will be too large for the recipient to reasonably receive. For example, sending 5MB of images to someone who uses a dial-up connection is probably not a good thing to do

4. If you want the titles and comments to be included with the images, check the Titles and Comments check boxes, respectively.

5. Click Compose. A progress window appears as iPhoto prepares the images. When this process is complete, the email application you selected opens and a new message is created. The images you selected are attachments to the email message (see Figure 15.19). By default, the subject of the message is *x* great iPhotos, where *x* is the number of images you selected.

Figure 15.19
Sending images from iPhoto is simple; all that remains is to address the message and add some text!

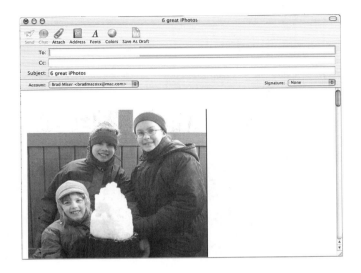

6. Address the message, add some text to it, and send it as you would any other email you write.

ORDERING PRINTS AND BOOKS

Although most of us have an inkjet printer that is capable of printing fairly nice photos, printing photos can be a bit of a pain, and the results you get aren't always the best. Plus, if you want to share those photos with other people, you have to go through the hassle of mailing them, which might be enough to stop you from sharing them.

To save you the hassle of printing or mailing images, you can order prints from Apple (the prints are actually provided by Kodak). The first time you order prints, you use or create an Apple account; after that, you can order prints with a single click by using the appropriately named 1-Click service.

The first time you use this service, you have to configure an account. When you click the Order Prints or Order Book button for the first time, you have to click the Set Up Account button. Then, follow the onscreen instructions to obtain and configure an account. If you already have an account at the Apple Store, you use the same account to order prints and books. After you have configured your account, use the following steps to order prints:

1. Select the photos for which you want to order prints (such as by selecting an album).

2. Click the Order Prints button to see the Order Prints dialog box (see Figure 15.20). Along the left side of the dialog box are the photos you have selected. You can scroll up and down in the dialog box to view all of them. In the right side of the window, you see the list of available sizes, the prices, and the quantity box.

15

Figure 15.20
The nicest thing about ordering prints is that they can be ordered and mailed right from your Mac.

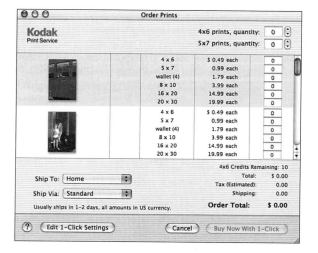

3. Enter the quantity of each size of photo you want to order. The total cost of your order appears at the bottom of the dialog box. If you want to order 4″×6″ or 5″×7″ photos of all the selected images, use the quantity boxes at the very top of the dialog box.

4. If you haven't used this service before, open the Ship To pop-up menu, select Add New Address, and create an address. Add addresses for everyone to whom you will send photos.

5. Select the address to which you want the current order sent on the Ship To pop-up menu.

6. Select the shipping method on the Ship Via pop-up menu. Your choices are Standard or Express. Obviously, Express is faster and is also more expensive.

7. When you are ready to order, click the Buy Now button.

8. Follow the onscreen instructions to complete the order. Your photos are printed and shipped, and Apple keeps you notified of the status of your order via email.

In the Order Prints dialog box, you see the cost of each size of print you can order. Most of these costs are quite reasonable when compared to the cost of the ink and paper required to print images on an inkjet printer. The shipping costs are also reasonable given that you don't have to do any work to get the order shipped anywhere you'd like. However, because ordering prints is so easy, you might find yourself going overboard the first time or two you order. So, before you click the Buy Now button, take a moment to double-check what you are ordering.

CAUTION

If images in a group you select in an album or individually are low resolution, they have the low-resolution warning icon placed on them. This icon is a yellow triangle with an exclamation point inside it. An image with this icon might or might not print well in prints or in a book you order. Be cautious about including low-resolution images in your orders; otherwise, you might be disappointed with the results you get. If you do want to print low-resolution images, print them in a smaller size to make them look as good as possible.

You can also order professionally printed and bound books by using the same service you use to order prints. The process is also quite similar to ordering prints of your photos:

1. Build the book you want to have printed.

NOTE

A printed book has to be at least 10 pages long, and it will be whether you have images on all 10 pages or not. So, make sure you have at least 10 pages of content before you print a book; otherwise, your book will be printed with blank pages.

2. Print your book and check it. Use the draft or black-and-white mode of your printer to make the process faster and less expensive.

3. When you are sure that your book is right, click Order Book. Your book is then assembled. Depending on the number of images and pages in your book, this process can take a few minutes. If your book contains low-resolution images or fewer than 10 pages, you will be warned. When the process is complete, you see the Order Book dialog box. This dialog box is similar to the Order Prints dialog box and works in the same way.

4. Select a cover for your book on the Cover Color pop-up menu.

5. Use the Ship To and Ship Via pop-up menus to enter the shipping information. Use the quantity box and arrows to set the number of books you want to order.

6. When you are ready to order, click the Buy Now button and follow the onscreen instructions.

Be aware that ordering books is a relatively expensive proposition. The first 10 pages cost $29.99, and additional pages are $3 per page. Shipping for a book is also relatively expensive at $7.99. Take plenty of time to design and check your book before you order it unless you don't mind $40 "experiments."

CREATING A .MAC IMAGE HOMEPAGE

If you have a .Mac Web site, posting a group of images on that Web site is simple:

> **NOTE**
>
> You must have a .Mac account to publish an image Web page.

→ To learn how to create a .Mac Web site, **see** "Using a .Mac iDisk and HomePage to Create and Serve Your Web Pages," **p. 426**.

To post your images to your .Mac account, perform the following steps:

1. Select the images you want to place on the Web (such as selecting an album on the Source pane).

> **NOTE**
>
> You can't publish more than 48 images to a Web site at the same time.

2. Click the HomePage button. Your Mac connects to your .Mac account and you see the Publish HomePage dialog box (see Figure 15.21).
3. Select the title text at the top of the page and edit it. By default, the Web page's title is the name of the photo album, but you can change it to be anything you want.
4. Select the page text just below the title text and edit it. For example, you can include a few sentences to explain the images you are posting on the site.

Figure 15.21
Using iPhoto's HomePage button, you can create a Web page for your photos in mere seconds.

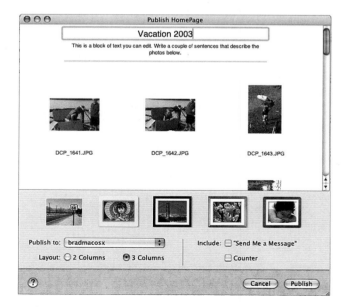

5. Select the title of the first image on the page and edit it, if necessary. By default, images are titled with the title they have within iPhoto. You can change this text as you desire (changing the titles on the Web page does not change the titles within iPhoto).

6. Repeat step 5 for each image on the page.

7. Click a frame style to apply that frame to all the images on the page

8. Select the .Mac account to which you want to publish the page on the Publish to pop-up menu.

9. Select the number of columns of images you want to include on the page by clicking the 2 Columns or 3 Columns radio button.

10. Check the Send Me a Message check box to include a link to your email address on the Web page. A visitor can click this link to send you an email message.

11. Check the Counter check box if you want the page to include a counter that counts the number of visitors to the Web page.

12. Click Publish; iPhoto connects to the Internet and transfers your photos to your .Mac account. When the process is complete, you see a completion dialog box that provides the URL to the page you just created.

13. Click the Visit Page Now button and enjoy (see Figure 15.22).

On the Web page you create with the HomePage tool, you can click an image or click the Start Slideshow link to display the images in a slideshow. In the resulting slideshow, you can click on images to see larger versions in separate Web browser windows.

Figure 15.22
Putting images online is a great way to share them with others.

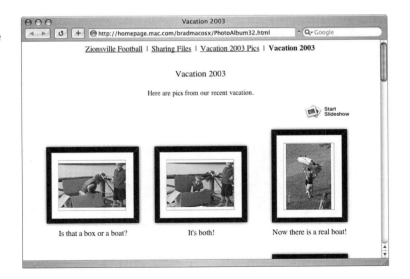

PUBLISHING IMAGES AS .MAC SLIDES

You can publish a set of iPhoto images as a .Mac slideshow—this enables other people to use your slideshow as their screensavers.

NOTE

You must have a .Mac account to publish iPhoto images for others to access.

→ To learn how to obtain and use a .Mac account, **see** "Using a .Mac iDisk and HomePage to Create and Serve Your Web Pages," **p. 426**.

To publish images as .Mac slides, do the following:

1. Select the images you want to publish (such as selecting a photo album on the Source pane).
2. Click the .Mac Slides button in the Tool pane. Your Mac connects your .Mac account and you see a warning dialog box asking whether you are sure you want to publish a set of .Mac slides.
3. Click the Publish button to see a progress window that shows each image as it is uploaded. When the process is complete, you see the confirmation dialog box.
4. If you want to inform others that your slides are available, click the Announce Slideshow button and you'll see an email message that contains information about how the slides can be accessed. If not, click the Quit button and skip step 5.
5. Address the email message and send it.

Anyone who uses Mac OS X version 10.2 or later can use your slides as her screensaver by subscribing to it. As you make changes to the slides by republishing them, the changes you make are automatically made for everyone who has subscribed to the slideshow.

→ To learn how to subscribe to .Mac slides to use them as a screen saver, **see** "Customizing the Mac OS X Desktop," **p. 121**.

USING YOUR iPHOTO IMAGES ON THE DESKTOP AND AS A SCREEN SAVER

You can easily add images in your iPhoto Library to your desktop. The images you add are used both as the desktop image and as a screensaver:

1. Select the images you want to use on the desktop, such as by selecting a photo album on the Source pane, and click the Desktop button. The Screen Effects dialog box opens (see Figure 15.23). The image source you selected is shown on the pop-up menu.

TIP

You can optimize images for your desktop by cropping them using the Desktop option on the Constrain pop-up menu.

Figure 15.23
You can easily apply your photos to the desktop and as a screensaver from within iPhoto.

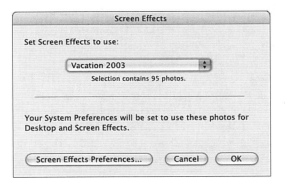

2. If you don't want to use the image source shown on the pop-up menu, open it and choose a different source. This menu contains each photo album you have created along with the All Albums choice that takes photos from all your photo albums. (You can't select your Photo Library.)

3. Click the Screen Effects Preferences button.

4. Use the Desktop & Screen Saver pane to configure your desktop images.

5. Click the Screen Saver tab and use its controls to configure a screen saver.

6. Move back into iPhoto and click the OK button to close the Screen Effects dialog box.

→ To learn how to configure desktop images and a screensaver, **see** "Customizing the Mac OS X Desktop," **p. 121**.

PUTTING IMAGES ON CD OR DVD

iPhoto makes putting images on CD or DVD easy. For example, you can back up your images on disc for safekeeping or perhaps to send those photos to someone else:

1. Select the images and photo albums you want to put on a CD or DVD, such as selecting a photo album to put its images on a disc.

2. Click the Burn button. It becomes active (it fills with a color radioactive symbol). You are then prompted to insert a blank disc.

3. Do so and click OK. The Burn button begins to pulse, indicating that you are ready to burn the disc.

4. Click the Burn button again; the Burn Disc dialog box appears. In this dialog box, the number of albums and photos you have selected to burn is shown.

5. Click the Burn button. A progress window appears, and you can use it to monitor the process. When the CD or DVD has been burned and verified, the progress window disappears, the disc is ejected, and you hear the disc complete tone.

6. Insert the disc back into your Mac.

The CD or DVD is mounted and you see it as a source in the iPhoto Source pane. You can click the Expansion triangle next to the CD icon to expand it. When you do, you see all the photo albums it contains.

If you provide the disc you burned to someone who uses iPhoto, he can mount the disc and access the photos it contains from the iPhoto Source pane. For example, he can drag the images from the CD onto his Photo Library to import them into his own Photo Library. The files can also be accessed directly from the Finder by opening the CD in a Finder window if the recipient doesn't have or use iPhoto. (Be aware that the somewhat confusing naming and hierarchy structure iPhoto uses to store images makes this process somewhat cumbersome. If the recipient doesn't use iPhoto, consider exporting the images as a Web site, as you will learn how to do in the next section).

EXPORTING IMAGES FROM IPHOTO

There are various ways you can export images from iPhoto for different purposes. You can export images as separate files so you can work with them in other applications or to send those files to other people. Or you can export a set of images as a Web site. Another option is to export a set of images as a QuickTime movie.

If you want to use iPhoto photos in other applications, you might need to export those images as individual files:

1. Select the images you want to export as files, such as by selecting an album.

2. Select File, Export or press Shift-⌘-E. You see the Export Photos dialog box.

3. Click the File Export tab if it isn't already selected.

4. Select the file format into which you want the images exported from the Format pop-up menu.

5. Click the "Full-size images" radio button to export the files at their current resolution, or click the "Scale images no larger than" radio button and enter the resolution at which you want the image files to be exported.

6. Click the "Use filename" radio button if you want iPhoto to generate filenames for you. Check the "Use title" radio button if you want the filenames to be the image titles. Click "Use album name" if you want the album name to be used in the figures' filenames.

7. If you want iPhoto to add the appropriate filename extension, which you should, check the "Use extension" check box.

8. Click Export.

9. Use the resulting sheet to choose a location in which to save the images and click OK. Each image is saved as a file with the format you selected (such as TIFF) in the location you selected.

Earlier, you saw how easily you can create a Web page containing photos via .Mac's HomePage. You also can easily create a separate Web site for your photos from within iPhoto so that you can view them on your hard drive, publish the site on a local network, or publish it to a Web site you host with a different Web hosting service:

1. Select the images you want to include in the Web site, for example, by selecting an album.

2. Select File, Export.

3. Click the Web Page tab of the Export Photos dialog box.

4. Enter the title of the page you are creating in the Title box.

5. Select the number of rows and columns in which you want the images to be displayed on the Web site. The number of pages in the site is calculated for you.

6. Use the Color radio button and bar to set the page background to a color (it is white by default) or the Image radio button and Set button to select an image as a background for the page.

7. Use the Text Color box to select the color of the text on the Web page.

8. Use the Thumbnail "Max width" and "Max height" boxes to set the maximum size of the thumbnails of each image.

9. If you want the titles or comments displayed, check the "Show title" or "Show comment" check boxes.

10. Use the Image boxes to set the maximum size of the images when the viewer clicks them on the Web site's Home page.

11. Use the "Show titles" and "Show comment" check boxes to determine whether the viewer sees titles and comments when viewing the large version of an image from the Web site.

12. Click Export.

13. Select a location to which to save the Web site and click OK. Note that you have to select a specific folder in which to store the Web site. The Web site is created in the location you specified.

14. Open the folder you selected in step 13 and open the *pagename*.html file, where *pagename* is the name of the Web site you entered in step 4 (iPhoto removes spaces from the name). You see the page in a Web browser. You can use this site as a stand-alone site or add it to other Web sites you have created. You can also edit the site using your favorite Web application.

You can also export images as a QuickTime movie. The steps to do this are similar to the steps to export image files or a Web page:

1. Select the images you want to include in the Web site—for example, by selecting an album.

2. Select File, Export.

3. Click the QuickTime tab of the Export Images dialog box.

4. Use the Width and Height boxes to enter the size of the QuickTime movie you are creating.

5. Enter the amount of time you want each image to be displayed in the "Display image for" box.

6. Use the Background tools to select a color or image for the slideshow's background.

7. Check the "Add currently selected music" check box if you want the current music soundtrack to be exported with the movie.

8. Click Export and use the Export Photos sheet to name the movie and select a location in which to save it. You can view the slideshow with any application capable of playing QuickTime movies.

WORKING WITH PREVIEW

You can preview most digital images using Mac OS X's Preview application. Although you can't make many changes in the images you preview, you can get a quick view of images in various formats. Using Preview is simple.

NOTE

> Preview might or might not be the default application for viewing image files. If not, you can open any specific image file by first opening the application and using the Open command or by setting Preview to the application associated with a specific image file.

→ To learn how to associate files with an application, **see** "Determining the Application That Opens When You Open a Document," **p. 169**.

When you open an image in Preview, the image fills the screen by default. You can control the magnification of the image using the Preview's Display menu. You can also rotate the image if you need to.

One of the nice things that Preview does for you is enables you to convert an image from one format to another. You can do this using the Export command on the File menu. In the Export sheet, you can select the file format and the options for the format you choose.

TROUBLESHOOTING

THE DIGITAL CAMERA IS NOT RECOGNIZED BY IMAGE CAPTURE OR iPHOTO

When I connect a digital camera to my Mac, neither Image Capture nor iPhoto recognizes the camera, so I can't download images.

This situation occurs when Mac OS X does not support the camera you are using, most likely because your camera does not use PTP. In this case, you can try two options:

- **Obtain Mac OS X–compatible software for your camera and use that to download images**—If your camera does not support PTP, you must use its own software to download images.

- **If you can, start up in Mac OS 9 and use the camera's Mac OS 9 software to download images**—Assuming your camera does offer Mac-compatible software, you can always restart under Mac OS 9 and use that version of the software to download images from the camera. Periodically check the manufacturer's Web site to see whether Mac OS X software is available.

In some rare cases, a cable or hardware problem might exist. Use the Apple System Profiler to ensure that your Mac is capable of communicating with the camera.

→ To learn how to use the System Profiler, **see** "Using the System Profiler to Create a System Profile," **p. 920**.

Mac OS X to the Max: Going All Out with iPhoto Keyboard Shortcuts

Table 15.2 provides a list of some of the more useful iPhoto commands along with their keyboard shortcuts.

TABLE 15.2   USEFUL iPHOTO COMMANDS AND KEYBOARD SHORTCUTS

Menu	Command	Keyboard Shortcut	What It Does
iPhoto	Preferences	⌘-,	Opens the iPhoto Preferences dialog box.
File	New Album	⌘-N	Creates a new photo album.
File	Import	Shift-⌘-I	Enables you to import images from sources other than a digital camera.
File	Export	Shift-⌘-E	Enables you to export images outside of iPhoto.
File	Show Photo Info	⌘-I	Opens the photo information window that provides detailed information about an image.
File	Duplicate	⌘-D	Creates a copy of selected images.
File	Revert to Original	None	Returns an image you have edited to its original condition.
File	Move to Trash	⌘-Delete	Moves selected images to the Trash.

TABLE 15.2   CONTINUED

Menu	Command	Keyboard Shortcut	What It Does
File	Empty Trash	None	Empties the Trash.
Edit	Select All	⌘-A	Selects all the images in the Contents pane.
Edit	Deselect All	Shift-⌘-A	Deselects all images in the Contents pane.
Edit	Rotate Counterclockwise	⌘-R	Rotates selected images in the counter clockwise direction.
Edit	Rotate Clockwise	Shift-⌘-R	Rotates selected images in the clock-wise direction.
Edit	Set Title To	None	Enables you to choose the information you want displayed as the selected images' title. The options are Empty (no title), Roll info, Filename, and Date/Time. If you select the Date/Time option, you can select the format of the date and time used in the title.
Edit	Keywords	⌘-K	Opens the Keywords dialog box that enables you to assign keywords to images and search for images by key words or other data.
View	Titles	Shift-⌘-T	Displays titles next to the image thumbnails in the Contents pane.
View	Keywords	Shift-⌘-K	Displays keywords next to the image thumbnails in the Contents pane.
View	Film Rolls	Shift-⌘-F	Displays film rolls next to the image thumbnails in the Contents pane. (In iPhoto, the film roll is the number of the import session in which you added an image to the Photo Library.)
View	Arrange Photos	None	Enables you to group images in the Contents pane by Film Roll, Date, Title, or Manually.
Help	iPhoto Help	⌘-?	Opens the Help Viewer application, showing iPhoto help.

CHAPTER 16

LISTENING TO AND WORKING WITH MUSIC

In this chapter

UNDERSTANDING MUSIC ON THE MAC

Music is an important part of the digital lifestyle. From listening to tunes while you work or play to creating customized audio tracks for your iMovie movies, music adds tremendously to your Mac life. In addition to the simple act of listening to music, the Mac enables you to customize your music in almost every respect.

iTunes is Mac OS X's amazing digital music application that enables you to truly master your music. For example, you can do the following:

- Listen to audio CDs
- Store and listen to all your music on your Mac so it is only a click away
- Convert music into a variety of formats
- Browse and purchase music using the Apple Music Store
- Customize music playback
- Create and manage custom playlists
- Create custom audio CDs
- Manage music on a portable music player, the best of which is Apple's iPod
- Share your music on a network
- Listen to audio streams from the Internet

> **NOTE**
>
> By default, iTunes is installed when you install Mac OS X. If iTunes isn't installed on your Mac, you can download a copy from www.apple.com/itunes/.

> **NOTE**
>
> You can also use iTunes to listen to audio books and other content from Audible.com. This service offers many audio books you can load into iTunes and listen to or transfer to a music player to take with you. Explaining how to work with Audible content is beyond the scope of this chapter. To learn about this, visit www.apple.com/itunes/audiobooks.html.

EXPLORING ITUNES

When you launch iTunes, the iTunes window opens (see Figure 16.1). If you read through the previous chapter, this window should look familiar to you; iTunes and iPhoto share many interface features.

> **TIP**
>
> If you don't see the Browse pane, click the Browse button to open it.

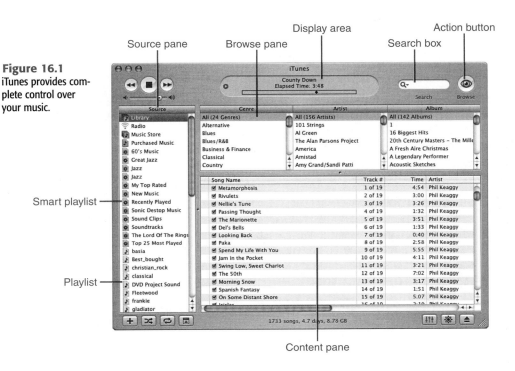

Figure 16.1
iTunes provides complete control over your music.

The iTunes window consists of three panes—Source, Browse, and Content—and the control and display area that surrounds those panes. The Browse pane can be hidden or shown; the other panes are shown at all times (unless you minimize the iTunes window, which you will see later in this chapter).

The first time any user launches iTunes, the iTunes Setup Assistant opens and configures iTunes for that user. For example, the assistant asks you to accept the license agreement, configure iTunes for playback of Internet music, determine whether iTunes should automatically connect to the Internet to download song information, and automatically locate relevant files on your Mac and add them to your Music Library.

THE SOURCE PANE

The Source pane shows the available music sources. When you want to work with a source, for example to listen to it, you select that source on the Source pane. As you work with iTunes, you will see the following sources:

- **Library**—The Library contains all the music you have added to iTunes and enables you to access any of your music quickly and easily. Because you can import audio CDs to your Mac, you can add all your music to the Library—no more fussing with individual CDs. You can also add music from the Apple Store and the Internet to your Library. You can browse and search the contents of the Library and play any music it contains.

- **Radio**—The Radio Source enables you to listen to Internet radio broadcasts.

- **Audio CD**—When an audio CD is inserted in your Mac, you see its icon in the Source pane. You can listen to it and add it to your Library, which iTunes calls *importing*, so you never have to use the CD itself again.

- **Playlists**—*Playlists* are collections of songs you create and listen to. They enable you to create your own music collections that contain exactly the songs you want to listen to in the order in which you want to listen to them. You can add any music from your Library to playlists, and you can have as many playlists as you want.

- **Smart Playlists**—Smart playlists use a set of expressions you create to collect songs in a group (unlike playlists, which you create by manually adding music to). You define the expressions used for each smart playlist you create. Smart playlists can be dynamic, meaning songs can be automatically added to them based on the expressions you create.

- **Music Store**—Apple's Music Store enables you to find and purchase music online. You can preview music and then buy it. When you do so, that music is downloaded to your Mac and added to your Music Library. You can buy entire CDs or individual songs.

- **Purchased Music**—This is a special playlist that contains all the music you have purchased from the Apple Music Store.

- **Shared Music**—With iTunes, you can share music with other people on your network and other people can share music in their Libraries with you. When you select a shared source, you can listen to music in other people's Libraries.

- **Music Player**—You can use iTunes to manage music players, such as MP3 players and, more importantly, an Apple iPod. When you connect a music player to your Mac, it appears as a source.

> **TIP**
>
> You can change the relative size of any of the panes by dragging its resize handle, which is a small circle in the center of the border between the panes.

THE BROWSE PANE

The Browse pane provides a way for you to browse your music by genre, artist, and album (refer to Figure 16.1). When you select a source, you can browse that source in the Browse pane. As you select items in the pane, the contents of what you select are shown in the Content pane (explained in the next section). The more specific you make the Browse pane, the more specific the selection of song results in the Content pane. For example, if you click a specific genre, the artists associated with that genre are shown in the Artist column. Similarly, if you select an artist in the Artist pane, that artist's albums are shown in the Album pane. When you select an album, that album's songs are shown in the Content pane.

The Browse pane can be shown or hidden for different sources. And you can choose to show or hide the Genre column within the Browse pane.

To show the Genre column when you are browsing a source, do the following steps:

1. Select iTunes, Preferences or press ⌘-,.

2. Click the General tab if it isn't selected already.

3. Check the "Show genre when browsing" check box.

4. Click OK. Whenever you browse a source, the Genre column is shown.

TIP

> You can use the Source Text and Song Text pop-up menus on the General pane of the iTunes Preferences window to set the relative size of the text used in the Source pane and Content pane, respectively.

To show or hide the Browse pane for a source, select that source and select Edit, Show Browser or Edit, Hide Browser, respectively. When the Browse pane is hidden, the Content pane expands to fill the right side of the iTunes window (see Figure 16.2).

Figure 16.2
Press ⌘-B to show or hide the Browse pane (also called the Browser); compare this figure to Figure 16.1.

The Content Pane

The Content pane displays the contents (the songs) of the source selected in the Source or Browse pane. Along with song name, the Content pane can show a variety of other information for each song, including track number, time, artist, album, genre, and much more. You can choose to display different columns for each source.

To customize the information for a source, do the following steps:

1. Select the source whose Content pane you want to customize by clicking it in the Source or Browse pane. Its contents are displayed in the Content pane.

2. Select Edit, View Options or press ⌘-J. The View Options dialog box appears (see Figure 16.3). The name of the selected source appears at the top of the dialog box, as does a check box for each column that can be displayed in the Content pane.

Figure 16.3
Using the View Options dialog box, you can customize the information displayed in the Content pane for any source.

3. Check the check box for each column you want to be displayed when you are viewing the contents of the selected source.

4. Click OK. Each time you view the source, the columns you selected are shown.

NOTE

The first column in the Content pane does not have a column title and always appears. It is the Playback Order column, which indicates the order in which the songs will be played in the selected source. Because you can reorder the songs in playlists (and even for CDs), this is not to be confused with the track number.

The columns in the Content pane work similarly to those in a Finder window in the List view. You can sort the pane by a specific column (such as Track #) by clicking its column title (the column title by which the pane is sorted is highlighted in blue). You can drag columns to the left or right to change the order in which they appear, and you can resize a column by dragging its right border. Just like the view options you set, the changes you make to the columns themselves are retained for each source.

In many cases, you have to use the Content pane's scrollbars to see all the information it contains.

NOTE

One of the nice features of iTunes is that it automatically connects to the Internet and downloads information about CDs you play; music you purchase from the Apple Music Store includes this information, too. You can add or edit a song's information manually as well. This information enables you to understand many aspects of your music and more easily customize your music.

CONTROLS AND DISPLAY AREA

Surrounding the panes on the top and bottom is the control and display area. In this area, you see various controls you use to perform actions, along with the display area that presents information about what you are doing (see Figure 16.4).

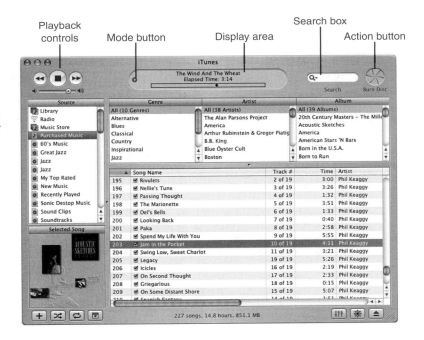

Figure 16.4
Surrounding the panes of the iTunes window are the controls and displays you use to work with your music.

In the upper-left corner of the window are the playback controls, which include rewind/jump to previous track; play, stop, or pause; fast forward/jump to the next track; and the volume slider. These are self-explanatory, and they change depending on the context (for example, when you are playing a CD, the Stop button appears, but when you stop the music, it becomes the Play button).

In the top center part of the window is the display area. This area shows information about what you are doing at any moment in time. For example, when you are listening to music, it shows information about the song that is currently playing. When you are importing music into your Library, it shows information about the importing process.

The display area also has several modes; you can change these using the Mode button. What this button does depends on the action you are performing at that particular time. For example, when you are listening to music, one mode displays a graphic equalizer representation of the music playing. In another mode, it shows the title of the track that is playing along with a progress bar. When you are importing a song, the display area shows a progress bar for the import process. In certain situations, this area also contains a Stop button you can use to stop what is happening (such as when you are importing MP3 files). You will see examples of these modes in the various figures in this chapter.

TIP

> When you are playing music, the name of the track, artist, and album it comes from rotate above the time display; you can change from one to the other by clicking the text. You can also switch from the remaining time display to the total time display or elapsed time by clicking the time being displayed.

To the right of the display area is the Search tool. You can use this to narrow the results shown in the Content pane for any source you select, such as your Library or a CD:

1. Select the source in which you want to search.
2. Click the Magnifying Glass icon and select the attribute by which you want to search. Your options are All (the default), Artists, Albums, Composers, and Songs.
3. Start to type in the Search tool. As you type, the results shown in the Content pane are narrowed down so it shows only songs that contain the text you type (the text can be in any of the columns shown in the pane). The more letters you type, the more specific the search becomes.

For example, to find all the songs in your Library that have the word *strange* somehow connected with them, you would leave All selected and type **strange** in the Search box. The Content pane would then show only those items whose name, artist, or other data contain that text. In this example, if you had selected a source containing the song "Strangers in the Night" and also had a song by Eddie Strange, both of these songs would appear in the Content pane.

TIP

> After you perform a search, the Clear button (which is a circle containing an *x*) appears at the right end of the Search tool. Click this button to clear the search and cause the Content pane to display all the contents of the selected source.

In the upper-right corner of the iTunes window is the Action button, which changes depending on the source selected. When an audio CD is selected, the Action button becomes the Import button, which enables you to add songs from the CD to your Library. When a playlist is selected, it becomes the Burn CD button, which enables you to burn a

CD from a selected playlist. When the Library, Music Store, or Shared Music is selected, it is the Browse button that shows or hides the Browse pane.

Along the bottom of the window are more controls and information (see Figure 16.5).

Figure 16.5
iTunes provides all the tools you need to get the most out of your music.

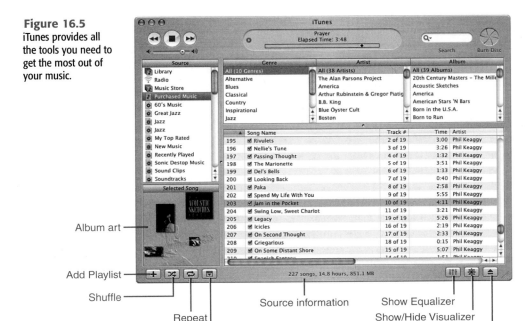

At the bottom of the window, the following features are available (from left to right):

- **New Playlist**—Click this to create a new playlist. If you hold down the Option key while you click it, you create a new smart playlist. You will learn much more about playlists later in this chapter.

- **Shuffle**—When you click this, the tracks of the selected source are played in a random order. This is reflected in the Content pane because the songs are reshuffled to reflect the random order in which they will be played. Click the button again to return the selected source back to its previous order.

> **TIP**
>
> To determine whether iTunes shuffles by song or album, use the Song or Album radio button on the Advanced pane of the iTunes Preferences dialog box.

- **Repeat**—The Repeat button enables you to repeat whatever you are playing. If you click this button once, the source repeats until you stop it. If you click this button twice, the source repeats one time.

- **Show/Hide Album Art**—When you click this, the Album Art window appears underneath the Source pane. The album art associated with the currently playing song is shown in this window. Music you purchase from the Apple Music Store has album art associated with it. You can also add graphics to this field for any music in your Library.

- **Source Information**—In the center of the bottom of the iTunes window information about the currently selected source is shown. You can see how many songs are included in the source, the total playing time, and the total file size of the source's tracks. This information is especially useful when you are burning CDs or managing a music player.

- **Show Equalizer**—This opens the iTunes Equalizer that enables you to control how music sounds. You will learn how to use this later in this chapter.

- **Show/Hide Visualizer**—This opens a funky, 60s-style window that displays visuals to accompany your music. More on this shortly.

- **Eject**—As you can probably guess, this ejects the selected source, such as an audio CD or a music player.

> **TIP**
>
> If you have an Apple Pro keyboard or are using a PowerBook or iBook, you can eject a selected source by pressing its Eject key.

When a music player is connected to your Mac, you see additional buttons related to that player, such as the iPod Options button. You will learn about these later in the chapter.

The commands for many of iTunes' controls, such as Shuffle, Repeat, and Eject, also appear on the Controls menu along with additional controls, including Volume Up, Volume Down, and Mute. Also, keyboard shortcuts are available for many of them (you will see these in the "Mac OS X to the Max" section at the end of this chapter).

To the left of the Eject button is the Show Visualizer button. If you click this button, the center part of the iTunes window becomes a throwback to the 1960s and you see visual effects while the music plays (see Figure 16.6). You can control the size of the Visualizer and turn it off or on by selecting the commands on the Visualizer menu. You can also add additional visual effects to iTunes and switch among them.

When you display the Visualizer, the Action button becomes Options. If you click this, you can set various preferences relating to the appearance of the Visualizer, such as the frame rate, whether song information is displayed, and so on.

When iTunes was originally released, Apple hyped this as one of the application's big features. Although it looks cool for about 10 seconds, I have never used it for longer than that period of time. Perhaps if you like to look at something while you listen to music, you might find this feature more useful than I do.

Figure 16.6
If you want to see as well as hear your music, use iTunes Visualizer mode.

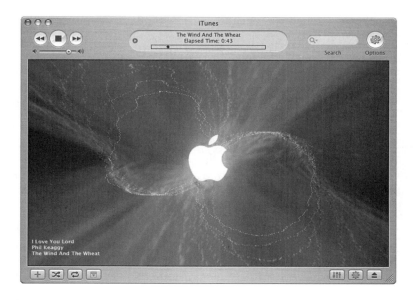

16

TIP

If you leave iTunes open and Visualizer on, but no music playing, you get some pretty interesting visual effects.

LISTENING TO AUDIO CDS WITH ITUNES

The most basic task for which you use iTunes is to listen to audio CDs. In addition to the capabilities provided by a "regular" CD player, iTunes provides many other features.

CAUTION

Some audio CDs use copyright protection schemes that prevent you from listening to the CD on a computer (with the idea being that you won't be able to make MP3 versions of the songs for illegal purposes). Unfortunately, not only do these CDs not work in your Mac, but they can actually cause damage. Before playing a CD in your Mac, check the label carefully to make sure its label doesn't contain any warnings about playing the CD in a computer or that the CD is copy-protected. If it does have such warnings, don't try to use the CD in your Mac.

PLAYING AN AUDIO CD

Playing an audio CD is straightforward. The following steps give you a quick run-through of the process for launching iTunes and playing a CD:

1. Insert the audio CD. By default, iTunes opens (if it isn't open already) and moves to the front. A message telling you that iTunes is looking up the CD on the CDDB database appears. Depending on how you connect to the Internet, this process can take a few

moments. If multiple matches are found for the CD, you are prompted to select the correct one. Do so, and then click OK. (This is done only the first time you listen to a CD because iTunes remembers CDs as you listen to them.)

If you have turned off the preference allowing iTunes to automatically check for information, this step is skipped. Also, if you have a dial-up connection and you don't allow applications to automatically connect, you have to make the connection manually for this to work.

The CD is mounted and appears in the Source pane.

2. The CD should be selected as the source automatically; if it isn't, select the CD as the source. Its contents appear in the Content pane. You might have to resize the window and the columns to be able to see all the CD's information. The Source Information area shows information about the CD's contents, such as the number of tracks and total playing time.

3. Click the Play button and use the other playback controls to control the music.

Playing an audio CD is as easy as pie (whatever that means). Here are a few tips for you:

- You can play a track by double-clicking it.

- If you uncheck the box next to a track's title, it is skipped.

- You can change the order in which tracks play by dragging them up and down in the window; iTunes remembers this order and the next time you insert the CD, the same order is used.

- The track currently playing is marked with a speaker icon in the Content pane. You can jump to the current song by selecting Edit, Show Current Song (⌘-L).

CONFIGURING iTUNES TO WORK WITH AUDIO CDs

By default, iTunes launches automatically when you insert an audio CD and then looks up its information. However, you can configure what happens when you insert an audio CD into your Mac by using the following steps:

1. Open the System Preferences application and click the CDs & DVDs button.

2. On the "When you insert a music CD" pop-up menu, select the action you want your Mac to take. By default, this is Open iTunes. Your other choices are "Open other application," which enables you to select a different application to launch when you insert an audio CD; "Run script," which enables you to choose an AppleScript to be executed; and Ignore, which causes your Mac to do nothing.

3. Quit the System Preferences application.

4. Back in iTunes, select iTunes, Preferences.

5. Click the General tab if it isn't selected already.

6. Using the On CD Insert pop-up menu, select the action you want iTunes to take when you insert an audio CD. The options are the following:

- **Show Songs**—The CD becomes available in the Source pane, but no action is taken.
- **Begin Playing**—The CD begins playing automatically.
- **Import Songs**—The tracks on the CD are added to your Library. (More about this later.)
- **Import Songs and Eject**—The tracks on the CD are added to your Library. When that process is complete, the CD is ejected.

7. If you don't want iTunes to connect to the Internet when it needs to, such as to look up a CD's information or access the Apple Music Store, uncheck the "Connect to Internet when needed" check box.

8. Click OK. The CD actions you selected become active.

CONTROLLING MUSIC PLAYBACK FROM THE DOCK

You can control iTunes from the Dock by opening its menu (see Figure 16.7). In addition to playback controls, you can see the name and artist of the current track, rate it, and so on.

Figure 16.7
The iTunes Dock menu enables you to get information about and control the music you are playing.

NOTE

I have included information on controlling music playback in the section about playing audio CDs, but it is equally applicable to listening to music from any source.

ADDING MUSIC FROM AUDIO CDS AND THE INTERNET TO YOUR iTUNES MUSIC LIBRARY

Listening to audio CDs with iTunes is fine, but for that purpose, any old CD player works just as well. iTunes' real power comes when you add all your music to the Library so it is always available to you. In addition to letting you find and listen to your music more easily, after it is in the Library, you can do all sorts of cool things with it, such as creating custom playlists and CDs.

CONVERTING AUDIO CDS INTO THE MP3 FORMAT AND ADDING THEM TO YOUR MUSIC LIBRARY

The MP3 format was the one that really started the digital music revolution. Although newer and somewhat better formats are available now, MP3 remains an important player in the digital music world.

UNDERSTANDING THE MP3 FORMAT

MP3 is the acronym for the audio compression scheme called *Moving Picture Experts Group (MPEG)* audio layer 3. The revolutionary aspect of the MP3 encoding scheme is that music data can be stored in files that are only about one twelfth the size of unencoded digital music without a noticeable degradation in the quality of the music. A typical music CD consumes about 650MB of storage space, but the same music encoded in the MP3 format shrinks down to about 55MB. Put another way, a single 3.5-minute song shrinks from its 35MB on audio CD down to a paltry 3MB or so. This small file size opens up a world of possibilities.

The other aspect of MP3 that has made it so amazingly popular is that converting different music formats into MP3 is very easy.

These two factors alone have forever changed the way music is made, distributed, and listened to.

The first, and most famous (or infamous depending on your point of view), is the capability to move music files over the Internet. Although downloading a 35MB file is prohibitive for everyone except those who have access to high-bandwidth connections, moving a 3MB MP3 file is practical for just about everyone. In addition to the controversial practice of sharing music (sometimes copyrighted music), MP3 over the Internet also has more legitimate uses. Artists can create MP3 music and distribute it over the Internet without requiring that they sign with a record company. This makes self-promotion possible and can eliminate the middleman from the music arena. As never before, music can move directly from the musician to anyone anywhere in the world.

Copyright Conscious

Musicians creating their own MP3 files and distributing them over the Net is certainly legitimate. However, it is not legitimate to create MP3 files of someone else's music and distribute them without the appropriate legal permission to do so.

Napster and other music sharing sites violate the letter and spirit of copyright laws because people other than those who own the rights to the music are distributing it.

When you are dealing with music, you need to be very conscious of the copyright status of any music with which you work. Although copyright laws are complex, the basic idea behind them is not. Simply put, you cannot distribute material to which someone else holds a copyright without (written) permission to do so.

Unless you create the music yourself (not simply encoding it yourself), you should not distribute it in any form. The exceptions are when you have received a license to use that music or when the music is in the public domain.

A second benefit of MP3 files' small size is that storing an entire music collection in a relatively small amount of disk space is possible, thus eliminating the need to bother with individual CDs. An entire music collection can be easily stored, organized, and accessed with a few clicks of a mouse. By using playlists, that music can be listened to in many ways.

Third, MP3 created a new class of portable music devices. Because MP3 files can be stored in small amounts of memory, devices with no moving parts can store and play a decent amount of music. Other devices contain small hard drives and can store huge amounts of music, enabling you to take your entire music collection with you wherever you go. These devices are extremely small and lightweight, and their contents can be easily managed.

Following are the two main sources of MP3 music to which you can listen:

- Music you encode yourself from your own audio CDs
- MP3 files you download from the Internet

The more important source of MP3 files for your iTunes Library is your own audio CD collection. You can encode the music on your audio CDs into the MP3 format and add those MP3 files to your music Library (and then add the songs to any playlists you want). In iTunes lingo, this is called *importing music*. In more general lingo, this process is called *ripping tracks*. Either way, creating MP3 tracks from your audio CDs is really powerful.

CAUTION

> Some audio CDs use copyright protection schemes that prevent you from listening to the CD on a computer (with the idea being that you won't be able to make MP3 versions of the songs for illegal purposes). Unfortunately, not only do these CDs not work in your Mac, but they can actually cause damage. Before playing a CD in your Mac, check the label carefully to make sure its label doesn't contain any warnings about playing the CD in a computer or that the CD is copy-protected. If it does, don't try to use the CD in your Mac.

Encoding audio CDs into MP3 files is straightforward. The only complexity you will encounter is the choice of specific encoding settings you want to use.

SETTING MP3 IMPORT PREFERENCES

Although the default MP3 encoding settings are probably fine, you should understand that you can make adjustments to the particular encoding settings iTunes uses to convert your music to MP3. The reason you might want to do this is to get the smallest file sizes possible while retaining an acceptable quality of playback.

The quality of encoded music is determined by the amount of data stored in the MP3 file per second of music playback. This is measured in kilobits per second (Kbps). The higher the number of Kbps, the better the music sounds. Of course, this means that the file size is larger as well. The goal of MP3 encoding is to obtain an acceptable quality of playback while minimizing the size of the resulting MP3 files.

The encoding level you should use depends on several factors, which include the following:

- **Your sensitivity to imperfections**—If you dislike minor imperfections in music playback, you should use higher-quality encoding settings. If you don't mind the occasional "bump" in the flow of the music, you can probably get away with lower-quality settings.

- **The music you listen to**—Some music hides flaws better than others. For example, you are less likely to notice subtle problems in the music while listening to grinding heavy metal music than when you listen to classical music.

- **How you listen to music**—If you use a low-quality sound system with poor speakers, you probably won't notice any difference between high-quality and low-quality encoding. If your Mac is connected to a high-fidelity speakers, the differences in music quality will be more noticeable.

iTunes provides three standard levels of encoding: good quality, high quality, and higher quality. As an experiment, I encoded the same 4-minute song using each of these levels; the results are shown in Table 16.1. These results might or might not match the particular encoding you do, but they should give you some idea of the effect of quality level settings on file sizes. In this case, I couldn't detect much difference between the quality levels in the sound of the music, so I could save almost 0.5MB per minute of music by using the good quality level.

TABLE 16.1   DEFAULT ENCODING LEVELS VERSUS FILE SIZE

Quality Level	Data Rate (Kbps)	File Size (MB)
Good	128	3.8
High	160	4.8
Higher	192	5.7

You can also use custom encoding levels if the standard levels aren't suitable for you.

The encoding settings iTunes uses are accessed with the Preferences command:

1. Select iTunes, Preferences.

2. Click the Importing button (see Figure 16.8).

Figure 16.8
The Importing pane of the Preferences dialog box enables you to control the encoding settings used for your music.

3. Use the Import Using pop-up menu to select the particular encoder you want to use. You have four options: MP3, AAC, AIFF, and WAV. Obviously, you should choose MP3 to create MP3 files.

> **NOTE**
>
> You can also use iTunes to convert or import songs in the AIFF or WAV formats. Audio Interchange File Format (AIFF) is a standard audio format used to move audio content among applications. Waveform Audio File (WAV) is a standard audio file format on the PC. iTunes can work with either of these file formats just as well as it can work with MP3 and AAC files. However, because MP3 and AAC are the formats most widely used for music, those formats are the focus of this chapter.

4. Use the Setting pop-up menu to select the quality level of the encoding—for example, select Good Quality to create smaller files. The Details area of the window provides information about the encoding level you have selected.

5. Check the "Play songs while importing" check box if you want to hear music as you import it. The encoding process finishes much earlier than the playing process so music continues to play after the encoding is done. This can be a bit confusing.

> **TIP**
>
> If you select the Import Songs and Eject option on the On CD Insert pop-up menu in the General pane of the iTunes Preferences window, the CD is ejected when the encoding is done. This is a good reminder that you can encode the next CD. (The music from the previous CD continues to play.)

6. Check the "Create file names with track number" check box if you want the MP3 files iTunes creates to have the track number included as a prefix in the filename.

7. Click OK. The next time you import music into the Library, it is encoded according to the settings you selected.

TIP

> You can vary the quality level you use from album to album or even from song to song. For example, if you want to play certain songs on a portable MP3 player, you might want to use a lower level for those songs so you can download more of them to the player.
>
> You might want to create one version of the tracks at low-quality levels and another version at high-quality levels. You could then create a lower-quality playlist to import to an MP3 player.

You can also create and use custom encoding levels if the standard choices aren't suitable. You configure custom encoding with the same steps you use for standard encoding. The difference is that you select Custom on the Setting pop-up menu. When you do that, the MP3 Encoder dialog box appears. This enables you to configure the following:

- **Stereo Bit Rate**—You can control the bit rate for stereo encoding. You can select rates between 8Kbps and 320Kbps. The higher the bit rate, the better the quality and the larger the file size will be.

- **Variable Bit Rate Encoding**—With this option turned on, the encoder uses a guaranteed minimum bit rate. You can set the level of this encoding using a secondary Quality setting that ranges from Lowest to Highest.

- **Sample Rate**—Music is encoded by taking a sample of the bits that make up specific instances in the music at various speeds. The rate at which these samples are captured, called the *sample rate*, affects the quality of the music. Higher sample rates result in higher-quality music (again, more data is collected per second of music). You can select a specific sample rate from the Sample Rate pop-up menu, or you can leave the default Auto setting (which enables iTunes to choose the sample rate).

- **Channels**—You can choose to capture one channel of music (Mono), both channels (Stereo), or let iTunes decide which to use (Auto).

- **Stereo Mode**—Your choices here are Normal, which causes each track's information to be stored independently, and Joint Stereo, which causes information that is the same in both tracks to be stored in one track while the unique information is stored in another. According to Apple, this mode improves sound quality when encoding at 128 kbps or below.

- **Smart Encoding Adjustments**—This setting enables iTunes to adjust the encoding rates as necessary to maintain the optimal ratio of music quality to file size. Unless you have a specific reason not to use this feature, you should leave it turned on.

■ **Filter Frequencies Below 10 Hz**—Music frequencies below 10Hz are not audible, so there is really no reason to include them in the encoding process because it wastes disk space. This feature should be left on as well.

ADDING MUSIC IN THE MP3 FORMAT TO YOUR LIBRARY

To encode music from an audio CD into the MP3 format, use the following steps:

1. Insert the CD containing the songs you want to encode. iTunes connects to the Internet and identifies the CD (again, assuming that you haven't disabled this feature or haven't listened to the CD before).

2. Select the CD in the Source pane (if you just inserted it, it is selected by default).

3. Uncheck the box next to the title of each song you don't want to encode—by default, every track is selected and is therefore imported. You can use the boxes to "unchoose" songs you don't want to import.

4. Click the Import action button. iTunes begins to encode the songs you selected. Depending on how fast your Mac is and the number of songs you selected, this process can take from a minute or two to half an hour or so. You can see the progress of the encoding process in the iTunes display window (see Figure 16.9).

Figure 16.9
This iTunes window shows a CD being imported; information about the song currently being encoded is shown in the Display area.

When the encoding process is completed, the song is marked with a green circle containing a check mark. The resulting MP3 files are added to your Library, and you can listen to them from there and add them to playlists.

Following are some pointers to improve your importing experiences:

- When you first start building your Library, set iTunes to Import Songs and Eject a CD when you insert it (use the On CD Insert pop-up menu on the General pane of the iTunes Preferences dialog box). When you insert an audio CD, iTunes imports it automatically. After iTunes finishes importing a CD, it ejects it. Then you can insert another and add it to the Library. After you have built your Library, select a different CD insert option; otherwise, you might end up with multiple versions of the same song in your Library (iTunes enables you to create multiple versions of the same songs in case you want to have songs encoded with different quality levels or in different formats).

- You can cancel the encoding process by clicking the small x at the right end of the encoding progress bar in the display area.

- You can listen to the music you are encoding while you are encoding it. Because the encoding process moves faster than real time, the import process is done before the selected songs stop playing. This can be confusing because it seems natural that both should stop at the same time. If you set CDs to eject after they are imported (using the On CD Insert pop-up menu), the end of the importing process is quite clear (because the CD is ejected).

- You can also listen to other songs in your Library or playlists at the same time you are importing songs from a CD.

- After the import process is complete, you can find the location of the encoded file for any song in your Library by selecting it and selecting File, Show Song File (⌘-R). A Finder window containing the file you imported opens, and the file is highlighted.

DOWNLOADING MP3 FILES FROM THE INTERNET AND ADDING THEM TO YOUR ITUNES MUSIC LIBRARY

Although illegal sharing of MP3 files is done over the Internet, there are also many legitimate sites from which you can download MP3 files to listen to. You might wonder why musicians would post their music in MP3 format on such sites. One reason is that they feel a desire to freely share their music with the world. Another reason is that musicians hope that, when you listen to their music, you will like it so much that you will purchase more of it (usually on audio CDs). Either way, you win because plenty of great music is available in the MP3 format that you can listen to.

DOWNLOADING MP3 MUSIC

To find sites from which you can download MP3 files, I recommend that you start at www.mp3.com. This site has thousands of songs you can listen to online and download to your Mac. You can browse music by genre and search for music. Whichever way you do it, you are likely to find more music to listen to than you have time to listen to!

TIP

The mp3.com music site enables you to preview songs before you download them. You should take advantage of this to prevent wasting the time required to download music you don't like and will end up deleting later anyway.

Downloading MP3 files is done in the same way as other files.

→ To learn how to download files from the Web, **see** "Downloading and Preparing Files," **p. 411**.

CONFIGURING ITUNES TO KEEP YOUR MUSIC ORGANIZED

Later in this chapter, you'll learn in detail how and where iTunes stores the music you add to your Library. For now, know that you should have iTunes store files you download in the same way as those you encode yourself. Here's how:

1. Select iTunes, Preferences.
2. Click the Advanced icon.
3. Check the "Keep iTunes Music folder organized" check box if it isn't already checked.
4. Check the "Copy files to iTunes Music folder when adding to library" check box if it isn't already checked. This causes iTunes to place copies of songs you have downloaded in the appropriate iTunes Music folders.
5. Click OK.

ADDING DOWNLOADED MUSIC TO THE LIBRARY

After you have configured iTunes to store the music you add in an organized way, add the music to your library:

1. Select File, Add to Library.
2. In the Add To Library dialog box, move to the MP3 files you want to add to your Library, select them, and click Choose. The files are added to your Library and you can work with them just like tracks you have imported.

NOTE

If you have unchecked the "Copy files to iTunes Music folder when adding to library" check box for some reason, you see a dialog box explaining that iTunes doesn't actually move the files but uses a reference to the files you choose. (If this check box is checked, iTunes does make a copy and places it in the appropriate location.) Just read the information in the dialog box and click OK.

TIP

You can also add music to the iTunes Library by dragging song files onto the iTunes icon on the Dock.

CONVERTING AUDIO CDS INTO THE AAC FORMAT AND ADDING THEM TO YOUR MUSIC LIBRARY

Like most other file formats, there are more than one digital music file format. One of the newest formats is the AAC format.

UNDERSTANDING THE AAC FORMAT

With the release of iTunes version 4, Apple introduced a new audio format called Advanced Audio Coding (AAC). The AAC format is part of the larger MPEG-4 specification. The basic purpose of it is the same as the MP3 format: to deliver excellent sound quality while keeping file sizes small. However, the AAC format produces files that have better quality than MP3 at even smaller file sizes.

Also like MP3, you can easily convert audio CD files into the AAC format.

One of the most important aspects of the AAC format is that all the music in the Apple Music Store is stored in this format; when you purchase music from the store, it is downloaded in this format.

AAC files have the .m4p filename extension.

Functionally, you aren't likely to notice any difference between AAC music files and MP3 files except in one area—most music players (such as MP3 players) don't support AAC-formatted music. The Apple iPod is a notable exception, so any music you purchase from the Apple Music Store can be placed on an iPod for playing on the move. You can also convert music in the AAC format into the MP3 format to put that music on regular MP3 players. (You'll learn how to do this later in this chapter.)

SETTING AAC IMPORT PREFERENCES

Also similar to MP3, various settings can be configured to adjust the way in which files are imported in the AAC format. Unlike MP3, there are only two choices for AAC importing options: High Quality and Custom. Do the following:

1. Select iTunes, Preferences.

2. Click the Importing icon.

3. Use the Import Using pop-up menu to select AAC Encoder.

4. Use the Setting pop-up menu to choose the quality level of the encoding. Select High Quality or Custom.

5. If you chose Custom, use the AAC Encoder dialog box to see the Stereo Bit Rate, Sample Rate, and Channels options. The Stereo Bit Rate and Sample Rate options are analogous to the same properties of MP3 files. The Channels setting enables you to select Mono or Stereo. After you have configured the settings, click OK to close the dialog box.

6. Check the "Play songs while importing" check box if you want to hear music as you import it. The encoding process finishes much earlier than the playing process so music continues to play after the encoding is done. This can be a bit confusing.

7. Check the "Create file names with track number" check box if you want the AAC files iTunes creates to have the track number included as a prefix in the filename.

8. Click OK. The next time you import music into the Library, it is encoded in the AAC format according to the settings you selected.

IMPORTING MUSIC FROM AUDIO CDs IN THE AAC FORMAT TO YOUR LIBRARY

After you have selected and configured the Import preferences, the steps to import music from Audio CDs in the AAC format into your Library are exactly the same as those you use to import tracks in the MP3 format.

→ To learn how to import tracks from audio CDs to your Library, **see** "Adding Downloaded Music to the Library," **p. 535**.

ADDING MUSIC FROM THE APPLE MUSIC STORE TO YOUR iTUNES MUSIC LIBRARY

With version 4.0 of iTunes, Apple introduced the amazing Music Store. This is an online source of hundreds of thousands of songs and albums you can search and browse for music in which you are interested. When you find music you want to add to your Library, you can purchase that music and download it with a couple of mouse clicks. Because you access the Music Store from within iTunes, it is very convenient to use. And because songs are only 99¢ (and sometimes even less when you purchase albums), adding music from the Music Store is an economical way to build your Library.

What's the Catch?

Because of copyright concerns, there are some limitations on the music you purchase from the Music Store. Fortunately, these limitations aren't likely to ever be noticeable to you. The only two meaningful restrictions are the following.

You can play music you purchase on only three Macs at the same time. The Mac on which you play music from the Music Store must be authorized to play it; this is done by configuring a Mac with a Music Store account. You can deauthorize a Mac when you want to use the music on a different machine, sell it, and so on so it doesn't count against the three-Mac limitation.

You can burn the same playlist that contains music you have purchased from the Apple Music Store onto only 10 CDs. However, you can always change the playlist and burn it onto additional discs or add a song to a different playlist to put it onto a CD.

UNDERSTANDING THE iTUNES MUSIC STORE

Two sources appear in the Source pane related to the Music Store. One is the Music Store itself. When you click this source, the Music Store appears inside the Content pane. The other is the Purchased Music playlist; all the music you download is added to this playlist so you can easily see the music you have purchased (it is also added to your Library).

If you use the Shopping Cart preference (explained later in this chapter), the Music Store source contains the Shopping Cart and the Purchased Music playlist.

NOTE

All music in the Music Store is in the AAC format, which means standard MP3 players won't be capable of playing that music. However, the Apple iPod can play AAC music, and putting your music on an iPod does not count against the three-Mac limit.

CREATING AND CONFIGURING AN APPLE STORE ACCOUNT AND SHOPPING PREFERENCES

To purchase music from the Apple Store, you need to configure an account on it. If you already have an account at the Apple Store (via its Web site), you already have an account for the Music Store because they use the same account. If not, you must obtain an Apple Store account.

NOTE

It is probably clear already, but to use the iTunes Music Store, your Mac must be capable of connecting to the Internet.

You don't have to have an account to browse and search the Apple Music Store, so you can check it out before you bother creating an account.

To sign in to an existing account or create a new one, use the following steps:

1. Click the Music Store source in the Source pane. The Music Store fills the Contents pane (see Figure 16.10).

2. Click the Sign In button in the upper-right corner of the Music Store window to see the Sign In account dialog box. This dialog box presents two options. In the upper part of the dialog box, you can click the Create Account button to create a new account. In the lower part of the dialog box, you can enter your existing Apple ID and password to sign in to your current account.

3. If you need to create an account, click the Create Account button and follow the onscreen instructions to do so.

4. If you need to sign in to your existing account, enter your Apple ID and password and click Sign In.

After you have signed in to your account, your Apple ID appears in the Account box to show you the account to which you are currently logged in. When you see this information, you are ready to shop.

Figure 16.10
The iTunes Music Store enables me to do something I have always wanted to be able to do—buy songs individually!

Following are the two ways you can make purchases from the Apple Music Store:

- With the 1-Click method, you select and purchase songs or albums with a single mouse click (thus, the method's name) and they are immediately downloaded to your Mac. This method is designed for people who use a fast Internet connection, such as DSL or a cable modem.

- With the Shopping Cart method, you select songs and albums and they are added to your shopping cart. When you are ready to purchase that music, you check out of the store and all the music in your cart is downloaded to your Mac at the same time. This method is designed for slow Internet connections because downloading music inhibits shopping for other music at the same time. If you prefer to be able to select music and think about it before purchasing it, this can also be a useful option.

You can configure your shopping preferences on the Store pane of the iTunes Preferences dialog box:

1. Open the iTunes Preferences dialog box and click the Store button. The Store preferences appear (see Figure 16.11).

2. To disable the Music Store, uncheck the Show iTunes Music Store check box. If you do this, the Music Store source does not appear in the Source pane and you can't access the store. If you select this option, you are missing out on some good stuff.

3. To use the 1-Click shopping method, click the "Buy and download using 1-Click" radio button; to use the Shopping Cart method, click the "Buy using a Shopping Cart" radio button.

Figure 16.11
Using the Store preferences, you can configure your shopping experience.

4. If you want songs to play immediately after you download them from the store, check the "Play songs after downloading" check box.

5. If you use a slow Internet connection, check the "Load complete preview before playing" check box. You can listen to a 30-second preview of the songs available in the iTunes Music Store. This enables you to check out music before you decide to buy it. If you check this box, the preview is downloaded to your Mac before it begins to play. This option is useful when you use a slow Internet connection because the preview plays smoothly if it has been downloaded to your Mac, whereas it might not if you try to listen to it while it is being downloaded.

6. Click OK to set your preferences.

BROWSING, SEARCHING, AND PREVIEWING MUSIC IN THE ITUNES MUSIC STORE

The Music Store works just like most other Web sites you have seen. You click links, make choices on pop-up menus, and search to move around. You can search for music, browse genres, and so on to find music in which you are interested. When it comes to the Music Store, if you can see it, you can probably click it to move to some music.

To search for music in the iTunes Music Store do the following steps:

1. Select the Music Store source. The Music Store fills the Content pane.

2. Click the Magnifying Glass icon in the Search Music Store box.

3. On the resulting pop-up menu, select the criteria by which you want to search, such as All (to search all fields), Artist (to search for a specific artist), and so on.

TIP

If you select Power Search, the Music Store is replaced by an advanced search window that enables you to perform very precise searches.

4. Type the text for which you want to search in the Search field. As you type, the music that meets your criteria is shown in the Contents pane (see Figure 16.12). At the top of the Contents pane are albums that correspond to the search, top songs related to the search, and top artists related to the search. In the lower part of the pane are the songs that meet the criteria you entered.

Figure 16.12
Like Johnny Cash?
With the iTunes Music Store, finding a lot of his music is easy.

5. Double-click a song to listen to a preview.

You can also browse the store by clicking the links that appear at the top of Content pane. For example, click the House button to move back to the Music Store home page. As you view specific content, a hierarchical list appears; you can click any of the links in this list to move to that location, such as all the music by an artist. You can view album covers to see a list of their contents. You can also click song names in "top" lists to see albums that contain those songs.

PURCHASING MUSIC FROM THE ITUNES MUSIC STORE

When you find music you want to buy, how you buy it depends on the method you use.

To buy music with the 1-Click method, simply click the Buy Album button next to an album you want to buy or the Buy Song button to buy that song. The album or song is immediately purchased, downloaded to your Mac, and added to your Library.

To buy music using the Shopping Cart method, use the following steps:

1. Click the Add button next to the song or album you want to buy. The song or album you selected is added to your Shopping Cart.

2. Continue adding songs or albums to the Shopping Cart.

3. When you are ready to purchase the music, click the Buy Now button. All the music in the Shopping Cart is purchased and downloaded to your Library.

After you have purchased music, Apple sends you a receipt via email (the receipt contains information about purchases you made in a certain period of time rather than listing only individual purchases).

LISTENING TO MUSIC YOU PURCHASED AT THE ITUNES MUSIC STORE

After you purchase music, it is just like any other music in your Library (with the restrictions listed earlier in this section).

Click the Purchased Music playlist to see and listen to the music you have purchased. Of course, you can browse and search in your Library to work with your purchased music. Here are some other points about the Music Store to consider:

■ You can move songs you purchased to other Macs by copying them across a network, putting them on a CD, and so on. After you have moved the music to the next Mac, you can add it to the Library using the Add to Library command. However, to play purchased music on a different Mac, you must authorize that Mac (see the next section for more information). You can authorize music on up to three Macs at the same time.

■ If a download is interrupted before all the music has been downloaded to your Mac, select Advanced, Check for Purchased Music. This enables you to recover any music you have purchased but have not downloaded.

■ You can download music only one time! This means that, if something happens to the Mac on which your purchased music is stored, you can't download it again without paying for it again. You should always back up your purchased music on a DVD, a CD, or another Mac.

AUTHORIZING AND DEAUTHORIZING A MAC TO PLAY MUSIC FROM THE MUSIC STORE

To play music from the iTunes Music Store on a Mac, that Mac must be authorized to play it. This happens when you sign in to your Music Store account.

If you want to deauthorize a Mac so it doesn't count against the three-Mac limit, select Advanced, Deauthorize Computer. After you confirm your choice by entering your account name and password, that Mac is no longer capable of playing any music purchased from the Apple Music Store.

Music on Multiple Macs

If you have more than one Mac, you might want to install your music Library on each Mac so you can access it from that machine (if your Macs are connected over a network, you can share music from one machine to the others instead). To copy music from one Mac to another, put that music on a CD or DVD and copy it to each

Mac. Or, you can use file sharing to copy the music files from one machine to another. Then, use the Add to Library command to add that music to the iTunes Library on the Mac.

> **TIP**
>
> You can replicate a music Library on another Mac, or for another user on the same Mac, by copying the iTunes folder in the Music folder under one user's Home folder and using it to replace another iTunes folder under a different user account. The Mac to which it is copied must also be authorized for it to play any music purchased from the Apple Store.

ORGANIZING YOUR MUSIC WITH THE iTUNES LIBRARY, STANDARD PLAYLISTS, AND SMART PLAYLISTS

So far, listening to music with iTunes isn't that much different from using a regular CD player (aside from the ability to store all your music in one place and download music from the Internet and the iTunes Music Store, that is). The real power of iTunes is in the capability to completely customize your music.

UNDERSTANDING WHERE iTUNES STORES YOUR MUSIC

Before getting into how to do that, it can be helpful to understand how and where iTunes stores the music you have added to the Library.

The Library doesn't actually contain any music—its contents consist of a listing of pointers to MP3, AAC, and other files stored on your Mac. However, each track is actually a file stored on your machine. The files that make up the iTunes Library are organized by artist and album and by default are stored in the following directory:

Home/Music/iTunes/iTunes Music/

You can find the location of any song in your Library by selecting it and selecting File, Show Song File (⌘-R). A Finder window showing the song's file opens and the file is highlighted.

> **TIP**
>
> If you have added songs to your library that are scattered all over your Mac, select Advanced, Consolidate Library to have iTunes place copies of all your music in the iTunes folder. This organizes all your music files in a single step.

KEEPING MUSIC FILES ORGANIZED

The music files you download from the Internet are stored wherever you have set files to be downloaded. You should organize music you download in a central location. If you are going to add the songs you download into iTunes, you should store them in the iTunes Music folder, just as iTunes would do if it encoded the files for you. This helps keep your music organized in a consistent fashion.

You can use the iTunes Music Folder Location preference on the Advanced pane of the iTunes Preferences dialog box to change the location of your iTunes Music folder. For example, if you want to share the music you encode with other users of your Mac, you should store it in your Public folder. Other users can then add that music to their iTunes Libraries and create their own playlists. Or, you might want to do this if your startup volume doesn't have a lot of room and you want to store your music elsewhere, such as on an external drive.

A couple of other preferences on the Advanced pane are related to keeping your music well organized. Set these with the following steps:

1. Open the iTunes Preferences dialog and click the Advanced button to open the Advanced pane (see Figure 16.13).

Figure 16.13
Use the settings on the Advanced pane of the iTunes Preferences dialog box to keep your iTunes music organized.

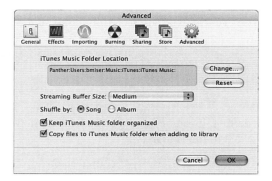

2. If you want to change the location in which iTunes stores music in the Library, click the Change button. Use the resulting Change Music Folder Location dialog box to move to and select a new folder. Click Open. From that point forward, iTunes will store music in the folder you selected.

TIP

If you want to change where your existing iTunes Music folder is located, copy it to the new location before you do step 2. Then, when you do step 2, select the Music folder you just copied. After you have confirmed that the new folder contains all your music, you can delete the original one.

3. Make sure the "Keep iTunes Music folder organized" preference is selected. This keeps all your music organized according to the standard iTunes scheme.

4. Check the "Copy files to iTunes Music folder when adding to library" check box. This causes iTunes to make a copy of any tracks you add to the Library (rather than importing them) and place the copies in the iTunes folder just like music you import.

5. Click OK.

TIP

> To return the Music folder to its default location, move your music folder to the original location and click the Reset button on the Advanced pane of the Preferences dialog box.

LISTENING TO THE LIBRARY

After you have added songs to your Library, you listen to them just like songs on an audio CD:

1. Select the Library as the source.

2. Click the Browse action button to place iTunes in the Browse mode if it isn't already.

3. Select the Genre in which you are interested; leave All selected if you want to browse all genres of music in your Library.

4. Click an artist or album that contains the songs you want to hear. The lower pane of the window shows the contents of whatever you select in the upper pane of the window. For example, to see all the albums by an artist, click that artist's name. In the Album pane, all the albums for that artist are shown. To see the tracks on that album, click its name in the Album column. In the Content pane of the window, all the tracks on the selected album are listed. To see all the contents of a selected item again, click All.

5. In the lower pane, select the song you want to listen to and click the Play button, or just double-click the song.

TIP

> In the panes of the Browse window, you see All at the top of each list. When you select All, all the items in that part of the window are selected (and played if you click the Play button). For example, if you select an artist in the Artist column, select All in the Album column, and click Play, all the albums by that artist are played. Similarly, if you select All in the Album window and then click Play, all your albums are played.

The other controls work just as they do for a CD, such as the check box, Shuffle button, and so on. You can also use the check box to skip songs and play a song by double-clicking it just as you can when you listen to a CD.

 If iTunes can't find a song you have added to the Library, see "iTunes Can't Find a Song in My Library" in the "Troubleshooting" section at the end of this chapter.

UNDERSTANDING PLAYLISTS

The benefit of creating and using pointers to music files in the Library is that you can create customized sublibraries, called *playlists*, of songs you want to hear. These playlists act like albums—they contain specific sets of songs.

There are two types of playlists: playlists and smart playlists. *Playlists* contain a fixed set of songs you select. *Smart playlists* use a set of criteria you define to select a playlist's contents, and the contents of smart playlists can be dynamic, meaning they change over time.

CREATING AND USING PLAYLISTS

You can create your own playlists and add any songs in your Library to them. The contents of a playlist remain the same until you change them manually. You can add the same song to more than one playlist and add the song to the same playlist more than one time. To create a playlist and add music to it, do the following:

1. Click the New Playlist button or select File, New Playlist (press ⌘-N). You see a new, untitled playlist in the Source pane.

2. Name the new playlist—the name is highlighted and ready to edit immediately after you create it. (You can also edit playlist names by clicking them and waiting a second or so until the name becomes highlighted.)

> **TIP**
>
> A great way to get a playlist started is to select the songs you want it to contain and then select File, New Playlist From Selection (or press Shift-⌘-N). A new playlist is created and the songs you selected are added to it.

3. Click Library to select it as the source.

4. Browse or search your Library to locate songs you want to add to the new playlist.

5. Drag the tracks you want to add from the Content pane of the Library onto the name of the playlist you created (the playlist is highlighted when the track is on top of it).

6. Continue adding tracks to the playlist.

7. Select the playlist in the Source pane to see its contents (see Figure 16.14).

Figure 16.14
This playlist contains songs from several movie soundtracks.

8. Set the order in which the tracks will play by dragging them up or down in the Content pane.

NOTE

As you can see in Figure 16.14, iTunes doesn't always get correct information, especially for music collections and movie soundtracks. (The artist shown for the music from the movie *Braveheart* in Figure 16.14 is Various Artists when it should be the soundtrack's creator.) If the incorrect information bothers you, use the Info window to correct it (you'll learn about that later in this chapter).

16

At the bottom of the iTunes window, the number of songs in the playlist, their total playing time, and the size of the files you have referenced in the playlist are shown. Because a playlist contains only pointers to tracks, its file size is quite small. However, this size information for the files it references is useful when you want to place the playlist on a portable MP3 device or when you want to burn a CD. You can use the size information to ensure that the playlist will fit in the device's available memory.

Listening to a playlist is just like listening to a CD. Select the playlist you want to hear and use the iTunes playback controls to listen to it.

You can delete entire playlists, delete specific songs from a playlist, or remove songs from the Library by selecting the items you want to remove and pressing Delete. You then see a warning dialog box; if you click OK, the playlist or song is removed (when you remove a song from a playlist, the original file is not affected). If you select a track in the Library to remove the related file you created using iTunes, you see a second dialog box asking whether you want iTunes to place the original file in the Trash. If you click OK, the file is also moved to the Trash. If you click Cancel, the original file remains on your Mac (you can add it back to the Library if you want to listen to it again).

Creating and Using Smart Playlists

Playlists are cool because they enable you to create custom albums for your listening pleasure. However, listening to the same playlists over and over can get a bit dull. This is where smart playlists come in. These playlists are generated by defining a set of criteria for the music you want to be included in the playlist rather than selecting individual songs. Even better, each time you play that playlist, the specific songs included can be determined dynamically by applying the playlist's criteria to your library. For example, iTunes comes with the Recently Played smart playlist. By default, this playlist contains the songs you have played in the past two weeks. The contents of this playlist change over time as you listen to different music, and, unless you listen only to this playlist, it will never be exactly the same twice.

The criteria you use for a smart playlist can be based on one or more attributes, and you can limit the size of the playlists to a specific number of songs.

Different icons are used to differentiate smart playlists from standard ones (see Figure 16.1).

To create a smart playlist, follow these steps:

1. Hold down the Option key and click the New Playlist button; select File, New Smart Playlist; or press Option-⌘-N. The Smart Playlist window appears (see Figure 16.15).

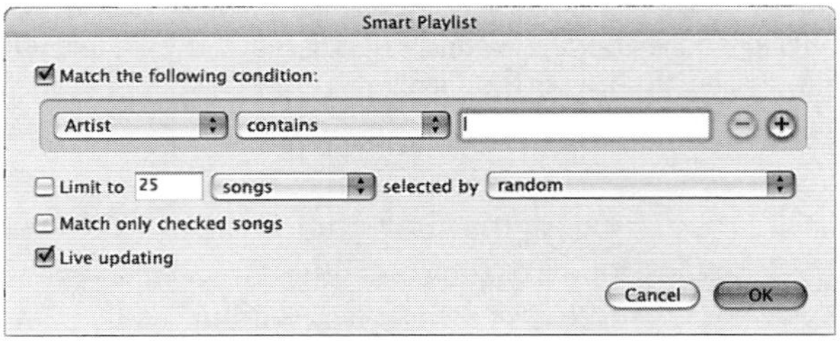

Figure 16.15
The Smart Playlist dialog box enables you to create a complex playlist based on multiple criteria.

2. Check the "Match xx of the following condition" check box. The pop-up menus and text box become active.

3. Select the criterion on which you want to base the condition on the first pop-up menu. For example, select Genre to base it on the condition on the music's genre.

4. Select the operand on which you want to base the condition on the second pop-up menu. The operands available depend on the condition you selected. For example, if you choose a text condition, such as Genre, your choices include contains, is, is not, and so on. If you choose a numeric condition, such as time, your choices include is, is not, is greater than, is in the range, and so on.

5. Enter the text or numbers for the condition in the check box. For example, if you selected Genre, you could enter Jazz or Rock. If you selected time, you could enter the length of the songs you want to be included.

6. Click the Plus sign. Another condition is added to the smart playlist. A new pop-up menu appears next to the check box at the top of the window.

7. On the new pop-up menu, select All if you want all the criteria to be met or select any if only one of the criteria has to be met for a song to be included in the playlist.

8. Repeat steps 3–5 to configure the new condition.

9. If you want to add another condition, click the plus sign again.

10. Repeat steps 3–5 to configure that condition.

> **T I P**
>
> To remove a condition from a smart playlist, click the minus sign next to that condition.

11. Keep adding and configuring conditions until you have added all that you want to include.

12. If you want to limit the playlist to a certain number of songs, amount of time, or file size, check the "Limit to" check box. Enter the value you want to use for the limit. Select the parameter by which you want to limit the playlist on the pop-up menu (for example, select songs to limit it to a specific number of songs), and then choose how you want the songs to be selected on the "selected by" pop-up menu. Suppose you want to include only 50 songs in the playlist and want them selected by those that are most played. Your input would be 50 in the text box, songs on the first pop-up menu, and most played on the second pop-up menu.

13. If you want the playlist to include songs you have skipped (by unchecking their check boxes), uncheck the "Match only checked songs" box. If this check box is checked, skipped songs are also skipped by the playlist.

14. If you want the content of the playlist to change over time, check the Live Updating check box. Each time you play the playlist, iTunes selects the songs it plays based on the latest information. For example, if the playlist is based on genre and you add a new album from the genre to your Library, that album would be added to the playlist automatically.

    If you don't check this check box, the playlist contains songs based on the music as it existed in your Library when you created the playlist.

15. Review the conditions to make sure you have defined them as you want them (see Figure 16.16).

Figure 16.16
This smart playlist plays 50 jazz songs I have rated four or five stars and have played most recently. Because it is updated live, as I listen to music that meets the criteria, that music is added to the playlist automatically.

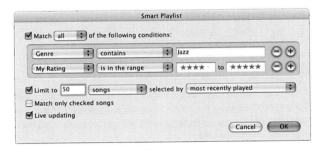

16. Click OK, and a new smart playlist appears in the Source pane.

17. Rename the smart playlist as needed (iTunes attempts to name the playlist based on its conditions; this might or might not result in the name you want to use).

18. Select the playlist. Its current contents are displayed in the Contents pane (see Figure 16.17).

You can also edit the default smart playlists Apple has provided for you or smart playlists you create:

1. Select the smart playlist you want to edit.

Figure 16.17
The current contents of the selected playlist are shown in the Content pane. Because it is updated live, the tracks included in the playlist change over time.

2. Select File, Get Info (⌘-I) or select File, Edit Smart Playlist. The Smart Playlist dialog box appears.

3. Use the controls to edit a smart playlist in the same way as when you create a smart playlist.

4. When you are done making changes, click OK. The playlist uses the updated conditions the next time you play it.

> **NOTE**
>
> The Purchased Music source is actually a smart playlist that collects all the music you have purchased from the Music Store. As you purchase music, each song you buy is added to the Purchased Music playlist automatically. (In case you are wondering, you can change this playlist.)

BROWSING PLAYLISTS

You can browse playlists just as you browse your entire library:

1. Select the playlist you want to browse.

2. Select Edit, Show Browser (or press ⌘-B). The Browse pane appears at the top of the window, and you can view the genre, artist, and album information for the songs included in the playlist.

OPENING PLAYLISTS

If you double-click a playlist, it opens in a separate and independent iTunes window. This makes working with playlists easy, especially when you are building them. You can open a playlist's window and more easily drag tracks from the iTunes window onto the playlist's window to add them to it. You can also use a playlist window to reorganize it, play it, and perform other playlist tasks.

CONFIGURING VIEWS FOR SOURCES

You can customize the columns shown for each source in the Source pane, including playlists, CDs, and so on:

1. Select the source whose view you want to configure.
2. Select Edit, View Options (or press ⌘-J). The View Options dialog box appears; the name of the selected source appears at the top of the dialog box.
3. Check the check boxes for the columns you want to see in the Content pane when you select that source. You can select from among many options, including Album, Artist, Comment, Date Added, Genre, and so on.
4. Uncheck the check boxes for those columns you don't want to see.
5. Click OK. When you select the source, you see only the columns you selected.

> **TIP**
>
> You can also customize the view for a source by holding down the Control key while you click in a column heading. A pop-up menu appears and you can quickly add or remove individual columns. You can also have iTunes automatically size one or all columns in the window.

The custom view you create is saved and returns each time you select that source. You can have different view options for each source you view (meaning your library, every playlist, each CD, and so on).

USING THE iTUNES INFORMATION WINDOW

The iTunes Information window is a powerful tool you can use to get information about tracks and control specific aspects of those tracks. For example, you can associate an Equalizer preset with a specific song, among many other things.

The Information window contains the following panes (see Figure 16.18):

- **Summary**—Use this tab to get general information about the song, such as title, artist, album, encoding method, and so on.
- **Info**—This tab enables you to apply various tags to the song, such as its artist, album, year, track number, and genre. You can also add comments about the song. The tags are what are searched when you perform a search using the iTunes Search tool.

■ **Options**—Using this tab, you can change the relative volume level of the song, apply an Equalizer preset, and control the start and stop playback time.

■ **Artwork**—This tab shows any artwork associated with the song. For example, when you purchase music from the Music Store, the album artwork is downloaded along with the song. You can also add artwork to or remove artwork from a song by using the Add or Delete button on the Artwork tab. You can even associate multiple graphics with the same song and cycle through them with the slider.

Figure 16.18
The iTunes Information window enables you to add or change information related to music in your Library.

TIP

If you open the Artwork pane located under the Source pane and artwork is associated with the song currently playing, it appears in this pane.

To access a song's information, use the following steps:

1. Select a song.

2. Select File, Get Info, (⌘-I). (You can also point to the song, Control-click, and select Get Info from the contextual menu.) The Song Information window opens.

3. Click the Summary tab if it isn't selected already. Information about the selected song appears (refer to Figure 16.18). The Summary tab provides detailed information (despite being called the Summary tab) about a song, such as where it is stored and the technical information related to how it was encoded.

4. To see the next or previous song in the selected source, click the Previous or Next button, respectively.

5. Click OK when you are done viewing this information. The Information window closes.

To make browsing and searching efficient, you should ensure that your music has the appropriate information associated with it. If you need to edit a song's information, use the following steps:

1. Select a song.

2. Select File, Get Info (⌘-I). (You can also point to the song, Control-click, and select Get Info from the contextual menu.) The Song Information window opens.

3. Click the Info tab to see the information that is currently applied to the selected song (see Figure 16.19). If you have imported the song from a CD or purchased it from the iTunes Music Store, the name of the song (which appears at the top of the Song Information window), artist, album, track number, and genre were likely filled in when you added the song to your Library. In many cases, that is all the information you need.

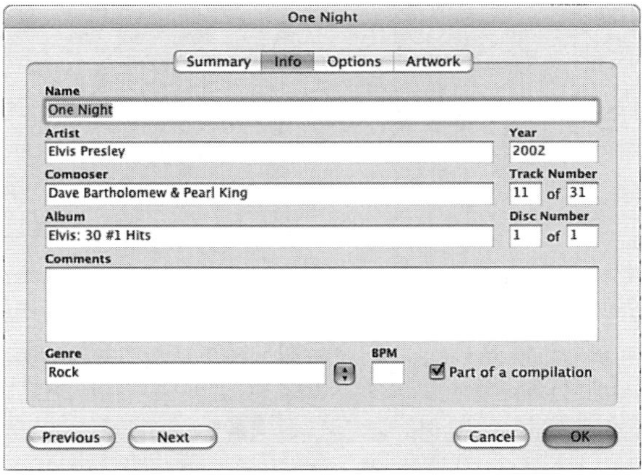

Figure 16.19
The Info tab of the Song Information window provides detailed tags for a song; these are useful for categorizing your music.

4. To change any of the song's tags, enter or edit the information shown in the various fields. For example, you can change the song's name or add comments about the song in the Comments field.

5. You can associate the song with a genre by selecting a genre on the Genre pop-up menu.

TIP

You can add your own genres to the Genre pop-up menu. Open the menu and select Custom. The Genre field then becomes editable, and you can type the genre you want to add. It is added to the menu, and you can associate it with songs just like the genres included by default.

6. Click OK to save your changes

You can configure some specific options for a song by using the Options tab of the Song Information window:

1. Open the Song Information window for a song and click the Options tab (see Figure 16.20).

Figure 16.20
The Options tab enables you to set a song's relative volume, equalizer, and other settings.

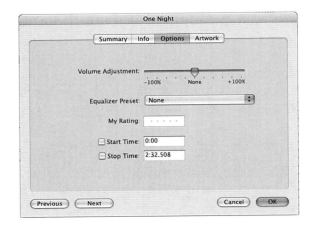

2. To change the relative volume of the song, drag the Volume Adjustment slider to the right to make the song play louder than normal or to the left to make the song play quieter than normal. This is especially useful when you include songs in playlists from a variety of sources because you can equalize the relative volume levels of those songs.

3. To apply an Equalizer preset to the song, use the Equalizer Preset pop-up menu. (You'll learn more about the Equalizer later in this chapter.)

4. To apply a rating to the song, click the dot in the My Rating field for the number of stars you want to give the song, from one to five.

> **N O T E**
>
> You can apply a rating to the songs in your Library to indicate how much you like or dislike them. You can use these ratings to sort the Contents pane, and you can use them in smart playlists. To rate a song from the iTunes window, Control-click it and select My Ratings on the contextual menu. Select your rating for the song (from one to five stars).

5. To start playing the song at some point other than its beginning, check the Start Time check box and enter the start time in minutes and seconds. When you play the song, it starts at the time you input. Using the Start Time option is a great way to get rid of interviews or talking at the start of a track. This content can be interesting once or twice, but probably not every time you hear the song. Just set the song to start when the talking is done and you won't ever have to hear it again.

6. To stop playing the song before it reaches its end, check the Stop Time check box and enter the time at which you want the song to stop in minutes and seconds. When the song reaches this point, it stops playing.

7. Click OK to apply the options to the song.

TIP

> Many of the items in the Song Information window can be applied to multiple songs simultaneously. For example, you can select several songs, open the Song Information window, and apply a genre to all the selected songs at the same time (you are prompted to make sure you understand you are changing multiple songs). Doing this saves a lot time when you need to apply the same information to a group of songs.

16

CUSTOMIZING MUSIC PLAYBACK

iTunes provides extensive control over how its window looks and how your music sounds when you play it. You can customize the iTunes window itself, and there are two general ways you can control how your music sounds. You can configure the iTunes effects preferences, and you can use the built-in iTunes Equalizer.

CONFIGURING THE ITUNES WINDOW

There are several ways in which you can customize iTunes for music playback.

TIP

> Remember that you can control iTunes from the Dock. Sometimes, hiding iTunes and just using the Dock controls to control your tunes is most convenient.

If you click the Maximize button (the green one), the iTunes window shrinks down so that only the playback controls and display area are shown (see Figure 16.21). You can use the resize handle to reduce the size of the window even further until only the playback, window, and volume controls are shown. Click the Maximize button again to restore the iTunes window to its full size.

Of course, in the full-size mode, you can manually resize the window by dragging its resize handle. Making it larger displays more information; making it smaller displays less. The window has a minimum size that is quite a bit larger than the reduced size you get with the Maximize button.

TIP

> If you click the Close button in the iTunes window, its window disappears but the music continues to play. When you move from iTunes into another application, such as the Finder, and then back into iTunes, its window appears again. You can also display the window by selecting Window, iTunes.

Figure 16.21
In this mode, the iTunes window takes up much less screen real estate.

16

USING iTUNES EFFECTS

iTunes includes three effects preferences you can set to control how music sounds. These effects are configured on the Effects pane of the iTunes Preferences dialog box:

1. Open the iTunes Preferences and click the Effects icon.

2. Use the Crossfade Playback check box and slider to control the amount of silent time between songs in your playlists. To control this time, check the box and use the slider to set the amount of silent time. If the slider is set to 0, there will be no silence; one song will fade directly into the next. Set the slider to a value up to 12 seconds to have that amount of silence between tracks.

3. The Sound Enhancer check box and slider enable iTunes to apply digital effects to your music to improve its quality (that is a matter of opinion, of course). To use this feature, check the Sound Enhancer check box and use the slider to set the relative amount of enhancing iTunes does.

4. To have iTunes automatically adjust the volume of each song as it plays to the same level, check the Sound Check check box. This avoids dramatic changes in volume level when you listen to various music.

5. Click OK. The effects you configured are applied to all your music as you play it.

USING THE iTUNES EQUALIZER

iTunes includes a graphic equalizer you can use to fine-tune the music you listen to. As with hardware graphic equalizers, you can adjust the relative volume levels of various audio frequencies to suit your preferences. Unlike with hardware graphic equalizers, you can select different preset configurations and create your own configurations. You can apply an equalizer configuration to your music even down to individual songs so each tune can have its own equalization.

To work with the Equalizer, perform the following steps:

1. Click the Equalizer button or select Window, Equalizer(⌘-2). The Equalizer window appears (see Figure 16.22).

2. To activate the Equalizer, check the On check box (it is on by default).

3. Select the Equalizer preset configuration you want from the pop-up menu. All iTunes music you play is adjusted according to the preset you selected.

Figure 16.22
These Equalizer settings are designed to maximize bass and emphasize treble frequencies.

Use the following ideas as you equalize your own music:

- Use the Preamp slider to change the relative volume level for every song. This is useful when a piece of music is recorded at a particularly high or low volume level.

- Create your own Equalizer settings by first selecting Manual from the pop-up menu. Then drag the slider for each frequency to the volume level at which you want that frequency to be played.

- Add your custom Equalizer settings to the pop-up menu by configuring the Equalizer and selecting Make Preset from the pop-up menu. In the Make Preset dialog box, name your preset and click OK. Your preset is added to the list and you can choose it just as you can one of the iTunes default settings.

- Edit the list of presets by selecting Edit List from the pop-up menu. The Edit Presets dialog box appears. You can use this to rename or delete any of the presets, including the default presets.

You can also associate Equalizer presets with specific songs:

1. Select the song to which you want to apply a preset.
2. Select File, Get Info (⌘-I). The Song Information window appears.
3. Click the Options tab.
4. On the Equalizer Preset pop-up menu, select the preset you want to be used for that song.
5. Click OK. When that song plays, the preset selected is used.

If you frequently apply equalizer presets to songs, use the View Options dialog box to have the Equalizer column displayed in the Content pane. This column includes an Equalizer preset pop-up menu from which you can choose a preset for a song.

MAKING YOUR MUSIC MOBILE

With all this great music, you aren't likely to want to limit your listening pleasure to those times when you are working at your Mac. There are two ways in which you can make your iTunes music mobile: by creating your own music CDs or by using a portable MP3 player.

USING iTUNES TO CREATE CUSTOM MUSIC CDs

With a Mac and a supported CD recordable drive, you can use iTunes to create your own music CDs. These CDs can contain specific playlists you can then listen to in your car, on portable CD players, and so on.

CAUTION

> If you have a CD recording application installed on your Mac, such as Adaptec's popular Toast, you might have trouble getting iTunes to record CDs. If you experience problems when you attempt to record CDs using iTunes, remove any other CD writing applications you have installed.

The general steps to use iTunes to record a custom CD are the following:

1. Install and configure your CD recorder.

→ For information about installing and using CD-R and CD-RW drives, **see** "Finding, Installing, and Using a CD Writer," **p. 790**.

2. Create the playlist from which you want to create a CD.
3. Configure iTunes for CD burning.
4. Record the CD.

NOTE

> The process of recording a CD is more commonly called *burning a CD*, which is the terminology iTunes uses.

Steps 1 and 3 have to be done only once, so after your system is properly configured, you can easily burn subsequent CDs.

CONFIGURING YOUR CD RECORDER IN iTUNES

Before you can burn a CD, you need to ensure that your CD recorder is properly configured:

1. Turn on your CD recorder (if it is an external model).
2. Open the iTunes Preferences dialog box and click the Burning icon.
3. Ensure that your CD recorder appears next to the CD Burner text at the top of the Burning pane, which means iTunes recognizes and can burn to the device. If you have more than one CD burner available, select the one you want to use on the CD Burner pop-up menu.

If iTunes does not recognize that you have a supported CD-R or CD-RW drive, see "iTunes Can't Find My CD Recorder" in the "Troubleshooting" section at the end of this chapter.

4. Use the Preferred Speed pop-up menu to set the burn speed to the appropriate speed. Try Maximum Possible to get the fastest burns. If recording doesn't work properly, reduce the speed. A safe recoding speed is 2x. Unless you are in a tremendous hurry to get a CD done, this will probably be plenty fast for you.

5. To record an audio CD that will be compatible with standard audio CD players, click the Audio CD radio button and set the amount of quiet time between tracks on the CD by using the Gap Between Songs pop-up menu.

6. To record an MP3 CD, click the MP3 CD radio button. CDs recorded in this format play only on devices that support the MP3 format. The benefit of these CDs is that you can fit many more tracks on a single CD than you can when you use the Audio CD format.

7. To record the tunes on a data CD or DVD, click the Data CD or DVD radio button. These discs are typically limited to playback on computers; putting tunes on a DVD is a great way to back them up.

16

> **N O T E**
>
> If your Mac doesn't have a DVD-R drive, the radio button will be labeled Data CD.

8. Click OK.

Each time you burn a CD or DVD, it is burned in the selected format. If you want to change the format of a disc, just use the previous steps to select a different format.

> **T I P**
>
> You should back up any music you purchase from the iTunes Music Store. A great way to do this is to periodically burn the Purchased Music playlist onto a CD, or after your music collection grows such that your purchased music won't fit on a CD or DVD.

BURNING AN AUDIO CD

When your system is configured properly, you are ready to create the CD:

1. Create the playlist you want to put on the CD. Make sure the songs are in the order in which you want to listen to them. Also be sure that the playlist contains fewer minutes of music than your CD-R media is rated for—select the playlist and look at the bottom of the iTunes window. Most CD-R media is rated for 70–80 minutes so your playlist should be less than this.

2. Select the playlist you want to place on the CD.

3. Click the Burn CD action button; you are prompted to insert a blank CD.

4. Insert the blank CD and close the drive (unless you have a slot-loading CD-RW drive, in which case this isn't necessary). In a moment, the Burn CD button is in color and

starts pulsing to indicate that you are ready to burn. iTunes checks to make sure that everything is ready to go. When these checks are complete, you are prompted to click the Burn CD button.

5. Click the Burn CD button again to burn the CD.

CAUTION

> Use CD-R discs for audio CDs you create rather than CD-RW discs, especially if you will be using the CDs you create in noncomputer CD players. If you create an audio CD using a CD-RW disc, you probably won't be able to play it using any CD player except the one on which you created it (which wouldn't be very useful).

When iTunes records your playlist to a CD, it first translates the music into the standard Audio CD format (assuming you elected to create an audio CD rather than an MP3 or data CD, of course). The application translates each of the songs on the CD prior to burning them. This process takes several minutes to complete. Watch the display area for progress and status messages. When it is done, iTunes begins recording the CD.

CAUTION

> The spinning Burn CD icon gives you a clue as to how fast data is being transferred to the CD recorder. The faster the icon spins, the higher the data transfer rate is being achieved. If the icon slows considerably or stops altogether, you might experience errors because data isn't flowing fast enough to keep the CD burning process fed properly. If this happens, quit all applications that might be accessing any disks on your Mac and make sure that you aren't playing any music in iTunes. This ensures that the maximum amount of system resources is available for the CD burning process. You can also lower the burn speed to reduce the data flow requirements—doing so often alleviates this problem.

Depending on the speed at which your recorder works and the amount of data to record, this process can take only a couple of minutes or quite a while. When it is complete, iTunes plays a sound to indicate that the process is done. The CD you created is mounted on your Mac and is selected as the current source.

 If iTunes stops the process before it is complete, see "iTunes Stops Recording Before the Process Is Complete" in the "Troubleshooting" section at the end of this chapter.

If the CD you create can't be read on standard CD players, such as those in your car, see "The CDs I Make Won't Play in My Noncomputer CD Player" in the "Troubleshooting" section at the end of this chapter.

USING ITUNES WITH AN APPLE IPOD

Although the Apple iPod is an MP3 player, it is much more than most MP3 players. Whereas many MP3 players are limited to 64MB or 128MB of memory, the iPod includes its own hard drive with 10GB, 20GB, or even 40GB of storage space. This means you can store an entire music collection on the iPod (about 10,000 songs for the 40GB model), which eliminates the chore of selecting a small subset of your library to take on the road with you. The iPod uses the FireWire interface to communicate with your Mac, so data transfers to and from the iPod much more quickly than it does with most other MP3 players (because most use USB 1, which is much slower than FireWire). In addition, iTunes is designed to make managing your mobile music with the iPod even easier than it is with standard MP3 players. For example, you can set up the iPod so it is automatically synced with your iTunes music collection, including the songs in your Library, playlists, and so on. Additionally, iPods can play music in the AAC format, which means you can also take music with you that you purchased from the iTunes Music Store without any additional steps.

NOTE

> You even use an iPod to display your contacts and appointments.

The iPod's only downside is its cost, which is higher than that of many MP3 players. At press time, the iPod costs $299 for the 10GB model, $399 for the 20GB model, or $499 for the 40GB model. However, if you consider that the iPod is actually a very small FireWire hard drive and includes an 8-hour rechargeable battery, its price doesn't seem as high. Also, keep in mind that you would have to buy many, many memory cards for most players for them to even approach the amount of music you can store on the iPod.

Another nice feature of the iPod is that its battery can be recharged through the FireWire port. So, you can recharge your iPod just by connecting it to your Mac.

iTunes is designed to keep the iPod in sync with your music Library. Here's how:

1. Connect the iPod to your Mac using the supplied FireWire cable. Your Mac recognizes the iPod as a new source, and iTunes begins to download all the music in your Library to the iPod. During this process, the iTunes Information window displays the progress of the process, as well warning you *not* to unplug the iPod while the update is in process. As songs are downloaded, the refresh icon next to them disappears.

NOTE

> If your iTunes library contains more music than can be stored on the iPod, you must manually configure the music on the iPod. You will learn how to do that shortly.

2. When the process is complete, disconnect the iPod. Your entire iTunes music library is ready to go with you.

TIP

> iTunes contains a complete online help system for the iPod. To access it, select Help, iPod Help.

When an iPod is connected to your Mac, it is mounted on the desktop and is available as a source in the Source pane (see Figure 16.23). You can work with an iPod as a source in ways that are similar to other sources.

iPod source

Figure 16.23
When an iPod is connected to your Mac, it appears on the Source pane.

Player Options button

As you add music to your Library, create playlists, remove songs, and so on, you should keep your iPod current with your iTunes Library. You can control how this is done by setting preferences for the iPod using the Player Options button, which looks like the iPod itself.

When you click this button, the iPod Preferences window opens (see Figure 16.24). The options you have in this window are explained in the following list:

- **Automatically update all songs and playlists**—When this option is selected, the entire iTunes music Library is synchronized with the music on the iPod each time you connect the iPod to your Mac. This means the iPod contains a mirror image of the music you are managing in iTunes. Of course, your iPod must be capable of storing all the music you have in your iTunes Library for you to use this option.

- **Automatically update selected playlists only**—When you select this option, you select the playlists you want to be updated. When you connect the iPod to your Mac, only the selected playlists are synchronized. This option is useful if there is music in iTunes that you don't really want to carry with you or when you can't fit your entire iTunes Library on the iPod. Create the playlists you want to keep on the iPod and then have them synchronized automatically.

■ **Manually manage songs and playlists**—With this option, you must manually move songs to the iPod; you do this just as you do for regular MP3 players. To add playlists or songs to the iPod, drag them onto the iPod icon in the Source pane.

> **TIP**
>
> You can double-click the iPod icon in the Source pane to open it in its own window.

■ **Open iTunes when attached**—With this check box selected, iTunes opens when you attach an iPod to your Mac.

■ **Enable FireWire disk use**—You can use your iPod as an external FireWire hard disk. To do so, check this box and also the "Manually manage songs and playlists" radio button. When you attach the iPod to your Mac, you can work with it just like other hard disks. (You can't use this method to transfer music to the iPod, though; instead you must use iTunes to do that.)

■ **Only update checked songs**—This option enables you to prevent songs from being copied to the iPod. Check this box and then uncheck the box next to any songs you don't want to be copied to the iPod.

Figure 16.24
The Player Options button enables you to configure how your iPod is synchronized with your iTunes music library.

SHARING iTUNES MUSIC ON A NETWORK

You can share music in your iTunes Library with other Macs with which you are networked. You can also listen to music that is being shared with you.

CONFIGURING YOUR MAC TO SHARE MUSIC

To share your music with other Macs on your network, you just need to set your sharing preferences:

16

1. Open the iTunes Preferences dialog box and click the Sharing button.

2. Click the "Share my music" radio button.

3. Click the "Share entire library" radio button to share all the music in your Library, or click the "Share selected playlists" radio button and check the box next to each playlist you want to share to share only those playlists.

4. Give your shared music a name by typing a name in the Shared Name field. This is the name of the source others will select to access your music.

5. If you want to require a password for people to be able to share your music, check the "Require password" box and enter a password in the field.

6. Click OK.

7. If you required a password, provide it to the people with whom you want to share your music.

After you have shared your music, people can access it using the same steps you use to access music being shared with you.

NOTE

> For your music to be accessible on the network, your Mac must remain awake. If you turn it off or it goes to sleep, others won't be able to access your shared music any more.

LISTENING TO MUSIC BEING SHARED WITH YOU

To search your network for music being shared with you, open the Sharing pane of the iTunes Preferences dialog box and check the "Look for shared music" check box. When you close the Preferences window, iTunes looks for any sources being shared with you. When it finds them, they appear in the Source pane. Shared sources have a blue icon with a single note symbol. Do the following:

1. Select the shared source that you want to listen to.

2. If it requires a password, enter the password at the prompt and click OK. The shared source becomes available.

3. Click the Expansion triangle next to the source to see the playlists that have been shared with you.

4. Listen to the shared source just as you listen to your own playlists.

NOTE

> You can't move music from a shared source into your Library from within iTunes.

TROUBLESHOOTING

iTunes Can't Find a Song in My Library

I try to play a song in the iTunes Library, but I see a message stating the song can't be used because the original file can't be found.

iTunes doesn't actually store music files in the Library, but rather contains pointers to music files. If the original file is moved around or deleted from your machine, iTunes can't find it and doesn't know how to play that song. When you see this dialog box, you can attempt to locate the file yourself. If you are successful, iTunes restores its link in the Library and it works as before. If you can't find the file, you have to re-create it and add it to the Library again.

iTunes Can't Find My CD Recorder

When I start up iTunes for the first time, I see a message stating that no supported CD recorders were found. Or, my CD recorder is not recognized when I try to record a CD.

This problem occurs when iTunes doesn't detect a supported CD-R or CD-RW drive in your Mac system. To be supported, iTunes must have the appropriate device software incorporated into it. This can also occur if your CD-R or CD-RW drive is not properly connected to and working with your Mac.

The first step is to ensure that your drive can work with at least one other application on your Mac. For example, if the CD writing software included with your drive is Toast, use Toast to record a CD. If that works, you know that the problem is related to iTunes. If it doesn't work, you need to troubleshoot your CD-R or CD-RW drive before trying to use it with iTunes.

The second step is relatively easy, but if it doesn't work, there isn't much you can do. Go to the Apple iTunes Web site (www.apple.com/itunes) to see whether a newer version of iTunes is available. If so, download and install it and try again. Apple will continue to add support for various CD-R or CD-RW mechanisms to iTunes, and if you get lucky, yours will be one of them.

If neither of these steps works, you still have several options. One is to buy a CD-R or CD-RW drive supported by iTunes (hey, you needed a good reason to buy a new Mac, right?). The other is to use another application to create the CD. For example, Toast also enables you to create audio CDs.

iTunes Stops Recording Before the Process Is Complete

The CD I am attempting to record is ejected before the process is finished. What is causing this?

When you see a message stating that iTunes is stopping the burn process, some error has prevented iTunes from completing the CD. You usually see an error dialog box; unfortunately, such a dialog box almost always contains an indecipherable message.

The most likely cause of such errors is the inability of iTunes to write data to the drive fast enough. If pauses occur in the data stream that is being recorded to the CD, the process sometimes fails. Make the following changes to attempt to correct the problem:

1. Stop all other applications except iTunes. Although Mac OS X provides iTunes with protected memory, other applications might be accessing other drives in your system. This can slow the data being transferred to the CD recorder.

2. Reconfigure iTunes so it uses a slow burn speed because slower burn speeds are easier to maintain.

After making these changes, try to burn the disc again. If it still doesn't work, try Apple's support site and search for the specific error message you are seeing.

THE CDs I MAKE WON'T PLAY IN MY NONCOMPUTER CD PLAYER

When I install a CD I have burned in a regular CD player, such as that in my car, either the disc is ejected and won't play or the player acts as if no CD is in the player at all.

There are a couple of causes for this problem. One possibility is that the CD you burned was a CD-RW disc rather than a CD-R disc. Standard CD players (noncomputer CD players) are usually incapable of reading CD-RW discs. You should always create audio CDs that you intend to play in other CD players using CD-R discs.

The other possibility is that the standard CD player you are trying to use does not recognize the format of the CD-R disc. This usually happens only when the CD player is relatively old. The only solution to this is to use a different CD player.

MAC OS X TO THE MAX: MORE MUSIC

In this section, you will see a list of iTunes keyboard shortcuts, get an overview of using iTunes to listen to music on the Internet, and learn about some commands on the Advanced menu.

USING ITUNES KEYBOARD SHORTCUTS

Table 16.2 lists helpful iTunes keyboard shortcuts.

TABLE 16.2   ITUNES KEYBOARD SHORTCUTS

Action	Shortcut
Add to Library	⌘-O
Eject Disc	⌘-E
Full Screen (visual)	⌘-F
Get Info	⌘-I

Action	Shortcut
Hide/Show Browser	⌘-B
Hide/Show iTunes Window	⌘-1
Higher Volume	⌘-up arrow
Lower Volume	⌘-down arrow
Mute	⌘-Option-down arrow
New Playlist	⌘-N
New Playlist From Selection	Shift-⌘-N
New Smart Playlist	Option-⌘-N
Next Song	⌘-right arrow
Open Stream	⌘-U
Play/Pause	Spacebar
Preferences	⌘-,
Previous Song	⌘-left arrow
Select All	⌘-A
Select None	Shift-⌘-A
Show Current Song	⌘-L
Show Song File	⌘-R
Turn Visual On/Off	⌘-T
View Options	⌘-J

USING ITUNES TO LISTEN TO INTERNET RADIO

You can use iTunes to listen to various Internet radio broadcasts. To do so, follow these steps:

1. Select Radio as the source. The application downloads the current list of available genres and presents them in the Content pane.

2. Click the Expansion triangle next to a genre to view the channels available in that genre.

3. Select the channel you want to play and press the spacebar.

The selected channel begins to stream to your Mac; when the prebuffer is full, it begins to play.

When you first select the Radio source, iTunes downloads the list of available genres and channels. You can refresh this list at any time by clicking the Action button, which is called Refresh when the Radio Tuner source is selected.

When iTunes plays audio from the Internet, it first stores it in a buffer so it can play back smoothly even if your Internet connection is slow or is getting interrupted. If you experience starting and stopping when listening to Internet sources, adjust the size of the iTunes buffer. Do this by using the Streaming Buffer Size pop-up menu on the Advanced tab of the iTunes Preferences window.

Some of the channels are live, whereas some are just large playlists stored on the Internet. When you listen to one that is a playlist, it is repeated until you stop playing it.

USING iTUNES ADVANCED COMMANDS

The iTunes Advanced menu contains the following commands:

- **Open Stream**—This command enables you to enter the URL of an audio stream to listen to it.

- **Convert Selection to *Format***—Use this command to convert audio files to the format indicated by *Format*. The format shown on the menu is determined by the encoding format you have selected on the Importing tab of the iTunes Preferences window. To convert a track into this format, select it and select the command.

- **Consolidate Library**—Use this command to move copies of all the music you are managing in iTunes but that is currently stored outside the iTunes folder into the iTunes folder.

- **Get CD Track Names**—When you select an audio CD, use this command to update its song information from the Internet.

- **Submit CD Track Names**—If iTunes is unable to find a CD, you can use this command to submit track information to the database.

- **Join CD Tracks**—Use this command to combine tracks on a CD into a single track with no gaps between the songs. Select the tracks you want to join and then select the command. The tracks are played as a unit.

- **Remove Audible Account**—Use this command to remove the Audible.com account from your Mac. If you haven't configured any Audible content on your machine, you won't see this command.

- **Deauthorize Computer**—Use this command when you want to remove the current Mac from being one of three allowed to play music you have purchased from the Apple Music Store.

- **Check for Purchased Music**—Use this to ensure that you have downloaded all the music you have purchased, such as when your Internet connection is interrupted while you are downloading music from the store.

- **Convert ID3 Tags**—This command is used to convert the tag information among various formats. If the tags for songs you add to your Library are incorrect, you can try this command to see whether you can correct them. You can also use this command if you want to share music with an application that doesn't use the same tag format iTunes does.

MAKING DIGITAL MOVIE MAGIC WITH iMOVIE

Working with Digital Video

Digital video (DV) technology enables you to capture high-quality footage and then transform that raw footage into a movie that people will actually enjoy watching. With Mac OS X, a digital video camera, and iMovie, you can express yourself in ways that are limited only by your own imagination. Your movies can have plots, transitions, sound effects, music, special effects, and more. And you can distribute and watch your movies in many ways, such as on DVD, videotape, or the Web.

To create DV movies, you should have the following tools:

- A Mac capable of running iMovie (because you have Mac OS X, you have this)
- iMovie (iMovie comes with Mac OS X)
- QuickTime Pro (this is an optional but highly recommended addition to your movie toolkit)
- Digital video camera

→ To learn more about QuickTime Pro, **see** Chapter 19, "Viewing, Editing, and Creating QuickTime Movies," **p. 641**.

Choosing and Using a DV Camcorder

A DV camera enables you to capture your own video and easily import clips into iMovie via FireWire. Obtaining a DV camera can be a baffling and sometimes intimidating process. There are many brands, and each offers many models with dozens of different features. This adds up to more choices than you might want to deal with.

However, by assessing a few specific factors, you can quickly reduce the dozens of choices you have to just a few:

- **iMovie compatibility**—Compatibility with iMovie should be the most important factor you consider when you choose a DV camera. What does iMovie compatibility mean? Basically, it means you have the easiest time and get the best results using that camera with iMovie. This is because you can control the camera from within iMovie, which makes transferring clips from the camera into iMovie a snap.

  Apple maintains a list of iMovie-compatible cameras on the iMovie Web page. To see this list, go to www.apple.com/imovie/compatibility/camcorder.html. You will have the best results if the camera you choose is on this list.

- **Format**—Many video camera formats are available; the good news is that you need to consider only two formats: Digital8 and MiniDV. The difference between them is, as you probably surmised, size. Digital8 cameras use a digital tape the same physical size as an 8mm tape. MiniDV tapes are considerably smaller, and MiniDV cameras tend to be considerably smaller, as well. Because of the size benefits and the fact that MiniDV has become the standard for DV camcorders, I recommend you consider only cameras that use the MiniDV format.

■ **Cost**—How much you have to pay for a camera is likely to be one of the first things you think about. And it might indeed be the most important factor of all. To quickly find out how much specific models cost, make a note of some of the models you see on the camcorder compatibility list. Go to your favorite retail Web site—try www.smalldog.com—and search for the models you noted to see how much they cost.

■ **Magnification**—The power of the lens determines how close you must be to shoot something. Two values are quoted for DV cameras. One value is for optical zoom, and the other is for digital zoom. Optical zoom uses the physical lenses to achieve magnification; digital zoom uses digital enhancements to make the image larger. Optical zoom provides higher quality, but both are useful. For both values, bigger numbers are better (for example, a 20X optical zoom is better than a 10X optical zoom).

■ **Input and output ports**—In addition to the FireWire port, other ports are available to get information into or out of the camera. These include a microphone jack so you can connect and use a higher-quality or focusable microphone, additional audio/video input/output ports, and so on.

NOTE

Make sure the DV camera you get has a port that enables you to record from an external source. This is usually called an A/V port. Often, this is the same port used to export video from the camera (the same jack is used to record from a source as is used to export the video to a VCR). This feature enables you to use an analog source to capture clips for your movies (in effect, such camcorders function as digitizers). For example, you can record from a VCR and then use FireWire to transfer that footage through the DV camera into iMovie so you can use it in your movies. This is easy to do, and the quality is very good (better than with most consumer-level digitizing devices). Even better is a model that enables you to pass-through a signal so you don't even have to record it with your DV camera because the signal passes through the DV camera into your Mac (via FireWire). This means you get a higher-quality first-generation recording in your movie rather than a second-generation recording (as you would if you have to record the video on the DV camcorder before you import it into iMovie).

After you have obtained a digital video camera, using one is very similar to using an analog camcorder. Hopefully, you will use a script or storyboard to plan the shooting you will do with it to get the clips from which you will build your movie.

After you have captured a collection of video clips, you are ready to get into iMovie to begin making a movie.

NOTE

Before you start making DV movies, you should ensure that you have a lot of disk space in which to store your iMovie project. If you have 2GB or more available, you have enough to get started; however, you won't be able to store very many minutes of DV footage. If the free space is between 1GB and 2GB, you can get started, but you will have to carefully manage your disk space as you work. If you have less than 1GB of free space, you need to move some of your files off your disk because you won't have enough room for anything except the briefest of movie projects.

WORKING WITH iMOVIE

The iMovie window contains five main areas, only four of which you can see at the same time (see Figure 17.1).

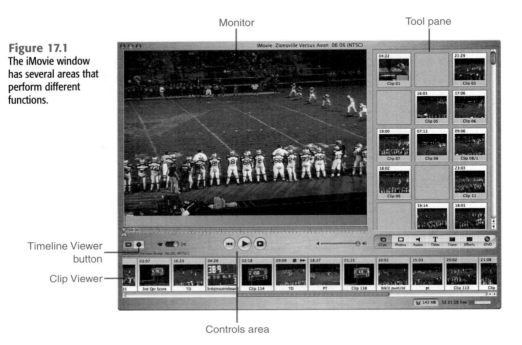

Figure 17.1
The iMovie window has several areas that perform different functions.

In the upper-left corner of the window is the Monitor. Here, you preview and edit your movie, as well as the clips from which you build that movie. In the upper-right is the iMovie Tool pane. At the bottom of the Tool pane are seven buttons, with each button opening a palette of tools in the pane. Just under the Monitor are the controls area that includes various buttons you use to control playback and editing functions. Underneath that area are the two viewers, the Clip Viewer and the Timeline Viewer (you can see only one viewer at a time). In the bottom-right corner of the window are the disk space tools you use to manage the disk space associated with your project.

iMovie has two basic modes in which you operate: Camera and Edit. The mode you are in is determined by the position of the Camera/Edit mode switch located in the Controls area (refer to Figure 17.1). When the switch is to the left (toward the camera icon), iMovie is in the Camera mode. In this mode, you work with a DV camera attached to your Mac to import video clips from which you will build your movie. When the switch is to the right (toward the scissors icon), iMovie is in the Edit mode and you can work with video clips to preview them, edit them, and so on. You will spend most of your iMovie time in Edit mode.

BUILDING A BASIC VIDEO TRACK

Start a new project by selecting File, New Project. In the Create New Project dialog box, name your movie. Move to the volume on which you are going to store it and click Create. Unlike many other applications, what you create is not a file but rather a folder that contains all the elements of your project.

NOTE

> Be sure to choose a volume with plenty of free space to store your iMovie project on. If you have a partitioned hard disk, you might need to move outside your Home directory to store your project to have enough room. In the ideal situation, you will have a dedicated hard disk or volume on which to store your project.

Save your project. Then, move to the Finder and open the project folder you just created to see three items: a folder called Media, an iMovie file, and a QuickTime movie with the same name as the project (see Figure 17.2). The media folder is used to store the clips, images, additional sounds (such as a music track), and other components you use in your project. The iMovie file, which has the same name as your project, is a small pointer file that contains references to all the files in the media folder you are using. If you want to open your project by double-clicking something, this is the file you double-click. The QuickTime movie file contains references to the QuickTime movie of the project.

Figure 17.2
When you create a new iMovie project, you create a folder that contains the Media folder, an iMovie reference file, and a QuickTime file.

Now you are ready to build your movie; you need to fill the iMovie Clips pane (also called the *Shelf*). To open the Clips pane, click the Clips button. The Clips pane is a holding area for the video clips, QuickTime movies, imported images, and other content you use in your movie. You drag clips from the Shelf to the Clip Viewer to place them in your movie. You can also drag clips from your movie and place them on the Shelf again. There's more on getting clips to and from the Shelf and the Clip Viewer later in this chapter.

IMPORTING CLIPS FROM A DIGITAL VIDEO CAMERA

Setting up a FireWire camera to work with iMovie is a snap. Power up your Mac, and then turn on the camera to its output setting (this is sometimes labeled VCR or VTR). Connect the FireWire cable to the DV camcorder and your Mac. iMovie switches into the Camera mode automatically.

CAUTION

> If the FireWire plug doesn't slip in easily, take a closer look. FireWire connectors are relatively fragile, so don't push too hard.

A message appears in iMovie's Monitor window confirming that iMovie is in touch with your DV camcorder. In addition to the "Camera Connected" message, notice that the button just under the Monitor is now Import. This means you are ready to begin importing your clips into iMovie.

The really cool part about an iMovie-compatible DV camcorder is that you can control your DV camcorder using iMovie's controls. The Play, Fast Forward, Stop, and other buttons in the iMovie Monitor control your DV camcorder. If you aren't using an iMovie-compatible camera, you have to control the camera using its controls and manually control iMovie as well.

 If you aren't able to control your camera from within iMovie, see "Nothing Happens with My Camera When I Use iMovie" in the "Troubleshooting" section at the end of this chapter.

To begin playing the tape in your camcorder, click the iMovie Play button (see Figure 17.3). The clips on the tape begin playing in the Monitor. Use the iMovie controls to move to the point on your tape at which you want to begin capturing clips from the tape.

TIP

> If, for some reason, you aren't getting the screen shown in Figure 17.3, check the Camera/Edit Mode switch and make sure its in Camera mode.

Following are the controls iMovie provides (from left to right and bottom to top):

- **Import**—You use this when you want to import clips to the Clips pane.
- **Camera/Edit Mode**—This switches iMovie between the Camera mode (which you are in now) and the Edit mode, which is the mode you use to edit your movie.
- **Rewind/Review**—When the tape is not playing, the Rewind button rewinds the tape at top speed. When the tape is playing, it plays the tape backward (you see the video, but there is no audio). In the Review mode, you have to "hold" down the button to keep the review going (in other words, if you let up on the button, it goes back into Play mode).
- **Pause**—This one freezes the video at a specific frame.
- **Play**—This plays the tape in the camera.
- **Stop**—The Stop button halts whatever is happening with the camcorder.

- **Fast Forward/Preview**—When the tape is not playing, the Fast Forward button moves the tape forward at top speed. When the tape is playing, it plays the tape forward at a high speed (you see video but don't hear any audio).
- **Volume**—Drag the slider to the right to increase the volume and to the left to decrease it. Note that this affects only the playback volume and doesn't actually change the movie at all.

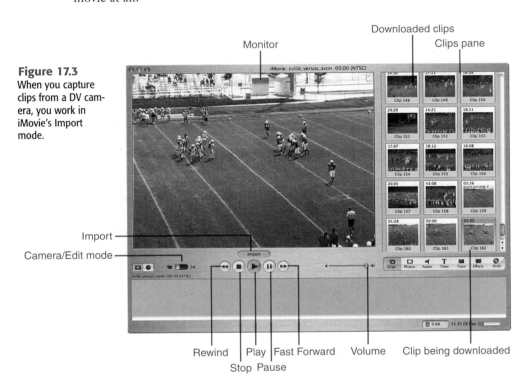

Figure 17.3
When you capture clips from a DV camera, you work in iMovie's Import mode.

Click the Import button (or press the spacebar); iMovie starts the camcorder and begins capturing the clips. It stores the first clip in the first available slot on the Shelf. When it gets to a scene break (the point at which you pressed the Stop button while filming with the DV camcorder), it stops that clip and immediately begins capturing the next scene, which it places in the next available slot on the Shelf.

iMovie continues this process until it runs out of video to import or out of disk space to store clips, whichever comes first. If you don't want to wait that long, click Import again to stop the capture process (or press the spacebar).

As you import clips into iMovie, keep a close eye on the Disk Gauge in the bottom-right corner of the iMovie window. This gauge shows you how much free space is available on the disk where your project is stored. When you are in good shape spacewise, the gauge shows green. When it turns yellow, you are starting to run out of room. When it turns red, the disk you are using is full and you need to clear more space on it to continue capturing clips.

 If the Disk Gauge turns red, see "Why Has the Disk Gauge Turned Red?" in the "Troubleshooting" section at the end of this chapter.

Use the iMovie controls to move the tape to the next set of scenes you want to capture, and begin again. Continue until you capture all the scenes your script and storyboards call for, your disk runs out of space, or the Clips pane is so full of clips that you have trouble dealing with so many. The Clips pane now has some nice clips (and probably some not-so-nice ones), ready for you to edit and use in your movie.

When you are done, disconnect your camera and turn it off.

Deleting Clips

As you capture clips, you will realize that some of them just aren't any good and you won't end up using them. That is the time to get rid of the worthless clip so it doesn't consume any precious disk space. On the Clips pane, click the clip you want to dump to select it. Drag it to the Trash (or press Delete)—it disappears from the Clips pane.

Placing a clip in the Trash gets it off the Shelf, but the clip still consumes disk space. To free up that disk space, you must empty the Trash. To do so, select File, Empty Trash. Depending on how big the clips in the Trash are, you might see a dialog box asking you to confirm that you want to empty the Trash. Click OK and the contents of the Trash are deleted. The space this junk consumed on the disk is free for other purposes. (The increased free space is reflected on the Disk Gauge.)

TIP

If you want to control how clips are broken instead of letting iMovie do it for you, uncheck the Automatically start new clip at scene break check box in the Import area of the iMovie Preferences dialog box. When you import video, the clips come in as one continuous chunk unless you start and stop the importing process manually. Frankly, dealing with one large clip is much more difficult than letting iMovie break up the clips for you. But if you have recorded your movie using very short multiple clips of the same scene, you might choose to have them come in as one long clip instead.

IMPORTING QUICKTIME MOVIES AND IMAGES

In addition to clips you capture from a DV camcorder, you can also import QuickTime movies and images onto the Clips pane for use in your movies.

NOTE

You can import image files in all the common Mac image file formats, such as JPEG, TIFF, PICT, and so on. For best results, you should size your images so they have a resolution of exactly 640×480 because iMovie scales them to that size anyway, which can result in some distortion if the original image's size is much different from this.

TIP

> You can access photos in your iPhoto Photo Library directly from within iMovie. You will learn how to do this later in this section.

To import content into iMovie, perform the following steps:

1. Select File, Import (Shift-⌘-I).

2. In the resulting Import sheet, move to and select the file you want to add to the iMovie project and click Open.

   The Import Files dialog box opens showing how the import is moving along. If your clip is fairly lengthy, this process can take a few moments. When the import process is complete, the clip or images appear on the Clips pane.

From this point on, imported content behaves in the same way as any other clip on the Clips pane.

PREVIEWING YOUR CLIPS

Select a clip by clicking it on the Clips pane. The clip is highlighted with a blue border—this means the clip is selected. More telling is the first frame of the clip the Monitor shows. Notice that when you select a clip, iMovie also moves into the Edit mode, in which you can manipulate your clips (if it isn't in the Edit mode, slide the Camera/Edit Mode switch to the right). In the Edit mode, the iMovie window features the controls shown in Figure 17.4 and described in the following list:

- **Scrubber bar**—The Scrubber bar is a visual representation of the timeline for a clip, a group of clips, or your movie (depending on what you have selected).

- **Timecode**—The precise location of the Playhead is shown by the timecode that floats next to the Playhead. As its name implies, the timecode provides information about the time aspects of a clip or movie. Timecodes appear in the following format:

  Minutes:Seconds:Frames

  If a clip or movie is less than a minute, you see only two sets of numbers: Seconds and Frames.

  The Frames part of the timecode is a counter that measures the number of frames in a single second of the clip. Most clips you capture with a camcorder have 30 frames per second, which results in smooth onscreen motion. Within each second of the clip, the frames are numbered from 00 to 29 (for a total of 30 frames). The Frames part of the timecode tells you where in each second of the clip you are. For example, a timecode of 36:21 means the clip is 36 seconds long and has gone 21 frames into the 37th second (so it is actually almost 37 seconds long).

TIP

As you start editing, the timecode becomes very useful, especially when you are able to interpret it immediately. The first few times it can be a bit confusing, but just keep remembering that the last number in the timecode is the frame number; timecodes will become second nature to you as you gain iMovie experience.

- **Playhead**—The Playhead is a pointer on the Scrubber bar that shows you the relative location of the frame that currently appears in the Monitor. You use the Playhead to determine where you are in a clip or in your movie. As a clip or movie plays, the Playhead moves across the Scrubber bar. You can also drag the Playhead to move in a clip or in your movie.

- **Start Crop Marker/End Crop Marker**—As with most Mac applications, you select the material you want to change in some way (in this case, frames of a video clip) and then perform some action on them, such as cutting them out of a clip. You use the crop markers to select the frames with which you want to work. The Start Crop Marker indicates the first frame you select, whereas the End Crop Marker indicates the last frame in the selection.

- **Selected frames**—The selected frames are indicated by the gold highlighting between the two markers. The action you select is performed on these frames. For example, if you select Cut, the selected frames are removed from the clip or movie.

- **Move to Start**—Clicking this moves you to the start of your movie and unselects any selected clips.

- **Play/Pause**—Click Play to watch and hear selected clips. Click Play again to pause the action. You can also start and stop play by pressing the spacebar.

- **View in Full Screen**—Plays the selected clips in full-screen mode in which you see only the clips; the iMovie interface disappears. Click the mouse button or press the Space bar to exit the full-screen mode.

- **Volume**—This slider adjusts the playback volume. Note that this affects only the current volume of the clip or movie and in no way changes the clip or the movie itself.

Click Play to watch and hear the selected clip. Click Play again to pause the clip. You can also start and stop play by pressing the spacebar. As the clip plays, notice that the Playhead moves across the Scrubber bar.

NAVIGATING CLIPS IN iMOVIE

As you edit, you are constantly moving around a clip to get to specific areas to edit. There are several ways to do this.

Click the Playhead and drag it to the right to move forward in the clip or to the left to move backward in the clip. When you release the mouse button, the Playhead is at the exact position where you left it and you can see the frame indicated by the timecode. Use this method for gross but quick movements in the clip, such as moving from the beginning to the middle.

Figure 17.4
Getting comfortable with iMovie's Editing tools probably won't take very long.

Timecode
Playhead
Selected frames
Start crop marker
End crop marker

Move to Start
Play/Pause
Scrubber bar
View in Full Screen
Volume

You can also move the Playhead much more precisely using the keyboard; this is essential when you get to detailed editing because you can move by increments as small as a single frame. To move the Playhead one frame at a time, use the left- and right-arrow keys. As you probably guessed, the right-arrow key moves the Playhead forward one frame, and the left-arrow key moves you backward one frame.

You can also move the Playhead forward or backward 10 frames at a time by holding down the Shift key while you press the left- or right-arrow keys. This movement is also very useful when you are doing detailed editing because it enables you to quickly move to a precise location in the clip, but you get there more quickly than by moving one frame at a time.

A fast preview technique is to select a clip and fast-forward through it (press ⌘-]) so you get a good idea of what it contains. If it looks as if it contains no usable footage, delete it. If it looks promising, watch it again at regular speed.

EDITING A CLIP

Editing clips is one of the most important tasks you will do. When you edit a clip, you remove everything from that clip that will detract from, rather than add to, your movie. Editing your clips is fundamental to creating good movies.

You can edit clips at any time, but in my opinion you are better off if you edit your clips *before* you place them in a movie. Building a movie from edited clips gets you to a completed movie more quickly because you deal with less unwanted material when you actually build your movie.

When you edit a clip, you select the frames you want to take action on by using the start and end crop markers. You use these markers to select video clips much like you use the mouse or keyboard to select text within a document.

REMOVING FRAMES FROM A CLIP

One of the most fundamental tasks is removing frames from a clip, such as removing them from the beginning or end of a clip. However, you can remove frames from anywhere in a clip with the same steps:

1. Click the clip you want to edit on the Clips pane to select it; the clip appears in the Monitor.

2. Preview the clip and locate a part of the clip that should be removed.

3. Click the End Crop Maker and drag it to the approximate point at which you want to stop removing frames from the clip. When you click the crop marker, it becomes dark blue to indicate it is selected, the Playhead sticks to it, and you see the frame at which both are currently located in the Monitor. The gold bar that appears between the crop markers indicates the frames you have selected. As you drag a crop marker, you can see the frames through which you are moving.

    While the Playhead is stuck to the end crop marker, you can move it one frame at a time by pressing the right-arrow key to add one frame to the selection or by holding down the Shift key and pressing the right-arrow key to add 10 frames to the selection. Similarly, if you press the left-arrow key, you remove 1 or 10 frames from the selection. Use this technique to position the end crop marker on the exact end frame you want to select.

4. Click the Start Crop Marker (it becomes highlighted in dark blue and the Playhead jumps and sticks to it); then drag the start crop marker to the approximate location at which you want to start selecting frames. (If you want to start selecting frames at the first frame, you don't need to move the start crop marker because it is positioned there by default.)

    While the Playhead is stuck to the start crop marker, you can move it one frame at a time by pressing the right-arrow key to remove one frame of the selection or by holding down the Shift key and pressing the right-arrow key to remove 10 frames of the selection. Similarly, if you press the left-arrow key, you add 1 or 10 frames to the selection. Use this technique to position the start crop marker on the exact start frame you want to select.

    The frames you have selected are represented by a gold bar on the Scrubber bar (see Figure 17.5).

Figure 17.5
Selecting frames is the most important step when editing a clip.

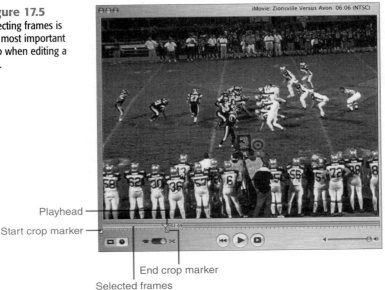

Playhead

Start crop marker

End crop marker

Selected frames

17

5. To remove the selected frames from the clip, select Edit, Cut (⌘-X). The crop markers are reset to the beginning of the clip, and the selected frames are removed from the clip.

> **TIP**
>
> You can also remove frames by selecting them and pressing the Delete key or selecting Edit, Clear. The Clear command removes selected frames without placing them on the Clipboard. Technically speaking, you should use Clear rather than Cut because memory resources aren't wasted by placing the selected frames on your Mac's Clipboard. However, I prefer to use Cut because it has a keyboard shortcut, whereas Clear does not. And practically speaking, you won't notice any performance problems if you leave frames on your Clipboard.

6. Play the clip to see how it is without the frames you just removed. If you don't like the result, you can undo it by selecting Edit, Undo (⌘-Z) and selecting a different set of frames to remove.

7. Preview the edited clip and continue editing it until you have removed all the frames you don't want to include in the movie.

CROPPING A CLIP

You can also crop a clip to remove everything from it except the frames you have selected. This is a good way to remove frames at the beginning and end of a clip at the same time:

1. Use the selection techniques you learned in the previous steps to select the frames that you want to remain in the clip.

2. Select Edit, Crop (⌘-K). The frames that were not included in the selection are removed from the clip.

3. Preview the clip. If you don't like the results of the crop, undo it.

SPLITTING A CLIP

You might want to split a clip so you can work with each part independently. For example, you might want to use one part of the clip at one location in a movie and another part of the clip later in a movie. When you split a clip, the two resulting clips behave just like clips you have created by capturing them from a DV camera or by importing them. Do the following steps:

1. Select the clip you want to split. It appears in the Monitor.

2. Drag the Playhead to the point at which you want to split the clip.

3. Select Edit, Split Video Clip at Playhead (⌘-T). The clip is split into two clips at the point in the clip at which the Playhead was located. A new clip with /1 is appended to the first segment's name and is added to the Clips pane (for example, if the clip's name was Clip 43, the new clip is named Clip 43/1). You can treat the two clips independently because they are now separate clips.

BUILDING A MOVIE FROM CLIPS ON THE CLIPS PANE

After you have done the rough editing of your clips, you can begin creating your movie. You assemble your movie by placing clips on the Clip Viewer in the order you want them to be in the movie.

Click the Clip Viewer button, which is the rectangular shape just under the Scrubber bar, to bring the Clip Viewer to the front (it will probably be in the front already). To begin assembling your movie, simply drag clips from the Clips pane onto the Clip Viewer (see Figure 17.6). Drag them onto the Clip Viewer in the order in which you want them to appear; you can reshuffle them later if you want.

When you select one or more clips on the Clip Viewer, the Monitor shows the clips you have selected. Vertical lines in the Scrubber Bar mark the boundaries of each clip. If you don't have any clips selected, the Monitor shows the contents of all the clips on the Clip Viewer—in other words, your entire movie.

If the Clip Viewer gets full, use its scrollbar to reveal empty space for more clips.

Press Shift-⌘-A to deselect any clips that are selected. Press the Home key to move to the start of your movie. To preview your movie, press the spacebar. Your movie plays. You can use the same movement and editing controls with an entire movie as you can when dealing with an individual clip (such as fast forward). (You can play a single clip again by selecting it on the Clip Viewer.)

Figure 17.6
I have moved clips from the Shelf to the Clip Viewer; the Clip Viewer shows the sequence in which the clips will be played in the movie.

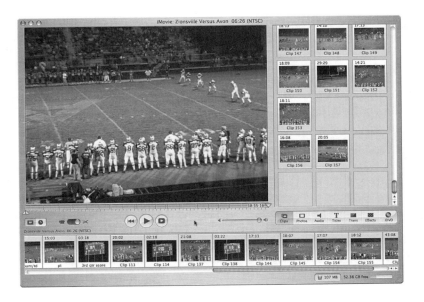

You can change the order of clips by dragging them from one location on the Clip Viewer to another. As you move a clip between two other clips, the clips move apart to show where your clip will be placed when you release the mouse button.

You can remove a clip from your movie and place it back on the Clips pane by dragging it from the Clip Viewer to the Shelf. You can delete a clip by selecting it and then pressing Delete.

To see your movie in full-screen mode, click the Play Full Screen button. Your movie plays back so it takes up the entire screen. This helps you focus on your movie without any distractions from the iMovie interface. To stop your movie and return to iMovie before your movie has finished, click the mouse button or press the spacebar.

Continue placing clips in the Clip Viewer until you have all the clips you want to appear in your movie. You don't have to use all the clips on the Clips pane; you can leave clips there for later use or delete them when you are sure you won't use them in this movie.

ADDING iPHOTO IMAGES TO A MOVIE

You can add your iPhoto images to a movie, or you can create a movie consisting entirely of iPhoto images to create a slideshow. When you add images from iPhoto to a movie, you can configure motion effects for the images you add; in iMovie, these effects are called the Ken Burns Effect. This effect—taken from the treatment of images Ken Burns uses in his excellent documentaries, such as *Civil War*—applies motion and zoom effects to the image. You can configure the effect for each image you add to the movie, from no effect at all to a maximum effect.

NOTE

> When you import images into iMovie, they appear on the Clips pane just like video clips. You add images on the Clips pane to a movie by dragging them to the Clip Viewer.

For all images you add, regardless of whether you choose to use the Ken Burns Effect, you can set the image duration and zoom. The image's duration setting determines how long the image appears on the screen, and the zoom determines which part of the image is displayed.

To add iPhoto images to a movie, perform the following steps:

1. Click the Photos button to open the iPhoto pane.

2. On the Source pop-up menu, select the iPhoto source, such as a photo album, that contains the images you want to add to the movie on the pop-up menu. The images contained in the selected photo album appear in the Preview window in the lower part of the palette (see Figure 17.7). To the right of the pop-up menu the number of images contained in the selected photo album is shown.

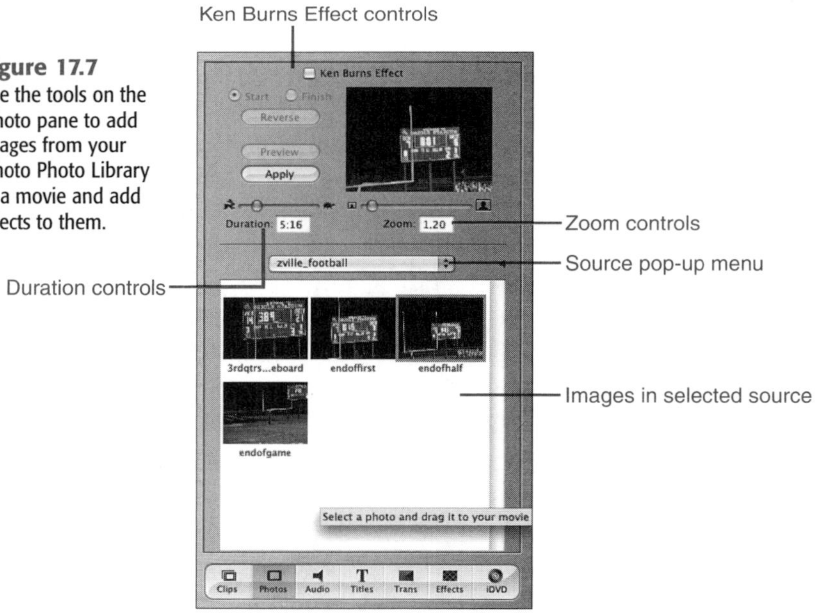

Figure 17.7
Use the tools on the iPhoto pane to add images from your iPhoto Photo Library to a movie and add effects to them.

3. Select the image you want to add to the movie. A preview of the image with the current motion effects appears in the image Preview window located at the top of the pane.

TIP

If you are configuring an image you placed in a movie from the Clips pane, you don't need to do steps 2 and 3. Just select the image in the Clip Viewer before you click the Photos button. When you click the Photos button, the image you selected appears in the Preview window and you can work with it just like an image located in your iPhoto Photo Library.

4. If you want to apply the Ken Burns Effect to the image, click the Ken Burns Effect check box. The Ken Burns Effect controls become active and you see a preview of the image with the effect applied in the Preview window. If you don't check this box, only the Duration and Zoom controls are active.

5. Click the Start radio button. This enables you to configure the starting location of the motion effect. Skip this step if you aren't using the Ken Burns Effect.

6. Use the Zoom slider to set the amount of magnification applied to the image at the start of its clip if you apply the Ken Burns Effect or throughout the image clip if you don't apply the effect. Drag the slider to the left to show more of the photo or to the right to show less of it.

7. Move the pointer over the image in the Preview window. The cursor turns into a hand.

8. Hold down the mouse button and drag the image until the part of the image you want to be shown at the start of the image clip (with the Ken Burns Effect applied) or throughout the image clip (without the effect) is shown in the Preview window.

9. Click the Finish radio button. The image jumps to its ending location and zoom settings.

10. Use the Zoom slider to set the amount of magnification applied to the image at the end of its clip. Drag the slider to the left to show more of the photo or to the right to show less of it.

TIP

You can also enter the zoom and duration values by typing a duration (in the timecode format) or zoom (in zoom amount) directly in their respective boxes.

11. Move the pointer over the image in the preview window. The cursor turns into a hand.

12. Hold down the mouse button and drag the image until the part of the image you want to be shown at the end of the image clip is shown in the Preview window.

13. Use the Duration slider to set the length of time for the image clip. Drag the slider to the left to make the clip shorter (which makes the motion effect faster if you have applied it to the image) or to the right to make the clip last longer (to make the motion effect slower if you have applied it to the image). (If you don't apply the Ken Burns Effect to an image, setting its duration only changes the length of time that image appears onscreen.) When you release the mouse button, a preview of the image and motion effect appears in the Preview window.

14. Click Preview to see the image clip as you have configured it in the Preview window. (If you don't apply the Ken Burns Effect, the Preview button is inactive because there is no point in previewing a static image—what you see is what you get.)

TIP

> If you want the motion effect to be applied in the opposite direction, click the Reverse button. A preview of the motion effect moving in the opposite direction (zooming in instead of zooming out) is shown in the Preview window.

15. Make changes to the image settings until you are satisfied, and then click Apply. The motion effect, duration, and zoom settings are applied to the image, and the image clip is placed at the end of the Clip Viewer. When the image appears on the Clip Viewer, the image is rendered and selected so it appears in the Monitor.

16. Drag the image clip to the location on the Clip Viewer at the point in the movie where you want it to appear.

ADDING TRANSITIONS

The segment between two clips in a movie is called the *transition*. You can use different transitions to smooth the flow from one clip into the next so your series of individual clips doesn't look like a series of clips, but rather a movie that flows smoothly from one scene to the next. All video uses transitions of one sort or another.

The three most common types of transitions are the *Straight Cut*, *Cross Dissolve*, and *Fade To* or *From Black*. The Straight Cut isn't a transition you have to apply; this is what happens when you don't add a transition. A Straight Cut transition occurs when one scene runs right into another. As long as the adjacent scenes are similar enough, the straight cut seems natural and you don't even notice it. The Cross Dissolve, in which one scene dissolves into the next, is also common. This transition can be useful when the adjacent scenes are somewhat similar but different enough that a straight cut is a bit jarring. The Fade To and From Black are two of the more useful transitions. With the fade, one scene fades to black or fades in from a black screen.

iMovie enables you to add a variety of transition effects to your movies with a simple drag and drop.

To get started, open the Transitions pane by clicking the Trans button. The Transitions pane appears and you see the Transitions tools (see Figure 17.8).

The tools on the Transitions pane are the following:

■ **Preview window**—When you select a transition on the list of available transitions, a preview of that transition plays in the Preview window. You can use this to get a quick idea of what the transition looks like. You see the transition applied to the clip you have selected; if you don't have a clip selected, you see that transition applied to the first clip in your movie.

■ **Preview button**—When you click the Preview button, you see a preview of the selected transition in the Monitor. This makes the effect of the transition easier to see because it appears much larger, but it also takes longer to preview.

■ **Update**—You use this button to change a transition that has been placed in a movie. You select the transition clip, use the Transitions tools to make changes to it, and then click the Update button to apply those changes to the transition clip in the movie.

■ **Direction arrows**—When a transition has a directional component, such as a push effect, you use the direction arrows to set the direction of the transition. For example, when you use the Push transition (where one clip "pushes" the previous one off the screen), you click the arrow for the direction in which you want the push to occur.

■ **Speed**—You use this slider to control the amount of time over which the transition effect is displayed. Moving the slider to the left makes the transition last a shorter amount of time. Moving it to the right stretches the transition out so it takes longer to play. After you release the slider, you immediately see the transition in the Preview window.

■ **Available Transitions**—This list shows the transition effects currently available. To work with a transition, select it on the list.

Figure 17.8
Use the Transitions pane to apply transition effects to a movie.

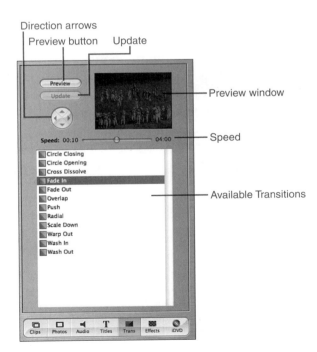

Applying a transition can be done in just a few steps, as the following example of applying a scale down shows:

1. In the Clip Viewer, select the clip after which you want the scale down transition to appear and move the Playhead to the end of the clip.

2. Click Scale Down to select it and then watch the preview in the Preview window.

3. Set the transition's duration with the slider; try placing the slider in the middle of its range. If that is too long or too short, use the slider to set the proper amount of time for the transition.

4. When the timing looks close, click Preview to see how it looks on the Monitor.

5. After you are satisfied with the transition, drag the transition from the Transitions palette to the Clip Viewer and drop it between the two clips you want to transition between. The transition appears as a green box with arrowheads that indicate the direction of the transition (see Figure 17.9).

Figure 17.9
Adding a transition is similar to adding a clip; the main difference is that transitions have to be rendered.

Rendering progress ⎤   Transition clip

Transitions are fairly sophisticated effects and require your Mac to do a lot of work to apply them to a clip. This process is called *rendering*. When your Mac renders a clip, it applies the proper amount of transition effect to each frame of the affected section of the clip. Applying a complex transition with a long duration can take a while. Fortunately, you can continue to work while your Mac renders transition effects.

When you place a transition on the Clip Viewer, your Mac immediately begins to render it; you see the small rendering progress bar at the bottom of the transition clip (refer to

Figure 17.9). When the rendering process is complete, the progress bar disappears. While a transition is being rendered, you can preview the transition or move on to something else.

If you want to make adjustments to the transition, select it in the Clip Viewer and either use the time slider on the palette to change its duration or use one of the transition's other controls to adjust it. Click Update to apply the change to the transition. (The clip will be rendered again.)

NOTE

You can place two transitions adjacent to one another. For example, to have one clip fade out and then the next fade in, place a Fade Out and a Fade In between two clips.

Don't feel as though you need to have a transition before and after every clip. Sometimes the default Straight Cut works just fine. This is where your creativity comes in, so experiment until you achieve an outcome that is pleasing to you.

TIP

You can play only portions of your movie by selecting the clips you want to play in the Clip Viewer (including transitions). When you press the Play button (or the spacebar), only the selected parts of your movie play. This saves time and helps you focus on particular parts of your movie. To play the whole movie again, deselect all the clips by pressing Shift-⌘-A.

ADDING TITLES

When it comes to titles, credits, and other text, your iMovie movies can certainly hold their own. You can add many title effects to your movies in almost limitless ways. You will be amazed at how much improvement you can make to your movies with the right title effects.

Although adding onscreen text is called *titling*, this term refers to much more than just the movie's name. Basically, titling is iMovie's term for overlaying all sorts of text on the screen. The titles you might want to use in your movies include the following:

- **Captions**—As with figure captions, you can use clip captions to add information to the image onscreen. You might want to add some explanation of what is happening on the screen or the date on which the clip was captured; you can even add subtitles if you want. *Captions* is the term for basically any informative text relating to a scene that you want the viewer to see. Captions can appear anywhere in your movie.

- **Credits**—I'm sure you are familiar with credits because most modern movies have several minutes of credits at the end. Credits are just what the term implies: the opportunity to take, or give, credit for something in the movie. For example, you can list all the people who appear in the movie. Or, if someone helps you with the movie, you might want to give him some fame by mentioning his name. Even though you can use credits anywhere in the movie, most credits appear at the end.

■ **Titles**—Titles are text that can introduce a movie, a scene, or anything else you think warrants an introduction. Titles normally appear at the beginning of something, whether it be a movie or scene.

iMovie provides various titling tools you can use to add almost any type of text to your movie. Titles are added using tools similar to the Transitions tools. You add and manipulate titles using the Titles pane. Click the Titles button to open the Titles pane (see Figure 17.10).

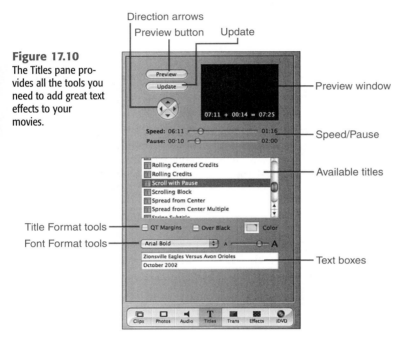

Figure 17.10
The Titles pane provides all the tools you need to add great text effects to your movies.

The following tools are included on the Titles pane:

■ **Preview window**—This works just as it does on the Transitions pane. When you click a title style, you see a preview of it in the preview window. You also see a preview whenever you make changes to the title.

■ **Preview button**—When you click this, you see a preview of your title in the Monitor.

■ **Update button**—If you make changes to a title you have already placed in your movie, click this button to update the title to include the changes you have made.

■ **Direction arrows**—Some styles involve motion for which you can set the direction. You select a direction by clicking one of the active direction arrows.

■ **Sliders**—Just like transitions, all titles have a set amount of time that it takes for the title effect to occur. You use the duration sliders to set this time. The Speed slider controls the overall length of the text effect. The Pause slider determines how long a text effect pauses on the screen (if applicable), and the Wave slider controls the amount of the wave (if applicable).

- **Title style**—You click a title style to use it. The tools that are active on the palette change, depending on the style you select.

- **QT Margins check box**—A QuickTime movie has proportions different from a standard TV screen. For title styles that appear on the bottom edge of the screen, this can be a problem because those titles can get cut off when the movie is viewed on a TV. Unchecking the QT Margins check box moves the title up on the screen so it won't be cut off when you show the movie on a TV. Checking it moves the title back down again so it appears in a better location on the screen when viewing the movie in the QuickTime Player. You should leave this unchecked unless the style you use leaves text at the bottom of the screen. The only styles for which you need to use this are Music Video and Stripe Subtitle.

- **Over Black check box**—By default, when you place a title, it's applied over the selected clip on which you drop the title. When you place the title on a clip, the clip might be split in such a way that there are two clips. One contains the title effect, and the other contains the remainder of the clip. If you want the title to appear in the first part of the clip, drop the title on the left side of the clip. If you want the title to appear on the end of the clip, drop it on the right side of the clip. The adjacent clips slide apart to indicate where the title clip is placed.

  If you prefer the title to appear over a black background, you can check the Over Black check box. Instead of being applied to a clip in your movie, the title appears in a new black clip that is added to your movie wherever you drop the title.

- **Color button**—Click this to change the color of the text in the title (it also affects the stripe color in Stripe Subtitle).

- **Font Family menu**—You can select a font family for a title using this pop-up menu.

- **Font Size slider**—This slider enables you to make the selected font larger (drag it to the right) or smaller (drag it to the left).

- **Text blocks**—You type the text for your title in the text blocks that appear on the palette. You see two or more styles of text block, depending on what style you use. Most styles use single lines of text, but others use a larger text block into which you can place a fair amount of text.

- **Add/Remove buttons**—Some styles allow you to add text blocks to the title. When the Add button (the +) is active, click it to add text blocks to your title. Click Remove (the –) to remove text blocks.

You see different tools and options on the palette, depending on the title style you use. Some styles (for example, Centered Multiple) enable you to add more lines or blocks of text. With these styles, the Add button is active. Other styles (for example, Scrolling Block) involve motion for which you can set the direction; the direction arrows are active for these types.

Following are the general steps you use to add titles to your movies:

1. Decide which type of text you want to add (caption, credit, date, or title) and to which clip you want to apply the text (or whether you want to apply it to a black background).

2. Based on the type of text you add and where you apply it, decide on a title style to use.

3. Open the Titles pane and click a title style to select it.

4. Type your text in the text boxes for that style. Use the Add button (if available) if you want to add more text blocks to the title.

5. Select a font, color, and size for the title.

6. Set the direction of the motion (if applicable).

7. Set the speed, pause (if applicable), and wave (if applicable) of the title.

8. Preview the title in the Preview window, and click the Preview button to preview it in the Monitor.

9. Make adjustments to the title until it is right.

10. Place the title in your movie by dragging it to the Clip Viewer.

11. View the section of your movie that contains the title to ensure it works the way you want it to.

12. If it doesn't, select the title and make changes to it using the Titles pane; then click Update to update the title.

Even though you do most of these steps, you might choose to do them in a different order than I suggest. Just experiment to find the order that suits you best.

Just as the transitions effects have to be rendered before they can be added to your movie, titles must be rendered before they appear onscreen. Rendering can take a while, so use the Preview function to get your titles in great shape before you actually add them to your movie. Just as with transition effects, you see a red progress bar in the title clips as they are rendered. If you update a title, its clip must be rerendered.

NOTE

> Sometimes, existing transitions block you from adding a title clip. If this happens, delete the transition, add the title clip, and after the title has been rendered add the transition back in. If you are going to use many titles in your movie, adding the titles before you add transitions might be easier.

ADDING SPECIAL EFFECTS

You can add all sorts of interesting visual effects to make your movie look better and even more interesting.

MAKING A CLIP PLAY IN REVERSE

You can make a clip play in reverse in your movie. Why would you want to do this? There are several possible reasons. One is for comedic effect. Another might be to create an instant replay type of effect (you will want to increase the speed of the clip to do this, and you learn how later in this section). Do the following:

1. Select the clip you want to play in reverse.

2. Select Advanced, Reverse Clip Direction (⌘-R). On the Clip Viewer, a direction arrow appears indicating that the clip plays from right to left.

> **N O T E**
>
> Reversing a clip also reverses its audio. You can mute the audio of any clip, as you will learn later in this chapter.

The first scene of the clip becomes the last one in the movie, and the thumbnail view you see becomes the last frame (which is now the first frame).

> **N O T E**
>
> A transition impacts the clips to which it is attached. If you reverse a clip that has an attached transition, a warning dialog box appears and tells you that reversing the clip invalidates the transition. It then asks whether you want to rerender the transition. If you proceed with the reversal, the affected transitions are rerendered.

You can restore a clip to its proper direction by selecting it and using the Reverse Clip Direction command again.

APPLYING SPECIAL EFFECTS TO YOUR MOVIE

The Effects pane contains a number of other special effects you can apply to your clips (see Figure 17.11).

The Effects pane includes the following tools:

- **Preview window**—When you select an effect, you see a preview of it in the Preview window.

- **Preview button**—Click this button to see a preview of the selected effect in the Monitor.

- **Apply**—Click this button to apply the selected effect to the selected clip.

- **Effect In**—The Effect In slider controls the number of frames over which the effect is applied. When the slider is all the way to the left, the effect is applied in full force from the start of the clip. As the slider is moved to the right, the effect fades in and is applied gradually over the time selected on the slider up to the maximum amount of time on the slider (10 seconds). For example, if you wanted to apply the black-and-white effect to a clip surrounded by two color clips, you might want the color of the clip to slowly fade away so the transition to black-and-white isn't jarring.

- **Effect Out**—The Effect Out slider controls the time over which the effect fades out. When the slider is all the way to the right, the effect remains in full force until the end of the clip. As the slider is moved to the left, the effect begins to fade out from the point at which the slider is set (the maximum amount is 10 seconds before the end of the clip).

- **Available Effects**—This area contains the list of effects from which you can choose. You can use the scroll tools to see all the available effects.

- **Configuration tools**—Various sliders appear when you select certain effects; these sliders enable you to change some aspect of the effect. For example, when you select the Ghost Trails effect, you see three sliders that enable you to configure that effect. Some effects don't have configuration tools; these effects are either on or off.

Figure 17.11
You can use the Effects pane to apply a variety of special effects to your clips.

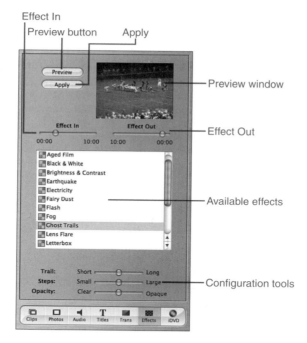

The Effects pane is a bit different from the Transitions and Titles tool panes. The tools on the Effects pane are related to each other only in that they are effects you apply to the video track. This differs from the tools on the Transitions pane, for example, on which all the tools are related to creating transitions.

EXPLORING THE iMOVIE EFFECTS

Although they do different things, all these effects work similarly—after you use some of them, you can easily use all of them. Table 17.1 lists the effects on the default Effects pane and provides some examples of when you might want to apply them.

TABLE 17.1   iMOVIE SPECIAL EFFECTS TOOLS

Effect	What It Does	When to Use It
Adjust Colors	Enables you to adjust the hue, color, and lightness of a clip.	When a clip has poor color or seems somewhat dingy
Aged Film	Makes the clip look old by adding scratches, jitters, and other artifacts that appear in video captured with old cameras.	For artistic effects
Black & White	Converts a clip into black-and-white.	For artistic effects
Brightness & Contrast	Enables you to adjust the brightness and contrast of a clip.	When a clip is too dark, too bright, or has poor contrast.
Earthquake	Causes the clip to "shake."	For artistic effects
Electricity	Causes an "electric" line to appear at the top of the clip as if it is being hit by lightning or a Tessla Coil.	For artistic effects
Fairy Dust	Causes a trail of "fairy dust" to move across the screen.	For artistic effects
Flash	Makes a flash of light wash out the clip for a time.	For artistic effects
Fog	Shrouds the clip in digital fog.	For artistic effects
Ghost Trails	Causes the clip to be ghosted so objects are trailed by faint copies of themselves as they move.	For artistic effects
Lens Flare	Causes a spot of light to appear as if the camera were pointed toward the sun when the clip was captured.	For artistic effects
Letterbox	Places black bars at the top and bottom of the screen to simulate the Letterbox format. This effect actually cuts off the top and bottom part of the clip rather than reformatting it into the true letterbox format.	For artistic effects

17

TABLE 17.1 CONTINUED

Effect	What It Does	When to Use It
Mirror	Makes the clip appear with a mirror image of itself.	For artistic effects
N-Square	Makes the clip play in each of multiple squares on the screen; you set how many squares appear onscreen.	For artistic effects
Rain	If rainy days and Mondays get you down, you won't like this one.	For artistic effects
Sepia Tone	Applies a wood grain texture to the clip.	For artistic effects (often used to make a clip appear as if it were filmed in the past)
Sharpen	Adjusts a clip's sharpness.	When a clip is too fuzzy
Soft Focus	Applies a blur to the images in a clip.	For artistic effects

N O T E

Be careful about using the Brightness & Contrast controls on your clips. The relative brightness levels of video can vary depending on the device you use to show your movie. For example, you might find that a clip appears slightly darker in iMovie than it does when you export it to videotape. Thus, if you make it brighter in iMovie, it might appear washed out when you view it on a TV. You should do some testing on your setup and how you will view your movie (such as exporting a sample to videotape) before you make many of these adjustments.

APPLYING EFFECTS TO CLIPS

The general steps to apply a special effect are the following:

1. Select a clip to which you want to apply an effect.
2. Select the effect you want to apply.
3. Set the time it takes for the effect to be applied and the time over which it disappears.
4. Use the effect's other controls to adjust that effect's properties, while previewing the effect along the way.
5. Apply the effect to the clip.

You change a clip that has an effect applied to it by updating the effect:

1. Select the clip that has an effect applied to it. You then see the clip in the Monitor.
2. On the Effects pane, select the effect you want to change and use the Effects tools to configure it.
3. Click Apply, and the effect is applied to the clip; the clip is rendered again.

When you apply an effect to a clip, iMovie renders that clip using the effect you apply. However, it also saves the original clip so you can go back to it if you want:

1. Select the clip that has an effect applied to it.

2. Select Advanced, Restore Clip. The clip is restored to its previous condition.

You can restore a clip only until you empty the iMovie Trash. This is because the original version of the clip is stored in the Trash when you apply an effect to it. When the original version is removed from iMovie (by emptying the Trash), it is no longer available to be restored. Don't empty the iMovie Trash until you are sure you won't want to restore any of the modified clips to their original conditions.

iMovie's effects are interesting and fun to apply. Here are some more tips about effects:

■ You can apply multiple special effects to the same clip. When you apply two or more special effects to the same clip, the number of effects you have applied is indicated by the number next to the special effects icon.

■ If you apply multiple special effects to a clip and want to restore it to its original condition, you have to use the Restore Clip command once for each effect you applied to the clip to get it back to its original condition. For example, if you applied two effects to a clip, you must use this command twice to restore the clip to its original state.

■ As with transitions, you shouldn't add special effects just because you can—which might be a temptation because they are fun to play with. A few special effects go a long way.

Working with the Timeline Viewer

To this point, you have used only one of iMovie's two viewers. The Clip Viewer is a good place to focus on the video track of your movie. But as you get into finer levels of detail in the editing process and start working with audio, you switch over to the Timeline Viewer. This view provides a more detailed view of your movie, and you "see" all the tracks that make up your movie.

To switch to the Timeline Viewer, click its button (it has a clock icon) to see the Timeline Viewer (see Figure 17.12). This viewer looks more complicated than the Clip Viewer, and it is. This complexity enables you to do lots of great things, especially with your movie's audio track.

The Timeline Viewer has the following tools:

■ **Timeline Viewer**—This viewer shows all the details of a movie's contents and enables you to configure them.

■ **Video track**—The top track on the Timeline Viewer displays the video track for the movie. You can see each clip in the movie, including video clips, transitions, and titles. This information is exactly the same as in the Clip Viewer, although it looks a bit different. The video track also includes the audio that is part of the video.

Figure 17.12
The Timeline Viewer enables you to see all the tracks in your movie.

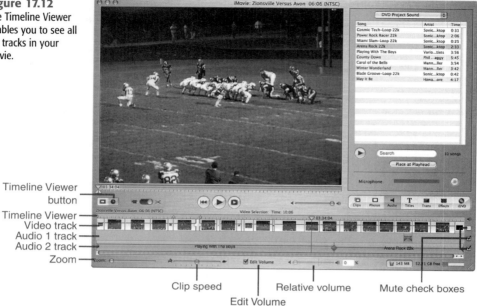

Timeline Viewer button
Timeline Viewer
Video track
Audio 1 track
Audio 2 track
Zoom

Clip speed
Edit Volume
Relative volume
Mute check boxes

- **Audio 1 track**—You can place any sound on the Audio 1 track, including sound effects, sound you record, and music. The sound on the track is represented by blue blocks when the sound is a sound effect or by an orange bar when the sound is recorded sound or music.

- **Audio 2 track**—The Audio 2 track is the same in function as the Audio 1 track. Its purpose is to make working with multiple sounds easier because you can separate sounds on the audio tracks to make them easier to manipulate.

- **Zoom**—You can select the magnification of the Timeline Viewer using the Zoom slider. When the slider is to the left, you see more of the movie's timeline but the elements you see are smaller and more difficult to work with. When you move the slider to the right, you zoom in and can see elements in greater detail. As you edit a movie, you can use this slider to change the view to be appropriate for the task you are doing. For example, when you are synchronizing sound, you might want a close-up view so you can position objects in precise relative positions. When you are recording sound from an audio CD, you might want to see more of the movie to see how much longer the sound you are recording will play relative to the movie's length.

- **Clip Speed**—This slider enables you to change the speed at which a clip plays. Moving the slider to the left (toward the rabbit) makes the clip play more quickly and provides a fast-forward effect. Moving the slider in the other direction (toward the turtle) makes the clip play more slowly in a slow-motion effect. When the slider is in the center, the clip plays at its original speed.

■ **Edit Volume**—When this check box is checked, a line representing the volume level of an audio clip appears in the clip. You can change the volume level of the clip by moving the line up or down at various points. For example, to fade the sound out, you drag the line to the bottom of the clip. The angle of the line indicates how rapid the fade out is. You can change the volume at multiple points in any clip.

■ **Relative Volume**—This slider and text box enable you to set the relative volume of clips. For example, you might want narration in your movie to be louder than the music score. You move the slider or enter a percentage in the box to set the relative volume levels of various audio elements. Unlike the Volume slider in the Monitor, this slider does change the movie. It is called Relative Volume because you change only the relative volume levels of elements in your movie, not the actual volume of the movie itself (which is controlled by the viewer when your movie is played).

■ **Mute check boxes**—The Mute check boxes determine whether the audio contained in a track is audible or silent. When a track's Mute box is checked, the sound contained in that track is heard. Conversely, to mute a track's sound, you uncheck its Mute box.

NOTE

You can do everything on the Timeline Viewer that you can on the Clip Viewer. You click a clip to select it. The clip is highlighted in blue, and then you can apply effects, transitions, and titles to it. You can also edit in the Monitor just as you can when you select a clip on the Shelf or in the Clip Viewer. Use the Clip Viewer when you want to make large changes to your movie, such as placing and moving clips, adding transitions, and so on. For finer work, such as adding sound effects, use the Timeline Viewer.

CHANGING THE SPEED OF A CLIP

One special effect is located on the Timeline Viewer. This is the Clip Speed slider, which you can use to make a clip play more quickly than normal or more slowly than normal.

Using the slider is trivially easy. Select a clip in the Timeline Viewer and drag the slider to change its speed. To make the clip play more quickly, drag the slider to the left. When you play the clip, it plays at the faster speed. It appears as compressed on the Timeline Viewer to show that it requires less time to play than it did originally. To slow down the clip, drag the slider to the right. Now, when you play the clip, it plays more slowly. The clip expands on the Timeline Viewer. Put the slider back in the center to return the clip to its normal speed.

When you apply speed effects to a clip, the fast forward or the play slow symbol appears on that clip in the Clip Viewer.

TIP

> You can combine the direction and speed effects to add an instant replay to your movie. Select the portion of the clip you want to replay and copy it. Paste it twice so you have the three copies of the clip in a row. Select the middle copy and make it play in reverse. Use the Clip Speed slider to make this rewind quickly. When you play this section, it appears as if the clip were rewound at high speed before replaying, thus looking just like instant replay.

USING SOUND IN YOUR MOVIES

Using iMovie, you can create rich, full soundtracks for your movies. You can include four types of sound in your movies, which are the following:

- **Native sounds**—When you import clips into iMovie, any sound that was part of those clips comes in, too. If your clips had sound, you've already heard it numerous times while you were assembling your movie from those clips. You can use iMovie tools to control some aspects of your movie's native sounds.

- **Sound effects**—You can add sound effects to your movie to bring it to life. You can use iMovie's built-in sound effects, and you can import other sound effects to use.

- **Narration and other recorded sound**—If you want to explain what is happening in a movie or add your own commentary, you can record narration for your movie. You can also use the narration tool to record sounds from a tape player or other audio device.

- **Music**—The right music makes a movie a better experience. You can import music to your movies from many sources, such as your iTunes Music Library, audio CDs, MP3 files, and so on.

You use the Timeline Viewer to control the audio portion of your movie. As you saw in an earlier section, the Timeline Viewer enables you to see all the tracks that are part of your movie.

Each track on the Timeline Viewer is used to create and edit one of the three audio tracks you can have in your movie. The top track displays the native sound in your clips. Typically, the Audio 1 track is used for sound effects and narration, and the Audio 2 track is used for music. Functionally, there is no difference between these tracks, and you can use them however you want.

The tracks you see are all time-based views of your movie. The left side of the tracks represents the beginning of your movie, and the right side represents the end. You also see the Playhead, which works the same way it does in the Clip Viewer and the Monitor. For example, you can move it in the same ways, and the timecode shows its location in the movie. The frame at which the Playhead is currently located appears in the Monitor window.

You use the tools on the Audio pane to work with a movie's soundtracks (see Figure 17.13).

Figure 17.13
You can use the
Audio pane to add
sound to a movie.

This pane includes the following tools:

- **Source pop-up menu**—This pop-up menu enables you to select the source of sound you want to use. Its three fundamental options are iTunes Library, which lets you access the music and sounds you have stored in iTunes (you can select a playlist to work with the songs it contains); iMovie Sound Effects, which enables you to add sound effects to a movie; and Audio CD, which enables you to record audio from a CD.

- **Sounds in selected source**—When you select a source on the Source pop-up menu, the sounds contained in that source are listed in the center part of the pane. For example, when you select a playlist, the songs in that playlist are shown. You can select a sound (such as a song or sound effect) to work with it.

- **Play**—Click this button to hear a sound you have selected.

- **Search tool**—Use this tool to search for sounds. As you type text in the Search box, the list of sounds is reduced to include only those items that contain the text you type.

- **Place at Playhead**—When you select a sound and click this button, that sound is inserted at the current location of the Playhead.

- **Recording tool**—You can use this tool to record sound, such as from a microphone connected to your Mac. An obvious use of this tool is to add narration to a project. However, you can also connect other devices, such as a tape recorder, to record sound from that source.

WORKING WITH NATIVE SOUND

Your movie probably has some sound that came with the video clips. If you recorded your clips with a DV camcorder, these sounds are whatever you recorded, for better or worse. Each clip has its own soundtrack, which is what you see represented in the Native track of the Timeline Viewer. The bars you see show the beginning and end of each audio clip (and by no coincidence, each video clip).

MUTING NATIVE SOUNDS

The most basic change you can make is to mute the Native track so you don't hear any of its sounds. To mute the Native track, uncheck the Mute check box located on the right end of the Native track. Now when you play your movie, you don't hear any Native sound from it. To hear the native sounds again, check the Mute box.

CHANGING RELATIVE VOLUME LEVELS

Because your clips probably came from different sources or were recorded under different conditions, the sound level from one clip to the next might vary quite a bit. Although some variation is natural (you expect the roar of a jet plane to be louder than a cat walking across the road), too much variation (or the wrong variation, such as if the cat is louder than the airplane) can be annoying or distracting.

Use the Relative Volume slider to set the relative sound levels of the various sound clips on the Native track:

1. On the Native track (the top track on the Timeline Viewer), select a clip that should be at the average volume level of your movie; after you do so, the clip's bar on the track is highlighted in blue to show it is selected.

2. Make sure the Relative Volume slider is set to the 100% position, which is marked by a vertical line through the slider. This sets the volume level of the selected clip at the average level.

> **TIP**
>
> You can also set the relative volume levels as percentages by typing a number in the percent box next to the slider. The position of the slider is always indicated by the percentage displayed in the box. When you move the slider, the percentage changes, and when you input a percentage, the slider moves accordingly.

3. Select another clip in the Video track.

4. Use the Relative Volume slider to set its volume relative to the average clip you selected in step 1. If you want the sound of the selected clip to be louder than the sound level of your average clip, drag the Relative Volume slider to the right of the 100% position; you can make the sound as loud as 150% of the average sound. If you

want it to be quieter, move the slider to the left of the 100% position. Or, if you want it to be about the same, leave the slider in the 100% position, which is the default for all sound.

5. Repeat steps 3 and 4 for each clip in the Video track.

6. Preview your movie to hear the results of your work. Hopefully, all the sound makes sense. Loud sounds should be loud and quiet sounds should be quiet. If not, continue with the previous steps until the native soundtrack is what you want it to be.

> **TIP**
>
> You can change the relative sound levels for several clips at once by holding down the Shift or ⌘ key while you select the clips. With the clips selected, move the Relative Volume slider. The relative volume of all the selected clips is set at the level you choose.

FADING SOUNDS

You can use iMovie's Edit Volume tool to make the sound of a clip fade in or out smoothly. If you make a clip's sound fade in, it starts completely silently and smoothly increases to the level you set. Similarly, if you fade out a sound, its volume smoothly becomes quieter until by the end of the clip, when it has faded to silence.

> **NOTE**
>
> If you add a Fade Out or Fade In transition to a clip, its sound also fades, so you don't need to use the Edit Volume tool to fade the sound for that clip.

To fade sound, perform the following steps:

1. Select the sound clip you want to fade, such as one of the clips on the Video track that contains sound.

2. Check the Edit Volume check box. The Volume Level bar appears through each clip in the track you selected (see Figure 17.14). This line represents the volume level at each point in each sound clip in that track. By default, this line is at the 100% position (relative position, that is).

3. Click the Volume Level bar at a point at the end of the clip whose sound you want to fade out. A handle (a yellow dot) appears, and a segment of the Volume Level bar is highlighted in yellow to indicate which portion of the clip will be affected by the change you make. A smaller dot appears at the start of the segment to show you where the fade will begin.

> **TIP**
>
> Getting a marker to appear exactly where you want it to be can be difficult. If the Volume Level bar moves at the start of the next clip instead of the end of the one you are trying to fade, you clicked in the wrong clip. Press ⌘-Z to undo the marker creation and try again.

Figure 17.14
You can use an audio clip's volume level bar to set its volume at any point.

Volume level bar

4. Drag the yellow handle until it is at the bottom of the clip; this represents the zero volume level. A nice fade out effect is created, and the clip's volume smoothly fades out at the end of the clip.

> **TIP**
>
> Instead of dragging the marker, you can use the Relative Volume slider to set the location of the marker, or you can type a percentage in the percentage box (such as 0 to make the sound silent).

5. Move to the beginning of clip whose sound you want to fade in.
6. Click the Volume Level bar at the beginning of the clip; a marker appears.
7. Drag the handle to the bottom of the clip, move the Relative Volume slider all the way to the left, or type **0** in the percentage box. The clip's sound is now silent at the start.
8. Click the Volume Level bar at the point at which you want the clip's volume to reach its 100% level. Another handle appears.

> **TIP**
>
> Before you can move a marker, you must select it. When a marker is selected, it is yellow. When it isn't selected, it is purple.

9. Drag the handle to the 100% point, move the Relative Volume slider to the 100% line, or type **100** in the percentage box. The clip's sound now fades in smoothly (see Figure 17.15).

Figure 17.15
You can use the volume level bar to set the sound level of an audio clip.

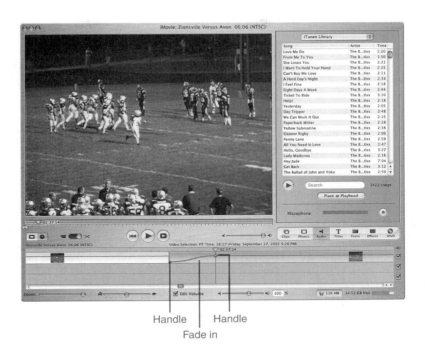

Handle | Handle
Fade in

NOTE

To remove a marker (thus returning the Volume Level bar to its previous location), select the marker and press the Delete key.

EDITING A CLIP'S NATIVE SOUND

As you learned when you began editing clips, whatever you do to a clip's video, you do to the clip's sound. This works the other way, too; changing the sound affects the video—unless you extract the sound from the clip (you learn how to do this in the next section). You should play each clip and listen carefully to its sound. Crop or trim the clips as needed to eliminate sounds you don't want or to include sounds you do want (without messing up the video).

EXTRACTING A CLIP'S NATIVE SOUND

You can extract the audio portion of the clip to work with it independently from the video clip. Extracting the audio from a clip also enables you to move it relative to the video clip. This is useful if you don't want to use all the audio but want to keep all the video in a clip.

One of the best uses for the extracting audio feature is when you have a clip containing background music that should be at least somewhat synchronized with the video, such as a ballet performance. You can extract the audio, and then you can edit the video part of the clip without hacking up the music that goes with it. You can then spread the extracted music so the single music clip covers all the video. Although the music might not exactly match what is happening in the video anymore, this is much less distracting than music that jumps around as the edited scenes play.

To extract a clip's sound track, select that clip on the Timeline Viewer. Then select Advanced, Extract Audio. The audio portion of the clip is extracted and placed on the Audio 1 track. When you extract it, it's still in sync with the video clip from whence it came.

After the audio clip is extracted, you can use the audio-editing techniques you've learned about in this chapter to work with it. For example, you can move it around, lock it in place, and so on.

When you extract audio from a video clip, the audio actually is copied to the audio track rather than cut from the video clip. The volume of the audio that is part of the video clip is set to zero so you never hear it again. Does this matter? Not really, but you shouldn't extract an audio clip unless you really need to. Because it is not actually removed from the video clip, your movie file is larger than if you didn't extract the audio (because iMovie carries two versions of that sound around). If you want to mute only a specific audio clip, set its relative volume to zero instead of extracting it.

This also means you can hear the sound of a video clip from which you have extracted the sound by selecting that clip and using the Relative Volume slider to increase the sound of the clip again. You can use this for some interesting sound effects because you can have multiple versions of the sound playing at the same time, with each being slightly out of sync with the others.

TIP

> You can lock audio to a video clip so that when you move the video, the audio goes along for the ride and always remains in sync with the video. When a clip is locked, you see the locked icons. One appears at the beginning of the locked audio, and the other appears at the point at which the audio is locked on the corresponding video clip.

ADDING SOUND EFFECTS TO YOUR MOVIE

One of the more fun aspects of making a movie is adding sound effects to it. You can use the tools on the Audio pane to add sound effects to a movie.

To work with sound effects, open the Audio pane and select iMovie Sound Effects on the Source pop-up menu. The list in the middle of the pane shows all the built-in sound effects. To hear one, click it. The effect you click plays so you can preview it. Continue clicking sounds until you find one you want to use in your movie.

When you find the perfect sound effect, drag the sound effect from the Audio pane and drop it onto the Audio 1 track. When you move it over the track, a yellow line appears on the track where the clip will be placed when you release the mouse button; this line indicates the point at which the sound effect will start playing. In other words, where you place the effect on the track determines where in the movie the effect is heard. When you release the mouse button, a small square appears on the track. This square represents the sound effect you have added (see Figure 17.16). You can work with the sound effect just as you can with the other elements in a track.

Figure 17.16
A sound effect has been added to the movie.

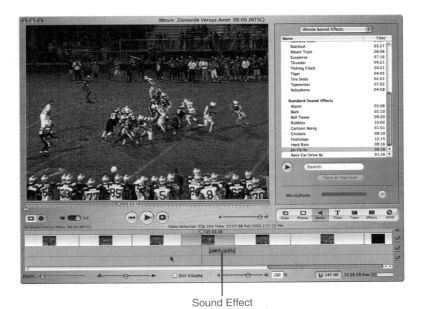

Sound Effect

Drag the Playhead to the left of the sound effect you just placed and press the spacebar to preview it. To move the sound effect, click it to select it (its box darkens to indicate it is selected), and drag it to a new location. When you select the effect, the Playhead jumps to the beginning of the sound effect. At that point, the Playhead sticks to the sound effect, and you can move it frame by frame using the left- and right-arrow keys (hold down the Shift key to move it 10 frames at a time).

When you have the effect positioned so it plays at the perfect point in the video, you should lock it to that spot so that, if you move the video, the sound effect still plays at the right time. To do so, select the effect and select Advanced, Lock Audio Clip at Playhead (⌘-L). You see the locked indicators and, from that point on, the sound stays at the relative location of the Playhead when you used the command.

If you want to move the sound relative to the video track again, select the clip and select Advanced, Unlock Audio Clip (⌘-L).

NOTE

> The Fade and Relative Volume slider controls work on sound effects just as they do on native clips.

You can also overlap sound effects. To do so, simply drag one effect on top of another. At those moments where the sound effects overlap, both effects play. You can more easily manage overlapped sound effects by placing one in the Audio 1 track and the overlapping sound in the Audio 2 track.

TIP

> You can add other sound effects by importing audio files, such as WAV, AIFF, or MP3. When you import a sound file, it is placed on the Audio 2 track at the current location of the Playhead.

RECORDING SOUND FOR YOUR MOVIE

Using the Audio pane, you can record your own sounds to play during your movie. One obvious use for this is to add narration to various parts of your movie.

To record sound from an external source, you need to have some sort of microphone attached to your Mac. Some Macs have built-in microphones; other Macs have microphone jacks (although these sometimes require that you use a PlainTalk microphone). One of the best ways to record sound is to use a USB microphone. To record narration, use a headset-type microphone, such as those included with voice recognition software. Or add a USB sound input device that enables you to connect a standard microphone to it (many headphone-type microphones include such a port).

To record narration or other sound for a movie, perform the following steps:

1. Click the Audio button to open the Audio pane. At the bottom of the pane is the recording tool. It includes an input level monitor and the Record button.

2. Drag the Playhead to the point in your movie at which you want to begin recording.

3. Test your microphone setup by speaking into it or making the other type of sound you will be recording, such as by playing a tape player connected to your Mac. If everything is working, you see a sound level bar in the input level monitor that shows the level of the sound being input. This bar should be moving to levels at least above halfway across the bar, but it should remain in green. If the level gets into the yellow, the input level is probably too high. If it gets in the red, it is definitely too high.

4. Click the Record button (the button with the red dot in it). Your movie begins playing. Speak into the microphone or make the sound you are recording, such as by playing an external audio device. A purple bar appears on the Audio 1 track to represent the sound you are recording. The sound you record is labeled *Voice #*, where # is a sequential number (each time you click the Record button, this number increases by one).

5. When you have recorded all the sound you want, click Record.

6. Edit the recorded sound using the same techniques you use for other sound, such as native sound and music.

ADDING MUSIC TO YOUR MOVIE

A music sound track can help you convey a full range of emotions or simply make your movies more enjoyable to watch. There's just something about music; we love to hear it, even when our main purpose is to watch something.

Because working with music is much like the other sounds you have already learned about, you already understand almost everything you need to know about adding music to one of iMovie's audio tracks. You can use the Audio 2 track to store the music you want to play during all—or parts—of your movie. You can use several different pieces during your movie, or you can have one piece play throughout.

There are three ways to add music to a movie. The easiest way is to use music from your iTunes Music Library. You can record from an audio CD and import music as well. Because using music from your iTunes Music Library is the best way, it is the only one covered in this chapter. Frankly, because iTunes enables you to manage all the music with which you work, you aren't likely to use one of the other methods anyway.

To add music from your iTunes Library to a movie, perform the following steps:

1. Click the Audio button to open the Audio pane.
2. Move the Playhead to the location in the movie at which you want the music to start playing.
3. On the Source pop-up menu, select iTunes Library or select the playlist that includes the music you want to add to the movie. The Content window shows a list of every song in your iTunes Library or the contents of the playlist you selected, respectively.
4. Scroll or search in the Contents pane to find the music you want to add to the movie. Searching works just like it does in other areas.

TIP

> You can double-click a song or select it and click the Play Sound button to hear it. To stop the music, click the Play button again.

5. Click Place at Playhead. The music is imported into iMovie and placed on Audio track 2 at the location of the Playhead. You see the name of the song in the music clip (see Figure 17.17).
6. Play the movie to hear the music playing as the movie does.

MIXING AUDIO TRACKS

After you have added all the audio to your movie, play it. Listen to the individual tracks (use the Mute buttons to turn off tracks) and then listen to how the various sounds interact. Use the editing controls to change the relative volumes of the tracks. For example, your music should be quieter than any sound effects you want your audience to hear. You can use the Relative Volume slider to make this happen.

17

Figure 17.17
The song called "Playing with the Boys" has been added to this movie's soundtrack.

You can also move music and sound effects between the two Audio tracks. This can be especially useful if you want to use part of one track but mute the rest of it. You can drag the sound from one track to the other and mute the track you don't want to hear.

NOTE

> If any of your sound tracks extend beyond the end of your video track, it continues to play while the video track shows a black screen. When you change video after you have added audio, be sure to preview the entire movie again.

The audio tools you learned how to use throughout this section work on all types of audio. For example, you can use the fade tools to fade a song, use the Relative Volume slider to set the relative volume of narration to music, and so on. Use these tools to blend all the sound in the soundtrack together.

One editing tool that hasn't been covered yet is cropping audio. To crop an audio clip, use the following steps:

1. Select the sound you want to crop. It becomes highlighted.

2. Drag the Crop Marker at the end of the audio clip to where you want the sound to stop. The Playhead sticks to the crop marker so you can easily see where it will end (and you can use the Arrow keys to position it precisely). The sound that remains is shown by the darkened area, and the sound that is not selected is indicated by the light part of the sound clip bar.

3. Move the Playhead to the point just to the left of the crop marker.

4. Play the movie to hear where the sound stops.

5. Adjust the crop marker if necessary.

6. Repeat steps 2–5 for the crop marker at the beginning of the sound clip if you want to crop sound from the beginning as well.

7. Select Edit, Crop. The sound outside the crop markers is removed from the clip and the movie. The clip shortens to indicate that the sound has been removed.

TIP

> You don't actually have to use the Crop command if you want to leave the sound clip intact for some reason. Any sound outside a clip's crop markers won't be heard when you play or export the movie. However, you should crop out unused sound clips to save disk space after you are sure you won't need that sound any more.

DISTRIBUTING YOUR MOVIE

17

Watching a movie in iMovie is okay, but iMovie is not really intended to be a viewing application. After you have finished your movie and are ready to release it to the world, you export your movie from iMovie. What you export it to depends on how you want your viewers to be able to watch your movie.

People can watch your movie in three primary ways. You can record your movie on videotape that others can watch with a VCR. You can also export your movie to a QuickTime file that can be viewed on a computer—you then transmit your movie file to others in a variety of ways, including by email, on the Web, or on CD-ROM. The third, and definitely coolest, way is to use iDVD to record your movies on a DVD that can be played in a standard DVD player. The good news is that you can export the same movie using any or all of these methods to get your movie to as many people as possible.

DISTRIBUTING YOUR MOVIE ON VIDEOTAPE

Distributing your movie on videotape offers several benefits. The first is that the quality of your movie appears to be higher because you don't have file size or other technical limitations to deal with (as you do when you want your movie to be viewed on a computer). The second is that almost everyone has access to a VCR and TV, and watching a videotape is easy. A third benefit is that storing a movie on videotape is easy (a tape doesn't hog valuable disk space, for example). Using videotape results in good viewing quality, as well as easy viewing and storage.

The first step to getting your movie on videotape is to export your movie from iMovie to your DV camcorder. This process works similarly to getting clips from the DV camcorder into iMovie.

Follow these steps to export your movie:

1. Connect the FireWire port on your camcorder to the FireWire port on your Mac (this is the same setup you used to import clips from the camcorder into iMovie).

2. Open your iMovie project; the Monitor displays the Camera Connected message.

3. Use the iMovie controls to move the tape in the video camera to the point at which you want to begin recording your movie.

4. Select File, Export.

5. In the Export pop-up menu, select To Camera (it is probably selected already).

6. If you want more than the default 1 second of black to appear before your movie begins and after it ends, increase the value in the Add _ seconds of black before movie and the Add _ seconds of black to end of movie fields.

7. Click Export.

Several things happen, all of which are automatic, so you can sit back and relax. iMovie sets your camcorder to record and then waits a few seconds to ensure that your camcorder is ready. The camcorder begins recording while displaying 1 second (unless you set it to a different amount) of black screen. After the black screen, your movie begins to play and your camcorder records it. A progress bar shows how much longer you have to go (because your whole movie plays, the process takes as much time as your movie is long). You won't hear any sound while your movie is being recorded—this is normal operation.

When your movie is finished, iMovie stops your camcorder. Your movie is now captured on the camcorder; from here on, you can treat it just like any other movie you have recorded. For example, you can connect the camera to a VCR and record your movie to a VHS videotape.

NOTE

> Some DV camcorders enable you to pass through a signal. This means you can output to VCR at the same time you are inputting to the DV camcorder through FireWire. This is good because you can make a first-generation recording directly on the VCR at the same time you record it on your DV camcorder. In fact, you might not even have to record it on the DV camcorder at all. To find out whether your DV camcorder has this feature, connect it to a VCR at the same time as you connect it to your Mac. If you see a picture through the VCR while you export the movie to the DV camcorder, you can pass on through.

DISTRIBUTING YOUR MOVIE ELECTRONICALLY

You can also distribute your movie as a QuickTime file for viewing on a computer. The primary advantage of this method is that it is an easier and much less expensive way to get your movie to many people than using videotape.

The primary disadvantage to viewing your movie on a computer is that the quality is largely dependent on the computer being used and the technical savvy of the person to whom you have sent the movie. (Although it's easy, playing a QuickTime movie requires a bit more knowledge than playing a videotape does.)

The steps to create a QuickTime version of your movie are the following:

1. Select File, Export.

2. Select To QuickTime from the Export pop-up menu. You see the Export Movie window, which now has a Formats pop-up menu. You can use this menu to choose a format in which to export your movie.

3. Click the Formats pop-up menu. You have several options to select for the format of the movie you want to export.

4. Select the format you want to use. The format you select determines the size of the QuickTime file as well as its playback quality.

5. Click Export to see the Export QuickTime Movie dialog box.

6. Name your movie, select a location in which to save it, and click Save.

iMovie begins to export your movie, and a progress bar that gives you an idea of where you are in the process appears onscreen. The Playhead also moves and the movie plays in the Monitor in the background. Unless your movie is really short, the export process takes a long time, so plan on doing something else for a while. Eventually, the progress bar goes away. When it does, you are finished exporting the movie. This QuickTime movie can be viewed just like any other QuickTime movie (for example, in the QuickTime Player or on the Web) .

→ To learn about viewing QuickTime movies, **see** "Viewing QuickTime Movies," **p. 652**.

The only complicated part of this process is choosing the format in which you want to export the movie. When exporting to QuickTime, you must always trade off file size versus quality. The better the quality of your movie, the bigger the file is (and the more resources it consumes to send or store).

When choosing quality and file size, always keep the recipient of the movie in mind. If you know that the person to whom you plan on emailing it uses a 56K modem, keeping the file size small is important. If you are using a CD, maximize quality; it doesn't matter how big the file is (as long as it isn't bigger than the amount of space on the disc, of course).

> **TIP**
>
> You can decrease the size of the QuickTime file by muting soundtracks before you export the movie (muted soundtracks are not exported).

After you have created the QuickTime version you want to distribute, you can distribute it in many ways, including the following:

- Attach it to an email message.
- Post it to a Web site.
- Burn it on a CD.

→ To learn about using Mail to send attachments, **see** "Sending and Receiving Files with Email," **p. 378**.

→ To learn about creating a Web site, **see** Chapter 14, "Putting Yourself on the Web," **p. 423**.

→ To learn about burning CDs, **see** "Finding, Installing, and Using a CD Writer," **p. 790**.

NOTE

> You might want to create multiple QuickTime versions of your movie and distribute it in more than one way.

TIP

> If you select the Expert Settings format option, you can configure custom export settings. Covering these is beyond the scope of this chapter, but at least you know they are available.

EXPORTING YOUR MOVIE TO DVD

Using the iDVD application and a DVD-R drive, you can put your iMovie projects on DVDs that can be played in a standard DVD player.

→ To get an overview of iDVD, **see** Chapter 18, "Watching and Creating DVD Movies," **p. 621**.

The iDVD pane enables you to add chapter markers to a movie and then send a movie to an iDVD project (see Figure 17.18).

Figure 17.18
You can use the iDVD pane to add chapters markers and send a movie to iDVD.

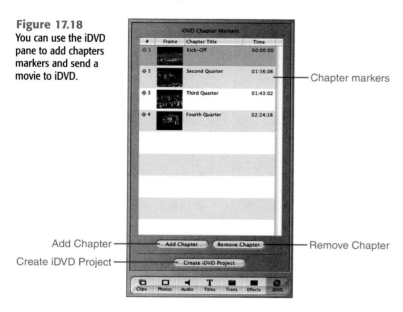

An overview of the tools on the iDVD pane is provided in the following list:

- **Chapter markers**—When you add a chapter marker to a movie, that marker is added to the list of chapter markers at the top of the iDVD pane. In addition to a thumbnail of the frame where the marker is placed, the name of the marker (which is the name of the related button on the chapter selection menu) and the timecode of the frame at which the marker is located are shown.

- **Add Chapter**—This button adds a new chapter marker to the movie at the current location of the Playhead.

- **Remove Chapter**—When you select a chapter marker shown on the list and then click this button, that marker is removed from the movie.

- **Create iDVD Project**—When you click this button, a new iDVD project is created and the current iMovie project is added to it.

To add chapter markers to a movie, perform the following steps:

1. Click the iDVD button to open the iDVD pane.

2. Move the Playhead to the point where you want to place the first chapter marker.

3. Click Add Chapter. The new marker is shown at the top of the iDVD pane. For each marker, the first frame, the chapter title, and the timecode at which the chapter starts are shown.

4. Edit the chapter's title. This is the text that appears next to the chapter on the DVD.

5. Repeat steps 2–4 for each chapter you want to create.

After you have added chapter markers, click the Create iDVD Project button to open iDVD, create a new iDVD project, and add the movie to it.

> **TIP**
>
> You can also add a movie to an iDVD project by dragging the QuickTime reference version from the movie project's folder onto a menu within iDVD.

TROUBLESHOOTING

NOTHING HAPPENS WITH MY CAMERA WHEN I USE IMOVIE

When I connect my digital video camera to my Mac, iMovie is not able to access it or iMovie can't control it.

If you don't see the "Camera Connected" message when you have your digital video camera connected to your Mac while iMovie is open, iMovie is unable to communicate with your camera for some reason.

Check the FireWire cable to ensure that it is plugged in properly. Make sure your camera is turned on and in the output mode.

If these steps don't help, make sure your camera is on Apple's iMovie compatibility list. If it is on the list, a problem might exist with the FireWire port on your Mac; try another device in the port if you can. If your camera is not iMovie compatible, you might need to try a different DV application.

WHY HAS THE DISK GAUGE TURNED RED?

When I'm editing my movie, why does the disk gauge turn red?

This means the volume on which you have stored your iMovie project is getting full and you need to clear more space on the volume on which you are working. Try one of the following actions to get more working room:

- Delete unused clips from the Shelf.
- Select clips to which you have applied special effects and click the Commit button.
- Empty the iMovie Trash.
- Using the Finder, move files off the volume on which your project is stored.
- Move the iMovie project to another volume that has more space.

MAC OS X TO THE MAX: iMOVIE EDITING SHORTCUTS

Table 17.3 lists the name, keyboard shortcut, and a brief description of each iMovie command.

TABLE 17.3   iMOVIE SHORTCUTS

Menu	Command	Keyboard Shortcut	What It Does
iMovie	Preferences	⌘-,	Opens the iMovie Preferences dialog box.
File	New Project	⌘-N	Creates a new iMovie project.
File	Open Project	⌘-O	Opens an existing iMovie project.
File	Save Frame As	⌘-F	Saves the frame currently displayed on the Monitor as an image file outside of iMovie. This enables you to capture frames from a movie as a graphic.
File	Import	Shift-⌘-I	Enables you to import content into an iMovie project, such as graphic files, audio files, and so on.
File	Export	Shift-⌘-E	Enables you to export an iMovie project to videotape, to QuickTime, or for DVD.

Menu	Command	Keyboard Shortcut	What It Does
File	Show Info	⌘-I	Opens the Clip Info window that provides information about a selected clip.
File	Empty Trash	None	Empties the iMovie Trash.
Edit	Select All	⌘-A	Selects all the clips in the Clips pane or on one of the viewers.
Edit	Select None	Shift-⌘-A	Unselects any selected clips; this causes your entire movie to be shown in the Monitor.
Edit	Crop	⌘-K	Removes all frames that are outside the crop markers.
Edit	Split Video Clip at Playhead	⌘-T	Creates two clips from the current clip. The clips are separated at the location of the Playhead when the command is used.
Edit	Create Still Frame	Shift-⌘-S	Creates a still image of the current frame and places that image on the Clips pane, from which you can add it to a movie.
Advanced	Extract Audio	⌘-J	Extracts the audio track from a selected video clip and places it on one of the Audio tracks where it becomes just like any other audio; for example, you can move it on the timeline, crop it, and so on.
Advanced	Paste Over at Playhead	Shift-⌘-V	Pastes selected frames over frames in the selected clip starting at the current location of the Playhead. Use this command to replace some of the video in a clip.
Advanced	Lock/Unlock Audio Clip at Playhead	⌘-L	Locks an audio clip to the current location of the Playhead, such as when you place it at the beginning of a video clip when you want the audio to always remain in sync with the video clip, even if you move the video clip on the timeline. If you select a locked audio clip and use the command, the clip becomes unlocked again.

17

TABLE 17.3   CONTINUED

Menu	Command	Keyboard Shortcut	What It Does
Advanced	Reverse Clip Direction	⌘-R	Causes the selected clip to play in the opposite direction.
Advanced	Restore Clip	None	Causes a clip to which you have applied special effects to be returned to the condition it was in when you imported it into iMovie (except for any edits you made, such as removing frames).
None	Decrease volume	Down arrow	Decreases the playback volume.
None	Fast Forward (Camera mode)	⌘-]	Makes the camera play in fast forward.
None	Increase Volume	Up arrow	Increases the playback volume.
None	Move audio clip backward by 1 frameof audio clips precisely.	Click audio clip; then left arrow	Enables you to move the location
None	Move audio clip backward by 10 frames	Click Audio clip; then Shift-left arrow	Enables you to move audio clips in 10-frame increments.
None	Move audio clip forward by 1 frame	Click audio clip; then right arrow	Enables you to move an audio clip forward by one frame.
None	Move audio clip forward by 10 frames	Click audio clip; then Shift-right arrow	Enables you to move an audio clip forward by 10 frames.
None	Move backward 1 frame	Left arrow	Moves the Playhead back one frame.
None	Move backward 10 frames	Shift-left arrow	Moves the Playhead back by 10 frames.
None	Move Crop Marker backward by 1 frame	Click crop marker; then left arrow	Moves the selected crop marker back one frame, adding one frame to the currently selected frames if you selected the start crop marker or removing it if you selected the end crop marker.

17

Menu	Command	Keyboard Shortcut	What It Does
None	Move Crop Marker backward by 10 frames	Click Crop Marker; then Shift-left arrow	Moves the selected crop marker back 10 frames, adding 10 frames to the currently selected frames if you selected the start crop marker or removing 10 frames if you selected the end crop marker.
None	Move Crop Marker forward by 1 frame	Click Crop Marker; then right arrow	Moves the selected crop marker ahead one frame, adding one frame to the currently selected frames if you selected the end crop marker or removing it if you selected the start crop marker.
None	Move Crop Marker forward by 10 frames	Click Crop Marker; then Shift-right arrow	Moves the selected crop marker ahead 10 frames, adding 10 frames to the currently selected frames if you selected the end crop marker or removing 10 frames if you selected the start crop marker.
None	Move forward 1 frame	Right arrow	Moves the Playhead forward by one frame.
None	Move forward 10 frames	Shift-right arrow	Moves the Playhead forward by 10 frames.
None	Move Playhead to beginning of clip/movie	Home	Moves the Playhead to the beginning of a clip if a clip is selected or to the beginning of the movie if no clip is selected.
None	Move Playhead to end of clip/movie	End	Moves the Playhead to the end of a clip if a clip is selected or to the end of the movie if no clip is selected.
None	Play/Stop (Edit mode)	Spacebar	Starts or stops playback of either a clip if one is selected or the movie if no clips are selected.
None	Rewind (Camera mode)		Cmd-[Rewinds the camera.
None	Start/Stop Import (Camera mode)	Spacebar	Starts or stops the import process.

17

CHAPTER 18

WATCHING AND CREATING DVD MOVIES

In this chapter

TAKING ADVANTAGE OF DVD ON THE MAC

There are two purposes for which you can put DVD technology to use on your Mac. The first is to enjoy all the great content available in the DVD format, that being everything from your favorite movies and TV shows to documentaries and music videos. Any Mac OS X Macintosh that includes a DVD-ROM drive, which most modern Macs do, can display DVD discs through the DVD Player application. The second, and even more fascinating, way to benefit from DVD is by creating your own DVDs to view on the DVD player in your Mac or on most standard DVD players (those used to view DVD content via a television or home theater system). Macs equipped with a DVD-R or DVD–RW drive, such as Apple's SuperDrive, can use the amazing iDVD application to place content on DVDs. The DVDs you create with iDVD can include motion menus and other great effects so they act just like the latest DVDs from Hollywood. You can place movies you create with iMovie, QuickTime movies, slideshows, and other content on DVD just by dragging and dropping. You can create slideshow content using iDVD, too.

WATCHING DVD MOVIES ON THE MAC

DVD movies are the latest and best way to watch movies. Because they are digital, the image and sound quality of DVD movies is superb. And the digital format enables special features that can't be duplicated with other means, such as videotape. For example, with DVD movies, you can get true 5-, 6-, or even 7-track soundtracks to provide unbelievable surround sound and sound fidelity. Plus, DVDs usually have a lot of features—missing scenes, trailers, and so on.

NOTE

> Watching DVD movies from a desktop Mac is okay, but DVD movies on the Mac really shine when you use a PowerBook or iBook. Forget the crummy selection of movies usually shown on airplanes (when there even are movies) that you can't see or hear anyway. With a DVD-equipped Mac OS X mobile Mac, you can watch movies anytime, anywhere. If you travel a lot, you might find this reason enough to get your own mobile Mac. And waiting for just about anything will never be the same. With a mobile Mac and your favorite DVD, time is never wasted.

Mac OS X supports the playback of DVD movies with the DVD Player application.

USING DVD PLAYER TO WATCH MOVIES

The DVD Player application has the following three windows (see Figure 18.1):

- **Viewer**—This is the window in which you watch the DVD content.
- **Controller**—This window provides the controls for movie playback.
- **Info**—This window provides information about the disc you are playing.

Figure 18.1
With DVD Player, you can enjoy all the amazing content available on DVD, such as complete seasons of your favorite TV shows.

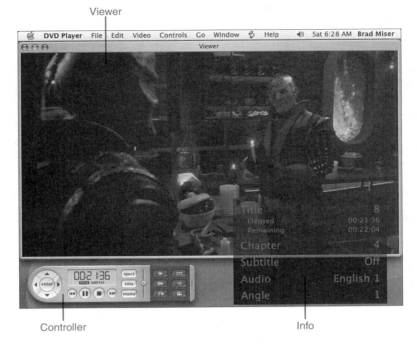

Viewer

Controller

Info

18

NOTE

> If you try to capture screenshots of a DVD using the Mac's built-in tools, such as the Grab application, you won't be allowed to or all you will get is a black screen. To capture DVD content in a screenshot, you need to use the excellent Snapz X Pro on a Mac equipped with an NVIDIA graphics card.

The Viewer window is straightforward. The DVD's content appears in this window; you can choose various sizes for the window from Half Size to Full Screen. In Full Screen mode, the Mac OS interface disappears and you can see only the DVD content and the DVD windows you choose to display.

The Controller window contains the controls you use to watch movies. It has two orientations, which are vertical and horizontal. It is in the horizontal mode by default (see Figure 18.2). You can change the orientation to vertical by selecting Controls, Use Vertical Controller. To change the Controller back to the horizontal orientation, select Controls, Use Horizontal Controller.

The Controller has additional controls in the Control Drawer, which you can close or open (see Figure 18.3). To open or close the Control Drawer, select Controls, Open Control Drawer or Controls, Hide Control Drawer. You can also open or close the Drawer by dragging its resize handle.

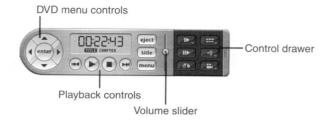

Figure 18.2
The Controller does just what you think: It enables you to control DVD playback.

DVD menu controls

Control drawer

Playback controls

Volume slider

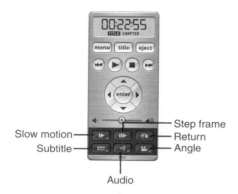

Figure 18.3
The Control Drawer contains controls you aren't likely to use as often as those on the main Controller.

Slow motion

Subtitle

Step frame

Return

Angle

Audio

If you have used a standard DVD player or VCR, the DVD Player controls will be easy to understand. To play and control a movie, use the following steps:

1. Insert the DVD into your Mac's DVD drive. After a moment, the DVD is mounted on the machine. By default, DVD Player opens and begins to play the DVD. Depending on the DVD, the disc's main menu might appear or you might be prompted to select a soundtrack or other features.

 If you see a message about the DVD's region code, see "When I Play a Movie, I See a Message About the Region Code Needing to Be Set" in the "Troubleshooting" section at the end of this chapter.

TIP

> To configure what action your Mac takes when you insert a DVD, use the CDs & DVDs pane of the System Preferences utility.

2. Select the menu option you want, such as Play. The movie begins to play in the Viewer window. In the upper-left corner of the window is text for a moment that shows the control you used most recently (such as Play).

18

TIP

Click in the Information window on the Controller to cycle through the available data, such as chapter, remaining time, and so on. Click the Title or Chapter text to change the display to the related information.

3. Use the commands on the Video menu to control the size of the Viewer. If you select Full Screen, the image becomes as large as possible and the Mac OS interface is hidden. After a designated time passes, the Controller disappears, too.

4. To bring the Controller back, move the pointer, press a key, or press Shift-Ctrl-C.

NOTE

If you minimize the Viewer, it moves into the Dock and the movie continues to play. Unlike QuickTime movies, you can't see the movie in the Dock icon, however.

5. To see information about the movie you are watching, select Window, Show Info. The Info window appears and you can see where you are in the movie and the features that are being used, including subtitles, the angle being shown, and so on (see Figure 18.4).

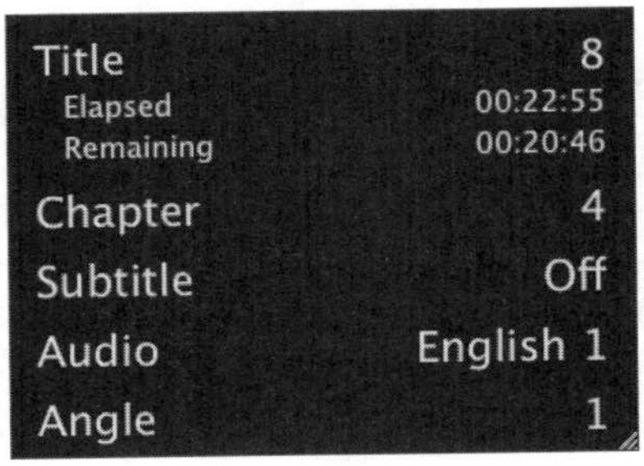

Figure 18.4
The Info window provides information about a movie you are watching.

Title	8
Elapsed	00:22:55
Remaining	00:20:46
Chapter	4
Subtitle	Off
Audio	English 1
Angle	1

TIP

You can resize the Info window by dragging its resize handle.

 If you see the NOT PERMITTED message when you use a control, see "An Action I Try Isn't Permitted" in the "Troubleshooting" section at the end of this chapter.

If you see a green screen when you attempt to view a disc, see "When I View a DVD, I See a Green Screen" in the "Troubleshooting" section at the end of this chapter.

6. To change the orientation of the Info window to better fit a widescreen, select Controls, Use Wide Info Window.

NOTE

Use the commands on the Window menu to show or hide the Viewer, Controller, and Info windows.

7. Use the other controls on the Controller to watch the movie.

TIP

You can also control a movie by pointing to onscreen controls with the mouse.

Following are some other DVD playback notes:

- **DVD menus**—All DVD movies include a menu that provides access to the content of the disc and its special features. You can highlight and select commands on these menus using the keyboard's arrow buttons, using the mouse to point to them, or using the mouse to point to them on the Controller.

- **Use the controls in the Control Drawer to quickly change the movie's settings**—For example, you can control subtitles using the Subtitles button.

- **Scan forward or backward**—When you scan forward or backward, you can control the rate of the scan by selecting Controls, Scan Rate, and then the rate at which you want to scan (such as 8x speed). DVD Player supports scan rates up to 32x, which is really flying.

- **Go menu**—Many commands are available on this menu that you can use to quickly access various areas on the DVD, including the DVD menu, the beginning of the disc, the content you were viewing the last time you played the disc, and so on.

- **Bookmarks**—You can use this feature to mark specific areas of a DVD so you can quickly return to them. When viewing content to which you want to add a bookmark, select Controls, Add Bookmark. In the Add Bookmark dialog box, name the bookmark (the current time is the default name) and click OK. You can return to that bookmark by selecting Go, Bookmarks, *Bookmarkname*, where *Bookmarkname* is the name of a bookmark you have created. Select Controls, Edit Bookmarks to open the Edit Bookmark dialog box, which you can use to change existing bookmarks.

- **Keyboard commands work best**—As you watch movies, you will find that the best way to control them is using the keyboard. Most of the major functions in the player have keyboard shortcuts. For the best DVD experience, learn to use these shortcuts.

→ To learn the many keyboard shortcuts for playback and configuration DVD Player offers, **see** "DVD Player Keyboard Shortcuts," **p. 638**.

CONFIGURING DVD PLAYER

DVD Player is a relatively simple application, but you can do some configuration to make it work the way you want it to. The DVD Player preferences window has four panes: Player,

Disc Setup, Full Screen, and Windows (see Figure 18.5). These preference settings are summarized in Table 18.1.

NOTE

You can't control a movie while the Preferences dialog box is open.

Figure 18.5
You can configure DVD Player using its Preferences dialog box.

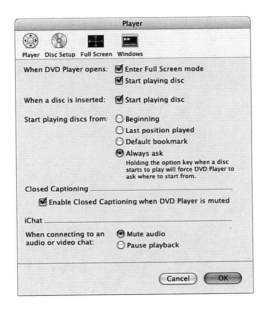

18

TABLE 18.1   DVD PLAYER PREFERENCES

Pane	Preference	Effect
Player	When DVD Player opens: Enter Full Screen mode Start playing disc	These determine which action DVD Player takes when it opens. Because when you watch a movie, it is typically in the Full Screen mode, this preference selects the Full Screen mode when a DVD is mounted on your desktop and DVD Player starts up (which it does by default when a DVD containing movie content is mounted on your Mac). If you want discs to start playing when DVD Player opens, make sure the Start playing disc check box is checked.

TABLE 18.1   CONTINUED

Pane	Preference	Effect
Player	When a disc is inserted: Start playing disc	With this enabled, a DVD starts to play when you insert it into your Mac.
Player	Start playing discs from: Beginning Last position played Default bookmark Always ask	Use these radio buttons to determine where discs start to play. The Last position played is a useful option because a disc resumes playing at the location you last viewed it.
Player	Closed Captioning: Enable Close Captioning when DVD Player is muted	With this option enabled, when you mute a DVD, the Closed Captioning window appears.
Player	iChat When connected to an audio or video chat: Mute audio Pause playback	Use these radio buttons to determine which action DVD Player takes when you enter a chat session.
Disc Setup	Language Audio Subtitle DVD Menu	Use these pop-up menus to determine the default settings for these areas.
Disc Setup	Internet: Enable DVD@ccess web links	Many DVDs offer content on the Web. Use this preference to enable or disable these links.
Disc Setup	Audio Audio output: System Sound Output Digital Out Disable Dolby dynamic range compression	If your Mac supports digital audio out, use the pop-up menu to select Digital Out to take advantage of that output, such as 5.1 digital surround sound. Use the check box to determine whether dynamic range compression is used (this evens out the volume level of a disc).
Full Screen	Viewer Default viewer size: Half Normal Maximum Current Enable view resizing	Select the default size of the Viewer window. If you want to resize the Viewer window by dragging its resize handle, check the check box.

18

Pane	Preference	Effect
Full Screen	Controller Hide Controller If Inactive For __ Seconds	Use this to control the automatic hiding of the Controller when you aren't using it. By default, the Controller is hidden after 10 seconds. You can change this time or turn off the feature if you want to manually hide and show the Controller.
Full Screen	Displays: Dim other displays while playing Remain in full screen when DVD Player is active Disable menu bar (kiosk mode)	If multiple monitors are connected to your Mac, use the Dim other displays while playing check box to cause all the displays except the one on which the DVD is playing to dim. If you want DVD Player to remain in Full Screen mode whenever it is inactive, check the middle check box. By default, DVD Player switches to Maximum Size mode when you move to the Finder or another application. Check the Disable menu bar (kiosk mode) check box if you want to disable the DVD Player menu bar.
Windows	Options Display status information Fade controller when hiding	The status information appears at the top of the Viewer and provides information about what is happening, such as when you press a control. Uncheck the Display status information check box to hide this information. To have the Controller fade slowly out of existence when it hides, check the Fade controller when hiding check box. With this unchecked, the Controller blinks out of existence.
Windows	Floating Overlays: Info display Close Captioning	Use these controls to set the color of information display and transparency of the Info and Closed Captioning windows.

18

NOTE

> Most DVDs that claim to offer DVD-ROM or Web content are not compatible with the Mac. However, you can often open these DVDs via the Finder to access some of this additional content.

CREATING YOUR OWN DVDS

Watching DVDs others create is fun, but because you use a Mac, you aren't limited to taking what others give. With a Mac equipped with a DVD-R drive, such as an Apple SuperDrive, and Mac OS X, you can use the iDVD application to put your own content on DVD. You can view these DVDs on your Mac using the DVD Player application. But even better, you can play the DVDs you create on most standard DVD players, such as the DVD player connected to your TV.

You can place the following two general types of content on DVD:

- Movies you have created with iMovie or QuickTime movies you have created or obtained from other sources
- Slideshows made up of images from iPhoto or other sources

In addition to being able to place this content on DVDs, with iDVD you can create motion menus and buttons that enable you to showcase your content from the DVD's main menu; these menus work just like the menus on commercially produced DVDs.

Unfortunately, iDVD is not part of the standard Mac OS X installation. It is included on all new Macs that have the SuperDrive; otherwise, you have to purchase a copy as part of the iLife package Apple sells. Fortunately, this package sells for only $49 (iTunes, iPhoto, and iMovie are included as well).

Because iDVD is not part of the standard Mac OS X installation (and because if this book gets any bigger, it might be dangerous to lift), I don't have room to provide detailed instructions for working with iDVD. What follows is a brief overview of the application so you have a general idea of how it works.

UNDERSTANDING THE iDVD WINDOW

When you launch iDVD, you see the iDVD window (see Figure 18.6). Similar to iMovie, iDVD automatically opens the last project on which you worked. If you haven't used iDVD before, you can create a new project.

The top and largest pane of the window is the Contents pane. What you see and do in this area depends on the mode in which iDVD is operating (you'll learn more about these modes in the next section). When you are in the Design or Preview mode, the Contents pane shows a menu of buttons on the DVD. Buttons represent each project that has been placed on the DVD, or they can lead to another menu. When viewing a DVD, you click a button to view the content or menu with which it is associated. Each menu can include up to six buttons.

Figure 18.6
Don't let the simple appearance of the iDVD mislead you; iDVD is a powerful application.

Contents pane   Movie, slideshow, and menu buttons

iDVD controls

Each menu also has a theme that determines how the menu looks and sounds. At the most basic, a *theme* is simply a static image that is the menu's background. However, menus can contain motion, which means a movie can play as the menu's background while the menu appears onscreen (if you have watched DVD movies, you have no doubt seen examples of motion menus). Motion menus can include a movie with sound, a movie without sound, or a static image with sound. You can apply one of iDVD's default themes to your menus, and you can create and save your own themes.

Buttons can also have motion, which means the content accessed by that button plays within the button itself while the button is being viewed. This type of motion provides a preview of the content without the viewer having to actually open it. (Again, if you have viewed commercially produced DVD movies, sometimes the chapter buttons contain motion and show you part of the chapter associated with the button).

Along the bottom of the iDVD window is the toolbar that contains six buttons (see Figure 18.7). Each of these enables you to perform a specific task.

The available iDVD buttons are

- **Customize**—This button opens the iDVD Drawer (also called the Customize Panel). You'll learn more about this in the next section.
- **Folder**—This button adds a folder button, which represents a menu on the DVD. After you add a folder, you can place content on the menu that the folder button represents.
- **Slideshow**—This button adds a slideshow to the menu you are currently viewing.
- **Motion**—This button turns background and button effects, called *motion effects*, on or off. When the button is green, motion effects are on and are displayed on the screen. When the button is gray, motion effects are off and aren't displayed.

- **Preview**—When you click this button, iDVD moves into the Preview mode (you'll read more about this mode later in this chapter).

- **Burn**—When you are ready to create a DVD, you click this button to write the project to a DVD.

Figure 18.7
The buttons along the bottom of the iDVD window provide access to its tools.

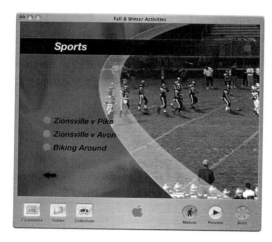

When you click the Customize button, the iDVD Drawer appears (see Figure 18.8). The Drawer contains controls and information you use while you design and build a DVD.

Figure 18.8
The Customize pane enables you customize various aspects of an iDVD project.

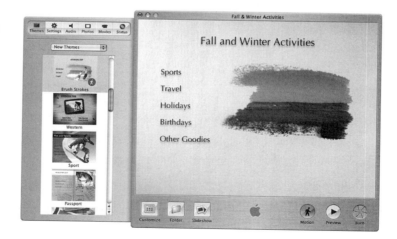

Along the top of the Customize panel are six buttons:

- **Themes**—*Themes* are sets of formatting options you can apply to a menu by clicking the theme you want to use. A number of standard themes are provided with iDVD. You can also create and save your own themes and use them just like iDVD's standard themes.

- **Settings**—The Settings tools enable you to customize the appearance of a menu from adding background images or movies and sound to formatting the menu's title to formatting the buttons' locations and titles.

- **Audio**—You use the Audio tools to access the music stored in your iTunes Music Library. You can add this music as background to any menu on a DVD and you use it to add soundtracks to slideshows on a DVD.

- **Photos**—You use the Photos tools to access the images stored in your iPhoto Photo Library. You can use these images as backgrounds for any menu on a DVD and create slideshows from them.

- **Movies**—You can use the Movies tools to add iMovie and QuickTime movies to a DVD.

- **Status**—The Status tools enable you to assess the status of the content you place on a DVD. This includes both the movies you add to the DVD as well as any other files you want to include on it, such as high-resolution versions of the images contained in a DVD's slideshows. You also use the Status tools to add content to the DVD-ROM portion of a DVD (the additional files that can be used when the DVD is inserted into a computer).

UNDERSTANDING iDVD MODES

iDVD has different modes for different parts of the DVD creation process. The following sections give you an overview of each of these modes.

UNDERSTANDING THE DESIGN MODE

The Design mode is the one in which you add movies and other content to a DVD. You also use this mode when you are designing the look and feel of a DVD by applying background images, background sounds, titles, motion effects, and so on to a DVD on which you are working. Some of the major elements of the iDVD window in the Design mode are shown in Figure 18.9 and explained in the following list:

- **Project title**—The project title is the name under which you save the iDVD project file. This is the name of the file you open to open a project. It does not actually appear when the DVD is viewed.

- **Menu**—The Contents pane of the iDVD window represents a menu that appears onscreen when the DVD is viewed.

- **Menu title**—Each menu can have a title to identify it. You can format menu titles in a variety of ways.

- **Menu background**—Each menu can have an image as its background. Or you can use a movie as a background; when the menu appears onscreen, the background movie plays. You can also add background sounds to any menu.

- **Buttons**—Onscreen buttons represent movies, slideshows, or other menus on a DVD. Buttons can be text; images; or previews of the content to which a button points, such as a movie.

18

■ **Button titles**—Each button is identified by a title. When a button contains an image or a preview, the title appears next to the button; when a button is text only, the button title is the button itself. You can format button titles in a number of ways.

■ **Drop zone**—Some menus contain a drop zone in which you can place images or movies that are displayed while the menu that contains the drop zone is onscreen.

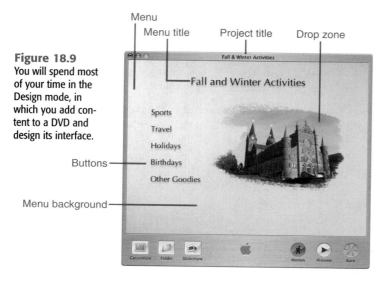

Figure 18.9
You will spend most of your time in the Design mode, in which you add content to a DVD and design its interface.

DVDs that you produce with iDVD, just like those produced commercially, can include multiple levels of menus. Each menu can contain content buttons (such as for movies or slideshows) or menu buttons that lead to other menus. All DVDs contain at least the main menu, which is the menu that appears when the DVD is played. The main menu is also the one that appears when you open an iDVD project.

You can add menus to the main menu and then add submenus to those menus to build a multitiered structure for a DVD.

Each menu can contain up to six buttons, with each button representing either content (a movie or slideshow) or a submenu. A DVD can contain up to 36 menus—you aren't likely to want to actually include that many, however.

In the Design mode, you can move among menus using the folder, Back, and Forward buttons.

UNDERSTANDING THE SLIDESHOW MODE

In the Slideshow mode, you can create slideshows from images contained in your iPhoto Photo Library or anywhere else on your Mac. You can control the order in which the images appear, the amount of time each image appears onscreen, and the soundtrack that plays while the slideshow plays. In the Slideshow mode, the iDVD window provides the tools you need to create your slideshows, as shown in Figure 18.10 and explained in the following list:

- **Images**—The images contained in the slideshow are displayed in the upper part of the window in the order in which they will appear during the slideshow.

- **Scroll tools**—You can use the scroll tools to browse the images shown in the window.

- **Configuration controls**—You use these controls to configure specific aspects of the slideshow.

- **Audio well**—You place the sound file you want to use as the slideshow's soundtrack here.

- **Return button**—Click this button to move back to the menu on which the slideshow is contained; it also returns iDVD to the Design mode.

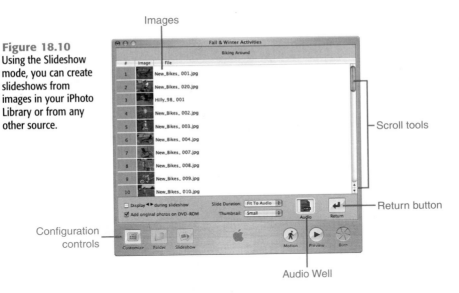

Figure 18.10
Using the Slideshow mode, you can create slideshows from images in your iPhoto Library or from any other source.

UNDERSTANDING THE PREVIEW MODE

iDVD enables you to preview a DVD before you burn it. In the Preview mode, iDVD behaves just like a DVD player; it even presents an onscreen remote control you use to control the DVD. You use the Preview mode to watch a DVD before you actually burn it to a disc. Previewing a DVD enables you to find and fix mistakes so you don't waste time and money burning discs that have problems. In the Preview mode, the iDVD window looks like that shown in Figure 18.11 and contains the elements explained in the following list:

- **Content window**—This window contains the content displayed onscreen when the DVD is played on a standard DVD player or on a computer.

- **Remote control**—The iDVD remote control simulates the remote controls used by many DVD players and includes most of the primary controls you use to view the DVD.

- **Menu controls**—These buttons perform menu tasks; for example, click the Menu button to move to a DVD's main menu.

- **Playback controls**—Use these buttons to play a DVD.

- **Cursor controls**—Use these controls to make selections in the DVD window. You can use the direction arrows to move the cursor and the Enter button to choose what you have selected.

- **Volume slider**—Drag this to the right to increase the volume or to the left to decrease it.

Figure 18.11
Using the Preview mode can prevent you from creating coasters.

18

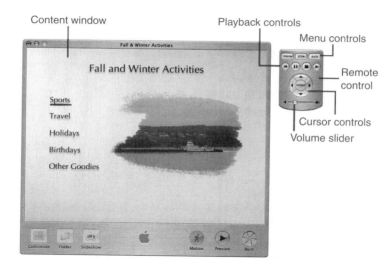

UNDERSTANDING THE BURN MODE

This is the mode you use when you burn a DVD. In this mode, the iDVD window displays a progress bar that shows you the current status of the burn process (see Figure 18.12).

UNDERSTANDING iDVD PROJECTS

Similar to iMovie, when you create a DVD, you first create a project. The project determines what content will appear on the DVD as well as its look and feel.

The content you place on a DVD consists of either movies or slideshows. Because you can place any iMovie or QuickTime content on DVD, there is really no limit to the movie content you can place on a DVD. You can create slideshows from still images in the usual image formats, such as JPEG, TIFF, and so on. Again, because iDVD supports all the standard formats, you can add just about any image to an iDVD slideshow.

Figure 18.12
Burning a DVD with iDVD is a simple matter of clicking the Burn button.

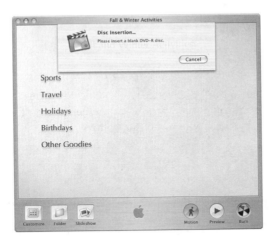

When you place content on a DVD (by adding to a project), it is encoded into the MPEG-2 format, which is the standard for DVD. MPEG-2 provides very high quality with relatively small file sizes (thus making digital movies on DVD possible). Fortunately, iDVD manages the encoding process for you and does so automatically.

A DVD created with iDVD can contain up to 90 minutes of content. However, iDVD uses a higher-quality encoding scheme when the content in a DVD project is 60 minutes or less—you should try to keep your DVDs within this limit, if possible. (You might think that 60 minutes isn't much, but you will find that creating 60 minutes of *good* content takes a bit of doing.) Again, iDVD manages this for you; the application selects the 90-min. or 60-min. format for you automatically.

TROUBLESHOOTING

WHEN I PLAY A MOVIE, I SEE A MESSAGE ABOUT THE REGION CODE NEEDING TO BE SET

When I try to play a DVD movie, I get a message about region codes.

All DVD movies contain a code so they play in only one of six regions in the world. This ensures that the format is supported by the display systems in that part of the world and also helps with piracy issues.

If you try to play a movie that has a code other than the one with which your player is set, you will see a dialog box enabling you to change the code for your player (in this case, the DVD drive in your Mac). If you choose to change the code, your DVD drive's code is changed. However, you can make this change only five times. At that point, the drive's code becomes permanent. I don't recommend that you change your drive's region code unless you are sure that most of the DVDs you will play in the future will have that code. If a code different from most of your movies becomes permanently set for your drive, you will be able to play only movies with that region code.

AN ACTION I TRY ISN'T PERMITTED

When I try to use a control, a NOT PERMITTED message appears onscreen.

The controls for a DVD movie can be activated only at specific times. For example, sometimes you can't scan forward through the warnings at the beginning of every DVD. The only solution is to wait until you are able to use the control.

WHEN I VIEW A DVD, I SEE A GREEN SCREEN

When I try to view a DVD, all I see is a green screen.

This can happen for two reasons. One is that you are viewing a disc in the wrong region; the other is that DVD Player sometimes suffers from an occasional glitch. Try resizing the Viewer window with one of the commands on the Video menu. Most of the time, this clears any temporary problems DVD Player is having. If this doesn't work, the region code is the culprit.

MAC OS X TO THE MAX: AND DVD FOR ALL

This section contains some additional information for your DVD enjoyment.

DVD PLAYER KEYBOARD SHORTCUTS

Table 18.2 contains keyboard shortcuts for DVD Player.

TABLE 18.2 KEYBOARD SHORTCUTS FOR DVD PLAYER

Action	Keyboard Shortcut
Add bookmark	⌘-=
Edit bookmarks	Option-⌘-B
Close/Open Control Drawer	⌘-]
Closed captioning on	Option-⌘-T
Closed captioning, separate window	Option-⌘-W
Closed captioning, over video	Option-⌘-V
DVD menu	⌘-'
Eject	⌘-E

Action	Keyboard Shortcut
Highlight DVD menu options	Up, down, left, right arrows; Tab; Shift-Tab
Next chapter	Right arrow
Previous chapter	Left arrow
Play/Pause	Spacebar
Play from the beginning of the disc	Shift-⌘-D
Play from the position the last time the disc was played	Shift-⌘-L
Play from default bookmark	Shift-⌘-B
Preferences	⌘-,
Viewer size to half	⌘-1
Viewer size to normal	⌘-2
Viewer size to maximum	⌘-3
Viewer size to full screen	⌘-0
Scan backward	Shift-⌘-left arrow
Scan forward	Shift-⌘-right arrow
Select DVD menu options	Return
Show/Hide controller	Shift-⌘-C
Show/Hide Info window	Shift-⌘-I
Show/Hide viewer	Shift-⌘-V
Stop	⌘-.
Switch to Finder	Shift-_⌘-F
Mute	Option-⌘-down arrow
Use horizontal/vertical controller	Option-⌘-C
Use wide/standard Info window	Option-⌘-I
Volume up	⌘-up arrow
Volume down	⌘-down arrow

18

TIP

When scanning, each time you press the related key combination, the scan rate increases.

TURNING YOUR MAC INTO A HOME THEATER SYSTEM

Unless you have an Apple Cinema Display (and even if you do have one), you might want to use your Mac to see movies at a larger size than what your monitor provides. After all, even with a 23″ monitor, viewing movies on a Mac is not practical for more than one or two people.

The solution to this is to add a projector to your system. You can attach a projector to any Mac that has a video out port (which all modern Macs have). Then you can project your movies to almost-theater size for an even better movie experience. You can also project the Web to that size along with any other tasks you do on your Mac.

NOTE

> A PowerBook or an iBook and a portable projector make an instant movie theater wherever you are.

And just as easily as you can project your movies, you can project the Web, your iMovies, slideshows, images, and anything else you work with.

Although projectors are fairly expensive, they are comparably priced to big-screen HDTV televisions. By adding an HDTV tuner, you can also project HDTV images with many projectors, so the projector can be used with various sources in addition to your Mac.

To add better sound to your Mac theater, you can route the sound output of your Mac to your sound system, or if your Mac can accept PCI cards, you can install a surround sound card to achieve digital sound.

If you have a PowerMac G5, you can take advantage of its digital audio output to listen to movies in full 5.1 digital surround sound.

CHAPTER 19

VIEWING, EDITING, AND CREATING QUICKTIME MOVIES

In this chapter

UNDERSTANDING QUICKTIME AND QUICKTIME PRO

Apple's QuickTime is the technology your Mac uses to handle time-synchronized data. *Time-synchronized data* simply means data that must be managed so that its components remain "in sync" with each other. For example, when you're playing digital video, the video image must remain in sync with the sound track. When you're watching an animation or video, sound effects need to occur at the correct moments.

Since its introduction, Apple's QuickTime has been one of the most successful multimedia standards on any platform. In fact, it has been so successful that it is also widely used on Windows computers; QuickTime movies on Windows play the same way they do on the Mac. QuickTime has also been widely adopted on the Web. Many Web sites serve video and animation files as QuickTime movies.

Although it is natural to think of QuickTime in terms of video, you should also remember that QuickTime can be used for sound, animation, and other dynamic data (such as audio) as well. And not all components have to be present at all times; for example, you can have a QuickTime movie that consists only of a soundtrack.

You will encounter QuickTime movies in many places, including interactive games, reference titles, entertainment titles, learning tools, and, of course, Web pages.

MAC OS X QUICKTIME RESOURCES

Various files, folders, and resources are part of Mac OS X's implementation of QuickTime. These include the following:

- **QuickTime Preferences**—The QuickTime pane of the System Preferences utility enables you to configure various aspects of how QuickTime works. The QuickTime preference file is stored in each user's Preferences folder within the user's Library folder.

- **QuickTime Player**—As with previous versions of QuickTime, the QuickTime Player is the basic application you use to watch, create, and edit QuickTime movies. It is located in the Applications folder.

- **QuickTime Updater**—Apple regularly updates QuickTime; this application can be used to ensure that all the QuickTime components on your Mac are in the current version. You can run the Updater from inside QuickTime Player, or you can run it from the Update tab of the QuickTime pane of the System Preferences utility.

NOTE

> *Streaming* is the capability to play QuickTime movies as they download from the Web—rather than having to wait until the movie is downloaded to your Mac before you can play it. If you have a fast Internet connection, streaming is very nice because viewing QuickTime movies on the Web is about as responsive as watching TV. If you use a phone modem, you still have to wait a while for most QuickTime movies.

- **QuickTime.framework folder**—This folder provides the framework files for QuickTime (`Mac OS X/System/Library/Frameworks/QuickTime.framework`, where `Mac OS X` is the name of your Mac OS X startup volume).

→ To learn about Mac OS X's framework structure, **see** "Mac OS X Architecture and Terminology," **p. 12**.

- **QuickTime Plug-in**—This plug-in (located in `Mac OS X/Library/Internet Plug-Ins`, where `Mac OS X` is the name of your Mac OS X startup volume) enables you to view QuickTime movies on the Web from within a Web browser.

QUICKTIME VERSUS QUICKTIME PRO

Way back in version 3.0 of QuickTime (which was introduced as part of Mac OS 8.5), Apple added a new scheme for QuickTime distribution. QuickTime comes in two flavors: QuickTime and QuickTime Pro. With QuickTime, you get a basic set of capabilities that enable you to watch all sorts of QuickTime movies. But that is about all you can do with it. QuickTime Pro, on the other hand, enables you to create and edit QuickTime movies, along with various other useful things.

QUICKTIME "BASIC"

With the version of QuickTime included as part Mac OS X, you'll get substantive QuickTime capabilities. These features include the following:

- Viewing all flavors of QuickTime movies on and off the Internet
- Working with more than 30 audio and video file formats
- Changing the size at which movies are played
- Printing frames of movies
- Watching QuickTime TV

QUICKTIME PRO

When you pay for the QuickTime Pro upgrade, you'll get many more features. One of the most important features is the ability to create and edit your own QuickTime movies. QuickTime Pro provides you with all the capabilities of QuickTime "basic," plus much more, including the following:

- Playing full-screen video
- Viewing files in a wider variety of formats
- Creating your own QuickTime movies
- Editing and saving movies in various formats

NOTE

> If you do much work with multimedia files, just the ability to save files that you can open in QuickTime into other file formats makes the upgrade worthwhile.

19

- Copying and pasting material from various formats into QuickTime movies
- Preparing QuickTime movies for streaming delivery via the Web
- Using sharpening, color tinting, and embossing filters on movies and images
- Creating slideshows from a series of still images

TIP

The additional features in QuickTime Pro become part of the QuickTime framework. Therefore, any applications that use that framework, such as iTunes, iMovie, iPhoto, iDVD, Final Cut Express, and so on, also benefit from the additional QuickTime Pro features, such as the capability to apply custom compression schemes. In fact, a QuickTime Pro license is included with Apple's professional applications, such as Final Cut Pro.

FACTORS AFFECTING QUICKTIME MOVIE QUALITY

As with other forms of multimedia, certain parameters govern how QuickTime movies appear on your Mac. To be comfortable with QuickTime, you should understand some of these basic specifications, which are described in the following sections.

RESOLUTION

QuickTime movies are composed with specific resolutions, just as still images are. The *resolution* of QuickTime movies is specified similarly to the way the resolution of your monitor is, that being X pixels wide by Y pixels high.

Although a QuickTime movie looks best in its default resolution, you can resize it in the QuickTime Player. Just as with still images, if you try to increase the resolution of a movie by making it larger, your Mac has to create pixels that aren't really there. This usually makes the movie look *pixilated*. Making a movie smaller usually does not detract from the way it looks because the Mac only has to remove pixels.

QuickTime movies created with larger resolution are better because they have a larger image to view and better definition of those images. The trade-off is in the frame rate at which the movie will play back (covered later in this chapter) and the size of the QuickTime movie file. The larger the resolution, the more information your Mac has to work with, and thus the harder it has to work to play back the movie and the larger the file sizes are. Sample resolutions for QuickTime movies are shown in Table 19.1.

TABLE 19.1 COMMON RESOLUTIONS FOR QUICKTIME MOVIES	
Resolution	**Approximate Viewing Size on 800×600 Desktop (21" Monitor)**
130×160	2.75"×3"
160×120	3"×2.75"
320×240	5.75"×5"
640×480	11.5"×9"

Not So "Quick" Time

When QuickTime first appeared on the Mac, Mac hardware was underpowered; thus, the early QuickTime movies had to be pretty small so that playback could even approach smooth motion. The standard resolution for a QuickTime movie in those days was a paltry 160×120 pixels. This earned QuickTime the label of "postage stamp" size movies by its critics. A bit of an exaggeration perhaps, but the first QuickTime movies were awfully small. Fortunately, both Mac hardware and QuickTime technology have improved so that larger QuickTime movies are practical. In fact, with Web streaming and a broadband Internet connection, QuickTime movies can be full-screen and still have very fluid motion.

COLOR DEPTH

Just like still images, QuickTime movies are created with a specific color depth. Movies with a larger number of colors require more processing power and have larger file sizes. Plus, some Macs are limited in the color depth they can view, so creating a movie in 24-bit color can cause it to look different on those machines that cannot work with that many colors. Therefore, these Macs have to reduce the number of colors in the movie before the movie is played.

FRAME RATE

QuickTime movies—just like their analog counterparts—are actually a series of still images that are slightly different from one another. As these images are shown onscreen, you see the illusion of motion—QuickTime is really just the digital age equivalent of the flipbook. The faster these images "flip" on the screen, the smoother and more lifelike the movie appears. The speed at which the movie plays is called the *frame rate*.

As with all other aspects of QuickTime movies, there is a trade-off between the quality of the movie and the resources it requires to be played. The higher the frame rate, the smoother and better the movie appears. However, QuickTime movies with higher frame rates require more processing power to view and the files are larger, thus requiring more disk space and download time.

19

NOTE

> The resolution, color depth, and frame rate aren't the only factors that determine how well a movie plays. Other factors include processing power, video display hardware, hard disk or CD-ROM speed, and especially connection speed (for a movie over the Internet).

NOTE

> Apple maintains an extensive Web site dedicated to QuickTime. This site includes software and updates you can download, information on how QuickTime works, links to QuickTime showcases, and so on. The site is at www.apple.com/quicktime and has some great samples of QuickTime movies you can view.

QUICKTIME MOVIE TRACKS

QuickTime movies can contain multiple *tracks*, where each track contains certain information. For example, a movie can have a video track, text track, and soundtrack. You can also have multiple tracks of the same type in a single movie. Or, you can have a movie with only one track (for example, a music track can be its own "movie"). Using QuickTime Pro, you can manipulate the individual tracks of a movie.

MULTIMEDIA TYPES SUPPORTED BY QUICKTIME PRO

In addition to its native format, QuickTime Pro works with various other formats, including the following:

CAUTION

> The following list is for QuickTime Pro. The basic version of QuickTime can work with some of these file formats, but certainly not all of them.

- **Video**—QuickTime can work with various video formats, including QuickTime, Audio Video Interleave (AVI, which is the Windows standard video format), Moving Picture Experts Group-1 (MPEG-1), MPEG-4, and Digital Video (DV).

- **Audio**—QuickTime supports many audio formats, such as Audio Interchange File Format (AIFF), AAC, WAV (the PC audio standard), MP3, and more.

- **Image**—Of course, QuickTime supports PICT and other Mac graphic formats, but it can also display BMP (Windows Bitmap), JPEG, and GIF images.

- **Animation**—QuickTime also supports several standard animation formats, such as PICS files.

UNDERSTANDING QUICKTIME VERSION 6

Mac OS X version 10.2 was the first version to include QuickTime version 6. Version 6 of QuickTime introduced support for MPEG-4. MPEG-4 is a revolutionary new compression scheme capable of delivering very high-quality video and audio in much smaller file sizes than is possible with other schemes. Plus, MPEG-4 is scalable, meaning that various quality and file-size trade-offs are possible. At its best, MPEG-4 provides quality equivalent to MPEG-2, which is the scheme primarily used for DVD movies. MPEG-4 can be used in many situations, but the most significant benefit—at least initially—is for movies broadcast over the Internet. MPEG-4 allows movies to be played over the Net in very high quality, even over relatively low-speed connections. In the not-so-distant future, MPEG-4 is likely to become a dominant standard for many aspects of video and audio content.

When you use the Pro version of QuickTime 6, you can produce content in the MPEG-4 format.

UPGRADING AND CONFIGURING QUICKTIME

Before you start watching and editing movies, you need to do some configuration of QuickTime so you get the best results on your system. Because you are serious about using a Mac (if you weren't, I assume you wouldn't have purchased this book), I suggest that you upgrade to QuickTime Pro. With all the additional capability that it brings to your system, it is a very worthwhile investment.

Going Pro

The Pro upgrade helps you in all digital lifestyle areas, not just QuickTime movies. For example, you can use QuickTime Pro to save QuickTime and other content in various formats for use in your projects. You can also use QuickTime Pro to save QuickTime movies you find on the Web to your Mac. In fact, QuickTime Pro's benefits are too numerous to list in detail. But even the brief list here should be enough to help you see that it is a worthwhile upgrade.

UPGRADING TO QUICKTIME PRO

Upgrading to QuickTime Pro does not require any additional software installation; all you need is a registration code. That code unlocks the additional features of QuickTime Pro. There are several ways to obtain your QuickTime Pro registration code:

- Go to www.apple.com/quicktime/download and click the Upgrade Now link.
- Open the QuickTime Player application, and select QuickTime Player, Preferences, Registration. Then, click Registration and finally the Register Online button.
- Open the System Preferences utility, open the QuickTime pane, click Registration, and then click Register Online. You will move onto the registration Web site.
- Call Apple at 1-888-295-0648 to order the upgrade by phone.

NOTE

At the time of this writing, the QuickTime Pro upgrade was about $30. After you have used it for a while, you will no doubt agree that this is a real bargain.

19

Using the Web site to upgrade is quite simple—just follow the onscreen instructions. You will receive your registration code via the order confirmation Web page or via the phone, depending on how you order the upgrade. Save this code because you will need it each time you have to configure QuickTime Pro.

CAUTION

From this point forward, I assume that you have upgraded to QuickTime Pro. If you haven't upgraded to QuickTime Pro, the material beyond basic viewing of QuickTime movies won't work for you.

CONFIGURING QUICKTIME

You'll need to do some basic configuration of QuickTime to customize it for your system. This configuration is done with the QuickTime pane of the System Preferences utility. Open the System Preferences utility and click the QuickTime icon to open the QuickTime pane. Across the top of the pane, you see the following tabs: Plug-in, Connection, Music, Media Keys, and Update.

THE PLUG-IN PANE

This pane has three check boxes and one button. The "Play movies automatically" check box controls whether QuickTime movies automatically play in your Web browser. This should usually be checked. Check the "Save movies in disk cache" check box if you want movies you view on the Web to be saved in your browser's disk cache. This is a useful option if you like to view a movie more than once during a single browsing session; subsequent viewings are much faster because the movie is read from your disk rather than being downloaded from the Web again. Most users should check this box as well. The "Enable kiosk mode" check box hides some QuickTime Player commands so that movies being viewed can't be saved and other changes can't be made. This option is useful if others will be using your Mac to view movies and you don't want them mucking around with your QuickTime settings or saving movies that they view.

The MIME settings button enables you to choose the types of files handled by QuickTime when you encounter them on the Internet. Click the MIME settings button, and you will see the MIME settings sheet. In that sheet, you will see a listing of various groups of file formats, such as Streaming, Video, and so on. Click the Expansion triangle next to each group to see the file formats it contains. Check the box next to the file formats you want to be handled in QuickTime; to have QuickTime handle all the formats in a group, check the group's check box. Click OK.

> NOTE
>
> *MIME* is the acronym for Multipurpose Internet Mail Extensions. As you might guess, MIME was originally developed as a means of exchanging files via email. Now, the term refers to the general encoding schemes used to encode files transferred over the Internet.

THE CONNECTION PANE

This pane enables you to configure the speed at which you connect to the Internet. This is important because the speed at which you connect to the Net has a huge impact on how movies appear to you when you view them on the Web. Use the Connection Speed pop-up menu to choose your connection speed. If you have a slow connection, such as a 56K modem, the "Allow multiple simultaneous streams" check box becomes active (it is disabled for high-speed connections). This option allows QuickTime to download and play multiple

QuickTime streams at the same time. With a high-speed connection, this isn't a problem so the check box is disabled (the feature is enabled at all times for fast connections). However, if you use a slow connection, you should uncheck this because the performance will be very poor when your Mac tries to download more than one stream at a time.

NOTE

> Some sites check the speed of connection you have set for QuickTime and provide the movie size the provider feels is appropriate for the connection speed you have selected. If you can't access the size you want, try changing the connection speed to a higher value, even if your connection isn't capable of that speed.

The Instant-On button enables you to configure how streaming movies are played when you view them from the Net or from some other streaming source. When you enable the Instant-On feature, you can set the amount of delay that occurs before a movie starts playing. With a shorter delay, movies start playing faster but less buffered data is stored on your Mac. Thus, should some network congestion occur and the download process be slowed, interruptions in movie playback will be more likely.

In most cases, the Instant-On feature is beneficial, especially if you have a fast Internet connection. To enable this feature, click the Instant-On button. In the resulting sheet, check the "Enable Instant-On" check box. Then, drag the slider to set the amount of delay before streams begin playing. With the slider all the way to the left, movies begin playing immediately. Moving the slider to the right causes a delay in playback, which might lower the amount of interruption you experience while increasing the amount of time you wait before the movie actually starts playing. You should experiment with various levels of delay until you achieve fast playback with few or no interruptions. When you have set the slider, click OK to close the sheet.

The Transport Setup button enables you to change the protocol and port QuickTime uses to download QuickTime streams from the Internet (see Figure 19.1). Your choices are User Datagram Protocol (UDP) or Hypertext Transfer Protocol (HTTP). UDP is a good choice because it does less work (such as providing error correction services) and so is likely to provide a better data stream. The port is the logical (rather than physical) connection that is made to your Mac; all services have a unique port. The default UDP port is 554; unless you use another service that uses this same port, there is little reason to change it. If you use HTTP, the default port is 80.

QuickTime automatically configures the protocol and port for you. However, if you need to set them manually for some reason (such as a conflict with your current configuration), click the Transport Setup button. The Streaming Transport Setup window will appear. Use the pop-up menu to choose the protocol to use and the radio buttons and text field to set the port. You can also reset the automatic configuration by clicking the Auto Configure button. When you are done, close the Streaming Transport Setup window.

19

Figure 19.1
The Transport
Protocol sheet
enables you to
change the transport
protocol and port
used for QuickTime
streaming (if you
need to—most users
won't need to change
these).

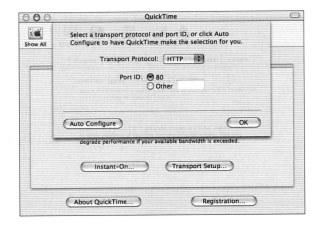

> **NOTE**
>
> If your Mac is behind a firewall or uses unusual ports to connect to the Internet, you
> might need to use the Streaming Transport Setup dialog box to configure QuickTime for
> your connection.

THE MUSIC PANE

QuickTime can play music using different synthesizers (a synthesizer transforms digital or
other signals into specific musical notes, tones, and so on). This pane is useful if you work
with a Musical Instrument Digital Interface (MIDI) device. By default, the standard
QuickTime Music Synthesizer is used. However, you can install various synthesizers and use
them to produce the music that is part of QuickTime movie files. If you are involved in creating MIDI files or using a MIDI instrument, you can use this area to select the default synthesizer that should be used.

> **NOTE**
>
>
>
> Working with MIDI devices and other synthesizers is beyond the scope of this book. If
> you want to learn more about MIDI, check out `http://dir.yahoo.com/`
> `Entertainment/Music/Computer_Generated/MIDI/`.

THE MEDIA KEYS PANE

Media keys enable you to manage your access to protected data files. If you need to get to
QuickTime files that are sensitive, you need to use a password (called a *key*) to access the
files. Individual tracks can also be secured with a key. If you use such secured QuickTime
files, you can enter the keys needed to play them in this pane of the window.

NOTE

> To work with secured QuickTime information, you need its key. You must get the key from the provider of the QuickTime file. Conversely, if you send secured QuickTime files to someone, make sure that you give him the appropriate keys.

To add a media key, click the Add button. In the sheet that appears, enter the category and key information and then click OK. The key appears in the Media Keys pane. You can view any QuickTime information that is secured with this key. You can also delete keys using the Delete button or change them using the Edit button.

NOTE

> Using the security features of QuickTime is beyond the scope of this book. Search the Apple Web site if you need to create or use secured QuickTime files.

THE UPDATE PANE

The Update pane enables you to control how updates to QuickTime are handled and to add third-party QuickTime software to your system.

Click the Update Now button to have your Mac check for updates to the QuickTime software. Check the "Check for updates automatically" check box if you want your Mac to check for QuickTime updates when you use QuickTime. If you use a high-speed Internet connection, this option is useful. However, if you use a low-speed connection, you probably won't want to have QuickTime check for updates automatically, so uncheck this check box.

If you click the "Install new 3rd-party QuickTime software" radio button and then click Update Now, your Mac checks for updates to non-Apple QuickTime software.

NOTE

> The Software Update feature of Mac OS X also manages QuickTime updates.

THE REGISTRATION BUTTON

Click the Registration button; the Registration sheet appears (see Figure 19.2). Enter your name, organization, and QuickTime Pro registration code that Apple provided to you. When you are finished entering your information, click OK.

Verify that the upgrade was successful by clicking the Registration button again. The version information should now reflect that you are using the Pro version.

 If the registration was not successful, you will see an error dialog box; or if, when you return to the Registration sheet, you still see that the version is Basic, see "My Attempt to Upgrade to QuickTime Pro Failed" in the "Troubleshooting" section at the end of this chapter for help.

19
.

Figure 19.2
You upgrade QuickTime to QuickTime Pro using the Registration sheet (the current version of QuickTime is shown in the middle of the sheet; after you upgrade, this will show that you are using the Pro Edition).

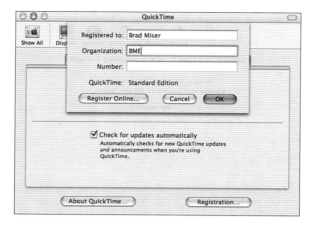

NOTE

The QuickTime Pro registration information is part of the preferences for each user account you have created for your Mac. If you enter this information for only one user, only that user will have access to QuickTime Pro's features. Other users will still be able to use the Basic version of QuickTime. If you want specific users to have access to QuickTime Pro, you will need to repeat the registration process when logged in under those user accounts.

The other information, such as connection speed, is also dependent on the user account that is logged in. You need to configure QuickTime for each user for which you create an account on a single Mac OS X machine.

VIEWING QUICKTIME MOVIES

You can view QuickTime movies in various contexts, such as from your hard drive, CD-ROMs, the Web, using QuickTime TV, and so on. Although the appearance of the QuickTime Player controls varies a bit between these contexts, the viewing controls work similarly.

NOTE

You can watch QuickTime movies without upgrading to the Pro version. However, if you don't upgrade, you will see a dialog box urging you to upgrade the first time you open QuickTime Player each day. You can choose to upgrade later, or you can use this dialog box to upgrade immediately. Not having to see this dialog box might be one of the best reasons to upgrade!

SETTING QUICKTIME PLAYER PREFERENCES

QuickTime Player is the basic application you use to view and edit QuickTime movies. There are some preferences you might want to set by selecting QuickTime Player,

Preferences, Player Preferences. The options in the resulting Player Preferences dialog box are as shown here:

- **Open Movie**—If you check the "Open movie in new players" check box, each movie you open appears in a new QuickTime Player window rather than replacing the current movie. When you edit movies, you will probably have several open at the same time, so you should check this box so that you don't have to keep opening and closing the movies with which you are working.

- **Auto-Play**—If you check the "Automatically play movies when opened" check box, movies begin to play as soon as you open them.

- **Only Front Movie Plays Sound**—If the "Play sound in frontmost player only" check box is checked and you have more than one movie playing, only the movie in the frontmost QuickTime Player window produces sound.

- **Play Sound in Background**—When the "Play sound when application is in background" check box is checked, a movie's sound continues to play when you move a movie into the background.

- **Show Equalizer**—When the "Show equalizer" check box is checked, you will see the QuickTime Player equalizer.

- **Hot Picks**—Checking the "Show Hot Picks movie automatically" check box means that when you launch QuickTime Player, it goes to the Internet to check for an Apple "hot pick" movie and displays that movie in the window (you can choose to watch it or not). This is checked by default. If you don't want to see the hot pick each time you launch the application, you should uncheck the box.

- **Fast User Switching**—If the Fast User Switching feature is enabled, users can log in to your Mac without other users having to completely log out first. If you check the "Pause movies when logged out" check box, movies that are playing when another user logs in are paused until the previous user logs back in.

WATCHING QUICKTIME MOVIES FROM YOUR HARD DRIVE OR CD-ROM

If you use a VCR, CD, or DVD player, you won't have any trouble using the basic QuickTime Player controls (see Figure 19.3). Find a QuickTime movie that is on your hard drive or a CD-ROM and open it.

TIP

> QuickTime movie files use the extension .mov. If you don't know where a QuickTime movie is, use the Finder to search for files with this extension.

→ To use the Finder to search for files, **see** "Finding Files and Folders on Your Mac," **p. 114**.

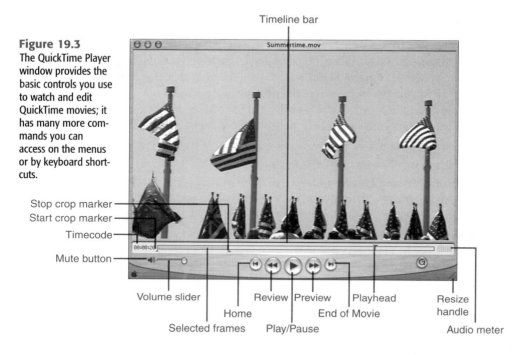

Figure 19.3
The QuickTime Player window provides the basic controls you use to watch and edit QuickTime movies; it has many more commands you can access on the menus or by keyboard shortcuts.

NOTE

If the Hot Pick option is enabled, when you open the QuickTime Player, it searches for the current hot pick movie and displays that movie (or a few frames of the movie) in the window. Usually, you can click the image to move to the Web to view the movie in its entirety. If the hot pick movies annoy you, disable them using the QuickTime Player preferences setting.

A QuickTime Player window appears and the movie is displayed (refer to Figure 19.3).

Most of the controls in the QuickTime Player window are easily understood. For example, the Review button plays the movie in reverse, the Preview button plays the movie in fast forward mode, and so on.

However, you need to become familiar with the less obvious parts of the QuickTime Player window, especially if you have never worked with digital video before. The current frame is shown in the viewing window (if you haven't played the movie, it is the first frame in the movie). Just below the viewing window is the movie's Timeline bar (also known as the Scrubber bar). This represents the total length of the movie. The location of the Playhead shows where in the movie the current frame is located. As you play a movie, the Playhead moves to the right in the Timeline bar so that it always shows the location of the frame being shown in the viewing window.

At the left edge of the Timeline bar, you see the timecode. The timecode represents the location of the Playhead in the following format: Minutes:Seconds:FrameNumber. For example, if you see 2:34:10, the Playhead is located on the 10th frame of the 34th second of the second minute of the movie.

The crop markers are used to select parts of a movie when you are editing it. The Start (or left) crop marker shows the start of a selection, and the Stop (or right) crop marker shows the end of the selection. The shaded area between the crop markers shows the frames that have been selected.

Control the size of the movie using the commands on the Movie menu. Increasing the size of a movie beyond the size at which it was created sometimes decreases its image quality and frame rate. With some movies, this is hardly noticeable; with others, increasing the size can make the movie unwatchable. You can experiment to see which size is the best compromise for a particular movie on your specific system.

TIP

> You can also change the size of the QuickTime Player window using the Resize handle. The window remains in proportion to the size in which the movie was created. If you hold down the Shift key, you can resize the window any way you want (with sometimes amusing effects on the movie itself). You can quickly return a movie to its default size by selecting Movie, Normal Size or by pressing ⌘-1.

Click the Play button to view the movie and use the Volume slider to adjust its sound level.

→ QuickTime Player offers many keyboard shortcuts; to learn what shortcuts are available, **see** "Using QuickTime Player Keyboard Shortcuts," **p. 673**.

You can get more control over the sound using the Sound controls; display them by selecting Movie, Show Sound Controls. The Timeline bar is replaced by sliders for balance, bass, and treble. Use the sliders to make the changes you want. Select Movie, Hide Sound Commands to return to the Timeline bar view.

19

TIP

> To mute a movie, click the speaker icon at the left edge of the Volume slider.

Similarly, you can control the brightness of the movie using the Video controls; select Movie, Show Video Controls to display the Brightness bar. Click and drag the Brightness bar to the right to make the movie brighter or to the left to make it less bright; select Movie, Hide Video Controls when you are done.

NOTE

> When you minimize a movie, it moves onto the Dock and continues to play.

That's about all there is to viewing movies. However, you can fine-tune your movie experience by using some of the other playback commands listed in Table 19.2.

TABLE 19.2   SUMMARY OF QUICKTIME PLAYER PLAYBACK CONTROLS

Command	Keyboard Command	What It Does
Movie, Loop	⌘-L	Makes the movie play in a continuous loop. Choose the command again to make the movie "unloop."
Movie, Loop Back and Forth	None	Makes movie play in a continuous loop, but it plays forward until it reaches the end of the movie. Then it plays in reverse. When it reaches the beginning again, it plays forward.
Movie, Size commands	⌘-0 through ⌘-1 ⌘-2 ⌘-F	Changes the size of the movie window. The choices are Half Size, Normal Size (the size at which the movie was created), Double Size, and Full Screen.
Movie, Present Movie	Shift-⌘-F	The Present Movie dialog box will appear. Select the movie size from the pop-up menu, select the Normal or Slide Show option, and click Play. When the movie plays, the QuickTime Player window will disappear (as will your desktop) and all you will see is the movie itself. When the movie is done, you will return to the QuickTime Player window. If you select the Slideshow mode, you have to click the mouse button or Spacebar to move through each frame of the movie.
Movie, Play Selection Only	⌘-T	Plays only the frames you have selected using the crop markers.
Movie, Play All Frames	None	Causes the entire movie to play, regardless of the frames you have selected.
Movie, Play All Movies	None	Plays all the movies you have open.
Movie, Go to Poster Frame	None	Every QuickTime movie has a poster frame; this is the frame that appears when the movie is first opened. By default, this is the first frame in the movie. Choosing this command moves you to the poster frame for the current movie.
Movie, Set Poster Frame	None	Sets the poster frame for the current movie.
Movie, Choose Language	None	QuickTime movies can contain tracks that provide different languages. If the movie you are watching has multiple language tracks, use this command to choose the one you want to hear.

TIP

> If you use multiple monitors and select the Full Screen option, you can select the monitor on which the movie plays in the Present Movie dialog box.

NOTE

> QuickTime movies can also be inserted into many types of documents, such as Word files, PowerPoint presentations, and so on. When you view such a file, you will see a "mini" QuickTime controller that enables you to watch the movie that is embedded in a particular document. Applications can add or remove controls to customize the interface you see in that application, but when you understand how to view movies with the QuickTime Player, you won't have any trouble with these other controllers.

WATCHING QUICKTIME MOVIES ON THE WEB

QuickTime is a major format for movies on the Web. Using the QuickTime plug-in, you can watch QuickTime movies from within a Web browser, such as Safari. When you do so, you use controls that are similar to those in the QuickTime Player application.

One of the best places to view QuickTime movies is at Apple's Movie Trailer site. Here, you can view trailers for the latest creations from Hollywood.

CAUTION

> If you use a slow Internet connection, watching movies, such as the movie trailers on the Apple Web site, can be an exercise in patience. High-quality movie files are *big*. Watching them on the Web, even with the streaming feature and the MPEG-4 format, can take more time than it is worth. If you use a dial-up account, try watching some movies to see whether you can tolerate the length of time it takes to download enough of the movie so that you can begin watching it. If you can, great. If not, you might have to find smaller movies to watch or, even better, move up to a high-bandwidth connection. You can also use the Instant-On preference to configure the delay before a movie begins to play.

19

To view some cool trailers online, do the following steps:

1. Go to www.apple.com/trailers.
2. Click a trailer to view it. What happens next depends on how the particular trailer has been created. Related to the previous caution, many of the trailers on the Apple site are offered in different versions, which are sized to be appropriate for various connection speeds. Usually, there are three choices: low (for dial-up connections), medium (for DSL, slower cable, or ISDN connections), and high (for faster cable modem or T-1 connections).
3. Click the size your connection supports. You will see a window that contains QuickTime controls you can use to watch the trailer (see Figure 19.4).

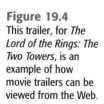

Figure 19.4
This trailer, for *The Lord of the Rings: The Two Towers*, is an example of how movie trailers can be viewed from the Web.

4. Some movies display a link labeled "Click Here to Play Movie." If so, click that link to begin the movie streaming. Other movies begin to stream as soon as the new window opens.

   The movie begins to play as soon as enough has been downloaded to your Mac so that the trailer plays continuously. If you use a fast connection and use the Instant-On feature, this happens quickly. If you use a slow dial-up connection or have configured a delay using the Instant-On slider, it can take longer. You can see how much of a movie has been downloaded by looking at the dark shaded part of the Timeline bar.

> **TIP**
>
> You can start a movie at any time by pressing the spacebar. If you don't wait for the automatic start, the movie might stop before it finishes if it "runs out" of downloaded movie before it gets to the end.

5. Use the QuickTime controls listed in Table 19.3 to control playback.

 If you can only download a QuickTime movie from the Web rather than being able to view it, see "I Can't View QuickTime Movies on the Web" in the "Troubleshooting" section at the end of this chapter.

TABLE 19.3   QUICKTIME CONTROLS FOR WEB MOVIES

Control	Function
Volume	Click the volume button and a slider will pop up. Use the slider to set the volume level.
Play/Pause	Use this to play or pause the movie. The spacebar does the same thing.
Slider	Drag this to move to any point in the movie.
Step backward/Step forward	Moves back or ahead in the movie by one frame.
QuickTime controls	Pops up a menu of additional commands.

If you have upgraded to QuickTime Pro and click the QuickTime controls button, you will see a pop-up menu with some or all of the following commands on it:

- **About QuickTime Plug-in**—Shows you the version of the QuickTime plug-in you are using.

- **Open This Link**—Opens a link.

- **Save As Source**—What this does depends on the item you are viewing. For .mov files, this does the same thing as Save As QuickTime Movie.

- **Save As QuickTime Movie**—This command enables you to save a movie you are viewing to your hard drive so you can view it later. When you save it to your hard drive, it becomes just like any other QuickTime movie on your Mac (you view or edit it using QuickTime Player). This feature is disabled for some movies.

- **Plug-in Settings**—Enables you to configure your plug-in by opening the QuickTime pane of the System Preferences utility.

- **Connection Speed**—Enables you to set your connection speed (you should have already set this using the QuickTime pane in the System Preferences utility).

- **QuickTime Language**—If the movie has tracks for different languages, you can select the language in which you want to hear the movie.

NOTE

If you aren't using QuickTime Pro, you will see only a subset of these commands. For example, you won't be able to save a QuickTime movie to your local disk. And, depending on the content you are viewing, some of the commands might be disabled.

EXPLORING A QUICKTIME VR MOVIE

QuickTime Virtual Reality (VR) enables you to interact with movies that simulate panoramic, virtual worlds. You can move around within a movie, and you can even closely examine objects within that movie. QuickTime VR is widely used on the Web so you can examine products, museums, and other interesting things.

19

If you have never used it before, you might not have any QuickTime VR files on your Mac. If you don't, go to www.apple.com/quicktime/whatson/ and look in the News & Entertainment area. There will no doubt be some VR movies for you to view.

Find the movie you want to explore and click it. You won't see the usual QuickTime controls. Instead, you will see special cursors that indicate what you can do with the movie. The standard cursor is a small circle with a dot in the center. When you see this, you know that you are looking at a QuickTime VR movie.

To move around the image, simply hold down the mouse button and drag (the cursor will show an arrow to indicate which way you are moving). The image will move accordingly, and you can explore to your heart's content.

NOTE

You have probably noticed by now, but just in case, www.apple.com/quicktime contains many resources for QuickTime. You will find anything you need to understand and use QuickTime at this site.

CREATING AND EDITING A MOVIE WITH QUICKTIME PRO

Watching QuickTime movies is great, but you can go beyond just watching QuickTime content. With QuickTime Pro, you can create and edit your own QuickTime movies. Editing movies with QuickTime Player is pretty easy because it works just like most other Mac applications. You can select portions of a movie and paste them into other movies, cut them, or duplicate them. Working with QuickTime content is very similar to working with text or graphics.

CAUTION

You can't edit QuickTime movies unless you upgrade to QuickTime Pro. And, after you upgrade, you sometimes need to quit QuickTime Player to make the upgrade effective. To check this, open the QuickTime Player and open the File menu. If you see any Save commands, you are using QuickTime Player Pro. If you don't see any Save commands, you are still using the Basic version. You need to restart QuickTime Player to get the Pro features.

CREATING A NEW QUICKTIME MOVIE AND ADDING CLIPS TO IT

You can create a movie by pasting clips from other movies into it:

1. Launch QuickTime Player.
2. Select File, New Player. You will see an empty QuickTime movie. There isn't anything in the viewing area, so it is collapsed—all you see are the QuickTime Player controls.

3. Open a movie from which you want to copy a clip to paste into your new movie.

4. Drag the left crop marker to where you want the copy to start and the right crop marker to where you want the copy to end. The shaded area between the crop markers represents the frames of the movie you have selected (see Figure 19.5).

Frame at location
of Playhead

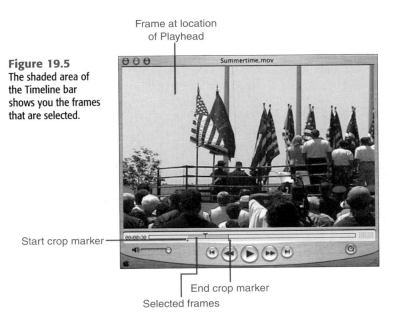

Figure 19.5
The shaded area of the Timeline bar shows you the frames that are selected.

Start crop marker

End crop marker
Selected frames

5. Select Movie, Play Selection Only and then click the Play button (or press ⌘-T and press the spacebar) to play only the frames you have selected.

6. Fine-tune your selection by placing the Playhead over a crop marker. When you do so, the Playhead "sticks" to the crop marker. Hold down the Shift key and use the right- and left-arrow keys to move the crop marker by single frames in either direction.

7. Repeat the previous step to fine-tune the location of the other crop marker.

8. Play the selection again and continue to fine-tune it until it has the exact frames you want to copy into the new movie.

9. Press ⌘-C to copy the selected frames.

10. Move back to the new movie you created in step 2.

11. Press ⌘-V to paste the clip into the new movie. The previously empty movie will now show the clip you pasted into it. Play the clip by pressing the spacebar.

19

NOTE

> The new movie takes on the default resolution of the clip you paste into it, even if the movie was not being displayed at its default size when you used the Copy command. For example, if the movie you copied from was at half size, the new movie will be the normal size of the movie from which you copied the clip. You can change the playback size of the new movie, but its default resolution (its normal size) is based on the largest resolution clip you paste into it.

12. Open another movie and copy a clip from it (or copy a different clip from the same movie).

TIP

> You can move the Playhead rapidly while moving a crop marker by holding down the Shift-⌘ keys while you press the left or right arrow.

13. Go back into your new movie and move the Playhead to where you want the next clip to be pasted. You can paste another clip at the beginning, at the end, or in the middle of your new movie.

14. Press ⌘-V to paste the second clip in the new movie. The frames you paste remain selected in the new movie. If you don't like the results of the paste, undo it or cut the new frames.

15. Jump to the front of the movie and play it.

16. Keep pasting clips into your movie until it has all the clips you want in it.

17. Select File, Save As.

18. In the Save dialog box, click the "Make movie self-contained" radio button, name the movie, select where you want it to be saved, and click Save. Your new movie is complete.

Transition

A *transition* is the means by which one clip moves into the other. Many types of transitions are used when creating videos. The most common is the cross fade, in which one scene gradually fades into the next. Many more are possible, such as spinning transitions, in which one clip spins into the next, and shade transitions, in which one scene rolls up like a window shade, and so on.

Unfortunately, you can do only one kind of transition with QuickTime Player: the straight cut. This means that one scene ends and the next begins with no transition effect. If you are careful with the clips you paste together and you judiciously use the Step button to cut your clips, you can make the transitions work fairly well (remember that if your clip has a soundtrack, it goes along with the video and is cut in the same way). The better way to add transitions is to use iMovie.

→ To learn how to use iMovie, **see** Chapter 17, "Making Digital Movie Magic with iMovie," **p. 569**.

When you use resources from one QuickTime movie in another, QuickTime can refer to that information rather than physically placing the material in the movie—this is what happens when you save a movie normally (allowing the movie to depend on the other clip, which QuickTime calls a *dependency*). This is similar to using an alias to a file. The advantage of this is that the movie file will be much smaller because it is storing only the pointer to the material rather than the material itself in the file. The disadvantage is that if you move the movies around, such as when you email them, the pointer can become invalid, and the movie won't be able to find the referenced material.

If you save a movie with the "Make movie self-contained" radio button selected, the pasted material is actually stored in the file. This means that the movie does not depend on any references. You can move it wherever you want to, and it will work fine.

If you are sure that you won't be moving the clips you are using, use the "Save normally" option. If you think you might move one or more of the clips, use the "Make movie self-contained" option.

To learn about the movie you have created, select Window, Show Movie Info. The Movie Info window will appear. Use the Expansion triangle to show all the information in the window (see Figure 19.6).

Figure 19.6
The Movie Info window provides detailed information about your movie, such as its normal size and format.

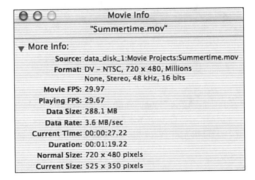

ADDING, ENABLING, AND DISABLING TRACKS

As you learned earlier, QuickTime movies can contain different tracks, and those tracks can contain video, text, sound, and so on. You can have multiple tracks in a movie, and you can even have multiple tracks of the same type in a movie, for example, multiple sound tracks.

Adding different kinds of information to your movie automatically adds a new track to the movie. As an example, you can quickly add a text track that displays a bar containing the text across the bottom of the window. Here's how:

1. Use a word processor to create the text you want to add.

2. Use the font size controls to make the text the size you want it to be and copy the text.

3. Open the movie to which you want to add the text track.

4. Use the Crop Markers to select the portion of the movie over which you want the track to appear.

5. Select Edit, Add Scaled.

The text track is scaled to appear across all the frames you selected. For example, if you selected the entire movie, the text track will appear the whole time that the movie plays (see Figure 19.7).

Figure 19.7
You can see the text track that I added at the bottom of this movie; you can see the text that I copied in the TextEdit window in the background.

NOTE

Unfortunately, with QuickTime Player you have no control over the background color of the text (black), nor can you change the color of the text track (white). However, the text you paste will maintain the other formatting you applied in the application you used to create it, such as size, italic, and so on.

View the tracks your movie contains by selecting Edit, Enable Tracks. The Enable Tracks window appears, and you see all the tracks contained in your movie. You can disable a track so that it doesn't play in your movie by clicking it (the On or Off icon next to the track's title indicates whether the track is enabled or disabled). Click OK to close the Enable Tracks dialog box.

Tracks are a very powerful feature of QuickTime, and I have shown you only a bit of what you can do with them. For example, you can add additional sound tracks, video tracks, graphics, and any other content in the same way you added a text track. That is the nice thing about QuickTime—it works in a similar way no matter what kind of data you work with.

USING OTHER EDITING COMMANDS

QuickTime Player has more editing commands you can use. These commands appear on the Edit menu and include the following:

- **Select All**—Use this to select all the frames in a movie.
- **Select None**—Use this to quickly unselect any selection.
- **Add**—The Add Scaled command scales what you paste to the selection in which you are pasting it, but Add just pastes it in and lets the length fall where it may. For example, if you add a sound track to a movie, the sound will play for its default length. If you use the Add Scaled command instead, it will be scaled so that it plays only as long as the frames you have selected do when you paste it.
- **Replace**—When you use this command, the frames you have copied or cut replace the frames that are selected when you use the Paste command instead of being added to them.
- **Trim**—When you use the Trim command, everything *outside* the crop markers is removed from the movie.

N O T E

Trim is more commonly called Crop in other applications.

- **Extract Tracks**—Use this command to extract a track from a movie. When you do so, the track is copied from the current movie and placed in a new QuickTime Player window (in which it will be the only track).
- **Delete Tracks**—Use this when you want to remove a track from a movie.

CREATING A QUICKTIME SLIDESHOW

One of the best ways to display your digital images is to create a QuickTime movie from them. This movie becomes a nice slideshow that you show on your Mac. You can also add sound or other tracks, just as you can with other kinds of movies. Follow these steps:

1. Put all the images you want to appear in the slideshow in a single folder.
2. Name the files and add a sequential number at the end of the name (for example, picture1, picture2, and so on).
3. Open QuickTime Player and create a new player.
4. Select File, Open Image Sequence.
5. In the Open dialog box, select the first image in the series that you want to appear in the slideshow and click Open. You will see the Image Sequence Settings dialog box.

19

6. Select a frame rate from the pop-up menu. This rate determines how long each image stays onscreen. Although video frame rate is measured in multiple frames per second, you want the frames of a slideshow (which are the individual images you want in the show) to be onscreen for at least a few seconds. A good frame rate for a slideshow is about 3 seconds per frame. This keeps the images onscreen long enough to be seen but not long enough to get tiresome.

7. After you have chosen a frame rate, click OK. The images will be imported into the movie in the sequence of the numbers in the names of the files.

> **N O T E**
>
> The resolution of the slideshow is taken from the resolution of the images you place in it. QuickTime Player will attempt to make all the images the same size—that being the size of the largest image in the sequence. This can result in some very bad distortion if the application scales an image to any significant degree. You should use an image-editing application to make all the images the same resolution before you import them into QuickTime Player.

8. Press the spacebar to see the slideshow. Each image will be shown for the amount of time you set when you set the frame rate.

9. Select File, Save As. Name the movie, select either the "Save normally" or the "Make movie self-contained" option, select a location, and click Save. Your slideshow is now saved as a QuickTime movie.

You can also add a sound track (such as music in an MP3 file) to your slideshow to make it even more impressive:

1. Locate the MP3 file you want to use as a soundtrack.

2. From QuickTime Player, open the MP3 file. It will appear as a movie with no video track.

3. Play the music so that you are sure it is what you want.

4. Use the Info window for the slideshow to figure out how much music you need.

5. Select the portion of the music you want to use as the soundtrack and copy it.

> **T I P**
>
> Use the timecode to determine exactly how much music you are selecting.

6. Switch back into the slideshow and select the entire movie.

7. Use the Add command to add the music track to the slideshow. The music will be added as a soundtrack and will play when you play the slideshow.

NOTE

> You can't fade music using the QuickTime Player, so unless you choose your music and work the timing carefully, you might end up with a jarring ending to the soundtrack. You need to use a more capable application, such as iMovie, to be able to fade the soundtrack for a movie.

NOTE

> If you use iPhoto, you can also export a group of images as a QuickTime slideshow. In addition, you can create a slideshow from a group of images using iDVD.

→ To learn how to use iPhoto, **see** "Using iPhoto to Master Digital Images," **p. 470**.

→ To learn how to create DVD slideshows, **see** "Creating Your Own DVDs," **p. 630**.

CUSTOMIZING YOUR QUICKTIME MOVIES

One of the most powerful editing features in QuickTime Player is not very obvious—the Movie Properties tool. The tool is somewhat hidden by being placed on the Movie menu, rather than on the Edit menu where it belongs.

To open the tool, select Movie, Get Movie Properties (or press ⌘-J). The Movie Properties tool will appear and, at first, you might not be too impressed (see Figure 19.8).

Figure 19.8
Hidden under a rather plain interface is one of the most powerful parts of the QuickTime Player.

The tool has two pop-up menus at the top of the window. From the left pop-up menu, you choose the element with which you want to work. If you open the menu, you will see Movie, which enables you to work with the movie as a whole, and a listing of each track in the movie (such as Video Track and Sound Track). From the right pop-up menu, you select the aspect of that element that you want to learn more about or that you want to change. The information to view or the controls you can use appear in the lower pane of the window.

The Movie Properties tool is very powerful, and it can help you with many tasks. Although I don't have room to cover it in all its detail in this chapter, a few examples will help you understand how it works. You can explore on your own from there.

NOTE

> You can use the Movie selection in the left pop-up menu to control various aspects of the movie itself. For example, you can set the movie to play automatically when it is opened by selecting Auto Play on the right pop-up menu and checking the Auto Play Enabled check box. And, you can use the Controller option to choose a different movie controller (or to display no controller at all).

CHANGING THE SIZE OF A MOVIE

You can use Movie Properties to change many aspects of a movie's appearance, including its size and orientation. This is important for many reasons. For example, if your viewer will be using a different monitor resolution than that on which you originally created the movie (its normal size), your movie might not fit on the viewer's screen, or it might appear in postage stamp size. Do the following:

1. Open the movie you want to change and select Movie, Get Movie Properties. The Movie Properties tool will open.

2. Select the Video Track from the left pop-up menu.

3. Select Size from the right pop-up menu (see Figure 19.9).

Figure 19.9
You can change the size of a movie by using the Size command for the video track.

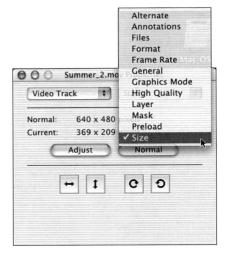

The lower part of the window will now show controls you can use to resize the movie as well as change its orientation.

4. Click Adjust. The movie window will have resizing handles you can use to change the movie's size (see Figure 19.10). Drag the handle in any corner of the window to resize the movie. As you move the handles, the size shown in the Properties window will be updated.

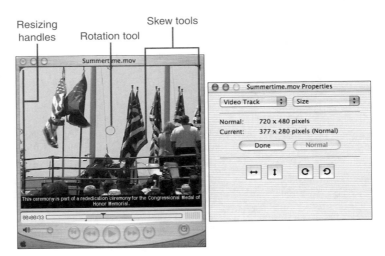

Figure 19.10
You can use the resize handles and other tools in the Movie Properties dialog box to change the size and orientation of the movie.

5. Click the Rotation tool in the center of the window and drag to rotate the image.

6. Click and drag the Skew tools on each side of the movie to skew it in either direction.

TIP

You can "flip" the image horizontally, vertically, counterclockwise, or clockwise using the buttons at the bottom of the Movie Properties window.

7. After the size and orientation are correct, click Done.

8. Save your movie.

The next time the movie is opened, it will be at the size you set it (the size you set becomes the movie's normal size).

As you saw in Figure 19.9, there are many other choices for the video track. Take some time to explore them.

CHANGING THE VOLUME OF A MOVIE'S SOUNDTRACK

There are also many controls you can use to manipulate a movie's soundtrack. They work similarly to the tools you can use for the video track. As an example, you can change the volume of any soundtrack as well as adjust its balance. You might want to do this to change the relative balance of different soundtracks when you have more than one in the same movie. You can make the background music quieter and narration louder, for example:

1. Open the movie and then the Movie Properties tool.

2. Select the sound track you want to change from the left pop-up menu and open the right pop-up menu (see Figure 19.11).

Figure 19.11
You can see that there are also many tools you can use to work with a movie's sound-track.

NOTE

If you have more than one sound track in a movie, you can select each one to work with them individually.

3. Select Volume from the right pop-up menu. The window will contain controls that enable you to change the volume levels of the sound track (see Figure 19.12).

Figure 19.12
Using these volume controls is a matter of setting the various levels by dragging in the bars.

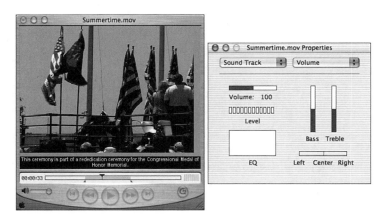

4. Drag in the Volume bar to change the relative volume level of the track.

TIP

> If you increase the volume over the default 100 reading, the bar turns red to show that you have overloaded the volume level.

5. Adjust the bass and treble levels using the Bass and Treble bars; they work just like the Volume bar (just drag in the bar to set the level).

6. Change the balance of the sound track using the Balance slider in the lower-right corner of the window.

7. Play the movie to see whether the levels you set are appropriate. When the movie plays, you can see the relative volume levels for the various sound frequencies in the Equalizer area of the window.

8. Save the movie.

As with the video tools, there are many more sound track tools you can explore to make the most of your movie's sound tracks.

NOTE

> If you have a text or other type of track, you will see controls for that specific kind of track as well. They work similarly to the controls for the video and sound tracks.

TROUBLESHOOTING

MY ATTEMPT TO UPGRADE TO QUICKTIME PRO FAILED

When I entered my QuickTime Pro registration information, I saw an error dialog box stating that the registration information is not correct. Or, it appeared to work, but when I returned to the Registration sheet, the Basic version was still shown and no registration information appeared in the sheet.

The QuickTime Pro registration code is tied to the name you used when you obtained it. You must enter this name exactly as you used it; otherwise, the registration code will not be accepted. Also, double-check the registration code you entered; these codes are long and complex, so it is easy to make a mistake. The code and name are case-sensitive, so make sure you enter them exactly as shown in the information you receive from Apple.

I CAN'T VIEW QUICKTIME MOVIES ON THE WEB

When I attempt to view a QuickTime movie on the Web, I'm unable to do so and am forced to download the file to my Mac instead.

This happens if the QuickTime plug-in has been moved or damaged. To reinstall the plug-in, you need to update QuickTime. When the updater runs, it will reinstall the plug-in in the appropriate location and you will be able to use it with your Web browser. To update

QuickTime, open the QuickTime Player application and select QuickTime Player, Update Existing Software. The appropriate files will be downloaded and installed on your Mac. Restart your Mac and you should be able to view QuickTime movies on the Web.

MAC OS X TO THE MAX: TAKING QUICKTIME FURTHER

You've learned a lot about QuickTime, but even so, there is a lot more you can do. In this section, you'll get some tips to help you go even further with QuickTime.

USING QUICKTIME PRO TO CONVERT FILES INTO OTHER FORMATS

QuickTime supports many types of file formats that you are likely to encounter on the Internet as well as on CD-ROMs and other sources of multimedia files. These files can contain all sorts of content, everything from videos to sounds to still images and combinations of all of these. One of the most powerful features of QuickTime Pro is the ability to use it to convert files into different formats. You can import many file types into QuickTime Player and then export them or save them in a different format.

To import non-QuickTime movie content into QuickTime Player, use the Import command on the File menu.

Table 19.4 lists some of the more useful files you can create using the Export command on QuickTime Player's File menu. In the "Save exported file as" dialog box, you can use the Export pop-up menu to choose many formats, including those listed in Table 19.4. After you choose a format, you can set the options used for the export with the Use pop-up menu and Options button.

TABLE 19.4   USEFUL FILE FORMATS TO WHICH QUICKTIME PLAYER CAN EXPORT CONTENT

Export to Format	Use
Movie to AVI	This exports a movie to the Windows AVI format. The AVI format is a standard on the PC side of things, so this is useful if you want to provide movies for Windows users (although they would be better off using the Windows version of QuickTime).
Movie to BMP	You can convert frames of a movie into the BMP format, which is the Windows bitmap image format.
Movie to DV Stream	This is an extremely useful function because it enables you to export QuickTime movies in the DV format so that you can then import them into a digital video editing application.
Movie to MPEG-4	This creates an MPEG-4 version of the movie, which will have high quality and relatively small file size. The only downside is that the recipient's movie player has to be capable of handling MPEG-4 content, which not all do.

Export to Format	Use
Sound to AIFF	This option enables you to save the movie's sound in the AIFF format, which can be used in almost any application that works with sound. You can also export sounds from your movies in this format to use as system sounds.
Sound to Wave	This is a sound format that is common on Windows PCs.

When you select one of these export formats, you can use the Options button to configure the specifications to export the file with. In the resulting Settings dialog box, you can configure the format you are exporting. For example, when you export a movie as a DV Stream, you can choose the video format and the audio format. If you use the MPEG-4 format, you will see a Settings dialog box with five tabs that enable you to configure various aspects of the resulting MPEG-4 movie, such as its size, video and audio quality, streaming properties, and compatibility. Although covering the options for specific formats is beyond the scope of this book, you should take a look at the options that are available for specific export formats that you use.

USING QUICKTIME PLAYER KEYBOARD SHORTCUTS

QuickTime Player keyboard shortcuts are shown in Table 19.5.

TABLE 19.5   KEYBOARD SHORTCUTS FOR QUICKTIME PLAYER

Action	Keyboard Shortcut
Add	Option-⌘-V
Add Movie As Favorite	⌘-D
Add Scaled (scale frames to selection)	Option-Shift-⌘-C
Close Player window	⌘-W
Export	⌘-E
Find	⌘-R
Find Again	⌘-G
Get movie properties	⌘-J
Jump crop markers to Playhead, play movie forward, and begin selecting frames	Shift-⌘-right arrow; hold down Shift-⌘ keys to continue process
Loop	⌘-L
Move to next crop marker or to end of movie	Shift-Option-left arrow
Move to next crop marker or to start of movie	Shift-Option-right arrow
Move Playhead backward one frame	Left arrow
Move Playhead and crop marker backward one frame	Shift-left arrow

19

TABLE 19.5   CONTINUED

Action	Keyboard Shortcut
Move Playhead forward one frame	Right arrow
Move Playhead and crop marker forward one frame	Shift-right arrow
New Player Window	⌘-N
Open URL	⌘-U
Pause movie (movie playing)	Spacebar or Return
Play movie (movie paused)	Spacebar or Return
Play movie at double size	⌘-2
Play movie at half size	⌘-0
Play movie at normal size	⌘-1
Play movie backward (review)	⌘-left arrow
Play movie forward at higher speed	⌘-right arrow
Play movie in Full Screen mode	⌘-F
Play movie in reverse while moving right crop marker to deselect frames	Shift-⌘-left arrow; hold down Shift-⌘ keys to continue process
Play Selected Frames Only	⌘-T
Replace selected frames	Shift-Option-V
Select All Frames	⌘-A
Select None (no frames)	⌘-B
Show Movie Info	⌘-I
Turn down volume	⌘-down arrow
Turn volume to maximum	Shift-Option-up arrow
Turn volume to minimum	Shift-Option-down arrow
Turn up volume	⌘-up arrow

19

CHAPTER 20

USING THE OTHER *i* APPLICATIONS

In this chapter

WORKING WITH iCAL, iSYNC, AND iCHAT

Although the three applications that are the topic of this chapter might not be quite as exciting as the other *i* applications, they are very useful and you might find yourself using them even more regularly than you do the others. Here's a quick summary of these "other" *i* applications:

- **iCal**—Enables you to do the tasks you would expect from a calendar application, including creating events, managing a to-do list, and so on. However, where iCal separates itself from other calendar applications is the ease with which you can make your calendar available to others over the Web and access calendars that others make available to you.

- **iSync**—Serves a single purpose, which is to keep two things in sync. What is amazing about this application is how diverse those two things can be. Along with keeping computers on the same page, you can also synchronize other devices, such as a Bluetooth Palm PDA with your iCal calendar and Address Book.

- **iChat**—When you need to communicate with someone else in real time, there's no easier or more powerful way to do it than with iChat. Of course, you can also use it to do text instant messages. Although somewhat useful, that isn't anything to write home about. However, with iChat, a broadband Internet connection, and a FireWire camera, you can use iChat to conduct videoconferencing and audioconferencing. And that is something to write home about, or actually, that is something to have a videoconference with home about.

MANAGING YOUR CALENDAR WITH iCAL

We all have busy lives and, if you are like me, you have trouble remembering where you are supposed to be and when you are supposed to be there. Fortunately, Mac OS X's iCal calendar application can help you keep your schedule under control. With this tool, you can maintain multiple calendars at the same time, such as a work calendar, family calendar, and so on. Even better, you can share your calendar with others so coordinating activities is much easier. You can also access other people's calendars to see how your schedule meshes with theirs.

CONFIGURING iCAL

You don't need to configure many preferences in iCal, but if you open iCal Preferences, you will see the following options (see Figure 20.1):

- **Week**—Use the "Days per week" and "Start week on" pop-up menus to configure how iCal manages and displays weeks. You can select 7- or 5-day weeks and set the start day of the week.

- **Day**—Use the pop-up menus in this area to set the start and end times for your days and to chose how many hours are displayed at a time.

- **Month**—The "Show time in month view" check box determines whether the time is displayed next to events when you are viewing your calendar in the Month view.

- **Time Zone**—iCal's Time Zone Support feature enables the application to add time zone information to your calendar. You can then associate events with specific time zones and change the time zone for which you are viewing events. This feature is most useful when you are using iCal while traveling. As you change time zones, you can set iCal to use the time zone you are currently in. Then, it adjusts the time for each event so it is appropriate to the time zone you are in. If you leave this check box unchecked, time zone is ignored.

- **Events and To Do items**—Use these tools to configure how events and To Do items are managed. Use the "Sort To Do items by" pop-up menu to choose how To Do items are sorted; your options are due date, priority, and summary. Use the "Delete events and To Do items after" check box and text box to determine whether iCal deletes these items and, if so, the number of days after they occur that must pass before these items are deleted from your calendar. The "Hide To Do items with due dates outside the calendar view" check box enables you to hide any To Do items that don't need to be done during the period you are currently viewing. The "Hide To Do items" check box and text box enable you to have iCal hide To Do items after they are completed and to set the number of days that must pass until completed items are hidden.

Figure 20.1
Configuring iCal isn't hard to do.

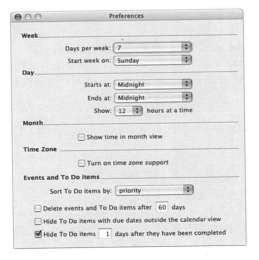

USING ICAL

Like other *i* applications, iCal is pretty simple to use. If you have used other calendar applications, you probably will have an easy time moving to iCal. By default, the iCal window has three panes (see Figure 20.2).

Subscribed-to calendar

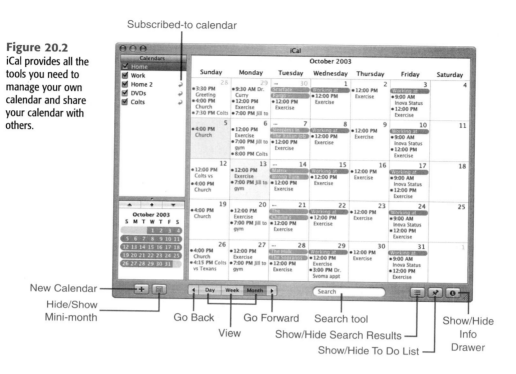

Figure 20.2
iCal provides all the tools you need to manage your own calendar and share your calendar with others.

New Calendar

Hide/Show Mini-month

Go Back

View

Go Forward

Search tool

Show/Hide Search Results

Show/Hide To Do List

Show/Hide Info Drawer

Along the upper-left side of the window is the Calendars pane. In this pane, you see each calendar you have created along with those to which you have subscribed. If a calendar's check box is checked, its events are being displayed. If not, they are hidden.

The lower-left pane contains the Mini-month tool, which shows you a month at a glance.

In the right pane is the calendar itself. There are three views for this: Day, Week, and Month.

Along the bottom of the window are the following tools:

- **New Calendar**—Click this to create a new calendar.
- **Hide/Show Mini-month**—This shows or hides the mini-month tool. When you are viewing the mini-month, you can move back in time by clicking the Back button (the upward-facing arrowhead above the mini-month), forward by clicking the Forward button (the downward-facing arrowhead), or to the current month by clicking the Current Month button (the diamond).
- **Go Back**—Use this to go back by a day, week, or month (whichever is currently displayed).
- **View**—Use these three buttons to change the view of the calendar window.
- **Go Forward**—Use this to go forward by a day, week, or month (whichever is currently displayed).

20

- **Search tool**—Use this to search for events. This tool works similarly to the Search tool in other areas, such as iTunes or the Finder. One difference is that when you enter search text, iCal's Search Results pane opens automatically, which leads right into the next bullet.

- **Show/Hide Search Results**—Click this to open the search results pane, which appears just under the calendar pane (see Figure 20.3). This pane lists all the events that meet your search criterion.

Figure 20.3
Here, I have searched for items related to the Indianapolis Colts; because I have subscribed to the Colts calendar online, I see all the vital game information.

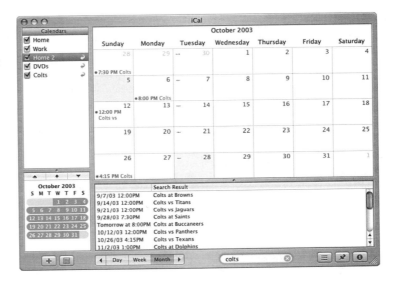

- **Show/Hide To Do List**—This button opens the To Do Items pane, which shows the To Do items on your plate.

- **Show/Hide Info Drawer**—Clicking this opens the Info Drawer that provides detailed information about a calendar, an event, or a To Do item you have selected (see Figure 20.4).

TIP

If you turn on the Time Zone preference, the Time Zone pop-up menu appears in the upper-right corner of the iCal window. Use this to select the time zone for the current calendar. The default is the time zone set in the System Preferences application. You can select Other on the pop-up menu to open the "Change time zone" window and use its tools to change the time zone for the calendar.

CREATING, CONFIGURING, AND WORKING WITH CALENDARS

As you read earlier, you can manage multiple calendars within the iCal application. For example, you might want to create separate calendars for home and work activities, for special projects, and so on. Each calendar can include its own events and To Do items. To create a new calendar, do the following steps:

1. Click the New Calendar button. A new, untitled calendar appears on the Calendar list.

2. Enter the name of the new calendar and press Return.

3. Select Window, Show Info (⌘-I), or click the Show Info button. The Info drawer opens. At the top of the Drawer, the name of the calendar is shown so that you know which calendar you are getting information about.

4. Click the word `Description` and enter a description of the calendar.

5. Use the Color pop-up menu to associate a color with the calendar. When you add events to the calendar, they appear in the color your select. Having different colors for different calendars is useful because you can easily see which events came from which calendars when you are viewing multiple calendars at the same time.

Figure 20.4
In this example, I have selected a very important item on my To Do list and opened the Info Drawer so I can see and configure the details for that event.

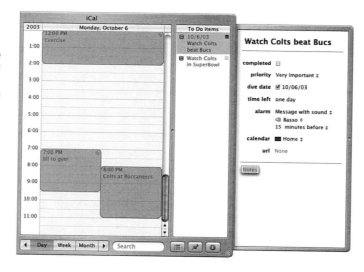

To include a calendar's events and To Do items in the calendar being displayed, check its check box. If you uncheck a calendar's box, its events and To Do items are hidden.

WORKING WITH EVENTS

You can use iCal to track life events of all kinds. You can associate events with specific calendars, set reminders, and so on. To create an event, do the following steps:

1. Select the calendar and then the day on which you want the event to appear.

2. Select File, New Event (⌘-N), or open the contextual menu over the day on which you want the event to appear. A new event appears on the selected date.

3. Type the name of the event and press Return.

4. Open the Info Drawer by selecting Window, Show Info (⌘-I). The Info Drawer shows the new event you have created.

5. Enter information about the location of the event by replacing the word location that appears under the event's title.

6. Check the "all-day" check box if the event is an all-day event.

7. If it isn't an all-day event, use the "from" and "to" fields to set a start and end time for the event.

TIP

> You can also change or set the date of the event using the "from" and "to" fields.

8. Enter attendees for the event in the "attendees" field. You can type in names or drag them from your Address Book. To show people in your Address Book, select Window, Show People (Option-⌘-A). You can drag people from the People window onto the "attendees" list. To enter multiple attendees, press Return after each name.

9. Assign a status to the event using the "status" pop-up menu.

10. If you want the event to repeat, use the "repeat" pop-up menu. You can choose a standard frequency for the event or select Custom to set a custom frequency. When you choose a frequency, the "end" pop-up menu appears. Use this to choose an end date for the repeating event.

11. If you want to set an alarm for the event, use the "alarm" pop-up menu. Your options for the alarm are the following: None, which has no alarm; Message, which displays a text message; "Message with sound," which displays a text message and plays a sound; Email, which causes an email to be sent to you; and "Open file," which opens a file of your choice. If you select an alarm with sound, the sound pop-up menu appears. If you choose any type of alarm, a pop-up menu that enables you to set the alarm time appears. If you select Email, a pop-up menu that enables you to select the email address to which the alarm should be set appears.

TIP

> The email addresses that appear on the "alert" pop-up menus for events or To Do items are those that are on your card in the Address Book application. To add more addresses, add them to your card.

20

12. Select the sound for the alarm if applicable and the amount of time before the event that you want the alarm to be activated.

13. If you want to change the calendar on which the event appears, use the "calendar" pop-up menu to do so.

14. If a URL is associated with the event, enter it in the "url" field.

15. Enter any notes about the event in the Notes field.

16. Review the event and make any necessary changes; then close the Info window if you want to (see Figure 20.5).

Figure 20.5
Here's an event worthy of being in iCal.

To view or change the details of an event, click the event in the calendar and then click the Show Info button (if the Info Drawer is closed). Make changes to the event as needed and the changes are saved automatically.

Here are some additional tips for working with events:

- You can change the date on which an event occurs by dragging it from one date in the calendar to another.

- You can change the calendar on which an event occurs by opening its contextual menu (Control-click the event) and selecting the event's new calendar.

- You can duplicate an event by opening its contextual menu and selecting Duplicate; selecting Edit, Duplicate; or pressing ⌘-D. You can drag the copy onto a different date.

- You can email an event to others by opening its contextual menu and selecting "Mail event." Your default email application opens and the event is included as an attachment (see Figure 20.6). The recipient can then drag the attachment, which has the extension `.ics`, onto iCal to add it to his calendar.

- If you have turned on the time zone feature, the "time zone" pop-up menu appears in the Info Drawer when you view the event. You can use this to set the time zone for the event. This is especially useful if you will be inviting people who are not in your current time zone.

Figure 20.6
You can email events to other so they can easily add them to their own calendars.

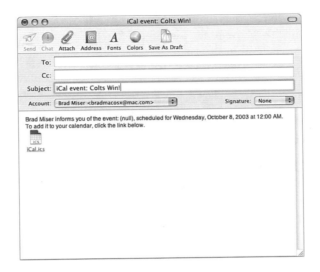

WORKING WITH YOUR TO DO LIST

To create a To Do item, use the following steps:

1. Either open the To Do pane, open its contextual menu, and select New To Do or select File, New To Do (⌘-K). A new To Do item appears on the To Do list.

2. Type the name of the To Do item and press Return.

3. Open the Info Drawer if it isn't open already. Information about the event appears.

4. Use the "priority" pop-up menu to set the To Do item's priority.

5. If the event has a due date, check the "due date" check box and use the date field that appears to set the due date.

6. If you want to set an alarm for the event, open the "alarm" pop-up menu and select the alarm you want to set. The options are the same as those for an event.

7. Select the calendar with which the To Do item should be associated on the "calendar" pop-up menu.

8. If a URL is associated with the To Do item, enter it in the "url" field.

9. Enter any notes for the To Do item in the Notes field.

Following are some tips for working with To Do items:

- You can change a To Do item by selecting it and opening the Info Drawer. Then use the tools to change the item's information; these work just like when you create a To Do item.

- When you have completed a To Do item, mark it as complete by checking the box next to its name or by checking the "completed" box on the Info Drawer.

■ The priority of a To Do item is indicated by the number of bars that appear to the right of its name on the To Do items list (see Figure 20.7).

Figure 20.7
You can use iCal to manage your To Do list (hopefully, your list has more meaningful items than mine does).

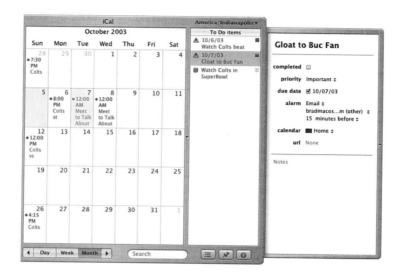

■ Open a To Do item's contextual menu to duplicate it, change the calendar with which it is associated, mark its priority, email it, or change the sort order for the To Do items pane.

■ When the due date for an item passes, its complete check box becomes a warning icon to indicate that the item is overdue.

TIP

> When you email an event or a To Do item to someone, the recipient can add the item to his calendar by clicking its link or by dragging it onto the iCal window.

PRINTING FROM ICAL

From iCal, you can print calendars, To Do lists, and mini-months. When you open the Print dialog box, select iCal on the third pop-up menu. This opens the iCal print controls (see Figure 20.8). You can use these controls to choose the iCal items you want to print and set the date window for which you want to print the selected items.

SYNCHRONIZING YOUR CALENDAR IN MULTIPLE LOCATIONS

If you use more than one Mac, you will probably want to keep your iCal calendar on each machine synchronized. To do this, you use iSync.

→ To learn how to synchronize information on multiple machines, **see** "Synchronizing with iSync," **p. 689**.

Figure 20.8
iCal offers flexible printing options.

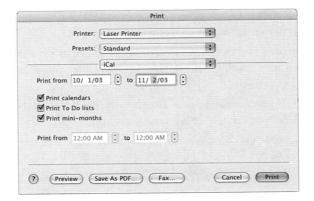

SHARING YOUR ICAL CALENDAR

One of the cool things about iCal is that you can publish your calendars online so other people can view them. You can choose to share an iCal calendar via your .Mac account or use any other WebDAV server.

TIP

> Because you can access a shared calendar over the Web, sharing your calendar provides a way for you to view your calendar even if your Mac isn't available. As long as you can access the Web, you can get to and view your calendar.

To publish your calendar, use the following steps:

1. Select the calendar you want to share.
2. Select Calendar, Publish. The Publish sheet appears (see Figure 20.9).

Figure 20.9
You can easily publish your calendars via .Mac.

3. Type the name of the calendar as you want it to appear online; by default the calendar's name is entered, but you can change this if you want to.

4. If you want changes you make to your calendar to be published automatically, check the "Publish changes automatically" check box. In most cases, you should check this so your calendar is always up-to-date.

5. If you want both the subject and notes associated with an item to be published, check the "Publish subjects and notes" check box.

6. If you want the alarms and To Do items to be published, check the "Publish alarms" and "Publish To Do items" check boxes.

7. Choose how you want to publish the calendar on the "Publish calendar" pop-up menu. Select "on .Mac" to use your .Mac account or "on a WebDAV server" to choose a different server. If you chose the latter option, you need to enter the server's URL along with your username and password for that server.

NOTE

If you haven't configured your .Mac account when you start to publish your calendar, you are prompted to do so.

8. Click Publish. When the calendar has been published, you see the confirmation dialog box. This dialog box provides the URL for the calendar and enables you to visit the calendar online or send an email announcing the calendar (see Figure 20.10).

Figure 20.10
Even though this shared calendar isn't too interesting, it can be viewed on the Web at any time.

Following are some more pointers on sharing your calendars online:

■ When a calendar is shared, the shared icon (which looks like a dot radiating waves) appears next to the calendar's name.

■ If you open a shared calendar's contextual menu, you see several interesting commands. These include Unpublish, which removes the calendar from the Web; Send publish email, which enables you to send an email announcing the published calendar and its URL; Copy URL to Clipboard, which copies the calendar's URL to the Clipboard so you can easily paste it into documents; Refresh, which publishes any changes you have made to the calendar; and Change Location, which enables you to move the calendar to a different site.

■ People can subscribe to your shared calendars so they appear in their iCal windows. More on this in the next section.

■ You can view your own shared calendar at any time from any computer by moving to its URL. This is a great way to maintain access to your own calendar when you aren't at your Mac.

■ You can change a shared calendar by selecting and opening the Info Drawer. Use the controls in the Drawer to make changes to the calendar's settings.

SUBSCRIBING TO OTHER CALENDARS

You can subscribe to other calendars to add them to your iCal window. You can also subscribe to other personal calendars or public calendars.

SUBSCRIBING TO PERSONAL CALENDARS

You can add other personal calendars to your iCal window by doing the following steps:

1. Select Calendar, Subscribe (Option-⌘-S). The Subscribe sheet appears.

2. Enter the URL for the calendar to which you want to subscribe.

3. If you want the calendar's information to be refreshed automatically, check the Refresh check box and select the frequency at which you want the refresh to occur on the pop-up menu.

4. If you don't want the calendar's alarms to appear in your iCal window, check the "Remove alarms" check box.

5. If you don't want the calendar's To Do items to show up in your iCal window, check the "Remove To Do items" check box. You usually don't want to display the To Do items on a calendar to which you are subscribing unless you have To Do items on it.

6. Click Subscribe. The calendar is added to your iCal window and you can view it just like your own calendars. iCal indicates that it is a subscribed-to calendar by the curved arrow icon next to the calendar's name. If you set the calendar to be refreshed automatically (refer to step 3), it is kept current.

20

TIP

> If you don't set a calendar to be refreshed automatically, you can refresh it manually by opening its contextual menu and selecting Refresh.

NOTE

> You can't make any changes to a calendar to which you are subscribed. You can only view it.

SUBSCRIBING TO PUBLIC CALENDARS

Many public calendars are available to which you can subscribe. For example, most professional sports teams have calendars that show games and other events. You can also find DVD release calendars, TV schedules, and many other types of calendars to subscribe to. Just like personal calendars, when you subscribe to public calendars, the events on those calendars are shown in your iCal window. To find and subscribe to public calendars, do the following steps:

1. Select Calendar, Find Shared Calendars. Your default Web browser opens showing Apple's Calendar library (see Figure 20.11).

Figure 20.11
This Web page provides all sorts of interesting calendars to which you can subscribe.

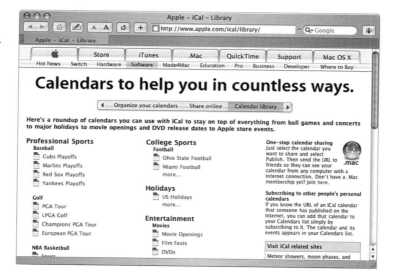

2. Click the calendar to which you want to subscribe. You move into iCal and the Subscribe To sheet appears. The relevant information is filled in automatically.
3. Review the subscribe options and change them as needed.
4. Click Subscribe. The calendar is added to your iCal window and you can view its events.

TIP

On the iCal Library page, click the iCalShare.com link to move to a page with even more calendars to which you can subscribe.

SYNCHRONIZING WITH ISYNC

iSync enables you to synchronize calendar, Safari bookmark, and contact information among multiple computers and other devices, such as PDAs or cell phones. To use iSync among a group of computers, you need to have a .Mac account. However, you can use iSync to synchronize other devices without a .Mac account.

CONFIGURING ISYNC PREFERENCES

Configure the relevant iSync preferences with the following steps:

1. Launch iSync (Applications folder) and open the iSync Preferences dialog box by selecting iSync, Preferences (⌘-,).

2. To show the iSync menu in the menu bar, check the "Show iSync in menu bar" check box.

3. If you want iSync to warn you when you attempt to sync a Palm device, check the "Display Palm HotSync warning" check box. When you attempt to synchronize a Palm device, you are instructed to use the HotSync software instead (you will learn how to configure iSync for Palm devices in a later section).

4. If you want to be alerted when data changes on your Mac, check the "Show Data Change Alert when" pop-up menu and select the amount of data that must be changed before you see a warning. Your options are "any," "more than 1%," "more than 5%," or "more than 10%."

5. Close the Preferences dialog box.

SYNCHRONIZING MACS WITH ISYNC

Before you can use iSync, you need to set up each Mac you will synchronize with it. To do this, use the following steps:

NOTE

Before configuring iSync, make sure your .Mac account is configured on the Mac.

1. On one of the Macs you want to synchronize, launch iSync.

2. Click the .mac button in the upper-left corner of the iSync window.

3. Click the Register button in the lower-right corner of the resulting sheet.

4. Enter a name for the Mac you are registering—use a unique name for each machine.

20

5. Click Continue. Your Mac signs on to the .Mac server and registers itself. When that process is complete, the Synchronization Setup dialog box appears (see Figure 20.12).

Figure 20.12
Use this window to configure how iSync synchronizes the information on this Mac.

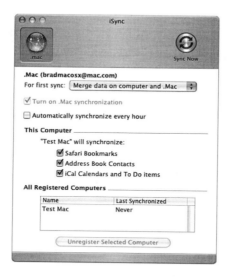

6. On the "For first sync" pop-up menu, select the option you want to use for the first synchronization for the Mac on which you are working. Select "Merge data on computer and .Mac" if you want the data on your Mac to be uploaded to the .Mac server and the data on the server to be downloaded to your Mac. Select "Erase data on .Mac and the sync" if you want the data on your Mac to replace any data stored on the .Mac site. Select "Erase data on computer then sync" if you want the data on your Mac to be replaced by the data on the .Mac server.

7. If you want synchronization to occur automatically every hour, check the "Automatically synchronize every hour" check box.

8. Check the boxes for the data you want to be synchronized. Your choices are Safari Bookmarks, Address Book Contacts, and iCal Calendars and To Do items.

9. Click the Sync Now button. Your Mac takes the action you indicated in step 6, and the progress of the process is shown in the iSync window (see Figure 20.13). If you set an alert to display, it is shown when the amount of data you selected (of each type, such as Contacts) is changed (see Figure 20.14). Click Proceed to finish the process for that data type. When the process is complete, the same data exists on the .Mac server and on the Mac.

TIP

Click the Cancel Sync button to stop the synchronize process.

Figure 20.13
This progress bar shows you how the synchronize process is going.

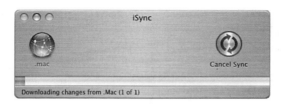

Figure 20.14
When you see this dialog box, you know that some data on your Mac is going to be changed.

10. Repeat steps 1–9 for each Mac you want to synchronize. Make sure you don't choose to erase the data on the .Mac server after you have synced at least one machine to it. After you have synchronized all your Macs, each Mac contains the same set of data.

If you have set each Mac to synchronize automatically, you don't need to do anything because iSync manages the process for you. If you don't have a Mac set to be synchronized automatically, either open iSync and click the Sync Now button or select Devices, Sync Now (⌘-T).

Following are some iSync pointers:

■ You can view a log showing each synchronization by selecting Window, Show Logs (⌘-L). In the resulting Log window, you see each synchronization that has been done.

■ To see a list of all the Macs you are synchronizing with iSync, open iSync and click the .mac button. At the bottom of the window, you see each Mac you have registered.

■ To stop synchronization on a specific machine, open iSync, click the .mac button, and uncheck the "Turn on .Mac synchronization" check box. That Mac is no longer synchronized. Check the box again to turn synchronization back on.

■ To remove a Mac from the list of registered computers, select it on the list of registered machines and click Unregister This Computer for the current Mac or Unregister Selected Computer to unregister a different one.

■ If you installed the iSync menu on the menu bar, you can see the time of the last synchronization on that Mac. You can also perform synchronization by selecting Sync Now or open iSync by selecting Open iSync.

■ To create a backup of the data on a Mac, open iSync and select Devices, Back Up My Data. This creates a backup copy of the data on your Mac. You can restore this data by selecting Devices, Revert to Backup.

20

■ You can revert to the most recent synchronization by opening iSync and selecting Devices, Revert to Last Sync.

NOTE

> If you use iCal to manage your To Do list, make sure you keep all the Macs you synchronize up-to-date by using the automatic synchronization option or by performing regular manual synchronizations. Otherwise, you might see alarms for To Do items you have already completed.

TIP

> You can also use iSync to synchronize contact and calendar data on an iPod with your Mac.

SYNCHRONIZING A MAC WITH A PALM PDA

One of the most useful things you can do with iSync is synchronize a Palm PDA so that its information is transferred to your iCal and Address Book on your Mac and vice versa. Unfortunately, iSync doesn't support this by default. Before you can synch with a Palm device using iSync, you must complete the following setup steps:

1. Go to www.apple.com/isync/tipsandtricks.html.
2. Download the iSync Palm Conduit.
3. Install the iSync Palm Conduit.
4. Open the HotSync Manager application that was part of the PDA's software installation.
5. Select Hot Sync, Conduit Settings. The Conduit Settings window appears.
6. On the resulting sheet, check the "Enable iSync for this Palm device" check box.
7. Click OK.

NOTE

> Before synchronizing your Palm device with iSync, synchronize it with the Palm software and cradle or Bluetooth first. This ensures that the device is properly configured. Then, you can use iSync to manage the synchronization of the device.

To synchronize the Palm device with your Mac, do the following steps:

1. Open iSync. The Palm device appears at the top of the iSync window (see Figure 20.15).
2. Click the Palm icon. The Palm synchronization sheet appears (see Figure 20.16).

Figure 20.15
After you install the iSync conduit, your Palm device appears in the iSync window.

Figure 20.16
You can use this sheet to configure how your Palm device is synced with your Mac.

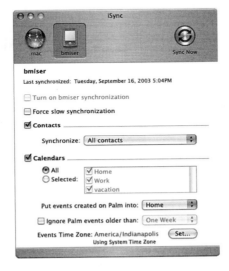

3. If you want to synchronize your contact information on the Palm device with your Address Book, check the Contacts check box and select the contacts on the Synchronize pop-up menu. Select "All contacts" to have all the information synchronized, or select specific groups in your Address Book.

4. If you want your iCal calendars to be synchronized, check the Calendars check box. Then, click the All radio button to have all your calendars synchronized or the Selected radio button to have only selected calendars synchronized. If you choose Selected, check the box for each calendar you want to include in the synchronization.

5. Select the iCal calendar on which you want events created on the Palm to be placed from the "Put events created on Palm into" pop-up menu.

6. If you want old events on the Palm to be ignored, check the "Ignore Palm events older than" check box and select the period of time within which events must fall to be included in the synchronization on the pop-up menu.

7. If you want to set the time zone for events, click the Set button and use the resulting sheet to select a time zone.

After you have configured the Palm device for synchronization, you can synchronize it by pressing its HotSync button. iSync launches and you see the progress of the synchronization process in the iSync window.

20

If problems occur when syncing the information on the Palm device and your Mac, you see the Conflict Resolver (see Figure 20.17). Two versions of the information are shown. One version is labeled "This computer," whereas the other is labeled with the name of the Palm device. Click the version you want to keep and click Continue. Keep working through the data until you have resolved all the problems.

Figure 20.17
Use the Conflict Resolver to fix problems when synchronizing data between a Mac and a Palm device.

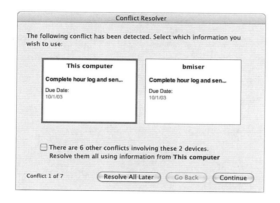

After you have synchronized your PDA and your Mac, your schedule and contacts are available from both locations.

COMMUNICATING WITH iCHAT AV

 iChat is Mac OS X's instant messaging and video/audio conferencing application. Although it enables you to text chat with others, you can now have audio- and videoconferences via iChat AV.

To text chat, each person must have an iChat, a .Mac, or an AOL Instant Messenger account. To chat with audio or video, both parties must be using a .Mac account.

CONFIGURING iCHAT

If you are going to use iChat to have audio- and videoconferences, you must have a FireWire camera attached to your Mac. You can use an Apple iSight camera, shown in Figure 20.18, or some FireWire camcorders for this purpose. You also need a broadband connection to the Internet.

NOTE

To use a camcorder for chatting, the camera must support play through, meaning the input coming through the camera's lens must play through the FireWire out port at the same time. If your camera doesn't offer this, you won't be able to use it to chat. Fortunately, most camcorders work with iChat.

Figure 20.18
An iSight camera is an inexpensive way to add AV capabilities to your Mac.

Connect the camera you are going to use to your Mac. If it is a camcorder, power it up and prepare it to capture footage by placing it in the camera mode.

If you don't have a FireWire camera or a broadband connection to the Internet, you can still use iChat for text chatting.

NOTE

Many camcorders are set to go to sleep after a certain period of inactivity passes. When you are using a camcorder during a video conference, it thinks it is inactive because you aren't recording. When it goes to sleep, your conference suddenly ends. Use your camcorder's controls to set its sleep to a large value or to turn off its sleep mode.

To get started, launch iChat and use the following steps to configure it:

1. Review the information in the welcome screen and click Continue. The "Set up a new iChat Account" window appears. If you have a .Mac account configured for the current user account, the account information is configured automatically. If not, enter the .Mac or AIM account information in the window and click Continue.

TIP

If you want to apply for an iChat account, click the Get an iChat Account button and follow the onscreen instructions to register for a trial .Mac account. The accompanying iChat account remains valid even if you let the .Mac account expire.

2. After you have completed the account configuration, click Continue. The "Set up Rendezvous Messaging" window opens.

3. If other Macs are on a network with which you can communicate, click the "Use Rendezvous messaging" radio button. This enables you to chat with others on your local network because all Rendezvous devices are found automatically. If you use a wireless network in a public place, you might want to leave this off.

4. Click Continue to see the "Set up iChat AV" window. During this step, iChat attempts to connect to a camera connected to your Mac. If it finds one, the image being broadcast by that camera is shown. Just under the image is a volume level indicator that displays the relative volume of the source's audio input. If a camera is not found, a message stating that there is no camera attached to the computer is shown.

5. Click Continue to see the Conclusion screen.

6. Click Done. The basic configuration of iChat is complete.

iChat offers a number of preferences you can use to configure the way it works. The general preferences you can configure and a description of some specific preferences that might interest include

■ **General**—Use the General tab of the iChat Preferences dialog box to configure some general iChat behaviors (see Figure 20.19). The Settings check boxes enable you to configure various settings. For example, you can set iChat to automatically log you in when you open iChat. You can also add the iChat status to the menu bar. Use the radio buttons to determine what happens when you log in to your user account and your iChat status is Away; for example, you might want your status to be updated to Available automatically. Use the "Save received files to" pop-up menu to select a location in which you save files you receive via iChat.

Figure 20.19
Use the General pane to configure various iChat settings.

- **Accounts**—Use the Accounts pane to configure the account over which you want to chat.

- **Messages**—The Messages pane enables you to set various formatting options for your messages (see Figure 20.20). Use the Set Font button to configure the font in which you want to view text messages. Use the balloon and font color pop-up menus to choose the color of those items. Check the "Reformat incoming messages" check box and use the corresponding Set Font button and pop-up menus to have iChat reformat text you receive according to your preferences. If you want text to be sent as you type it (when you are using Rendezvous messaging), check the "Send text as I type" check box. Use the "Confirm before sending files" check box if you want to confirm a command to send a file before it is sent. If you want to save the transcript for chat messages, check the "Automatically save chat transcripts" check box and use the Open Folder button to choose the location in which you want the transcripts to be stored.

Figure 20.20
Using the Messages preferences, you can control the formatting used for chatting.

- **Alerts**—Use the Alerts pane to set the alerts and notifications iChat uses to get your attention. Select the event for which you want to configure an alert on the Event pop-up menu and then select the specific alert on the check boxes and pop-up menus to configure it. Repeat these steps for each event for which you want to set an alert.

- **Privacy**—Use the radio buttons to set access levels to your iChat account. If you select one of the Specific People options, use the Edit List button to create a list of people who should be allowed or denied access. Use the check boxes at the bottom of the pane to block others from seeing that you are idle or to prevent Rendezvous users from seeing your email and AIM addresses.

- **Video**—Use these preferences to configure AV conferencing (see Figure 20.21). In this pane, you see the current image being received from the camera connected to your Mac. Just under the image is an audio meter that provides a graphic representation of

20

the volume level being received. If you want to set a bandwidth limit for conferencing, use the Bandwidth Limit pop-up menu to do so. Check the "Automatically open iChat when camera is turned on" check box to have iChat launch when you turn on your camera. Check the "Play repeated ring sound when invited to a conference" to be notified via a ringing sound when someone wants to conference with you.

Figure 20.21
Use the Video pane to configure AV conferencing.

SETTING UP CHATTING BUDDIES

There are two sources of people with whom you can chat; in iChat lingo these are called *buddies*. One source is the people who your Mac can see via Rendezvous. The other source is people who are configured in your Address Book and have either a .Mac email address or an AIM screen name.

When you open iChat, you see two windows: One is titled Rendezvous, and the other is labeled Buddy List (see Figure 20.22). The people shown on the Rendezvous list are found automatically when your Mac searches your local network for Rendezvous users. You add people with whom you want to chat on the Buddy List. You can chat with people on either of these lists in the same way.

NOTE

If you haven't enabled Rendezvous messaging, you don't see the Rendezvous pane.

To add people to your Buddy list, do the following steps:

1. Add the person you want to place on your Buddy List to your Address Book; include either a .Mac address or an AIM username.

2. In iChat, click the Add Buddy button located in the lower-left corner of the Buddy List window. The resulting sheet shows all the people in your Address Book. Search or browse in the list to find the person you want to add to your Buddy List.

3. Select the person you want to add to your Buddy List and click the Select Buddy button. You move back to the Buddy List and the person you selected is shown on the list.

4. Repeat steps 2 and 3 to add more people to your list.

Figure 20.22
The Rendezvous window shows users who are available to chat on your local network, whereas the Buddy List shows users who have been added to your permanent Buddy List.

CHATTING WITH TEXT

You can text chat with others by using the following steps:

1. Select the person in the Rendezvous window or on the Buddy List with whom you want to chat.

2. Click the Text Chat button, which is the A located at the bottom of the respective window. An empty Instant Message window appears.

3. Type your message.

4. When you are done, press Return to see the message you typed near your name at the top of the window. It is sent to the person with whom you are chatting.

   Your message appears in a text bubble on that user's desktop. When the user clicks the bubble, she is able to type a reply and send it you.

   When you receive a reply to your message, you see the person's picture along with the text she sent.

5. Type your response in the message box at the bottom of the window and press Return.

TIP

Click the emoticon icon at the end of the text box to include a smiley with your text.

20

6. Continue chatting to your heart's content (see Figure 20.23).

Figure 20.23
Hopefully, your iChats will be more meaningful than this one!

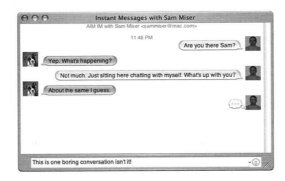

7. When you are done chatting, close the Instant Message window.

CONFERENCING WITH VIDEO AND SOUND

If a person you want to talk to and see meets the requirements for AV chatting, click the camera icon next to the person with whom you want to conference. A request for conference is sent to that person. You also see a Video Chat window that shows the image being transmitted by your camera.

The person with whom you are trying to communicate sees a Video Chat invitation window. If he clicks your name in that window, it expands to show a Video Chat window on his machine. He can then select to Accept or Deny your request.

If he accepts, you see a message that video conferencing is starting.

When the conference starts, two windows open within the video chat window. The larger window shows the image being transmitted, and the smaller window shows the image you are transmitting.

TIP

> You can move the smaller window around by dragging it. You can click the full-screen mode button (the square with two arrows in it) to make the Video Chat window fill the screen.

Speak normally, and you should keep your movements a bit slower than usual so the motion is smoother on the other end. Depending on how many servers the data has to flow through and how fast each person's connection is, considerable delay might occur. You need to adjust your speech and movement to fit the specific conference in which you are participating. In most cases, this delay won't be a problem for you. When you are done with your conference, close the window.

20

Mac OS X: Expanding Your System

CHAPTER 21

UNDERSTANDING INPUT AND OUTPUT TECHNOLOGY

In this chapter

UNDERSTANDING INTERFACE TECHNOLOGY

The heart of any computer is its processor. For this processor to be capable of doing anything, it has to have data on which to operate. There are many ways in which data is moved into, out of, and within your Mac. Just to use a Mac, you do not need to understand the various technologies involved in data transfers. However, if you add enhancements to your machine—whether they are external peripherals or internal system upgrades—you do need to understand these technologies.

In this chapter, you will gain a fundamental understanding of the various input and output technologies your Mac uses to move data. This understanding will help you when the time comes to add devices or other improvements to your system.

NOTE

> The term *interface* refers to the location at which two devices are physically connected. The term also refers to the technology that particular interface uses. For example, when someone refers to devices that use a USB interface, this implies that a specific physical connector is used (a USB connector) over which data following the USB specification is communicated.

On your Mac, there are two general types of input and output interfaces: those with external interfaces (ports) and those whose interfaces are internal to the machine.

CAUTION

> Obviously, the types of interfaces available depend on the model of Mac you are using and whether you have added components to it. This chapter focuses on modern Mac models, such as the Power Mac G5, Power Mac G4, PowerBook G4, and so on. Newer machines generally support newer and better technologies. For example, the Power Mac G5 offers faster interface technologies than the Power Mac G4 does. Similarly, newer models of machines of the same class also support faster technologies. For example, later models of the Power Mac G4 added support for FireWire 800, whereas earlier models do not support this. In this chapter, you will find information on the more common interfaces used on modern Macintosh computers, but this chapter is not intended to explain all the interfaces that can be used. To be familiar with the technologies your specific Mac supports, you should study the specifications included with it.

WORKING WITH EXTERNAL INTERFACES

The most obvious data input and output interfaces are those whose ports are located on the outside of the machine. Modern Macs have a number of built-in interfaces you can use to move data into or take data out of the machine.

NOTE

All data that travels around your Mac eventually moves from one device to another. When data "crosses over," it is said to have crossed a bus. A data *bus* is simply a channel through which data flows. Many buses exist inside your Mac, and all devices have at least one bus (the point at which data enters or leaves the device).

NOTE

If you want to really dive into the details of computer buses and other technology, check out www.pcguide.com/ref/. Although this site is PC-focused, it does contain lots of great general information that is equally applicable to the Mac. For example, you can learn all you need to know about the various hard drive technologies at this site in addition to finding detailed information on memory buses, monitors, and just about anything else about which you want to learn.

ETHERNET

Ethernet is the interface that is used for almost all local area networks (LANs). Ethernet is designed for hub-based networks, which means information flowing across the network is controlled to some extent by a central Ethernet hub.

All modern Macs have built-in Ethernet ports to enable you to network with other machines; Ethernet on all modern Macs uses an RJ-45 connector, which looks like an overgrown telephone connector (see Figure 21.1).

Figure 21.1
All modern Macs have an Ethernet port. The only variation is in the speed the port supports.

21

Three different speeds of Ethernet are supported by the Mac. These are the following:

- **10 megabits per second (Mbps)**—This was the speed of the "original" Ethernet.

- **100BASE-T**—This flavor of Ethernet is 10 times as fast as the original and is also known as *Fast Ethernet*. It communicates at speeds up to 100Mbps. All modern Macs support at least 100BASE-T Ethernet.

- **Gigabit Ethernet**—The newest Ethernet standard can communicate at 1,000Mbps. Newer Power Mac G4, Power Mac G5, and Newer PowerBook G4 machines support Gigabit Ethernet.

NOTE

> The Power Mac G4 was the first PC to support Gigabit Ethernet as a standard feature. It follows in the tradition of earlier Macs, which were the first to provide built-in Ethernet support as standard equipment.

Ethernet-capable devices can communicate at various levels of speed up to their maximum speeds (such as Gigabit Ethernet). Higher-speed devices can communicate at lower speeds, but lower-speed devices can't communicate at the higher speeds. Therefore, the speed at which devices communicate over Ethernet connections always defaults to the maximum speed of the lower-speed device.

A *protocol* is the "language" in which data is communicated over a particular interface at a particular time. The physical interface might be capable of transmitting data in more than one protocol. For example, Ethernet can be used to transmit data in the AppleTalk protocol as well as using the Transmission Control Protocol/Internet Protocol (TCP/IP).

All Ethernet devices are designed to work with an Ethernet hub (or router) that acts as a traffic controller for the data being communicated among the attached devices.

Ethernet is used exclusively for networking computers to hubs, routers, or other computers.

→ To learn more about Ethernet hubs, **see** "Finding and Installing an Ethernet Hub," **p. 808**.

→ To learn more about creating and using an Ethernet network, **see** Chapter 26, "Building and Using a Network," **p. 821**.

Direct Connect Ethernet

Because Ethernet is designed to be used with hubs, you can't simply connect two Ethernet ports together to connect two machines. Instead, you have to use a special Ethernet cable, called a *crossover cable*. Using such a cable, you can connect any two Ethernet devices directly. If you use a standard Ethernet cable, the devices must be connected with an Ethernet hub.

An exception to this is the Ethernet port on some modern Mac models. It can sense whether it is connected to another device or a hub and configure itself appropriately for either situation using a standard Ethernet cable.

21

FIREWIRE 400

FireWire 400 (more commonly referred to as just *FireWire*) is a fast technology that provides an interface for many types of peripheral devices. FireWire was designed to enable very high data rate transfers (it communicates at 400Mbps), such as those required to move digital video data. At least one FireWire 400 port is available on all modern Mac models.

> **NOTE**
>
> FireWire is Apple's brand name for an industry-standard interface definition. The actual specification for the interface is IEEE 1394. Other companies use specific names for their implementations of the interface, such as Sony's term for it: i.Link.

FireWire offers several major advantages, which are the following:

- **High speed**—FireWire is capable of communicating at up to 400Mbps, making it suitable for many high-bandwidth applications.
- **Chainable**—FireWire devices can be chained together; the interface supports up to 63 devices per port.
- **Hot-swappable**—FireWire devices can be connected to and disconnected from your Mac while the Mac is running.
- **Powered connection**—The FireWire interface is capable of providing power to a peripheral device through the bus. Devices that use the capability don't require a separate power supply. Also, this enables some FireWire devices that have batteries, such as an iPod, to be charged by the Mac while it is connected.

FireWire connectors are an unusual shape and consist of a rectangle with a triangular top section (see Figure 21.2). FireWire ports are marked with a high-tech-looking *Y*.

Figure 21.2
FireWire ports can be used for various devices, the most prominent of which are digital video cameras.

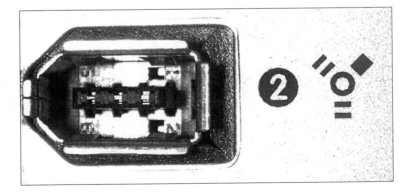

The connector shown in Figure 21.2 is that used to connect FireWire devices to your Mac. Consumer and other FireWire-equipped devices can use differently configured FireWire ports. For example, you won't find a port like that shown in Figure 21.2 on a DV camera.

Because of size limitations, DV cameras use a much smaller FireWire port that looks quite different from the FireWire ports on a Mac. Typically, these devices include the specialized cable you need to attach their ports to the FireWire port on your Mac.

CAUTION

> FireWire connectors are relatively delicate. You should always exercise care when connecting a FireWire device to a FireWire port. The pins in the connector are somewhat fragile and can be bent if you attempt to insert the connector when it is not aligned properly.

Because of its capability to move large amounts of data quickly, the FireWire interface is used for many devices, including the following:

- Digital video cameras
- External hard drives
- External drives, including CD-RW, DVD-R, and tape drives
- Other devices, such as iPods
- Scanners

Competition

Apple's implementation of FireWire has led the industry. For example, Apple is almost single-handedly responsible for the dramatic rise in the use of digital video technology. Most other computers still require that a separate card be added to be able to use devices that transfer data via the FireWire interface.

FireWire's competitor is the USB 2 interface. USB 2 is much faster than the previous USB specifications and is slightly faster than FireWire 400. Although support for FireWire is built in to Macs, it isn't built in to all Windows PCs. Most Windows PCs have USB 2 support by default, which means the market for USB 2 devices is much larger than for FireWire devices. Want some good news? Many modern Macs also support USB 2 and FireWire 800, which is much faster than USB 2. As usual, when it comes to leading technologies, the Mac is leading the way.

FIREWIRE 800

FireWire 800, as you can probably guess from its name, is faster than FireWire 400. As you can also probably guess, FireWire 800 communicates at 800Mbps. FireWire 800 supports similar devices such as hard drives but can move data at twice the rate of FireWire 400 devices. Currently, FireWire 800 devices are mostly limited to data storage, such as hard drives, but as the technology matures, it can be expected to enable other devices as well.

Another advantage of FireWire 800 over FireWire 400 is the length over which data can be communicated. FireWire 800 works over distances up to 100 meters.

FireWire 800 uses a different port than does FireWire 400 (see Figure 21.3).

Figure 21.3
FireWire 800 and FireWire 400 cables are not interchangeable, as you can see in this photo.

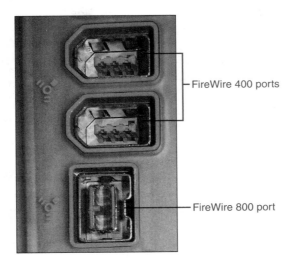

FireWire 400 ports

FireWire 800 port

USB 1.1

The universal serial bus (USB) is an interface that also provides access to external peripheral devices for your Mac. USB 1.1 is a fairly slow interface and is capable of transferring data at the rate of 12Mbps (compared to 400Mbps for FireWire 400). Although slower than many other interfaces, this speed is more than adequate for many peripheral devices.

USB ports on Macs have a thin rectangular shape (see Figure 21.4).

Figure 21.4
USB ports enable you to connect your Mac to a large variety of devices.

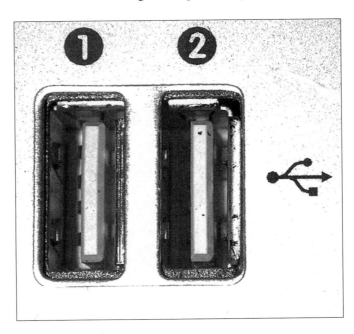

21

NOTE

Similar to FireWire, the USB ports on peripheral devices can look quite different from the USB ports on a Mac. Many USB devices have a USB port that is almost square; others have specialized shapes (such as those on digital still cameras that tend to be small).

USB offers advantages similar to those offered by FireWire, including

- **Chainable**—As with FireWire, USB devices can be chained together. A single USB port can support up to 127 devices. Many FireWire devices have two ports; one is an input port that you connect to a Mac's FireWire port or another FireWire device and the other is an output port that enables you to connect another FireWire device. This enables you to add multiple devices to a single FireWire port on a Mac without a hub.

- **Hot-swappable**—USB devices can be connected to or disconnected from your Mac while it is running.

- **Self-powered**—The USB interface can also provide power to a peripheral device, so that such devices do not require a separate power supply.

Apple Leads Again

Adoption of the USB interface across the entire computer industry can also be largely attributed to Apple. Although USB is an industry-standard interface, it was not widely used until Apple released the iMac. The success of the iMac encouraged other computer manufacturers to more strongly support the adoption of USB. All PCs are now also equipped with USB ports. Eventually, USB will replace several different ports on the PC (such as the parallel port) as it has on the Mac.

Because USB is an industry-standard interface, Macs can use the same USB hardware as PCs do. The manufacturer only has to provide Mac-specific software for the device to be Mac compatible.

All modern Macs are equipped with at least one USB port, and most have two or more. To connect more USB devices, you can install a USB hub for your system.

→ To learn more about USB hubs, **see** "Finding, Installing, and Using a USB Hub," **p. 813**.

Numerous devices can use the USB interface, including the following:

- Mice
- Keyboards
- USB hubs
- Printers
- Digital cameras
- Microphones
- Speakers
- CD-R and CD-RW drives
- Cradles for Palm OS devices
- Scanners

N O T E

Although USB supports up to 127 devices and FireWire supports up to 63, these are somewhat theoretical limits. The actual number of devices you can connect to these ports depends on the power requirements of the devices. For example, you could not connect 127 USB devices that get their power from the USB interface to a single Mac because the bus could not provide enough power for all those devices.

USB 2

USB 2 is a much faster implementation of the USB interface. It communicates at 480Mbps, which is even faster than FireWire 400. In fact, USB 2 is so fast that it is suitable for hard drives and other high data rate transfer devices.

USB 2 is supported by many modern Macs, and USB 2 has become a standard on Windows PCs. USB and USB 2 share the same hardware, so USB 2 and USB 1 devices can exist on the same USB chain. In fact, from the outside, you can't tell whether a Mac supports USB 2 or not (because the ports are the same as those used for USB 1). To determine whether your Mac supports USB 2, check the technical information provided with the machine.

If your Mac does support USB 2, many USB 2 devices are available, most of which your Mac can use even if they are not designed for the Mac. This is the benefit of supporting dominant technologies on Windows PCs—little to no development has to be done for a device to support Macs and Windows PCs. (Of course, if software is required to support the device, Mac OS X must be available for you to use that device with a Mac.)

PCI

Peripheral component interconnect (PCI) is actually an internal interface that is used to provide additional external interfaces for specific purposes through PCI cards. These cards are plugged in to available PCI slots inside the Mac, and then the ports provided by that card become available for you to use (see Figure 21.5).

N O T E

AGP is the abbreviation for *accelerated graphics port*. On Macs that include PCI slots, the AGP slot is filled with the graphics card that is installed in the Mac when it is built.

Adding PCI cards to a Mac is rather straightforward. You open the Mac's case, remove a blank cover from an available slot, insert the card into an available slot, and replace the screw that holds it in place. After any required software is installed, the ports provided by that card become available.

One of the best applications of a PCI card is to add a second monitor to your Mac by adding a second graphics card to it. On newer Power Mac G4s and G5s, the video card already supports dual monitors, but on those machines, you can add more graphics cards to add even more monitors.

21

Figure 21.5
This photo shows the three open PCI slots in a Power Mac G4; a graphics card occupies the AGP slot located toward the bottom of the photo.

Open PCI slots

Graphics card installed in the AGP PCI slot

→ To learn more about installing a second monitor for your Mac, **see** "Installing and Using a Second Monitor," **p. 749**.

Many PCI cards are available for your Mac, including the following:

- Graphics cards
- Video digitizers
- Other interfaces (such as SCSI)
- Advanced audio cards

Earlier Power Mac G4 models came with four PCI slots; one was occupied by the graphics card installed by Apple, leaving three open slots as shown previously in Figure 21.5. Beginning with the models released in January 2001, Power Mac G4s have four open PCI slots plus the AGP slot occupied by a graphics card.

NOTE

> PCI is also an industry-standard interface. Earlier in the Mac's history, Apple used a proprietary interface, called NuBus, to accomplish the same purpose. Because NuBus cards were unique to the Mac, fewer types were available and those that were available were also expensive. Wisely, Apple adopted the PCI standard, which means that Macs can use the same PCI cards as PCs can. Developers need only provide Mac-specific software to enable their devices to work with the Mac.

21

PCI-X

Power Mac G5s introduced support for PCI-X (PCI extended) cards. This technology performs the same function as PCI but provides higher data rates, up to 1Gbps. PCI-X cards are mostly used for high-end digital video and audio tasks. PCI-X slots are backward compatible, so you can install a standard PCI card in a PCI-X slot.

AIRPORT

All modern Mac models provide an AirPort card slot in which you can install an AirPort card to add wireless networking capabilities to the machine. There are two types of AirPort: AirPort and AirPort Extreme. The primary difference between these is the speed at which they communicate.

→ To learn more about AirPort, **see** Chapter 11, "Using an AirPort Network to Connect to the Internet," **p. 297**.

> **NOTE**
>
> Power Mac G5s include Bluetooth and AirPort antenna ports to which you attach antennas for these wireless technologies.

BLUETOOTH

Bluetooth is a wireless standard for communicating with peripheral devices, such as PDAs, cell phones, printers, mouse devices, and so on; Bluetooth is similar to USB 1 only in that it is wireless.

Mac OS X has built-in support for Bluetooth devices, but to use this capability, your Mac must have the hardware required to communicate via Bluetooth. This can be obtained in two ways. One is to add a USB Bluetooth adapter to one of your Mac's USB ports (see Figure 21.6). The other is to order a Power Mac or PowerBook with a Bluetooth adapter built-in (Power Mac G5s require you to use a Bluetooth antenna that is included when you choose to have the Bluetooth module included).

The most common uses of Bluetooth are the following:

- **Synchronize contact information with cell phones and PDAs**—Using Bluetooth, iSync, and Address Book, you can manage your contact information among several devices and synchronize them easily.
- **Print wirelessly**—You can also add Bluetooth adapters to many types of printers so you can communicate with them without using wires.
- **Use wireless keyboards and mice.**
- **Transfer photos from a digital camera to your Mac without wires.**

Over time, you will likely connect to most low-speed peripheral devices wirelessly using Bluetooth.

21

Figure 21.6
A Bluetooth adapter enables any Mac OS X Mac to communicate with Bluetooth devices.

> **NOTE**
> Bluetooth is an electronics industry standard, so many wireless devices are Bluetooth compatible.

MODEM

A modem (modulator-demodulator) is another interface device that provides networking services to your Mac. The great benefit of a modem is that it can provide these services over standard phone lines, thus enabling the age of online services—most importantly, the Internet.

Specific modem hardware implements a specific communication standard, with more modern standards providing higher-speed connections. The current dial-up modem standard is V.92. Modems supporting this standard are capable of communicating at 56,700 bits per second (bps, more commonly referred to as 56K). Although dial-up modem speed has increased significantly over the past few years, it is still relatively slow, especially for data-intensive applications such as video.

All modern Macs include a built-in modem capable of 56K speeds.

> **NOTE**
> As with Ethernet, the actual speed obtained with a dial-up modem depends on each side of the connection. The communication speed between two devices is the highest speed at which they both can communicate. Because dial-up modems use phone lines, they are also greatly affected by the noise that is prevalent in most telephone architectures. Unless the phone lines used are exceptionally clean, modem communication is unlikely to occur at the maximum speed possible.

21

Other types of modems are available as well, including cable, DSL, and so on. These modems provide much greater speed and reliability but depend on the respective service being available.

→ For more on modems, **see** "Choosing a Modem," **p. 817**.

VIDEO

The video interface in the Mac provides the video output of the machine to a monitor or other device. Depending on the particular Mac model you are dealing with, several types of video interfaces might be available. On Power Mac G5s and G4s, you can add more video options through PCI or PCI-X cards.

Power Mac G5s and Power Mac G4s have at least one built-in graphics card (in the Power Mac G4, this card occupies the AGP 4x slot, and in the Power Mac G5 this has been improved to be an AGP 8x slot) to which you attach a monitor or other display device. Although PowerBooks, eMacs, iMacs, and iBooks have built-in monitors, the PowerBook, eMac, iMac, and newer iBooks also have external video interfaces so you can connect them to external displays, projectors, and other display devices. (You can also attach a USB video device to enable Macs to provide output to external displays.)

APPLE DISPLAY CONNECTOR

The Power Mac G5 and G4 include the Apple Display Connector (ADC), shown in Figure 21.7. This video connector is proprietary to Apple and was designed for its Cinema Displays. The ADC carries several data streams, those being analog video, digital video, USB, and power. This enables ADC-equipped machines to take advantage of all the features of Apple's digital flat-panel monitors.

→ For information about working with ADC devices, **see** "Finding, Installing, and Using a Monitor," **p. 744**.

> **NOTE**
>
> In Figure 21.7, you can also see that the three PCI slots are still available (the "blanks" are still installed). If other PCI cards were installed, you would see the additional ports those cards would provide.

> **NOTE**
>
> The graphics cards in Power Mac G5s and newer Power Mac G4s include an ADC port and a DVI port. These machines support two monitors out of the box. All you have to do is connect a monitor to each port.

MINI D-SUB VGA CONNECTOR

Several Mac models provide a standard video graphics array (VGA) port to which you can attach a monitor or another display device (refer to Figure 21.7). The benefit of the VGA port is that VGA is the video standard for the PC as well, so you can use just about any

21

monitor with a Mac that has a VGA port. Over the recent past, monitors are becoming digital, which means they use the DVI interface. Monitors that support the VGA standard are moving toward extinction. Eventually, as all video devices support the DVI interface, VGA devices will no longer exist. Until then, the most likely uses you have for VGA ports will be to connect an external monitor or projector to a Mac that has one.

Apple Display connector   Standard VGA connector

Figure 21.7
The ADC interface provides video, USB, and power so you can take advantage of the advanced features of Apple's Cinema Displays.

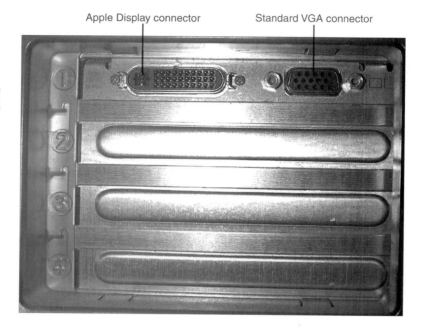

NOTE

Some Macs, such as iMacs and eMacs, provide only a "duplicate" image through the VGA port to that of the desktop. For example, when you connect an external monitor or projector to an iMac, the image you see on that device is the same as that on the iMac's monitor. This is called *video mirroring*.

DVI

The digital video interface (DVI) is designed for flat-panel digital displays. The DVI interface is standard on all digital flat-panel displays—except Apple's, which use the ADC interface. Power Mac G5s and modern Power Mac G4s include video cards that offer both ADC and DVI ports so you can use either type of display. You can also connect a display to each port to let you have two monitors available. (To use dual Apple Cinema displays, you must connect one of them through a DVI/ADC adapter.)

21

NOTE

> Interestingly, support for VGA or analog monitors for Power Mac G5s and modern G4s requires an adapter. The age of analog monitors on Macs is mostly over (the exception is eMacs that include a flat CRT monitor).

S-VIDEO CONNECTOR

Some Macs, such as the PowerBook G4, include an S-video output port. S-video provides a high-quality video signal and can be connected to television monitors, VCRs, and other video devices.

NOTE

> The list of video interfaces in this section is by no means exhaustive. For example, many PCI video digitizing cards provide other video ports, such as those for standard RCA video inputs and outputs.

ANALOG AUDIO

Several basic analog audio interfaces are provided on specific Mac models. Some models, such as the iBook, have only one audio interface (the headphone jack). However, many audio devices use the USB or FireWire interfaces (such as microphones, speakers, and so on), so even the lack of audio ports does not really limit you too much.

Standard audio ports available on various Mac models include the following:

- **Headphone jacks**—You connect standard headphone mini-jack connectors to these.
- **Speaker jacks**—You can attach speakers to these. The difference between a headphone jack and a speaker jack is that a headphone jack provides amplified signals, but a speaker jack generally does not (most computer speakers are externally powered).
- **Microphone jacks**—You can attach microphones to these. Strictly speaking, you are supposed to use PlainTalk-style microphones in the microphone jacks in Macs. These microphones have longer plugs that make contact in different places than a standard mic jack does. However, for some uses and with some Macs, a standard microphone will work just fine. You can also obtain adapters or use a USB microphone.

NOTE

> Some Mac models, such as iMacs and PowerBooks, have built-in microphones.

→ For information on speakers, **see** "Finding, Installing, and Using Speakers," **p. 754**.

21

As with video, many PCI cards provide additional audio interfaces.

DIGITAL AUDIO

Power Mac G5s support optical digital audio and provide input and output ports to enable advanced audio features. These ports enable you to connect receivers, digital instruments, and other audio devices. And, Power Mac G5s support digital 5.1 surround sound speakers with no additional hardware (finally!).

PC CARD

PowerBooks support the PC card interface. This interface provides a slot into which you can plug PC cards to add additional capability to the PowerBook.

TECHNOLOGIES SUPPORTED BY OS X, BUT NOT PART OF MODERN MACS

When Apple moved to USB and FireWire as the primary external interfaces, it left behind some of its previously standard interfaces. Some older Macs, such as beige Power Mac G3s, might have these interfaces, and they are supported by Mac OS X:

- **Apple desktop bus (ADB)**—The ADB port was used to connect mice, keyboards, and other input devices to the Mac. ADB devices were sometimes difficult to work with because they were not hot-swappable; removing an ADB device from or attaching such a device to a running Mac could cause major problems (in some cases, doing so wrecked the machine's motherboard).

- **Serial bus**—Previous-generation Macs used two serial ports: the Modem port and the Printer port. These ports were actually functionally identical and provided an interface to printers, modems, digital cameras, and other devices.

- **SCSI**—The small computer system interface (SCSI, which is pronounced *scuzzy*) is a general interface for attaching various devices to a computer. Older-generation Macs included an external SCSI port to which you could attach a chain of SCSI devices. The SCSI interface is a relatively fast one, but it is also relatively difficult to work with. Each device has to have a unique identifier, and each SCSI bus is limited to seven devices. Creating SCSI device conflicts is easy to do, and the cables and connectors are large and can be hard to work with.

TIP

> You can add an external SCSI interface to Power Mac G5s and G4s by adding a SCSI PCI card. This enables you to connect and use external SCSI devices, such as hard drives, scanners, and so on. Of course, you will need the appropriate Mac OS X drivers to use such devices.

→ For more on SCSI, **see** "SCSI," **p. 720**.

21

NOTE

A great resource on the Net from which you can learn about various interface technologies is http://webopedia.internet.com/. In addition to plenty of information about input and output technologies, you can find information on just about any computer-related terminology you encounter. When you find a term, you are also presented with links to additional sites at which you can get more detailed information.

USING INTERNAL INTERFACES

There are numerous types of internal interfaces you will never deal with—unless you build your own Mac or do complex repairs. However, some of the internal interfaces are important to understand because you use them to expand your system.

ATA

The AT attachment (ATA) interface is a PC standard specification for hard disk drives and has been adopted on modern Macs. The ATA interface provides high-speed communication, and because it is a PC standard, ATA hard drives are inexpensive.

As with other specifications, there are various "flavors" of the interface, with each offering a specific speed. For example, modern PowerMac G4s use the Ultra ATA/100 standard, which means the throughput of devices using this standard is 100 megabytes per second (MBps). If you add internal hard drives to a Power Mac G5 or PowerMac G4 or replace an existing drive with a larger one, make sure the drive uses the ATA standard your Mac supports.

NOTE

When you deal with internal devices, you might also hear the term *IDE*, which stands for *integrated drive electronics*. IDE devices are those on which the controller is integrated into the device rather than provided by the computer. This term is often used as a synonym for ATA because ATA devices are also IDE devices. But IDE refers to the general technology, whereas ATA refers to a specific specification.

TIP

If your Mac supports FireWire 400 or 800, it is often better to add an external FireWire drive than to add more internal drives.

DIMM, SO-DIMM, AND DDR SDRAM

The dual inline memory module (DIMM) interface is the standard for RAM chips in many modern Macs, such as the Power Mac G4. DIMM chips use a 64-bit path. You use this interface when you want to expand the RAM capability of one of these Macs.

PowerBooks and iBooks use small outline DIMM (SODIMM), which is a physically smaller interface that provides the same capabilities as the full-size DIMM.

21

The newest Macs, such as Power Mac G5s, use double data rate synchronous dynamic random access memory (DDR SDRAM) modules. This technology offers improved performance over previous Mac models.

In all cases, when you expand your Mac's RAM (which is one of the best things you can do), you need to ensure that you get memory modules that are the type and speed your Mac supports. See your Mac's documentation to determine the type of memory modules you need for it.

SCSI

Earlier in this chapter, you read that SCSI was once a standard external interface. Because of its speed advantages, it was also a standard internal interface that was used for all Mac hard drives. In fact, Apple was the only manufacturer that included the SCSI interface and drives as standard equipment. This speed advantage was one reason the Mac became popular with graphics professionals and others who needed to move a lot of data quickly.

In an effort to cut the cost of its machines, Apple did away with the SCSI interface as the standard one for internal data communication. At the same time, the speed of the PC standard interface, ATA, increased such that this imposes little to no performance penalty for modern Macs. (FireWire replaced SCSI to connect external devices.)

There is more than one SCSI standard, each of which offers a specific speed along with other specifications. Some examples are the following:

- **Fast SCSI**—Supports speeds up to 10MBps
- **Ultra SCSI**—Supports speeds to 20MBps
- **Ultra Wide SCSI**—Supports speeds up to 40MBps

The various SCSI specifications use various connectors and cables—you usually can't connect a device using one standard to an interface that uses another. As with other interfaces, the actual speed of communication across a SCSI interface defaults to the maximum speed of the lowest-speed device connected to the interface.

CHAPTER **22**

WORKING WITH INPUT DEVICES

In this chapter

22

CHOOSING AN INPUT DEVICE

Technically speaking, an *input device* is any device you use to move data into your Mac. Some input devices enable you to input data to create documents, images, movies, and so on. The other type of data input devices enables you to control your Mac.

In the context of this chapter, the term *input device* refers to the essential devices you use to input data and to control your Mac. Other sorts of input devices used only for data input, such as cameras, scanners, and so on, are covered elsewhere in the book.

→ To learn about digital cameras and scanners, **see** Chapter 15, "Creating and Editing Digital Images," **p. 457**.

→ To learn about digital video cameras, **see** Chapter 17, "Making Digital Movie Magic with iMovie," **p. 569**.

There are two types of essential input devices: keyboards and mouse devices. However, many varieties of each device exist, and in the case of mouse devices, some of the varieties are hardly recognizable as being a device of that type. There are other types of input devices you might want to use, such as a graphics tablet.

NOTE

> Many of the devices described in this chapter use the USB interface.

→ To learn more about USB, **see** "USB 1.1," **p. 709**.

Introduced in Mac OS X version 10.2 is the built-in handwriting-recognition system called Ink. With Ink, you can use a tablet to write or draw and the Ink system converts your writing into text and graphics.

Also introduced in Mac OS X version 10.2 but expanded for 10.3 is the Mac's capability to support wireless devices that use Bluetooth technology. Many of these devices are available, including keyboards, mouse devices, PDAs, cell phones, and so on. Bluetooth enables your Mac to wirelessly communicate with multiple devices at the same time.

FINDING, INSTALLING, AND CONFIGURING A KEYBOARD

The keyboard is one of the most fundamental, and at the same time, simplest devices in your system. You are likely to spend most of your "Mac" time pounding on its keys, so it pays to make sure you have a keyboard you like.

CHOOSING AND INSTALLING A KEYBOARD

All Macs come with a keyboard of one type or another, so if you are happy with the keyboard that came with your Mac, there is no need to consider another type. The most recent Apple keyboard, the Apple Pro Keyboard, is widely recognized as an excellent keyboard because it combines a very nice feel with good ergonomics and features. The Apple Pro Keyboard also provides several control keys, which are the mute, volume, and eject keys; these are located along the top of the number pad. And it looks pretty cool, too.

However, other types of keyboards are available, such as those designed for maximum ergonomics, to provide additional controls (such as an Internet button), and so on.

NOTE

You can check out available keyboards by visiting the peripherals section at www.smalldog.com.

Many modern keyboards use the USB interface, so installing a keyboard is a trivial matter of plugging it in to an available USB port. (And remember that, as you read in Chapter 21, "Understanding Input and Output Technology," USB devices are hot-swappable so you can connect and disconnect them without turning off the power to your Mac.)

Some keyboards are wireless; two basic types of these devices are available. One type includes a transmitter you plug in to an USB port. The other type, such as the Apple Wireless Keyboard, uses Bluetooth. The advantage of Bluetooth is that you don't consume a USB port and can communicate with many Bluetooth devices at the same time. The disadvantage is that your Mac must have a Bluetooth adapter installed.

If at all possible, you should obtain a wireless keyboard; being without wires is very freeing, especially if you move your keyboard or mouse around much. And who needs all the clutter that so many wires bring?

If you use a USB-based wireless keyboard, you connect its transmitter to a USB port and then use its controls to get the transmitter and keyboard communicating. If you use a Bluetooth keyboard, you use the Bluetooth configuration tools to install and configure it.

→ To learn more about Bluetooth devices, **see** "Finding, Installing, and Using Bluetooth Devices," **p. 735**.

If the keyboard you select includes additional features, such as additional buttons and controls, it probably also includes software you need to install. This typically adds a new pane to the System Preferences application you use to configure the device. An example of this is provided in the next section.

CONFIGURING A KEYBOARD

With Mac OS X, you can change the key repeat rate and the delay-until-repeat time. You can also configure the function keys and set the language in which your keyboard is configured. Here's how:

1. Open the System Preferences utility, click the Keyboard & Mouse icon to open the Keyboard & Mouse pane, and click the Keyboard tab if it isn't selected already (see Figure 22.1).

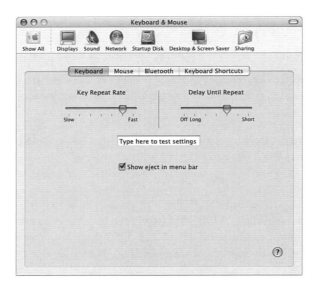

Figure 22.1
Use the four tabs of the Keyboard & Mouse preferences pane to configure your mouse and keyboard.

> **N O T E**
>
> If you don't have a Bluetooth adapter installed in your Mac, the Bluetooth tab won't appear on the Mouse & Keyboard pane.

2. Use the Key Repeat Rate slider to set how fast a key repeats itself. Move the slider to the right to cause keys to repeat more quickly.

3. Use the Delay Until Repeat slider to set the amount of time it takes for a key to repeat itself. You can test your settings in the text area below the sliders.

4. Use the steps in the next section to configure keyboard shortcuts.

CONFIGURING YOUR KEYBOARD SHORTCUTS

One of the best things you can do to increase your personal productivity is to learn to use keyboard shortcuts. In the "OS X to the Max" sections of other chapters in this book, you will find many keyboard shortcuts. You should take the time to learn and practice the shortcuts for the OS, as well as shortcuts for any applications you use frequently. The Mac Help Center also lists some keyboard shortcuts.

 Using the Keyboard Shortcuts tab of the Keyboard & Mouse, you can configure many of the available keyboard shortcuts. You can enable or disable some of the standard keyboard shortcuts and add keyboard shortcuts for commands in applications you use.

If you turn on the Full Keyboard Access feature, you can access the interface elements with the designated keys. Open the Keyboard & Mouse pane of the System Preferences application and click the Keyboard Shortcuts tab (see Figure 22.2). You will see a list of standard

OS keyboard shortcuts in a number of areas, such as screen capture, universal access, keyboard navigation, and so on.

Figure 22.2
Use the Keyboard Shortcuts tab to configure your own keyboard shortcuts.

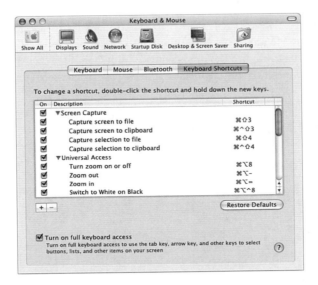

Disable any of the listed shortcuts by unchecking the shortcut's On button. Typically, you would do this when that shortcut conflicts with a shortcut in an application you use. For example, the default shortcut to capture the screen to a file is Shift-⌘-3. The screenshot application I use, Snapz Pro X, also uses this shortcut by default. Because I don't use the Mac OS X's built-in shortcut, I changed the default screenshot shortcut to be something different so it wouldn't interfere with the default Snapz Pro X shortcut.

If you don't want to be able to use the keyboard to select control items for some reason, uncheck the "Turn on full keyboard access" check box to turn off this feature. Because it can be faster and easier to select items using the keyboard than the mouse, you should leave this on and learn to use these shortcuts.

→ To see an explanation of the standard keyboard shortcuts you can configure and use, **see** "Getting the Most from Keyboard Shortcuts," **p. 739**.

Use the steps in the next section to configure your keyboard's language preferences.

CONFIGURING YOUR KEYBOARD'S LANGUAGE SETTINGS AND THE INPUT MENU

You can configure the languages you use for the keyboard along with other input preferences using the International pane of the System Preferences application. You can also configure the Input menu, which enables you to quickly choose among languages and select some other keyboard tools:

22

1. Open the International pane of the System Preferences application.

2. On the Language tab, move the language you want to be the default to the top of the list by dragging it there. Move the other languages on the list to set the order in which they are used.

3. Click the Input Menu tab. You use this area to show the Keyboard menu on the Finder menu bar and to configure the items you see on it (see Figure 22.3). The default language, which was set when you installed Mac OS X, is checked in the pane.

Figure 22.3
You can configure the Input menu with the Input Menu tab of the International pane.

4. Check the "Show input menu in the menu bar" check box.

5. Check the boxes next to the other languages you want to be available on the Input menu.

6. Check the Character Palette check box to add that to the menu. You can use this to select, configure, and use custom characters.

7. Check the Keyboard Viewer check box to add that to the menu. This viewer shows you the keys for a selected font.

8. Click the Options button to see a sheet that enables you to set several options relating to the languages you are using.

9. Set the options you want and click OK.

When you open the Keyboard menu, which is indicated by a flag representing the language you have made the default, you see the items you configured there (see Figure 22.4).

Figure 22.4
The Input menu enables you to select the language setting for your keyboard and open palettes and viewers related to the keyboard.

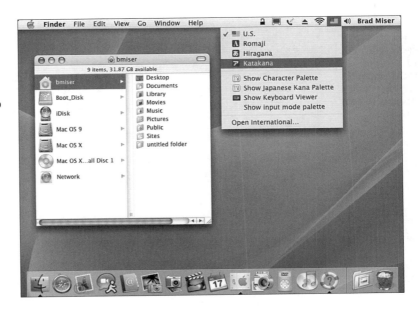

TIP

> If you select "Show input mode palette," the languages you have selected on the Input Menu tab appear in a palette that is always visible on the desktop. You can click a language on this palette to select it.

CONFIGURING YOUR INPUT DEVICE'S SOFTWARE

If you use a non-Apple keyboard and it includes software, you can use it to configure that keyboard.

Open the System Preferences application and then open the pane relating to the keyboard you are using (see Figure 22.5).

Use the controls provided by that pane to configure the device.

Figure 22.5
I use a Logitech Cordless Elite keyboard and mouse; the Logitech Control Center pane enables me to configure many aspects of these devices.

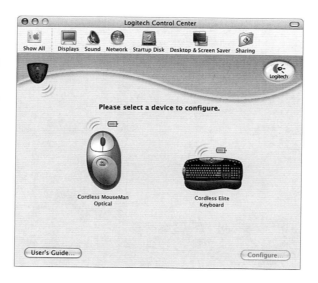

FINDING, INSTALLING, AND CONFIGURING A MOUSE

When the Mac was first introduced, its mouse separated it from all the computers that came before it, and those that came after it, for a long time. Until Windows and other platforms adopted the mouse as one of their primary input devices, the Mac and its mouse really stood out from the crowd.

CHOOSING AND INSTALLING A MOUSE

All desktop Macs come with the Apple Pro Mouse. This is an optical mouse, which means it uses light to translate your movements into input information (as opposed to the rolling ball in previous generations of mouse devices). Optical mouse devices eliminate the frequent cleaning required by the ball-based ancestors. The Apple Pro Mouse uses the entire top half as its "button," which makes using it even easier (if that is even possible). And it shares the same clear or white plastic look as the Apple Pro Keyboard.

NOTE

> Schools love the Apple Pro Mouse, too. In schools, kids often take the balls out of "regular" mouse devices, thus rendering the mouse unusable until a replacement ball is located or the mouse is replaced. By switching to the optical mouse, some school districts have saved several hundreds of dollar that they would have otherwise spent because of missing mouse balls.

There are three main considerations when choosing a mouse.

One is its comfort in your hand. Mouse devices come in various shapes and sizes. Using one that is suited to your own hand cuts down on fatigue in your hand and lower arm.

Another factor is the number of buttons and other features on the mouse. Apple's mouse devices all provide a single mouse button, but other mouse devices come with two or more buttons. These buttons can be programmed to accomplish specific tasks, such as opening contextual menus. Also, some mouse devices include a scroll wheel that enables you to scroll in a window, such as a Web page, without moving the mouse.

NEW Because support for a two-button mouse with a scroll wheel is built in to the OS, (even though you won't find this indicated on the Mouse tab of the Keyboard & Mouse pane of the System Preferences application), you should get at least a two-button mouse. This makes opening contextual menus, which are used throughout the OS and in most applications, much easier. Even better, get a mouse that includes a scroll wheel. This makes scrolling much more convenient and faster at the same time.

Third, you need to decide whether you want a wireless mouse. Because of the amount of time you spend moving a mouse, you should really consider a wireless mouse. Getting rid of the wire provides much more freedom of movement for you. As with keyboards, two types of wireless mouse devices are available—those that use a USB transmitter and those that use Bluetooth (such as Apple's Wireless Mouse).

Like installing a keyboard, installing a mouse isn't hard.

If you use a wired mouse, just plug it in to an available USB port.

If you use a USB-based wireless mouse, plug its transmitter in to an available USB port and use its controls to get the mouse and transmitter communicating.

If you use a Bluetooth mouse, use the Bluetooth configuration controls to set it up.

→ To learn more about Bluetooth devices, **see** "Finding, Installing, and Using Bluetooth Devices," **p. 735**.

N O T E

> Apple's wireless keyboard and mouse use Bluetooth to communicate with a Mac. You must purchase these devices separately. Hopefully, someday soon Apple will build Bluetooth support into all Macs and include the wireless keyboard and mouse. Even better, maybe someday Apple will replace its mouse design with a two-button (or more) version that includes a scroll wheel.

CONFIGURING A MOUSE

Configuring a mouse is much like configuring a keyboard; however, if you use a mouse that offers additional features, you need to install and configure the software that comes with that device first to take advantage of all its features. Without this software, your mouse might default to acting like a standard one-button mouse. (However, if it includes a second button and scroll wheel, these will likely work as you expect without any additional software installation.)

22

To configure a mouse, do the following:

1. Open the Keyboard & Mouse pane of the System Preferences application.
2. Click the Mouse tab (see Figure 22.6).

Figure 22.6
Configuring a mouse isn't hard to do.

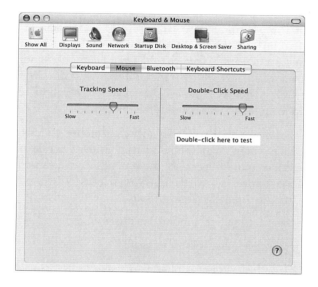

3. Use the Tracking Speed slider to set the tracking speed of the mouse. A faster tracking speed means that the pointer moves farther with less movement of the mouse.

> **TIP**
>
> If your mouse includes a Scroll wheel, you will also see the Scrolling Speed slider. Use this slider to set the speed at which the wheel scrolls.

4. Use the Double-Click Speed slider to set the rate at which you have to click the mouse button to register a double-click. You can use the test area to check out the click speed you have set.
5. Quit the System Preferences utility.

Unfortunately, even though Mac OS X supports a second mouse button and wheel for most devices, you can't configure them, such as setting the action that occurs when you click the second button or the speed at which you scroll using the Mouse tab. To configure those aspects of a mouse, you must use the software that came with it (see Figure 22.7).

Figure 22.7
If you use a mouse with a second (or third) button and a scroll wheel, use its software to configure it.

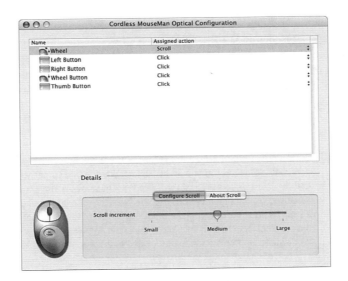

> **NOTE**
>
> PowerBooks and iBooks use a trackpad instead of a mouse (although you can connect a mouse to one of these machines just as you can any other Mac).

→ For information about working with a trackpad, **see** "Using and Configuring the Trackpad," **p. 988**.

INSTALLING AND USING AN INK DEVICE

Since version 10.2, Mac OS X has supported handwriting recognition, meaning you can input text and graphics using a pen and tablet device. This is accomplished through Mac OS X's Ink technology. When you install an Ink-compatible device, an Ink pane appears in the System Preferences utility; you use this to configure how you want handwriting recognition to work. Then, you can input directly into most applications or input into the InkPad application and paste the content into another application.

INSTALLING A TABLET

Tablet devices enable you to input information and execute control using a pen-type mouse you use to "write" on the tablet.

> **NOTE**
>
> Check out all the details about Wacom tablets on www.wacom.com. You can purchase a tablet at the Wacom site or at www.smalldog.com.

22

Installing a tablet is no more complicated than installing any other device. You simply connect the tablet to an available USB port. However, because the tablet needs power to operate, you must connect it using a USB port that provides power to peripheral devices. You can connect it to a USB port on the Mac itself, one on an ADC display, or one on a powered USB hub. You can't connect it to a USB port on the keyboard, though.

Then you install the software provided with the tablet. That is all there is to it.

NOTE

Because Ink support is built in to Mac OS X, you might wonder why you need to install additional software. You should install the software that comes with the tablet to ensure that the latest drivers are installed. The Wacom software also provides access to advanced configuration options that are beyond those you can configure with Mac OS X's Ink technology. Covering the details of advanced configuration of a tablet is beyond the scope of this chapter. To explore the tablet software, open the Wacom Tablet application installed in the Wacom folder located in the Applications folder.

CONFIGURING INK

Before you get started with Ink, you need to understand that getting handwriting recognition to work reliably takes some time and experimentation. Unless you have picture-perfect penmanship, you will have to do some trial and error to get it to work reliably. Expect to spend some time and effort configuring and experimenting with Ink. Make adjustments to Ink, and then try writing. Then, make more adjustments and try again. Eventually, you will be able to make it work pretty well.

After you have installed a tablet, you need to turn on handwriting recognition and configure it:

1. Open the System Preferences utility. Click the Ink button to open the Ink pane (see Figure 22.8).

Figure 22.8
You use the Ink pane of the System Preferences utility to configure handwriting recognition.

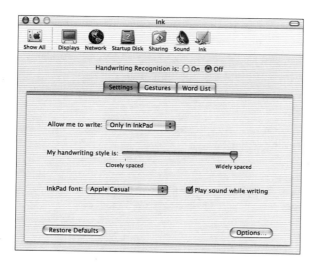

2. Turn on handwriting recognition by clicking the On radio button.

3. Use the "Allow me to write" pop-up menu to determine where you want to be able to make input via the tablet.

TIP

If you select Anywhere on the pop-up menu, the Mode button on the InkPad toolbar becomes a Pen to indicate that you can write anywhere. You can click the Mode button to switch back and forth between these modes.

4. To configure the input sensitivity for your handwriting style, use the slider labeled "My handwriting style is."

5. Use the InkPad font pop-up menu to select the font that is used in the InkPad writing window.

6. If you want to hear sounds while you write, leave the "Play sound while writing" check box checked.

You can access additional controls by clicking the Options button on the Settings tab (see Figure 22.9).

Figure 22.9
Use these options to fine-tune Ink to match your handwriting style.

Continue experimenting with writing in the InkPad and making adjustments until your writing is recognized reliably. This will take some time and patience, but if you continue refining the adjustments, you can make it work fairly reliably.

22

NOTE

There are numerous adjustments you can make to the tablet, pen, and mouse using the Wacom Tablet application. For example, you can configure the mouse's buttons and the pen's button. Covering the details of this application is beyond the scope of this chapter. If you are going to use a tablet, you should explore this application to better configure your tablet.

USING INK

After you have configured Ink to reliably recognize your handwriting, there are two general ways you can use it.

One is to make all input via the InkPad application by switching to the InkPad window when you are in another application. For example you can use Ink to write an email message. When you click the Send button the text you input is pasted into the active document window. You can then edit it just like text you typed. You can also write directly in many applications:

1. Open the Ink pane of the System Preferences utility and select Anywhere on the "Allow me to write" pop-up menu. (You can also click the mode button in the InkPad toolbar.)

2. Open an application and create a new document, such as a new email message.

3. Move the pointer into the blank document and start writing. As you write, an InkPad window pops up and shows you the text you are writing. When you release the pressure on the pen, Ink recognizes what you wrote and enters that text in the document (see Figure 22.10).

Figure 22.10
Here I am entering text directly into an email message.

Not all applications recognize Ink input, but most OS X applications do. The best way to figure out whether an application you use supports Ink is to try it. If an application doesn't support direct entry using Ink, you can always use the InkPad to enter text.

TIP

If you click the Graphic mode button (the star) at the bottom of the InkPad window, you can also draw in the window and paste the result into your documents.

NOTE

The most advanced tablets are incorporated into LCD monitors so you can input directly onto the images on which you are working. Check them out at www.wacom.com/lcdtablets/index.cfm.

FINDING, INSTALLING, AND USING BLUETOOTH DEVICES

Bluetooth is a wireless communication standard used by many devices, including computers, keyboards, mouse devices, personal digital assistants (PDAs), cell phones, printers, and so on. Mac OS X is designed to be Bluetooth capable so your Mac can communicate with Bluetooth devices, such as to synchronize your iCal calendar on your Mac with the calendar on your Palm PDA.

PREPARING FOR BLUETOOTH

Two elements are required for Bluetooth.

One is the software component, which is installed as part of Mac OS X version 10.3.

The other is the transmitter and receiver that sends and receives Bluetooth signals. Some Mac models have this device built in. For those models, you don't need anything else. For models without this, however, you need to obtain and install a Bluetooth USB adapter. This device connects to a USB port and enables a Mac to send and receive Bluetooth signals.

NOTE

You can learn more about Bluetooth on the Mac at www.apple.com/bluetooth/.

Bluetooth communication is set up between two devices—a single device can be communicating with more than one other Bluetooth device at the same time. Each device with which your Mac communicates over Bluetooth must be configured separately so your Mac recognizes that device and that device recognizes your Mac.

Two steps are involved in setting up Bluetooth. First, you configure Bluetooth for your Mac using the Bluetooth pane of the System Preferences application. Then you configure your Mac to work with each Bluetooth device you want to use.

CONFIGURING BLUETOOTH ON YOUR MAC

When your Mac recognizes that is has the capability to communicate via Bluetooth, the Bluetooth pane appears in the System Preferences application (see Figure 22.11). You use this to configure the general aspects of Bluetooth on your Mac and to see the list of devices your Mac recognizes.

Figure 22.11
Use the Bluetooth pane of the System Preferences application to control general aspects of Bluetooth on your Mac.

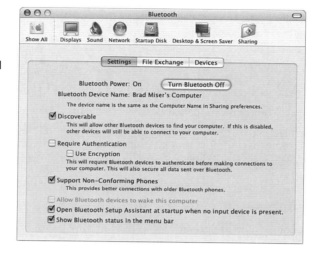

You use the Settings tab to configure your Mac's Bluetooth configuration. It includes the following controls:

TIP

> In most cases, the default settings will work for you. You should try to configure a Bluetooth device before you adjust your Mac's Bluetooth settings. If it doesn't work properly, come back to these controls to make adjustments.

- **On/Off**—Use the button at the top of the pane to turn Bluetooth services on or off.
- **Discoverable**—This makes your Mac "discoverable" by other devices because your Mac transmits signals that other devices can detect. If you don't want this, you can uncheck the check box. For example, if you work in a area in which there are many Bluetooth devices, you might want to hide your Mac so other devices won't be able to detect it. You can still connect to your configured Bluetooth devices when this box is unchecked; your Mac just won't be capable of being detected by other devices.
- **Authentication**—If you check the Require Authentication and Use Encryption check boxes, your Mac uses encrypted signals to communicate. You might want to use this option if you operate in an area in which there are other Bluetooth devices.

- **Non-conforming Phones**—If you use an older Bluetooth-capable cell phone, checking this box should provide better results.

- **Wake**—If you check the "Allow Bluetooth devices to wake this computer" check box and your Mac is sleeping, Bluetooth devices can wake it up when they need to communicate with it.

- **Setup Assistant**—The Bluetooth Setup Assistant helps you connect to and configure devices. If you check the "Open Bluetooth Setup Assistant at startup when no input device is present" box, the assistant launches if no devices are configured on your Mac when it starts up.

- **Bluetooth menu**—Check the "Show Bluetooth status in the menu bar" check box to add the Bluetooth menu to the menu bar.

Many Bluetooth interactions involve the transfer of files between the devices. You can configure how these transfers occur by using the File Exchange tab (see Figure 22.12).

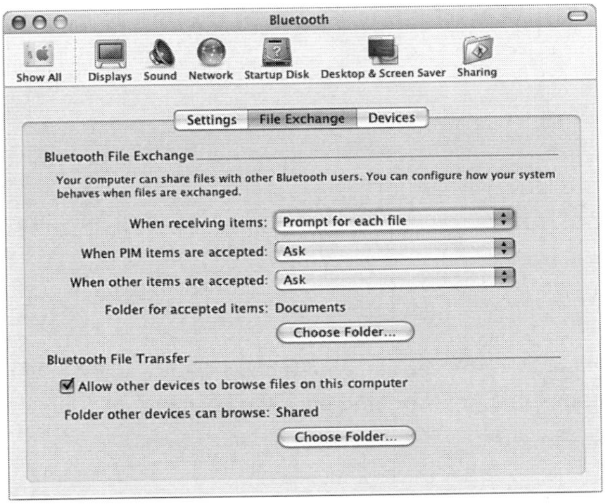

Figure 22.12
Use the File Exchange tab to configure file transfers over Bluetooth.

In the Bluetooth File Exchange section, you can choose how your Mac accepts files from other devices and where those files are stored.

In the Bluetooth File Transfer section, you can enable other devices to browse your Mac. If you enable this, you can choose the specific folder other devices will be able to see.

On the Devices tab, you can see the devices that are currently configured on your Mac. You can also remove those devices and set up a new device.

INSTALLING A NEW BLUETOOTH DEVICE

Before you can communicate with a Bluetooth device, that device must be configured on your Mac. And because Bluetooth devices are paired, your Mac must also be configured on

22

the Bluetooth device with which you are communicating. After you have establish a pair, your Mac can communicate with its partner, and vice versa.

To set up a new device, you use the Bluetooth Setup Assistant. The general steps to do this are the following:

1. Open the Bluetooth Setup Assistant by either clicking the Set Up New Device button on the Devices tab of the Bluetooth pane of the System Preferences application or selecting Set Up Bluetooth Device on the Bluetooth menu. The Bluetooth Setup Assistant opens (see Figure 22.13).

Figure 22.13
The Bluetooth Setup Assistant walks you through the steps required to set up a Bluetooth device.

2. Click Continue.

3. Select the type of Bluetooth device you want to set up, such as Mouse, Keyboard, Mobile Phone, or Other Device, and click Continue. Your Mac searches for available Bluetooth devices.

NOTE

The Bluetooth device you are configuring must be discoverable for your Mac to be capable of finding it, just as your Mac must be discoverable for other devices to be capable of finding your Mac.

4. Select the device you want to configure and click Continue.

5. Follow the onscreen instructions to configure the device. When the process is complete, the devices can communicate.

NOTE

When Bluetooth devices are connected as a trusted pair, the same passkey is required on each device for those devices to communicate.

22

WORKING WITH BLUETOOTH DEVICES

After you have configured a Bluetooth device to work with your Mac, you use the device's applications or controls to communicate with your Mac or use a Mac application to work with the device.

For example, one of the most useful Bluetooth devices is a Palm PDA. You can use the iSync application to synchronize the PDA's calendar and contact list with your iCal calendar and Address Book so that you have the same information available on both devices. Because you can communicate wirelessly, you don't need to bother connecting any wires or even putting the PDA into a cradle to synchronize. You can also transfer files between the two devices, such as to install applications on the Palm.

→ To learn how to use iSync, **see** "Synchronizing with iSync," **p. 689**.

Although synchronizing a PDA wirelessly is one of the most useful Bluetooth-enabled tasks, it isn't the only one. Consider the following examples:

- Using wireless keyboards and mouse devices
- Printing wirelessly
- Connecting to the Internet through a Bluetooth modem
- Communicating with other Bluetooth-equipped Macs to share files
- Transferring photos wirelessly from a Bluetooth digital camera
- Keeping your contact list on a Bluetooth cell phone in synch with your Address Book

MAC OS X TO THE MAX: INPUTTING MORE BETTER AND FASTER

No matter what you do, you will be inputting information constantly. Use the information in this section to do that better and faster.

GETTING THE MOST FROM KEYBOARD SHORTCUTS

Using keyboard shortcuts is a great way to work both faster and smarter. Mac OS X includes support for many keyboard shortcuts by default. As you have seen throughout this book, many areas of the OS and within applications provide keyboard shortcuts you can use.

USING KEYBOARD NAVIGATION

One of the least used, but most useful, aspects of using keyboard shortcuts is keyboard navigation. You can use the keyboard to access almost any area on your Mac in any application, including the Finder. For example, you can open any menu item by using only keys even if that item does not have a keyboard shortcut assigned to it.

First, configure keyboard navigation:

1. Open the Keyboard Shortcuts tab of the Keyboard & Mouse pane of the System Preferences application.

2. Make sure the "Turn on full keyboard access" check box is checked.

3. Review the list of Keyboard Navigation and Dock shortcuts to make sure the ones you want to use are enabled (see Table 22.1 for the details).

4. If you want to use a keyboard shortcut that is different from the default, double-click the default and change it to a new combination.

5. Quit the System Preferences application.

TABLE 22.1   KEYBOARD NAVIGATION AND DOCK KEYBOARD SHORTCUTS

Shortcut	What It Does	Default Keyboard Shortcut
Turn keyboard access on or off	Enables or disables the use of certain keys, such as the Tab key, to navigate.	Control-F1
Focus on Menu	Opens the first menu on the current menu bar; use the Tab or arrow keys to move to other menu items.	Control-F2
Focus on Dock	Makes the Dock active; use the Tab or arrow keys to move to icons on the Dock.	Control-F3
Focus on Window (active) or new window	Moves into the currently active window or takes you to the next window if you are already in a window.	Control-F4
Focus on Toolbar	If you are using an application with a toolbar, such as the System Preferences application, this makes the toolbar active. Use the Tab or arrow keys to select a button on the toolbar.	Control-F5
Focus on Utility window (palette)	Moves you into the first tool palette, and then each palette in order.	Control-F6
Rotate Windows	Moves you among the open windows in any application, such as he Finder, Word, and so on.	⌘-`
Toggle focus for any control within windows	Moves you to the next control within a window, such as to a pop-up menu, text box, and so on.	Control-F7
Automatically hide and show the Dock	Hides or shows the Dock.	⌘-Option-D

Using the shortcuts in Table 22.1, you can move to and select just about anything you can see. For example, to select a menu command, press the Focus on Menu shortcut (Control-F2 by default) and use the right-arrow or Tab key to move to the menu on which the command is located. As you do, that menu opens. Use the down-arrow key to move to the command you want to select and press Return to activate the command.

As another example, when you are working with an application that has a toolbar, press the shortcut for the Focus on Toolbar command, use the Tab key to select the tool you want to use, and press Return to use it.

> **NOTE**
>
> Some applications don't support all aspects of keyboard navigation. For example, in Microsoft Word, you can't select radio button options using the arrow keys, which is too bad.

ADDING KEYBOARD SHORTCUTS FOR APPLICATION COMMANDS

 You can add keyboard shortcuts to commands within Mac OS X applications using the following steps:

1. Open the Keyboard Shortcuts tab of the Keyboard & Mouse pane of the System Preferences application.

2. Click the Add Shortcut button (+) at the bottom of the window. The Add Application sheet appears.

3. Select the application for which you want to create a shortcut on the Application pop-up menu. If the application isn't listed, select Other and use the Open Application dialog box to choose the application. To set a shortcut for all applications, select All Applications.

4. In the Menu Title box, type the exact command name for which you want to create a shortcut. If the command contains an ellipsis, you need to include that as well.

> **TIP**
>
> To type an ellipsis, use the Character palette.

5. In the Keyboard Shortcut field, enter the shortcut for the command.

6. Click Add. When you return to the Keyboard Shortcuts tab, the shortcut you added is listed under the related application under the Application Keyboard Shortcuts section.

> **NOTE**
>
> At the time this book went to press, this feature was still not working properly in the final release of OS X Panther, but this is how it *should* work. Hopefully, this will be fixed in a point release soon!

22

Get Serious

If you want to make keyboard shortcuts work even better, consider adding a macro application to your Mac. My favorite is QuicKeys. Using this application, you can create macros to perform almost any series of steps and then activate the macro with a keyboard shortcut or by clicking a button on a toolbar.

Using QuicKeys you can easily create a keyboard shortcut for any action or series of actions you want to perform. For example, you can record a series of steps and perform those steps by pressing the keyboard shortcut you assign to the macro you create. If you want to take your personal and your Mac's productivity to the next level, get a copy of QuicKeys as soon as you can.

NOTE

To learn more about QuicKeys, visit `www.cesoft.com/products/quickeys.html`.

CHAPTER 23

FINDING, INSTALLING, AND USING OUTPUT DEVICES

In this chapter

WORKING WITH OUTPUT DEVICES

Your Mac's output devices determine how the data you are manipulating appears and sounds to you and, in the case of a printer, to the world. Using high-quality output devices can make your Mac experience more enjoyable and productive.

In this chapter, you will learn about the following output devices:

- Monitors
- Speakers
- Printers

In addition to these hardware items, you will also learn about a significant output mechanism that isn't hardware: Portable Document Format (PDF). PDF offers many benefits; the most important is that you can distribute electronic versions of your documents—the viewer does not have to have the same application or fonts you used to create the document to be able to view the document. The PDF appears to the viewer just as it does on your computer. Even better, support for creating PDF documents is built in to Mac OS X.

Finally, because color is such an important part of Mac OS X, you will learn about synchronizing color across multiple output devices.

FINDING, INSTALLING, AND USING A MONITOR

Next to your Mac itself, your monitor might be the most important element of your system. Having the correct type and size of monitor can make working with your Mac more efficient and more enjoyable.

CHOOSING A MONITOR

The fundamental factors you need to take into account when choosing a monitor are detailed in the following sections.

DISPLAY TYPE

There are two options in the way a monitor displays information. With a *cathode-ray tube (CRT)* monitor, information appears on the screen as the result of an electron gun spraying electrons against the inside of the monitor screen, which is covered with phosphors that glow when struck by those electrons. The other choice is a *liquid crystal display (LCD)*, which uses a liquid-based display medium. This technology enables the viewing area to be very thin and light, which is why all laptops are equipped with LCDs.

The image quality of both types of displays is very good. Until recently, the cost of LCDs prevented their use except where nothing else would work because of size limitations, such as in a laptop. Recently, the cost of LCD monitors has decreased, so you can now purchase affordable LCD monitors for desktop machines as well.

LCD monitors offer many benefits over CRTs. One is their size and weight; a comparably sized LCD display is much smaller and lighter than a CRT monitor. And a high-quality LCD monitor has a sharper and more vibrant picture than its CRT cousin. Because of these reasons, LCD monitors now dominate the computer landscape, so much so that the eMac is the only production Mac that features a CRT. All the monitors Apple produces are now LCDs.

Unless you really need to spend the least amount of money possible, you should only consider LCD displays for your system. That is, unless you use a Mac whose external monitor support is limited to VGA output, in which case a CRT display can make sense. Being limited to VGA does not limit you to a CRT; some LCD monitors offer VGA ports.

23

DISPLAY SIZE

Display size might be the single most important factor when considering a monitor. Various sizes of display area are available. The most common CRT monitor sizes are 15'', 17'', 19'', and 21''. Common LCD monitor sizes are 15'', 17'', and 18'' along with Apple's spectacular Cinema Displays, which come in a 17'' and 20'' and a 23'' high-definition model. When it comes to display size, bigger is better. You should get a quality monitor in the largest size you can afford because more display space yields more working area.

INTERFACE TYPE

On modern Macs, there are three interfaces to which you connect a monitor: VGA, DVI, and Apple Display Connector (ADC). Various Mac models provide different types of video interface ports. For example, many Power Mac G4s and Power Mac G5s have an ADC and a DVI port on their built-in AGP graphics card. Some models with built-in monitors support external VGA monitors along with their built-in displays (flat panel LCD in the case of PowerBooks, iBooks, and iMacs; CRT in the case of the eMac). Regardless of a machine's built-in ports, using adapters, you can connect other types of monitors to them as well.

→ To learn more about video interfaces, **see** "Video," **p. 715**.

All these interface types provide excellent image quality, and each offers its own benefits. The primary benefit of VGA is that it was the standard interface for PC monitors, so you can use almost any CRT monitor with your Mac. The Digital Video Interface (DVI) offers superior digital signal quality and direct interface to many types of flat-panel displays. Among the benefits of ADC is that it is a digital signal and an Apple ADC display offers other features, such as including two additional USB ports, requiring only one cable (from the Mac to the monitor), and enabling you to power up your Mac and make it sleep or wake up.

TIP

If you use an Apple ADC monitor (one of its flat-panel displays), you can power up your Mac by pressing the Power button on the monitor and put your Mac to sleep by pressing the Power button again. Press the Power button while your Mac sleeps, and it will wake up.

Dot Pitch

On CRT monitors, the electron gun sprays electrons on a metallic grid on the inside of the glass. The smaller the distance between the holes in this grid is, the finer an image the monitor can display. Monitors with smaller pitches are better than those with larger pitches, all other things being equal. Typical pitch sizes range from .24mm to .28mm. Dot pitch is not applicable to flat-panel displays.

Picking a Display

Choosing a monitor can be difficult because of the number of choices that are available. However, you can use several factors to quickly narrow down the options to a few monitors that meet your criteria. First, decide how much you can afford to spend. You can spend as little as $100 for a 14″ CRT to around $1,999 for the top-of-the-line Apple Cinema HD Display. Second, decide whether you want a CRT or an LCD display. If you use a newer Power Mac G4 or a Power Mac G5 or own another model and can afford to spend a bit more, I strongly recommend that you consider an LCD display. In addition to the size and weight advantages, the display quality of some of the LCDs is amazing. Additionally, many offer special features such as additional ports. Third, choose the largest size in a quality brand of the type you choose that fits your budget.

NOTE

> The monitor issue is not just for Power Mac G4 or Power Mac G5 users to consider. All modern Macs that include a built-in monitor have a DVI or VGA output port. For example, you can connect a monitor to an iMac's VGA port to use an external monitor with it. The image you see is the same as that shown on the iMac's internal display, but you can use a larger monitor that way, or you can show the same image to several people at the same time (such as for a presentation).

NOTE

> Before you invest in an Apple flat-panel display, make sure your Mac supports the ADC interface. Some of the earliest Power Mac G4 machines don't.

I hate to sound like a commercial here, but Apple's displays are the best available. If you have a Mac with the ADC interface, you should really consider either the flat-panel 17″ Apple Studio Display or one of the Apple Cinema Displays, which are the largest flat-panel screens available that use the ADC interface. Although the 17″ version might seem sort of small, its amazing clarity and brightness more than make up for giving up a bit of screen real estate. Additionally, the Apple Cinema Displays are magnificent. Currently, I have the 22″ cinema display and an older 15″ Studio display (no longer produced) connected to my Power Mac G4. For the maximum in size and image quality, consider the 23″ Cinema HD display that supports high-definition output.

NOTE

> Some Macs, such as the iMac, require an adapter to be capable of connecting a VGA monitor to its video output port.

Apple has converted its entire monitor line to LCD displays, so that is clearly the future for Mac users. The only machine Apple currently produces that uses CRTs is the eMac.

INSTALLING A MONITOR

Installing a monitor requires two steps. First, connect the appropriate cables to the monitor and the Mac (in the case of ADC displays, only one cable is required). Second, install any software that was provided with the monitor. Some monitors include a ColorSync profile; if yours does, you should install and use it. If you are adding a second monitor to your Mac and have to install an additional graphics card, the graphics card you install might also have software that provides its special features.

→ To learn more about ColorSync, **see** "Synchronizing Color Among Devices," **p. 776**.

NOTE

> You can find an adapter to enable you to attach almost any type of display to almost any type of video port. For example, some Power Mac G4s include two video output ports. One is ADC, whereas the other is DVI. If you want to connect an Apple ADC display to both ports, you need a DVI/ADC adapter.

CONFIGURING A MONITOR

After you have installed a monitor, use the Displays pane of the System Preferences utility to configure it. If you use a single monitor, this pane has two tabs—Display and Color. If you use multiple monitors, the pane also includes the Arrangement tab (see Figure 23.1). You use the Display tab to configure the resolution, color depth, refresh rate, and brightness of the display. The specific options you have depend on the graphics card and monitor you are using. In any case, use the menus, sliders, pop-up menus, and other controls to configure the display. Generally, you should use the highest resolution that is comfortable for you to view. Then, choose the largest color depth and highest refresh rate that are supported at that resolution. Finally, set the brightness to a comfortable level for you.

Setting the resolution of a display is a matter of personal preference, but generally you can tolerate higher resolutions on larger monitors. For example, on the 21" Apple Cinema Display, a resolution of 1600×1024 is comfortable for many people. On smaller monitors, 1024×768 might be appropriate. The resolution also depends on the sharpness and clarity of the display. For example, on the Apple 17" flat-panel, a resolution of 1024×768 is very comfortable, but that same resolution might not be comfortable on a lower-quality CRT display.

Figure 23.1
The Display pane of the System Preferences utility for an Apple 20" cinema display; the Arrangement tab indicates that this machine is using multiple monitors.

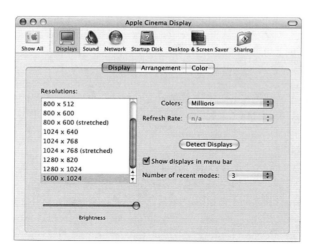

Because your Mac can resize the resolution on-the-fly (you don't have to restart), trying different resolutions to see which works best for you is easy. The trade-off is between more screen space at higher resolutions versus everything appearing smaller. Find the best fit for the type of data you work with and your eyesight.

Some monitors support a "stretched" resolution, such as 1024×768 (stretched). This takes the standard 1024×768 resolution and "stretches" pixels in the horizontal direction so the image fills a widescreen display. (If you use a nonstretched resolution on these displays, black vertical bars appear on each side of the screen.)

NOTE

> The "standard" resolution for Macs has continued to increase along with the size and clarity of monitors. For most of the Mac's early life, the standard display resolution was 640×480 (which also happens to be the resolution of non-HD television by the way). When Macs included larger screens and bigger monitors became available, this increased to 800×600. Currently, the minimum resolution you will likely use on most displays is 1024×768. In fact, some applications won't even run at 800×600 or less.

After you have selected a resolution, select the color depth on the Colors pop-up menu. In almost all cases, you should select Millions. However, if you use an older graphics card and display, you might have to settle for Thousands.

If you use a CRT, select the highest refresh rate available on the Refresh Rate pop-up menu. Using higher refresh rates makes the image flicker less and results in less strain on your eyes.

NOTE

If you use an Apple or other flat-panel display, the Refresh Rate pop-up menu is grayed out because refresh rate isn't applicable to these displays.

If you want your Mac to detect the ADC displays you have attached to it, click the Detect Displays button. The name shown at the top of the System Preferences application and each Display settings dialog box (there will be one for each monitor) should identify the display you are using. (This button does not appear when you are using other types of displays.)

Use the "Show displays in menu bar" check box to turn on the Displays menu in the menu bar. You can configure a display, such as setting its resolution, by selecting the resolution you want to use from the Displays menu.

If you display this menu, use the "Number of recent modes" pop-up menu on the Display pane of the System Preferences application to set the number of resolution settings to display on the menu. For example, if you select 3 on this pop-up menu, the Displays menu on the menu bar shows the most recent three settings you have selected. This makes changing among your most commonly used resolution settings even easier.

Some monitors support software brightness controls, in which case you will see a Brightness slider on the Displays pane. If you don't see this, use the display's physical controls to set its brightness (and contrast, if applicable).

→ For more information on resolution and color depth, **see** Chapter 15, "Creating and Editing Digital Images," **p. 457**.

After you have configured the Display tab, use the Color tab to select a ColorSync profile for your display.

→ To learn more about ColorSync, **see** "Synchronizing Color Among Devices," **p. 776**.

INSTALLING AND USING A SECOND MONITOR

To create the ultimate amount of desktop working space, consider adding multiple monitors to your system. With the Mac OS, you have always been able to have two or more monitors working at the same time, with each monitor displaying different portions of the desktop. For example, you can display a document on which you are working on one monitor and all the toolbars and palettes you are using on a second. Or you might want to have a document open on one screen and your email application open on the other.

NOTE

Most Power Mac G4 and all Power Mac G5 models offer support for multiple monitors out of the box. These machines include an ADC port and a DVI port on the AGP graphics card so you can connect one of each type of monitor to take advantage of multiple monitors. You can also use a DVI/ADC adapter to attach two ADC displays to the same machine. All you need to do is add the second display (and an adapter if needed), and you are good to go.

To have multiple monitors installed on a machine without out-of-the-box multiple monitor support or to add even more monitors to a machine that already supports multiple monitors, you need to install a PCI or PCI-X graphics card for each monitor.

NOTE

> Modern Power Mac G4s and Power Mac G5s feature an accelerated graphics port (AGP) slot in which the preconfigured graphics card is installed. This slot offers the greatest video performance and is where the RADEON or NVIDIA graphics card is installed. When you add a second monitor, you install additional graphics cards in the PCI or PCI-X slots that are available. Because only one AGP slot exists, you aren't able to achieve the same level of performance from the video cards installed in the PCI slots. However, you can still achieve very good performance with PCI- or PCI-X-based graphics cards. And you can always configure your system so you work with applications and documents that require the maximum performance on the displays that use the AGP slot. You can use the other displays for less graphics-intensive applications.

Choosing a PCI or PCI-X Graphics Card

Many graphics cards are available, each offering differing levels of performance and special features. When choosing a graphics card, consider the following factors:

- **Mac OS X compatibility**—Not all graphics cards are Mac OS X–compatible, so any that you consider should be.

- **Performance**—Graphics cards offer varying levels of performance, such as 2D and 3D acceleration and the display resolution they support. The amount of memory installed on a card is a large determinant of this performance, with more memory being better. Common memory amounts are 32MB, 64MB, or 128MB. Generally, you should obtain the highest performance you can afford.

- **Video interface support**—Many graphics cards support VGA monitors. Almost all modern cards support the DVI interface used by most non-Apple flat-panel displays. Some offer support for both interfaces. If you are going to add a flat-panel display as a second monitor, get a card that supports DVI (assuming that the monitor does) because it will result in better image quality and enable you to use the monitor's special features.

- **Special features**—These include video digitizers that enable you to digitize video from analog sources, TV tuners that enable you to watch TV or the output from a VCR on your display, and other features for which you might have a use.

NOTE

> You can also replace the default AGP video card in your Mac with one that offers better performance. Just make sure that the card you get is compatible with your Mac. Replacing the AGP card is similar to installing a PCI or PCI-X card.

Installing a Graphics Card

Installing a PCI or PCI-X graphics card is a relatively easy process.

CAUTION

> The following steps are an example of how a typical graphics card is installed on a Power Mac G4. You should follow the instructions that came with your Mac and the graphics card you are adding.

NOTE

> If software is provided for the card, such as drivers and applications, you should install the software before you install the card. However, check with the instructions that came with the card to see the order in which the manufacturer recommends the items be installed.

23

To install a new or additional graphics card, do the following:

1. Power down your Mac.
2. Open the case.
3. Locate the PCI or PCI-X slot in which you want to install the card. You can use any open PCI slot; they are functionally identical. In Power Mac G5s, you should use the slot that matches the performance of the card you are installing.
4. Remove the blank cover from the PCI or PCI-X slot you are using.
5. Install the PCI or PCI-X card in the slot and secure it with the screw that was used to hold the blank cover in place.
6. Close the case.
7. Attach a monitor to the VGA or DVI output of the graphics card.
8. Restart your Mac.

→ To learn where the PCI slots are located in a Power Mac G4, **see** "PCI," **p. 711**.

WORKING WITH TWO (OR MORE) MONITORS

If you have installed an additional graphics card and connected it to a monitor or you have a Mac that supports multiple monitors, you need to configure the displays to work together. When you have more than one monitor installed, one of the monitors must be the primary monitor. This is the monitor on which the menu bar, Dock, mounted volumes, and other desktop items are displayed. The rest of the monitors contain windows that you place on them.

To display items on more than one monitor, do the following:

1. Open the Display pane of the System Preferences Utility. When you do so, you see a Displays pane on each monitor. On the primary monitor, this is included in the System Preferences application window. On the other monitors, this is an independent window with the name of the monitor at the top of the window. The settings shown in each Displays pane are those that are currently being used for that monitor. On the primary

display, a third tab called Arrangement appears in the Displays pane (see Figure 23.2). The Displays pane on the other monitors contains the normal tabs, but it does not contain any part of the System Preferences interface (see Figure 23.3).

2. Set the resolution, color depth, and refresh rates for each monitor using its Displays pane. You can use different settings for each monitor; for example, if one monitor is larger than the other, you might want a higher resolution on the larger monitor.

3. Click the Arrange tab on the primary monitor's Display pane. You will see a graphical representation of the monitors attached to your system (see Figure 23.4). The primary monitor is indicated by the menu bar across the top of the monitor window (on the left display in Figure 23.4).

Figure 23.2
This Display pane contains the Arrangement tab, which means it is for the primary display.

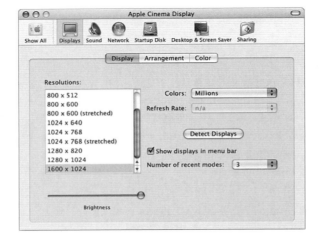

Figure 23.3
This Displays pane is on a secondary monitor; note that the resolution setting is different from that of the primary display shown in Figure 23.2.

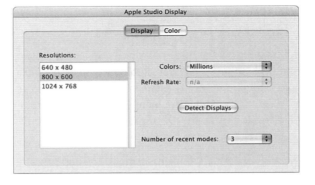

Figure 23.4
This system has two monitors attached to it; the relative resolution settings are indicated by the size of the monitors in this pane. The primary monitor, located on the left, is set to a higher resolution than the one on the right.

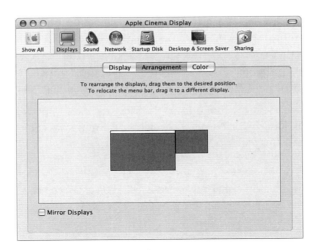

23

4. Organize the monitors by dragging them on the pane. For example, drag the monitor you want to display "to your left" to the left side of the pane. This configures the virtual desktop so you move the mouse/pointer to the left to work on the left display. The monitor icons should be in the same orientation as the physical monitors on your desktop.

5. Set the primary monitor by dragging the menu bar onto it.

6. Quit the System Preferences utility.

 If you can't get both monitors working, see "My Second Monitor Doesn't Work" in the "Troubleshooting" section at the end of this chapter.

Because the desktop stretches across all the monitors connected to your system, they act as one large desktop. You can drag windows and palettes from one monitor to another by moving them from one side of the desktop to the other. You can move between the monitors by moving the pointer "across" the divide between them. For example, you might have an image open in Photoshop on one monitor and all the Photoshop palettes on the other. Or, you can have a Word document open on one monitor and a Web browser on another. After you use multiple monitors for even a short time, you might find that you can never get along with just one again.

NOTE

You can drag windows between the monitors, but the menu bar, Dock, and other desktop items always remain on the primary display.

You can have multiple monitors display the same image by turning on display mirroring. In this case, each monitor displays the same desktop. You are limited to the same amount of working space, but that same space is displayed on multiple displays. This is especially useful when you connect a projector to one video port and use a display on the other. You can work using the display while the audience sees what you are doing via the projected image.

To configure mirroring, set the monitors to the same resolution. In the Arrange tab of the Display pane, check the Mirror Displays check box. All monitors connected to the machine then display the same image.

NOTE

> If you connect a display or projector to the VGA or DVI port on a PowerBook, iBook, iMac, or eMac, you can only use video mirroring.

If you add the Displays menu to your menu bar, you can control display mirroring, the resolution, and the color depth of each monitor by choosing the setting you want on the menu. You can also open the Displays pane of the System Preferences utility from the menu (see Figure 23.5).

Figure 23.5
Control the resolution and other settings of all the displays attached to your Mac from the Displays menu in the Mac OS X menu bar.

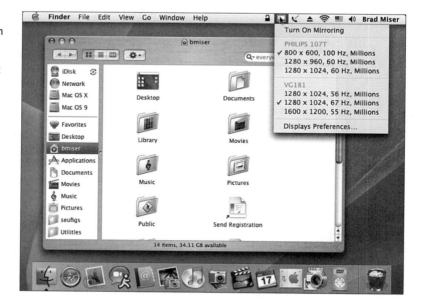

FINDING, INSTALLING, AND USING SPEAKERS

Sound is an important part of the Mac experience. Adding speakers to your system is a good way to enhance the experience of music, movies, games, and other multimedia.

The five basic types of speakers you might be able to use with your Mac include

- **Built-in**—The built-in speakers on eMacs and older iMacs provide fairly good sound. The built-in speakers in PowerBooks and iBooks are okay as long as you are on the move and can't use anything better. But the built-in speakers on other Macs are pretty sorry.

- **Analog**—Analog speakers connect to the Mac's headphone or speaker jack. You can find very high-quality computer speakers, some of which rival their home stereo counterparts in sound quality.

- **Apple Pro**—Some Macs, such as the iMac, include a jack for Apple Pro speakers. These machines include a pair of Apple Pro speakers, also known as *eyeball speakers*. These are analog speakers that offer decent sound quality and a very stylish design.

- **USB**—Digital speakers use the USB interface to connect to your Mac. USB speakers also offer excellent quality.

- **Digital 5.1 Surround Sound**—If you are lucky enough to have a Power Mac G5 or you install a 5.1 audio card in a Power Mac G4, you can use digital 5.1 surround sound speakers. These provide the ultimate in sound quality and enable your Mac to match a home theater's sound output.

Digital Surround Sound Is Lacking

It's a shame that only the Power Mac G5 supports digital surround sound. After many years of providing unmatched audio out of the box, the Mac has trailed Windows machines for some time in the area of audio. Many more 5.1 surround sound cards are available for Windows machines, and many Windows desktops support 5.1 out of the box. With its emphasis on leading-edge digital media capabilities, it is too bad that most Macs are limited to simple stereo audio. (For example, when you watch a DVD on all Macs except the G5, you are limited to stereo sound output and the cool surround sound effects enabled by DVD are missed.) Hopefully, Apple will introduce 5.1 support in all Mac models soon.

CHOOSING AND INSTALLING SPEAKERS

As with other system components, choosing speakers is primarily a task of balancing how much you want to spend versus how demanding you are in terms of quality. In either analog or USB, speaker sets come with a number of speakers. A basic set has two speakers; however, unless you have a very small budget, you should get a set that also includes a subwoofer. More advanced digital 5.1 speaker sets can have six speakers to provide full surround sound.

NOTE

As mentioned earlier, surround sound is an area in which Macs trail PCs. Sound cards that provide true surround sound are available for PCs, but at the time of this writing, few are available for the Mac.

A good choice for many systems is Harman Multimedia SoundSticks (see Figure 23.6). These USB speakers provide excellent sound, and they are among the best-looking speakers around. Because they are USB based, all modern Macs can use them.

Figure 23.6
SoundSticks sound as good as they look.

23

If you have a Power Mac G5, you should get a set of speakers that takes advantage of the advanced audio capabilities of these machines to provide true 5.1 digital surround sound.

Installing speakers requires that you provide power to the subwoofer, attach all the satellite speakers to it, and then connect the subwoofer to your Mac (via the headphone or speaker jack, via a USB port, or to the digital audio out port). If you use Apple Pro speakers, you attach them to the Apple Pro speaker port.

USING SPEAKERS

You can control the audio output of your system in several ways.

Some speakers come with volume and other controls on one of the satellites.

You can control the system volume of your Mac through the keyboard volume controls on the Apple Pro keyboard or on the PowerBook's and iBook's built-in keyboard. Other keyboards, such as the excellent Logitech Duos, provide volume wheels that you use to control your system's volume.

You can also use the Sound pane of the System Preferences utility to set sound levels. At the bottom of the pane, you can use the Output volume slider to set the general sound level for your system, including muting it. You can also choose to install the Volume menu on the Mac OS X menu bar. If you do so, you can set the volume level by clicking the speaker icon on the menu bar and setting the volume level with the slider.

NOTE

> You can also control volume using controls within specific applications, such as iTunes or iMovie. When you do so, the volume control in the application changes the volume of that application's output relative to the system volume level.
>
> When you use the volume controls on an Apple Pro keyboard, you change the system volume level.

NEW The Sound pane of the System Preferences application has three tabs: Sound Effects, Output, and Input.

On the Sound Effects tab, you can set the relative volume level of alert sounds, the alert sound you want to use, the audio controller through which alert sounds play, whether user interface sound effects play, and whether you hear feedback when you change the volume level using the keys on the Apple Pro or other keyboard.

Select the alert sound you want to use by clicking it on the list. You then hear a sample of the sound you select. When your Mac needs to get your attention, it plays this sound.

One of the nice features of Mac OS X is that, with some speakers such as USB SoundSticks, you can set the alert sound to play through the Mac's internal speaker while the rest of the sound plays through the external speakers. You do this by setting "Internal speakers" on the "Play alerts and sound effects through" pop-up menu. This means that alert sounds play through the Mac's built-in speaker(s) rather than through the external speakers, such as SoundSticks. This prevents you from being jarred by an alert sound when listening to loud music or movies.

NOTE

> If you use external analog speakers that get their output from the speaker jack on your Mac, you can't choose those speakers separately from the Mac's built-in audio controller because the Mac's controller controls the output to the speaker jack. Only when you use USB or digital speakers, such as the SoundSticks, or when you install a PCI sound card, can you configure separate sound output devices.

Set the volume level of alerts by using the "Alert volume" slider. If you do have alerts play through internal speakers while other sound plays through external speakers, you likely need to set the alert volume level relatively high to be able to hear it over the sound coming from the external speakers.

If you check the "Play user interface sound effects" check box, you will hear sound effects for various actions, such as when you empty the Trash.

If you check the "Play feedback when volume keys are pressed" check box, you will hear a sound when you change the system volume level using the volume keys on your keyboard. The louder the volume setting, the louder the feedback sound.

23

Use the Output tab to select the output devices you want to use to play sound other than system alerts (see Figure 23.7). When you install additional devices, such as SoundSticks, you see each device in the output device list. Choose the device you want to use to play sound and then configure the settings for that device. The settings you have depend on the device you have installed. For example, with SoundSticks, you can control the balance of the satellite speakers.

Figure 23.7
The Output tab of the Sound pane of the System Preferences utility enables you to configure the balance of SoundSticks satellite speakers.

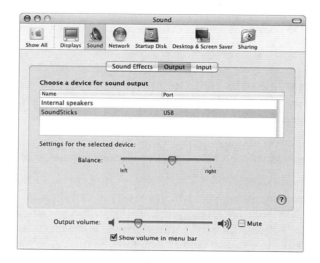

Use the Input tab to configure sound input devices, such as the audio in port or USB microphones (see Figure 23.8). A list of all sound input devices appears in the upper part of the pane. You can use the "Input volume" slider to set the input volume level for the selected device. Use the "Input level" display to monitor the input volume being received by the input device. The "blips" show you how "loud" the input sound is. A blip remains at the highest level of sound input to show you where the maximum is. Generally, you should set the level so that most of the sound is coming in at the middle of the range.

Figure 23.8
You can use the input sound to set the input volume for USB microphones and other input devices.

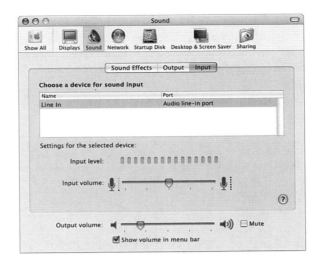

FINDING, INSTALLING, AND USING PRINTERS

If you want to get your work out on paper, you can use many types of printers to get the job done. Under Mac OS X, you install and manage printers using the Printer Setup Utility application. And Mac OS X includes support for a large number of printers by default.

Four basic categories of printers are available, based on the technology the printer uses to imprint the paper:

- **Inkjet**—Inkjet printers spray small dots of ink on the paper to form images and text. Inkjet printers produce excellent quality text and good-to-excellent quality graphics. For personal printers or those shared by only a few people, inkjets are hard to beat. A good quality inkjet printer costs less than $150, so they are also an excellent value. Support for many Hewlett-Packard, Epson, and Canon inkjet printers is built in to Mac OS X.

- **Laser**—Laser printers produce superb quality for both text and graphics. They are also very fast and are the best choice for network printing. Lower-end laser printers are affordable enough to also be a good choice for a personal printer. Unfortunately, all reasonably priced (for home or home office use) laser printers are black-and-white only.

23

- **Color laser**—Color laser printers produce excellent text and graphics and also have color capability. Unfortunately, color laser printers are very expensive and are unlikely to be an option for you unless high-quality color printing and network support are required and you have a business that can justify their expense.

- **Other printers**—Beyond color laser printers are dye-sublimation and other higher-quality printers that are used in graphic design and other high-end businesses.

NOTE

A factor to consider when selecting a printer is that inkjets use a lot of ink and cartridges are expensive. If you do much black-and-white printing, a laser printer can be a less expensive option in the long run when you consider the cost of the consumable supplies (ink versus toner).

There are two ways you can connect a printer to your Mac: directly or through a network. To connect a printer directly to your Mac, you simply attach the printer cable to the appropriate port on your Mac (USB or Ethernet for newer Macs; serial or Ethernet for older Macs). How you connect a printer to your network depends on the type of network you are using. If you are using an Ethernet network, you can attach a cable from the nearest hub or print server to your printer. You can also choose to share either type of printer over a wired or wireless network.

Mac OS X supports several printer communication protocols, including AppleTalk, IP Printing, Open Directory, Rendezvous, direct connection through USB, and Windows Printing.

Mac OS X also enables you to share printers over a wired or wireless network.

CHOOSING A PRINTER

Covering the mind-boggling variety of printers available is beyond the scope of this book. However, we can identify some printer classes you might want to consider, including

- **Inkjet**—A good-quality inkjet printer will serve almost everyone. Even the inexpensive models can do a great job with text and graphics, including printing photos and other high-resolution images. If your page quantity needs are fairly modest, an inkjet printer is a good choice, especially if you need color output.

- **Laser**—If you have higher quantity demands or your printer needs to support several users, a laser printer might be a better choice. Laser printers are faster and less expensive per page than are inkjets. Many laser printers are networkable so supporting your local network with a single printer is easy.

- **Other options**—If you have the need for a color laser printer or dye-sub printer, you are probably in a company that has an IT staff that handles obtaining and installing these devices. As long as the printer uses standard network printer drivers, Mac OS X machines will be capable of printing to them just fine.

Mac OS X includes support for Rendezvous; this technology enables your Mac to actively seek devices to which it is networked. In the case of Rendezvous printers, your Mac can discover the printers it can access and automatically configure itself to use those printers. No configuration on your part is required. However, printers have to be Rendezvous capable for this to work. Even though Rendezvous has been supported since Mac OS X version 10.2, few printers support this technology.

INSTALLING PRINTERS

There are many types of printers you can install, configure, and use with Mac OS X. In this section, you will learn how to work with the most common types of printers.

INSTALLING A LOCAL USB PRINTER

As long as it offers Mac OS X–compatible drivers, you can install and use just about any USB printer. Using such devices is relatively straightforward:

1. Connect the printer to the power supply and to your Mac's USB port.

2. Install the printer driver software, if necessary. If the printer you are using is an inkjet from HP, Lexmark, Canon, or Epson, the drivers are probably already built in to Mac OS X.

> **TIP**
>
> To see which specific printer models are supported natively by Mac OS X, open `Mac OS X/Library/Printers`, where `Mac OS X` is the name of your Mac OS X startup volume. You will see folders for each brand of printer you elected to install when you install Mac OS X. Open the folder for the printer brand in which you are interested. The supported models have a `.plugin` file.

3. Configure the printer in the Mac OS X Printer Setup Utility.

Support for many inkjet printers is built in to Mac OS X. For example, you can use the following steps to install, configure, and use an Epson 740i inkjet. Other models of inkjet printers work similarly:

1. Connect power to the printer.

2. Connect the printer's USB cable to a USB port on your Mac.

> **NOTE**
>
> If support for the specific model of printer you are using is not built in to Mac OS X, you need to install its specific software prior to configuring the printer on your Mac.

3. If the printer has Mac OS X–compatible software, install it—support for several printers is built in to the operating system.

4. Open the Printer Setup Utility (Applications/Utilities).

5. In the Printer List window's toolbar, click Add. The Printer List sheet appears. At the top of this sheet is a pop-up menu on which you select the type of printer connection for the printer you are configuring. By default, Rendezvous is selected.

6. Select the type of printer configuration you want to add from the pop-up menu (see Figure 23.9). The choices on the pop-up menu are AppleTalk, IP Printing, Open Directory, Rendezvous, USB, and Windows Printing. At the bottom of the pop-up menu, you will also see various options that relate to any printers that were installed when you installed Mac OS X.

Figure 23.9
When you open the pop-up menu at the top of the Printer List sheet, you see all the printer connection methods your Mac supports.

When you make a selection on the pop-up menu, two things happen. First, you return to the Printer List sheet that is reconfigured to reflect the selection you made. Second, the connection method you select, such as USB, is scanned for available printers.

For example, if you select USB, the USB buses are scanned and the available USB printers are listed in the window. A list of possible printers for the configuration you selected is shown.

7. Select the printer you want to add from the list of available printers.

8. On the Printer Model pop-up menu, select the specific printer model you are configuring, if it isn't selected by default.

> **TIP**
>
> If a specific model isn't selected, you see the Auto Select option. This enables Mac OS X to automatically select the model it thinks is the best match.

9. Click Add to return to the Printer List; the printer you added is listed in the window (see Figure 23.10).

Figure 23.10
An Epson Stylus Color
740 has been
installed on this Mac.

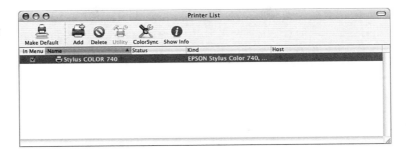

10. To make the printer you added the default, select it and click the Make Default button.

11. Select the printer and click the Show Info button. The Printer Info window appears.

At the top of the window is a pop-up menu that enables you to choose the aspect of the printer about which you want to see information. The options are Name & Location, Printer Model, and Installable Options (see Figure 23.11).

Figure 23.11
You can use the
Printer Info window
to see information
about a printer and
configure specific
properties, such as its
name.

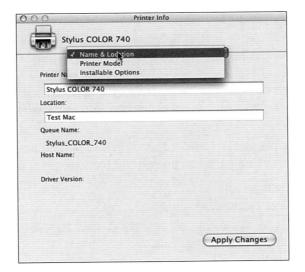

12. Select Name & Location on the pop-up menu.

13. If you want to name the printer something other than its default name, enter the name in the Printer Name field.

14. In the Location field, enter location information for the printer—by default, this is the name of the Mac to which it is connected. You might want to provide a more descriptive location if you will be sharing the printer with people via a network.

15. Select Printer Model on the pop-up menu. At the top of the window is the same list of printer models you used earlier to select the printer. You can choose a different model if you want to try one of the other options.

16. Select Installable Options on the pop-up menu. You can see any additional options that are available for the printer you are configuring. Select the options you want to install.

17. Click Apply Changes, and the information and options you entered are applied to the printer.

18. Close the Printer Info window.

19. Quit the Printer Setup Utility.

> **TIP**
>
> If you hold down the ⌘ key and click the Hide/Show Toolbar button in the Printer List window, you cycle through toolbar configurations, including various icon sizes and a text-only toolbar.

INSTALLING A NETWORK PRINTER

Using a network printer is a good way to share a printer among multiple users; with the rise of home networks, installing a networked printer in a home or home office is also a practical option.

Installing a network printer is similar to installing a local printer. The specific steps you use depend on the network you are using and the particular printer model. Support for most laser printers is built in to Mac OS X.

In the following example, an HP LaserJet 2200DN is installed on a small Ethernet network. The steps to install other printers on different types of networks are similar:

1. Connect power to the printer.

2. Connect the printer to an Ethernet hub.

3. If the printer has Mac OS X–compatible software, install it—support for most laser printers is built in to the operating system.

4. Open the Printer Setup Utility(Applications/Utilities).

5. In the Printer List window's toolbar, click Add. The Printer List sheet appears.

6. Select the type of printer you want to add from the pop-up menu at the top of the Printer List sheet. The choices on the pop-up menu are AppleTalk, IP Printing, Open Directory, Rendezvous, USB, and Windows Printing. At the bottom of the pop-up menu the various options that relate to any printers installed when you installed Mac OS X are listed. For most small Ethernet networks and printers, AppleTalk will work; select AppleTalk on the pop-up menu.

7. On the lower pop-up menu, select the AppleTalk zone you want to access. In many cases, the Local AppleTalk Zone option is what you want to choose. If the printer is installed on a different AppleTalk zone, you must select that zone instead.

The network is scanned and the available printers are listed in the Printer List sheet (see Figure 23.12).

Figure 23.12
This AppleTalk network includes one LaserJet printer.

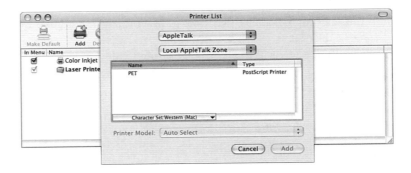

8. Select the printer (and driver on the Printer Model pop-up menu, if necessary) that you want to add, and click Add. You return to the Printer List, the connection to the printer is opened and configured, and the printer you added is listed in the window (see Figure 23.13).

Figure 23.13
Two printers are now available in the Printer Setup Utility; the PET printer is a laser printer installed on the network.

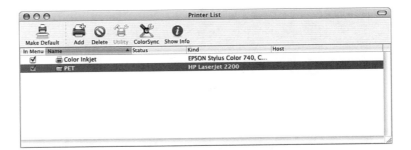

NOTE

If the exact printer model has a driver in Mac OS X, the Printer Model pop-up menu is inactive (because the driver for the specific model was found). If the specific model of printer you have selected does not have a corresponding driver installed, the Printer Model pop-up menu becomes active. Select the brand of printer you are installing and then choose the specific driver you want installed on this menu. If you leave the option Auto Select selected, Mac OS X chooses the driver it thinks is the best match.

9. Select the printer and click the Show Info button. The Printer Info window appears.

At the top of the window is a pop-up menu that enables you to choose the aspect of the printer about which you want to see information. The options are Name & Location, Printer Model, and Installable Options.

10. Select Name & Location on the pop-up menu.

11. If you want to name the printer something other than its default name, enter the name in the Printer Name field.

12. In the Location field, enter location information for the printer; by default, this is the name of the Mac to which it is connected. You might want to provide a more descriptive location if you will be sharing the printer with people via a network.

13. Select Printer Model on the pop-up menu. At the top of the window is the same list of printer models you used earlier to select the printer. You can select a different model if you want to try one of the other options.

14. Select Installable Options on the pop-up menu to see any additional options available for the printer you are configuring (see Figure 23.14). Select the options you want to install.

Figure 23.14
This LaserJet printer has several installable options.

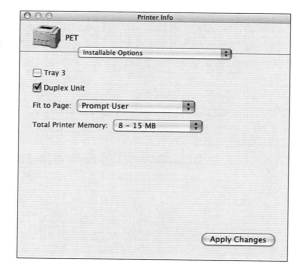

15. Click Apply Changes. The information and options you entered are applied to the printer.

16. Close the Printer Info window. The list of available printers as you installed and configured them appears (see Figure 23.15).

17. Quit the Printer Setup Utility.

TIP

In the Printer List window, the default printer is indicated by its name appearing in bold. To set the default printer, select it in the Printer List window and click the Make Default button.

Figure 23.15
This Mac now has
two printing options.

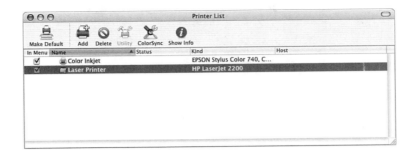

INSTALLING OTHER TYPES OF PRINTERS

As you can see on the pop-up menu on the Printer List sheet, Mac OS X supports several types of printer connections. Installing and configuring each type is slightly different. Covering all these options is beyond the scope of this chapter; however, you can use the steps in the previous sections as a general guide for configuring any type of printer.

TIP

> If you want to hide a printer that is connected to your Mac so it can't be used, uncheck the In Menu check box in the Printer List window. This removes the printer from the list of available printers on the Print dialog box so it can't be used. To make the printer available again, check its In Menu check box.

PRINTING WITH BLUETOOTH

Bluetooth wireless technology enables you to print to and share a wireless printer among many Bluetooth-equipped devices. To do so, you set up a Bluetooth printer much like you set up a Bluetooth PDA or other device. Then, you can choose that printer and print to it just like printers physically attached to or networked to your machine.

In addition, Bluetooth adapters are available for many models of printers. These adapters connect to one of the printer's standard ports and enable that printer to communicate via Bluetooth. For example, the MPI Tech Bluetooth Printer Adapter connects to the parallel port on HP printers to enable those printers to communicate via Bluetooth (see Figure 23.16). These adapters also enable you to print from other Bluetooth devices, such as PDAs and cell phones.

In some cases, you won't choose a Bluetooth printer using Mac OS X's normal Printer Setup and Print dialog box tools. Rather, you'll use the Output Options (covered later in this chapter) to print a PostScript file. Then, you'll send that file to the printer to print it.

→ To learn how to configure Bluetooth devices, **see** "Finding, Installing, and Using Bluetooth Devices," **p. 735**.

Figure 23.16
Using a Bluetooth adapter, you can enable a printer to communicate wirelessly.

CONFIGURING PRINT OPTIONS AND SHARING A PRINTER

Under Mac OS X, version 10.3, you can share printers connected to your Mac over wired and wireless networks, as well as those connected directly to your Mac through USB. You can also configure a couple of aspects of how a printer is configured when the Print command is issued:

1. Open the Print & Fax pane of the System Preferences utility.

> **TIP**
>
> If you click the Set Up Printers button, the Printer Setup Utility opens.

2. Click the Printing tab if it isn't selected already (see Figure 23.17).
3. Select a printer from the "Selected printer in Print Dialog" pop-up menu. One option is "Last printer used," which causes the most recently used printer to be selected. Each printer you have installed on your Mac is also listed on this pop-up menu.
4. Configure the default paper size by selecting it on the "Default paper size in Page Setup" pop-up menu.
5. Check the "Share my printers with other computers" check box to share all your Mac's printers with other machines that can connect to yours through a wired or wireless network.
6. Quit the System Preferences utility.

Figure 23.17
You can use the Print & Fax preferences to configure print options and printer sharing.

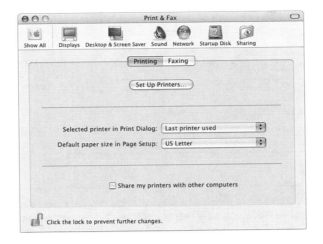

TIP

> You can also turn on printer sharing by checking the Printer Sharing check box on the Services tab of the Sharing pane of the System Preferences application.

If you share your printers, any printers connected to your Mac are available for others. For example, if you provide an AirPort network, users of that network can print to a USB printer connected directly to your Mac.

TIP

> If your network includes an AirPort Extreme Base Station, you can connect a USB printer to the Base Station to share it.

CONFIGURING AND ACCESSING SHARED PRINTERS

To access printers being shared on a network, use the following steps:

1. Open the Printer Setup Utility. The list of printers installed on your Mac contains Shared Printers.

2. Click the Expansion triangle next to the Shared Printers item. A list of all printers being shared on your network appears (see Figure 23.18). You also see the name, type, and host for each printer.

3. Check the In Menu check box for each printer you want to appear in Print dialog boxes.

4. Quit the Printer Setup Utility.

Figure 23.18
Two printers are
being shared on the
network.

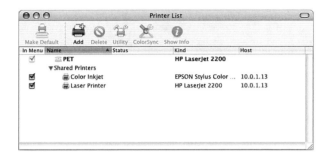

TIP

> You don't have to perform the previous steps; they just make selecting a shared printer a
> bit easier. You can actually choose any shared printer via the Print dialog box by first
> selecting Shared Printers on the list of available printers and then selecting the specific
> printer to which you want to print.

PRINTING UNDER MAC OS X

When you print a document, you see the print dialog box for the default printer. You can
choose any other printers that are installed by using the Printer pop-up menu (see
Figure 23.19). The Print dialog box contains a variety of pop-up menus and other tools
you can use to configure a print job.

Figure 23.19
The list of printers
available to your Mac,
including any that are
being shared with you
over a network, are
shown on the Printer
pop-up menu.

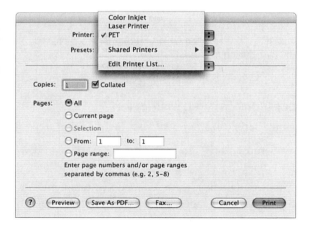

The specific options you see in the Print dialog box depend on the printer you are using.
You select the settings you want to configure from the third pop-up menu (counting the
Printer and Preset pop-up menus as the first and second) and then configure those settings
with the controls that appear in the lower part of the dialog box. Depending on the printer
you select, you might have the following options:

- **Printer**—You can use this pop-up menu to select a printer to which to print. You can also open the Printer Setup Utility by selecting Edit Printer List. You can check for any updates to printer software by selecting Check For Printer Updates.

- **Presets**—You can switch between the standard settings for the selected printer, or you can save a custom configuration and switch to that one.

- **Copies & Pages**—These controls enable you to set the number of pages you want to print and choose the part of a document you want to print.

- **Duplex**—If a printer is capable of duplexing, you use these controls to configure it, such as by printing on both sides of the paper.

- **Layout**—These commands enable you to control how many pages print per sheet of paper, the direction in which your document layout prints, and whether a border is printed.

- **Output Options**—This pane enables you to print the document as a PDF or PostScript file.

- **Scheduler**—This pane enables you to schedule a print job.

- **Paper Feed**—These controls enable you to select a paper tray for the print job, or you can choose to do a manual feed.

- **Print Settings**—Controls in this pane enable you to choose a paper type and select from the print modes offered by a printer (such as color, black and white, draft, and so on).

- **Image Quality**—These controls enable you to determine the quality with which images are printed—to save toner, for example.

- **Printer Features**—This pane can contain various commands, such as halftoning, flipping horizontal, and other specialized settings.

- **ColorSync**—This pane enables you to choose ColorSync options for the selected printer.

- **Summary**—The Summary area displays a description of the print job you have currently configured. This can be useful if you have configured a complex print job and want to check it before you run it.

> **TIP**
>
> In the Copies & Pages dialog box for most printers, you have the option to collate documents. If you have ever had to hand-collate a large document, you will really appreciate this feature.

You can preview a print job by clicking the Preview button. When you are ready to print, click Print or press Return.

You can check the status of a print job by double-clicking the printer on the Printer List; when a job is sent to a printer, the Printer's icon opens on the Dock and begins to bounce; you can click this to open a printer to access its status window (see Figure 23.20). You can use the commands on the Jobs menu to control print jobs. You can also sort the jobs in the queue by Status or Name. You can even use the buttons on the printer window's toolbar to control the printer, such as the Delete button to delete any print jobs that are selected in the window.

Figure 23.20
You can monitor the status of print jobs by double-clicking a printer in the Printer List or by clicking the Printer's icon on the Dock to open the monitor window for that printer.

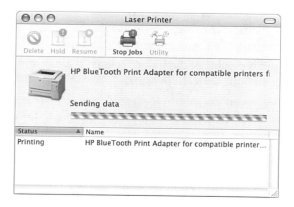

USING A PRINTER FROM THE CLASSIC ENVIRONMENT

Printing from the Classic environment can be a bit problematic because Classic has trouble interfacing properly with the USB ports. Some printers work fine from within Classic, but others do not.

To print from within Classic, you need to first install the printer's software in the Classic environment. Then you use the Classic Chooser to select the printer to which you want to print. You will probably have more luck printing to network printers than you will printing to USB or other local printers.

The only way to figure out whether the printer you want to use will print under Classic is to give it a try. I had mixed results. An Epson 740i printer could not be selected because Classic Chooser did not find the USB ports—printing to my HP PSC 750 was also unsuccessful because the USB port could not be found. However, I was able to print to a networked laser printer.

 If you are unable to print to a printer in Classic, see "I Can't Print Under Classic" in the "Troubleshooting" section at the end of this chapter.

WORKING WITH MAC OS X'S BUILT-IN FAX CAPABILITY

 With Mac OS X version 10.3, the capability to send and receive faxes is built in to your Mac. Of course, to use this capability, your Mac must have a modem installed and that modem must be connected to a working phone line.

RECEIVING FAXES ON YOUR MAC

To configure your Mac to receive faxes, do the following steps:

1. Connect your Mac's modem to a working phone line.

2. Open the Print & Fax pane of the System Preferences application.

3. Click the Faxing tab (see Figure 23.21).

Figure 23.21
With a Mac OS X-equipped Mac, you can get rid of your fax machine.

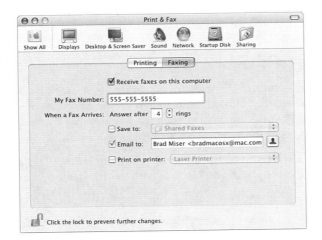

4. Check the "Receive faxes on this computer" check box. The other controls in the pane become active.

5. Enter the phone number to which you have connected your Mac in the My Fax Number field.

6. Use the "Answer after" field to set the number of rings before your Mac answers the phone.

7. If you want the fax to be saved as a file, check the "Save to" check box and select the location in which you want fax files to be saved on the pop-up menu.

8. If you want the fax to be emailed, check the "Email to" check box and enter the address to which you want it be to mailed in the field.

> **TIP**
>
> Click the Address Book button to select an email address to which to send the fax.

9. If you want the fax to be printed, click the "Print on printer" check box and select the printer to which it should be printed on the pop-up menu.

10. Quit the System Preferences application.

When the phone number to which your Mac is connected receives a call and the number of rings you set have occurred, your Mac answers the phone and attempts to receive a fax. If it receives one, it is saved, emailed, or printed as indicated by your configuration choices.

SENDING FAXES FROM YOUR MAC

You can send faxes from within any application on your Mac as easily as you can receive them.

→ To learn how to fax documents, **see** "Faxing Documents," **p. 180**.

23

WORKING WITH PDFS

Portable Document Format (PDF) files are one of the most useful ways to output documents for electronic viewing. Any PDF document can be easily read by anyone using any computer platform. PDF documents maintain their appearance because they do not rely on fonts and other aspects of the system on which they are viewed.

Under Mac OS X, PDFs are a native file format. You can create PDFs from within any Mac OS X application, and you can read PDF files with the Preview application.

> **NOTE**
>
> The free Adobe Reader application is also available for Mac OS X. This application offers more features for viewing PDFs than does Preview, but either application will get the job done. To download a copy of Adobe Reader, visit www.adobe.com/products/acrobat/readstep2.html.

CREATING PDF FILES

Creating PDF files is an extremely simple task:

1. Open the document for which you want to create a PDF.
2. Select File, Print.

> **TIP**
> You can also click the Save As PDF button instead of performing steps 3 and 4.

3. Select Output Options on the Options pop-up menu.
4. Check the "Save as File" check box and select PDF on the Format menu.

> **TIP**
> The other option on this menu is PostScript. This creates a PostScript version of the file you are printing. This can be useful for a number of tasks, such as sending to a Bluetooth printer or printing service.

5. Click Save.

6. Name the document and select a location in which to save it. Use the filename extension .pdf.

7. Click Save.

> **NOTE**
>
> When you do a print preview under Mac OS X, the preview is in PDF. You can also create a PDF file by previewing a file; when the preview window appears, select File, Save As PDF.

Creating a PDF using the Output Options command does not create or preserve any hyperlinks in a document. For example, if you create a PDF of a Web page, the links on that page will not be functional. Similarly, if you create a text document that contains a table of contents in which the entries are hyperlinked to the sections in the document, the resulting PDF will not contain active links. Basically, creating a PDF using the Print command simply replicates a paper document without adding any features of an electronic document. Even so, being able to create a PDF from any document using the Print command is useful when you want to send your documents to other people.

> **TIP**
>
> Creating a PDF version of a document is also a great way to capture versions of that document at specific points in time for archival purposes.

To create PDFs that contain hyperlinks and other electronic document features, you need to use a more sophisticated application. For example, Adobe applications can save documents in PDF format and preserve hyperlinks within those documents. Or, you can use the full Acrobat application to create more sophisticated PDFs from any application.

> **NOTE**
>
> You can't use the Print dialog box to create PDFs from Classic applications. You either must open the document using a Mac OS application or create the PDF using Acrobat or another application capable of creating PDFs (such as Adobe FrameMaker).

VIEWING PDFs WITH PREVIEW

To view the document you created, open it. Unless you have configured PDFs to open in a different application, Preview launches and you can view the PDF. Use the commands on the View menu to navigate in and control the appearance of the PDF. For example, use the Zoom In command (⌘-+) to magnify the PDF file.

TIP

> Because Adobe Reader enables you to take advantage of all the features PDF documents offer, you might want to designate it as the default application for all PDF documents so it opens automatically when you view PDFs.

→ To learn how to associate file types with applications, **see** "Determining the Application That Opens When You Open a Document," **p. 169**.

NOTE

> If you are serious about creating PDFs, consider getting a copy of Adobe Acrobat. With this application, you can create full-featured PDFs that can contain hyperlinks, hot-linked indexes, and so on.

SYNCHRONIZING COLOR AMONG DEVICES

One of the most challenging aspects of creating color documents for output on paper or electronically is maintaining consistent color among the images and text in those documents. Each device you use, such as monitors, printers, scanners, cameras, and so on, can have a slightly different interpretation of particular colors and can use a different color space. This makes creating a document that contains the colors you really want difficult.

Apple's *ColorSync* technology is an attempt to solve this problem. With ColorSync, you configure a ColorSync profile for each device with which you work. If all your devices use a ColorSync profile, the colors across the elements of your document should be consistent because ColorSync translates colors across different color spaces.

The two general steps to use ColorSync are the following:

1. Use the ColorSync Utility to select and configure a ColorSync profile for each device you will use.
2. Use the color management features of the application you want to use to create a document to select the ColorSync workflow for that project.

CONFIGURING COLORSYNC

To configure a ColorSync profile for your devices, do the following:

NOTE

> To use ColorSync, a device must have a ColorSync profile installed. For many devices, this profile is built in to Mac OS X. For others, the profile is installed when you install software related to that device.

1. Open the ColorSync Utility (Applications/Utilities).
2. Click the Preferences button if it isn't selected already, and then click the Default Profiles tab (see Figure 23.22).

Figure 23.22
Use ColorSync to match the colors on various devices with which you work.

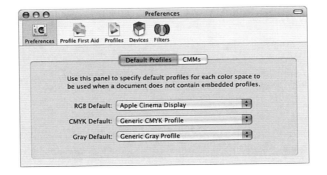

3. Use the pop-up menus to select default profiles for the RGB, CMYK, and Gray color spaces. If you can't find the profile for the device you are using, you need to install its ColorSync profile or select a generic profile.
4. Click the CMMs tab and select the color-matching method you want to use. If you haven't installed additional CMMs, your choices are Automatic or Apple CMM.
5. To see the profiles installed, click the Profiles button and expand the area, such as System or Computer, to see the profiles that have been installed for that area.
6. To see the devices for which ColorSync profiles have been installed, click the Devices button and expand each type of device listed in the window (see Figure 23.23). You can select a device to see more detailed information and configuration options in the right side of the window.

Figure 23.23
This machine has several ColorSync profiles installed for various devices.

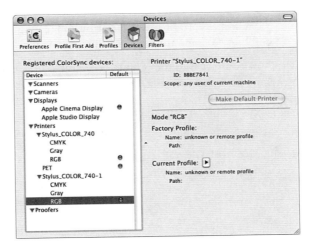

7. Click the Filters button to view and configure ColorSync filters.

8. Quit the ColorSync utility.

TIP

> The Profile First Aid tab enables you to verify and repair the profiles installed on your Mac.

If you can't find profiles for the devices you want to use, see "I Don't See a ColorSync Profile for My Device" in the "Troubleshooting" section at the end of this chapter.

NOTE

> Understanding and using ColorSync effectively is a very complex topic. For detailed information, see Apple's ColorSync Web site located at `www.apple.com/colorsync`.

USING COLORSYNC

After you have installed and configured your device profiles and workflows, the way you use ColorSync depends on the particular applications you use. For example, you can employ the ColorSync profiles when you print a document by using the ColorSync option on the Options pop-up menu in the Print dialog box. Other applications, such as Photoshop, enable you to employ more sophisticated ColorSync features.

TROUBLESHOOTING

MY SECOND MONITOR DOESN'T WORK

When I install and connect a second monitor, it remains dark when I restart my Mac. Why isn't the second monitor working?

Isolate the problem to the graphics card or the monitor by connecting the monitor that is working to the second graphics card and the monitor that isn't working to the first card.

If the second monitor (now connected to the original graphics card) works but the other monitor does not, you know that the problem is related to the graphics card. The most likely cause is an incompatible card. Check the manufacturer's Web site to ensure that card is supported on Mac OS X. Download and install any updated drivers for that card. Finally, make sure that the card is properly seated in the PCI slot.

If the second monitor doesn't work when it is connected to the original graphics card, you know the problem lies with the monitor itself.

I Can't Print Under Classic

When I try to print from a Classic application, errors are generated and I am not able to print.

First, ensure that you have installed the printer software under the Classic environment you are using. Next, make sure that printer is selected in the Classic Chooser.

If you still can't print, you must restart in Mac OS 9 and print from there, assuming your Mac is capable of starting up under Mac OS 9 of course.

I Don't See a ColorSync Profile for My Device

I don't see a profile for a specific device I want to use. How do I obtain the correct profile?

For you to be able to choose a profile for a device, that profile has to be installed. It should have been installed when you installed that device's software. However, if it wasn't, check the Web site of the manufacturer of the device. Locate a ColorSync profile and download it. Install it in the `Library/ColorSync/Profiles` directory in your Home directory.

If you still can't find a profile, the profile might be damaged. Run the ColorSync Utility (Applications/Utilities) to verify and repair your profiles.

CHAPTER 24

UNDERSTANDING AND USING DATA STORAGE DEVICES

In this chapter

UNDERSTANDING DATA STORAGE OPTIONS

A general law of Mac use—especially when you start using DV, digital music, digital images, and other digital media technologies—is that you can never have too much room in which to store your data. In this chapter, you will learn more about the following types of data storage devices:

- Hard drives
- CD writers
- Apple's SuperDrive
- Other removable media drives
- Tape drives

CHOOSING, INSTALLING, AND USING A HARD DRIVE

Your Mac's hard drive is one of its most important devices, and its performance and operation have a major impact on the performance and operation of your system. At some point, you will probably want to increase the amount of hard disk space available to you. Adding more hard drive space is relatively simple in most cases and offers many benefits to you.

CHOOSING A HARD DRIVE

When it comes to choosing a hard drive, you should consider the following factors:

- **Will your Mac support additional internal hard drives?**—If you use a Power Mac G5, Power Mac G4, or other desktop Mac, the answer to this question is yes. If you have an iMac, an eMac, a Power Mac G4 Cube, a PowerBook, or an iBook, the answer is no.

- **Should you add an external drive?**—If your Mac won't support the addition of another internal hard drive, you will likely want to add more hard drive space by using an external hard drive. Even if your Mac can handle an additional internal hard drive, you might choose to get an external drive instead because external drives are simpler to install and easier to use with different machines. For example, you can share the same external hard drive among several Macs. Because FireWire offers acceptable performance for all but the most demanding tasks, you won't face much of a performance penalty if you use an external hard drive.

- **Which drive interface does your Mac use?**—For internal drives, the choices are ATA or SCSI. For external drives, the choices are FireWire, FireWire 800, USB 2, or SCSI.

NOTE

> Some external hard drives use the USB 2 interface, which is a dominant interface on Windows computers and is supported on some Mac models. However, in most cases, FireWire external drives should be your first choice. FireWire (both varieties, but especially FireWire 800) offers excellent performance and you won't have to use a USB port on your Mac (which is good because you tend to need more USB ports than FireWire ports).

- **What size drive do you need?**—Drives come in various sizes; generally, you should get the largest drive you can afford in the format you select.

- **Does your Mac need to meet specific performance requirements?**—If you intend to use the drive for high data rate work, such as DV, typically, you need to get a drive that spins at least 7,200rpm. Some drives spin even faster, which means they can transfer data at a greater rate. (Some drives that spin at slower rates are also acceptable; check with the drive's manufacturer to see what data rate the drive can sustain.)

NOTE

> If you have a Mac with room for only one internal hard drive, you can replace that drive with one of a higher capacity. For PowerBooks and iBooks, this is a relatively simple operation. For iMacs, this is a more complex task and is not recommended unless you are very comfortable working with hardware.

→ To learn about the various interfaces related to hard drives, **see** Chapter 21, "Understanding Input and Output Technology," **p. 703**.

After you have answered these questions, you should have a good idea about the type of drive you need, such as an external FireWire hard drive with at least 45GB that offers performance suitable for DV work.

Head to your favorite retail site (one of mine is `www.smalldog.com`) to research or purchase hard drives (see Figure 24.1).

CAUTION

> Before you purchase a drive, check the owner's manual for your Mac to ensure that the specifications for the drive are compatible with your Mac.

To begin using a drive, you must install the drive, and then initialize and partition the drive.

Figure 24.1
Check out this LaCie 250GB FireWire 800 USB 2 external drive for a lot of storage space and excellent performance (of course, your Mac has to support either technology to be able to use this drive).

INSTALLING AN EXTERNAL HARD DRIVE

Installing an external hard drive is about as simple as things get. You connect the power supply to the drive, if needed (some drives take their power from the interface). Then, you connect the FireWire, USB 2, or SCSI cable to the drive and your Mac.

If you install a SCSI drive, you must make sure that it has a unique SCSI ID number for the external SCSI bus to which you are attaching it. You also need to ensure that the drive is properly terminated. (Most modern Macs require a SCSI PCI card to be added to be capable of using external SCSI drives. Unless you specifically need SCSI for some reason, a FireWire drive is a better choice.)

After you have connected the drive and powered it up, the installation part is complete (easy installation is a good reason to use an external drive).

 If you're having trouble getting your Mac restarted after connecting a SCSI drive to it, see "My Mac Won't Start Up After I Connect a Drive to It" in the "Troubleshooting" section at the end of this chapter.

→ For more information about SCSI, **see** "SCSI," **p. 720**.

CAUTION

Remember that SCSI devices, unlike FireWire or USB devices, are not hot-swappable. You must power down your system before adding or removing a SCSI drive.

INSTALLING AN INTERNAL HARD DRIVE

Installing an internal hard drive is a bit more complicated than installing an external drive, but it is still relatively easy to do.

NOTE

> Because I don't recommend that most users replace a hard drive in most Macs, this section provides information only on adding additional hard drives to a Power Mac G4 or G5. If you are comfortable enough working inside a Mac to be able to replace a hard drive, you probably don't need any help doing so.
>
> The following steps describe how to install an internal ATA drive in a Power Mac G4. Installing a SCSI drive is similar, although it uses the SCSI interface and cables rather than ATA cables as this example shows. These steps are provided only as an example; you should follow the instructions provided with your Mac.

Before you get started, read through the instructions contained in your Mac's user manual. Then do the following:

1. Get the drive ready to install by configuring it as a slave drive (if necessary); see the instructions that came with the drive for help with this. Typically, this involves configuring jumper clips on specific pins at the back of the drive (see Figure 24.2). Most of the time, these pins are already set in the appropriate configuration.

Figure 24.2
This photo shows the back of a hard drive; the jumper clips are configured to make this drive the slave.

Jumper clips

2. Back up the data on your Mac (just in case).

3. Power down your Mac.

4. Open the case.

5. Locate the bay in which you are going to install the drive; in Power Mac G4s, this bay is located at the bottom of the machine toward the back (see Figure 24.3).

6. Unplug the power cable from the motherboard and both cables from the existing drive.

7. Remove the screw that holds the driver carrier in place.

Drive Bay

Figure 24.3
The hard drive that came with this G4 Power Mac is installed in the lower part of the drive carrier located in the drive bay; an additional drive can be added to the upper part of the carrier.

PCI Slots

8. Install the new drive in the upper part of the drive carrier; use the screws that were included in the accessory kit that came with your Mac.

9. Install the drive carrier back in the Mac.

10. Connect the power and data cables to each drive.

11. Reconnect the power cable to the motherboard.

12. Close the Mac and power it up.

The Mac should restart normally. When it boots up, you won't notice any difference because you can't use the drive until you initialize it.

INITIALIZING AND PARTITIONING A HARD DRIVE

Before you can use a hard drive, whether it is internal or external, you must initialize it. You can also partition it to create multiple volumes on a single drive (for example, you might want to be able to install more than one version of the Mac OS on a single disk).

NOTE

Most external hard drives come initialized, in which case you can use them without doing the following steps. However, even in those cases, you might want to partition the drive, especially if it is a large one.

To initialize and partition a disk, perform the following steps:

1. Launch Disk Utility (Applications/Utilities). In the Disk Utility window, you will see two panes. In the left pane, you see the drives installed in your system (the drives are labeled by their capacities and types).

2. Select the drive with which you want to work. At the top of the right pane are five tabs; each tab enables you to view data about a drive or to perform a specific action. Under the drive icon in the Source pane, you will see the partitions each drive currently contains (see Figure 24.4).

Figure 24.4
Disk Utility can see two drives; the upper drive is the machine's internal drive that has two partitions, and the lower drive is a 60GB FireWire drive.

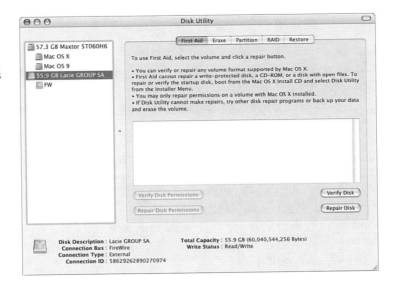

3. Click the Partition tab.

4. Select the number of partitions you want to have on the drive by using the Volume Scheme pop-up menu. Each partition is represented by a box in the Volumes pane of the window. The partitions are called `Untitled`, `Untitled 2`, and so on.

5. Select a volume by clicking it on the Volumes pane. The information for that volume is shown in the Volume Information area.

> **TIP**
> You can divide a volume into two partitions of the same size by selecting the partition and clicking the Split button.

6. Name the selected volume by typing a name in the Name box.

7. Select the format type from the Format pop-up menu. You should almost always select Mac OS Extended (Journaled) or Mac OS Extended. The journaling option is the best choice if it is available because it improves Mac OS X's capability to recover from unexpected power losses and other such circumstances.

> **NOTE**
>
> The other format options are Unix File System and Free Space. These are useful in some special circumstances. For example, if you are going to run a Unix OS system (apart from Mac OS X) on your machine, you might want to use the Unix File System for one partition.

8. Enter the size of the volume in the Size box.

   You can also set the size of a partition by dragging its Resize handle in the Volumes pane.

   If you check the "Locked for editing" check box, the information is reset and locked (you won't be able to change it).

9. If you are going to use the partition while booted up under Mac OS 9, leave the "Install Mac OS 9 Disk Drivers" box checked. If you are using the partition for Mac OS X only, as a Unix drive, or for some other special purpose that doesn't involve Mac OS 9, you should uncheck this box.

   The status of the disk with which you are working is shown in the bottom pane of the window. For example, if you can initialize the disk, you will see a status message stating the Write Status is Read/Write.

10. Select the next partition.

11. Repeat steps 6–10 for each of the volumes (see Figure 24.5).

Figure 24.5
This drive contains two volumes after it has been partitioned; one is called Book Projects and is about 30GB, and the other is called DV Projects and is about 26GB.

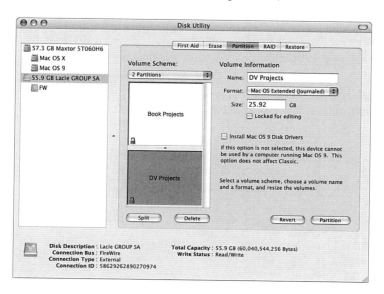

CAUTION

> Partitioning a drive erases all the data on it.

12. Click Partition.

13. If you are sure that you want to initialize and partition the drive, click Partition in the Warning dialog box. You will see a progress window showing how things are proceeding. After a few moments, you will return to the Disk Utility window.

14. Select the drive you partitioned. Confirm that the drive has been partitioned properly (see Figure 24.6).

Figure 24.6
The selected drive now has two partitions on it.

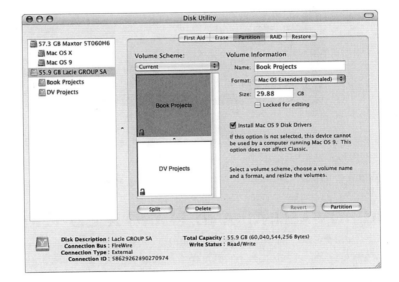

15. Select one of the partitions you just created. The Information pane at the bottom of the window reveals details about that partition, such as the format, capacity, available space (which will be about the same as capacity immediately after you partition a drive), and so on.

16. Explore each partition to ensure that they are configured properly.

17. Quit Disk Utility.

When you return to your desktop, you will see the new volumes that are ready for your data (see Figure 24.7).

 Disk Utility can't see your new drive? See "Disk Utility Can't See My Drive" in the "Troubleshooting" section at the end of this chapter.

Figure 24.7
The Book Projects and DV Projects volumes are ready to use.

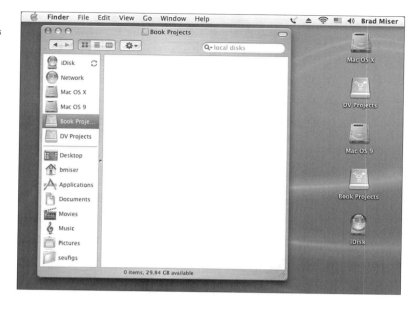

You can also use Disk Utility for various other tasks, such as erasing a disk or a volume, disk maintenance, and creating a RAID disk.

→ To learn how to use Disk Utility for disk maintenance tasks, **see** "Maintaining Your Hard Disks," **p. 878**.

FINDING, INSTALLING, AND USING A CD WRITER

Writing data to CDs has many useful applications, such as general data storage, sending large amounts of data to other people, creating custom audio CDs, and so on. Writing to CDs requires that you have a compact disc recordable (CD-R) or compact disc recordable rewritable (CD-RW) drive and a CD-burning application.

A CD-RW drive can write to CD-R and CD-RW discs. The difference between these two technologies is that CD-RW discs can be erased and reused, whereas CD-R discs can be filled only once (depending on the application you use, you can sometimes fill a disc in multiple recording sessions). Because CD-RW discs are more expensive (about $1 per disc) when compared with CD-R discs (less than $.50 per disc), you typically use a CD-RW disc to create a CD for test purposes. When you are sure that the CD will be created properly, you burn a CD-R disc.

NOTE

> CD-R drives have largely gone by the wayside. CD-RW drives can do everything that CD-R drives can do plus write on CD-RW discs, so there is no real reason to use a CD-R drive (you probably couldn't find one to buy even if you wanted to).

CHOOSING AND INSTALLING A CD WRITER

Most modern Macs include CD-RW drives as standard equipment; if you have a machine that is so equipped, you don't need to think about this type of drive any further. However, if your Mac doesn't have an internal CD-RW drive, you can easily add an external CD writer.

NOTE

> Apple's SuperDrive is a combination DVD-R and CD-RW drive. This drive is included with most high-end Mac models. Apple's Combo drive is a CD-RW and DVD-ROM drive. All modern Macs have this drive.

When choosing a CD-RW drive, you have three basic options, which are based on the interface the drive uses. Any of the options work well for most users:

- **USB**—CD-RW drives that use the USB interface are slower and less expensive than the other options. All modern Macs offer at least one USB port so you can add a USB CD writer to any system.
- **FireWire**—CD-RW drives that use FireWire are a bit better because of the higher data transfer rate, which can sometimes prevent problems when creating discs for certain types of data. FireWire CD writers are also slightly more expensive than USB drives. Most modern Macs feature at least one FireWire port and so are compatible with FireWire CD-RW drives.
- **SCSI**—Some CD-RW drives use the SCSI interface. Older Macs or those to which a SCSI PCI card has been added are candidates for a SCSI CD-RW drive. However, I recommend that you stick with one of the other interface types if you can because they are standard on all current Macs.

In addition to the interface, you should consider several other factors:

- **Mac OS X compatibility**—Although USB or FireWire drive hardware is the same for any platform, the software they use is not. Make sure that the drive you choose includes Mac OS X–compatible software.
- **Speed**—CD-RW drives can burn CDs at various rates of speed; faster drives take less time to burn a CD. If burning a CD quickly is important to you because you will do it frequently, get the fastest drive you can afford. Otherwise, if you burn CDs only occasionally, speed is not a very important factor.
- **Portability**—If you have a PowerBook or iBook, look for a portable CD-RW drive, preferably one that gets its power from the interface so you have only one cable to connect. You will then be able to burn CDs while away from a power supply.
- **Software**—All CD-RW drives include the software you need to burn CDs. Various CD-burning applications are available. If you have a preference for one of them, look for a drive that features that application. However, because you can burn CDs from the

24

Finder and from iTunes directly, you probably don't need a specific burning application. Some of these applications, though, offer features that aren't found in the Mac's built-in burning software.

NOTE

If you intend to use your CD-RW drive to back up your Mac, try to get one that comes with the Dantz Retrospect backup application.

First, select the interface you want to use. If your Mac has FireWire ports and you can pay a bit more for the drive, head to your favorite retailer and check out the FireWire offerings for Mac OS X-compatibility, speed, portability, and software. If you need to go USB, consider the same issues. Any drive you choose will likely work pretty well.

If there is a specific CD burning application you want to be able to use, such as Apple's iTunes, check the software publisher's or Apple's Web site to ensure that the drive you are considering is supported by that application. Not all drive mechanisms are supported by all applications, so you need to make sure the mechanism you get is supported by the applications you want to use.

Of course, you can also install an internal CD-RW drive in a machine that doesn't have one. This usually involves replacing the machine's current CD or DVD drive. The process for doing this is quite similar to installing an internal hard drive.

INSTALLING AN EXTERNAL CD WRITER

Installing an external CD writer involves two steps. First, you physically connect the drive to your Mac using a FireWire, USB, or SCSI cable and then connect the power supply to the drive (if required). Second, you install any software provided with the drive.

TIP

If you install a USB drive, connect it to a port that is as close to the Mac as possible. For example, if you use a USB hub, it is better to plug the drive in to one of the ports on your Mac. Sometimes, sending data through a hub can slow it slightly and, in rare cases, this can cause CD writing problems. This is especially important if the drive also gets its power from the USB port.

CAUTION

If you use a SCSI drive, you must ensure that the drive has a unique SCSI ID and that it is terminated properly.

USING A CD WRITER

Using a CD-RW drive is dependent on the particular application you use to create CDs. Several applications are available that serve this purpose, and most of them offer unique benefits.

One of the easiest to use is Apple's own Disc Burner application that is built in to the Mac OS X Finder. Disc Burner enables you to create CDs from the Finder by using drag and drop. This is about as simple as it gets.

NOTE

Disc Burner does not support recording to a CD in more than one session. You have to place all the files you want on a disc at the same time.

If you are unable to create CDs, see "I Can't Create a CD" in the "Troubleshooting" section at the end of this chapter.

TIP

If your CD-burning application can create disc images, you should do this before b urning a CD. You can create and then test the disc image. If it works, go ahead and burn it to a CD.

24

CONFIGURING MAC OS X TO BURN CDs

Before burning CDs from the Finder, you should configure Mac OS X to work with the drive you have installed. You do this through the CDs & DVDs pane of the System Preferences utility.

Open the System Preferences utility and click the CDs & DVDs icon to open that pane (see Figure 24.8).

Figure 24.8
You use the CDs & DVDs pane of the System Preferences utility to configure the actions your Mac takes when you insert CDs and DVDs of various types.

Use the "When you insert a blank CD" pop-up menu to select the action you want your Mac to take when you put a blank CD into your machine. You have the following options:

- **Ask what to do**—When you insert a blank CD, your Mac prompts you and provides a list of possible actions from which you can choose (see Figure 24.9). The Action pop-up menu contains a similar set of choices to those on the "When you insert a blank

CD" pop-up menu on the CDs & DVDs pane, such as Open Finder and Open iTunes. From this dialog box, you can also name the CD by entering its name in the Name field. You can make the action you select on the Action pop-up menu to be the default (checking the "Make this action the default" check box in the prompt window does the same thing as selecting that option in the CDs & DVDs pane). The Eject, Ignore, and OK buttons in the dialog box do what you expect (eject the disc, ignore it, or implement the changes you make, respectively). Because this option provides the most flexibility, I recommend that you choose it. However, for specific situations, the other choices might be more appropriate for you.

Figure 24.9
When the "Ask what to do" option is selected, you see this prompt when you insert blank CD media into your Mac's drive.

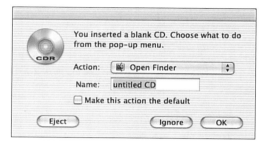

- **Open Finder**—When this option is the default or if you select it in the prompt, the blank CD is mounted and the Finder becomes the active application. You can then use the Finder to name the CD, add contents, and burn it. If you usually burn CDs from the Finder and don't like to be interrupted by the prompt, this option is probably for you.

- **Open iTunes**—When a disc is mounted, iTunes becomes the active application. If you mostly burn audio CDs, this setting can make the process more convenient.

- **Open other application**—If you choose this option, you are prompted to select the application you want to open. That application is then opened when you insert a blank CD. This is the option you want if you use a third-party application, such as Toast, to burn CDs.

- **Run script**—With this option, an AppleScript you select is launched when you insert a blank CD. After you select the script you want to launch, it appears on the "When you insert a blank CD" pop-up menu. If you have a custom burn process implemented through an AppleScript, this is the option you should choose.

- **Ignore**—When you insert a blank CD, your Mac takes no action. In fact, this disc is not even mounted in the Finder. You have to manually take some action later, such as opening an application that can burn CDs, to do something with the disc. If you prefer to keep blank CDs in your Mac and don't want to be interrupted when you insert them, this might be the option you want to choose.

BURNING CDs FROM THE FINDER

After you have configured your Mac, burning CDs from the Finder is very straightforward, as the following steps demonstrate (these steps assume that you have selected the "Ask me what to do" option; however, using the Open Finder option works similarly). Do the following:

1. Insert a CD-R or CD-RW disc into the drive. You will be prompted to select an action (refer to Figure 24.9).

2. Select Open Finder on the Action pop-up menu.

3. Enter the name of the CD you are burning in the Name field. You can name CDs just as you name other volumes on your Mac, such as hard drives. The one area of caution should be if you intend to share the disc with other users. If so, you should keep the name short (eight characters or fewer) and avoid spaces or special characters to prevent problems on other computers.

4. Click OK. You move into the Finder and see that the CD you just named is mounted. You also see the Burn action button in the Places sidebar to indicate that the CD can be burned.

5. Drag the files you want on the CD to the mounted CD-R or CD-RW disc, just like any other volume to which you can copy or move files. The files are copied to the CD and you see the standard move/copy progress window.

6. Arrange and organize the files as you want them to be on the CD (see Figure 24.10).

Figure 24.10
Here, I have moved files for this book onto the CD (note the CD icon in the Finder window's title bar).

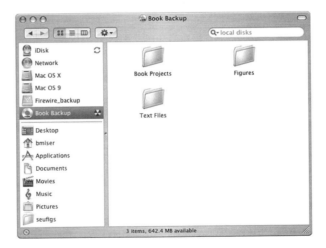

CAUTION

> Because burning CDs from the Finder is a single session, you can burn to a CD-R disc only once. After it has been burned, you won't be able to add files to it. Make sure you have all the files on the CD that you want before you burn it. If you want to be able to burn in multiple sessions, you need to use a different application to create CDs, such as Disk Utility.

→ To learn how use Disk Utility, **see** "Burning CDs/DVDs with Disk Utility," **p. 799**.

7. Select the CD and select File, Burn Disc, or click the Burn action button next to the CD in a Finder window.

8. In the resulting dialog box, select the speed at which you want to burn the disc. In most cases, Maximum is the best choice. However, if you are having problems burning discs at your drive's maximum speed, you can open the Burn Speed pop-up menu and choose a slower speed.

9. Click Burn to see a progress window as the data is prepared and the disc is recorded and verified. When the process is complete, the CD is mounted on the desktop and ready to use (see Figure 24.11). You will notice that its Action button is now Eject instead of Burn.

TIP

> In the CD Burn progress window, click the Expansion triangle to see detailed progress information.

Figure 24.11
The CD called Book Backup has been recorded and can be used. Note that its Action button is now the Eject button, whereas in the previous figure it had the Burn button.

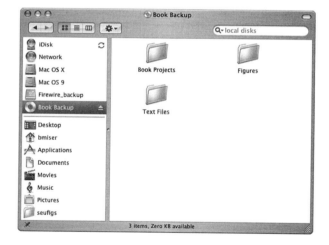

Burning CDs from the Finder is just that simple. In fact, burning CDs is just as easy as using floppy drives was back in the old days—except CDs hold about 500 times more data, of course.

BURNING DVDS WITH APPLE'S SUPERDRIVE

Apple's SuperDrive is a special case because, along with CD-RW and CD-R discs, it can also burn DVD-R discs that can be used to record data and be mounted on the desktop or played in consumer DVD players when you burn them using iDVD or another DVD-creating application. This drive is available (at least as an option) on all Mac models.

NOTE

Just as with CD-RW drives, third-party DVD-R/DVD-RW hardware and software are available. However, because Apple's DVD-R technology works so well and is included with Mac hardware and as part of Mac OS X, Apple's technology is the focus of this section.

One downside to this technology is the expense of DVD-R discs, which currently cost about $3 per disc for 2x discs or $4 per disc for 4x discs. Of course, when you compare that cost on a per-MB basis, DVD-Rs seem not to be so expensive after all.

Creating a data DVD is very similar to creating a data CD, except that you can store up to 4.7GB of data on a single disc (compared to about 750MB on a CD).

First, configure your Mac for the action you want it to take when you insert a blank DVD-R disc.

Open the System Preferences utility and click the CDs & DVDs icon to open that pane. Use the "When you insert a blank DVD" pop-up menu to select the action you want your Mac to take when you put a blank DVD into your machine. You have the following options:

- **Ask what to do**—When you insert a blank DVD, your Mac prompts you and provides a list of possible actions from which you can choose. The Action pop-up menu contains a set of choices similar to those on the "When you insert a blank DVD" pop-up menu on the DVDs & DVDs pane, such as Open Finder and Open iDVD. From this dialog box, you can also name the DVD by entering its name in the Name field. You can make the action you select on the Action pop-up menu be the default (checking the "Make this action the default" check box in the prompt window does the same thing as selecting that option in the DVDs & DVDs pane). The Eject, Ignore, and OK buttons in the dialog box do what you expect (eject the disc, ignore it, or implement the changes you make, respectively). Because this option provides the most flexibility, I recommend that you choose this option. However, for specific situations, the other choices might be more appropriate for you.

- **Open Finder**—When this option is the default or if you select it in the prompt, the blank DVD is mounted and the Finder becomes the active application. You can then use the Finder to name the DVD, add contents, and burn it. If you usually burn DVDs from the Finder and don't like to be interrupted by the prompt, this option is probably for you.

- **Open iDVD**—When a disc is mounted, iDVD becomes the active application. If you mostly burn DVDs using iDVD, this setting can make the process more convenient.

- **Open other application**—You can use this option to select a different application to open when a DVD is inserted.

- **Run script**—With this option, an AppleScript you select is launched when you insert a blank DVD. After you select the script you want to launch, it appears on the "When you insert a blank DVD" pop-up menu. If you have a custom burn process implemented through an AppleScript, this is the option you should choose.

- **Ignore**—When you insert a blank DVD, your Mac takes no action. In fact, this disc is not even mounted in the Finder. You have to manually take some action later, such as opening an application that can burn DVDs, to do something with the disc. If you prefer to keep blank DVDs in your Mac and don't want to be interrupted when you insert them, this might be the option you want to choose.

After you have configured your Mac, burning DVDs from the Finder is very straightforward, as the following steps demonstrate (these steps assume that you have selected the "Ask me what to do" option; however, using the Open Finder option works similarly):

1. Insert a DVD-R disc into the drive. You are prompted to select an action.
2. Select Open Finder on the Action pop-up menu.
3. Enter the name of the DVD you are burning in the Name field. You can name DVDs just as you name other volumes on your Mac, such as hard drives. The one area of caution should be if you intend to share the disc with other users. If so, you should keep the name short (eight characters or fewer) and avoid spaces or special characters to prevent problems on other computers.
4. Click OK. You move into the Finder and will see that the DVD you just named is mounted.
5. Drag the files you want on the DVD to the mounted DVD-R disc, just like any other volume to which you can copy or move files. The files are copied to the DVD and you see the standard move/copy progress window.
6. Arrange and organize the files as you want them to be on the DVD.

CAUTION

> Because burning DVDs from the Finder is a single session, you can burn to a DVD-R disc only once. After it has been burned, you won't be able to add files to it. Make sure you have all the files on the DVD that you want before you burn it. If you want to burn to a DVD in more than one session, use Disk Utility instead.

→ To learn how use Disk Utility, **see** "Burning CDs/DVDs with Disk Utility," **p. 799**.

7. Select the DVD and select File, Burn Disc.
8. In the resulting dialog box, select the speed at which you want to burn the disc. In most cases, Maximum is the best choice. However, if you are having problems burning discs at your drive's maximum speed, you can open the Burn Speed pop-up menu and choose a slower speed.

9. Click Burn. You will see a progress window as the data is prepared and the disc is recorded. When the process is complete, the DVD is mounted on the desktop and ready to use.

To create a DVD for video, images, and other multimedia content, you can use Apple's iDVD application, which enables you to drag and drop QuickTime movies, images, and other multimedia files to create a custom DVD, including DVD motion menus.

→ To learn how to use iDVD, **see** "Creating Your Own DVDs," **p. 630**.

NOTE

Apple also offers DVD Studio Pro, which is a professional-quality DVD creation application.

CAUTION

DVD-R drives are currently in their infancy and several formats are competing for domi-nance. If you are considering a third-party DVD-R drive, make sure it is compatible with iDVD and other Apple DVD applications—not all drives are compatible. Eventually, DVD-RW drives will likely take the place of CD-RW drives, but for the next few years, you can expect some turbulence in this area.

BURNING CDs/DVDs WITH DISK UTILITY

In addition to helping you maintain your disks, the Disk Utility application can also help you burn CDs and DVDs. It is especially useful when you want to burn a CD or DVD from a disk image file. This creates a CD or DVD from the disk image. Another great use of this is to back up image files for the applications you download from the Internet; rather than keeping a folder of these items on your hard drive, you can use Disk Utility to burn a folder of images onto a CD or DVD.

NOTE

Disk Utility under Mac OS X version 10.3 combines the functionality of Disk Utility in pre-vious versions with the Disk Copy application (which no longer exists as a separate appli-cation).

The benefit to burning a disk image onto a CD using Disk Utility rather than just using the Finder is that, when you use Disk Utility, the image is mounted when you insert the CD—you don't have to first open the disk image file to mount it.

TIP

One of the best reasons to use Disk Utility to burn CDs or DVDs is that you can leave a disc open so you can burn to it multiple times. When you use the Finder, you can have only one recording session for a disc. When you use Disk Utility, you can choose to make a disc *appendable*, meaning you can burn to it more than one time.

BURNING A SINGLE DISK IMAGE ON CD OR DVD

To put a single disc image on CD or DVD using Disk Utility, do the following:

1. Locate the disk image file you want to put on CD. (To mount a disk image file, double-click it.)
2. Launch Disk Utility.
3. Select Images, Burn.
4. Move to and select the disk image you want to put on CD.
5. Click Open to see the Burn Disc dialog box.
6. Insert the disc on which you want to burn the image.
7. Click the Expand button to open the Burn dialog box (see Figure 24.12).
8. Set the burn speed by using the Speed pop-up menu. In most cases, Maximum is the best choice. However, if you have problems burning discs, a slower speed might help.
9. If you are burning to an erasable disc, check the "Erase disc before burning" check box to erase the disc before you burn to it.

Figure 24.12
Expanding the Burn Disc dialog box in Disk Utility opens up some very useful options, especially the "Leave disc appendable" option.

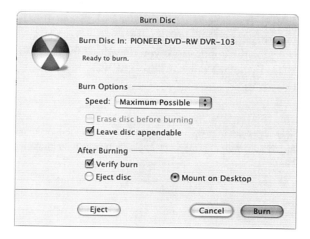

10. If you want to be able to add more data to the disc at a later time, check the "Leave disc appendable" box.

11. Make sure the "Verify burn" check box is checked to have your Mac verify the disc after the burn is complete; if you are confident and want to save some time, you can uncheck this box.

12. Click the "Eject disc" radio button if you want the disc ejected when it has been burned or the "Mount on Desktop" radio button if you want the disc to be mounted.

13. Click Burn or press Return. You will see the Progress window that displays the progress of the burn. When the process is complete, the disc is ejected or mounted on the desktop, depending on the option you selected in step 12 (see Figure 24.13).

Figure 24.13
Here, I have placed the disk image for software associated with a Logitech keyboard and mouse on a CD; notice that it looks just like a CD containing an application you might buy, even to the CD name and custom icon.

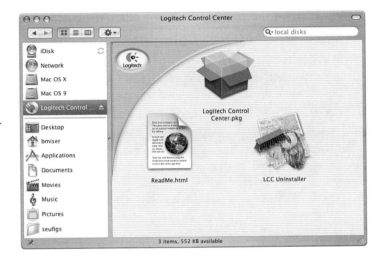

If you left the disc appendable, you can repeat these steps to add more files to it. When you append files to a disc, the Burn button becomes the Append button to indicate that you are adding files to the disc.

CAUTION

If you want a disk image to mount when you insert the CD on which you want it burned, burn only one disk image on the disc. If you add multiple disk images to the same disc, only the one you most recently burned is accessible in the Finder. You should use the multiple session option only when you are burning other types of files onto a disc.

TIP

You can use Disk Utility to erase CD-RW or DVD-RW discs. To do so, launch the application, insert the CD-RW or DVD-RW you want to erase, click the Erase tab, and use the tab's tools to erase the disc.

24

BURNING MULTIPLE FILES ON CD OR DVD

You can also burn multiple files onto a CD or DVD, for various reasons, such as backing up files or a folder. First, you create a disk image of the items you want to place on the disc. Then, you burn the disc from the disk image you created.

BURNING A FOLDER ON CD OR DVD

You can create a disk image from a folder and then burn that image onto a disc:

1. Gather all the files you want to put onto a disc in a single folder.

2. Open Disk Utility.

3. Select Images, New, Image from Folder.

4. Move to and select the folder from which you want to create an image.

5. Click Open. You will see the Convert Image dialog box (see Figure 24.14). Use this dialog box to name the disk image and choose the options for the image.

6. Name the disk image file and select the location in which you want to store it.

7. On the Image Format pop-up menu, select a format for the image you are creating. The read/write option creates an image you can add more files to later. The read-only option creates a "closed" image to which files can't be added later. The compressed option creates a compressed version of the folder so you can get more files in a smaller space. The DVD/CD master creates a disk image ready to be put on disc.

8. Use the Encryption pop-up menu to choose an encryption scheme for the image file if you want to protect the data it contains. If you select none, the image is not encrypted.

9. Click Save. You will see a Progress window as the image file is created. When the process is complete, the disk image you created is shown in the Source pane.

Figure 24.14
The Convert Image dialog box enables you to configure a disk image you are creating.

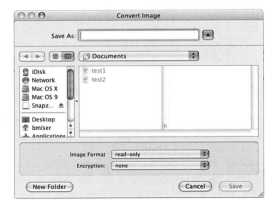

10. Select the disk image you just created and follow the steps in the previous section to put that image on disc.

BURNING A VOLUME ON CD OR DVD

You can also create a disk image from an entire volume. Then you can place that image on a disc for backup or other purposes. The steps you follow are very similar to those in the previous section. The only difference is that you select the volume from which you want to create a disk image and then select Images, New, Image from *device* where *device* is the name of the volume you selected. That volume is then selected and you move to the Convert Image dialog box.

USING A TAPE DRIVE

Tape drives offer a tremendous amount of storage space at a relatively low cost. However, because of the slow rate at which they can read and write data, tape drives are limited to a single purpose: data archival and backup. However, for these functions, a tape drive is very useful.

→ To learn about tape drives and backing up your Mac, **see** "Backing Up Your System," **p. 887**.

WORKING WITH OTHER REMOVABLE MEDIA DRIVES

Quite a few other data storage options are available. Table 24.1 summarizes several of them.

TABLE 24.1   REMOVABLE MEDIA DRIVE OPTIONS FOR MODERN MACS

Technology	Configuration	Comments
USB Flash	USB	Various USB flash devices are available. These small devices, usually attached to a keychain or other portable item, plug in to a USB port, and you can store data on them. They offer various storage capacities and behave like other volumes you mount on your desktop. If you need to "carry" data with you among various computers, these devices can be a great option.
DVD-RAM	FireWire, External SCSI, External	Uses dual-sided DVD-RAM discs that can store up to 5.2GB of data. These discs cost about $20 each. This is a good choice as a backup drive on which you can also store working files. At one point, Apple included DVD-RAM as an option on new machines but has abandoned this option in favor of CD-RW and DVD-R drives. This is a technology that seemed promising in the beginning but has been abandoned.

24

TABLE 24.1 CONTINUED

Technology	Configuration	Comments
Floppy	USB, External	The good old floppy is still around. These drives enable you to read and write standard 3.5" floppy disks. Some also enable you to read and write to 120MB "super" floppy disks. With the rise of CD-RW and USB flash, there isn't really any reason to keep using this technology. Apple long ago abandoned it; the PC world is finally letting go of it as well.
Zip	ATA, Internal FireWire, External USB, External SCSI, External	The Zip drive uses a 250MB or 100MB removable disk that costs about $12 per disk. At one point, Zip drives were extremely popular and were standard equipment on Power Macs. However, with the rise of the CD-RW and DVD-R drives, there isn't really any reason to use a Zip drive. Because a CD-R disc is only about $0.25 and holds nearly as much as three Zip disks, CD-R makes much more sense for most purposes. The rapid fall of Zip drives from a once-prominent place was amazing to see.
Jaz	SCSI, External	Jaz drives use a 2GB disk. However, a 2GB disk costs more than $100, so this technology can't compete very well with DVD-R (for which a 4.7GB disc costs less than $5) or CD-R for general data storage. This is another format that was extremely popular for a while, but has since gone the way of all obsolete technologies.

24

TROUBLESHOOTING

MY MAC WON'T START UP AFTER I CONNECT A DRIVE TO IT

After I connect a SCSI drive to my Mac, it won't start up.

Every SCSI device on each SCSI bus must have a unique SCSI ID on that bus; SCSI devices can have an ID number between zero and seven. When you connect a SCSI device that has the same SCSI ID number as a device currently on the same SCSI bus, your Mac will be unable to start. Do the following:

1. Remove the drive from your Mac.
2. Launch System Profiler and click the SCSI tab.
3. Check the device numbers of the SCSI devices on the bus to which you are attaching the drive; there might be more than one SCSI bus, so make sure you are looking at the right one.

CAUTION

> Make sure you power down all devices before changing the SCSI ID.

4. Reset the SCSI ID to an unused number between zero and seven.
5. Reattach the drive and start up your Mac.

If the Mac restarts, you can initialize the drive.

If your Mac still won't restart, the drive you have attached has not been properly terminated. Check the manual that came with the drive to see how to terminate it. If the drive is not self-terminating, you have to add a SCSI terminating cable to it.

DISK UTILITY CAN'T SEE MY DRIVE

When I launch Disk Utility, it does not recognize the drive I installed.

The fundamental problem is that your new drive is not registering with your Mac. There can be many causes for this problem, but the most likely are the following:

- **The drive is incompatible with your Mac**—Double-check the drive's specifications against those in your Mac's owner's manual.

- **The drive is improperly installed**—Repeat the installation steps to ensure that the drive is installed and connected properly.

- **An internal drive is not set to be the slave**—You must set any additional drive to be the slave; your Mac's "first" preinstalled drive must be the primary drive. See the instructions that came with your drive to see how to set it as the slave.

NOTE

> Different Mac configurations might require slightly different configurations of drives. Check the user's manual for your Mac before installing an internal drive.

I CAN'T CREATE A CD

When I try to create a CD, the CD-RW drive can't be found or the process is never completed.

Creating CDs can be a finicky process.

One complexity associated with using CD-burning software is that these applications support only specific CD-RW drives. If a particular drive isn't supported by the application you want to use, it won't work. Your only option is to find a version that will support your drive or find another application that will.

CD-burning applications can also interfere with one another. If you have more than one CD-burning application installed on your Mac and have trouble creating CDs, remove all the applications but one.

You can also have data transfer speed problems. Most CD-RW drives include a buffer to which data is written before it is placed on the CD. This buffer ensures that a steady stream of data is written to the CD. If this stream is interrupted and the buffer becomes empty, the process will fail or it will appear to finish, but the CD will be unusable. If this happens, make sure no other applications are running before you attempt to create CDs.

CHAPTER 25

INSTALLING AND CONFIGURING CONNECTING DEVICES

In this chapter

USING HUBS TO CONNECT YOUR MAC TO NETWORKS OR PERIPHERAL DEVICES

Some devices serve the purpose of connecting your Mac to networks or peripheral devices. In the case of networks, you use an Ethernet hub to enable your Mac to communicate with other computers, printers, network file servers, and the Internet. In the case of peripheral devices, you can use a USB or FireWire hub to expand the number of peripheral devices, such as printers, cameras, scanners, and so on, that you can connect to your Mac at the same time. Hubs are usually simple to install and configure (in fact, they often don't require much configuration at all).

NOTE

> One of the best ways to connect Macs to one another is through an AirPort Base Station, which acts as a network hub. You can also install AirPort Base Stations on wired networks, such as those connected through an Ethernet hub, and the station can "cross over" the data from the wired to the wireless network.

→ To learn how to install and configure an AirPort network, **see** Chapter 11, "Using an AirPort Network to Connect to the Internet," **p. 297**.

FINDING AND INSTALLING AN ETHERNET HUB

Ethernet is a hub-based network architecture, meaning that all the data that flows through an Ethernet network must flow through a hub of one type or another.

NOTE

> There are two exceptions to this rule. One is using an Ethernet crossover cable to connect two devices. This special cable acts as a very basic hub, so you don't need to use a specific hub device. The other is that some Macs support direct computer-to-computer Ethernet connections using a standard Ethernet cable.

→ To learn more about Ethernet, **see** "Ethernet," **p. 705**.

UNDERSTANDING ETHERNET HUBS

The basic function of an Ethernet hub is to enable data to flow through an Ethernet network. The three basic types of Ethernet hubs are as follows:

- **Passive, or *dumb*, hubs**—These hubs don't do anything but allow data to be passed back and forth between the devices to which they are connected. All the traffic through a passive hub goes to every device on the network, thus compromising the performance of the network because much of the data being communicated is wasted.

- **Intelligent or manageable hubs**—In addition to the basic function, which is to connect various Ethernet devices, these hubs offer features that can be used to monitor and manage the data flowing through the network.

- **Switching hubs**—This type of hub is the most active; it actually directs the flow of each packet of information based on the destination of that packet. Because data is sent only where it is actually needed, the data flow on the network is efficient. Switching hubs offer the best performance of any hub type.

  These hubs can also accomplish *load balancing*, which means they analyze the flow of information and direct information such that the load on various devices on the network is balanced. This prevents particular devices from being overloaded while others sit idle. Load balancing is particularly important for situations in which active Web or other servers are on a network. A Web server can easily generate large amounts of traffic; load balancing can smooth the data flow around such servers so that no one server gets overwhelmed, thus slowing network traffic to a crawl.

In addition to the core features of enabling the communication of data to multiple devices on a network, many hubs also offer additional features, which include the following:

- **Support for multiple speeds**—Hubs can support the various speeds of Ethernet; many hubs support multiple speeds and can intelligently switch between speeds so that you can have both low- and high-speed devices attached to the same network. The hub manages the differences in speeds to prevent bottlenecks and other performance problems.

- **Number of ports**—Every Ethernet hub offers a specific number of ports, such as 5 or 10. The more ports a hub has, the more devices it can support. Hubs can also be attached to other hubs to enable even more devices to be attached to a network.

- **Firewall**—Some hubs can act as firewalls to protect the networks to which they are connected from outside attack.

→ To learn more about hubs that provide a firewall, **see** "Defending Your Mac from Net Attacks," **p. 908**.

- **Internet account sharing**—Hubs offering this feature enable everyone on a network to share a single Internet account. Such hubs usually include a DHCP server and often offer firewall protection, too.

- **Network analysis and management software**—Some hubs include software you can use to analyze the traffic flow on the network to which they are attached so you can identify problems, such as a bottleneck (which is a spot on the network at which point the data flow is slowed, usually because of a device being overloaded).

CHOOSING AND INSTALLING AN ETHERNET HUB

Choosing the right Ethernet hub for your network is a matter of identifying the features you need and then locating a hub that offers those features. Some features to consider are the following:

25

- **Speed**—All modern Macs can communicate at speeds of at least 100Mbps, so you should make sure that the hub you get can handle this speed. Many modern Macs support speeds up to 1000Mbps (more commonly called gigabit), so if you have at least one of these Macs on your network, you should look for hubs that support Gigabit Ethernet. Most hubs are capable of switching speeds and are rated with the speeds they support, such as 10/100 for a hub that can support 10Mbps and 100Mbps.

- **Number of ports**—Hubs support multiple devices through the ports they offer. You need a port for each device on the network, such as each Mac, AirPort Base Station, printer, cable modem, and so on. Generally, you should get a hub with more ports than you think you will need to allow room for your network to grow.

- **Internet account sharing**—If you plan on sharing an Internet account, you need to find a hub that supports this.

NOTE

Internet account sharing is built in to the Mac OS X. However, using a hub to share an account is often a better choice because a Mac that provides account sharing always has to be on, and it takes a performance hit to share an account. Sharing hubs are dedicated devices and are always on by design. Because such hubs are inexpensive and easy to use, they are usually the best choice.

- **Firewall**—If you connect your network to the Internet, you should use a hub that offers a firewall—such hubs often support sharing an Internet account as well.

NOTE

Configuring Mac OS X's built-in firewall to protect individual machines is simple. However, if you have other machines that don't offer a firewall, you should ensure that the hub you use provides one.

→ To learn how to configure the Mac OS X firewall, **see** "Defending Your Mac Against Net Hackers," **p. 911**.

- **Mac OS X compatibility**—Because Ethernet is not platform specific, most hubs support Macs, Windows, and other machines. However, some hubs offer particular features that are platform specific.

- **Other features**—If there are specific features you need, such as network management software, look for hubs that offer those features.

Hubs generally fall into two camps: those designed for small networks with few or no features (see Figure 25.1) and those designed to support a larger number of devices or that offer other features (see Figure 25.2).

Figure 25.1
This Asante hub is an example of a basic Ethernet hub that is designed for small networks.

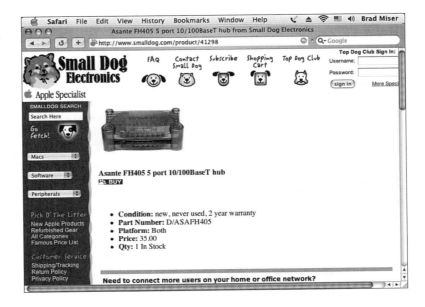

Figure 25.2
This Linksys hub includes 24 ports and is designed for a larger network.

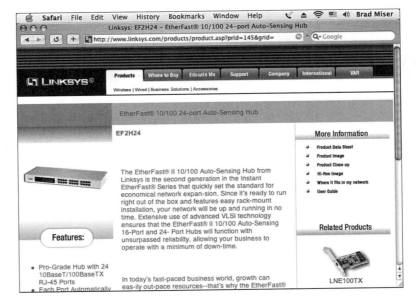

Typically, if you evaluate the list of factors provided previously, the type of hub you need becomes clear fairly quickly. Then it is a matter of choosing among the brands that offer the type of hub you need.

In theory, installing an Ethernet hub is easy; you simply connect power to the hub and then connect each device (computers, printers, and so on) to it using Cat 5 Ethernet cables with

RJ-45 connectors at each end. In practice, routing the cables can be a major challenge, especially if you are covering large distances in a building that is not designed to allow easy routing of such cables.

Ethernet Cards

To attach a specific device to an Ethernet network, that device must have an Ethernet card installed in it. Although all Macs have Ethernet cards built in, other devices might not. For example, Ethernet cards are not installed in every printer, even those that are capable of being networked. Some Windows PCs do not include Ethernet as a standard configuration item, especially those that are designed for home use.

The type of Ethernet card you need to install in a device depends on the specific device you are installing on the network. For example, the interface card for a printer needs to match the specifications for a particular brand and model. On the other hand, devices that can use PCI cards can accept a standard Ethernet PCI card to enable that device to be attached to a network.

After an Ethernet hub is physically installed on the network, you might have to install some software or configure that hub (for example, if you will be sharing an Internet connection over it, you have to configure the hub's DHCP server).

NOTE

Most hubs include an *uplink* port to which you can attach other hubs. This enables you to expand a network by adding more devices to it than a single hub has ports. After you have filled the ports on one hub, you can attach another hub to the first hub's uplink port and begin using the ports on the second hub to add more devices to the network.

USING AN ETHERNET HUB

For most applications, after a hub is installed and configured, you don't need to think about it anymore. It simply does its work. If you use network-monitoring software, you run that from a device connected to the hub.

Most hubs offer a basic set of diagnostic lights you can use to monitor the traffic across each port on the hub. These lights can be useful if your network has problems you need to diagnose. One type of diagnostic light included for each port on most hubs is an activity light that illuminates when the hub senses activity from the device connected to that port. Most hubs also include a speed indicator light for each port to give you information about the speed of communication with a specific device; this light can help you ensure that each device is communicating with the network at the maximum possible speed.

→ To learn how to configure and use an Ethernet network for file sharing, **see** Chapter 26, "Building and Using a Network," **p. 821**.

→ To learn about using a hub to share an Internet account, **see** Chapter 27, "Sharing an Internet Connection," **p. 855**.

FINDING, INSTALLING, AND USING A USB HUB

Because so many peripheral devices use the USB interface, you will probably run out of available USB ports before you run out of devices you want to attach to your Mac. That's where a USB hub comes in.

→ To learn more about the USB interface, **see** "USB 1.1," **p. 709**.

UNDERSTANDING USB HUBS

A USB hub expands the number of USB ports available on your Mac; USB hubs are one of the simpler devices you will use. USB ports offer the following features:

■ **Number of ports**—The number of ports a USB hub offers determines the number of devices you can attach to it. Typical USB hubs offer four ports, but some offer more than that (such as seven ports).

CAUTION

> Sometimes the number of ports offered by a hub can be a bit deceiving. Remember that you have to use one port to connect the hub to your Mac or to another USB hub. Some hubs count this "upstream" port, but others do not. For example, some four-port hubs allow you to connect only three USB devices because one port is required to connect the hub to your Mac or to another hub. Other four-port hubs provide an additional port for the upstream connection so that you can actually connect four devices to them.

■ **USB 2 or USB 1 support**—The two types of USB are USB 1 and USB 2. USB 2 is faster than USB 1. If you are using USB 2 devices, you should get a hub that supports USB 2. USB 1 devices are mostly keyboards, mouse devices, and other low-bandwidth devices. USB 2 devices are typically hard drives, cameras, and other devices that require large amounts of data to be moved quickly. USB 2 hubs support USB 1, but USB 1 hubs do not support USB 2.

■ **Self-powered or bus-powered**—Some hubs get the power they need from an external power supply (they provide this power to the devices that are attached to them if needed). Others take power for the hub and the USB devices from the USB bus itself.

NOTE

> Although most Macs include two or more USB ports, you can often find additional ports in the other devices attached to your Mac. For example, the Apple Pro keyboard has two USB ports built in to it. Apple monitors, such as the 22" Apple Cinema Display, also include additional USB ports. Make sure that you account for these available ports before adding a dedicated USB hub to your system.

25

CHOOSING, INSTALLING, AND USING A USB HUB

Choosing a USB hub is mostly a matter of deciding if you need to be able to support USB 2 devices and the number of USB devices you want to be able to connect to your Mac at the same time (see Figure 25.3).

Figure 25.3
This Asante four-port hub is an example of a simple, inexpensive USB hub you can add to your system.

> **TIP**
>
> Remember that USB is hot-swappable, meaning you can connect and disconnect USB devices at any time. There are many devices you will need to connect only periodically, such as a digital camera. So you don't really need a USB port dedicated to every USB device you have—just those you want to always be available. Having one or more extra ports above that number enables you to add other devices as you need them.

Next, you should decide whether you want a self-powered or bus-powered hub. Because some devices take their power from the USB interface, you should get a USB hub that is capable of providing its own power (many hubs can operate either on their own power or on power from the USB bus). If you are going to use the hub primarily on the move, such as with your PowerBook, a bus-powered hub might be a better choice (it will be smaller than a powered hub).

Some hubs offer other features that aren't required but can be useful. For example, some hubs provide status lights for each port. These lights show you when a device is actively using the port; this can be helpful when you are troubleshooting problems with a specific peripheral device.

Installing a USB hub is quite simple. You just attach its uplink port to a USB hub on your Mac or on another USB hub. Then, attach each device to a port on the hub. If the hub is self-powered, you attach its power source. That's it.

NOTE

> USB 2 and USB 1 cables use the same connector so you can't tell the difference just by looking at the cables. Be sure you don't try to support a USB 2 device over a hub that supports only USB 1.

There isn't anything to using a USB hub, either. They just work.

NOTE

> *Bluetooth* is a wireless protocol designed for relatively low-speed peripheral devices such as mice, keyboards, printers, PDAs, and so on. Mac OS X supports Bluetooth, but to use this feature, a Mac must have a Bluetooth transmitter and receiver. Some Macs, such as Power Mac G5s, have the option to have the Bluetooth module built in and can connect to Bluetooth devices out of the box. For other Macs, you will need to add a Bluetooth adapter (usually to a USB port) to be able to communicate with Bluetooth devices. When a Mac has a Bluetooth adapter, it acts as a Bluetooth hub and can communicate with many Bluetooth devices at the same time.

→ To learn how to use Bluetooth, **see** "Finding, Installing, and Using Bluetooth Devices," **p. 735**.

FINDING, INSTALLING, AND USING A FIREWIRE HUB

A FireWire hub is analogous to a USB hub; its primary purpose is to provide additional FireWire ports to which you can connect FireWire devices (see Figure 25.4).

UNDERSTANDING FIREWIRE HUBS

Because many Macs include only two FireWire ports (most mobile Macs have only one), and peripheral devices such as keyboards and monitors don't include additional FireWire ports, you are more limited in the number of FireWire devices you can attach to your Mac than you are with USB out of the box.

→ For more information on FireWire, **see** "FireWire 400," **p. 707**.

Figure 25.4
This Orange Micro FireWire hub offers three additional ports (one port is required for the upstream connection).

25

Daisy-chaining on FireWire Hubs

FireWire supports daisy-chaining, which means some FireWire devices, such as hard drives, have two FireWire ports. One port receives the FireWire connection coming in, whereas the other can support a connection going out. You can link FireWire devices in this way so that you can support many devices from a single FireWire port. However, this can be problematic for some devices that require large amounts of data to flow smoothly, such as a digital camcorder. Because all the data in a FireWire chain flows across each device, the data flow can be turbulent when many devices are connected on a single chain. For best performance, devices with higher data speed requirements should be placed closer to the Mac, preferable actually connected to the Mac's FireWire port. A FireWire hub can help manage the data flow so you can connect more devices without the interference that can be experienced when you use a FireWire daisy-chain.

If you use multiple FireWire storage devices, such as a hard drive, tape drive, CD-RW, or other devices that you will want to be connected at all times, you probably need to add more FireWire ports to your system.

FireWire hubs work in a way that is similar to a USB hub, and you have similar parameters to choose from:

- FireWire or FireWire 800
- Number of available ports (most FireWire hubs include either three or six ports)
- Self-powered, bus-powered, or both

CHOOSING, INSTALLING, AND USING A FIREWIRE HUB

The process of choosing, installing, and using a FireWire hub is also analogous to the same tasks for a USB hub. First, determine whether you need to support FireWire 800. FireWire 800 is a faster protocol than FireWire so you need a hub that is capable of supporting it (you can't use FireWire devices with a FireWire 800 hub, and vice versa). Second, decide how many ports you need. Third, decide whether you need a more mobile hub that can take its power from the bus. Fourth, look for any special features you might need (there aren't many available, so this won't take much time).

NOTE

Remember that one port is used to connect the hub to the Mac or to another hub. Most of the time, you can connect one less device to a hub than the number of ports it offers. Because FireWire devices are also hot-swappable, you need only a dedicated port for those devices you want to be connected to your Mac at all times. As long as you have at least one available port for the devices you use only periodically, it isn't a big deal to connect and disconnect those devices.

Installing and using a FireWire hub is also as simple as installing and using a USB hub. Simply connect the hub to your Mac using a FireWire cable, connect its power supply (if applicable), and connect the FireWire devices to the hub.

The FireWire cable you use depends on the device and the type of FireWire being supported; FireWire 800 cables are different from standard FireWire cables. Many devices use a FireWire cable with a standard FireWire connector on each end, but some devices, such as digital video cameras, have a uniquely shaped FireWire port. The specialized cable you need for such devices is usually included with the device.

TIP

You can chain both USB and FireWire hubs. So, you can connect hubs of the same type to one another to continue to add devices to your system, up to the maximum number of devices supported by that interface.

CHOOSING A MODEM

The other major type of connecting device you are likely to use is a modem. Modems come in several flavors, depending on the type of connection through which the modem works. The major modem types are the following:

- **Phone line or dial-up**—All modern Macs include a built-in 56K modem as standard equipment. The only significant benefit of dial-up modems is that they work over any standard phone line, which makes them the only practical option for many people. However, dial-up modems are slow and are not as reliable as other modem types.

- **Cable**—Cable modem connections to the Internet are among the fastest and most reliable. Cable Internet service availability can be limited, but if it is an option for you, you should definitely consider it.

- **DSL**—Digital subscriber line modems offer benefits similar to those of a cable modem. However, in many areas, DSL connections are even less available than are cable modems.

- **ISDN**—At one point, it seemed as if integrated services digital network (ISDN) modems were going to be the best way to connect to the Net. However, with the rise of cable and DSL modems, ISDN modems are usually preferable only when those two options are not available. ISDN modems are faster than dial-up modems, but they aren't nearly as fast as cable or DSL. An ISDN account also tends to be more expensive than other options.

Choosing the kind of modem you will use depends on the type of Internet connection you will be using. Most cable, DSL, and ISDN providers offer modems with their service (although you usually have the option to provide your own modem as well).

Installing and configuring these modems is also dependent on the type of connection you are using.

→ To learn more about installing and configuring a modem, **see** Chapter 10, "Connecting Your Mac to the Internet," **p. 263**.

NOTE

> There are other ways to connect to the Internet, such as with a fractional T-1 line. However, if you are going to connect your system with technology like this, your provider usually handles the configuration and installation of the hub equipment you need.

Mac OS X: Living in a Networked World

CHAPTER 26

BUILDING AND USING A NETWORK

In this chapter

LOCAL AREA NETWORKING WITH MAC OS X

Wherever there is more than one computer (whether those machines are running the Mac OS, Windows, Linux, and so on) in the same general physical area, there is an opportunity to network those computers into a local area network (LAN). A LAN offers many benefits, including the following:

- Sharing devices, such as printers
- Sharing files
- Providing a local Web
- Sharing an Internet connection
- Providing FTP, email, and other services

A LAN can be as simple as two Macs (or a Mac and a network device such as a printer) connected together using an Ethernet crossover cable. And a LAN can be as complex as hundreds of computers, dozens of printers, and many other devices. Local networks can also be anything in between, from a small home office with a couple of Macs and a Windows machine to a workgroup that has 10 or more workstations in it.

Creating and managing a large Ethernet network (such as one with hundreds of devices on it) is a major task, coverage of which is beyond the scope of this book. This chapter assumes a more modest network that includes several Macs; a Windows PC or two; and a couple of network devices, such as printers. Not coincidentally, this is the environment in which Macs are most likely to be used. The principles of managing larger networks are the same, but the details are much more complicated.

Similarly, this chapter focuses on the two networking technologies for which support is built in to the Mac OS: Ethernet and AirPort. There are other means of networking machines together, but they are specialized and beyond the scope of this book. For most networks that you will manage with Mac OS X, Ethernet and AirPort are the best tools to create a LAN.

NETWORKING SERVICES SUPPORTED BY MAC OS X

More than any previous version of the Mac OS, Mac OS X supports a variety, in both range and depth, of network services. The network services supported by Mac OS X are summarized in Table 26.1.

26

TABLE 26.1 NETWORKING SERVICES PROVIDED BY MAC OS X

Service/Protocol	Abbreviation	Function
Apple File Protocol	AFP	Enables file sharing on machines running older versions of the Mac OS, such as Mac OS 8 and Mac OS 9.
AppleTalk	AppleTalk	Set of services used to communicate on Macs running older versions of the Mac OS or AppleTalk devices such as printers. AppleTalk continues to be supported under Mac OS X.
Bluetooth	Bluetooth	Enables Macs to communicate with various wireless devices, such as cell phones and PDAs.
Bootstrap Protocol	BOOTP	
Common Internet File System	CIFS	Provides remote file access on many play forms, such as Windows.
Dynamic Host Configuration Protocol	DHCP	Providesautomatic assignment of IP addresses to devices on a network.
File Transfer Protocol	FTP	Enables the fast transfer of files over TCP/IP networks.
Hypertext Transport Protocol	HTTP	Provides the transmission and translation of data between a Web server and Web client.
Internet Protocol	IP	Enables communication across a wide variety of devices and services.
Lightweight Directory Access Protocol	LDAP	Enables users to locate resources, such as files and hardware devices, on a network.
Network File Service	NFS	Enables file sharing on Unix-compatible devices, such as Mac OS X computers.
Network Time Protocol	NTP	Synchronizes time across devices on a network.
Open Transport	OT	Another set of networking protocols that was introduced under earlier versions of the Mac OS.
Point-to-Point Protocol	PPP; PPPoE	Provides TCP/IP services over dial-up connections (PPP) and over Ethernet (PPPoE).

26

TABLE 26.1   CONTINUED

Service/Protocol	Abbreviation	Function
Printer Access Protocol	PAP	Provides services necessary to print to network printers.
Rendezvous	Rendezvous	Enables Rendezvous-compatible devices on a network, such as computers and printers, to automatically discover and configure other Rendezvous-compatible devices.
Service Location Protocol	SLP	Enables devices on a network to be discovered automatically.
Short Message Block	SMB	Enables Macs to connect to Windows and Unix file servers.
Transmission Control Protocol/Internet Protocol; User Datagram Protocol/ Internet Protocol	TCP/IP; UDP/IP	Enables the transmission of data across extended networks, such as the Internet. These protocols do not provide services in themselves but are the means by which data is transmitted across networks.
Web-based Distributed Authoring and Versioning	WebDAV	Extends HTTP to provide collaboration and file management on remote Web servers.

NOTE

Support for SMB and CIFS enables you to integrate Macs onto Windows and Unix networks with no additional software installations. If you have ever been treated as a second-class citizen by a Windows network administrator, this feature alone makes Mac OS X a great thing.

All the services listed in Table 26.1 can be useful, but covering all of them is beyond the scope of this book. In this chapter, you will learn how to implement the two services you are most likely to use: file sharing and FTP. After you have learned to configure these, you can apply similar principles to configure additional services on your network.

→ To learn how to configure Mac OS X's built-in Web server to implement HTTP services, **see** "Using Mac OS X to Serve Web Pages," **p. 446**.

NOTE

The WebDAV standard is a relatively new one that is gaining wide use. It provides a much better environment for file sharing and other services across HTTP networks, primarily the Web. For example, when you use an iDisk under Mac OS X, you are using the WebDAV standard. This enables you to remain connected to the iDisk for long periods of time without being disconnected during idle periods.

IMPLEMENTING A NETWORK

To implement a network, you should do the following:

1. Design your network.
2. Build your network.
3. Configure the services that will be available on the network.
4. Monitor and administer your network.

DESIGNING A NETWORK

Before you implement a network, you need to design the network you want to create. As a starting point, answer the following questions:

- **What types of services do you want to provide over the network?**—Will you provide file serving? Do you want to share an Internet connection? How about FTP or Web services? The answers to these questions will drive the rest of your network design. For example, if you plan to share an Internet connection, you will most likely want to include a hub that can act as a DHCP server.

- **How many devices do you want to be on the network?**—The devices for which you plan must include all the workstations on the network as well as shared devices, such as printers, modems, and so on. The answer to this question determines how many access points into the network you will need to provide.

- **How will you connect the devices together?**—For example, will you use Ethernet for all devices or will you include an AirPort hub (hardware or software base station) in the network? The answers to these questions determine the connecting devices you will need to use, such as Ethernet hubs, AirPort base stations, and so on.

- **Who will need access to the services you are providing?**—How will they connect to the network? The answers to these questions help you identify the users on your network.

- **What are the security implications of the services you are providing on the network?**—This question should drive you to ensure that you protect machines that will have access to the network. For example, you need to be very careful about providing FTP access to machines on which sensitive or critical data is stored. There are security concerns with any network service you provide; you should understand these when you design your network so you know how to provide proper security for it.

→ To learn how to use a network to share an Internet connection, **see** Chapter 27, "Sharing an Internet Connection," **p. 855**.

→ To learn how to protect your network from attack, **see** "Defending Your Mac from Net Attacks," **p. 908**.

As you answer the previous questions, you should be ready to design your network. You should document your network design with at least a simple sketch of the network, the list of the devices you need to include on the network, and so on. Also, include the services you will be providing from specific machines on the network. An example of a design for a small office network is shown in Figure 26.1.

Figure 26.1
A simple network design document, such as this one for a small office network, can aid network design, implementation, and maintenance.

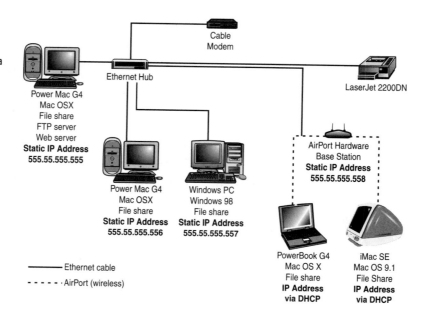

TIP

> Having your network design documented enables you to expand it more easily when you outgrow it. It is much simpler to determine what needs to be done to expand a network when you see it on paper than it is by looking at it in the real world. (Besides, unless all the machines are in the same room, you probably won't be able to see them all at the same time, anyway.)

BUILDING A NETWORK

After your network design is complete, you can start building that network.

Obtain the devices and cables you need and assemble the network.

Your network design document identifies the devices you need on the network. For example, you can determine the type of Ethernet hub you need by counting the number of devices you are connecting to it and determining whether it must provide services to the network, such as a DHCP server, so you can share a single Internet account among the devices. You also need to determine the types and length of cable you will need to attach the devices to the network, how the cables will be routed, and so on.

→ To learn more about Ethernet hubs, **see** "Finding and Installing an Ethernet Hub," **p. 808**.

After you have obtained the devices that will be installed on the network, you need to connect and configure those devices to access the network.

Connecting the devices to the network is simply a matter of attaching an Ethernet cable to the Ethernet hub and to each device. Of course, depending on the physical locations of the devices on the network, this can be quite a challenge, especially if you have to traverse long distances or connect machines located on different floors. If you are using AirPort on your network, you need to install AirPort cards in machines using AirPort services.

Configuring the devices attached to the network includes configuring the Internet access and firewall (if needed) for each machine, configuring an AirPort base station, and so on.

→ To learn how to configure Mac OS X machines for Internet access, **see** Chapter 10, "Connecting Your Mac to the Internet," **p. 263**.

→ To learn how to install and configure an AirPort network, **see** Chapter 11, "Using an AirPort Network to Connect to the Internet," **p. 297**.

→ To learn how to share an Internet connection among the devices on the network, **see** Chapter 27, "Sharing an Internet Connection," **p. 855**.

→ To learn how to protect machines on your network from Internet attacks, **see** "Defending Your Mac Against Net Hackers," **p. 911**.

> **NOTE**
> When you create a LAN, you are actually creating an intranet. You can provide most services on an intranet that are available on the Internet. The only difference is that you can control what happens on the intranet much more closely than you can control anything on the Internet.

As you install a device, be sure to test its basic access to the network by accessing various resources on the network, such as networked printers and Internet access if that is provided through the network. This step confirms that the physical aspects of the network are working properly and that the basic network configuration for Internet access is done properly.

After you have confirmed that the devices are correctly attached to and configured for the network, you need to configure the particular services each machine will use and the access that others on the network will have to those services; examples of such configuration are provided in the next section.

> **NOTE**
>
> Tutorials on creating and managing Ethernet networks are located at www.lantronix.com/learning/index.html.

CONFIGURING THE SERVICES ON A NETWORK

As you learned in Table 26.1, Mac OS X supports a large number of network services. To access these services, you must configure each machine that will be using them. This involves configuring the particular machine that will be providing those services (the *server*) and then enabling access to those services on various machines on the network that will be accessing those services (the *clients*).

Explaining how to configure each of the possible services is beyond the scope of this book. However, learning about some examples of services you are likely to use will enable you to configure the others.

Some services you'll want to take advantage of on most networks are the following:

- File sharing
- FTP server
- Windows file sharing
- Printer sharing
- Web server

→ To learn how to share files with Windows computers, **see** "Mac OS X to the Max: Networking Mac OS X with Windows Computers," **p. 853**.

→ To learn how to share the printers attached to a Mac OS X machine, **see** "Configuring Print Options and Sharing a Printer," **p. 768**.

→ To learn how to host Web sites from a Mac OS X machine, **see** "Using Mac OS X to Serve Web Pages," **p. 446**.

CONFIGURING AND USING FILE SHARING

The Mac OS has long provided peer-to-peer file-sharing capabilities to enable Macintosh computers on a network to share files. Support for such file sharing continues under Mac OS X, but be aware that the improved security features of Mac OS X make configuring and accessing files on a specific machine a bit more complicated than it was on previous versions of the Mac OS.

Under Mac OS X, file sharing is improved because, in addition to Mac OS X machines, you can also share files with Macs running OS 9 and earlier, Windows file servers, and Unix file servers. For other Macs, you can use AppleTalk for file sharing or use TCP/IP. For Windows and Unix, you can use SMB and CIFS services.

When connecting to other Macs for file sharing, the machines communicate through either TCP/IP or AppleTalk. To log in to a Mac OS X file-sharing machine serving files via TCP/IP, that machine must have an IP address. Typically, this IP address is assigned as part of connecting that machine to the Internet, such as by a DHCP server.

Mac OS X includes support for Rendezvous, which enables devices to seek out other Rendezvous-compatible devices on a network and configure automatically access to those devices. All Macs that have Mac OS X version 10.2 or later are Rendezvous aware and can therefore take advantage of this technology to easily and quickly connect to other Macs. However, other devices, such as printers, can also support Rendezvous, so those devices can be configured automatically as well.

AppleTalk is the Mac's original network protocol, and it continues to be supported in Mac OS X. When you are connecting to Macs running OS version 8.6 or earlier, you have to use AppleTalk as support for file sharing over TCP/IP, which was added in Mac OS 9.0.

In the next chapter, you will learn how to share an Internet account using a DHCP server. Such a server assigns IP addresses to the machines connected to it. The *D* stands for dynamic, meaning these addresses can change. This can make locating a specific machine by its IP address tough. Fortunately, with most DHCP servers, you can choose to manually assign IP addresses to the devices attached to it. When you do this, machines have the same IP address even though they are using a DHCP server to obtain that address.

With Rendezvous, you don't need to worry about the IP addresses of individual machines because your Mac seeks out the devices that are communicating on a network and automatically configures access to those devices.

NOTE

If other devices on your network, such as printers, have dynamic IP addresses assigned to them and you use the IP address to configure that device, you can lose the connection to those devices when the DHCP server assigns a new address to them. (This typically happens if the hub loses power for some reason or the device is removed from the network for a while.) In such cases, you need to reconfigure any computers that access the device with the new address assigned by the DHCP server. For such devices, consider assigning a static address that remains constant for that device.

To identify the current IP address of a Mac OS X machine, open the Sharing pane of the System Preferences application. Select and activate the service in which you are interested; the current address is shown at the bottom of the pane (see Figure 26.2).

26

Figure 26.2
When you select an active service, such as Personal File Sharing, the URL to connect to that service is shown at the bottom of the Sharing pane.

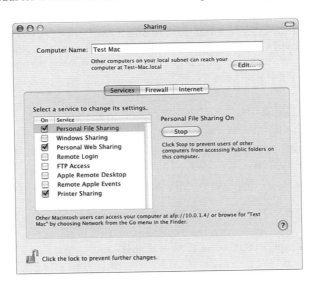

You can also use the machine's name to identify it from other machines that support Rendezvous. The machine name is shown in the Computer Name field at the top of the pane and also at the bottom of the pane as part of the address information (in Figure 26.2, you can see that the Mac's name is Test Mac).

TIP

> To identify the current IP address of a Mac OS 9 machine, open the File Sharing control panel.

CONFIGURING FILE SHARING

To share files from a Mac OS X machine, you must enable the Personal File Sharing service on that machine. This includes turning on the service, turning on AppleTalk (if you will be sharing files with Mac OS 9 machines), naming the machine, and so on.

TIP

> If your purpose in file sharing is one-way—for example, enabling others to download files from a specific machine but not to upload files—consider using FTP services on a machine rather than file sharing. You will learn how to provide FTP services in a later section of this chapter. You can also use Web sharing to enable people to download files from a Mac OS X machine.

What's in a Name?

Your Mac actually has two names associated with it. One is the computer name, which by default is a combination of the first user's name and the word *Computer*. The other name is that device's hostname, which is actually the name used when the device is accessed over a network.

By default, the hostname and the computer name are the same, except your Mac automatically removes any characters, such as spaces, that aren't permitted in a hostname. Any changes you make to the computer name are automatically made in the hostname. However, you can manually set the hostname for a machine to be something different from its computer name. To do this, click the Edit button at the top of the Sharing pane. In the resulting sheet, enter the hostname of the Mac.

The following steps assume that the Mac has access to the network (via Ethernet or AirPort) and that the default privileges are in place on the file-sharing machine. You can change the default privileges for items to share to make them more available. You learn how to do that in a later section.

To provide file sharing services from a Mac running Mac OS X, do the following steps:

1. Open the System Preferences utility.
2. Click the Sharing icon to open the Sharing pane (see Figure 26.3). At the top of the pane are the computer's name and its hostname.

Figure 26.3
You enable the network services a Mac provides by using the controls on the Services tab of the Sharing pane.

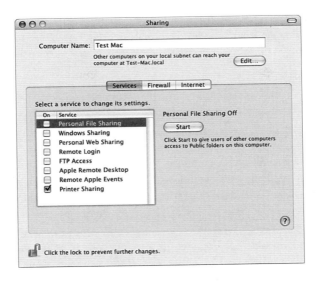

The Sharing pane has three tabs. The Services tab is used to view and configure the services the machine will provide. You use the Firewall tab to enable and configure the machine's firewall, and you use the Internet tab to enable a machine to share its Internet connection with other machines.

→ To learn how to configure a Mac's firewall, **see** "Defending Your Mac Against Net Hackers," **p. 911**.

→ To learn how to share an Internet connection among the devices on the network, **see** Chapter 27, "Sharing an Internet Connection," **p. 855**.

3. Provide the computer's name by entering a name in the Computer Name text box; use a name that will help others on the network easily identify the machine. The default computer name is the first user's name entered when the machine was registered, with an apostrophe, an *s*, and the word *Computer* tacked onto it. You can use the default computer name or change it to one you prefer.

After you provide a name, the machine's hostname is automatically created. Some characters aren't allowed in a hostname, which is the name by which the machine is identified on the network. If you enter such characters in the computer name, the machine name that people see on the network won't be exactly what you entered. For example, if you include a space in the computer name, it is replaced by a hyphen for the machine's network name. The Mac automatically removes and replaces any disallowed characters.

4. If you want to manually enter a hostname, click the Edit button; then, in the resulting sheet, enter the hostname for the machine. The extension .local is added to the hostname you type to indicate that the host is on the local network.

5. Select the service you want to activate on the machine, such as Personal File Sharing.

6. Click the Start button to turn on the selected service. If you have selected Personal File Sharing, that service is activated; after a moment or two its status becomes On and you

see the AFP address of the machine and the hostname at the bottom of the pane. When you select and enable other services, information related to those services is shown in the pane instead. When the service is running, the Start button becomes the Stop button.

TIP

> You can also start a service by clicking its On check box.

7. If you want to share files with Windows PCs (to enable Windows machines to access files stored on the Mac), select Windows Sharing and click the Start button. The address that Windows machines can use to access the Mac is shown at the bottom of the pane.

If you will be sharing files with Macs running a version of the Mac OS older than Mac OS X and those machines don't allow file sharing over TCP/IP, you need to make AppleTalk active on the Mac OS X machine. If the machines to which you will be providing file-sharing services do allow file sharing over TCP/IP, you don't need AppleTalk and can skip to step 13.

CAUTION

> If you don't need to use AppleTalk to use file sharing, leave it off. AppleTalk can sometimes interfere with other network services, such as TCP/IP services to the Internet. AppleTalk can also make your machine visible to a local or wide area AppleTalk network.

8. Open the Network pane of the System Preferences utility by clicking the Network icon on the toolbar.

9. Select the network port over which AppleTalk access will be provided on the Show menu. For example, select Built-in Ethernet to enable machines to use the AppleTalk protocol over Ethernet. Select AirPort to provide AppleTalk over an AirPort network.

NOTE

> You can provide AppleTalk over only a single network port at a time. For example, you can provide AppleTalk over Ethernet or over AirPort, but not both at the same time.

10. Click the AppleTalk tab and check the Make AppleTalk Active check box. The computer name you entered in the Sharing pane is shown next to the text Computer Name.

11. If you have AppleTalk zones on your network, select the zone from the AppleTalk Zone pop-up menu (if there aren't any zones, this pop-up menu is inactive). You can configure AppleTalk zones using the Configure pop-up menu (select Manually if you want to manually configure the network or Automatically to have your Mac configure it automatically).

12. Click Apply Now.

13. Review the services you have configured on the Sharing pane (see Figure 26.4).

Figure 26.4
This Mac is providing file-sharing services to Macs and Windows PCs and is sharing the printers connected to it.

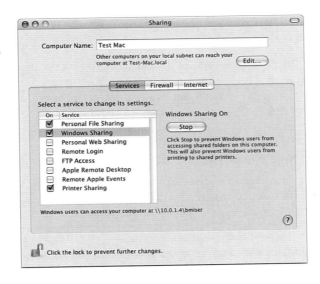

14. Close the System Preferences application.

USING FIREWALLS AND NETWORK SERVICES

If you have a firewall installed on the machine you are configuring as a server, you must configure that firewall to allow the type of access needed for others to access it from the network. For example, to enable the machine to provide file sharing services, you must configure the firewall to allow machines from the network to connect to the file server. With some firewalls, you can allow access to specific services, such as AFP, only from specific IP addresses. All other requests for services will be denied.

If you use the Mac OS X built-in firewall that you can enable on the Firewall tab, the services you enable on the Services tab are allowed automatically. You can use the Firewall tab of the Sharing pane to manually configure the services that are allowed if you need to.

If you use another type of firewall or configure the built-in firewall using another method (such as the Unix commands), you must enable access to the services you are providing through that firewall.

Similarly, if some machines on your network are connected through a Graphite AirPort base station, you won't be able to access those machines from machines connected outside the AirPort network, such as via Ethernet. Because an AirPort base station provides NAT protection of the machines it connects, machines outside the AirPort network can't see any

26

of the machines on the AirPort network unless the base station allows bridging between the wired and wireless networks. By default, you have to manually configure a Graphite base station to allow bridging.

On newer base stations, bridging is automatically provided when you connect the station's Ethernet port to the wired network.

Always be aware of the security settings of the networks you are configuring and using. Sometimes, you can waste a lot of time troubleshooting a network problem that is actually a case of things working just as planned (such as when you try to figure out why no one can connect to a machine protected by a firewall that isn't configured to allow those services to be accessed on the machine).

ACCESSING SHARED FILES FROM A MAC OS X COMPUTER

There are two basic ways you can access a server. One is to browse the network for available servers. The other is to move to the services on a machine directly using the URL for the specific service you want to access.

In either case, when you connect to a server, you must log in to that server to access its resources. You can log in under a user account that is valid for that server, or you can log in as a guest. When you log in under a valid user account, you have access to all the items on that machine just as if you were logged in to the machine directly (rather than over a network). If you are logged in as a guest, you can access only the items on the machine that allow public access, such as each user's Public folder.

NOTE

> To access a server by browsing, it must support Rendezvous or AppleTalk. If not, you have to access it by entering its URL via the Connect to Server command.

To access shared files stored on a Mac OS X file server from a Mac OS X machine by browsing the network, do the following steps:

1. Open a Finder window and select the Network directory on the Places sidebar. The Network directory appears (see Figure 26.5). This directory contains an icon for each machine that is providing services to the network along with the Servers icon.

NOTE

> The icon labeled Servers actually points to the current machine. If you open it, you see the computer on which you are working. If you open that, you jump to the Computer folder.

TIP

Server icons you access over a network have the globe icon that is similar to the icon for the Network directory. A server's icon also indicates its status. When the icon is in color, you are currently connected to that server and its resources are available to you. When the icon is shaded, you are not connected to the server.

Figure 26.5
The Network directory shows the machines providing services to the network.

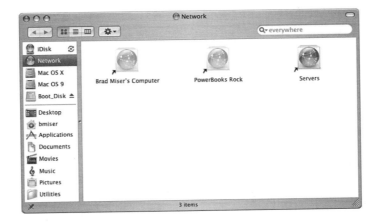

2. Double-click the server you want to access. The Connect To Server dialog box appears (see Figure 26.6).

Figure 26.6
You use this dialog box to log in to a server.

3. Enter the username and password for the account under which you want to log in and click either Connect or Guest. The server's resources that you can access appear in the Finder window (see Figure 26.7). The resources that appear depend on the user account under which you are logged in. If you logged in as a guest, you can access only public resources.

26

Figure 26.7
These volumes are being served by the machine called Brad Miser's Computer and are accessible over the local network.

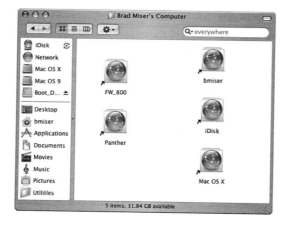

4. Open the resource you want to use and access its files. For example, you can open files, drag them to your Mac to copy them, and so on.

For more precise access to services on a Rendezvous machine or to access services on a machine that doesn't support Rendezvous, you can use a server's address to access it manually. To do so, perform the following steps:

1. From the Finder, select Go, Connect to Server (⌘-K). The Connect to Server dialog box appears (see Figure 26.8).

Figure 26.8
Use the Connect To Server dialog box to manually move to servers.

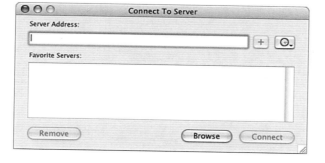

TIP

If you click the Browse button, you move to a Finder window showing the Network directory; this does the same thing as selecting Network on the Places sidebar.

2. Type the server address you want to access in the Server Address box. The address you use depends on how you want to access the server. For example, to open all of a server's resources, type its hostname, which is *hostname*.local, where *hostname* is the hostname

of the machine you are accessing. To access file-sharing services, use the URL for File Sharing services, which will be something such as `afp://10.0.1.4/`. You obtain the URL for the specific service you want to access on the Sharing pane of the System Preferences application on the server you are accessing.

3. Click Connect to see the "Connect to server" dialog box (see Figure 26.9).

Figure 26.9
Use this dialog box to log in to a network server.

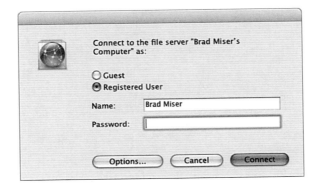

4. Enter the username and password for the account under which you want to log in and click either Connect or Guest. The server's volumes that you can access appear in the Select Volume dialog box (see Figure 26.10). The resources that appear depend on the user account under which you are logged in. If you logged in as a guest, you can access only public resources.

Figure 26.10
The machine called `Brad Miser's Computer` has a number of volumes that can be mounted on the machine being used to access that server.

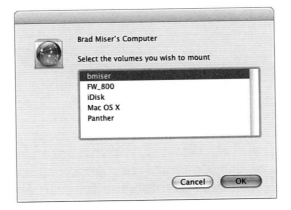

26

5. Select the volume you want to mount—hold down the Shift or ⌘ key to select multiple volumes—and click OK. A Finder window opens and the volumes you chose to access are shown in the Places sidebar (see Figure 26.11). If you have set mounted servers to appear on the desktop using the Finder preference, they appear on your desktop as well.

Figure 26.11
The volume called `bmiser` and the disk called `FW_800` are being accessed over the local network.

6. Access the network volumes just like those physically connected to your Mac.

If your preferences are set such that mounted volumes appear on your desktop, you will see the shared volumes there as well.

Following are some additional tips about using a Mac OS X machine to access file-sharing services via the Connect to Server command:

- When you sign on to a Mac OS X file-sharing machine as a registered user, meaning you have a username and password, the Options button in the Connect To Server dialog box is enabled. If you click this button, you can set some preferences related to accessing the file-sharing services on this machine. You can add the password for the file server to your keychain, allow a clear-text password (on by default), receive a warning when sending a password in clear text (also on by default), or allow secure connections using the SSH protocol. When you change these settings, you must click Save Preferences to save them. You can also change the password for the account under which you are logging in (if the account allows this) by clicking the Change Password button.

- When you are logged in to a file-sharing machine, you can quickly choose other volumes to mount by opening the Connect To Server dialog box (press ⌘-K), selecting the file server on which you are logged in, and pressing Return. You jump to the Select Volume dialog box (because you are already logged in), and you can select another volume to mount on your machine.

- The address to which you most recently connected is remembered in the Server Address box so you can reconnect to it.

- To log back in to the same file-sharing machine under a different user account, such as an administrator account, you must log off that machine and repeat the initial login process. You do this by ejecting all the mounted volumes provided by that server.

- At the upper-right corner of the Connect To Server dialog box is a pop-up menu (the Clock icon) that shows a list of the most recent servers you have accessed. You can select a server from this list to return to it, or you can clear the list by selecting Clear Recent Servers.

- In the lower part of the dialog box is the Favorite Servers list. You can add a server to your favorites list by entering its URL and clicking the Add to Favorites button (+). You can return to any favorite server by selecting it on the list and clicking Connect.

- You can place an alias to a networked volume on your Mac, such as by adding it to the Places sidebar. When you open such an alias, you are prompted to log in to the server and, upon doing so, you can access that volume. If you add the password to your key-chain, you can skip the login process.

 If you are unable to access the file server, see "I Can't See the File Server Using the Connect to Server Command" in the "Troubleshooting" section at the end of this chapter.

To log in to the same network server under a different user account, you must log out of that server and then reconnect to it. If you accessed a network resource by browsing, log off by selecting the server and selecting File, Eject. To log off a server from which you have mounted multiple volumes, you must eject each volume you have mounted on your Mac.

TIP

> You can add a network server to the Startup Items tab of the Accounts pane of the System Preferences application to mount that server each time you log in.

USING FILE SHARING WITH MAC OS 9 COMPUTERS

You can use file sharing with Mac OS 9 computers just as you can with Mac OS X machines.

The access you have to a Mac OS 9 machine from a Mac OS X machine is determined by the file-sharing settings of the Mac OS 9 machine.

NOTE

> Explaining setting up file sharing on a Mac OS 9 machine is beyond the scope of this chapter. For help, see my book *The Mac OS 9 Guide*.

When you enable access to a Mac OS X file-sharing machine from a Mac OS 9 machine, the user of the Mac OS 9 machine has the same options as someone who signs on to the file-sharing computer using a Mac OS X machine. For example, if he signs on under a guest account, he can mount any of the Public folders on the file-serving machine. If he logs in under a valid user account, he can use any volumes that user has permission to access on that machine.

26

If you have trouble using file sharing from a Mac OS 9 machine, see "My Mac OS 9 Machine Can't Share Files" in the "Troubleshooting" section at the end of this chapter.

NOTE

> Remember that Macs running older versions of the Mac OS must be configured to allow file sharing via TCP/IP; otherwise, you must turn on AppleTalk for the Mac OS X file server.

CONFIGURING AND USING FTP SERVICES

Among its other network services, Mac OS X also includes a built-in File Transfer Protocol (FTP) server. Using an FTP server can be an even more convenient way to enable others to access files stored on a particular machine. Other people can use a standard Web browser or FTP application to download files via the FTP services you enable on a machine.

CAUTION

> Granting FTP access to a machine has security implications that are beyond what I have room to cover in this chapter. If you intend to use the FTP services on a machine that has sensitive data on it, you should investigate the implications of running FTP services on a Mac under Mac OS X that has data on it you need to protect.
>
> You can sometimes move outside the particular Home directory for the account under which you log in to the FTP site, so be very careful about granting FTP access to a machine unless you are very sure about the person who will be using it.

Configuring FTP services under Mac OS X is similar to providing file-sharing services:

1. Open the Services tab on the Sharing pane of the System Preferences application.
2. Select the FTP Access service.
3. Click Start. FTP services start up, showing the FTP address for the machine at the bottom of the pane.
4. Quit the System Preferences application.

If you use the Mac OS X built-in firewall on the machine on which you are enabling FTP services, you must do a bit more configuration to allow FTP access across the firewall:

1. Open the Network pane of the System Preferences application.
2. Select the port through which the FTP machine is connected to the network on the Show pop-up menu.
3. Click the Proxies tab.
4. Check the "Use Passive FTP mode (PASV)" check box.

To access the FTP server, use a Web browser or an FTP client and use the URL `ftp://ip_address/`, where *ip_address* is the IP address of the machine providing FTP services (remember that the FTP URL for the machine is shown at the bottom of the Services tab when you select the FTP Access service). You are prompted to enter the username and password; enter the short name and the password for the user account whose Home directory you want to access. A Finder window appears, as does that user's Home folder. You can use it just as other FTP sites you have used (see Figure 26.12). You can browse the various directories shown and download any files you want. If you attempt to access a directory to which you don't have the required access privileges, your request is denied.

Figure 26.12
The volume called 10.0.1.4 is an FTP server being accessed over a network.

If you use a non-administrator account to log in to the FTP server, you have access to the entire Home directory for that user account. If you log in under an administrator account, you have wider access to files on the machine.

 If you can't access the FTP site on a machine, see "I Can't See the FTP Site" in the "Troubleshooting" section at the end of this chapter.

If you are initially able to enter the FTP site, but then it stops working, see "FTP Access Was Working but Now It Isn't" in the "Troubleshooting" section at the end of this chapter.

MONITORING AND ADMINISTERING A NETWORK

In addition to the tools you need to configure and start various network services, such as file sharing or FTP, Mac OS X includes tools you can use to monitor and administer your network. Two of these are the Network Utility, which enables you to diagnose your network connections, and the NetInfo Manager, which provides comprehensive control over many aspects of a Mac OS X machine.

USING THE NETWORK UTILITY TO ASSESS YOUR NETWORK

The Network Utility provides a set of tools you can use to assess the condition of communication across machines on your network as well as a set of tools that enable you to get information about various sites on your network and the Internet.

When you launch the Network Utility (Applications/Utilities), you see a window with nine tabs, one for each service the application provides (see Figure 26.13).

Figure 26.13
Ping is a useful way to test your connection to another machine (in this case, I pinged www. apple.com).

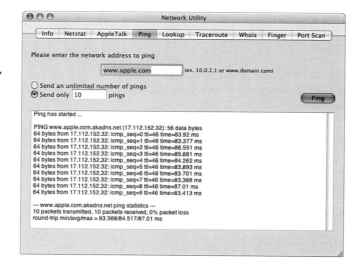

Table 26.2 summarizes the tabs in the Network Utility application.

TABLE 26.2   TABS IN THE NETWORK UTILITY APPLICATION

Tab	Function
Info	Provides information about the selected network interface. For example, you can get the IP address, connection speed, connection status, and hardware information. You also see the statistics about the transfers over the selected interface.
Netstat	Presents various statistics about the performance of the various network protocols. To access this data, select the Netstat tab, choose one of the options by selecting a radio button, and click Netstat. The data appears in the Netstat pane.
AppleTalk	Provides information about active AppleTalk services on the machine.
Ping	Contacts a specific server to assess network performance.
Lookup	Provides various information about a specific Internet address. For example, you can enter a URL and get the IP address for that site.
Traceroute	Traces a specific route between machines and provides statistics about that route, such as the maximum number of hops needed.
Whois	Enables you to look up information about a domain or an IP address, such as to whom it is registered.
Finger	Reports information about a specific individual based on the person's email address.
Port Scan	Enables you to scan for open access ports on a specific domain or IP address.

26

Covering each of these services in detail is beyond the scope of this chapter, but the next couple of examples should be helpful in getting you started.

CHECKING NETWORK CONNECTIONS WITH PING

Troubleshooting network problems can be difficult because identifying where the source of the problem is can be hard—for example, with the machine you are using, with the machine you are accessing, with an application, and so on. Ping is a way to check on the fundamental communication between two machines. If the ping is successful, you know that a valid communication path exists between two machines. If it isn't successful, you know that a fundamental problem exists with the communication between the machines, and this helps you know where to troubleshoot.

To ping a machine, perform the following steps:

1. Open the Network Utility and click the Ping tab.
2. Enter the IP address or URL for the machine you want to ping.
3. Click "Send an unlimited number of pings" to send a continuous number of pings, or click "Send only ___ pings" and enter the number of pings if you want to send a specific number.
4. Click Ping.

Watch the results in the lower part of the window. You can see your machine attempt to communicate with the machine whose address you entered. If they are able to successfully communicate, you see statistics about how fast the pings are (refer to Figure 26.13). If the pings are successful, you know the communication path between the machines is valid. If not, you know you have a fundamental connection problem between the two machines.

TRACING A ROUTE WITH TRACEROUTE

Sometimes looking at the specific route between two machines can help identify the source of problems you might be having:

1. Open the Network Utility and click the Traceroute tab.
2. Enter the domain name or IP address to which you want to trace a route, and click Trace. The window is filled with information that shows each step of the path from your machine to the one whose information you entered (see Figure 26.14).

UNDERSTANDING AND SETTING PERMISSIONS

Access to items on your Mac OS X machine, whether from the machine directly or over a network, is determined by the access privileges set for those items. Three levels of access privilege can be set for any item; these are the following:

- Owner
- Group
- Others

Figure 26.14
This Traceroute window shows the path from my machine to www.apple.com.

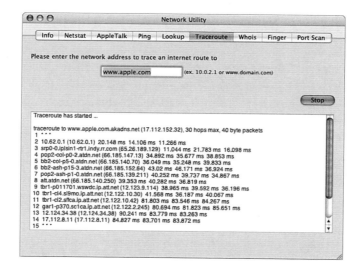

The owner is the owner of the item.

The group is a set of users. By default, Mac OS X includes several groups for which various permissions are assigned to different volumes and directories. Many of these default groups look odd, and some are even nonexistent (you see Members of group " ").

Others includes those users who are neither the owners nor members of a group.

Each level of access has four access options:

- **Read & Write**—This is the broadest level of access and lets the user to whom it is assigned read and write to the item to which it is assigned.

- **Read only**—This privilege lets a user see items in a directory but not change them.

- **Write only (Drop Box)**—With this access, a user can place items in a directory but can't see the contents of that directory.

- **No Access**—The user can't do anything with the item.

If you open the Info window for an item and expand the Ownership & Permissions area, the current access permissions for the item are shown. If you expand the Details area, the current permissions set for the owner, group, and others are displayed. For example, Figure 26.15 shows the Permissions information for the volume on which Mac OS X is installed, whereas Figure 26.16 shows similar information for a folder within the logged-in user's Home directory.

TIP

> To change permissions, click the Lock icon next to the Owner pop-up menu. When the Lock icon is unlocked, the pop-up menus become active.

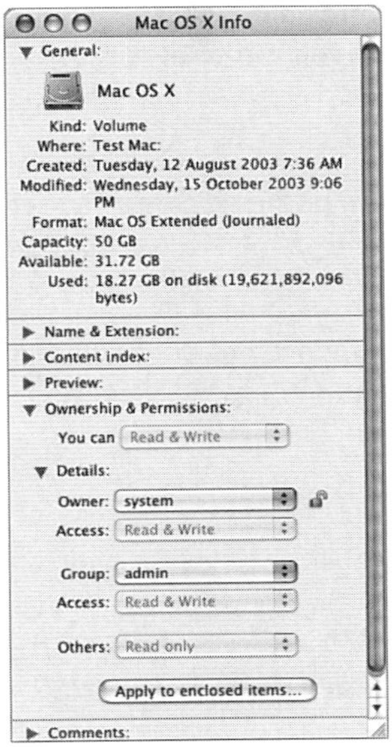

Figure 26.15
This Info window for the startup Mac OS X volume shows that the current user (You can) can read and write to the selected volume; the system admin and anyone in the admin group has the same access.

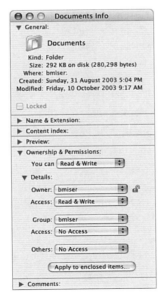

There are several things you need to know about the Ownership & Permissions information shown in the Info window.

First, unless you are logged in under the root or administrator account, you can't use the pop-up menus to change the permissions assigned to items on the Mac OS X startup volume above the current user's Home directory. However, when you open the Ownership &

Figure 26.16
This Info window is for the Documents folder within a user's Home directory; its pop-up menus are active and you can use them to set access permissions for the item.

Permissions area of the Info window for an item on another volume or within a user's Home directory, the pop-up menus become active and you can use them to change the privileges for the item.

Second, the groups you see in the Info window are default groups created when you install Mac OS X. The user accounts that are members of these groups can access the item with the group's privileges. You can't change the members of those groups from the Finder; you have to use the NetInfo Manager application, as you will see in the next section.

To configure access privileges for most items, you need to either be logged in as an administrator or authenticate yourself in the Info window. To do so, click the Lock icon and enter an administrator username and password.

To set the access privileges for all items, perform the following steps:

1. Log in under the account that is the owner of the items for which you want to change access permissions. For example, to change the access permissions for the items in a user's Home directory, log in under that user account. (You can see the owner for any item by opening the Details area of the Ownership & Permissions area of the Info window for that item.)

NOTE
> The owner for most items you will see is the original administrator account. The owner of items with the user directories is the user account for that directory, and the owner of system items is system, which is actually the root account.

→ To learn how to log in under the root account, **see** "Logging In As Root," **p. 236**.

2. Select the item for which you want to set permissions and press ⌘-I.

3. Expand the Ownership & Permissions section in the Info window and then expand the Details section.

Use the access permission pop-up menus to set the access privileges for each type of user. Different pop-up menus are active depending on the specific item for which you are setting access permissions and the user account you are using. If you aren't in a position to change an aspect of the permissions, the pop-up menus for that aspect are disabled.

4. If the Owner pop-up menu is active, use it to set the owner of the item. When you open this menu, you see each user account on the machine plus several other user accounts you probably have not seen before (see Figure 26.17). The primary ones you need to concern yourself with are system, which is the root account, and nobody, which makes no account the owner of an item. The current owner is indicated by a check mark.

Figure 26.17
You can use the Owner pop-up menu to set the owner for an item.

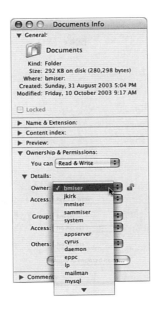

TIP

If you select Other on the Owner pop-up menu, you see the User Listing dialog box, which shows every user on your machine.

5. Use the Access pop-up menu under the Owner pop-up menu to configure the access the owner has to that item. Typically, the owner of an item is granted Read & Write access, which is the broadest access possible.

6. Open the Group pop-up menu and assign a group to the item. As with the Owner pop-up menu, all sorts of odd-looking groups appear on the Group pop-up menu. The staff group is selected for many items by default—you are a member of this group. The other groups you see have been created by default or by using the NetInfo Manager application. You can determine the members of the groups by using the NetInfo Manager application as well.

7. Use the Group Access pop-up menu to configure the access that members of the group you selected in the previous step have to the item. Usually, you should allow Read access for a group.

8. Use the Others pop-up menu to set the access everyone else (everyone who is not the assigned owner or a member of the assigned group) has. Typically, you allow either None or Write only (Drop Box) to others.

9. If you want the same privileges to apply to every item contained in the item you selected, click the button labeled "Apply to enclosed items." The same set of permissions are then applied to every item contained in the current item.

10. Continue setting permissions for other items as necessary.

Under Mac OS X, you can open multiple Info windows at the same time. This is a handy way to compare and contrast the permissions provided for different items.

USING THE NETINFO MANAGER TO ADMINISTER YOUR NETWORK

The NetInfo Manager application (Applications/Utilities) can be used to view and change an extensive amount of configuration information for a system. The application presents information based on a selected directory; by default, this is the information for the local-host directory, which is the machine on which Mac OS X is installed.

CAUTION

Using the NetInfo Manager application is not for the faint of heart. The information it presents and the controls it provides are complicated and can be quite dangerous to your system. This section can only scratch the surface of this application, and you should be careful if you explore the application on your own.

When you open the application, click the Lock icon and enter your administrator account information to enable changes to be made. A two-paned window with a toolbar appears (see Figure 26.18).

Figure 26.18
This NetInfo Manager window shows information for the base level of the localhost machine.

Networks and Complexity

As you explore networking, you might find yourself thinking that Mac OS X is much more complicated and less intuitive to set up and manage than previous versions. If you have these thoughts, I agree with you. Although under Mac OS 9, setting up users and groups and applying permissions to specific items to enable file sharing for anyone on the network is easy, the same tasks aren't so easy under Mac OS X. And under previous versions of the OS, you never had to deal with anything approaching the complexity of the NetInfo Manager application.

This complexity is part of the price paid for the additional capabilities and security of Mac OS X when compared to previous versions of the OS. Mac OS X is based on Unix, and the complexity of Unix comes to the forefront more in some specific areas of the OS than in others—networking is a prime example of where Unix really moves to the foreground. Fortunately, as you have seen, using the default configuration to provide basic services, such as file sharing, Web sites, and so on, is relatively easy. It is only when you are doing more complex tasks, such as changing the composition of the default user groups, that you have to get face-to-face with Unix.

In the upper pane is a browse window that works similarly to a Finder window in the Columns view. In the center column, you can browse the contents of an item selected in the left column. Similarly, in the far right column, you can browse the contents of an item selected in the center column.

In the lower pane are the details for the item you have selected in the upper pane. The specific details you see are related to what you have selected in the upper pane. For example, Figure 26.19 shows the details for the user account mmiser—selected in the upper pane—in the lower pane of the window.

Figure 26.19
You can use the NetInfo Manager to view and change information about the items you select.

When you have selected an item, you can change its information by editing the property and value data in the lower pane of the window.

NetInfo Manager is an extremely powerful utility, and you can administer many parts of your system with it. Because of space limitations, I can't cover it in much detail. However, a sample task will show you how it works in general.

You can change the members of a group through which access privileges are assigned by changing the members in that group. For example, you can add members to the group admin to change which user accounts have administrator privileges on your machine:

1. Open the NetInfo Manager application (Applications/Utilities).

2. Authenticate yourself as an administrator by clicking the Lock icon and entering an administrator username and password.

3. In the center column of the window, click groups and then select admin in the right column. The lower pane displays the various properties and their corresponding values.

4. Click the Expansion triangle next to the users property to expand it (see Figure 26.20). Each member is listed on a separate line. If you have created only one administrator account, that account and the root account appear in the list. If you have created more than one administrator account, each administrator account and the root account appear.

Figure 26.20
Expanding the users property by clicking its Expansion triangle reveals the members of the admin group (in this case, root, bmiser, and mmiser).

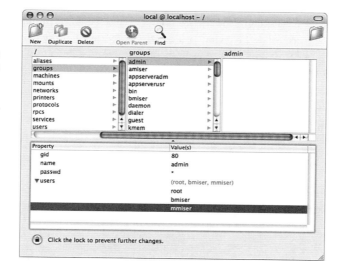

5. Select Directory, New Value. A new line is added to the users property; the value is `new_value`.

6. With the new value highlighted, change it to the short name of the user account you want to make a member of the admin group; then press Return.

7. Repeat the steps to add other members to the admin group.

8. Quit the application. In the Quit dialog box, click Review Unsaved, and then click Save in the Warning dialog box.

9. In the next dialog box, click the "Update this copy" button.

TIP

If the changes you make don't appear to be reflected, restart Mac OS X to force the new values to be implemented.

NOTE

You can make copies of directories so you can make changes to one and use it without writing over the previous version. This gives you a way to recover in case you mess something up.

The users you added to the admin group now have the privileges designated for this group. Opening the Accounts pane of the System Preferences application shows that the user accounts you added to the admin group are now designated as administrator accounts.

You can change the members of other groups you encounter in the same way.

NOTE

Of course, it would be a lot faster to use the Accounts pane of the System Preferences application to edit a user account to make it part of the admin group, but this example serves to show you generally how the NetInfo Manager application works. To change the members of other groups, you have to use the NetInfo Manager application; you can do so using the same steps as those to change the members of the admin group.

TROUBLESHOOTING

I CAN'T SEE THE FILE SERVER USING THE CONNECT TO SERVER COMMAND

I have configured file sharing on a machine on the network, but I am unable to access it using the Connect to Server command.

There can be many causes of this problem. The information in the following paragraphs should help you identify the source of the problem and solve it.

First, ensure that the file server can access the network. If Internet access is provided over the LAN, attempt to access Internet resources from the file server. If there is a printer or other network device, attempt to use that device from the file server. If that is successful, you know the problem lies with the configuration of the machine. If you can't access any network resources from the file server, a problem exists with the network connections for the file server. Check all the cabling to ensure that the machine is properly connected to the network.

Second, make sure that File Sharing is turned on.

Third, ensure that the file server's firewall is not blocking access to the service you are attempting to use. Mac OS X includes a built-in firewall you can use to protect your machine from attack. This firewall can block the very services you are attempting to access. If this is true, the machine won't be visible to the network.

→ To learn how to configure the firewall built in to Mac OS X, **see** "Defending Your Mac Against Net Hackers," **p. 911**.

MY MAC OS 9 MACHINE CAN'T SHARE FILES

When I try to access a Mac OS X file server from a Mac OS 9 machine, I can't see it in the Chooser.

Make sure the Mac OS 9 machine can access the network. Use the Chooser to select a network printer or other device. If that works, you know the problem lies with the configuration of the machine. If it doesn't, you have a networking problem. Check the cables and hubs to make sure everything is connected properly.

On the Mac OS 9 machine, turn off AppleTalk using the Chooser, assuming that the Mac OS 9 machine has an IP address. AppleTalk can cause problems with TCP/IP file sharing.

If the Mac OS 9 machine does not have an IP address, ensure that AppleTalk is turned on for the Mac OS X file server.

I CAN'T SEE THE FTP SITE

When I try to move to the FTP site, I get a connection refused or site not found error.

First, check whether any TCP/IP services are working. Turn on Web sharing for the machine you are attempting to use for FTP. If you can successfully connect to its Web site, a problem exists with the FTP services themselves. If you can't successfully connect, you have a network problem.

If the problem is related to the FTP service, make sure you don't have a firewall installed that blocks FTP services. Also, try shutting down the FTP machine and then starting it up again.

Even though enabling the Passive FTP mode on the Proxies tab of the Network pane of the System Preferences utility is supposed to enable FTP services through the Mac OS X firewall, I had trouble getting reliable access to machines on which the Mac OS X firewall was enabled, especially when using an AirPort connection. If you have trouble accessing an FTP site on a Mac OS X machine, try disabling the firewall on that machine (be sure you aren't connected directly to a broadband Internet connection with the firewall disabled) to see whether that is blocking access to the FTP services.

FTP ACCESS WAS WORKING, BUT NOW IT ISN'T

I have successfully accessed FTP services on a machine before, but now it isn't working.

If you are using a Web browser to access the FTP site, quit the browser, restart it, and try again.

If several unsuccessful logins to an FTP service have been attempted, subsequent logins will be denied. When this happens, restart the machine providing the FTP services.

MAC OS X TO THE MAX: NETWORKING MAC OS X WITH WINDOWS COMPUTERS

Because support for Windows and Unix file-sharing protocols is built in to Mac OS X, using a Mac on a Windows or Unix network is much easier under Mac OS X than it was under previous versions of the Mac OS.

SHARING FILES WITH WINDOWS COMPUTERS

You can use Mac OS X to access files provided on a network via the SMB protocol without doing any additional configuration. To use files provided on a Windows or Unix network that uses SMB, perform the following steps:

1. Connect your Mac OS X to the Windows or Unix network.

2. Open the Connect To Server dialog box and click Browse. Depending on the SMB servers on your network and how the network is configured, the SMB servers might or might not appear in the list of available servers when you browse the network, so you might have to enter the server address manually.

3. If you don't see the SMB server to which you want to connect, enter the address of the server to which you want to connect; the form of the address is smb://*ServerName*/ *ShareName*/. *ServerName* is the name of the server to which you are connecting; *ServerName* can be an IP address or a URL, and *ShareName* is the name of the item being shared with you, such as a disk or directory.

> **TIP**
>
> To determine the IP address (ServerName) for a Windows machine, open the Command Prompt window, type **ipconfig**, and press Enter. The IP address of the Windows machine will be shown.

26

4. Click Connect. You are prompted to enter your workgroup/domain, username, and password for that server.

5. Enter the required information and click OK. You are logged in to the shared resource and can use the files it contains just like a Mac that is acting as a file server (see Figure 26.21).

Connecting to Windows computers can be problematic depending on the specific network you are using. If the preceding steps don't enable you to connect to a Windows computer, try using the Apple support document located at the following address:

http://docs.info.apple.com/article.html?artnum=106660

To enable Windows users to access files stored on your Mac, carry out the following steps:

1. Open the Services tab of the Sharing pane of the System Preferences application.

2. Select the Windows Sharing service and click Start. The address to which Windows users need to connect is shown at the bottom of the pane. You need to provide this address to the Windows users you want to be able to access the machine.

3. Create a user account the Windows user can use to access your machine.

4. Provide the user account, password, and address to the Windows users you want to be able to log in.

Figure 26.21
The DDRIVE folder is located on a Windows XP machine on the local network.

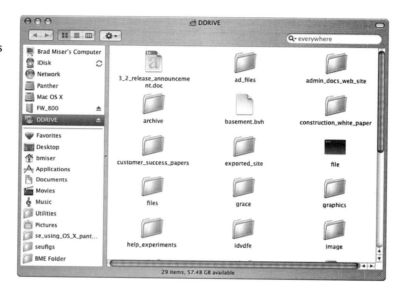

A Windows user can use the URL, username, and password you provided to log in to your Mac to share files just like Macs on your network (see Figure 26.22).

Figure 26.22
This Mac OS X folder is being accessed from a Windows XP computer.

CHAPTER 27

SHARING AN INTERNET CONNECTION

In this chapter

Enabling Multiple Macs to Use a Single Internet Account

One of the primary advantages of networking computers together is that they can share a single Internet account. This is especially useful for broadband accounts; however, you can share a dial-up connection, too.

> **NOTE**
>
> Dial-up accounts are relatively slow. Supplying several computers through slow access will divide that limited bandwidth and make the already-slow access even slower.

You can also share a single Internet account on mixed networks that include both Macintosh and Windows computers.

Most means of sharing an Internet account rely on the Dynamic Host Configuration Protocol (DHCP). This protocol enables IP addresses to be dynamically assigned to each device on a network. A DHCP server assigns and manages these addresses. This protocol means that each device doesn't have to have a unique IP address; the DHCP server has a unique address and assigns IP addresses to the machines under it, as they are needed.

> **NOTE**
>
> Each device for which a DHCP server provides an address must have a unique IP address; the DHCP server provides these addresses and ensures that they are unique. Most DHCP servers also provide network address translation (NAT) protection for the devices to which they provide services. When NAT protection is active, all the machines under the server appear to be from one IP address, which is that of the DHCP server. Using a DHCP server with NAT isolates the machines it serves from direct contact with other machines on the Internet and protects those machines from Internet attacks to a great degree.

In this chapter, you will learn how to share an Internet account using the following techniques:

- AirPort
- Mac OS X's built-in Internet sharing feature
- Multiple IP addresses for a single account
- A hardware DHCP server/hub

Using AirPort to Share an Internet Account

One of the easiest and best ways to share an Internet account is to use AirPort. In fact, using AirPort automatically enables you to share an Internet account among computers using an AirPort-compatible, wireless connection. You can also use an AirPort-equipped Mac to share an Internet connection with machines on an Ethernet network.

When you install and configure an AirPort hardware access point (also known as an *AirPort base station*), you can share the Internet account with which it is configured among AirPort-equipped Macs that can access that network. You can also share an Internet account among computers that are connected to the hardware access point via Ethernet. This is because the hardware access point is capable of acting as a DHCP server for the network and can provide that service to computers connected via AirPort and via Ethernet at the same time.

When used with a broadband connection, an AirPort hardware access point also provides your network with basic firewall protection when you use NAT (which is explained later in this chapter). Because the only thing directly connected to the Internet is the base station itself, hackers can't see the computers that are connecting to the Net through the base station. They can see the base station, but because it isn't a computer, there isn't much they can do to it.

Because AirPort is easy to install, configure, and maintain and because you also get wireless access for AirPort-equipped devices, using AirPort is one of the best ways to share an Internet account.

→ To learn how to install, configure, and use an AirPort network to share an Internet connection, **see** Chapter 11, "Using an AirPort Network to Connect to the Internet," **p. 297**.

NOTE

An AirPort base station is also a great way to share a dial-up Internet connection. Because the modem (if you use a dial-up account) and software required to maintain the dial-up connection are part of the base station, this method doesn't place any processing burden on the Macs using the AirPort network. Of course, to share a dial-up connection, an AirPort base station must include a dial-up modem, which is an option on newer base stations.

USING A MAC RUNNING OS X TO SHARE AN INTERNET ACCOUNT

Mac OS X includes a built-in DHCP server you can use to share a single Internet connection with other devices on your local network. And if the Macintosh on which you configure the DHCP server includes an AirPort card, you can also provide a wireless AirPort network without the use of an AirPort base station.

NOTE

The function of the DHCP server is to provide and manage IP addresses to devices on the network. The DHCP server doesn't actually provide the Internet access itself; that comes from the connection method you use (such as a cable modem). The DHCP server manages the traffic between the Internet connection and the other devices on the network.

One advantage of this approach is that you don't need to add dedicated Internet sharing hardware (such as a sharing hub or an AirPort base station) to your network. A standard Ethernet hub enables you to share an Internet account over an Ethernet network, and an AirPort card enables you to share an account over a wireless AirPort network. Another advantage is that it doesn't cost anything to share an account (assuming that you already have the connection hardware, such as for an Ethernet network).

NOTE

> You can use Mac OS X's built-in firewall to protect the DHCP machine from attacks from the Internet (and because it sits between the Internet and the other devices on your network, it protects those devices as well).

→ To learn how to configure the Mac OS X firewall, **see** "Defending Your Mac Against Net Hackers," **p. 911**.

This approach does have one significant disadvantage and one minor drawback, however. The significant disadvantage is that the Mac providing DHCP services must always be running for the machines that share its account to be capable of accessing the Internet. If the DHCP machine develops a problem, no device on the network can access the Internet. Similarly, if the machine from which the account is shared goes to sleep, the connection is lost by all the computers on the network. The less significant issue is that the DHCP services do require some processing power. These services will most likely not result in any noticeable performance decrease, but if your machine already runs at its limits, asking it to provide these services might slightly slow down other tasks.

NOTE

> DHCP servers are not platform specific. For example, if you have a DHCP server running on a Macintosh, you can connect a Windows computer to the network and use the same DHCP server to share the Internet account with it. Or, you can install a DHCP server on a Windows machine and use it to share the account with Macs on the network.

Configuring a Mac to provide DHCP services to a network requires the following general steps:

1. Connect the Mac to the Internet.
2. Install the network you will use to connect the Mac with other machines.
3. Configure the Mac to share its Internet account.

CONNECTING THE DHCP MAC TO THE INTERNET

It goes without saying (but I will say it anyway) that to use a Mac to share an Internet account, that Mac must be connected to the Internet. The method you use to connect to the Internet doesn't matter. You'll get the best results if you use a broadband connection, such as a cable DSL modem, but you can also share a dial-up connection if you want (don't expect speedy operation, though).

→ To learn how to connect a Mac to the Internet, **see** Chapter 10, "Connecting Your Mac to the Internet," **p. 263**.

INSTALLING THE DHCP MAC ON A NETWORK

The next step is to install the DHCP Mac on the network with which you are going to share the Internet connection. You can build a wired network using Ethernet, or you can install an AirPort card to connect the Mac to other AirPort-equipped Macs (you can share an account with other machines using both networking methods at the same time).

→ To learn how to install, configure, and use an AirPort network, **see** Chapter 11, "Using an AirPort Network to Connect to the Internet," **p. 297**.
→ To learn about Ethernet, **see** "Ethernet," **p. 705**.
→ To learn about Ethernet hubs, **see** "Finding and Installing an Ethernet Hub," **p. 808**.
→ To learn how to build and manage a network, **see** Chapter 26, "Building and Using a Network," **p. 821**.

CONFIGURING THE DHCP MAC TO SHARE AN ACCOUNT

After you have configured the Mac for Internet access and connected it to other computers (with or without wires), you need to configure the Internet sharing services on it.

The three possibilities when you configure Internet sharing on your Mac are as follows:

■ Your Mac is connected to the Internet via an Ethernet connection, and it has an AirPort card installed in it.

■ Your Mac is connected to the Internet via Ethernet but does not have an AirPort card installed in it.

■ Your Mac is connected to the Internet via an AirPort base station, in which case you can share the Internet account by connecting that Mac to other computers via Ethernet to share its account via an Ethernet network (you wouldn't need to share the Internet connection with the AirPort-equipped Macs because the base station does that).

NOTE

> AirPort base stations, except the original version, include an Ethernet port you can use to connect the base station to an Ethernet network. When you do this, the base station can also share a connection with machines connected to the Ethernet network. In that case, you don't need to use a Mac to share a connection.

When you configure Internet sharing on your Mac, it automatically determines which case is true for your machine and presents the appropriate options for you. To configure Internet sharing, use the following steps:

1. Open the System Preferences Utility and click the Sharing icon to open the Sharing pane.

2. Click the Internet tab. What you see depends on how the Mac is connected to the Internet. For example, in Figure 27.1, you see the Sharing Internet tab for a machine connected to the Internet via AirPort; you can tell this is so because AirPort is selected on the "Share your connection from" pop-up menu. In Figure 27.2, you see an example of a machine connected to the Internet via Ethernet. Because that machine also has an AirPort card installed in it, it can share its connection with other machines using both Built-in Ethernet and AirPort.

Figure 27.1
This Internet tab is for a computer connected to the Internet via AirPort.

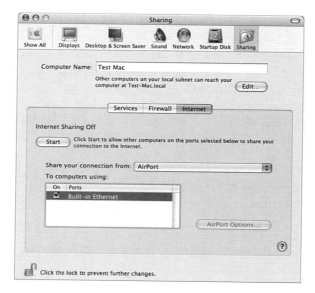

3. On the "Share your connection from" pop-up menu, select the Internet connection you want to share. In most cases, you will be connected by only one means, such as AirPort or Built-in Ethernet, so the choice should be obvious. However, if the Mac can connect in multiple ways, choose the option you want to share.

In the "To computers using" box are the choices you have for sharing the connection that you selected in step 3 with other computers. For example, in Figure 27.2, you can see that the Mac can share its connection with other machines over Ethernet and AirPort.

4. Mark the On check box for the ports over which you want to share the connection. For example, to share the Mac's connection with computers via AirPort, mark the On check box next to AirPort on the list of ports.

If you use an Ethernet port to share a connection, you might see a sheet warning you that activating sharing might cause problems for other ISP customers or violate your service agreement (some providers prohibit sharing an individual account on multiple machines, but most allow a reasonable amount of sharing such as with five or fewer computers). Read the dialog box and click OK to close it.

Figure 27.2
The Internet tab shows a machine that is currently connected to the Internet via Ethernet, but that also has an AirPort card installed in it.

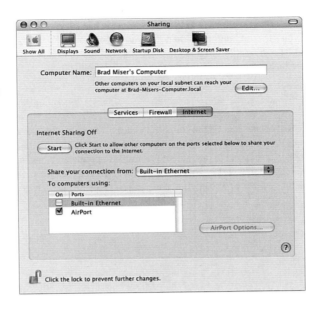

5. If you made an AirPort port active in step 4, select the AirPort port and click the AirPort Options button. Then configure the AirPort network you are creating using the resulting sheet. For example, you will name the network (if you don't want to use the default name), choose a channel and password, and so on. When you are done configuring the AirPort network, click OK.

→ To learn how to configure an AirPort network, **see** Chapter 11, "Using an AirPort Network to Connect to the Internet," **p. 297**.

6. Click Start (you can't click Start until you select at least one port on the "To computers using" list).

   You might see a warning sheet that explains that activating sharing might disrupt services on the network. If you are administering the network, click Start in the sheet. If someone else administers the network on which you are sharing your connection, make sure you coordinate with that person before starting Internet Sharing.

   Your connection will be shared with all the devices with which your Mac can communicate. For example, if your Mac is connected to a local network via Ethernet and you made that port active, other devices on the network can use the account via the DHCP services your Mac provides.

7. Quit the System Preferences Utility.

8. Configure the other devices on the network to use the Mac's DHCP server to access the Internet.

→ To learn how to install, configure, and use an AirPort network, **see** Chapter 11, "Using an AirPort Network to Connect to the Internet," **p. 297**.

→ To learn how to connect a Mac to the Internet, **see** Chapter 10, "Connecting Your Mac to the Internet," **p. 263**.

27

TIP

> If you share an Internet account over AirPort, an upward pointing arrow is added to the center of the AirPort icon in the menu bar. This indicates that the connection is shared and that you can access the sharing controls from the menu.

CAUTION

> If the machine sharing the connection goes to sleep, the Internet connection is lost on the network and no machine can access the Net. You should disable sleep using the Energy Saver pane of the System Preferences application when you use Internet Sharing. (In fact, when you start up sharing on a Mac that has sleep turned on, the Energy Saver button appears on the Internet pane so you can easily jump over and turn off sleep.)

If other machines with which you are sharing a connection are unable to connect to the Internet, see "The Machines with Which I Am Sharing a Connection from My Mac Can't Connect at All" in the "Troubleshooting" section at the end of this chapter.

If other machines with which you are sharing a connection lose the connection to the Internet, see "The Machines with Which I Am Sharing a Connection from My Mac Have Lost Internet Access" in the "Troubleshooting" section at the end of this chapter.

USING MULTIPLE IP ADDRESSES TO SHARE AN INTERNET ACCOUNT

With some broadband accounts, such as cable, you can purchase additional IP addresses (or DHCP names) so you can configure multiple machines to access the same account. The requirements to do this are an address for each device that will be using the account and an Ethernet or other network, which typically consists of a hub with the cable or DSL modem connected to the WAN port and each device connected to a LAN port.

NOTE

> Some ISPs use DHCP to provide IP addresses to you. In these cases, you assign a DHCP name to your computer. The ISP's DHCP server assigns IP addresses to you as you need them. To share an Internet account among several devices, you need a unique DHCP name for each device; you use this DHCP name to configure the network on each device.

To share an account using multiple IP addresses, do the following:

1. Contact your ISP to determine whether this option is available.

2. If it is, obtain additional addresses (or DHCP names); you will need one address for each machine or device (such as an AirPort base station) you want to share the account. You will probably need to pay an additional fee for each IP address you obtain.

3. Connect the cable or DSL modem to the WAN port on the hub for your network.

4. Connect each device to a LAN port on the hub.

5. Configure each machine with one of the available addresses (or DHCP names).

 If you can't use a device on your network because of an error message about the same IP address being used on more than one device, see "I Get an Error Message Telling Me That Multiple Devices Have the Same IP Address" in the "Troubleshooting" section at the end of this chapter.

One advantage to this method is that you can use a standard Ethernet hub to facilitate sharing the account; these hubs are quite inexpensive and are simple to install and use. Setting up each device to use its address is straightforward as well. You simply configure each machine as if it were the only one using the account. Another advantage is that you get maximum speed for each machine because each connects directly to the account; the traffic doesn't have to be managed by a DHCP server on your network. And, because there isn't any software on your network that has to manage the Internet traffic, as a DHCP server does, your connection for each device is dependent only on your modem and service, making it slightly more reliable than some of the other methods.

One possible disadvantage is that you might have to pay an additional fee for each address you use. The typical cost of additional addresses is $5–$7 per month per address on top of the address included with your base account. This can get expensive if you have several devices on your network; however, you can balance that cost against not needing a hub (Ethernet or AirPort) that has Internet account sharing built in.

Another disadvantage is that you don't get any special features, such as a built-in firewall. You have to add protection for each device on your network in some other way.

Typically, using a hub with built-in Internet sharing (such as an AirPort base station) or using a Mac to share its account is a better option. But, some providers require you to have a unique address for each machine that will be using the account, and this might be your only legal option.

→ For help choosing and installing an Ethernet hub, **see** "Finding and Installing an Ethernet Hub," **p. 808**.

→ For help installing and configuring a network, **see** Chapter 26, "Building and Using a Network," **p. 821**.

→ For help with protecting your Mac from Net attacks, **see** "Defending Your Mac from Net Attacks," **p. 908**.

USING A HARDWARE DHCP SERVER TO SHARE AN INTERNET ACCOUNT

One of the best ways to share an Internet account is to use a hub device that provides DHCP services to the network. These devices have the DHCP software built in and handle the administration of IP addresses for the network automatically.

In addition to basic DHCP services, some of these devices also include special features, such as built-in firewall protection for your network.

The general steps for installing and using such a device are the following:

1. Choose and obtain the device.

2. Install the device on your network.

3. Configure the device to connect to the Internet.

4. Attach the computers and other devices to the network and configure each device to use the DHCP server.

ISPs and Sharing a Connection

Not all ISPs support sharing a single Internet connection. Check the agreement you have with your provider to ensure that sharing an account is within your rights under that account. Some configurations can actually block access to your account by a hub or other sharing device, thus preventing you from sharing the account using a hardware device. Before you purchase a hub, make sure that it is acceptable under the terms of your Internet account; otherwise, you might end up wasting your money. Fortunately, most providers allow you to share the account on a reasonable number of machines.

Some providers use sort of a "don't ask, don't tell" policy. They provide support for one machine per account and make it clear that they don't support networks, in which case you are on your own if you have problems connecting through your own network. However, because using a sharing hub is so straightforward, this isn't really much of a drawback.

CHOOSING AND INSTALLING A DHCP HUB

Choosing a DHCP hub is similar to choosing an Ethernet hub. For example, these hubs offer different numbers of ports, different speeds, and so on. In addition to the DHCP services they provide, the major difference between standard Ethernet hubs and DHCP hubs is that DHCP hubs also offer a variety of other special features.

→ For help choosing and installing an Ethernet hub, **see** "Finding and Installing an Ethernet Hub," **p. 808**.

→ For help installing and configuring a network, **see** Chapter 26, "Building and Using a Network," **p. 821**.

→ For help with protecting your Mac from Net attacks, **see** "Defending Your Mac from Net Attacks," **p. 908**.

NOTE

> The AirPort hardware access point is a DHCP hub; its most special feature is that it can communicate with other devices wirelessly.

One of the most important of these special features is a firewall. Installing a DHCP hub that includes a firewall protects the devices on your network from being attacked by hackers coming to your network from the Internet.

One form of firewall is the NAT standard. Using NAT, there is one IP address for your network. The device providing NAT services shields the devices on your network by using a set of internal IP addresses for those devices. Thus, hackers trying to attack the only IP address that they can see get the hub device, which is typically immune to such attacks. Thus, your network is protected from external attack.

Many such devices are available, such as the Asante DSL/Cable Router.

Some of my favorite sharing and networking hubs are produced by Linksys (see Figure 27.3). Linksys hubs provide excellent features and are easy to install and configure. These hubs enable you to share an Internet account and provide NAT protection for your network.

Figure 27.3
Linksys produces excellent sharing hubs that are easy to install and configure.

Many sharing hubs also offer wireless services and so are similar to the AirPort base station. Because AirPort is based on standard wireless protocols, AirPort services are compatible with any wireless device that meets these same standards. However, because AirPort technology is integral to the Mac, I recommend that you stick with an AirPort base station if you want to obtain and use a wireless sharing hub.

NOTE

You can learn more about the Linksys products by visiting www.linksys.com.

27

Clumps of Data

When data is communicated across a network, it is done so in clumps of data. These clumps of data are more properly called *packets*. Each packet contains information that identifies its origin and destination (this is used to assemble all the packets together into a useful string of data). When a firewall filters IP packets, it examines each packet that comes into the network to ensure that it originated from the expected place. It rejects any packets that do not meet its requirements, thus protecting the network from unexpected traffic, which is likely to have been generated by hacking activity. Packet filtering adds an additional layer of protection for a network.

The XRouter Pro is another example of a sharing hub that is simple to install and configure. For most homes or home offices, the XRouter is an excellent choice.

NOTE

You can learn more about the XRouter Pro by visiting www.macsense.com.

Because of space limitations, I will be focusing on XRouter Pro in the remainder of this section. However, other devices, such as the Linksys hubs, can be installed and configured in a fashion similar to the XRouter Pro.

INSTALLING A DHCP SERVER

Installing a DHCP hub is similar to installing a standard Ethernet hub. Follow these steps:

1. Connect the output from the cable or DSL modem to the WAN port on the hub.
2. Connect the Ethernet cable from each computer to a port on the XRouter.
3. Connect the XRouter's power supply.

NOTE

You can attach the XRouter Pro to an existing Ethernet hub to provide its services to more than four devices at a time. To do so, connect one port on your current hub to the crossover port on the XRouter and use the crossover switch to select the crossover mode.

In the same way, you can also chain multiple hubs together to share an Internet account among more than four devices. For example, you can connect an AirPort base station to the hub to add AirPort-equipped devices to the network.

CONFIGURING MAC OS X MACS FOR DHCP SERVICES

After the physical connections are made, you need to configure each computer on the network to use DHCP for TCP/IP services.

NOTE

Consider creating a location for each TCP/IP configuration you use. This makes switching between configurations simple and fast.

→ To learn how to configure and use the Location Manager, **see** "Configuring and Using Locations," **p. 989**.

To configure machines on a network to connect to a DHCP server, follow these steps:

1. Open the Network pane of the System Preferences utility.
2. Select the location you want to configure from the Location pop-up menu.

3. On the Show pop-up menu, select the connection you want to configure, such as Built-in Ethernet or AirPort.

4. Click the Configure button.

5. Click the TCP/IP tab.

6. Select Using DHCP from the Configure IPv4 pop-up menu (see Figure 27.4).

Figure 27.4
Typically, configuring a Mac to use a DHCP server is simply a matter of selecting Using DHCP from the Configure IPv4 pop-up menu.

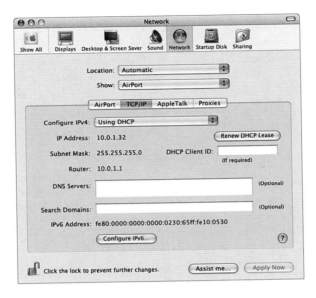

NOTE

Some DHCP servers require that you use a DHCP Client ID name. If so, enter that name in the DHCP Client ID field.

7. Click Apply Now to save the configuration.

8. Close the System Preferences utility.

9. Repeat these steps or use similar steps to configure the Macs on your network. For example, for Macs running Mac OS 9, use the TCP/IP control panel to select Using DHCP Server.

10. Configure the other devices on your network so that they use DHCP.

CONFIGURING A DHCP HUB

After the hub is physically connected to your network and the other devices are installed and configured, you need to configure the hub to connect to the Internet using your cable or DSL modem. How this is accomplished varies among devices, but most devices enable you to use a standard Web browser to configure the hub.

To install a typical DHCP hub, do the following:

1. Launch a Web browser.

2. Move to the IP address for the hub (the XRouter's IP address is 192.168.1.1).

3. When prompted, enter the username and password, and then click OK (the XRouter's username is blank and the password is admin). You will see the administration screen for the device.

4. Configure the hub following the instructions provided by the hub manufacturer and your ISP. You configure the hub using the same settings as you would for a computer with which you were accessing the Internet account. For example, if your ISP provides manual IP addresses, use the Static or Manual option to configure the hub. If your account is configured using DHCP, choose the "Get an IP address automatically" option.

→ For help configuring an Internet account, **see** Chapter 10, "Connecting Your Mac to the Internet," **p. 263**.

5. Save your changes and quit the Web browser.

Make sure you explore the configuration options your hub provides. For example, some hubs enable you to assign fixed IP addresses to certain devices. These addresses are provided in a range of addresses your hub provides (the first three sets of numbers in the IP address are the same for all the devices on the network, but you can choose the fourth set from a specific range of numbers). One use for this is to enable file sharing across those devices. Because you use IP addresses to share files under Mac OS X, having a fixed IP address enables you to connect to the same machine each time. If you allow the server to assign addresses, the address for each machine can change as machines connect to and disconnect from the network.

The machines on your network should be capable of accessing the Internet using a single account. If your hub provides NAT services, your network is relatively secure from outside attack because the internal IP addresses of devices are not exposed to the Internet.

TROUBLESHOOTING

THE MACHINES WITH WHICH I AM SHARING A CONNECTION FROM MY MAC CAN'T CONNECT AT ALL

I have started Internet Sharing on a Mac, but other devices on the network can't access the Internet.

Attempt to connect to the Internet from the Mac that is sharing the account. If that machine can't connect, something has happened to its Internet connection. If that machine can connect, check that Internet Sharing is configured properly.

Then, check the Internet connection settings for each machine to make sure they are set to connect via a DHCP server.

→ To learn how to connect a Mac to the Internet, **see** Chapter 10, "Connecting Your Mac to the Internet," **p. 263**.

→ To learn how to configure Internet Sharing, **see** "Configuring the DHCP Mac to Share an Account," **p. 859**.

THE MACHINES WITH WHICH I AM SHARING A CONNECTION FROM MY MAC HAVE LOST INTERNET ACCESS

The machines with which I am sharing an Internet connection were able to connect, but now they can't.

First, check whether all the machines with which the connection is being shared have this problem or only some do. If all the machines are unable to connect, the problem stems from the Mac sharing the account (see the next paragraph). If some of the machines with which the connection is being shared can access the Net, the problem lies with those machines. Check the configuration of those machines to ensure that they are configured to use a DHCP server. Also, check their network connections to make sure they are communicating with the network properly.

→ To learn how to connect a Mac to the Internet, **see** Chapter 10, "Connecting Your Mac to the Internet," **p. 263**.

→ To learn how to install, configure, and use an AirPort network, **see** Chapter 11, "Using an AirPort Network to Connect to the Internet," **p. 297**.

→ To learn how to build and manage a network, **see** Chapter 26, "Building and Using a Network," **p. 821**.

If none of the machines can access the Internet, something has happened to the Mac that is sharing the connection.

Make sure that the Mac is still running and that sleep is disabled. If both of these conditions are true, move to the next paragraph. If the Mac is shut down, restart it and restart Internet Sharing. If the Mac has gone to sleep, you need to wake it up and restart Internet Sharing.

Attempt to connect to the Internet from the Mac that is sharing the account. If that machine can't connect, something has happened to its Internet connection. If that machine can connect, reconfigure Internet Sharing.

→ To learn how to configure sleep, **see** "Managing Your Mobile Mac's Power," **p. 982**.

→ To learn how to connect a Mac to the Internet, **see** Chapter 10, "Connecting Your Mac to the Internet," **p. 263**.

→ To learn how to configure Internet Sharing, **see** "Configuring the DHCP Mac to Share an Account," **p. 859**.

I GET AN ERROR MESSAGE TELLING ME THAT MULTIPLE DEVICES HAVE THE SAME IP ADDRESS

When I attempt to start up one of the devices on my network, I see an alert stating that a device has already been assigned the IP address and that IP services are being shut down. How do I correct this problem?

Two devices on the same network cannot have the same IP address. If you start up one device and see this error message, you have two or more devices trying to use the same address. Check the configuration of each device to see which devices are using that address (for Mac OS X machines, use the TCP/IP tab of the Network pane of the System Preferences utility to see how the computer is configured). Check that each device has a unique address, including an AirPort base station or other device that is sharing the account.

Occasionally, your hub will "remember" the devices that are using specific IP addresses and you will see this error even though you made sure that each device had a unique address. If this happens, power down your entire network, including the hub and all other devices attached to it. Wait a few seconds and power up everything again. The error should be cleared as each device registers its unique address on the network.

MAC OS X TO THE MAX: TROUBLESHOOTING A NETWORK CONNECTION

Troubleshooting a network connection to the Internet can be quite challenging. Your approach should be to eliminate potential sources of the problem one by one until you find the specific problem you are having.

If you are unable to connect to the Internet after you have installed and configured an Internet Sharing hub, try the following steps:

1. Remove the hub again and return your configuration to the way it was before you installed the new hub.
2. Return one Mac to the condition it was in when you were able to access the Internet.
3. Check to see whether you can access the Internet. If you can, that means your modem is working properly and the configuration information is correct.
4. Attach that single computer and your modem to the DHCP hub again. This removes potential causes of problems that are due to the interaction of devices on the network.
5. Repeat the hub configuration and verify that the settings match those you used to connect the single Mac to the Internet.
6. Set the TCP/IP settings on the Mac to use a DHCP server.
7. Try to connect to the Internet. If you can connect, add your other machines back to the network. If the problem recurs, you know it is related to interaction among the devices.
8. In some cases, you might need to configure your hub to use media access control (MAC) address cloning. A MAC address uniquely identifies each node on a network. In some cases, you will need to clone, or copy, the MAC address of one of the computers on your network onto the router. See the instructions that came with the hub to learn how to configure MAC cloning on your router.
9. If you still can't connect, call your ISP for support.

PART VI

MAC OS X: PROTECTING, MAINTAINING, AND REPAIRING YOUR MAC

Maintaining and Protecting Your Mac

KEEPING YOUR MAC SAFE AND IN GOOD WORKING CONDITION

Time and effort you have to spend troubleshooting problems is time and effort you don't have available to accomplish what you want to accomplish. To avoid having to spend time solving problems, you should take specific steps to maintain and protect your Mac. In this chapter, the following preventive activities are described:

- Maintaining your Mac in good working condition
- Securing your Mac so people who use the machine or the network to which it is attached don't accidentally or maliciously cause problems
- Defending your Mac from attacks from the Internet

MAINTAINING YOUR MAC

Maintaining your Mac in good condition isn't terribly difficult, and the effort you do put in will pay off in having to spend less time and effort solving problems. In this section, you will learn about the following maintenance tasks:

- Maintaining your system software
- Maintaining your hard disks
- Backing up your system
- Maintaining alternative startup volumes and discs
- Building and maintaining a Mac toolkit
- Maintaining your applications

USING SOFTWARE UPDATE TO MAINTAIN YOUR SOFTWARE

Apple continuously updates the OS (and other applications) to solve problems, enhance performance, and introduce new features. Keeping track of the updates manually is time-consuming. Fortunately, you don't have to. You can use the Software Update tool (which consists of a pane in the System Preferences application and the Software Update application) to check, download, and install updates to Mac OS X and related software (such as firmware updates, updates to Apple applications you use, and so on).

CONFIGURING SOFTWARE UPDATE

To configure Software Update, follow these steps:

1. Open the System Preferences utility, and then open the Software Update pane (see Figure 28.1).

Figure 28.1
The frequency with which you check for updates depends on your connection to the Net; for most people, weekly updates are sufficient.

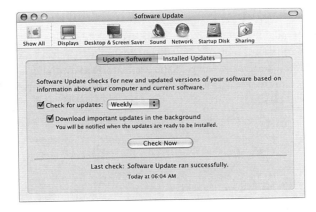

2. Use the check boxes, pop-up menu, and other buttons to configure the Software Update schedule (the options are described in the following bulleted list).

3. Quit the System Preferences utility.

When configuring Software Update, you have the following options:

- **Manual or Automatic Updates**—Use the "Check for updates" check box to determine whether your system will automatically check for updates when you have a network connection. If you check this box, use the pop-up menu to set the frequency with which this checking is done. Your choices are Daily, Weekly, and Monthly.

- **Download Updates in Background**—If you check the "Download important updates in the background" check box, Software Update automatically (you have to select the automatic option for this option to be available) downloads important updates (such as updates to the OS) without bothering you first. When the update has been downloaded and is ready to be installed, you are prompted to start the installation process manually.

- **Check Now**—You can click the Check Now button to manually check for updates.

- **Installed Updates tab**—Here you can see the history of all the updates Software Update has installed for you. Click the tab to see the list of files that were changed and when the changes were made. If you click the "Open as Log File" button, you will see a Console window that provides the same list, but in a different format and in a bit more detail.

NOTE

Immediately installing available updates is not always a good idea. Sometimes, the updates are flawed, in which case the problems become known pretty quickly. If you want to avoid early adopter problems, you might want to wait a few days after an update is available before you install it on your Mac.

28

Working with Software Update

When an update is available and you haven't selected the "download in background" option (whether you check for them manually or automatically), the Software Update application opens (see Figure 28.2). In the top pane of the application's window is a list of all available updates. If you select an update, information about that update appears in the lower pane of the window. You can download and install one or more updates by checking the box next to the update you want to install and clicking the Install button or choosing a specific option from the Update menu.

Figure 28.2
The Software Update application manages the download and installation of available updates for you.

TIP

You can jump straight into the Software Update application (without opening the Software Update pane first) by selecting Apple menu, Software Update.

NOTE

As with other application installs, you have to authenticate yourself as an administrator to be able to install updates via Software Update.

When you download updates, you can select one of the following download options from the Update menu:

- **Download only**—This option causes the update to be downloaded to your Mac. You have to run the installer manually to install it. Updates are provided as packages you can run just like other application installers. These packages are stored in the `Mac OS X/Library/Packages` folder, where `Mac OS X` is the name of your Mac OS X startup volume. When you want to install the update, open this folder and run the update's installer. After the file has been downloaded, a Finder window showing the installer is opened so you can run it easily.

■ **Install**—This one downloads and installs the update and then removes the package from your Mac.

■ **Install and Keep Package**—This option downloads and installs the update, but it also keeps the package so you can install the update again later if you need to. The update's installer is located in the `Mac OS X/Library/Packages` folder, where `Mac OS X` is the name of your Mac OS X startup volume. You can run the installer again from this location.

> **TIP**
>
> If you have more than one Mac, the first or third option can be a good choice because you can put the updater on a CD and install it from there on each machine rather than downloading it to each machine one at a time.

> **NOTE**
>
> When you click the Install button, the Install option is selected. To select one of the other options, you must use the Update menu.

If you selected the "download in background" option, you won't see the Software Update application until the updates have been downloaded to your Mac.

Occasionally, updates are released that are of no value to you, such as updates for languages you don't use, devices you don't have, and so on. Software Update regularly reminds you of these updates until you download them. However, if you see an update that you are sure you won't want to download and install, you can have Software Update ignore that specific update. To do so, use the following steps:

> **TIP**
>
> Ignoring an update removes it from this list. If you don't want to install a specific download, just uncheck its check box. To install that update, check its box before you click the Install button.

1. In the Software Update application, select the update you want to ignore.
2. Select Update, Ignore Update or press ⌘-delete.
3. Click OK in the resulting warning sheet. The update is removed and you will no longer be prompted to download the current or future versions of the update you ignored.

28

You can see ignored updates again by selecting Software Update, Reset Ignored Updates. All the updates you have ignored are added back to the Software Update application and you are prompted to download and install them again. You can't choose to restore a single update; you have to restore them all. Of course, you can choose to ignore specific updates again to remove them from the list.

NOTE

> Whether the "download in background" option is good for you or not mostly depends on the type of Internet connection you have. If you have a broadband connection, this option doesn't hurt because you aren't tying up your phone line while updates are downloading. You can just choose not to install any updates you don't want to. If you use a dial-up connection, it is better not to download updates in the background because some of the updates are quite large and you might tie up a phone line for a long time downloading an update you aren't going to install anyway.

After you have downloaded and installed an update, use the Installed Updates tab of the Software Update pane of the System Preferences application to verify that the updates were installed.

Seeing Installed Files

To view all installs that have been done on your Mac, including but not limited to software updates, open the folder `Mac OS X/Library/Receipts`, where `Mac OS X` is the name of your Mac OS X startup volume.

In this folder, you will see all the installs that have been performed on your Mac. Most are in `.pkg` files, but you can't open these to reinstall the software. Because they are receipts, they are for information purposes only.

NOTE

> If you want to manually check for Apple software updates, go to `www.apple.com/support`. Use the tools on the Apple Support pages to locate and download updates. For example, in the Downloads section, you will see a list of the current updates that are available.

Maintaining Your Hard Disks

Maintaining your disks will go a long way toward maximizing performance and preventing problems. You can use the Mac OS X Disk Utility application to do basic disk maintenance and repair. For maximum performance, you can also consider defragmenting and optimizing your disks.

Checking and Repairing Disks with the Disk Utility

Among other things, the Disk Utility application (located in the Applications/Utilities directory) enables you to check for problems with your disks and then repair problems that are found.

28

NOTE

> Under Mac OS 9 and earlier versions, the Disk Utility was called Disk First Aid. You can still see that heritage in the First Aid tab at the top of the Disk Utility window.

To check and repair a volume, perform the following steps:

1. Launch Disk Utility. In the left pane of the window are all the disks mounted on your Mac. Each volume on each disk is listed under the disk's icon. You will also see any disk images that have been mounted on the machine.

NOTE

> Even if a disk has only one volume on it, you will see that volume listed under the disk's icon.

2. Highlight the disk, volume on a disk, or disk image you want to check. When you select a volume, a number of tabs appear in the right pane of the window. How many appear depends on what you select.

   If you select a hard disk, the following five tabs appear: First Aid, Erase, Partition, RAID, and Restore.

   If you select a volume, you see the following tabs: First Aid, Erase, and Restore.

   If you select a CD, you see the First Aid, Erase, Partition, and Restore tabs.

   If you select a disk image, the First Aid and Restore tabs appear.

3. Check the bottom of the window for information about the disk, volume, disc, or image you selected. Again, what you see here depends on what you have selected.

   If you select a hard drive, you see the disk type, capacity, and S.M.A.R.T. status; for most disks, the latter provides an indication of the disk's health (Verified if the disk is in good working condition or About to Fail if the disk has problems).

   If you select a volume, you see various data about the volume, such as its format, number of folders, size, amount of space used, and the number of files it contains.

   If you select a DVD or CD drive, you see the drive's specifications and the types of discs with which the drive can work.

   If you select a disk image, you see its description, where it is located, and its current mount status (mounted or not).

4. Click the First Aid tab to see some information explaining how Disk Utility works.

NOTE

> You can't verify or repair a disk with open files, which means you can't do these tasks with your Mac OS X startup volume. To verify or repair that volume, restart your Mac from the Mac OS X installation CD and select Disk Utility from the Installer menu.

28

5. Click Verify Disk. The application checks the selected disk for problems. As it works, you will see progress messages in the First Aid pane. When the process is complete, a report of the results appears (see Figure 28.3).

Figure 28.3
The volume named Mac OS 9 appears to be okay.

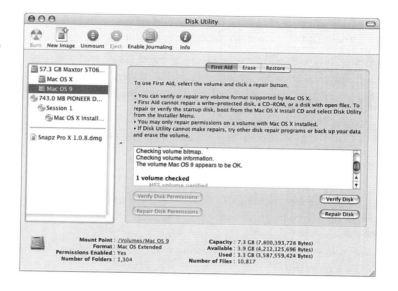

6. If problems are found, you are prompted to repair them. Do so.

7. Quit the application.

> **NOTE**
>
> For the Mac OS X startup volume, you never really need to run Disk First Aid. That is because the disk is checked and repaired during startup. You can also run a Unix disk repair utility during startup.

You can choose to repair a volume rather than to verify it. When you do so, repairs are made for any problems found immediately after the volume is checked. Generally, you should use the Repair button because it saves you a step.

→ To learn how to use the Disk Utility to initialize and partition hard disks, **see** "Initializing and Partitioning a Hard Drive," **p. 786**.

You can also use the Disk Utility to repair the permissions on the startup volume you are using. This can solve access problems with specific files on the machine when you don't have the required permissions. Do the following:

1. Select your current startup volume (you have to select the volume, not the disk on which the volume is stored).

28

2. Click Verify Disk Permissions. The utility begins checking the permissions for the startup volume. When the process is complete, you see the results in the information window on the First Aid tab.

3. If problems are found, you are prompted to repair them. You should choose to do so.

4. Quit the Disk Utility application.

You can use the Repair Disk Permissions button to verify and repair disk permissions in a single step.

TIP

> Disk Utility has a toolbar, which might be hidden by default. Click the Show Toolbar button in the upper-right corner of the window or select Window, Show Toolbar to view it. As with other Mac OS X toolbars, you can customize its contents as well.

ERASING DISKS WITH DISK UTILITY

You can also use Disk Utility to quickly erase and reformat volumes or erasable disks (such as CD-RW discs):

1. Select the disk or volume you want to erase.

2. Click the Erase tab.

3. Select the format you want to use for the volume on the Volume pop-up menu. For volumes on hard drives, your choices are Mac OS Extended (Journaled) and Mac OS Extended. If you select a disk, the options are Mac OS Extended (Journaled), Mac OS Extended, MS-DOS File System, and Unix File System.

4. Name the volume in the Name field.

5. If you selected a disk, click the Options button. The Erase Options sheet appears with two options. The "Zero all data" option writes zeros in all sectors on the disk. The "8 Way Random Write Format" writes random data over the entire disk eight times. The purpose of these options is to prevent data on the disk from being restored after you erase it. For example, if you were transferring a Mac to someone else, you would want to select one of these options so that the data you had on the disk could not be re-created. These options are really unnecessary unless you will be giving up control of the disk. If you want to use these options, select one or both and click OK.

6. If the Mac OS 9 Drivers Installed check box appears, uncheck it if you don't want Mac OS 9 drivers installed on the disk or volume. This setting affects only the ability to use the disk or volume when the Mac is booted up under Mac OS 9. Classic is not affected. If you want to be able to use the volume when running Mac OS 9, check the box.

7. Click Erase. The drive's or volume's data is erased and is formatted with the options you selected.

28

TIP

> You can get detailed information about a device or volume by selecting it and clicking the Info button on the toolbar.

ENABLING JOURNALING WITH DISK UTILITY

 Under Mac OS X version 10.3, disks can use the Mac OS (Journaled) file format. This format provides a journal function that tracks activity that has taken place in the main areas of the disk. This log helps re-create the data on the disk and makes repair operations more successful. In most cases, you should use this option because it gives you a better chance of recovering data and disks if you have problems. You can select the Journaled format when you erase a disk or volume, or you can enable journaling on an existing volume. To do the latter, use the following steps:

1. Select the volume on which you want to enable journaling.

2. Click the Enable Journaling button on the toolbar; select File, Enable Journaling; or press ⌘-J. The journaling information begins to be tracked for the selected disk or volume.

TIP

> You can disable journaling again by selecting File, Disable Journaling.

DEFRAGMENTING AND OPTIMIZING YOUR HARD DISKS

As you save files to a disk (again, this means any kind of disk you have mounted on your Mac, except for CD-ROMs, DVD-ROMs, and other locked disks from which you can only read data), data is written to the disk. The Mac is also frequently writing other sorts of data (such as preference changes and other system-level data) to the startup disk. As data is written to a disk, it is written in the next available space (called a *block*). After the data is laid down, the Mac returns to what it what was doing. When it is time to save more data, the next batch is written in the next open space, and so on. Think of this as the Mac putting all the data down in a straight line (yes, the disk is round, but it is easier to think of it this way), one chunk after another.

As files are opened and closed, data from different files is laid down in the next available space so that, instead of all the data from one file being in a continuous block, it can be stored in blocks located in various spots around the disk. In this state, the data is *fragmented*. Although fragmentation is a normal part of the way disk drives function, excessive fragmentation can slow down the disk. Things slow down because the drive head must read data from all the blocks that make up a particular file. As those blocks become more numerous and are spread out around the disk, it takes longer and longer to read all the data for that file.

You use a process called *defragmentation* to correct this condition. You need a disk maintenance program to do this, such as Tech Tool Pro. What the defragmentation process does is pick up all the data blocks for each particular file and write them in a continuous block. It does this for every file on the disk. After the data is laid out nice and neat, the drive performs faster because it doesn't have to move as far to read and write the data for a particular file.

NOTE  To learn more about Tech Tool Pro, visit `www.micromat.com`.

Because a hard drive is made up of a round disk that spins at a constant speed, it takes longer to read and write data to various parts of the disk. Data near the center is read more quickly than data out near the rim. Data can be written to the disk in such a way that the access speed of the drive is *optimized*.

To do this, the data that is used constantly but not changed much—such as the system software and applications—is stored near the center of the disk. The documents and other data that are infrequently used are stored out toward the edge of the disk. This arrangement speeds up the disk because access to the most frequently used data is faster, and keeping the static data together means it will not become fragmented. Thus, the data is read and written in an optimized (for speed) fashion. You also need a disk maintenance tool to optimize a disk.

Usually, defragmentation and optimization are done at the same time using the same tool. The steps to perform these tasks depend on the particular software you use. Generally, this is not complicated and is a matter of choosing the drives you want to defragment and optimize and clicking Start.

NOTE Defragmentation and optimization are somewhat controversial topics. Many experts believe they do little to no good, while others believe you can gain some performance and reliability improvements by performing these tasks on your disks regularly. Personally, I think you can better spend your time by keeping your disks well organized and using Disk Utility to check them every so often than worrying about squeezing a few microseconds of performance out of them.

CLEANING UP YOUR DRIVES

You can do a lot for the performance of your disks by simply keeping them cleaned up. The more data on your drive, the less room you have to store new files. If your disks get too full, their performance slows down significantly. More data means there is more information for your Mac to manage, and thus it has to work harder. You can also run into all kinds of problems if you try to save files to disks that are full to the brim; how full this is depends on the size of the files with which you are working.

28

Learn and practice good work habits such as deleting files you don't need, uninstalling software you don't use, and archiving files you are done with (such as on a CD-R disc).

NOTE

Many disk maintenance applications enable you to retrieve files you have deleted (an "undelete" or recover function). This is possible because during normal deletes (when you empty the Trash) the file is removed from the active system but might still exist on the disk in some form. The only way to be permanently rid of a file so it can't be recovered is to write over the area in which that file was stored with other data. To do this, you need an application that writes zeros or other bogus data over the location where the file you are deleting is stored. Typically, disk maintenance and other tools enable you to "really" delete files that you don't want to be able to be recovered. In Mac OS X version 10.3, you can also do this by using the Finder's Secure Empty Trash command.

MAINTAINING ALTERNATIVE STARTUP DISKS

One of the most important tasks you need to be able to do reliably and quickly is to start up from an alternative startup volume. In several situations you might need to do this. For example, if you find problems on your current startup volume, you will need to start up from another volume to repair that volume. If something happens to your startup volume such that your Mac can no longer use it, you need to use an alternative startup volume to get your Mac running.

Several possibilities exist for alternative startup volumes; you should maintain at least one, and preferably two, of the following options:

- **Your Mac OS X installation disc**—You can always use the disc that contains the Mac OS X installer as a startup volume. It contains the basic software you need to start up your system and repair the system software it contains. The downside to this is that any updates you have applied to your active system are not included in the version on the CD.

- **An alternative Mac OS X installation on a different volume**—You should install a backup installation of Mac OS X on a different volume from the one that you use for your primary system—if you can spare the disk space required to do so. Ideally, this alternative volume will be located on a separate disk (not just a separate volume) from your primary installation. For example, if you have an external FireWire hard drive, you can install Mac OS X on it so you can use it as a startup disk.

TIP

If you choose to install a backup version of Mac OS X on an alternative startup volume, you should delete any applications in that Mac OS X installation that you won't need when you are starting up from that volume. This will reduce the storage space it consumes. You also should start up from the volume and run Software Update every so often to keep the alternative startup volume current.

■ **Third-party application discs**—Many third-party applications, such as disk mainte-nance, antivirus, and backup software, include CDs that contain system software you can use to start up your Mac. These discs also enable you to run the application soft-ware with the idea that you will be able to correct a problem that has prevented you from starting up your system from the primary startup volume.

To start up your Mac from an alternative volume, restart the machine and hold down the Option key. After a few moments, each valid startup volume appears. Select the volume from which you want to start up and press Return (or click the right-facing arrow) .

> **TIP**
>
> You can refresh the list of available startup volumes by clicking the Refresh button (its icon is a curved line with an arrowhead).

> **NOTE**
>
> As always, you can start up your Mac from a CD by holding down the C key while the machine is starting up.

BUILDING AND MAINTAINING A MAC TOOLKIT

One of the best maintenance-related tasks you can do is to assemble and maintain a Mac toolkit. In times of trouble, this toolkit can enable you to get back to work quickly. Not having to find your tools in times of trouble also reduces the stress you experience. Following are some fundamental items you should keep in your toolkit:

■ **Your system configuration**—When you need help or are considering adding some-thing to your system, having a detailed understanding of your system is very important. Use the System Profiler application (in the Applications/Utilities folder) to generate a report on your system. Print that report and keep it handy (in case you can't generate it when you need it).

→ For more information about Apple System Profiler, **see** "Using the System Profiler to Create a System Profile," **p. 920**.

■ **Up-to-date backups**—Your toolkit should include everything you need to restore as much of your system as possible.

■ **A disk maintenance application**—You need one of these applications to solve disk problems you might encounter. Examples are Tech Tool Pro and Disk Warrior.

> **CAUTION**
>
> When selecting a disk maintenance application, make sure you get one that is written for Mac OS X. Using one designed for an older version of the OS can be harmful to your Mac and its data.

28

- **An antivirus application**—You'll need this to protect your machine from infection and in the event that your system becomes infected.

- **Your Mac OS X installation CD**—Sometimes, this is the only thing that will get your Mac started again.

- **Your original application installers on CD or DVD (even if you downloaded the installer originally), serial or registration numbers, and updates**—You should maintain the current versions of all your applications by maintaining the CDs on which they came. You should also create CDs or DVDs containing updates to those applications along with any applications you download from the Internet. Finally, be sure you have a list of the serial or registration numbers for your applications so you can restore them if needed. (You'll learn more about this in the next section.)

> **TIP**
>
> Consider devising some secure way to record passwords, usernames, serial numbers, and other critical data so you don't have to rely on memory to retrieve such information when you need it. Although keeping such information in hard copy is usually not advised, some people find it safer to develop and use some sort of code for this information and then have a hard copy of the encoded information handy.

MAINTAINING YOUR APPLICATIONS

Along with the system software, you should also maintain the applications you use. It is good practice to regularly check for updates for the applications on which you rely. There are several ways to do this, including the following:

> **NOTE**
>
> Many applications include the capability to go online to check for updates, either automatically or manually. For example, most Adobe applications can check for updates to keep you informed when new versions or patches are available.

- **Company mailing lists**—Some publishers maintain a mailing list for each application. Updates are announced in the mailing list, and the link to get to the update is provided.

- **Company Web sites**—Software publishers announce updates to their applications on their Web sites. Typically, you can check for and download updates from the Support area of a publisher's Web site.

- **Mac news**—Many Mac news sites and mailing lists include information about updates to popular applications.

- **Version Tracker**—Most Mac applications are listed on www.versiontracker.com. You should regularly check this site to look for application updates and patches.

NOTE

> As with the system software, it is sometimes wise to let a few days or a week pass after an update is released before you download and install it in case problems are introduced by the update.

You should also organize your applications and ensure that you have all the registration and serial number information you need for each application. It is amazing how easy it is to lose this information; getting it from the publisher can be a time-consuming task. Consider making a list of each application along with its serial number or registration number and keeping that list with the original CDs or the CDs containing the installers that you make for your applications. When you need to reinstall an application, this list will be a great time-saver.

Downloading Applications

If you obtain an application by downloading it rather than getting it on a CD, you should store the application installer so that you can reinstall it even if the publisher withdraws the installer for some reason (for example, sometimes the installer for one version is removed if a newer version is released). You can save hard drive space by placing these installers on a DVD-R or CD-R disc and storing that disc with your other application CDs.

You should also maintain the installer for any updates or patches you download and install so you can return the application to its current condition if anything happens to the version you have installed.

BACKING UP YOUR SYSTEM

If you use a computer, at some point, your system will crash, a disk will fail, or some other problem will happen and you will lose information you would rather not lose—maybe not today or tomorrow, but it *is* the inevitable nightmare. Think of the information you have on your Mac at this very moment that would be difficult—if not impossible—to reconstruct if your computer bombed and destroyed it. This data might be a report for work, a school project, your tax information, a complex spreadsheet, or even the great American novel on which you have been working. (For example, imagine that you have 2,000 photos in your iPhoto Library covering the last few years. Now imagine that the disk on which these images are stored dies. Losing all those images forever is not a pretty picture, is it?) Whatever the information, rest assured that some day, somewhere, somehow you will suddenly lose it. When that happens, you will want to be able to restore all the information on your Mac so you can quickly re-create your data. Backing up is the means by which you ensure that you can always preserve most of your work, no matter what happens to your Mac.

Backups: Insurance for Your Data

You need a good backup for more than just catastrophic failures of your hardware. I'll bet that you have accidentally deleted a file right before you needed it again. If you have a backup, you can quickly recover a document you accidentally delete. Or perhaps you edited a document and discovered that all your changes were actually worse than the original. You can use your backup to bring the file back to the way it was. If your Mac is ever stolen or destroyed, your backup enables you to recover from the disaster.

28

Although backing up your data is strongly recommended by computer authors, experts, and support personnel, it is a task that many Mac users never do for a variety of reasons. Some people don't back up data because they think their systems are infallible and won't crash. Still others are confused about how to make a backup of their system, or they lack the hardware and software necessary to maintain good backups. And then there are always those who simply don't believe that protecting their data is enough of a priority to waste their time on it.

However, because you are reading this book, I assume you are serious about your Mac and recognize the value of a good backup system.

There are four steps to creating and implementing a solid backup system. These steps are the following:

- **Define a strategy**—You need to define your own backup strategy; your strategy should define the types of data you will back up and how often you will back up your data. These choices will guide you as you decide on the type of hardware and software you use.

- **Obtain and learn to use backup hardware**—You need some kind of hardware on which to store the backed-up data. Many types of hardware can be used, including tape drives, removable media drives, additional hard drives, DVD-R drives, or CD-RW drives.

- **Obtain and learn to use backup software**—Ideally, you should use some sort of software to automate the backup process. The easier you make it on yourself, the more likely it is that your backup system will work reliably.

- **Maintain your backup system**—Like all other systems, you need to maintain your backup system and ensure that your data is safe.

DEFINING A BACKUP STRATEGY

One of the first things you need to decide is what data on your machine will be backed up.

The three general categories of data you should consider backing up are

- **Documents, photos, movies, music, and other important data you create**—These are, after all, the reason you use a Mac in the first place. You will want to back up all your own data because it doesn't exist anywhere other than on your computer. If you lose important data, it might be impossible to re-create. Even if you are able to re-create it, you will be wasting a lot of valuable time redoing what you have already done.

- **System files**—You probably have a CD-ROM that contains your Mac OS software, so you usually don't risk losing the Mac OS software itself. What you do risk losing is any customization you have done, updates you have installed, and so on. If you have adjusted any settings or added any third-party software, all the settings you have changed will be lost in the event of a major failure.

Additionally, don't forget about all the configuration information you have on your machine. For example, if you lose your system for some reason, you might lose all the configuration you have done to make your Mac connect to the Internet. You might also lose all the serial numbers of your software, which you will have to reenter if you need to reinstall it.

■ **Applications and other third-party software**—As with the OS software, you probably have CDs containing much of your third-party software. What you lose if you have a failure without a backup is the customization of those applications. Plus, you will have to reinstall that software—not an easy task if you have a lot of applications installed on your Mac. In any case, it can be very time-consuming to reinstall your applications.

NOTE

These days, you probably obtain a lot of your software by downloading it from the Net. If you lose the installers or patches you download without having a backup, you will have to download them again—assuming they are still available, of course. Sometimes, the version you want to use has been replaced by a newer version you don't want to use or pay for. (In my opinion, software companies should make older versions of applications available to download to handle cases where you need to reinstall it, but not all of them do.) And, occasionally, software moves from shareware to commercial, in which case it becomes unavailable to download again without paying for it. You should keep backup copies of any software installers or updates you download so you can reinstall that software if you need to—whether it is still available from the original source.

In conjunction with the kind of files you will back up, several types of backups you can make include

■ **Full backup**—In a full backup, you back up each and every file on your system. The advantage of doing full backups is that restoring your entire system, as well as just particular parts of it, is easy.

■ **Selected files only**—Using this scheme, you select particular files to back up; usually these are your important data (documents, photos, music, and so on) and some of your customization files (for example, preferences files). The advantage of this scheme is that you can make a backup quickly while protecting the most important files on your computer.

■ **Incremental backup**—This scheme combines the first two techniques in that all files are backed up the first time, but after that, only files that have changed are backed up until the next full backup. This scheme protects all your files but avoids the time and space requirements of doing a full backup each time.

What you decide about the type of data you will back up and how you will back it up should determine the type of backup system you develop and use. For example, if you decide that you don't mind having to reinstall applications and reconfigure settings or you mainly use small document files, you might be able to simply copy your document files onto a CD-RW or other removable media drive. If you have a great deal of data to protect, you will need to implement a more sophisticated system.

If you can assemble the hardware and software to do incremental backups, you should use this approach. It is the only one that is practical for frequent backups and also protects all your data.

Ideally, you want your backup system to work without any supervision or intervention by you. This is called an *unattended* backup because you don't even need to be there for the system to work. You can set the system to automatically back up during times when you are not working on your Mac. This is not only convenient, but it also means that because you don't have to *do* anything, you can't forget or be too lazy to keep your backups up-to-date.

CHOOSING BACKUP HARDWARE

The hardware you use for your backup system is important because having hardware that doesn't match the types of backups you want to make will doom your backup plan to failure. For example, if you go with a dedicated back-up hard drive or tape drive, you will be able to do frequent, incremental backups. The easier and better you make your backup system, the less work you have to do with it, and the more likely it is that you will *do* the backups. Table 28.1 lists the major types of backup hardware and summarizes their advantages and disadvantages.

TABLE 28.1 BACKUP HARDWARE

Drive Type	Backup Capability	Advantages	Disadvantages
CD-R and CD-RW	Can handle large amounts of data for full and incremental backups.	Drive has multiple uses (mastering CDs for distribution, creating audio CDs, and so on). Data is easy to share and recover because all computers have CD-ROM drives. Provides nearly permanent storage; this is a good choice for archival purposes. Backups can be stored away from your Mac. CD-RW drives are standard on many Macs. Media is very inexpensive.	Capacity of individual discs is limited so unattended backups are not always possible. It's relatively slow.

28

Drive Type	Backup Capability	Advantages	Disadvantages
DVD-R and DVD-RW	Can store large amounts of data on each disc.	Even so, you can't store enough to make full, unattended backups in most cases. Media can be mounted in most Macs. Data is easy to share because most computers can read DVD discs. Provides nearly permanent storage; this is a good choice for archival purposes. Backups can be stored away form your Mac. Apple's SuperDrive is available on all Mac models. DVD-R and DVD-RW drives can be used for many purposes (burning DVD movie discs, restoring disks, and so on).	DVD-R media is not reusable. Media is relatively expensive for backup use. It's relatively slow.
Hard drive	Depending on size, can handle large amounts of data for unattended full and incremental backups.	Very fast. Data is easily accessible. Drive can be mounted and used for other tasks.	High cost per MB of data storage. Data is harder to share. Unlikely to have sufficient storage space to make full backups. Backup drive is likely to be used for other purposes and thus might not be available for backing up. More difficult to store backups away from your Mac. Backup is subject to power surges and other outside causes of failure. Capacity can't be expanded.

28

TABLE 28.1   CONTINUED

Drive Type	Backup Capability	Advantages	Disadvantages
Tape	Can handle large amounts of data for full and incremental backups.	Large storage capability is perfect for unattended backups. Media is inexpensive (for example, a Travan 20GB tape costsas little as $34) Backups can be stored away from your Mac. Difficult to share with others because a tape drive of the same format must be available.	Tape can't be mounted; a tape drive is a single-purpose device. Tapes can be affected by magnetic forces and degrade over time. Relatively slow. Drives can be expensive.

Table 28.1 lists many options, but a careful review of the table should reveal that there are really only four choices for a serious backup system: tape, hard drive, DVD-R, or CD-RW.

The following list explains how I rate these options, in order of preference:

EXTERNAL FIREWIRE HARD DRIVES

Using a hard drive for backup provides the fastest performance, and you can usually get a drive large enough to store all the files needed to back up your primary drives (see Figure 28.4). You can easily configure automated backups so your data is constantly protected with no intervention on your part. And with FireWire, installing and using an external hard drive is literally a matter of connecting power to the drive, connecting the FireWire cable, and turning on the drive. That is all there is to it. Using a FireWire drive is simple. For performance and ease-of-use, a hard drive can't be beat.

There are several significant disadvantages to using a hard drive to back up data. One is that you can't archive data on a hard drive; a hard drive can be used only for your current backups. Another is that you can't store the backup in an alternative location, nor can you create multiple backups (unless you want to invest in multiple drives). Still another is that the capacity of the drive is fixed; the only way to expand the capacity of your system is to add more drives. And, hard drives can fail due to the same reasons that a drive in your Mac can fail, in which case your backup becomes worthless.

Another downside is that you will be tempted to use the backup drive for additional purposes when your other drives get full. You might delete the backup "temporarily" while you work on another project. Guess when something will go wrong and you will need your backup?

Still, even with these drawbacks, I find a hard drive the most convenient option for daily backups.

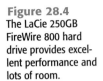

Figure 28.4
The LaCie 250GB FireWire 800 hard drive provides excellent performance and lots of room.

TAPE DRIVES

From a purist's viewpoint, this option wins by a mile. When it comes to the sole function of backing up, nothing comes close to a tape drive. Because the capacity of each tape is so large, a single tape drive can handle unattended backups for all but medium or large networks (in which a more sophisticated system is required). And the media for a tape drive is relatively cheap, can be reused, and is portable.

The downside of a tape drive is that it serves a sole purpose, which is backing up (of course, this is also a positive because you won't ever be tempted to use it for something else).

Tape drives are available in many format and interface options, but they all work in a similar way. If you want the best backup system, consider adding a tape drive to your Mac.

DVD-R DRIVES

DVD-R discs provide a good amount of storage space on each disc (4.7GB). This is enough room to do full and incremental backups, although you probably won't be able to store an entire backup on a single disc. Another plus is that many Macs include a SuperDrive so you don't need to spend money on additional hardware to back up your system. DVD-R is an excellent option for archiving data and should provide good long-term storage for the data you don't need to work on any longer.

Of course, a DVD-R drive is also very useful for other purposes, such as for creating DVDs with iDVD.

CD-RW DRIVES

This option takes a distant fourth place, in my opinion. These drives are also useful for backup purposes because CD-R media is so inexpensive (about $.50 or less for 650MB) and

28

because many Macs have a CD-RW drive built in. Plus, there are many other ways to use a CD-RW drive, such as creating audio CDs. Because every computer has a drive that can read CD-R discs, the data is very accessible.

However, even with these benefits, CD-RW drives are not an optimal choice for backing up. This is primarily because a CD holds only 650MB of data. Although that is a significant amount for everyday documents, it is inadequate for some types of projects. For example, when you consider iMovie projects, a single disc usually can't hold even one project. This means that unattended backups are usually not practical. Backing up an entire system on a CD-RW drive can take a long time, and you have to be there to swap new media in and out. And then, you have to manage the *many* discs that are required for your backups.

Still, if you already have a CD-RW, it is a good way to get your backup system started and to at least back up your documents.

Although you can make the other types of drives work in a backup system, they won't work that well over a long period of time. My recommendation is to go with one of the options in the previous list.

CHOOSING BACKUP SOFTWARE

Backup software enables you to define which files will be backed up and how often the backup will be updated. It also enables you to restore your data when the time comes. The software should enable you to automate the process as well.

Although there are many choices on the hardware side, there is one best option for Mac backup software: Dantz Corporation's Retrospect.

NOTE

> Note that Retrospect comes in various flavors depending on what you are backing up. Retrospect Express Backup is targeted to individual users with relatively simply backup needs, whereas Retrospect Workgroup Backup can back up a networked workgroup.

Retrospect does only one thing: It helps you create, implement, and maintain backups. Although limited in scope, Retrospect excels in function; it is a must-have piece of software. It is easy to use, yet it includes all the functions you need to establish and automate your backup strategy. If you intend to back up your Mac, you simply must use Retrospect.

Unfortunately, I don't have the space to explain how to use Retrospect, but suffice it to say that this software is extremely well designed and excellently implemented. After you install and configure it, it is so good that you won't have to deal with it very much (which should be a goal for any backup system).

Even better, many tape and other backup drives include this software, so you get everything you need for your backup system in one package.

28

To learn about Dantz and Retrospect, check out www.dantz.com (see Figure 28.5). You can get your questions about backing up your system answered there. I have been a customer for years and have been amazed by the exceptional support this company offers.

If you have a .Mac account, you can download and use Apple's Backup application. This application provides good backup capabilities. In addition to being able to back up to CD or DVD, you can back up your files to your iDisk (which takes the idea of remote storage of your data to a new level). You can also automate your backups. The application is simple to use and is free to anyone who has a .Mac account.

To learn about Backup, visit www.mac.com. If you have a .Mac account, you can download a copy of the software for free.

USING A BACKUP SYSTEM

I can't emphasize enough how important it is to maintain good backups for your data. Here are a few tips to keep in mind:

Figure 28.5
When it comes to Mac backup software, Dantz's Retrospect is as good as it gets.

- **Develop your own strategy based on the hardware and software you have or can afford to purchase**—At the least, make sure your critical data files are protected.
- **Make sure that backing up is easy**—If you have to do a lot of work to back up or if it takes a lot of your time, you won't end up keeping up-to-date backups. Ideally, you want to be able to do unattended backups; a hard or tape drive and a copy of Retrospect are your best bet.
- **Be consistent**—Whatever strategy you decide on, keep up with it. Old, out-of-date backups are not much better than no backups.

28

- **Always refresh your backups before you install any new software or make major changes to your system**—This will enable you to recover data if the changes you make to your system cause problems.

- **Be sure to test your backups regularly**—Try to restore a file or two to ensure that everything is working properly. If you don't, you might get a nasty surprise when you really need to restore some data.

- **Maintain your equipment**—Almost all equipment needs some kind of maintenance now and again, so follow the manufacturer's guidelines to keep your system in top condition.

- **Maintain more than one set of backups**—Create multiple copies of your backups in case something happens to one set.

- **Keep a set of backups offsite**—Keep a copy of your backups in a different location than your Mac is in. This will save you in the event of a catastrophic event such as fire or theft.

NOTE

> Archiving is slightly different from backing up. Backing up is done mostly for the "active" data on your Mac, whereas archiving is done with data you don't really need to work with anymore. Fortunately, you can use your backup system to archive data as well. For archiving smaller documents, a CD-RW drive is a good choice because the media is very cheap and relatively permanent. For larger amounts of data, a DVD-R disc is a good way to archive. When you archive, you should use a solution that won't degrade over time. In this case, an optical media is a better choice than magnetic media, such as a tape.

SECURING YOUR MAC

An important preventive maintenance task is to protect your Mac from other people who use it or from those who access its files from a network. You can also use the security pane of the System Preferences application, the secure delete trash function, and keychains to help you protect your Mac's security.

SECURING YOUR MAC WITH USER ACCOUNTS

You should create user accounts for everyone who uses your Mac. In addition to the features user accounts provide, such as a Web site and well-organized file storage, user accounts prevent unauthorized users from changing the system configuration of your machine.

→ To learn how to create and configure user accounts, **see** "Creating User Accounts," **p. 24**.

SECURING YOUR MAC WITH PRIVILEGES

For those who access your Mac over a network and for those who share your machine, you can control the access to specific items by setting privileges for those items. You can control

28

access in several levels of privilege from not being able to even see the item to being able to read and write to it.

→ To learn how to configure privileges, **see** Chapter 26, "Building and Using a Network," **p. 821**.

SECURING YOUR MAC WITH THE SECURITY PANE

 The new Security pane of the System Preferences application enables you to protect your Mac in a couple of ways. One is by using the FileVault feature that encrypts all the files in your Home folder; these files can't be used unless you input your login password or the master password for your Mac. The other way is by configuring various security settings for your Mac.

SECURING YOUR MAC WITH FILEVAULT

Mac OS X's FileVault feature encrypts all the files in your Home folder with 128-bit encryption. Such files can't be opened unless one of two passwords is entered. One password is the one you use to log in to your account. The other is a master password you set for your Mac; with this password, you can decrypt any encrypted files on your Mac, regardless of the user account with which those files are associated.

Once configured, FileVault works in the background and you won't notice it doing its job.

CAUTION

> According to Apple, FileVault can interfere with backups because it makes your Home folder appear as a single file to the backup system. This can make the individual files impossible to restore. When using FileVault, be sure you test your backup system to ensure that you can still recover files if you need to.

The following steps demonstrate how to configure FileVault:

1. Open the System Preferences application and click the Security icon. The Security pane appears (see Figure 28.6).
2. Click the Set Master Password button. The master password sheet appears. Generally, you should use this feature if there is some chance that any user of your Mac will forget his password; the master password enables you to decrypt encrypted files. However, you don't have to set a master password if you prefer not to. If not, skip the next three steps.
3. Enter the master password in the Master Password field and enter it again in the Verify field.
4. Enter a hint for the master password in the Hint field.
5. Click OK to return to the Security pane.
6. Click the Turn On FileVault button. The service starts up and you are prompted to enter your password.

Figure 28.6
Use the FileVault feature if you want to encrypt the files in your Home folder so they can't be used without a valid password.

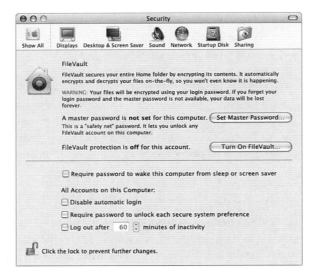

7. Enter your user account's login password and click OK. You will see a warning sheet that explains what you are doing and that activating this service can take a while (you can't log out of your account until the service has been turned on).

8. Click the Turn On FileVault button. The FileVault window appears; you can't do anything else on your Mac until FileVault has started up. This window shows you the progress of the encryption process. If you have a lot of data in your Home folder, this process can take quite some time. When the process is complete, you see the Login window.

NOTE

If you want this feature to be active for multiple user accounts, you must log in under each account and turn on FileVault.

9. Log back in to your account. You shouldn't notice any difference, but all your Home folder files will be encrypted and won't be accessible unless a valid encryption password has been entered.

CAUTION

FileVault applies only to each user account in which it is activated. And it works only on the files in each user's Home folder. Files stored outside the Home folders for which it is activated are not protected.

When you log in to your account, the files in your Home folder are decrypted automatically so you won't need to do anything else to access them. The value of FileVault is for those times when you aren't logged in to your account and someone else has access to your machine. For example, suppose someone steals your PowerBook. Although she can't access your user account without your login password, she could connect the machine to a FireWire drive with Mac OS X installed and start up from that volume. Because the files on your PowerBook's startup volume are not protected anymore (the OS on the FireWire drive is active), they are accessible. If FileVault is not on, these files are not encrypted and can be used, but if FileVault is on, these files are encrypted and are useless.

You can turn off FileVault again by clicking the Turn Off FileVault button and entering your login password.

If another user on your Mac turns on FileVault and subsequently forgets her password, you can use your Mac's master password (assuming you set one) to decrypt the files in that user's Home folder. You can provide the master password to the other user so they can decrypt their files. Then, change the master password to make sure only the "right" people have it.

SECURING YOUR MAC WITH SECURITY SETTINGS

Several other security settings are available on the Security pane (refer to Figure 28.6). These features are described in the following list:

- **Require password to wake this computer from sleep or screen saver**—If you enable this feature, a user account's login password is required to stop the screensaver or wake up the Mac from sleep.

- **Disable automatic login**—Check this box and the automatic login feature is turned off. This means that someone will have to log in into your Mac manually to be able to use it.

- **Require password to unlock each secure system preference**—When you check this box, a login password must be entered to make any changes that affect system security.

- **Log out after _ minutes of activity**—This feature logs out the current user account after the specified amount of inactivity has occurred. To use it, check the box and set the amount of time using the box. When the amount of inactive time passes, the current user is logged out automatically.

SECURING YOUR MAC BY REMOVING TRASH SECURELY

 Normally, when you delete files they are deleted from the system, but the data for those files might or might not be overwritten by other data. If not, files can sometimes be recovered by software restoration tools. If you want the files you delete to be overwritten with garbage so they can't be recovered, use the Secure Empty Trash command on the Finder's File menu instead of the normal Empty Trash command. This causes the files you delete to be overwritten so they can't be recovered.

SECURING YOUR MAC WITH KEYCHAINS

For security and other reasons (such as making online shopping more convenient), you need usernames and passwords to access network resources, whether those resources are on a local network or the Internet. After using even a few of these, you will have a large collection of usernames and passwords. Remembering these can be a challenge. Fortunately, your Mac lets you store all your usernames and passwords in a keychain. You can then apply your keychain to whatever resource you want, to use and the appropriate information is provided so you can access what you need. All you need to remember is the password that unlocks your keychain. By default, this is the same as your login password so that your keychain is used automatically. After you have added a password to your keychain, you can access the related resources without entering your keychain's password (because it is entered when you log in).

NOTE

NEW

The keychain functionality has been greatly improved for Mac OS X version 10.3, especially for Web resources you access via Safari. Although keychains worked unreliably under previous versions using Internet Explorer, they work very well under Safari. When you access a secured Web site, Safari prompts to see whether you want to add that site's username and password to your keychain. If you choose to do so, you don't have to enter this information again. When you return to the Web site, your username and password are entered automatically. This might very well be the most convenient feature of Mac OS X, version 10.3.

→ For more information about Safari and keychains, **see** "Browsing the Web with Safari," **p. 388**.

You can configure other keychains so that you can gain automatic access to secured resources during each working session. To secure those resources again, you can lock your keychain, which means the password must be entered for that keychain to be applied.

Before you can use a keychain, one has to be created. A keychain is created automatically for each user account you create. However, you can create additional keychains for specific purposes if you need to.

To use a keychain, it must be unlocked. To unlock a keychain, you enter its password when you are prompted to do so. When you log in to your user account, the default keychain for that account is unlocked automatically.

NOTE

You can store information that you want to secure using notes. For example, if you want to store your credit card information so it can't be accessed unless you are logged in to your user account, you can add it to your keychain. When you need that information, you can open the secured note in your keychain.

Many types of resources can be added to your keychain to enable you to access them, including the following:

- **AirPort network password**—When you add an Airport network password to your keychain, you can join the network by selecting it via the AirPort controls. The network's password is added automatically.

- **Application password**—Some applications require passwords to perform specific tasks. One notable example is the iTunes Music Store function. When you have your Music Store password added to your keychain, you can purchase songs with a single click of the mouse button (which can be a dangerous thing!).

- **AppleShare password**—Any passwords you use to access network volumes can also be added to your keychain.

- **Internet password**—When you need to enter passwords for Internet services, such as email accounts, adding them to your keychain makes accessing those services much more convenient because you never have to enter the password manually.

- **.Mac password**—When you enter your .Mac password in the .Mac pane of the System Preferences application, it is added to your keychain so you can work with your iDisk from the desktop without having to log in to your .Mac account.

- **Secure note**—These enable you to store information securely.

- **Web form password**—When you access your account on secure Web sites, you can add your usernames and passwords to your keychain. When you visit those sites again (via Safari), you can log in just by clicking the Login button because your username and password are entered automatically.

VIEWING AND CONFIGURING YOUR KEYCHAINS AND KEYCHAIN ITEMS

You access your keychains through the Keychain Access application by doing the following:

1. Open the Keychain Access application (Applications/Utilities folder). When the application opens, two panes appear (see Figure 28.7). In the right pane (the drawer) is a list of all the keychains that are installed. By default, you will see two of them. The login keychain is the default keychain for your user account. The System keychain is available to administrators and the root account (by default, it is empty). The contents of the selected keychain are shown in the upper-left pane of the application's window. In Figure 28.7, you can see the contents of my login keychain.

2. Select a keychain in the drawer and then a keychain item about which you want information and click the Attributes tab (see Figure 28.8). You will see information related to that keychain item, such as its name, its kind, the account to which it relates, address information, and comments you have entered about it, if any.

3. To see the item's password, check the Show Password check box. You are then prompted to confirm the keychain's password (you'll learn more about this in the next section).

28

Figure 28.7
This keychain can access the items listed in the upper pane of the window including email accounts and AppleShare volumes.

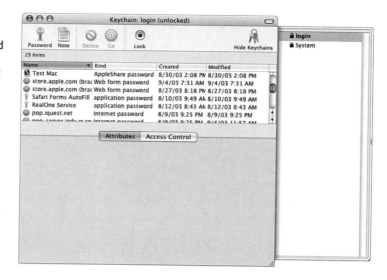

4. Confirm the password by entering it at the prompt and choosing to allow access to the item (the options you see are explained in the next section). When you return to the Attributes tab, you will see the item's password.

TIP

You can copy the password to the Clipboard by clicking the Copy Password to Clipboard button. This lets you easily paste the password where you need to use it.

Figure 28.8
You can use the Attributes tab to see information about an item installed in your keychain.

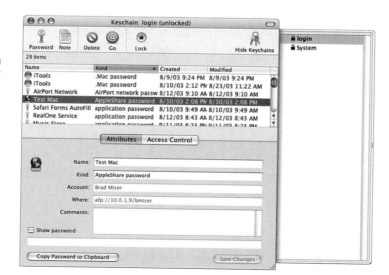

5. Click the Access Control tab. You will see a list of the applications that have access to the keychain item.

6. Use the access controls in the window to control which applications can access this item. In Figure 28.9, you can see that the Finder has access to the selected keychain item.

Figure 28.9
You can determine which applications can access a keychain item by using the Access Control tab.

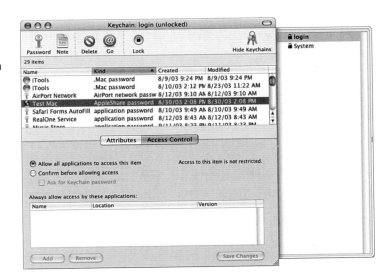

7. To allow access to the item without warning, check the "Allow all applications to access this item" radio button. You will see a warning that access to the item is not restricted.

8. To allow access but require confirmation, click the "Confirm before allowing access" radio button, and check the "Ask for Keychain password" check box if you want to be prompted for your keychain's password before access is allowed.

9. To enable an application to access the keychain item, click the Add button and select the application to which you want to provide access. Then use the preceding two steps to configure the access the application has to that item.

10. To remove an application's access to the item, select the application and click Remove.

11. Click Save Changes to save the changes to the keychain and its items.

ADDING ITEMS TO A KEYCHAIN

You can add items to a keychain in several ways, including the following:

■ When you access a resource that can provide access to a keychain, such as a file server, look for the "Add to Keychain" check box. When you check this, an item for that resource is added to your keychain. This is the most common and easiest way to add items to a keychain.

28

NOTE

> Sometimes you have to click the Options button to be able to add an item to your keychain. For example, when you mount a network volume, click Options to reveal the Add Password to Keychain check box.

- Drag a network server onto the Keychain Access window.
- Drag the Internet Resource Locator file for a Web page onto the Keychain Access window.
- Manually create an item.

CAUTION

> Not all applications support keychain access. If a particular application or resource doesn't support keychains, you won't be able to access that resource automatically. However, you can still use Keychain Access to store such an item's username and password for you, thus enabling you to recall that information easily. This also stores it more securely than writing it down on a piece of paper.

To manually add a password item to your keychain, perform the following steps:

1. Open Keychain Access (Applications/Utilities).
2. In the drawer, select the keychain to which you want to add the item (your default keychain is selected automatically).

TIP

> You can show or hide the drawer by clicking the Show Keychains or Hide Keychains button on the toolbar, respectively.

3. Select File, New Password Item; click the Password button on the toolbar; or press ⌘-N to see the New Password Item dialog box.
4. Enter the name of the item in the Name box. If you are adding an Internet resource, such as a Web page, enter its URL.
5. Enter the account name or username for the item in the Account box.
6. Enter the password for the item in the Password box.

TIP

> If you want to see the password as you type it, check the Show Typing check box. This helps you confirm you are entering the correct password. Otherwise, you see only bullets as you type.

28

7. Click Add to return to the keychain's window and see the new item you added. You will be able to access that item using your keychain. You can view and configure the new item using the steps in the previous section.

> **TIP**
>
> You can set the default keychain for your user account by opening the keychain you want to make the default one and selecting File, Make Keychain *keychainname* Default, where *keychainname* is the name of the keychain you have selected.

To add a secure note to a keychain, use the following steps:

1. Open Keychain Access.

2. In the drawer, select the keychain to which you want to add the note (your default keychain is selected automatically).

3. Select File, New Secure Note Item or click the Note button on the toolbar to see the New Secure Note Item dialog box.

4. Enter the name of the note in the Name box.

5. Enter the information you want to store in the Note box. This a freeform text field so you can enter anything you want.

6. Click Add to return to the keychain's window and see the new note you added.

7. To view the note, select it, click the Attributes tab, and click the "Show note" check box. You will see the note in the window.

> **TIP**
>
> Click the Copy Note to Clipboard button to copy the note to the Clipboard so you can paste it elsewhere.

ADDING A KEYCHAIN

You might want to add a keychain to your current account, which you can do using the following steps:

> **NOTE**
>
> You might want to move a keychain between user accounts so you don't have to re-create the items it contains.

1. Open Keychain Access (Applications/Utilities).

2. To add a keychain, select File, New Keychain or press Option-⌘-N. You will see the New Keychain dialog box.

28

3. Move to the location in which you want to save the keychain, name it, and click Create. (By default, keychains are stored in the Keychains folder in the Library folder in your Home folder. In most cases, you should store new keychains in this folder.) You are prompted to create the password for the keychain.

> **TIP**
>
> An exception to where you keep your keychains might be when you want to enable others to import your new keychain into their accounts, in which case you should store it in a location accessible to others, such as your Public folder. For example, you might want to create a keychain with Web site items on it. You could provide this to other users who would then be able to access the items contained in the keychains you install.

4. Enter the password for the keychain in the Password and Verify fields; then click OK. The new keychain is added to the list of available keychains, and you can work with it just like those already on this list.

USING KEYCHAINS

When you have a keychain configured for an account and it is unlocked, you can access the items it contains without entering your username or password. For example, when you open a server, it opens for you immediately.

> **NOTE**
>
> By the way, this is how Mac OS X can access your .Mac account without you having to log in each time. When you create a .Mac account, it is added to the keychain for the Mac OS X user account related to it. Mac OS X can use this keychain to access the .Mac account without requiring that you log in manually.

To prevent a keychain from being accessed, lock it. Do so by opening the Keychain Access application, selecting the keychain, and selecting File, Lock Keychain *keychainname*, where *keychainname* is the name of the keychain. You can also do so by pressing ⌘-L or clicking the Lock button on the toolbar.

To unlock a keychain again, select it, click the Unlock button on the toolbar, and enter the password for that keychain.

When an application must access a keychain item and is not configured to always allow access, the Confirm Access to Keychain dialog box opens and prompts you to enter a keychain's password and choose one of these three access options:

- **Deny**—If you click this, access to the item is prevented.
- **Allow Once**—A single access to the item is allowed. The next time you attempt to access it, you see the prompt again.
- **Always Allow**—Access to the item is always allowed.

NOTE

> The first time you access keychain items after the OS has been updated, such as through the Software Update application, you see the Confirm Access to Keychain prompt, even for those items for which you have selected the "always allow access" option (such as the first time you check your email after upgrading the OS). This is normal behavior. Just select the Always Allow option to reenable that behavior.

GOING FURTHER WITH KEYCHAINS

Keychain Access is actually a fairly complex application that can do more than just what I have room to show you in this section. Following are some pointers in case you are interested in exploring on your own:

- Your keychains are stored in the `Library/Keychains` folder in your Home directory. You can add a keychain from one account to another account by exporting the keychain file (use the File, Export command) to a location that can be accessed by the second account. (For example, you can copy your keychain into the Public folder of your Home directory to enable other users to add that keychain to their own accounts.) To add a keychain to a user account, open Keychain Access under that account and use the File, Import command. This is useful if you want to use the same keychain from several accounts.

- Delete a keychain either by selecting it and selecting File, Delete Keychain *keychainname*, where *keychainname* is the name of the keychain or by clicking the Delete button on the toolbar.

- If you select Edit, Change Settings for Keychain *keychainname*, where *keychainname* is the name of the keychain, you can set a keychain to lock after a specified period of time or lock when the Mac is asleep.

- If you select Edit, Change Password for Keychain *keychainname*, where *keychainname* is the name of the keychain, you can change a keychain's password.

- Select View, Show Status in Menu Bar to add a Keychain Access menu to the Finder toolbar. From this menu, you can lock or unlock keychains and access security preferences and the Keychain Access application.

- If you select Window, Keychain List or press Option-⌘-L, you see the Configure Keychain dialog box. You can use this to configure keychains for a user account or the system.

- If you select Window, Keychain First Aid or press Option-⌘-A, you see the Keychain First Aid dialog box. You can use this to verify keychains or repair a damaged keychain.

- You can access a keychain item for an Internet or network location by selecting the keychain item and clicking the Go button in the Keychain Access toolbar.

- In the keychain access prompt, you can click the Show Details button to expose the details of the keychain access being requested.

28

DEFENDING YOUR MAC FROM NET ATTACKS

The Internet is a major source of threat to the health and well-being of your Macs and the network to which they are connected. You face two fundamental types of threats: viruses and hackers. Although viruses receive more media attention, defending against viruses is easier than defending against attacks from hackers. However, with some relatively simple activity, you can protect yourself from both threats.

DEFENDING YOUR MAC FROM VIRUS ATTACKS

No matter what level of computer user you are, because of the extensive media hype about viruses, you are likely to be keenly aware of them. Although many viruses are relatively harmless, some viruses can do damage to your machine. Part of practicing smart computing is understanding viruses and taking appropriate steps to protect your machine from them.

CAUTION

> Under previous versions of the Mac OS, there were many fewer viruses on the Mac platform than for Windows or other operating systems. And, as of the release of Mac OS X, version 10.3, this is still the case. However, because Mac OS X is based on Unix, Unix viruses can be a threat to machines running Mac OS X. Until this threat is more fully understood, Mac OS X users would do well to pay additional attention to virus threats.

UNDERSTANDING THE TYPES OF VIRUSES

Although there are many types of individual viruses, there are two major groups of viruses of which you need to be aware:

- **Application viruses**—These viruses are applications that do *something* to your computer. What they do might be as harmless as displaying a silly message or as harmful as corrupting particular files on your hard drive.

- **Macro viruses**—A macro virus can be created in and launched by any application that supports macros (such as the Microsoft Office applications). When you open a file that has been infected by a macro virus, that virus (the macro) runs and performs its dirty deed.

Covering the multitude of viruses that are out there is beyond the scope of this book and, besides, there is no real need to become an expert on the viruses that exist. It is more important to understand how to protect yourself from these viruses and be able to recover from an infection should one occur.

PREVENTING VIRUS INFECTION

I hate to use this cliché, but when it comes to viruses, an ounce of prevention is indeed worth a pound of cure. The main way to avoid viruses is to avoid files that are likely to have viruses in them. Following are some practices to help you "stay clean":

- Find and use a good antivirus software program; keep the virus definitions for that application up-to-date.

- Be wary when you download files from any source, particularly email. Even if an email is apparently from someone you know, that doesn't mean the attachments it contains are safe. Some users will unknowingly transmit infected files to you (especially beginning users). Some viruses can use an email application to replicate themselves. Before you open any attachment, be sure it makes sense given who the recipient is.

- When you do download files, download them from reputable sites, such as magazine sites or directly from a software publisher's site. These sites scan files for viruses before making them available so your chances of getting an infected file are lower. Remember the expression, "Consider the source."

- After you download a file, run your antivirus software on it to ensure that it isn't infected. Most programs let you designate the folder into which you download files and automatically check files in this folder.

IDENTIFYING VIRUS INFECTION

Even with good preventive measures, you might occasionally become infected. Hopefully, you will find out you have been infected by being notified by your antivirus software—that means it is doing its job. But if you suddenly notice that your computer is acting peculiarly, you might have become infected. What does acting peculiarly mean? Viruses can have many different effects on your computer; some of the more common effects are the following:

- **Weird messages, dialog boxes, or other unexpected interface elements—** Sometimes viruses make themselves known by presenting something odd onscreen. So, if you suddenly see a strange dialog box, you might have stumbled across a virus (for example, one of the Word macro viruses causes a happy face to appear in Word's menu bar). They can also cause menu items to disappear or be changed in some way.

- **Loss in speed**—Viruses often make your computer work more slowly.

- **Disappearing files**—Some viruses cause files to be deleted or hidden.

- **Errors**—Many viruses cause various errors on your computer and prevent applications from working properly. If you haven't changed anything on your machine for a while and you suddenly start experiencing errors, you should check your computer for a possible infection.

USING ANTIVIRUS SOFTWARE

Although the best defense against viruses is being very careful about the files you transfer onto your machine, you should also obtain and use a good antivirus application. Good antivirus applications generally perform the following functions:

- Monitor activity on your computer to identify potential infection

- Periodically scan your drives to look for infections

28

- Notify you if an infection is discovered
- Repair the infected files and eliminate the virus
- Delete infected files if repairing them is impossible
- Enable you to identify particular folders that should be scanned automatically, such as the folder into which you download files
- Update themselves automatically

NOTE

Most viruses are identified by their code. The antivirus software knows about the virus's code through its virus definition file. As new viruses appear, this virus definition file needs to be updated so that the new viruses will be recognized as being viruses. You can usually obtain an updated virus definition file from the Web site of the manufacturer of your antivirus software. Most programs automate this process and can update the virus definition at intervals you set.

NOTE

One of the important things to look for in an antivirus program is that it can detect and repair macro viruses. Macro viruses are easy to create and spread, and some of them are quite nasty.

As with previous versions of the Mac OS, there are several major antivirus applications, including Norton AntiVirus for Mac and Virex.

These applications provide most of the features in the previous list, and they work well. You should obtain and use one of these applications to protect your Mac against viruses and to repair your Mac should it become infected.

If you have a .Mac account, you can download a free copy of Virex. When you download and install Virex, you can keep its virus definitions current and access other virus resources as well.

To get more information about Virex and to download it (if you have a .Mac account), visit www.mac.com and click the .Mac tab.

Viruses and You

Frankly, viruses are less of a problem than they appear to be from the tremendous amount of media hype they receive. Most of the time, you can protect yourself from viruses by being very careful about the files you receive in email or download from the Web. Because the only way for a virus to get onto your machine is for you to accept a file in which it is contained, you can protect yourself from most viruses by using common sense. For example, if you receive an email containing an oddly titled attachment (such as the famous I Love You file), you should either request more information from the sender before you open the file or simply delete the message.

This is one case is which being in the minority as a Mac user is beneficial. The vast majority of viruses are designed for Windows machines and have no affect on a Mac.

Adding and using an antivirus application makes your machine even safer, but if you are very careful about downloading files, you might find that you can get by just fine without one.

DEFENDING YOUR MAC AGAINST NET HACKERS

If you have a broadband connection to the Internet such as a cable or DSL modem, being attacked by hackers is a much more real threat than are viruses. And with a broadband connection, you *will* be attacked, daily if not hourly or even more frequently. Hackers are continuously looking for machines they can exploit, either to do damage to you or to use your machine to do damage to others (such as using your machine to launch a spam attack). Most of these attacks are carried out by applications, so they can be both automatic and continuous.

CAUTION

> Never expose a machine containing sensitive or production data to a broadband connection without protecting that machine from network attack. Doing so makes everything on such a machine vulnerable to exposure to a hacker, and the machine itself can be used to carry out attacks on other networks and machines.

There are two fundamental ways you can prevent your Mac from being hacked through your broadband Internet connection: Use a server/hub to isolate the machines on your network from the outside world or use a software firewall to protect each machine on the network from attack.

USING A SERVER AND FIREWALL TO PROTECT YOUR NETWORK

You can isolate the machines on your network from attack by placing a physical barrier between them and the public Internet. You can then use a Dynamic Host Configuration Protocol (DHCP) server that provides network address translation (NAT) protection for your network, or you can add or use a hub that contains a more sophisticated firewall to ensure that your network can't be violated. A benefit to these devices is that you can also use them to share a single Internet connection.

→ To learn how to install and use a DHCP server or firewall, **see** Chapter 27, "Sharing an Internet Connection," **p. 855**.

NOTE

> One of the easiest and best ways to protect machines on a local network from attack and to share an Internet connection is to install an AirPort hardware access point. These devices provide NAT protection of any computers that obtain Internet service through them, and for most users, this is an adequate level of protection from hacking.

28

USING A SOFTWARE FIREWALL TO PROTECT YOUR NETWORK

You can also install and use a software firewall; a software firewall prevents unexpected access to your Mac from the Internet. Software firewalls can be quite effective and might be the best solution if you have only a single Mac connected to the Internet.

CAUTION

> Unlike a hardware firewall or NAT hub, a software firewall must be installed on each computer attached to your network.

A software firewall works by blocking access to specific ports on your Mac; these ports are linked to specific services. If hackers can access these ports on your machine, they can use them to attack your machine directly to launch attacks on other computers, servers, and networks (such as denial-of-service attacks, in which a system is overloaded by repeated requests from many machines).

Because Mac OS X is based on Unix, it has built-in firewall protection. You can enable this firewall to protect a Mac from Net attacks by doing the following:

1. Open the System Preferences utility.
2. Click the Sharing icon to open the Sharing pane.
3. Click the Firewall tab.
4. Click the Start button. The firewall begins working and blocks inappropriate requests for access to your Mac (see Figure 28.10).

Figure 28.10
Enable Mac OS X's built-in firewall by clicking the Start button on the Firewall tab.

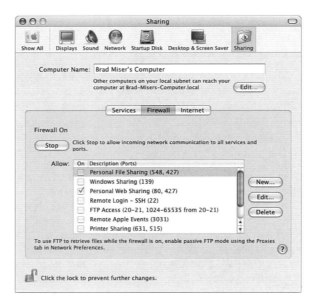

CAUTION

> To enable a service to access your Mac through the firewall, you need to enable the service on the Services tab first.

5. If you want to enable specific ports for a service that you are allowing access through the firewall, select the service and click Edit. (You can't change the ports for built-in services, such as personal file sharing.)

Only the services you allow will be permitted to access your Mac. All others will be denied. This provides more than adequate protection for most Mac users.

You can gain more specific control over the firewall if you choose to. However, configuring this firewall directly requires a fairly complete understanding of Unix and firewalls and requires more energy and time than most Mac users will care to spend on it. A better solution is to use an application that provides an interface for the firewall so it is much easier to configure.

MAC OS X TO THE MAX: GOING FURTHER WITH DISK UTILITY

Disk Utility is a very powerful and useful application. Unfortunately, covering all its functionality is beyond the scope of this chapter. Following are some hints about other tasks for which you can use it:

- **Create disk images**—You can create disk images from files, folders, or even drives and volumes. Just like other disk images you work with, you can easily put your disk images on CD, use them to quickly re-create a set of data in multiple locations, and so on. The commands you use to create and work with disk images are on the Images menu.

- **Burn CDs and DVDs**—Disk Utility enables you to burn CDs or DVDs from disk images. You can also use it to create multisession discs—something you can't do from the Finder's Burn command. Use the Burn button or the Burn command on the Images menu to access the application's burn functionality.

- **Work with disk images**—As you mount disk images in Disk Utility, it tracks those images in the lower part of the left pane so you can work with them again by selecting them. This makes accessing these images simple.

TIP

> To remove a disk image from Disk Utility, drag its icon out of the application window.

- **Mount, unmount, or eject volumes**—You can use the mount, unmount, and eject buttons and commands to perform those actions for disks, discs, volumes, and disk images.

28

- **Restore any folder, volume, or disk**—You can create a disk image from any source (such as a folder or volume) and use the application's command to restore that information on a disk. For example, if you want to replicate a set of software on multiple machines, you can create a disk image and use the Restore function on each machine to re-create that data. After you have created the disk image, use the Restore tab to restore it.

- **Access a log file**—As you perform actions with it, Disk Utility maintains a complete log of the actions it performs. To access this log, select File, Log or press ⌘-L. The Log opens and you can view its contents. This provides a complete history of your disk maintenance tasks.

- **Configure RAID disks**—Redundant array of independent disks (RAID) is a scheme whereby multiple disks can be linked to work together for performance and reliability reasons (for example, disks can be mirrored so the same information is always stored on more than one disk in case of disk failure). You can use the RAID tab in Disk Utility to configure RAID services on a machine.

- **Fix OS 9 permissions**—Mac OS 9 disks use slightly different permissions than do Mac OS X disks. Use the Fix OS 9 Permissions command on the File menu to repair the permissions on Mac OS 9 volumes and disks.

28

SOLVING MAC PROBLEMS

29

HANDLING MAC PROBLEMS

Even though Mac OS X is more stable than any previous version of the Mac OS, you will inevitably experience problems. You might experience crashes or hangs, or an application just might not work the way it is supposed to. You might even experience minor annoyances, such as having to do something in several steps that should require only one. In any case, one of these days, you will run into a situation that requires you to troubleshoot and solve a problem.

Dealing with a problem, especially related to Mac OS X, can be intimidating even if you are a power user because there is so much going on that you might not understand. Although the top-level Mac interface is still relatively simple and intuitive, the Unix underpinnings of the OS have added a tremendous amount of complexity to the operating system. Nowhere is this more apparent than when you are trying to solve a problem. As you use the various tools that are part of Mac OS X to diagnose and solve a problem, you are likely to run into information that doesn't make much sense to you—unless you have lived in the Unix world for a long time, in which case you'll feel right at home. However, the rest of us Mac users must do without most of the problem-solving tricks that worked so well in the OS in versions 9 and earlier. Instead, we need to learn a new bag of tricks for those times when things aren't going our way.

NOTE

> Some of the most common troubleshooting techniques under Mac OS 9 and earlier, such as rebuilding the desktop, managing RAM, and so on, are no longer applicable under Mac OS X.

Fortunately, you don't need to be a Unix expert to be able to troubleshoot and solve Mac OS X problems. Mostly, what is required is the ability to carefully observe what is happening and to follow logical trails. Being able to communicate clearly to others is also very important when you need to get help from someone else.

From the title of this chapter, you might be under the impression that you will be seeing many solutions to specific Mac problems you might encounter. If that is your expectation, I must be up front with you here. There simply isn't room in this book to provide lists of problems and solutions that would be detailed enough to help you with the specific problems you will face.

Instead, the purpose of this chapter is to help you learn *how* to troubleshoot Mac OS X problems in general. You can then apply the techniques and tools you will learn about in this chapter to any problems you face; these techniques will help you solve problems on your own. In the long run, the strategies you need to know to solve problems will be much more useful to you than lists of problems that might or might not include those you experience.

NOTE

> The goal of this chapter is to help you learn general problem-solving techniques, but solutions to some specific problems you might encounter are explained in the "Troubleshooting" sections in many chapters of this book.

UNDERSTANDING THE CAUSES OF PROBLEMS

The causes of the problems you experience will be one—or a combination—of five general types of problems:

- User error
- Bugs
- Conflicting software
- Attacks on your system
- Hardware failures

Each of these problems is detailed in the sections that follow.

USER ERROR

The results of many investigations into aviation accidents can often be summed up with the phrase "pilot error." Similarly, this is often the case with an "accident" in the Mac world. Many problems are the direct result of a user (this means you) doing something improperly—or not doing something properly. Some of the things you might do to cause problems for yourself are the following:

- **Not following instructions**—This is the big one. Many times, you will cause your own problems simply because you fail to follow the instructions provided with software or hardware. You should become a believer in the old adage "if all else fails, follow the instructions."

- **Operating a machine past its limits**—If you know that a particular application requires a computer with a G4 processor, but you try to run it on a G3-equipped Mac, you are bound to have troubles. If you live on the edge of your machine's capabilities, you will have more problems than you might with a more capable machine.

- **Not doing proper maintenance on your system**—If you don't keep an eye out for patches and updates to Mac OS X as well as the applications you use, you might experience more problems than you have to. Take advantage of the many ways in which you can keep your system up-to-date. For example, Mac OS X's Software Update feature can help you keep your system and all your Apple applications current.

- **Not keeping enough free space on a drive**—This is a fairly common cause of problems. All drives need to have free space to be capable of storing files, sometimes temporarily. If a drive is full, or very close to being full, you will have problems as you try

29

to store more data on it. This can be an even bigger problem under Mac OS X because virtual memory is always on—low disk space can cause problems related to insufficient RAM as well.

BUGS

Sometimes the cause of a problem is a bug inherent in the design of the products involved. The bug can be a design flaw, a manufacturing problem, or a conflict with some other part of your system. Although companies often do the best they can to prevent bugs, there is usually no way to prevent all the possible bugs in a product. Many bugs aren't revealed until a piece of software or hardware is combined with some other pieces of hardware or software.

CONFLICTING SOFTWARE

One of the most common causes of problems is conflicting software. Some programs just don't play well with others. Conflicts are often associated with system-level applications and resources because they modify the low-level operations of the system. However, applications can also conflict with one another and cause you headaches.

Because Mac OS X features protected memory, these types of conflicts are much less common under Mac OS X than they were under previous versions of the Mac OS. Because of protected memory, you aren't likely to experience any conflicts between applications. However, there is still the potential for conflict between software that modifies the system and the core OS.

ATTACKS ON YOUR SYSTEM

The two primary sources of attacks on your system come from the outside: viruses and hackers. Viruses can cause all sorts of problems from simple and silly messages appearing to strange dialog boxes to major system crashes and even data deletions or hard disk failures. However, viruses that do serious damage have traditionally been fairly rare on the Mac, but because Mac OS X is based on Unix, it remains to be seen whether viruses will be a more significant source of concern than they have been for Mac users. Fortunately, viruses are among the easier problems to avoid. On the other hand, if you use a broadband connection to the Internet, your Mac will be subjected to all sorts of hackers who want to do damage to you or others. These are definitely the more serious of the two possible sources of attacks.

NOTE

> Although attacks are normally associated with someone from outside your local network, this is not always the case. Sometimes, even unknowingly (such as in an email-based virus attack), users on your local network can wreak havoc on your system. The proper use of user accounts and permissions and a bit of paying attention will go a long way toward preventing incursions on your Mac from a local user.

→ To learn how to defend yourself against these attacks, **see** "Defending Your Mac from Net Attacks," **p. 908**.

HARDWARE FAILURES

The most unlikely cause of problems is a hardware failure. Although hardware does fail now and again, it doesn't happen very often. Hardware failures are most likely to occur immediately after you start using a new piece of hardware or close to the end of its useful life. Sometimes, you can induce a hardware failure when you upgrade a machine or perform some other type of maintenance on it—for example, if you install new RAM in a machine but fail to seat a RAM chip properly.

The most common problems associated with hardware devices are actually related to the device drivers that enable the OS to communicate with the device.

PREVENTING PROBLEMS

It is better to prevent problems than to try to solve them. Following are three techniques you can employ to minimize the problems you experience:

- **Maintain your Mac properly and protect it**—This will go a long way toward minimizing your problems.

→ For information about protecting and maintaining your Mac, **see** Chapter 28, "Maintaining and Protecting Your Mac," **p. 873**.

- **Be cautious about upgrades, updaters, and other changes to the system software or applications**—Generally, you should wait a period of time after an upgrade is released before putting it on your system. You should always carefully evaluate the benefits of a new version of an application versus the potential for problems it might introduce. This holds true for updaters and patches as well. If you are not experiencing the problems that are solved by an updater or a patch, you might be better off without it.

  You should try to keep a log that records the date and time when you make significant changes to your system, such as adding new software, changing network settings, and so on. Such a log can help you identify possible causes of problems when a time lag exists between when you make a change and when problems occur. Mac OS X's Software Update feature maintains such a log for you automatically. But when you make changes outside of that tool, you will have to record the relevant information manually.

TIP

> If you support more than one computer, you should have a test system on which you can install new software to test for a while before exposing other systems to it.

29

■ **Make as few changes as possible at one time**—There are at least two reasons you should make changes to your system (such as installing software, making major configuration changes, and so on) incrementally. The first and most important is that making multiple changes at one time can obscure the cause of problems. For example, if you install three or four applications at once and then experience problems, determining which of the applications you installed is causing the problem will be difficult. The second reason is that sometimes making multiple changes at once can cause problems for you. When you change something significant, go slowly and take one step at a time. Introduce changes only after you are fairly sure that the changes you previously introduced are working properly.

ASSESSING YOUR MAC

Key to troubleshooting and solving problems that you can't prevent is being able to accurately and precisely assess how your Mac is performing and knowing the specific configuration of your system. Mac OS X offers many more diagnostic tools than previous versions of the OS did; however, several of these tools are quite complicated. Still, even if you are not able to interpret all their output, people who are trying to help might be able to, so even in this case it is useful for you to know how to use them. You should understand how to use these tools before you need them.

NOTE

> If you choose Apple menu, About This Mac, you will see a window displaying the version of the Mac OS X you are running, the amount of RAM installed in your machine, and the specific processors it contains. You can also click the Software Update button to move to that pane in the System Preferences application or click More Info to move into the System Profiler. In Mac OS 9 and earlier, you could also get information about the RAM allocations for the applications running on your machine, switch among applications, and so on. Because Mac OS X manages RAM for you, this information is no longer valid, so the About This Mac window no longer serves the purposes it once did. However, for a quick insight into these major system parameters, it is a useful reference.

TIP

> If you click the Mac OS X version number shown in the About This Mac window, you will see the specific build number of the version you are using. Click this information and you will see your Mac's serial number.

USING THE SYSTEM PROFILER TO CREATE A SYSTEM PROFILE

For quite some time, the Mac OS has included the Apple System Profiler application, now just called System Profiler. This application enables you to get a detailed view into your system at a particular point in time.

29

To create a profile of your system, launch the System Profiler (Applications/Utilities directory). The System Profiler provides a window with two panes (see Figure 29.1). In the left pane is a list of areas about which you can get information, including Hardware, Software, Network, and Logs. The Hardware section is further organized into various aspects of your system, such as Memory, PCI/AGP cards, ATA, SCSI, and so on. The Software area is organized into Applications and Extensions. When you select an item in the left pane, detailed information about that item appears in the right pane. For example, in Figure 29.1, the Hardware item is selected, which provides an overview of a machine's hardware configuration.

Figure 29.1
The System Profiler provides detailed information about the hardware and software that make up your system.

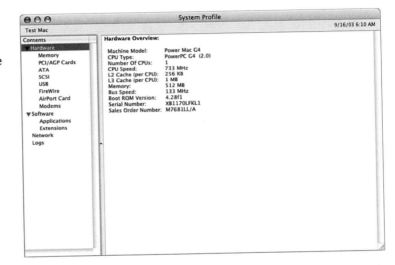

TIP

You can also open the System Profiler by clicking the More Info button that appears in the About This Mac widow.

Click the category for the part of the system about which you want information. For example, to see the memory configuration of your machine, click the Memory category. In the right pane is each memory slot the machine contains. When a chip is installed in a slot, you can select the chip and see detailed information about it in the lower part of the pane (see Figure 29.2).

Three views are available in System Profiler; you can select the view on the View menu. The Standard Report (press (⌘-2) is the default view, whereas the Short Report (press ⌘-1) hides the detail under the Software and the Logs categories. The Extended Report (press ⌘-3) adds the Framework category under Software; otherwise, it is the same as the Standard Report.

Figure 29.2
The Memory category enables you to get information about the memory configuration of your Mac.

29

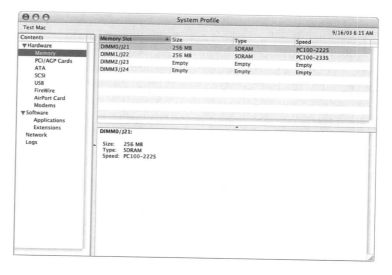

The categories available in System Profiler provide the following information:

- **Hardware**—This area provides an overview of the hardware that is part of your machine. You will see the type of Mac, the CPU(s) it includes, cache information, memory details, and other hardware information.

- **Hardware, Memory**—Use this category to view detailed information about the composition of your machine's memory.

- **Hardware, PCI/AGP Cards**—This category provides details about the PCI cards installed in a machine, such as the default graphics card. You can select a card in the upper window to get its details in the lower window.

- **Hardware, ATA**—Use this category to view detailed information about the hard drive and other drives installed in the machine. This information is organized by the various ATA buses in the machine. Again, select a device or volume in the upper pane to get detailed information about it in the lower pane (see Figure 29.3).

NOTE
> The drive on the ATA-3 bus in Figure 29.3 is an Apple SuperDrive, which is actually a Pioneer DVD-RW drive, model DVR-103.

- **Hardware, SCSI**—Here you see information about any SCSI devices included in your system.

- **Hardware, USB**—This particularly useful tab shows all the USB devices attached to your system. If you are having trouble with a specific device, use this information to see whether your Mac recognizes a device properly. You can also see the speed at which USB devices are communicating with your Mac.

Figure 29.3
Here you can see that this machine has a single hard drive on the ATA-4 bus and a DVD-RW drive in the ATA-3 bus.

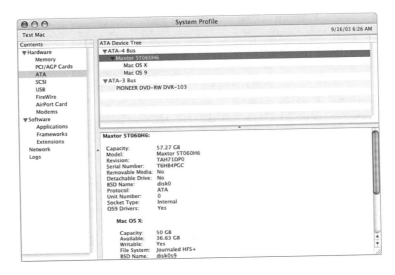

- **Hardware, FireWire**—This category displays information about the FireWire buses that are part of your Mac and shows details about any devices connected to them. If your Mac includes both FireWire 400 and FireWire 800, you will see each type listed in the window.

- **Hardware, AirPort Card**—View this to see the type of AirPort card installed in your Mac and the current AirPort network you are using, among other AirPort information.

- **Hardware, Modems**—If your Mac includes a modem, use this category to get information about it.

- **Software**—This provides an overview of your system software, including version and build, kernel version, boot volume (startup volume), computer name, and current user.

- **Software, Applications**—This category displays information about the applications installed on your startup volume. In the upper part of the pane is the application name, version number, and modification date. If you select an application, in the lower part of the pane you will see its version, modification date, location, and Info String (which is usually a copyright statement from the manufacturer).

- **Software, Frameworks**—This category lists the Mac OS X frameworks installed on your startup volume. In the upper pane, you see the name of the framework, its version, and when it was last modified. If you select a framework, in the lower part of the pane you will see its version, modification date, location, Info String (which can sometimes tell you more about the framework), and whether it is private.

- **Software, Extensions**—Here, you will see the Mac OS X extensions installed on your startup volume. The information available for each is similar to that available for frameworks. It also includes information about whether the extensions have been loaded and whether it is recognized as a valid and authenticated extension.

- **Network**—This category presents information about each network interface that is available, such as AirPort, built-in Ethernet, Bluetooth, an internal modem, and so on.

- **Logs**—This tab provides access to the Console and System logs. Each log can be selected to reveal its details. For example, in Figure 29.4, you can see the detailed information in the System log for September 14th. The information in these logs is quite technical. However, you can often review the logs for a specific point in time during which you were having trouble to assess what was happening with your system. For example, you can see significant events that occurred or didn't occur successfully. This can often reveal the source of a problem. Also, if you need to ask for help, accessing these logs can enable you to provide more specific information to the person trying to help you and might result in a problem being solved more quickly.

Figure 29.4
Log files, such as the system log, can be useful when you are troubleshooting problems.

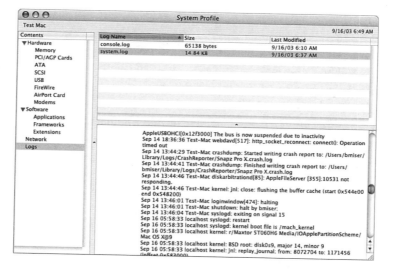

You should periodically export a Profiler report to disk and print it. If you need to get help with a problem, you can often email the report to the people trying to help you. If you have a problem that prevents your machine from starting up, you can use the hard copy version. To generate a profile for your system, do the following steps:

1. Launch the System Profiler.

2. Select File, Export, Rich Text or File, Export, Plain Text. The difference between these options is whether the report is formatted. Often, Plain Text is a better choice if you are going to email the information to someone else.

3. In the resulting Save sheet, name the file, choose a location in which to save it, and click Save. The profile is exported in the format you selected.

Open the report you exported to see the same information that was presented in the Profiler application (see Figure 29.5).

Figure 29.5
Keeping a recent Profiler report on hand can provide useful information when you are solving a problem yourself and when you need to ask for help.

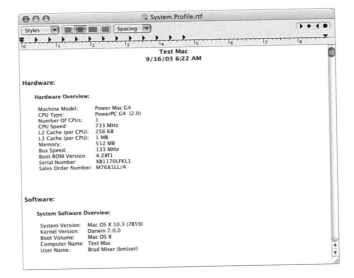

The System Profiler menus contain some additional commands that might be useful. For example, View, Refresh causes System Profiler to refresh all its information. If you select File, Save As, a report is saved in the System Profiler format, which means you can open it in the System Profiler application. You can select File, Print to print a hard copy of a report.

USING THE ACTIVITY MONITOR TO UNDERSTAND AND MANAGE PROCESSES

To provide services, your Mac runs many processes. These processes fall into many categories. User processes are those that are related to specific user accounts, such as running an application. Administrator (also called root) processes are those that are fundamental to the OS and are controlled by the OS, such as the Desktop database. NetBoot processes are those related to network services, such as Apple File Server.

29

NOTE

Under previous versions of Mac OS X, the functionality provided by Activity Monitor was provided by the Process Viewer and CPU Monitor. These applications are combined into the Activity Monitor.

The Activity Monitor application enables you to get detailed information about any process running on your Mac at any point in time. This information can be useful when it comes time to troubleshoot your system. You can also use the Activity Monitor to kill any running process.

The following steps walk you through using the Activity Monitor:

1. Open Activity Monitor (Applications/Utilities directory). You will see a window providing a listing of all the processes on the machine (see Figure 29.6).

Figure 29.6
Activity Monitor enables you to get detailed information about any process on your Mac.

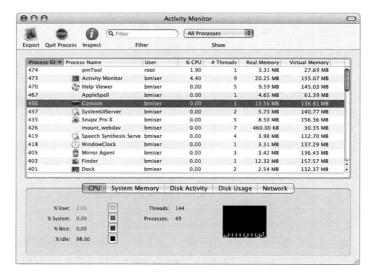

2. Select the category of process you want to view from the Show pop-up menu. There are many options from which to choose, and the option you choose will depend on the types of processes in which you are interested. For example, select My Processes to see the processes that are related to your user account. The processes shown in the window is refreshed according to the category you select.

For each process shown in the window, you can see the following information:

■ **Process ID**—Each process running on your Mac is assigned a unique ID number. This number can change each time the process is started.

■ **Process Name**—Unlike process number, a process's name is constant.

- **User**—This identifies the specific user running the process. In addition to the user accounts on your machine, you will see root processes.
- **% CPU**—This percentage indicates the amount of CPU processing that a process is consuming. This is one of the more useful pieces of data. Any process should be consuming a small percentage of the available CPU processing power. If a process is consuming a large amount, such as something more than 90%, that usually indicates the process is having trouble and should be stopped.
- **# Threads**—Processes can run in different threads within the processor. This column indicates how many threads a process is using. Unless you have a detailed understanding of how processors work, this isn't likely to be meaningful.
- **Real Memory**—This indicates how much physical RAM is being used by the process.
- **Virtual Memory**—This indicates how much virtual RAM is being used by the process.

The following list outlines some additional process tasks you can perform in Activity Monitor:

- **Open a sheet that enables you to quit the process normally or to force it to quit**—Select a running process and either click Stop Process or press Option-⌘-Q to open this sheet. You can use this to stop a process that is hung. For hung processes, use Force Quit; for processes that are running normally, use Quit.
- **Sort the processes shown in the window**—You do this by clicking the column by which you want them sorted. The current sort criterion is shown by the highlighted column name. You can reverse the direction of the sort with the sort order button that is located next to the column heading.

> **TIP**
>
> Sorting the window by the Real Memory or % CPU column is useful because you can see which processes are consuming the most system memory. If a process is consuming a large amount of memory (such as 80%), that can indicate something is wrong with the application. Sorting by process status can also be a useful way to identify processes that are currently hung.

- **Find specific processes**—You do this by typing in the Filter box. The list is reduced to only those processes that contain the text you type.
- **Open the Inspector window**—You double-click or select a process and then either click Inspect or press ⌘-I. The Inspector window opens and you see additional information about the process, including the parent process and recent hangs (see Figure 29.7). You can click the Memory tab to see detailed memory usage information for the process. Click the Statistics tab to get information about the threads, CPU time, and other technical specifications. Click Open Files to see the open files related to the process.

Figure 29.7
With the Process Inspector, no process can hide.

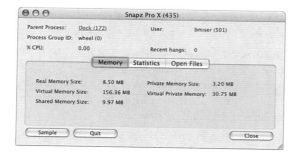

TIP

If you click the Sample button, you will see yet another window that provides even more technical information about a process.

- **Change the rate at which process information is updated**—You do this by selecting Monitor, Update Frequency; then you select the frequency you want to use, such as every 5 seconds. Increasing the sample rate provides data closer to real time.

USING THE ACTIVITY MONITOR TO MONITOR SYSTEM ACTIVITY

The Activity Monitor application also enables you to gain insight into the following system activities:

- **CPU Usage**—You can monitor the CPU activity of the processors in your Mac. This gives you a good idea of the resources being used at any moment in time. When CPU usage becomes close to the upper limit, this usually indicates a problem.

- **System Memory**—Using this tool, you can view the usage of various types of system memory, such as physical RAM and virtual memory. You can also view the free memory of your system, which can be useful to determine whether you need to add more memory resources to your Mac.

- **Disk Activity**—This tool enables you to view the performance of your machine when reading and writing data to disk.

- **Disk Usage**—This area enables you to see the space breakdown of a selected disk (see Figure 29.8).

- **Network**—This tool provides information about the communication across your network interface, such as via Ethernet.

To access this information, do the following:

1. Open Activity Monitor.
2. At the bottom of the window, click the tab for the information in which you are interested. The bottom part of the window displays the selected information.

29

Figure 29.8
The Disk Usage information shows that the disk called Mac OS X currently has about 37GB of free space.

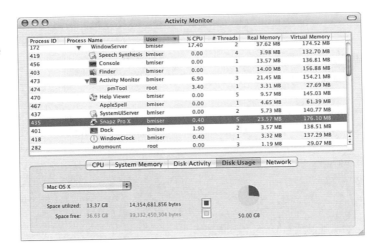

You can display system activity monitoring information on your desktop in a number of ways. For example, you can display CPU usage information on the desktop and display an icon showing other information on the Dock (see Figure 29.9). The monitoring options you have are listed in Table 29.1.

Figure 29.9
Several options are available for real-time performance monitoring from the desktop.

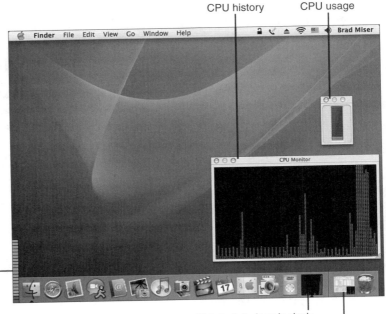

TABLE 29.1   MONITORING OPTIONS IN ACTIVITY MONITOR

Command	Keyboard Shortcut	What It Does
Monitor, Show Activity Monitor	⌘-1	Opens the Activity Monitor window.
Monitor, Show CPU Usage	⌘-2	Opens a window containing a bar for each processor that graphically displays its activity level.
Monitor, Floating CPU Window, Show Horizontally	⌘-4	Opens a bar showing activity for each processor. The bar is anchored in the lower-left corner of the desktop and is oriented horizontally.
Monitor, Floating CPU Window, Show Vertically	⌘-5	Opens a bar showing activity for each processor. The bar is anchored in the lower-left corner of the desktop and is oriented vertically.
Monitor, Floating CPU Window, Do not show		Closes the Floating CPU window.
Monitor, Show CPU History	⌘-3	Opens a window that tracks processor activity over time.
Monitor, Clear CPU History		Starts the CPU History window over again.
Monitor, Show CPU monitors on top of other windows		When this option is selected, all CPU monitor windows always appear on top of other windows. When not selected, the CPU monitoring windows can be hidden by other windows.
Monitor, Dock Icon, Show CPU Usage		Shows a CPU Usage window on the Dock.
Monitor, Dock Icon, Show CPU History		Shows a CPU History window on the Dock.
Monitor, Dock Icon, Show Network Usage		Shows a Network Usage window on the Dock.
Monitor, Dock Icon, Show Disk Activity		Shows a Disk Activity window on the Dock.
Monitor, Dock Icon, Show Memory Usage		Shows a Memory Usage window on the Dock.
Monitor, Dock Icon, Show Application Icon		Shows the Activity Monitor on the Dock instead of a monitoring window.

Command	Keyboard Shortcut	What It Does
Monitor, Update Frequency, Frequency		Changes the frequency at which the Activity Monitor monitors processors. The frequency can be .5 second, 1 second, 2 seconds, or 5 seconds.

TIP

When you choose a frequency, it affects only the monitor of processes. The monitors always display information in real time.

Monitoring is available only while Activity Monitor is running. When you quit the application, all monitoring disappears. If you want to display the monitoring tools but hide the Activity Monitor window itself, you must minimize or close the Activity Monitor window.

Viewing System Activity with Top

The Top window is a Unix window that provides detailed information about the current operation of your Mac. To access it, open a command-line application such as Terminal or X11, type **top**, and press Return.

The Top window provides detailed information about your system, although not in the most easily understood format (see Figure 29.10). At the top of the Top window, you see a summary of the activity on your machine; the lower part of the window lists all the running processes and detailed information about each.

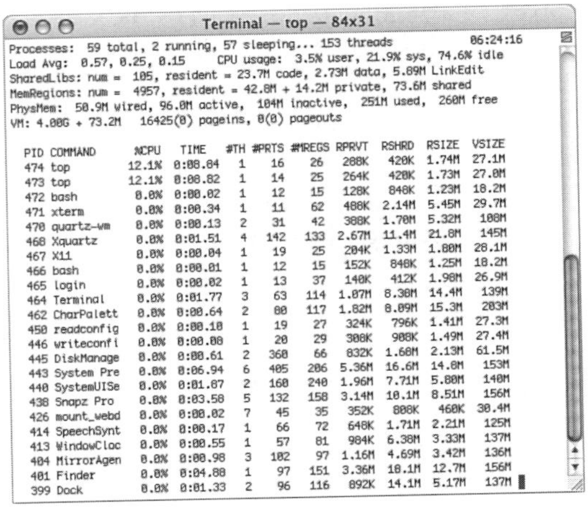

Figure 29.10
Using Top can be a bit intimidating, but the information it provides is worth getting to know.

In the summary area of the window, you can see how many processes are running versus the number sleeping, how many threads are running, the average loads, and the percentage of CPU usage of user processes versus system usage. The PhysMem information contains data about your RAM. For example, the amount shown as active is the RAM currently being used by running processes. The VM information provides data about the virtual memory being used.

NOTE

> You can get similar information in an easier-to-use format by using Activity Monitor.

In the lower part of the window, you see a table that provides data on each process that is similar to the information in the Activity Monitor. For example, you see the PID, which is the same Process ID as is displayed for a process in the Activity Monitor. You can also see the percentage of CPU use, the processor time, and other more technical information. Much of this information will probably not be useful to you unless you are quite technically oriented; however, it can be useful to others when you are trying to get help.

You can save the information seen in the Top window by selecting the information in the window and selecting File, Save Selected Text As. This text file can be useful or can be provided to someone else when you are getting help with a problem.

TIP

> To stop the Top process, press Ctrl-C.

USING THE CONSOLE TO VIEW LOGS

The Console application provides a window to which Mac OS X writes system messages you can view, most notably various logs your Mac creates as it works (or doesn't work as in the case of crash logs). These messages are mostly error messages; some of these can be useful when you are troubleshooting problems (see Figure 29.11). The messages you see are quite technical; unless you are a programmer or are extremely technically knowledgeable, you might not be able to understand all their detail. However, Console messages can be helpful to understand what was happening when something went wrong and when you are communicating a problem to someone else.

You can choose the log that is displayed in the Console window in a number of ways:

- **Click the Logs button in the toolbar**—You will see a list of all available logs organized into categories. You can expand a category to show the logs contained in that category. When you select a log, it appears in the Console window.
- **Select File, Open Console Log (or press Shift-⌘-O)**—This open that log. Or, you can select Open System Log (or press Option-⌘-O) to open the System log.

■ **Select File, Open Quickly**—Then choose the log you want to see on the hierarchical menu that appears.

Figure 29.11
Here the Console is displaying a crash log.

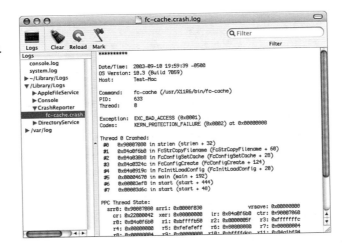

A number of logs is available through the Console, and each provides a specific type of information, as you can see in Table 29.2.

TABLE 29.2   LOGS AVAILABLE IN THE CONSOLE

Log Name	Information It Provides
console.log	This log lists events related to the core operation of your Mac, such as when specific events occurred. Reviewing this log can sometimes give you insight into failed processes that might be causing problems for you, but that you might not be aware of because an application didn't crash.
system.log	Whereas the console.log displays mostly errors, the system.log shows all events that have occurred for the system, such as when specific processes start up. You see the date and time for each event.
~/Library/Logs	This category of logs provides information related to your user account (indicated by the ~). The specific logs you see in this category depend on what you are running at any point in time. You will always see the CrashReporter log for each application that has crashed. You might also see logs for various processes, such as the MirrorAgent.log when you are using an iDisk that is synchronized on your Mac.
/Library/Logs	This category presents a set of logs related to the system. These include a system-level crash reporter along with many logs for various system services.
/var/log	This category contains many logs related to various processes. For example, you can choose the install.log to see a list of all installations you have done on your Mac or ftp.log to see information related to FTP access of your machine.

29

NOTE

You must be logged in under an account to see its logs. Even if another user is currently logged in while you are using your user account, you will still see only your logs.

You are most likely to use the Console to troubleshoot problems. To do so, use the following steps:

1. Open the Console and choose the log you want to view. For example, if an application has crashed, find that application's crash log, which will be located in the CrashReporter category within the ~/Library/Logs set of logs.

2. View the information you see. At the top of the log window, you will see summary information. Moving down the screen shows you the very technical log detail (see Figure 29.12).

Figure 29.12
This CrashReporter log shows information about a crash of the TextEdit application.

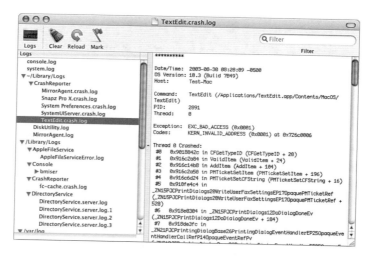

3. Save a copy of the log by selecting File, Save a Copy As.

4. Name the log, select a save location, and press Return.

5. In the Console, click the Clear button on the toolbar. The log's information is erased.

6. Repeat the steps that lead to the crash if you can. If not, just keeping doing what you were trying to do.

7. If the crash occurs again, repeat steps 1–4 to view the crash log. Compare the log to what you viewed in step 2. This might tell you whether it is the same problem or not.

8. If you can't solve the problem on your own, save the new log information so you can provide both logs to whomever you contact for help.

If you aren't very technically inclined, the information you see in the logs won't be understandable. However, you can still glean useful information such as the general cause of a problem and specific information about when it occurred. That information will often help you pinpoint exactly what was happening when a problem occurred, which is often critical to being able to solve it.

Here are a few other Console tips:

- You can open multiple Console windows at the same time by selecting File, New Log Window or pressing ⌘-N. This is useful when comparing different logs.
- You can reload the information in a log by viewing it and clicking the Reload button; by selecting File, Reload; or by pressing ⌘-R.
- You can use the Filter tool to search for specific log items.

SOLVING PROBLEMS

If you understand the general techniques you should use when troubleshooting, you will be able to handle almost all the problems you are likely to encounter. Having a good understanding of what you need to do will also make you more confident, which in turn will help you be more effective.

The general process of solving problems can be broken down into four phases, which are the following:

1. Implementing a workaround
2. Understanding and describing your problem
3. Fixing problems yourself
4. Getting help

You should work through these phases in the order in which they are listed. Doing so will help you solve your problem as efficiently as possible.

IMPLEMENTING A WORKAROUND

One of the tough things about troubleshooting is that you usually have to do it at an inconvenient time—for example, in the middle of a big project. At times like these, you are likely to feel stress, which can lead to frustration, which in turn often leads to hasty actions. Haste will often drive you down the wrong path.

Effective troubleshooting requires a cool head. The best approach when you are working under a deadline is to find a quick workaround for the problem that will enable you to complete the job you need to get done immediately. Then you can come back and really fix the problem later when you are more in a "troubleshooting" frame of mind.

There are many types of workarounds you might be able to implement to get you working well enough to meet your immediate needs. Some examples are the following:

- **Use a different application to complete the project**—If your trouble is with a specific application, use an alternative one to get the project done.

- **Log in from your clean user account**—Some problems are related to corrupted preferences and other files that are part of your user account. If you followed my recommendation to create a clean user account, log in under that account and try to complete your work.

- **Restart from an alternative startup volume**—If the problem is related to the system itself, use one of your alternative startup volumes until you have time to fix your current one.

- **Restart in Mac OS 9**—If the application you need is available under Mac OS 9 and you have a Mac that can be started up under Mac OS 9, restart your Mac in Mac OS 9 and get back to work. Not all Macs are capable of this, so it isn't an option for everyone.

- **Use a different Mac**—If you use your Mac for important work, you should consider having a backup machine so you can switch to it in times of trouble.

UNDERSTANDING AND DESCRIBING YOUR PROBLEM

When you start to troubleshoot, the most important thing you can do is to understand your problem in as much detail as possible. This understanding will enable you to know what you need to do to correct the problem. As you gain insight into your problem, you should be able to describe it in detail; this will help you get help from others if you are not able to solve the problem yourself.

Use the assessment tools, such as the Activity Monitor and the Console, that you learned about earlier in this chapter to help you understand what is happening.

PUTTING THE PROBLEM IN CONTEXT

Many problems are triggered by something you do (this doesn't mean you cause the problem, but that some action you take initiates the problem). When a problem happens, think about what you were doing immediately before the problem occurred. Following are some questions you need to answer:

- Which applications and processes were running (not only the particular one with which you were working)?

- What, specifically, were you trying to do (print, save, format, and so on)?

- Have you made any changes to the computer recently (installed software, changed settings, and so on)?

NOTE

If you create a system change log as was suggested earlier, answering the last question in the previous list will be much easier. Remember to use the Software Update logs to track changes to your Apple software, including those made to the OS itself. You can also view the install log as explained in the previous section to see which installers have been run recently.

The answers to these questions provide significant clues to help you figure out what is triggering the problem. Identifying the trigger goes a long way toward identifying the cause.

TRYING TO REPEAT THE PROBLEM

When a problem occurs, you should recover the best you can and then try to make the problem happen again. Try to re-create everything that was happening when the problem first appeared.

CAUTION

Obviously, you shouldn't intentionally re-create a problem in such a way that you will lose data. Make sure that your data is safe by having a good backup before you do much troubleshooting.

If you can replicate the problem, figuring out what is happening will be much easier. The hardest problems to fix are those that occur only occasionally or intermittently.

DESCRIBING THE PROBLEM IN DETAIL

After you have developed an understanding of how and when the problem is happening, write down a description of the problem. Be as detailed as you can. This description will help you decide on the best course of action, and if you are unable to solve the problem yourself, you will be in an excellent position to ask for help.

Use the Console to save logs related to the problem and the System Profiler to create a report about your system's configuration. This will create much of the detail that will enable you or someone else to solve the problem.

FIXING PROBLEMS YOURSELF

After you have described your problem, you should have some idea of where it lies. The four general areas in which you will experience problems are applications, system, hardware, and during startup.

CORRECTING APPLICATION ERRORS

Application errors usually fall into one of the following categories:

- **Hangs**—Sometimes application errors cause your application to hang. Fortunately, because Mac OS X has protected memory, a hung application usually affects only the application itself and your other applications continue to work normally. You are likely to lose unsaved data in the hung application, but at least your losses are limited to a single application.

- **Quits**—Sometimes, the application you are using suddenly quits. You might or might not get an error message saying something like, The application has unexpectedly quit because of an error. When this happens, you lose all the changes you made to the open document since the last time you saved it.

- **Won't do what it is supposed to do**—Many times, errors occur that prevent you from doing what you want to do—whether using a particular function of the software, printing, saving files, and so on.

> **NOTE**
>
> When you see an error alert that provides an error ID number, you should make a note of it. Although the number is not likely to be meaningful to you unless you have seen it before, it might be very meaningful to someone else when you ask for help.

Obviously, application problems are usually unpredictable. And when they happen, there isn't much you can do to recover your unsaved data (if you are saving frequently, you will limit your losses when the inevitable does happen). With an application problem, your real task is to figure out how to *prevent* future occurrences of the problem.

> **TIP**
>
> Some applications, such as Microsoft Office, have a recover feature that attempts to recover documents on which you were working when the application crashed or hung. This sometimes works and sometimes doesn't. However, you should take a look at recovered documents when you restart the application to see how much of your work you can restore.

Typically, there are many things you can try to correct an application error. Following are the general tasks you should attempt to get the application working properly again.

> **NOTE**
>
> **NEW**
>
> For version 10.3, Apple has added a crash reporter feature. When an application crashes, the crash reporter appears. At the top of this window, you can enter information about what you were doing at the time of the crash. When you have described this in as much detail as possible, you can send the information to Apple. Apple collects this information and uses it to identify problems that need to be fixed.

HUNG APPLICATION   When an application is hung, your only option is to force it to quit. You can do this by bringing up the Force Quit Applications window by pressing

Option-⌘-Esc. Select the application you want to force quit and click Force Quit. You can also use the Activity Monitor to force an application to quit—the benefit of the Activity Monitor is that you can see all the processes that are running along with their statuses. If other processes are also hung, you will be able to see them by looking at the Activity Monitor window. This can provide important clues as to the source of the problem (where two or three hung processes are gathered, there is likely a problem in their midst).

After you unhang the application, try to replicate the conditions under which it hung. If the problem is repeatable, it is either a bug in the application or a conflict with another part of the system.

Try running the application by itself while re-creating the situation in which the problem occurred (use your problem description to do this). If the hang doesn't occur again, you know that the problem is some type of conflict with another part of your system—be aware that this is much less likely to occur under Mac OS X than with previous versions of the OS.

If the hang is repeatable, the most likely solution is to install an update to the application. Visit the support area of the manufacturer's Web page to see whether the problem you have is a known one. If so, an update is probably available to correct it. If not, report the problem to tech support to see what the application's manufacturer recommends.

TIP

> When an error dialog box appears or an application hangs, it can be useful to capture a screenshot so you can reproduce it later when you are writing down the description of your problem. In the case of a hung application, capturing a screenshot can help you re-create at least a screen's worth of data if you lose it all. Sometimes this can be helpful (such as for a table of data). To capture a screenshot, use the Grab application or download and use the much more capable Snapz Pro X.

→ To learn how to capture screenshots, **see** "Capturing Screen Images with Grab," **p. 469**.

QUITS   When an application unexpectedly quits, you should do the same tasks as when it hangs—except that you don't need to force it to quit because it already has. The solution to most quits is to get an updated version of the application from the manufacturer.

TIP

> Applications under Mac OS X are like applications under other versions—they don't always work as they should and will sometimes crash or hang, in which case you lose any changes you have made since you last saved your document. Make it a practice to save your documents frequently; make sure you take advantage of auto-save features to automate this task, such as in Microsoft Office applications. You can also use automation tools, such as QuicKeys, to save any documents at regular intervals.

UNEXPECTED BEHAVIOR If the application isn't working as you expect it to, the most likely causes are that the application has a bug or you aren't using it in the way it was intended.

Eliminate the second possibility first. Check the application's documentation, help, or readme files to ensure that you are doing the task in the way the manufacturer intends. If you ask for help for something that is covered in the application's documentation, the responses you get might be embarrassing or unpleasant.

If you seem to be using the application properly, a likely cause is a bug and the solution is to get an update from the manufacturer.

> **TIP**
>
> Occasionally, an application's preferences can become corrupted, and cause problems for you. One way to eliminate this as a cause of a problem is to log on under an alternative user account. If the problem doesn't occur under that user account, the cause might be corrupted preference files. Log back into the previous user account and delete preferences related to the application that are stored in that user account's Library folder.

CORRECTING SYSTEM ERRORS

System errors can be tougher to solve because they are usually harder to isolate. Your goal should be to isolate the problem as much as you can. If you have carefully investigated and described your problem, you should have some idea where it originates.

Your first step should be to ensure that your system software is current—use the Software Update tool to check this.

The following list provides some general things to try for various sorts of system errors:

- If the problem seems to be related to a disk, run the Disk Utility or other disk maintenance application to correct it. The problem might be related to the disk being too full, so check that as well.

  Many Unix commands can be helpful when you are trying to solve system problems, such as getting rid of files you can't delete in the normal way and working with directories.

→ To learn how to use some basic Unix commands, **see** Chapter 9, "Unix: Working with the Command Line," **p. 243**.

- If the problem seems to be related to a specific user account, try repeating the same action under a different account. If the problem goes away, you know that something is wrong in the user account configuration.

  The best option for this is to use your clean user account to assess this. Because this account should have few or no third-party software installed, it often helps determine whether a problem is part of the system or is related to something happening under a specific user account.

Some troubleshooting tasks are possible only when you are logged in to your Mac as root. Logging in as Root can be dangerous, so you should know what you are doing before you try any action under the root account.

→ To learn about logging in as root, **see** "Logging In As Root," **p. 236**.

- If the problem is more general, you might have to reinstall the system or specific components of it.

→ For help maintaining and installing the OS, **see** Appendix A, "Installing and Maintaining Mac OS X," **p. 947**.

CORRECTING HARDWARE ERRORS

Hardware problems are almost always caused by one of the following two conditions: improperly installed hardware or problematic drivers.

Eliminate the first cause by reviewing the steps you took to install the hardware. Check out the instructions that came with the device to make sure you are following the manufacturer's recommendations.

If the hardware is an external device, check the cable you used to connect it; if you have another cable, try that. If the device is connected to a hub, reconnect it to a port on the Mac itself.

TIP

> A good way to check whether a device is successfully communicating with your Mac is to use the System Profiler. Use the bus type information (such as FireWire) for that device to see whether the device with which you are having trouble is listed.

If the hardware is internal, repeat the installation process to ensure that it is correct.

The most likely cause of hardware problems is a faulty or buggy driver. Your only solution to this problem is to get an updated driver from the manufacturer. Visit the manufacturer's Web site for help.

NOTE

> Many devices have a Mac OS 9 driver available. If the device you are using has an available driver and you can restart under Mac OS 9, consider restarting in Mac OS 9 and using the hardware from there until a better Mac OS X driver is available.

The hardware might simply be defective. Although this doesn't happen very often, it can occur. If none of the other solutions works, you might be left with this possibility, in which case all you can do is exchange the unit for a different one or repair it.

29

SOLVING THE STARTUP PROBLEM

One of the worst problems you can have is when your Mac won't start. This can be caused by many things, including software conflicts, buggy software, disk problems, failed hardware, or a combination of all of these. Instead of loading the system, the machine just sits there and flashes a broken folder icon, meaning your Mac can't find a suitable System Folder to use to start up the machine. (If the system doesn't try to start up at all, but you just hear the chimes of death, that means you definitely have a hardware problem.)

NOTE

> If you create and maintain at least one other valid startup volume, running Mac OS 9.2 or Mac OS X, you should be able to use that to start up in most cases. Although you won't be able to solve Mac OS X problems when you are booted up in the Mac OS 9 environment, you can at least get to work. And you should also be able to access the Internet to get help with the problem. If you have Mac OS X and Mac OS 9 installed on the same volume, a problem with that volume might prevent you from starting up in either system. That is one reason it is better to have the versions of the OS installed on separate volumes. You should also create an alternative Mac OS X startup volume.

In this case, start up from an alternative startup volume, such as a CD-ROM. Most likely, you will have to reinstall the OS on the volume you can't use to start up to correct the problem. However, before you do that, try running the Disk Utility on the disk containing Mac OS X to ensure that it isn't a disk problem.

NOTE

> If you have a backup of your entire system when it was working properly, you can restore that version instead of reinstalling a new one. The advantage of this is that you won't have to reinstall your third-party software.

MAC OS X TO THE MAX: GETTING HELP FOR YOUR PROBLEM

Unless you can instantly see how to solve your problem or one of your tools takes care of it, you will probably need to get help. There are plenty of sources for troubleshooting help, including the following:

- Manuals and online help
- Technical support from the manufacturer
- Web sites
- Newsgroups
- Magazines

- Troubleshooting software
- Mailing lists
- Co-workers and other people you know personally

When asking for help from people—regardless of the means you use, such as the telephone or email—be sure that you keep the following in mind:

- **Use basic manners**—You have no call to be rude to people who are trying to help you, even if they happen to work for the manufacturer of the software or hardware that is giving you trouble. Besides being the right thing to do, using good manners will probably get you better help. Manners are equally important when making requests via email or other online sources. "Please" and "thank you" go a long way toward encouraging people to help you. Sometimes this basic rule can be hard to remember when you are stressed out about a problem.

- **Give accurate, specific, and complete information**—Use the work you did earlier to provide a complete description of your problem. For example, provide information from logs you captured and be prepared to provide System Profiler information. Unless you give the person who is trying to help you a good idea of what is really going on, that person is unlikely to be able to help.

- **Don't wear out your welcome with someone who is only trying to help**—You need to be careful not to impose on people who are trying to help you only out of the goodness of their hearts. If you are asking a friend, co-worker, or even a complete stranger to help you with a problem, use her time efficiently. Be prepared to describe your situation. Be specific. And if the person can't help you after a reasonable amount of time, go to someone else. It is not fair to ask a volunteer to spend large amounts of her time trying to solve your problems. You can usually tell if someone is willing and able to help you quite quickly. If you sense that you are butting up against a dead-end, bow out gracefully and try another path.

Getting Help More Effectively

An ineffective request for help goes something like this, "I was printing and Word quit. Help!" This kind of question—which happens more than you might imagine—is just about impossible to answer.

A more effective question might be something like this: "I am using a 500MHz Power Mac G4 running Mac OS X version 10.3.1 that is connected to an Epson 740i. While I was trying to print from Microsoft Word for Mac OS X version 1.1, Word unexpectedly quit. I didn't get any sort of error message. I am able to print from other Mac OS X applications, and I have installed the latest printer drivers. Do you have any suggestions that might help?"

Table 29.3 lists some specific sources of online help with Mac OS X issues.

TABLE 29.3   SOURCES OF GENERAL HELP FOR PROBLEMS

Source	Contact Information	Comments
Apple	www.apple.com/support	Apple's support pages are a great source of information about problems, and you can download updates to system and other software. Check out the Tech Info Library to search for specific problems. You can also read manuals and have discussions about problems. If the problem you are having seems to be related to the OS, Apple hardware, or an Apple application, this should be your first stop.
MacFixIt	www.macfixit.com	This is a good source of information related to solving Mac problems. Access to this information is not free, but you can get help on literally every aspect of using a Mac. Most of the information comes from Mac users, and you can ask specific questions—although the answer to your question is probably already available. You can get access to current information free; however, you must pay to access older information maintained in an exhaustive set of archives. The fee is quite reasonable for the quality of the information to which you have access.
MacInTouch	www.macintouch.com	This site offers a lot of Mac news that can help you solve problems, especially if those problems are solved by a software update of which you are unaware.
Me	seusingmacosx@mac.com	You can email me to ask for help, and I will do my best to provide a solution for you or at least point you to a more helpful source if I can't help you directly.

Mac OS X: Appendixes

Installing and Maintaining Mac OS X

In this appendix

MOVING TO AND MAINTAINING MAC OS X

There are two basic paths to follow when you install Mac OS X version 10.3. One path is for those users who are currently using an earlier version of Mac OS X, such as version 10.1 or 10.2. The other path is for those users who are making the jump from Mac OS 9.x.x or earlier. Not coincidentally, two major sections in this appendix describe how to make the transition to version 10.3 via either path. The section called "Moving to Version 10.3 from Previous Versions of Mac OS X" will help you if you are already using a version of Mac OS X. The section called "Moving to Version 10.3 from Mac OS 9.x.x or Earlier" will guide you through the process of moving from older Mac OS versions to OS X. Obviously, you need to read whichever section is applicable to your situation.

After version 10.3 installation is complete, you should review the section titled "Updating Your Mac OS X Installation" regardless of which installation path you followed.

MOVING TO VERSION 10.3 FROM PREVIOUS VERSIONS OF MAC OS X

 The upgrade from previous versions of Mac OS X to version 10.3 involves a lot more than the change in number from 10.1 or 10.2 to 10.3 would indicate. Version 10.3 is a major update (in my opinion, it should have been called version 11), and moving to it requires some thought. It might take some time and effort to get into version 10.3's world, but the benefits are well worth the work.

This is especially true if you are running version 10.1.x. The move from 10.1 to 10.2 made extensive changes to some fundamental aspects of the OS and consequently, many applications that worked fine under 10.1 do not work under 10.2 without being updated. Most of these applications have been updated by now, but be aware that if you are currently running 10.1, you should check for updates to the applications you use if you haven't updated them recently.

WHAT YOU NEED TO KNOW BEFORE YOU INSTALL VERSION 10.3

Before you jump into the installation process, take a few moments to read through the following sections to ensure that you can make the transition smoothly.

ASSESSING YOUR SITUATION

The hardware requirements from previous versions of Mac OS X haven't changed all that much, so if you are currently running a previous version of Mac OS X, your hardware is more than likely Mac OS X version 10.3 compatible. (You might need to update your Mac's firmware; see the next section for information about doing this.)

Most major Mac applications that required an update for version 10.2 have already been updated. If you find that you use an application that has not been updated for 10.2 or 10.3, you might experience problems when you run it—if it runs at all. Check the software developers' Web sites and download and install any updates of your applications that were released for Mac OS X version 10.2 or later. Because significant changes were made for 10.2 (and carry over to 10.3), you might have to pay upgrade fees for some of these.

If applications you need are unavailable in version 10.3–compatible versions, check the software's Web site for the known issues when running the application under version 10.3. If you can live with those issues, proceed with the upgrade. If not, you might have to wait until those applications have been updated to install 10.3 or switch to an alternative application that has been made version 10.3 aware.

Fortunately, fewer applications require major updates to run under 10.3 versus 10.2 than were necessary for the change from 10.1 to 10.2.

CAUTION

> If you are moving from version 10.1 to 10.3, this is an important issue for you because many OS X applications that ran under 10.1.x were unable to run under 10.2 until they were updated. Make sure you have checked all your important applications for 10.3 compatibility before installing version 10.3.

Updating Your Mac's Firmware

Your Mac must have access to some basic software for it to start up. For example, it needs to know where to look for system software that it can use to start up. This software used to be permanently stored in hardware called read-only memory (ROM). This permanent ROM could not be updated, so what came with the Mac was as good as it could get. With modern Macs, the base software is stored in *firmware*, which is sort of a combination between software encoded in hardware and normal software. The advantage of this is that Apple can update the firmware on modern Macs to correct problems or improve performance.

CAUTION

> If your Mac's firmware needs to be updated for 10.3, the installation process will warn you and you will have to quit the installation and upgrade your firmware before you can continue.

Before installing Mac OS X version 10.3, you should ensure that your Mac's firmware is up-to-date. This is a simple task that might prevent problems later.

TIP

> To keep your Mac in top condition, you should check for firmware updates occasionally, whether you are upgrading the OS or not.

To update the firmware on your Mac, do the following steps:

1. Use a Web browser to go to Apple's software support page, which is located at www.apple.com/support/downloads.

2. To search for any firmware updates for your Mac, enter your Mac's model or processor and the word "firmware." For example, if you have a Power Mac G4, type `Power Mac G4 and firmware`. If you have an iMac, type `iMac and firmware`. The search will find all updates that meet your search criteria.

3. Find the most recent firmware update for your Mac and download it.

4. Double-click the updater to mount the disk image on your desktop.

5. Open the disk image.

6. If a text file is provided with the update, open the text file and read it. If the Update is provided as an installer, launch the installer. In either case, read the instructions to run the updater.

7. Follow the instructions to install the firmware update on your Mac.

Some firmware updates include a program that checks whether your Mac's firmware needs to be updated. If so, run the firmware installer. Typically, you launch the updater and then restart your machine while holding down the power button (until you hear a long tone). After the updater has finished, it restarts your Mac and will be using the updated firmware.

CHOOSING AN INSTALLATION METHOD

When you install version 10.3, there are three primary options, each with its own pros and cons:

- **Upgrade Mac OS X**—Using this option, you let the Mac OS X installer overwrite or revise your current Mac OS X installation as it sees fit. The benefit of this approach is that it is the easiest and most straightforward method. The downside is that the installation might not be as clean because the entire OS is not replaced. Consequently, there is a greater chance of the OS having problems or not working as well as it might with a clean install.

  The reported problems you might experience are related to specific situations, and there is no way to list all the possible conditions that might cause you problems. So, using this option is a bit of a crapshoot. However, if you don't usually perform a lot of system modifications and haven't installed third-party utilities, this option can save you some time because you shouldn't have to reconfigure your system as much as you might with the other options.

NOTE

If you install Mac OS X on a volume on which no version of Mac OS X has been installed, this option becomes Install Mac OS X.

- **Archive and Install**—Using this option, the installer creates a brand-new installation of Mac OS X and saves a copy of the current system (in a folder called Previous System" folder). This enables you to perform a clean installation of OS X version 10.3, while keeping files from the previous version in case you need to add them back into the system later. The benefit to this method is that the OS itself is likely to be installed better and cause you fewer problems. The downside is that you have to do some manual labor to finish the configuration.

  When you choose this method, you have the option to preserve users and network settings. When you choose this option, the current users, their Home folders, and your Mac's network settings are carried into the new system. This prevents you from having to work through the setup assistant application later, and it maintains all the files that currently reside in all Home folders on your machine.

- **Erase and Install**—When you select this option, the volume on which you install the OS is erased and reformatted and a clean install is performed. Because the volume is reformatted, you lose any data currently stored there. The benefit to this method is that you get a fresh start and rebuild your system from the ground up. The downside is that it requires the most work in that you have to reinstall all your applications, reconfigure your entire system, restore your documents, and so on.

In most cases, I recommend that you choose the Archive and Install method along with the option to preserve users and network settings. This both gets you a clean OS and maintains most of your current configuration, documents, and so on. In my book (and this is my book after all), this option results in the cleanest version of the OS and requires only a minimal amount of reconfiguration.

If you need to rebuild a volume, the Erase and Install option nets you the cleanest system. But, this option requires the most work because you basically have to start over from scratch and rebuild the volume, including all user accounts, documents, applications, system settings, and so on.

Frankly, I don't recommend the Upgrade Mac OS X option. Theoretically, this option should be the easiest because it attempts to maintain all of your current system configuration, including third-party software, users, documents, preferences, and so on. However, for the same reason, the resulting OS is not as cleanly installed as it is under the other options and the likelihood of problems or reduced performance is increased significantly. In some cases, it might be more work to solve problems introduced by upgrading the OS than would have been experienced with the Archive and Install option. However, if you haven't installed any third-party software that impacts the OS, this option might be the quickest path to Mac OS X version 10.3.

CREATING A BACKUP OF YOUR DATA AND APPLICATIONS

Although the risk of losing all your data during an upgrade is small (unless the data is on the volume on which you choose to use the Erase and Install option, in which case losing all the data is a certainty), the results of that happening could be unrecoverable if you don't have everything backed up properly. For example, imagine losing your iPhoto library. Without a backup, your photos would be gone forever. Performing the upgrade without a backup system is about like playing Russian roulette—the odds are with you, but if you lose, you lose big.

→ To learn more about backup options, **see** "Backing Up Your System," **p. 887**.

Before installing a new version of the OS, I urge you to make sure all your data is backed up. And, make sure you have CDs or installers for your applications in case they are damaged during the OS X 10.3 installation. You should also be sure you have paper copies of any setting information, such as the settings for your Internet connection, .Mac, and email accounts. Should you lose these configuration data, having them on hard copy will enable you recover with the least amount of fuss. Finally, be sure you also have copies of any updaters for your third-party applications so you can bring them to the latest version after you reinstall them (don't worry about Apple applications because you can update them via the Software Update application).

TIP

> If you have obtained software via downloads, put the installers on CD or on volumes other than the one on which you are installing Mac OS X. Some installers are removed when new versions are released, and you might not be able to download it again without paying for it again.

INSTALLING MAC OS X VERSION 10.3 WITH THE ARCHIVE AND INSTALL OPTION

As you read earlier, this method provides a good balance between having a clean installation and minimizing the reconfiguration work you have to do. Under this method, the installer archives your current system while it installs a clean version of Mac OS X version 10.3 on your machine. Then, you reinstall any system files you need from your current system in the 10.3 version. This method is a bit more work than the upgrade option, but you are also more likely to end up with better results. If you choose the Preserve Users and Network Settings option, all your user information (such as the contents of the Home folders) and most of your system configuration is carried over to the new OS.

There are two major parts to this upgrade process:

1. Perform the installation of Mac OS X version 10.3 on your current Mac OS X volume.
2. Move needed files from the previous version of Mac OS X to version 10.3.

INSTALLING MAC OS X USING THE ARCHIVE AND INSTALL OPTION

The first part is rather simple, as you can see in the following steps:

1. Start up from the first Mac OS X version 10.3 installation CD by inserting it into your Mac, launching the Install Mac OS X application, and clicking the Restart button at the

prompt. The Mac will restart from the installation CD and immediately enter the installation process. You can also insert the CD, restart your Mac, and hold the C key down while it is restarting.

> **NOTE**
>
> When your Mac is starting up under version 10.3, you won't see the Happy Mac icon as in version 10.1 and earlier. That icon has been replaced by the Apple logo. Apparently, Apple felt that the Happy Mac had outlived his usefulness and didn't look version 10.2/3–compatible. Oh well, rest in peace, Happy Mac!

A

As things begin to progress, you will see the Install Mac OS X Select Language window.

2. Select the language you want to use as the primary Mac OS X language and then click Continue. You will move into the Mac OS X Installer and see the welcome message.

3. Read the information in the next several windows; click Continue to move ahead in the process.

4. When you reach the Software License Agreement window, click Continue; then click Agree when prompted.

   The installer will check the volumes installed in your system. When it finishes, you will see the Select a Destination window. In this window, you will see all the volumes on your machine.

5. Choose the volume on which the current version of Mac OS X is installed. The volume you select will have a circle and green arrow on it to indicate that it is the currently selected volume. In the lower pane, you will see a message indicating how much free space is required for the installation and stating that you have elected to update Mac OS X on this disk.

6. Click Options. You will see the Install Options sheet.

7. Click the Archive and Install radio button.

8. Check the Preserve Users and Network Settings check box. This causes the installer to move all the existing user accounts, network configurations, and so on to the new version 10.3 installation. You should choose this option unless you have a very good reason not to do so, such as you want to start with a new set of user accounts. When you use this option, you will skip the Setup Assistant application because the installer will carry all that information over for you. (The rest of these steps assume that you have used this option. If not, you can review the "Erasing a Volume and Installing Mac OS X Version 10.3" section later in this appendix to help you work through the Setup Assistant.)

9. Click OK to close the sheet. In the Select a Destination window, you will see a message stating that you are installing a new version of 10.3 while saving the previous version and moving all user accounts to the new version.

10. Click Continue. You will see the Easy Install screen.

TIP

> If you aren't concerned about installing things you won't ever use, skip to step 16 to use the Easy Install option. This installs every possible file on your machine. It is an easy install, but you will probably end up storing several files you will never use (thus, wasting valuable disk space).

A

11. Click Customize to move to the Custom Install window. Use the tools in this window to deselect any files you don't want to install. I recommend you leave the BSD Subsystem and Additional Applications check boxes checked.

12. Click the Expansion Triangle next to the Printer Drivers check box to see a list of the printer brands Mac OS X supports. If you aren't ever going to want to use any of the brands of printers shown, uncheck their boxes to prevent the installation of those drivers.

13. Click the Expansion Triangle next to the Language Translations check box to see a list of the languages Mac OS X supports. If you aren't ever going to want to use any of the languages shown, uncheck their boxes. Or you can uncheck the Language Translations box to unselect all of them at once.

NOTE

> The language you choose in step 2 is always installed. The other languages Mac OS X supports are listed in the Language Translations section.

14. If you elected to install any of the other languages in step 13, expand the Fonts check box to ensure that the appropriate fonts are installed to support those languages.

15. Uncheck any of the other options you won't use.

16. Click Install. You will see a progress window that displays information about the various steps the installer goes through to install Mac OS X. This information includes an estimate of how long the process will take, but, of course, this is only an estimate. When the process is complete, your Mac will restart in Mac OS X version 10.3 and move into the Additional Software installation part of the process.

NOTE

> Mac OS X is packaged in a variety of ways depending on how you purchased it. For example, if you bought the complete upgrade package, you will have three Mac OS X CDs. If Mac OS X came with your Mac, you will have a variety of Software Install and Restore CDs (in which case, you won't have to do an initial install, but you might reinstall it some day). Just insert the appropriate CDs when prompted to do so.

17. At the prompt, remove the Mac OS X Installation CD and insert CD #2. The additional software will be installed and progress information will be displayed in the window.

18. If you are prompted to install any other CDs, do so and the installation process will continue.

When this process is complete, you will move to the Mac OS X 10.3 login window and be running under a clean version of Mac OS X version 10.3. In the login window, you will see the user accounts that existed in the previous version. (If you have only a single user account or if automatic login is enabled, you will move directly to the OS X desktop instead.)

NOTE

> If your accounts have pictures associated with them, you might see placeholders instead. Version 10.3 does not include the same set of images that previous versions did, so you might have to choose new images for some user accounts.

When you log in to version 10.3, you will find that most of your configuration from the previous version has been maintained, such as your login items, desktop photos, and Dock configuration. Some might not be (on some installs with early versions of the installer, I had to reconfigure some options). Usually, if you do have to reconfigure some aspects of the system, it takes only a few minutes to do so.

MOVING FILES FROM THE PREVIOUS SYSTEM TO THE NEW SYSTEM

The only downside of installing a clean version of the OS is that you have to move files you still need from the previous version to the new version. Mostly, these are the files related to specific third-party applications you have installed.

Before you bother looking for files to move, try to work with the system as it is. You might find that everything works just fine and you don't need to do the second part. After you are confident that you don't need the previous versions of the OS, you can trash the folder called Previous System located on your Mac OS X startup volume. If you do find some things that aren't working as you expect, proceed with the second part of the process.

If you do find that some third-party applications aren't working properly, reinstalling them from the original CDs or installers (that you, of course, saved on a CD or a different volume) is easiest. If you can't do this for some reason, or there are preference or configuration files that you need to retrieve from the old system, you have to find and move those files into the new system manually.

Finding and moving all the files you need from the old system to the new one can be a bit tricky, but with some patience and a bit of luck, you can work through it. (If you think installing a new OS is a bit tedious, try installing it dozens of times while writing a book!) Follow these steps:

1. Open the volume on which you installed version 10.3. In addition to the folder called System, you will see a folder called Previous Systems (see Figure A.1). This contains the previous versions of OS X that existed when you did the install.

Figure A.1
The Previous System folder contains, amazingly enough, previous versions of Mac OS X.

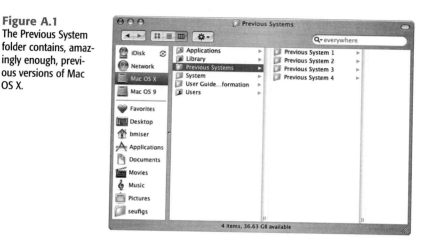

2. Open the Previous Systems folder and then open the most recent previous system folder contained within that folder. For example, if this is your first clean install, open the folder called Previous System 1. You will see the set of folders that were contained in that version of the OS (see Figure A.2).

Figure A.2
These folders contain files you might need to move to your clean installation of Mac OS X.

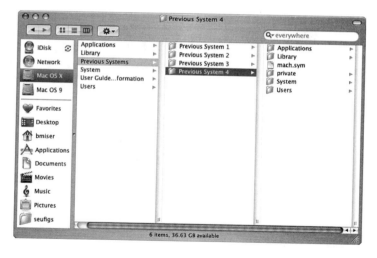

3. Drag the files you think you might need from the folder in the Previous System folder to the corresponding folder in the 10.3 System folder.

Whether you need any of these files and folders depends on your specific setup. In my testing, I found that my system worked fine without any of the old files, but in the event you need to move some files over, consider the following folders:

- **Applications**—This folder contains the previous versions of Apple applications that were part of the default installation. If you used the Additional Software install option, you will probably never need these older versions.

- **Library**—This folder contains the library files that provide functionality for various areas of the OS, such as Audio, Fonts, Java, and QuickTime.

- **System**—This folder contains only one folder, which is the system Library folder. In this folder are core application services and frameworks, such as Classic, Displays, and OpenSSL.

- **Users**—If you chose to move all user accounts to the clean installation, this folder is empty because you maintained the users in the new system. If you didn't preserve users, you can use the contents of this folder to re-create user folders.

Various third-party applications can store individual files within these folders as well, so if something doesn't seem to be working properly and you can't reinstall the application from an original installer, explore these folders to see whether you can find files for those applications. Then, move those files to the corresponding folders in 10.3 system folders.

After you have used 10.3 for some time and are confident it is working properly, you can dispose of the Previous System folders to recover disk space.

If an application does not work properly after you have installed Mac OS X, see "An Application Doesn't Work Under OS 10.3" in the "Troubleshooting" section at the end of this appendix.

If an application has lost your preferences after you install 10.3, see "An Application Lost My Preferences Under OS 10.3" in the "Troubleshooting" section at the end of this appendix.

UPDATING YOUR MAC OS X INSTALLATION

After you have completed the installation, use Software Update to update it.

→ To learn how to update the installation, **see** "Updating Your Mac OS X Installation," **p. 977**.

INSTALLING MAC OS X VERSION 10.3 WITH THE ERASE AND INSTALL OPTION

The Erase and Install option provides the cleanest installation of OS 10.3 and gives you the chance to rebuild the volume on which you install 10.3; this is a good thing because you have the chance to get rid of data and applications that you don't use anymore and that are just wasting space. The downsides to this method are that it requires you to back up all the data you do want to carry to the new 10.3 installation and is definitely the most work.

Following are the phases in this installation process:

1. Back up any data, including user Home folders and application installers and updaters, that you want to include in the 10.3 installation onto CD, DVD, or a different volume on a hard drive than the one on which you are installing Mac OS X version 10.3. Ensure that you have installers, updaters, and registration numbers for all your applications stored someplace besides the volume on which you are going to install Mac OS X.

2. If you want to partition a disk on which you are going to install Mac OS X, start up from the Mac OS X Installation CD and partition the drive.

3. Run the Mac OS X installer to install the OS and work through the Setup Assistant.

4. Create additional user accounts.

5. Copy data from the backups you made in step 1 into the new installation.

BACKING UP DATA TO TAKE INTO THE NEW SYSTEM

When you use the erase installation option, all the data on the volume on which you install Mac OS X is deleted, erased, removed, kaput, terminated, and so on. So, before you install, you need to save any data from your current Mac OS X installation some place other than the volume on which you are installing Mac OS X version 10.3. There are a number of ways to back up this data, including the following:

CAUTION

> If you are going to partition the drive on which you install Mac OS X, you need to save your data on a different drive (or CD or DVD) than the one on which you are going to install Mac OS X. When you partition a drive, you will destroy all the data on that drive.

- Burn the data on a CD or DVD.

- Copy the data to a different volume on the same or on a different hard drive (required if you are going to partition the drive).

- Copy the data onto tape.

→ To learn more about backup systems, **see** "Backing Up Your System," **p. 887**.

When backing up the data you want to "take with you," you should consider the following:

- **User Home folders**—The Home folders for each user account contain that user's documents, preferences, and other data. For example, the Music folder contains the iTunes Music Library, the Pictures folder contains the iPhoto Photo Library, and so on. The Library folder within the Home folder contains user preferences, email account information, Safari bookmarks, and so on. If you want to save any of this data, you need to back up the Home folders you want to save. You can be selective about these data; for example, you can choose to back up only parts of the Home folders, such as the Music and Pictures folders. In most cases, I recommend that you save the entire Home folder for each user account, unless you are not going to create that user account in the new system.

- **Application installers and updaters**—If you have installed or updated any of your applications from an installer that you downloaded, make sure you back up the application and its updaters. If you installed the application from CD, be sure you can locate the CDs and that you save a copy of any updates you downloaded and installed for that application.

You can also back up the applications themselves rather than the installers and reinstall the applications by dragging them from the backup into the Applications folder under the new system. However, this can sometimes result in the application not working properly because a system component wasn't installed properly. For most applications, I recommend that you reinstall them from the original installer and then apply any updates that are available.

You don't need to worry about Apple applications that are part of the Mac OS X installation, such as iMovie, iPhoto, etc. These are installed by the Mac OS X installer. One *i* application that you do have to back up is iDVD because it is not included on the Mac OS X installation CDs.

CAUTION

> In addition to the software installers and updaters, be sure you have any registration or serial numbers for any applications you are going to install in the new system. Losing this information can cost time and possible money if you have to reregister an application.

- **System Data**—If an application you use makes changes to the OS at a system level, you need to retrieve the files that application has saved in the current System folder so you can restore them. Typically, you need to do this only if you don't choose to reinstall the application from scratch.

After, and only after, you are sure you have backed up all the data you want to install in the new system, you can proceed with the rest of the steps of the installation process.

PARTITIONING A DRIVE BEFORE INSTALLING MAC OS X

You can partition a hard drive to make logical volumes on it; each volume acts like an independent hard drive. The time to do this is before you install Mac OS X because you must erase the entire disk, not just the volume on which you are going to install Mac OS X, to partition it.

CAUTION

> If you are going to use an existing volume to install Mac OS X, skip to the next section.

1. Insert the Mac OS X Installation CD 1 disc in your Mac, restart it, and press and hold down the C key while it starts up. When the Mac starts up, the installer application opens.
2. Select Installer, Open Disk Utility. The Disk Utility application opens.
3. Use the Disk Utility to partition the drive.

→ To learn how to use the Disk Utility to prepare and partition a disk to prepare a volume for Mac OS X, **see** "Choosing, Installing, and Using a Hard Drive," **p. 782**.

4. When you have partitioned the drive, quit the Disk Utility. You will return to the Mac OS X Installer.

STARTING THE MAC OS X VERSION 10.3 INSTALLATION

To install Mac OS X using the Erase and Install option, do the following steps:

1. Start up from the first Mac OS X version 10.3 installation CD by inserting it into your Mac, launching the Install Mac OS X application, and clicking the Restart button at the prompt. The Mac restarts from the installation CD and immediately enters the installation process.

   If you have partitioned the drive, you can skip this step because you will already be in the Installer.

   NOTE

   > When your Mac is starting up under version 10.3, you won't see the Happy Mac icon as in version 10.1 and earlier. That icon has been replaced by the Apple logo. Apparently, Apple felt that the Happy Mac had outlived his usefulness and didn't look version 10.2/3–compatible. Oh well, rest in peace, Happy Mac!

   As things begin to progress, you will see the Install Mac OS X Select Language window.

2. Select the language you want to use as the primary Mac OS X language and then click Continue. You will move into the Mac OS X Installer and see the welcome message.

3. Read the information in the next several windows; click Continue to move ahead in the process.

4. When you reach the Software License Agreement window, click Continue; then click Agree when prompted. (Of course, you should read the agreement to make sure you actually agree with it.)

   The installer checks the volumes installed in your system. When it finishes, you will see the Select a Destination window. In this window, you will see all the volumes on your machine.

5. Choose the volume you want to erase and install Mac OS X on. The volume you select will have a circle and green arrow on it to indicate that it is the currently selected volume. In the lower pane, you will see a message indicating how much free space is required for the installation and stating that you have elected to update Mac OS X on this disk.

   NOTE

   > If you have partitioned the drive, you will see that the drive is empty and that you have elected to install Mac OS X on the volume (rather than upgrade because there is nothing on the volume to upgrade).

6. Click Options. You will see the Install Options sheet.

7. Click the Erase and Install radio button.

> **NOTE**
>
> If you partitioned the drive, you can also select the Install Mac OS X option because there is no version of the OS on the disk. You can also select the Erase and Install option, but there is nothing to erase on the disk. When the disk is empty, these options do the same thing.

8. Select the format you want to use on the selected volume on the "Format disk as" pop-up menu. Generally, you should select the Mac OS Extended (Journaled) option, which is the default.

9. Click OK to close the sheet. In the Select a Destination window, you will see a message stating that you have selected to erase the volume and format according to the selection you made in the previous step.

10. Click Continue. You will see the Easy Install screen.

> **TIP**
>
> If you aren't concerned about installing things you won't ever use, skip to step 16 to use the Easy Install option. This installs every possible file on your machine. It is an easy install, but you will probably end up storing many files you will never use (thus, wasting valuable disk space).

11. Click Customize to move to the Custom Install window. Use the tools in this window to deselect any files you don't want to install. I recommend you leave the BSD Subsystem and Additional Applications check boxes checked.

12. Click the Expansion Triangle next to the Printer Drivers check box to see a list of the printer brands Mac OS X supports. If you aren't ever going to want to use any of the brands of printers shown, uncheck their boxes to prevent the installation of those drivers.

13. Click the Expansion Triangle next to the Language Translations check box to see a list of the languages Mac OS X supports. If you aren't ever going to want to use any of the languages shown, uncheck their boxes. Or you can uncheck the Language Translations box to unselect all of them at once.

> **NOTE**
>
> The language you choose in step 2 is always installed. The other languages Mac OS X supports are listed in the Language Translations section.

14. If you elected to install any of the other languages in step 13, expand the Fonts check box to ensure that the appropriate fonts are installed to support those languages.

15. Uncheck any of the other options you won't use.

CAUTION

> Before proceeding, make sure that you have backed up any data you want to save. All the data on the selected volume will be removed when you perform step 16. (If you partitioned the drive, it is already too late....)

16. Click Install. You will see a progress window that displays information about the various steps the installer goes through to install Mac OS X. This information includes an estimate of how long the process will take, but, of course, this is only an estimate. When the process is complete, your Mac restarts in Mac OS X version 10.3 and moves into the Additional Software installation part of the process (assuming that you chose to install some of the additional software of course).

NOTE

> Mac OS X is packaged in a variety of ways depending on how you purchased it. For example, if you bought the complete upgrade package, you have three Mac OS X CDs. If Mac OS X came with your Mac, you have a variety of Software Install and Restore CDs (in which case, you won't have to do an initial install, but you might reinstall it some day). Just insert the appropriate CDs when prompted to do so.

17. At the prompt, remove the Mac OS X Installation CD and insert CD #2. The additional software is installed and progress information is displayed in the window.

18. If you are prompted to install any other CDs, do so and the installation process continues.

    When this process is complete, you move into the Mac OS X 10.3 Setup Assistant (you'll know this has happened when you hear music and see the Welcome screen).

19. Follow the onscreen directions to work through the Setup Assistant. These steps include setting your personalized settings, entering or creating an Apple ID, registering your copy of Mac OS X, creating an administrator user account, choosing or configuring an Internet connection, setting up email accounts, selecting a time zone, and setting the time and date.

    The Setup Assistant is well-designed and does a good job of guiding you through the steps of configuring the basic aspects of Mac OS X, such as creating the first user account, configuring Internet access, and so on. You can use the information presented in other parts of this book to understand what the Assistant is asking you about and to reconfigure any settings you make via the Setup Assistant at a later time.

→ To learn about configuring Internet access under Mac OS X; **see** Chapter 10, "Connecting Your Mac to the Internet," **p. 263**.

TIP

> In most cases, just do the very basic amount of configuration in the Setup Assistant to get through it. Then do manual configurations, guided by the information in this book, of the system so you better understand what you have configured.

After the Setup Assistant has finished its work, you move to the Login window. Welcome to Mac OS X version 10.3!

CAUTION

> You should create additional user accounts and restore all the data you want before you do anything else, such as launching applications. This ensures that you don't create any new files in the Home folders and other locations that you will end up replacing when you restore data to the new system.

CREATING ADDITIONAL USER ACCOUNTS

After you have completed the Setup Assistant, log in and create user accounts for each user of your Mac; you will at least need one user account for each user whose data you are going to restore.

→ To learn how to create and configure user accounts, **see** "Creating User Accounts," **p. 24**, and "Testing and Configuring User Accounts," **p. 39**.

RESTORING DATA TO THE NEW SYSTEM

Restoring data from your backups can be somewhat time-consuming, but most of the process is not terribly complicated.

RESTORING USER HOME FOLDERS   There are two basic categories of data in users' Home folders that you might want to restore to the new system: data folders and files within the Library folder.

→ To learn about the contents of Home folders, **see** "Understanding the Home Folder," **p. 21**.

The default data folders in each user's Home folders include Desktop, Documents, Movies, Music, Pictures, and Public. (There might be additional folders if the user has created them.) These folders are very important because all the user's data is stored in them, such as their iTunes music and iPhoto Photo Library. To restore these folders, do the following steps:

1. Log in as the user whose folders you are going to restore.

2. Drag the folder you are restoring from the backup into the user's Home folder on the Mac OS X version 10.3 volume. If the folder already exists (such as the Pictures folder), you are warned that you are replacing an existing folder.

3. Click Replace to replace the current folder with the version you want to restore.

   Depending on how large the folder is (for example, the Music folder can be quite large if the user has added a lot of music to the iTunes Library), the copy process can take some time. Fortunately, you can copy multiple folders at the same time and continue to do other tasks while the copy proceeds.

4. Repeat step 2 for each folder you want to restore to the user's Home folder.

CAUTION

You can treat the Library folder just like the other default folders and replace it in its entirety. However, I don't recommend this because new versions of Mac OS X can store different files in the Library folder. It is better to be selective about what you replace in this folder so you replace only those files that are related to specific applications.

Restoring files from the user's Library folder is trickier and requires a bit more thought. Your goal should be to recover any of the user's personalized data, such as an address book, email accounts, bookmarks, application preferences, and so on.

NOTE

If you want the user to start over and create all new preferences, you can skip this part of the process.

The general steps to use are the following:

1. Open a Finder window showing the contents of the user's Library folder on the Mac OS X version 10.3 volume.

2. Open a second Finder window showing the contents of the user's Library folder on the backup volume, such as a DVD, CD, or hard drive.

3. Drag the files you want to restore from the backup volume into the same folder in the Library folder on the Mac OS X version 10.3 volume. If the file currently exists, you are prompted to replace it; elect to replace the file.

   Use Table A.1 to get an idea of the files you should replace.

4. Repeat step 3 for each Library file you want to move to the new installation.

TABLE A.1   EXAMPLES OF FILES WITHIN A USER'S LIBRARY FOLDER THAT MIGHT NEED TO BE RESTORED

Folder with a User's Library Folder	Filename or Folder Name	What It Restores
Application Support	AddressBook	The user's Address Book information.
Application Support	iCal	The user's calendar.

Folder with a User's Library Folder	Filename or Folder Name	What It Restores
Application Support	Other application folders	If there are other application folders, this restores them for each application the user will use.
Calendars		Any calendar files the user wants to maintain.
FontCollections		Any font collections the user wants to maintain.
Fonts		Any fonts the user wants to maintain.
iMovie		Any plug-ins or sound effects the user has added and wants to be available.
Internet Plug-ins		Any Internet plug-ins the user has installed that aren't included in the related application's installer.
Keychains		Any keychains the user has created.
Mail	All	The information related to the user's use of the Mail application, including account information and mail boxes.
Preferences		Any preferences for applications you will reinstall.
Safari	Bookmarks.plist	The user's Safari bookmarks.
Sounds		Any custom sounds the user has added to the system.

A

CAUTION

Table A.1 is not all-inclusive. There might be other files related to applications you have that are not included in the table. However, you should be able to locate those files by following similar patterns. For example, in the Preferences folder, look for files with the application's name. These are likely candidates for restoration.

RESTORING APPLICATIONS   After you have restored the appropriate Home folders, you should reinstall any applications you want to make available. While you can drag these from a backup, I recommend that you reinstall them from the CD or installer to ensure that any system files are installed properly. After you have installed an application, make sure you also apply any updates that are available for it.

RESTORING SYSTEM FILES   If there are specific system files, such as those associated with an application that you chose not to install with its installer, restore those from the backup to the new system.

UPDATING YOUR MAC OS X INSTALLATION

After you have completed the installation, use Software Update to update it.

→ To learn how to update the installation, **see** "Updating Your Mac OS X Installation," **p. 977**.

INSTALLING MAC OS X VERSION 10.3 WITH THE UPGRADE OPTION

As you read earlier, you can install version 10.3 directly over a previous version of Mac OS X. The installer manages all aspects of the upgrade for you and attempts to maintain as much of your current configuration as it can—however, don't expect perfection; some personalization might be lost. When this method works properly, this is an easy and fast way to upgrade. When it doesn't work, you can experience problems such as applications quitting unexpectedly. If you want to have the installer perform the upgrade, perform the following steps:

1. Start up in the Mac OS X environment you want to upgrade.

2. Insert the first Mac OS X version 10.3 installation CD.

3. Open the Install Mac OS X application.

4. Click Restart at the prompt.

5. Confirm that you are an Administrator for the machine. Your Mac restarts and boots from the installation CD, and you move into the Mac OS X installation process. The system goes through several checks that are different from the startup process under previous versions of the OS. Eventually, you see it begin to prepare the installation process.

> **N O T E**
>
> When your Mac is starting up under version 10.3, you won't see the Happy Mac icon as with previous versions of the OS earlier than Mac OS X 10.1. That icon has been replaced by the Apple logo. Apparently, Apple felt that the Happy Mac had outlived his usefulness and didn't look version 10.2/3–compatible. Oh well, rest in peace, Happy Mac!

As things begin to progress, you see the Install Mac OS X Select Language window.

6. Select the language you want to use as the primary Mac OS X language and then click Continue. You move into the Mac OS X Installer and see the welcome message.

7. Read the information in the next several windows; click Continue to move ahead in the process.

8. When you reach the Software License Agreement window, click Continue; then click Agree when prompted.

The installer checks the disks installed in your system. When it finishes, you see the Select a Destination window. In this window, you see all the volumes on your machine.

9. Choose the volume on which the current version of Mac OS X is installed. The volume you selected will have a circle and green arrow on it to indicate that it is the currently selected volume. In the lower pane, you will see a message indicating how much additional space is required to install the software and stating that you have elected to upgrade Mac OS X on this volume.

10. Click Continue. You will see the Easy Install screen.

> **TIP**
>
> If you aren't concerned about installing things you won't ever use, skip to step 16 to use the Easy Install option. This installs every possible file on your machine. It is an easy install, but you will probably end up storing several files you will never use (thus, wasting valuable disk space).

11. Click Customize to move to the Custom Install window. Use the tools in this window to deselect any files you don't want to install. I recommend you leave the BSD Subsystem and Additional Applications check boxes checked.

12. Click the Expansion Triangle next to the Printer Drivers check box to see a list of the printer brands Mac OS X supports. If you aren't ever going to want to use any of the brands of printers shown, uncheck their boxes to prevent the installation of those drivers.

13. Click the Expansion Triangle next to the Language Translations check box to see a list of the languages Mac OS X supports. If you aren't ever going to want to use any of the languages shown, uncheck their boxes. Or you can uncheck the Language Translations box to unselect all of them at once.

> **NOTE**
>
> The language you choose in step 6 is always installed. The other languages Mac OS X supports are listed in the Language Translations section.

14. If you elected to install any of the other languages in step 13, expand the Fonts check box to ensure that the appropriate fonts are installed to support those languages.

15. Uncheck any of the other options you won't use.

16. Click Upgrade. You will see a progress window that displays information about the various steps the installer goes through to install Mac OS X version 10.3. This information includes an estimate of how long the process will take, but, of course, this is only an estimate. When the process is complete, your Mac restarts in Mac OS X version 10.3 and moves into the Additional Software installation part of the process (assuming you chose to install some of the additional software of course).

A

NOTE

> Mac OS X is packaged in a variety of ways depending on how you purchased it. For example, if you bought the complete upgrade package, you have three Mac OS X CDs. If Mac OS X came with your Mac, you have a variety of Software Install and Restore CDs (in which case, you won't have to do an initial install, but you might reinstall it some day). Just insert the appropriate CDs when prompted to do so.

17. At the prompt, remove the Mac OS X Installation CD and insert CD #2. The additional software is installed and progress information is displayed in the window.

18. If you are prompted to install any other CDs, do so and the installation process continues.

    After the installation process is complete, you move to the Login window. Welcome to Mac OS X version 10.3!

 If your system is not working properly after installing 10.3 over a previous version of Mac OS X, see "The 10.3 System I Installed Is Not Working" in the "Troubleshooting" section at the end of this appendix.

UPDATING YOUR MAC OS X INSTALLATION

After you have completed the installation, use Software Update to update it.

→ To learn how to update the installation, **see** "Updating Your Mac OS X Installation," **p. 977**.

MOVING TO VERSION 10.3 FROM MAC OS 9.X.X OR EARLIER

Moving up to Mac OS X from earlier versions offers many benefits (you will learn about many of them throughout this book), but all this gain requires some pain, that being the pain of installing and learning to use a brand-new operating system. This appendix helps you with the first part, whereas the rest of the book helps you with the second. Following a logical sequence of steps results in the best chance for you to install Mac OS X without any problems. The major steps you should take are the following:

1. Assess your Mac to ensure that it can handle Mac OS X.
2. Make sure that your Mac's firmware is up-to-date (if not, update it).
3. Prepare a Mac OS X volume on which to install the OS.
4. Run the Mac OS X Installer.
5. Configure the OS.

After you install Mac OS X, you should maintain the OS with any updates Apple provides to keep it running as well as possible.

ASSESSING YOUR MAC'S CAPABILITY TO HANDLE MAC OS X

To minimize problems you might experience installing or using Mac OS X, ensure that your Mac meets the following minimum requirements as stated by Apple:

- **One of the following**—Power Mac G4, Power Mac G4 Cube, Power Mac G3 Blue & White, PowerBook G3 with built-in USB, PowerBook G4, iMac, eMac, or iBook.

CAUTION

> Although most iMacs and iBooks can run Mac OS X, if you have one of the original versions of either model, you might have trouble installing the OS, or if you are able to install it, it might not run very well. The original iMacs and iBooks are not really powerful enough (especially in terms of RAM) for Mac OS X. For example, a 233MHz or 266MHz G3 processor might not be fast enough to provide satisfactory performance for you. These machines typically came with only 32MB or 64MB of RAM, which is not adequate for Mac OS X. If you have one of these older machines, I recommend that you get a new Mac to take full advantage of Mac OS X.

- **At least 128MB of RAM**—At press time RAM was very inexpensive and providing 512MB of RAM could be done for only a few hundred dollars (less than $100 if you already have a couple hundred meg installed). Of course, your machine might not be able to take that much, but for all Macs, maximizing your Mac's RAM is one of the best investments you can make. Frankly, I don't think you will be pleased with the performance of a machine with Apple's minimum RAM installed; in my opinion, you should have at least 512MB of RAM, and preferably more, to get excellent performance.

- **A video card that has a Mac OS X–compatible driver**—If you have an Apple-supplied video card, such as an ATI or NVIDIA graphics card (the standard cards in modern Macs, including the options on the Power Mac G4), you meet this requirement. If you have installed a different card, be sure you have a drive that is compatible with Mac OS X, version 10.3.

- **At least 2GB of free disk space**—This is the minimum amount for just the OS. Because Mac OS X is designed to store all your documents and applications on the same volume on which the system is installed, you will need a lot more space on your Mac OS X startup volume than this. In fact, I recommend that you install it on partitions of 20GB or preferably even larger. This gives you plenty of room for your iTunes, iPhoto, and iMovie libraries, along with your applications and other documents.

If your Mac meets all these requirements, skip to the next section, "Updating Your Mac's Firmware."

If you don't have one of the Mac models listed, you are probably out of the Mac OS X game. For example, you can't even install Mac OS X on older Macs, such as those that use the 604 processor. If you have upgraded an older Mac's hardware so that it has a G3 or G4 processor, you might or might not be able to install Mac OS X. Installing a major system update on a system whose hardware has been upgraded is always a bit of a gamble. Some upgrades will handle the new OS okay, but others will balk at it. Before you try to install Mac OS X on an upgraded system, check with the manufacturer of that upgrade to see whether it is Mac OS X–compatible.

CAUTION

> Apple does not provide support for Mac OS X on machines on which you have installed an upgrade card.

You will have a much better Mac OS X experience if you install it on hardware that is on Apple's compatibility list.

If you have less than 256MB of RAM, you might be able to install and run Mac OS X, but you aren't too likely to be happy with its performance. You might be able to run Mac OS X with as little as 64MB of RAM, but you won't be able to use the Classic environment with this amount of memory. You should upgrade your Mac with as much RAM as it can handle or as much as you can afford—more RAM is better! Mac OS X manages its RAM much better than previous versions of the OS did, but you still need to provide plenty for it to work with.

Your Mac is very likely to meet the video card requirement. All Macs come with at least one Apple-installed video card. Unless you have done something unusual, such as replacing the card that came with your Mac with another one, you won't have trouble with the video card requirement.

CAUTION

> If you have multiple monitors attached to your Mac, you might need to remove any third-party video cards before you can install Mac OS X. If you leave the card installed and the Mac OS X installation is successful, the monitors connected to any third-party cards might not work. Until you install a Mac OS X–compatible driver for the video card, you aren't likely to be able to use any of its special features. I recommend that you remove third-party graphics cards that weren't installed by Apple before you install Mac OS X. After you have finished the installation, you can reinstall the additional cards.

Whether less than 2GB of free disk space will enable you to install Mac OS X is also a bit of a gamble. You might be able to get away with slightly less, but it isn't recommended. It depends on how much less you are trying to get away with. If you can free up at least 2GB on the volume on which you are going to install Mac OS X, you will be happier in the long run.

Because of the way Mac OS X is designed to store files (within user folders on the Mac OS X startup volume), you should have plenty of free hard drive space on the volume on which you will install Mac OS X. Mac OS X is designed so that you store all your documents and other files on the same volume as the system is installed on so you should have as much space on that drive as possible. (Don't worry—you aren't limited to storing documents on the same drive as the OS—you can store documents on any mounted volume, but not all Mac OS X's features will be available for other volumes.)

UPDATING YOUR MAC'S FIRMWARE

Your Mac must have access to some basic software for it to start up. For example, it needs to know where to look for system software it can use to start up. This software used to be permanently stored in hardware called read-only memory (ROM). This permanent ROM could not be updated, so what came with the Mac was as good as it could get. With modern Macs, the base software is stored in *firmware*, which is sort of a combination between software encoded in hardware and normal software. The advantage of this is that Apple can update the firmware on modern Macs to correct problems or improve performance.

NOTE If your Mac's firmware needs to be updated for 10.3, the installation process warns you and you must quit the installation and upgrade your firmware before you can continue. Things will go more smoothly if you check and update your firmware (if needed) before installing the OS.

Before installing Mac OS X version 10.3, you should make sure your Mac's firmware is up-to-date. This is a simple task that might prevent problems later.

TIP To keep your Mac in top condition, you should check for firmware updates every so often, whether you are upgrading the OS or not.

To update the firmware on your Mac, do the following steps:

1. Use a Web browser to go to Apple's software support page, which is located at `www.apple.com/support/downloads`.
2. To search for any firmware updates for your Mac, enter your Mac's model or processor and the word "firmware." For example, if you have a Power Mac G4, type `Power Mac G4 and firmware`. If you have an iMac, type `iMac and firmware`. The search will find all updates that meet your search criteria.
3. Find the most recent firmware update for your Mac and download it.
4. Double-click the updater to mount the disk image on your desktop.
5. Open the disk image.
6. If a text file is provided with the update, open the text file and read it. If the Update is provided as an installer, launch the installer. In either case, read the instructions to run the updater.
7. Follow the instructions to install the firmware update on your Mac.

Some firmware updates include a program that checks whether your Mac's firmware needs to be updated. If so, run the firmware installer. Typically, you launch the updater and then restart your machine while holding down the power button (until you hear a long tone). After the updater has finished, it restarts your Mac and will be using the updated firmware.

TIP

> You can also check for firmware updates by using the Software Update control panel under Mac OS 9.

PREPARING A VOLUME FOR MAC OS X

Because Mac OS X is such a radical change from previous versions of the Mac OS, it can also be a bit more complicated to install. Before you begin installing it, there is a fundamental decision you need to make about how you are going to install the new OS.

→ To learn more about disk partitions, **see** "Initializing and Partitioning a Hard Drive," **p. 786**.

CHOOSING A DISK CONFIGURATION OPTION

Ideally, you should install Mac OS X on a separate clean volume from where your current Mac OS 9 or earlier system lives. This enables you to more cleanly start your Mac in either Mac OS X or in a previous version of the operating system. This is advantageous because you can return to the older operating system in the event that something you need has not been ported to Mac OS X yet (such as a hardware device for which there is not yet a Mac OS X driver). This is somewhat complicated if you don't already have a system that has multiple volumes on which to install different versions of the OS.

The other option, which is not as desirable, is to install Mac OS X on the same volume as the current version of the OS. The advantage to this is that you don't need to worry about having multiple volumes on your Mac. You can simply install Mac OS X over the current OS. When you do this, the Mac OS X Installer installs Mac OS X on the same volume on which you have the current version of the Mac OS installed. This will likely work fine, but things are cleaner and more organized if you install each version of the operating system on its own volume.

If you already have more than one volume or one disk available, you should definitely install Mac OS X on a separate partition than the one that contains the current OS. If you have only one partition and aren't able to create multiple partitions, you must install Mac OS X on that partition. If either of these situations is the case for you, skip ahead to the section titled "Install Mac OS X."

If you can partition one or more drives in your system, it is worth the effort to do so before installing Mac OS X.

Before you get into the details of preparing a disk, you need to understand the following terms:

- **Initialize**—Before a disk can be used, it must be initialized. When a disk is *initialized*, the sectors on the disk are organized and the disk is prepared for use. All data on the disk is destroyed when the disk is initialized.

- **Partition**—When a disk is *partitioned*, it is separated into different logical volumes that act as if they were different disks. Each partition is independent of the others, at least to a point. You can install a unique OS on each partition and boot from that partition. Although partitions appear to be independent, they are part of the same physical disk. Therefore, you can't initialize or format a partition. Those tasks can be done only on an entire disk. However, you can erase and reformat a partition without affecting other volumes, even if they are on the same physical disk.

- **Volume**—A *volume* is an electronic construct that acts like a disk. A volume can be a disk, a partition on a disk, a network disk, a disk image, and so on. Anything that mounts on the desktop is a volume.

Using Mac OS 9 to Create Multiple Partitions on a Disk

Because this option enables you to start up your Mac in your current version of the Mac OS, you can always return to that version of the OS in the event that something you need does not work or does not work properly under Mac OS X. (This will most likely be necessary for any hardware devices for which you don't have Mac OS X–compatible drivers.)

CAUTION

> This section assumes you are installing Mac OS X on a system running some variation of Mac OS 9. If you are using an older version of the OS, the steps will be similar, although the details might be slightly different.

NOTE

> To use your Mac OS 9 installation for the Classic environment, you must install Mac OS 9.2.2.

When you partition a hard drive, you must *initialize* it, which means you destroy all the data on that disk. Before you partition a disk, make sure one of the following situations is true for you:

- You have all the original CDs for your software and can store your data files on some type of removable disk (such as a Zip disk or CD-R).

- You have a current backup of the disk you are going to partition.

Because you will erase the drive you are going to partition, you must rebuild it from scratch. The best way to do this is to have an effective backup system you can use to restore the contents and configuration of the drive. If you have to install the original software from CDs when you rebuild the drive's data, the process takes much longer.

NOTE

> For information on backing up Mac OS 9 machines, see my book *The Mac OS 9 Guide*.

To partition your drive, do the following steps:

1. Capture the current data on the disk (use your backup system or locate all your CDs and data disks).

CAUTION

> Don't blow through this step too quickly. Losing data is no fun.

2. Insert the CD containing the installer for the version of the Mac OS you are currently running. You should use your Mac OS 9.2 system software install or restore discs.

3. Restart your Mac, and as your Mac restarts, hold down the C key to boot from the Mac OS 9.2 CD-ROM.

4. After your Mac boots up, open the Utilities folder on the CD-ROM and then launch Drive Setup. You will see the Drive Setup window (see Figure A.3). Drive Setup looks for all the drives available on your system; they are listed in the window. Note that you might see some drives you cannot initialize, such as the DVD-ROM drive. You can also see the bus and ID numbers of all the drives connected to your system.

Figure A.3
Use Drive Setup for the previous version of the Mac OS that you use to partition a drive for Mac OS X.

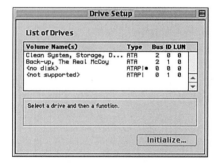

 If you don't see a drive that is installed in your Mac in the Drive Setup window, see "An Installed Disk Does Not Appear in the Mac OS 9 Drive Setup Window" in the "Troubleshooting" section at the end of this appendix.

CAUTION

> Some non-Apple drives are not compatible with Drive Setup. If you use a third-party drive, make sure that it is compatible with Drive Setup before you try to initialize it (you can launch Drive Setup and see whether it recognizes the drive, or you can check with the drive's manufacturer).
>
> If Drive Setup is not compatible with your drive, you will need a third-party drive utility such as FWB's Hard Disk Toolkit.

5. Select the drive you want to initialize and partition. If it is ready to be initialized and partitioned, you see a message saying so in the bottom of the window. If not, the software tells you what the problem is (for example, you can't initialize a disk that contains the active system software).

CAUTION

> Don't proceed unless you are sure that you have another copy of all the data on the disk you are going to partition.

A

6. Click Custom Setup to open the Custom Setup dialog box. You can see the disk's current name at the top of the window. Just under the Partitioning Scheme pop-up menu, you can see the capacity of the disk (see Figure A.4).

Figure A.4
You use this window to select the number and size of the partitions on a disk.

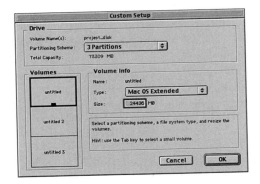

7. Choose the number of partitions you want on this disk from the Partitioning Scheme pop-up menu. In the Volumes area, you see a graphical representation of the volumes with the partitions applied.

Partition Guidelines
Although I can't tell you specifically how many partitions you should set up, I can give you some general guidelines. Unless you have a very specific purpose in mind or are working with a small disk, I wouldn't create any partitions smaller than 10GB, especially if you plan to install an OS or applications on it. You will need at least one partition for each version of the Mac OS in which you want to be able to independently start up.

If you plan on having one Mac OS 9 startup disk and one Mac OS X startup disk, you will need at least two partitions.

If you plan on using Mac OS X's disk organization to store all your data files and applications, be sure to create a large partition for it (preferably 20GB or larger).

8. Select the type of partition you want for the first partition from the Type pop-up menu. Unless you have a specific reason not to do so, select Mac OS Extended for all the partitions.

9. Enter the size for the first partition in the Size box or use the graphical representation of the volumes to adjust the size (drag the handle on the black box around the partition).

10. Continue selecting partition types and sizes until you have set up the total number of partitions you want on that disk (you have allocated the disk's entire capacity). You can have partitions with a different type on the same disk. In some cases, you might want to have a format that is more compatible with a specific purpose for the partition. For example, you might want to run Linux on a partition, in which case you should format that partition as a Unix disk.

    You should have at least two Mac Extended (also known as HFS+) partitions, with one being 20GB or more (the one on which you will install Mac OS X).

    When you are done, you see the completed dialog box and are ready to initialize the disk.

11. Click OK.

12. In the Initialize dialog box, click Initialize if you are sure you want to continue. You see the Drive Setup window again and can see the progress of the initialization and partitioning process. If the drive is large and requires a low-level format, this process takes a long time. If the disk is small or does not need a low-level format, the process is done fairly quickly. When it is complete, you see the partitions listed at the bottom of the Drive Setup window.

13. Quit Drive Setup to see the new volumes on your desktop.

14. Name the partitions you created. For example, name the partition on which you are going to install Mac OS X, Mac OS X. You might name the partition on which you are going to maintain Mac OS 9.2, Mac OS 9.2.

The volumes are now ready for your data. If you open them, you will see approximately the amount of free data you specified for the partition.

NOTE

> You won't ever get exactly the size of the partition that you set; usually, it is just a tad smaller than what you asked the Mac to create. That occurs because the structure of the drive itself requires some data to store, thus reducing the amount of free space on that volume. Plus, there are some invisible files on every partition, and they take space to store.

INSTALLING MAC OS 9.2

After you have created your partitions, install Mac OS 9.2 using the following steps:

1. Run the Mac OS 9.2 installer. If you haven't restarted your Mac since you partitioned your hard drive, you can run the installer from the CD that you used to run Drive Setup.

2. After the installation is complete, reinstall any third-party software (such as your Classic applications) on your Mac OS 9.2 partition.

3. Restart your Mac using the startup volume you created that contains Mac OS 9.2.

4. Configure Mac OS 9.2 so it meets your requirements (such as installing additional software).

After Mac OS 9.2 is configured properly, you are ready to install Mac OS X on another partition.

> **TIP**
>
> For help working with Mac OS 9, see my book *The Mac OS 9 Guide*.

INSTALLING MAC OS X

After you have prepared a volume for Mac OS X, install it using the following steps:

1. Insert the first Mac OS X CD in your Mac, restart your Mac, and hold down the C key to restart from the CD.

   The system goes through several checks that are different from the startup process under previous versions of the OS. Eventually, you will see it begin to prepare the installation process.

2. Follow the same steps as when you install the OS using the Erase and Install option, starting with step 2.

> **TIP**
>
> For best results, you should reformat the volume on which you are going to install Mac OS X using the HFS + with Journaling option.

→ To learn how to format a partition, **see** "Partitioning a Drive Before Installing Mac OS X," **p. 959**.

→ To learn how to install Mac OS X version 10.3 with the Erase and Install option, **see** "Installing Mac OS X Version 10.3 Using the Erase and Install Option," **p. 957**.

UPDATING YOUR MAC OS X INSTALLATION

As with the other software it produces, Apple frequently updates Mac OS X to improve security and reliability, fix bugs, add minor features, and so on. After you have installed and configured Mac OS X version 10.3, you should immediately check for and install updates to the OS and Apple applications that have been released since the version you installed. When you first start up under Mac OS X version 10.3, Software Update launches automatically. If it doesn't for some reason, or if you want to launch it manually, open the System Preferences application and click the Software Update icon to open the Software Update pane. In either case, use the Software Update tool to perform the update.

→ To learn how to use Software Update to update your software, **see** "Using Software Update to Maintain Your Software," **p. 874**.

TROUBLESHOOTING

AN APPLICATION DOESN'T WORK UNDER OS 10.3

After I installed Mac OS 10.3, an application that had worked under previous versions stopped working.

Two reasons that this can happen are the following:

- **The application is not version 10.3 compatible**—Version 10.3 includes many major changes from previous versions of Mac OS X. Some applications break when they run under 10.3. If an application does not work under 10.3, check the manufacturer's Web site to see whether the version you are running is compatible or whether a compatible version is available. Be sure to install any updates to the application you already had.

- **You did not move all required application files to your new Mac OS X installation**—If you performed a clean installation of 10.3, you need to ensure that any files the application installed in the system are moved from the previous version to the new version. The best way to do this is to reinstall the application from its original installer and updates.

→ To learn how to move files from the previous version of Mac OS X to 10.3, **see** "Installing Mac OS X Version 10.3 with the Archive and Install Option," **p. 952**.

If the version of the application you are using is supposed to be compatible with version 10.3 and you can't find any of that application's files in the previous version of Mac OS X's system, try reinstalling the application from the original CD or download the installer again. Make sure that you also reinstall any patches or updates that are available for it.

AN APPLICATION LOST MY PREFERENCES UNDER OS 10.3

After I installed Mac OS 10.3, an application lost my preferences.

This happens if you don't move application system preference files (user preference files are stored within a user's Home folder that is preserved if you use the Preserve Users option when you choose the Archive and Install installation method) from the previous version of the Mac OS X system to the 10.3 system. Check the previous version of the operating system to ensure that you have moved all the application's files over. If you have, you might just have to reconfigure the application's preferences.

AN INSTALLED DISK DOES NOT APPEAR IN THE MAC OS 9 DRIVE SETUP WINDOW

A disk installed in my Mac does not appear in the Drive Setup window, so I can't initialize or partition it.

This occurs when a disk is not installed properly, is not compatible with the bus to which it is attached, or the disk itself is defective. It can also occur with some disks that are not compatible with Apple's Drive Setup application.

If you have never used the disk before, the disk might not be installed properly.

If you installed the missing disk yourself, open your Mac and check the physical installation of the disk. Ensure that it is properly connected to the correct bus. You also need to ensure that the disk is the correct format for the bus to which it is attached. For example, if you are using an ATA bus, you must have an ATA disk rather than a SCSI disk. Make sure you have attached a power supply to the disk.

If you have used the drive in the same machine before or the installation checks out okay, the drive is probably not compatible with the Drive Setup application. You will need to obtain a different application, such as FWB's Hard Disk Toolkit, and attempt to format and partition the disk with that utility.

If neither of these steps solves the problem, the disk itself might be defective. The only options in this case are to replace the disk or have it repaired.

THE INSTALLER WON'T RECOGNIZE A PARTITION

I can't choose the volume on which I want to install Mac OS X because the volume is grayed out.

On some machines, the installer won't be able to install Mac OS X on a volume that is not contained entirely within the first 8GB of its ATA hard drive. Affected machines might include PowerBook G3, Power Macintosh G3, Macintosh Server G3, and iMacs with processors running at 333MHz or less.

On the affected machines, you must install Mac OS X on a volume that is completely contained within the first 8GB of its hard drive.

If you have a hard drive that is larger than 8GB, you must partition that drive so it contains a volume that is 8GB or less in the first 8GB of the drive. You can select that partition to install Mac OS X.

If you have a partitioned drive, one of the first partitions must be 8GB or less. If not, you have to repartition the drive so one of the first partitions is less than 8GB.

To partition a drive, use the Drive Setup application under Mac OS 9.x.x or the Disk Utility under Mac OS X.

If you are installing Mac OS X from an upgrade rather than a full version, you must have an earlier version of Mac OS X installed on the disk on which you want to install the update. If not, you won't be able to select the disk. If you have erased the previous version of Mac OS X from that volume for some reason, you will need to reinstall the previous version of Mac OS X and then run the Mac OS X upgrade installer again. When the installer detects a previous version of Mac OS X, you should be able to choose the disk on which the previous version is installed.

→ To learn how to partition a drive under Mac OS 9.x.x, **see** "Using Mac OS 9 to Create Multiple Partitions on a Disk," **p. 973**.

→ To learn how to partition a drive under Mac OS X, **see** "Initializing and Partitioning a Hard Drive," **p. 786**.

THE INSTALLER COULDN'T FINISH

The Mac OS X installer quits before it finishes the installation.

This problem can happen for two main reasons: Your Mac is not capable of running Mac OS X or a problem exists with the volume on which you are trying to install it.

If your Mac is not capable of running Mac OS X, the installer might not even start. However, it might start if you are running it on a machine that is one of the supported Macs but does not meet the minimum requirements, such as having at least 128MB of RAM. Your only option is to upgrade your Mac so it meets all the requirements or replace the Mac with a newer one.

The installer might also balk if a problem exists with the volume on which you chose to install it. Run the installer again and choose to erase and reformat the volume (if you didn't do so the first time). If you did choose to erase and reformat the volume, try to install it on another volume instead.

If none of this works, you should contact Apple for help.

THE 10.3 SYSTEM I INSTALLED IS NOT WORKING

After I installed Mac OS 10.3 over a previous version of Mac OS X, things are screwy.

If you are having problems (such as applications that worked fine before 10.3 that are now starting to quit unexpectedly) after installing Mac OS X 10.3 over a previous version, it probably means you are enjoying one of the situations in which the installer was incapable of properly upgrading your system. In this case, one of the following two solutions should get you running version 10.3 properly:

- **Use your backup to reinstall the previous version of Mac OS X, and then perform a clean install of Mac OS X version 10.3**—Assuming that you followed good practice and backed up your system before attempting the upgrade, you can restore your previous system. Then, upgrade your system using the Erase and Format option.

→ To learn how to perform a clean install of 10.3, **see** "Installing Mac OS X Version 10.3 with the Erase and Install Option," **p. 957**.

- **Prepare an empty volume and install Mac OS X on it**—Create an empty partition and install the OS on it. Then move any data you need from your backup system into your new system. This amounts to a total rebuild of your system, but sometimes, that is the only option you have.

→ To learn how to use Mac OS X tools to prepare and partition a disk, **see** "Choosing, Installing, and Using a Hard Drive," **p. 782**.

→ To learn how to perform a clean install of 10.3, **see** "Installing Mac OS X Version 10.3 with the Erase and Install Option," **p. 957**.

COMPUTING ON THE MOVE WITH POWERBOOKS AND iBOOKS

In this appendix

USING MAC OS X ON A MOBILE COMPUTER

Using Mac OS X on a laptop Mac, such as an iBook or a PowerBook, isn't much different from using it on a desk-bound machine. The two primary tasks unique to mobile Macs are the following:

- Managing your Mac's power
- Configuring and using the trackpad

Although managing locations isn't unique to mobile Macs, you are more likely to need to switch among network configurations when using a PowerBook or an iBook, so you should also understand how to use the Location Manager to make reconfiguring your Mac's network connections fast and easy.

Also not unique to a mobile Mac—but more likely to be used with one than with a stationary Mac—is synchronizing the files on multiple machines. Using iSync, you can ensure that the files on a mobile Mac are the same as those on a stationary Mac, and vice versa.

MANAGING YOUR MOBILE MAC'S POWER

The factor that makes a mobile Mac mobile is the capability to run using battery power. This is obviously an advantage, but it also adds another task for you, which is managing that power so you maximize your battery life and thus your working time while on the move.

When you run Mac OS X on a mobile Mac, by default you see the power management icon (see Figure B.1). If you click this icon, the power management menu appears. At the top of this menu is an icon that keeps you informed about the power state of your Mac. When the battery is fully charged and you are running on the AC adapter, you see the plug icon. When the battery is charging, you see the lightning bolt icon and an estimate of either the time or the percent until the battery is fully charged. If you open the menu, you see the percentage until charged if you are displaying the time (or vice versa), a menu you can use to change the displayed value, and the Open Energy Saver command to open the Energy Saver pane of the System Preferences utility.

NOTE

> The first item on the power management menu is always the opposite of what you have selected to display. For example, when you choose to display time on the icon, the percentage is shown on the menu, and vice versa. If you don't show time or percentage in the icon, you see time on the menu.

When you are running on battery power, the icon changes to a battery. The battery icon is filled proportionally to the amount of power you have left (see Figure B.2). At the top of the power management menu, you see the time or percentage remaining until you are out of power (you can also choose to show neither).

Figure B.1
The power management icon and menu on the menu bar keep you informed of the power state of your mobile Mac.

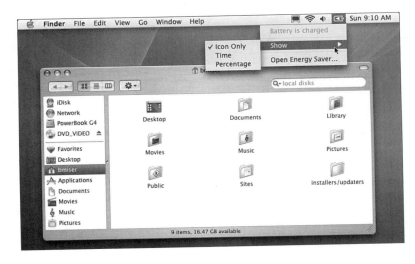

Figure B.2
This Mac is running on battery power and has 3 hours and 33 minutes of running time left at current power usage levels.

When you plug the power adapter back in to the Mac, the icon changes to a battery with a lightning bolt to indicate that the battery is charging.

> **NOTE**
>
> The battery icon takes a few seconds to update. For example, if you unplug the AC adapter and then immediately point to the icon, you still see the charging status information. While your Mac is calculating how much time you have left, you see the word `Calculating` next to the icon; just wait a few moments and the information shown is updated.

You can configure the power management icon on the menu bar in the following ways:

- Open the menu and select Show, Time to show the time remaining for the battery or for the charging process next to the icon.
- Open the menu and select Show, Percentage to show the percent of power/time remaining for the battery or for the charging process next to the icon.
- Return to the battery icon alone by selecting Show, Icon Only.
- Open the Energy Saver pane of the System Preferences utility by selecting Show, Open Energy Saver.

> **TIP**
>
> To remove the power management icon and menu from the menu bar, open the Energy Saver pane of the System Preferences utility and uncheck the "Show battery status in the menu bar" check box.

You should consider the following steps to maximize your battery life:

- **Dim your screen**—Your Mac's screen is a major source of power consumption. If you dim the screen, it requires less power and thus extends your battery life. To dim your screen, use the Brightness slider on the Displays pane of the System Preferences utility. Dim the display as much as you can while still being able to see it comfortably. For example, when you are traveling on a darkened airplane, you can set your display brightness to a lower level than when you are using it in a well-lit room.

> **TIP**
>
> Some PowerBooks and iBooks have dedicated function keys to control screen brightness. When you press one of these, an onscreen level indicator pops up to show you the relative brightness level.

- **Configure the Energy Saver pane for the work you are doing while you are on the move**—Use the Energy Saver pane to configure your mobile Mac's power usage to maximize battery life. You'll learn how a bit later in this appendix.
- **Avoid applications that constantly read from a CD or DVD**—The CD or DVD drive is another major source of power use. If you can copy files you need onto your hard drive and use them from there, you will use power at a lower rate than if your Mac is constantly accessing its removable media drive. In some cases, such as when you are watching a DVD movie, this isn't possible. At other times, you can store the files you need on the hard drive. For example, when you want to listen to music, you can add the songs to your iTunes Music Library so you don't need to use the CD or DVD drive.

■ **Put your Mac to sleep whenever you aren't actively using it**—You can put your Mac to sleep by selecting Apple menu, Sleep or by closing your mobile Mac's lid. Because Mac OS X manages sleep much better than previous versions of the Mac OS did, this isn't nearly as intrusive as it was. When you open your Mac or press a key, the Mac instantly wakes up as compared to 30 seconds or more of wake-up time for a Mac under previous versions of the OS.

One of the most important power management tasks is to actively use the Mac's Energy Saver pane of the System Preferences utility. This enables you to customize your Mac's energy settings to maximize battery life for the type of work you are doing.

You can do this in two ways. One is to use the pane's standard energy setting configurations. The other is to configure the details yourself.

To use the standard configurations, perform the following steps:

1. Open the System Preferences utility and click Energy Saver, or click the power management icon to open the power management menu and select Open Energy Saver. You will see the Energy Saver pane. At the top of this pane is the Optimize Energy Settings pop-up menu. This enables you to configure your Mac to use power settings appropriate for specific tasks.

2. Open the Optimize Energy Settings pop-up menu and select the settings you want to use. When you do so, a summary of those settings appears below the menu (see Figure B.3).

Figure B.3
You can use the Optimize Energy Settings pop-up menu to quickly configure your Mac's energy use.

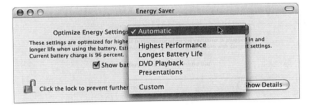

3. Quit or hide the System Preferences utility.

CAUTION

When your battery power starts getting low (about 10% remaining), you will start to see low-power warning dialog boxes. If you continue to use your Mac to lower power levels, eventually the screen dims. When your Mac is on its last electron, it goes to sleep. The only way to revive it is to connect it to the power adapter or change to a fresh battery. This (hopefully) prevents you from losing data because the Mac shuts off unexpectedly. Even in sleep mode, your Mac uses some power, so if it enters the sleep mode because of low battery power and you don't do anything about it, eventually, your Mac turns off. And poof, there goes any data you have left unsaved.

The default energy settings are the following:

- **Automatic**—These settings are optimized for performance when your Mac is plugged in and battery life when it isn't.

- **Highest Performance**—These settings are optimized for performance at all times.

- **Longest Battery Life**—These settings are optimized for battery life at all times.

- **DVD Playback**—These settings are optimized for DVD playback. For example, sleep is set for 3 hours so you can make it through most movies without your Mac going to sleep (if you have ever had the screen go dark during a movie, you know what a benefit this is).

- **Presentations**—These settings are optimized for presentations; your Mac never goes to sleep.

- **Custom**—These settings are those you configure.

If you prefer a more hands-on approach, you can use the Detail mode to customize the energy-saving settings yourself. Do the following:

1. Open the System Preferences utility and click Energy Saver, or open the power management menu and select Open Energy Saver.

2. Click the Show Details button. The pane expands and you see controls you can use to configure the energy-saving settings in detail (see Figure B.4). By default, the Sleep tab is selected; you use the controls on this tab to configure the sleep settings for your system.

Figure B.4
When you show details, you can adjust several aspects of the energy-saving settings independently.

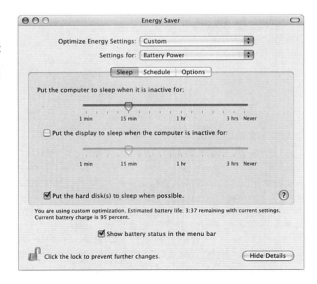

3. Select Custom on the Optimize Energy Settings pop-up menu.

TIP

> If you select one of the standard settings on the Optimize Energy Settings pop-up menu with the Details shown, you can see the details of that configuration. For example, select DVD Playback and you see that the sleep timer is set for 3 hours, display sleep is off, and hard disk sleep is on.

4. Choose the power source for which you want to configure energy savings on the Settings for pop-up menu; your choices are Power Adapter or Battery Power. You can have a separate configuration for each power mode. (The mode in which you are operating is selected by default.)

5. Use the top slider to control the amount of inactive time before the entire system goes to sleep.

6. Check the "Put the display to sleep when the computer is inactive for" check box and drag the slider to set the amount of inactive time before the screen goes dark.

   Because the screen is such a major consumer of power, you should have the display sleep after only a few minutes of inactivity when you configure your mobile Mac for operating in battery power. This also protects the flat-panel display in your mobile Mac from damage and early failure.

NOTE

> If you set the display sleep time to be less than the time at which your screen effects (such as the screensaver) activate, you will see a warning saying so and the Screen Effects button will appear. You can click this button to change your screen effects settings. Normally, when you are running on battery power at least, you want the screen to go dark rather than using the screensaver because the screensaver consumes battery power for processing and screen display.

7. Unless you have a very good reason not to, leave the "Put the hard disk(s) to sleep when possible" check box checked. The hard disk is another major consumer of power, and putting it to sleep saves significant amounts of energy.

8. Review the settings summary that appears just below the controls area to ensure that the settings are what you desire. If you are running on battery power, you will see an estimate of the time remaining.

9. Click the Schedule tab. You use this tab to set an automatic startup or shutdown/sleep time for the computer.

10. To set an automatic startup time, check the "Start up the computer" check box and choose the day (using the pop-up menu) and time (by typing a time or using the Up and Down arrow buttons) at which the machine should start. For example, you can set your Mac to start at a specific time everyday, on weekdays or weekends, or on a specific day only.

11. To set an automatic shutdown or sleep time, check the lower check box on the pane and select Shut Down or Sleep on the pop-up menu. Then select the day and time you want this action to happen on the Day pop-up menu and using the time box and arrow buttons.

12. Click the Options tab. Use the check boxes on this tab to further configure Energy Saver.

13. Using the two Wake check boxes, you can set wake options so that your Mac will wake up when it detects a call on its modem or when the network needs to access your machine.

14. Use the "Restart automatically after a power failure" check box if you want your Mac to restart after the power fails. Because your iBook or PowerBook has a battery, this option isn't as meaningful as it is for a desktop Mac.

15. Set the processor performance setting on the Processor Performance pop-up menu. Your choices are Highest and Reduced. Highest provides maximum performance and requires more power; Reduced lowers performance but also lowers power requirements. If you are configuring for battery operation, select Reduced and use your Mac for a while. If you don't notice performance problems, leave the setting as is. If you notice slow operation, increase the processor performance setting again.

16. Select the other power mode on the Settings for pop-up menu, and configure the Sleep and Options tabs for that mode. (The Schedule settings are the same for both modes.)

17. If you don't want it to appear, turn off the battery icon on the menu bar by unchecking the "Show battery status in menu bar" check box. You should usually leave this displayed because it provides important information when you are running on battery power.

18. Quit the System Preferences utility. Your energy settings will take effect.

Energy Saver settings are global, meaning they are the same for all user accounts on your Mac.

TIP

If you operate your mobile Mac on battery power frequently, consider getting a second battery. This effectively doubles your working time because you can swap out batteries without shutting down your Mac. Just put it to sleep and change the battery. As long as you are fairly quick about it, you can change the battery and go back to where you were.

USING AND CONFIGURING THE TRACKPAD

Configuring and using the trackpad is straightforward. You use the Keyboard & Mouse pane of the System Preferences utility to control how your trackpad works. When you are using a mobile Mac, the Trackpad tab becomes available. Follow these steps:

1. Open the Keyboard & Mouse pane of the System Preferences utility and click the Trackpad tab (see Figure B.5).

Figure B.5
When you are running Mac OS X on a mobile Mac, you can set the trackpad options using the Trackpad tab on the Keyboard & Mouse pane.

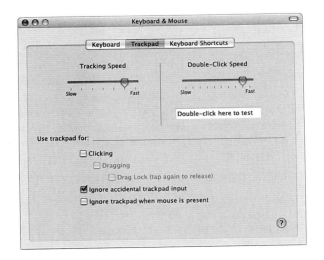

2. Use the Tracking Speed slider to set the speed at which the pointer moves relative to your finger speed on the pad.

3. Use the Double-Click Speed slider to control how fast you have to click the trackpad button or the trackpad itself to register a double-click.

4. If you want to be able to "click" the trackpad button by tapping on the trackpad, check the Clicking check box.

5. Use the Dragging and Drag Lock check boxes to control how you can drag items with the trackpad. If you turn on the clicking option and then check the Dragging check box, you can drag an item by touching your finger to the trackpad and dragging your finger across it. If you check the Drag Lock check box, the item continues to be locked to the cursor until you release it by tapping the trackpad again.

6. To disable the trackpad while you are typing, check the "Ignore accidental trackpad input" check box. This option prevents unwanted interference from the unintentional taps on the trackpad while you are typing or just moving your hand across the pad. When you stop typing, the trackpad becomes active again.

7. If you want the trackpad to be disabled when you connect an external mouse to your mobile Mac, check the "Ignore trackpad when mouse is present" check box.

8. Quit the System Preferences utility.

CONFIGURING AND USING LOCATIONS

As you move your mobile Mac around, you will probably want to connect to different networks from different locations. For example, you might use an AirPort network to connect to the Internet at home, an Ethernet network to connect when you are at work, and a dial-up connection when you are on the road.

The Mac OS X Location Manager feature enables you to configure multiple network configurations on your Mac. You can then switch among these configurations easily (rather than having to manually reconfigure your Mac each time you change locations).

NOTE

> You can have more than one active port on the same machine, meaning you can have different means of connecting to a network active at the same time (such as AirPort and Ethernet). You don't need to have a location for each active port. You should use locations when you want to have different *sets* of active ports that you want to be able to switch among easily.

To configure a new network location, use the following steps:

1. Open the Network pane of the System Preferences utility (see Figure B.6).

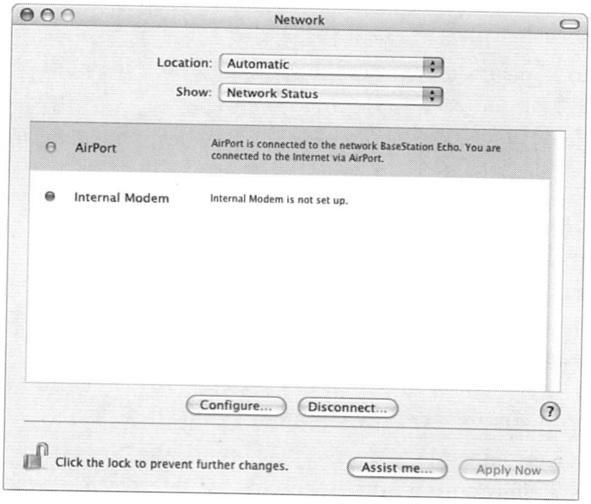

Figure B.6
If you regularly change networks, configure a location for each network you use so you can easily switch between them.

2. From the Location pop-up menu, select New Location.

3. Name the location and click OK. You return to the Network pane and the location you created appears in the Location pop-up menu.

4. On the Show pop-up menu, select Network Port Configurations.

5. Check the check box for each connection method you want to be active for the location you are configuring. Uncheck the check box for those connetion methods that you won't be using under this location.

6. Arrange the order of the connection methods in the list to be the order in which you want your Mac to try to connect to the network. Put the first method you want to be tried at the top of the list, the second one in the second spot, and so on. For example, if

you want to use Built-in Ethernet first and then AirPort, drag Built-in Ethernet to the top of the list and place AirPort underneath it. When your Mac connects to the network, it will try these connections in the order in which they are listed.

7. Use the Show pop-up menu to choose the first connection method you want to configure for this location—for example, Internal Modem to configure a dial-up connection.

8. Use the tabs in the Network pane to configure that connection method.

→ For help configuring an Internet connection, **see** Chapter 10, "Connecting Your Mac to the Internet," **p. 263**.

→ For help configuring an AirPort connection, **see** Chapter 11, "Using an Airport Network to Connect to the Internet," **p. 297**.

→ For help configuring a network connection, **see** Chapter 26, "Building and Using a Network," **p. 821**.

9. Repeat steps 7 and 8 for each connection method you made active in steps 4–6.

10. Quit the System Preferences utility. The network configuration you configured will be used.

The default location for your Mac is called Automatic. If you don't use any other locations, this might be okay, but you might want to rename it to be more meaningful. You can also remove locations from the machine by editing the location. Follow these steps:

1. Open the Network pane of the System Preferences utility.

> **TIP**
>
> You can quickly jump to the Network pane by selecting Apple menu, Location, Network Preferences.

2. Select Edit Locations from the Location pop-up menu.

3. Select the location you want to change.

4. Rename the location by clicking the Rename button, entering the new name, and pressing Return.

5. Delete a location you no longer use by selecting it and clicking Delete.

6. To duplicate a location, select it and click Duplicate; you can then rename it and modify it as needed.

7. Click Done.

8. Make any other changes to the location selected in the Location pop-up menu and click Apply Now.

9. Close the System Preferences utility.

Changing your network settings is as easy as selecting Apple menu, Location, and then the location you want to use (see Figure B.7). Your changes take effect immediately—you don't need to restart your Mac or even log out.

Figure B.7
The locations you configure will be available to all the users of your Mac.

Changing locations does not necessarily immediately disable configuration settings for other locations. For example, if you have a dial-up configuration for one location and an AirPort configuration for another location, switching from the location with the AirPort configuration to the location with the dial-up configuration does not disrupt your AirPort connection unless the dial-up location also has a different AirPort configuration.

In other words, settings under one location do not affect all the configuration settings for other locations. Only when you configure a specific network connection differently under one location does it affect that connection under the other location.

However, if you log out or restart your Mac, you lose access to the services you were using under a previous location.

> **TIP**
>
> To protect your mobile Mac's data in the event someone swipes it, use Mac OS X's FileVault feature to encrypt your data so any rat who takes your mobile Mac won't be able to use its data.

→ To learn how to use FileVault, **see** "Securing Your Mac with FileVault," **p. 897**.

KEEPING YOUR MOBILE MAC IN SYNC

Most mobile Mac users also have a desktop Mac with which they share files. Keeping the files on each machine in sync can be a challenge. Fortunately, the iSync application is designed to help you do just that. Although iSync works for any two or more Macs, it is especially useful to keep a mobile Mac and a desktop cousin in total harmony.

→ To learn how to use iSync, **see** "Synchronizing with iSync," **p. 689**.

INDEX

How can we make this index more useful? Email us at indexes@quepublishing.com

I

types (Console application), 933

Lookup tab (Network Utility), 842

lost files, viruses, 909

ls command, 251

M

.Mac service
accounts
accessing, 428-429
creating, 426-428
iDisk configuration, 430-431
iDisk default storage, 429-430
iDisk local copy, 431-432
iDisk synchronization, 432
email accounts, 426
HomePage service, 426
iCards, 426
iDisk, 426, 432-434
commands, 434-435
folders, 433
information sharing, 435-436
upgrading, 437
logging in, 429
logging out, 429
member sign-ins, troubleshooting, 453
pane
configuring, 283-284
System Preferences utility, 207
screen saver modules, 215-216
service
accounts, adding, 228
iDisk uses, 228
slides, images, publishing as, 508
software, 426
Web hosting, 426
Web sites
creating, 438
customizing, 443-444

HomePage templates, 438-443
images, posting, 506-507
pages, adding, 438-441
troubleshooting, 454

Mac news sites, 886

Mac OS 9, shared files on networks, 839-840

Mac OS 9.2
applications, 187
Classic applications, installing, 196-198
desktop folders, 187
documents, 187
installing, 976-977
restarting, 201
running, 200-201
system folders, 187

Mac OS 10.2, installing
assessments, 948-949
firmware updates, 949-950

Mac OS 10.3
applications
preferences, troubleshooting, 978
troubleshooting, 978
installing, 948
Archive and Install option, 952-957
backups, 952
Erase and Install option, 957-965
methods selection, 950-951
Upgrade option, 966-968
troubleshooting, installation upgrades, 980
upgrading from Mac OS 9.x.x or earlier, 968-973

Mac OS Standard Format (HFS), 14

Mac OS X
applications, 144
benefits, 10-12
configuring to serve Web sites, 451
digital cameras, compatibility, 459

hardware costs, 17-18
history, 10
installing, 977
Internet account sharing, 857-858
layers, 12
application subsystems, 16-17
Aqua user interface, 17
Darwin core, 14-15
graphics subsystems, 15-16
logging in, 32
logging out, 32
restarting, 32, 201
shared files on networks, 839
shutting down, 33
starting, 20
Home directory, 21-23
user accounts, 20
system requirements, 969-970
disk space, 969
firmware updates, 971-972
RAM, 969
video cards, 969
Web hosting, 425

Mac Setup Assistant, 192

Mac toolkit, 885
antivirus application, 886
disk maintenance application, 885
installation CD, 886
original CDs, 886
system configuration, 885
up-to-date backups, 885

MacFixIt Web site, troubleshooting resources, 944

Mach, 13-14
advanced virtual memory, 13
automatic memory, 13
preemptive multitasking, 13
protected memory, 13
virtual memory, 13

MacInTouch Web site, troubleshooting resources, 944

We're a 'buzz' with refurbished Macs!